Building AI Agents and Knowledge Graphs

A practical guide to autonomous and modern AI agents

Salvatore Raieli | Gabriele Iuculano

<packt>

Building AI Agents with LLMs, RAG, and Knowledge Graphs

Copyright © 2025 Packt Publishing

All rights reserved. No part of this book may be reproduced, stored in a retrieval system, or transmitted in any form or by any means, without the prior written permission of the publisher, except in the case of brief quotations embedded in critical articles or reviews.

Every effort has been made in the preparation of this book to ensure the accuracy of the information presented. However, the information contained in this book is sold without warranty, either express or implied. Neither the authors, nor Packt Publishing or its dealers and distributors, will be held liable for any damages caused or alleged to have been caused directly or indirectly by this book.

Packt Publishing has endeavored to provide trademark information about all of the companies and products mentioned in this book by the appropriate use of capitals. However, Packt Publishing cannot guarantee the accuracy of this information.

Portfolio Director: Gebin George

Relationship Lead: Ali Abdi

Project Manager: Prajakta Naik

Content Engineer: Mark D'Souza

Technical Editor: Irfa Ansari

Copy Editor: Safis Editing

Indexer: Tejal Soni

Production Designer: Alishon Falcon

Growth Lead: Kunal Sawant

First published: July 2025

Production reference: 1300625

Published by Packt Publishing Ltd.

Grosvenor House

11 St Paul's Square

Birmingham

B3 1RB, UK

ISBN 978-1-83508-706-0

www.packtpub.com

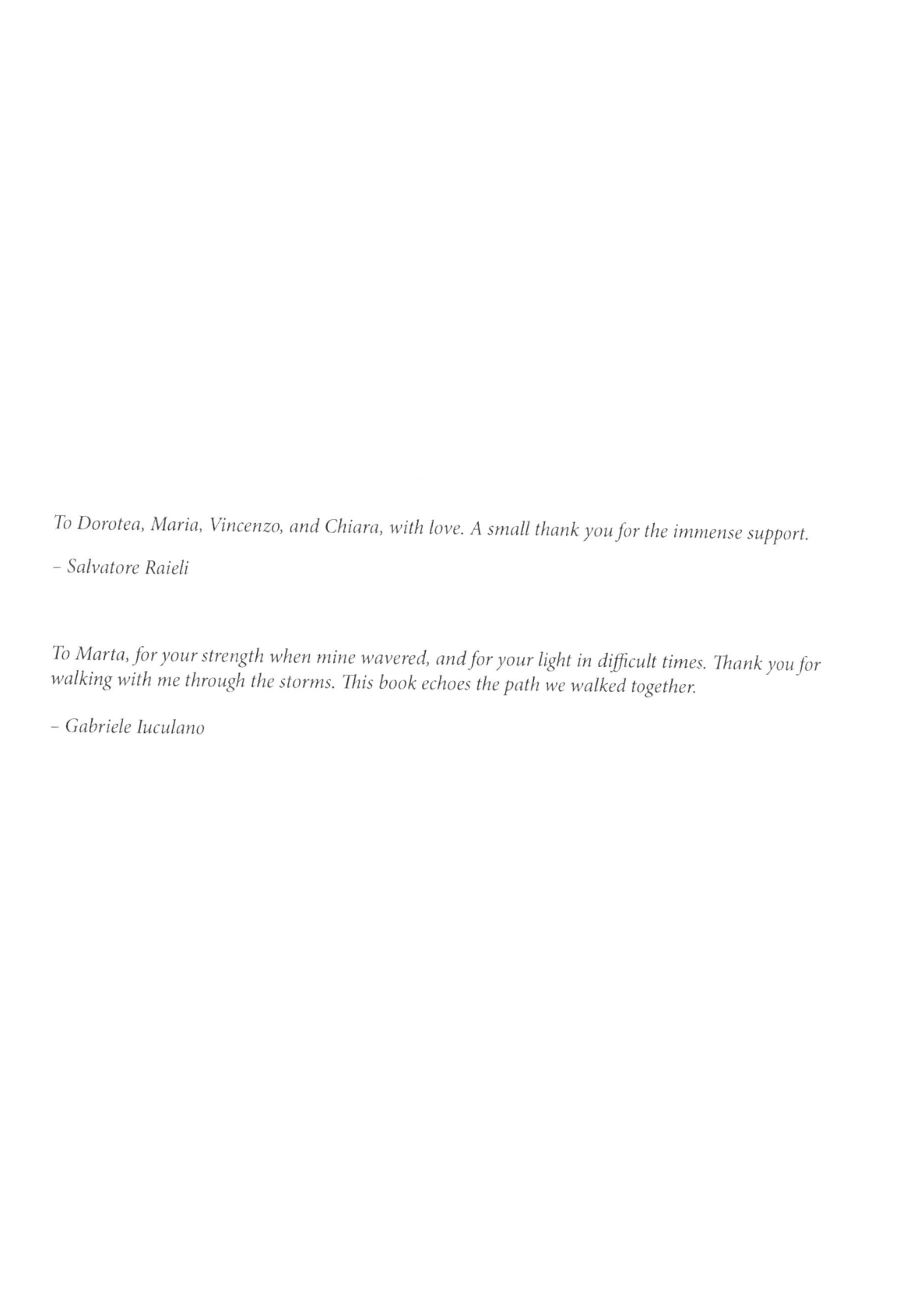

To Dorotea, Maria, Vincenzo, and Chiara, with love. A small thank you for the immense support.

– Salvatore Raieli

To Marta, for your strength when mine wavered, and for your light in difficult times. Thank you for walking with me through the storms. This book echoes the path we walked together.

– Gabriele Iuculano

The author acknowledges the use of cutting-edge AI, in this case, ChatGPT and Grammarly, with the sole aim of enhancing the language and clarity within the book, thereby ensuring a smooth reading experience for readers. It's important to note that the content itself has been crafted by the author and edited by a professional publishing team.

Contributors

About the authors

Salvatore Raieli is a senior data scientist in a pharmaceutical company with a focus on using AI for drug discovery against cancer. He has led different multidisciplinary projects with LLMs, agents, NLP, and other AI techniques. He has an MSc in AI and a PhD in immunology and has experience in building neural networks to solve complex problems with large datasets. He enjoys building AI applications for concrete challenges that can lead to societal benefits. In his spare time, he writes on his popularization blog on AI (on Medium).

Gabriele Iuculano boasts extensive expertise in embedded systems and AI. Leading a team as the test platform architect, Gabriele has been instrumental in architecting a sophisticated simulation system that underpins a cutting-edge test automation platform.

He is committed to integrating AI-driven solutions, focusing on predictive maintenance systems to anticipate needs and prevent downtimes. He obtained his MSc in AI from the University of Leeds, demonstrating expertise in leveraging AI for system efficiencies. Gabriele aims to revolutionize current business through the power of new disruptive technologies such as AI.

About the reviewers

Malhar Deshpande serves as the director and principal product owner of the AI Center of Excellence at Clean Harbors, where he leads AI initiatives, blending data science, machine learning, and generative AI to transform environmental services. With expertise in technology, innovation, and extensive experience in building AI teams, Malhar Deshpande is recognized for driving innovative solutions. He holds a Bachelor of Engineering, a master's in information systems, and an MBA from Northeastern University. As a technical reviewer, he is honored to contribute to this book, the AI and technology community, and the future of AI.

I am grateful to my parents, Mohan and Asha Deshpande, for their unwavering support and focus on education. Thanks to my wife, Shruti; my daughter, Tara; and my brother, Dr. Rupak, his wife, Dr. Riteeka, and their daughter, Samaira, for their love and encouragement throughout this journey.

Lalit Chourey is a seasoned software engineer with over a decade of experience in developing scalable backend services and distributed systems, specializing in AI infrastructure for LLM training. Currently a software engineer at Meta Platforms, Lalit leads a team in architecting robust systems for machine learning training. Previously at Microsoft, he led the development of several large-scale cloud services on Azure. Lalit holds a BTech in information technology from the National Institute of Technology, Bhopal, India.

Table of Contents

Preface   xiii

Part 1: The AI Agent Engine: From Text to Large Language Models

1

Analyzing Text Data with Deep Learning   3

Technical requirements	4	RNNs, LSTMs, GRUs, and CNNs for text	19
Representing text for AI	4		
One-hot encoding	4	RNNs	19
Bag-of-words	6	LSTMs	22
TF-IDF	8	GRUs	24
		CNNs for text	26
Embedding, application, and representation	11	Performing sentiment analysis with embedding and deep learning	28
Word2vec	12	Summary	33
A notion of similarity for text	15		
Properties of embeddings	17		

2

The Transformer: The Model Behind the Modern AI Revolution   35

Technical requirements	35	Visualizing internal mechanisms	52
Exploring attention and self-attention	36	Applying a transformer	57
Introducing the transformer model	42	Summary	64
Training a transformer	47		
Exploring masked language modeling	50		

3

Exploring LLMs as a Powerful AI Engine — 65

Technical requirements	65	Exploring smaller and more efficient LLMs	81
Discovering the evolution of LLMs	66	Exploring multimodal models	84
The scaling law	66	Understanding hallucinations and ethical and legal issues	93
Emergent properties	69		
Context length	71		
Mixture of experts	72	Prompt engineering	97
Instruction tuning, fine-tuning, and alignment	74	Summary	101
		Further reading	102

Part 2: AI Agents and Retrieval of Knowledge

4

Building a Web Scraping Agent with an LLM — 105

Technical requirements	106	LangChain	123
Understanding the brain, perception, and action paradigm	106	Haystack	124
		LlamaIndex	126
		Semantic Kernel	126
The brain	109	AutoGen	127
The perception	113	Choosing an LLM agent framework	128
Action	114		
Classifying AI agents	115	Creating an agent to search the web	129
Understanding the abilities of single-agent and multiple-agent systems	119	Summary	133
		Further reading	133
Exploring the principal libraries	122		

5

Extending Your Agent with RAG to Prevent Hallucinations — 135

Technical requirements	136	Retrieval, optimization, and augmentation	146
Exploring naïve RAG	136	Chunking strategies	146

Embedding strategies	149	tuning	161
Embedding databases	155	Using RAG to build a movie recommendation agent	163
Evaluating the output	158		
Comparison between RAG and fine-		Summary	167
		Further reading	167

Advanced RAG Techniques for Information Retrieval and Augmentation 169

Technical requirements	170	Training and training-free approaches	190
Discussing naïve RAG issues	170	Implementing an advanced RAG pipeline	193
Exploring the advanced RAG pipeline	172		
Hierarchical indexing	172	Understanding the scalability and performance of RAG	197
Hypothetical questions and HyDE	174		
Context enrichment	176	Data scalability, storage, and preprocessing	197
Query transformation	177	Parallel processing	199
Keyword-based search and hybrid search	178	Security and privacy	202
Query routing	179	Open questions and future perspectives	205
Reranking	180		
Response optimization	185	Summary	211
Modular RAG and its integration with other systems	188	Further reading	211

Creating and Connecting a Knowledge Graph to an AI Agent 213

Technical requirements	214	Creating a knowledge graph with an LLM	226
Introduction to knowledge graphs	214	Knowledge assessment	230
A formal definition of graphs and knowledge graphs	216	Knowledge cleaning	231
		Knowledge enrichment	232
Taxonomies and ontologies	220	Knowledge hosting and deployment	234
Creating a knowledge graph with your LLM	221	Retrieving information with a knowledge graph and an LLM	236
Knowledge creation	222	Graph-based indexing	238

Graph-guided retrieval	239	LLMs reasoning on knowledge graphs	249
GraphRAG applications	242	**Ongoing challenges in knowledge graphs and GraphRAG**	**252**
Understanding graph reasoning	**245**		
Knowledge graph embeddings	246	**Summary**	**254**
Graph neural networks	247	**Further reading**	**255**

8

Reinforcement Learning and AI Agents 257

Technical requirements	258	Challenges and future direction for deep RL	289
Introduction to reinforcement learning	**258**	Learning how to play a video game with reinforcement learning	290
The multi-armed bandit problem	262	**LLM interactions with RL models**	**304**
Markov decision processes	270	RL-enhanced LLMs	304
Deep reinforcement learning	**274**	LLM-enhanced RL	305
Model-free versus model-based approaches	275	**Key takeaways**	**312**
On-policy versus off-policy methods	276	**Summary**	**314**
Exploring deep RL in detail	277	**Further reading**	**314**

Part 3: Creating Sophisticated AI to Solve Complex Scenarios

9

Creating Single- and Multi-Agent Systems 319

Technical requirements	321	ChemAgent	342
Introduction to autonomous agents	**321**	Multi-agent for law	344
Toolformer	326	Multi-agent for healthcare applications	346
HuggingGPT	327	**Working with HuggingGPT**	**353**
ChemCrow	339	Using HuggingGPT locally	354
SwiftDossier	341	Using HuggingGPT on the web	361

Multi-agent system	365	Results as a Service (RaaS)	387
SaaS, MaaS, DaaS, and RaaS	377	A comparison of the different paradigms	389
Software as a Service (SaaS)	377	Summary	393
Model as a Service (MaaS)	380	Further reading	394
Data as a Service (DaaS)	385		

10

Building an AI Agent Application — 397

Technical requirements	398	Model training	438
Introduction to Streamlit	399	Model testing	441
Starting with Streamlit	399	Inference optimization	443
Caching the results	404	Handling errors in production	451
		Security considerations for production	452
Developing our frontend with Streamlit	409	Asynchronous programming	456
Adding the text elements	410	asyncio	461
Inserting images in a Streamlit app	411	Asynchronous programming and ML	465
Creating a dynamic app	413	Docker	470
Creating an application with Streamlit and AI agents	421	Kubernetes	472
		Docker with ML	473
Machine learning operations and LLM operations	432	Summary	476
Model development	435	Further reading	477

11

The Future Ahead — 479

AI agents in healthcare	479	Web agents	488
Biomedical AI agents	482	Challenges and open questions	489
AI agents in other sectors	484	Challenges in human-agent communication	489
Physical agents	485	No clear superiority of multi-agents	492
LLM agents for gaming	487	Limits of reasoning	495
		Creativity in LLM	501

Mechanistic interpretability	504	**Summary**	**518**
The road to artificial general intelligence	510	**Further reading**	**519**
Ethical questions	514		

Index 523

Other Books You May Enjoy 538

1
Analyzing Text Data with Deep Learning

Language is one of the most amazing abilities of human beings; it evolves during the individual's lifetime and is capable of conveying a message with complex meaning. Language in its natural form is not understandable to machines, and it is extremely challenging to develop an algorithm that can pick up the different nuances. Therefore, in this chapter, we will discuss how to represent text in a form that is digestible by machines.

In natural form, text cannot be directly fed to a **deep learning** model. In this chapter, we will discuss how text can be represented in a form that can be used by **machine learning** models. Starting with natural text, we will transform the text into numerical vectors that are increasingly sophisticated (one-hot encoding, **bag of words** (**BoW**), **term frequency-inverse document frequency** (**TF-IDF**)) until we create vectors of real numbers that represent the meaning of a word (or document) and allow us to conduct operations (word2vec). In this chapter, we introduce deep learning models, such as **recurrent neural networks** (**RNNs**), **long short-term memory** (**LSTM**), **gated recurrent units** (**GRUs**), and **convolutional neural network** (**CNNs**), to analyze sequences and discuss their strengths as well as the problems associated with them. Finally, we will assemble these models all together to conduct text classification, showing the power of the learned approaches.

By the end of this chapter, we will be able to take a corpus of text and use deep learning to analyze it. These are the bases that will help us understand how a **large language model** (**LLM**) (such as ChatGPT) works internally.

In this chapter, we'll be covering the following topics:

- Representing text for AI
- Embedding, application, and representation
- RNNs, LSTMs, GRUs, and CNNs for text
- Performing sentiment analysis with embedding and deep learning

Technical requirements

In this chapter, we will use standard libraries for Python. The necessary libraries can be found within each of the Jupyter notebooks that are in the GitHub repository for this chapter: https://github.com/PacktPublishing/Modern-AI-Agents/tree/main/chr1. The code can be executed on a CPU, but a GPU is advised.

Representing text for AI

Compared to other types of data (such as images or tables), it is much more challenging to represent text in a digestible representation for computers, especially because there is no unique relationship between the meaning of a word (signified) and the symbol that represents it (signifier). In fact, the meaning of a word changes from the context and the author's intentions in using it in a sentence. In addition, native text has to be transformed into a numerical representation to be ingested by an algorithm, which is not a trivial task. Nevertheless, several approaches were initially developed to be able to find a vector representation of a text. These vector representations have the advantage that they can then be used as input to a computer.

First, a collection of texts (**corpus**) should be divided into fundamental units (words). This process requires making certain decisions and process operations that collectively are called **text normalization**. A sentence, therefore, is divided into words by exploiting the natural division of spaces (**text segmentation**); each punctuation mark is also considered a single word. In fact, punctuation marks are considered to be the boundaries of sentences and convey important information (change of topic, questions, exclamations).

The second step is the definition of what a word is and whether some terms in the corpus should be directly joined under the same vocabulary instance. For example, "He" and "he" represent the same instance; the former is only capitalized. Since an algorithm does not include such nuances, one must normalize the text in lowercase. In some cases, we want to conduct more sophisticated normalizations such as **lemmatization** (joining words with the same root: "came" and "comes" are two forms of the verb) or **stemming** (stripping all suffixes of words).

Tokenization is the task of transforming a text into fundamental units. This is because, in addition to words, a text may also include percentages, numbers, websites, and other components. We will return to this later, but in the meantime, we will look at some simpler forms of tokenization.

One-hot encoding

In traditional **natural language processing** (**NLP**), text representation is conducted using discrete symbols. The simplest example is one-hot encoding. From a sequence of text in a corpus (consisting of n different words), we obtain an n-dimensional vector. In fact, the first step is to compute the set of different words present in the whole text corpus called vocabulary. For each word, we obtain a vector as long as the size of the vocabulary. Then for each word, we will have a long vector composed mainly of zeros and ones to represent the word (one-hot vectors). This system is mainly used when we want a matrix of features and then train a model. This process is also called **vectorization**; here's a sparse vector for the following two words:

$$restaurant = [0 \ 0 \ 0 \ 0 \ 0 \ 1 \ 0 \ 0 \ 0]$$

$$pizzeria \ \ = [0 \ 0 \ 1 \ 0 \ 0 \ 0 \ 0 \ 0 \ 0]$$

There are different problems associated with this representation. First, it captures only the presence (or the absence) of a word in a document. Thus, we are losing all the semantic relationships between the words. Second, an average language has about 200,000 words, so for each word, we would have a vector of length 200,000. This leads to very sparse and high-dimensional vectors. For large corpora, we need high memory to store the vectors and high computational capacity to handle them. In addition, there is no notion of similarity. The two words in the preceding example are two places that sell food, and we would like the vectors representing these words to encode this similarity. If the vectors had a notion of similarity, we could conduct clustering, and the synonyms would be in the same cluster.

In order to obtain such a matrix, we must do the following:

- Standardize the text before tokenization. In this case, we simply transform everything into lowercase.
- We construct a vocabulary constituted of unique words and save the vocabulary so that in a case from a vector, we can get the corresponding word.
- We create an array and then populate it with 1 at the index of the word in the vocabulary; 0s elsewhere.

Let's take a look at how this works in code:

```
import numpy as np

def one_hot_encoding(sentence):
    words = sentence.lower().split()
    vocabulary = sorted(set(words))
    word_to_index = {word: i for i,
        word in enumerate(vocabulary)}
    one_hot_matrix = np.zeros((
        len(words), len(vocabulary)), dtype=int)
    for i, word in enumerate(words):
        one_hot_matrix[i, word_to_index[word]] = 1

    return one_hot_matrix, vocabulary
```

Let's look at a specific example:

```
sentence = "Should we go to a pizzeria or do you prefer a restaurant?"
one_hot_matrix, vocabulary = one_hot_encoding(sentence)
print("Vocabulary:", vocabulary)
print("One-Hot Encoding Matrix:\n", one_hot_matrix)
```

We get the following output:

```
Vocabulary: ['a', 'do', 'go', 'or', 'pizzeria', 'prefer', 'restaurant?', 'should', 'to', 'we', 'you']
One-Hot Encoding Matrix:
 [[0 0 0 0 0 0 0 1 0 0 0]
 [0 0 0 0 0 0 0 0 0 1 0]
 [0 0 1 0 0 0 0 0 0 0 0]
 [0 0 0 0 0 0 0 0 1 0 0]
 [1 0 0 0 0 0 0 0 0 0 0]
 [0 0 0 0 1 0 0 0 0 0 0]
 [0 0 0 1 0 0 0 0 0 0 0]
 [0 1 0 0 0 0 0 0 0 0 0]
 [0 0 0 0 0 0 0 0 0 0 1]
 [1 0 0 0 0 0 0 0 0 0 0]
 [0 0 0 0 0 1 0 0 0 0 0]
 [1 0 0 0 0 0 0 0 0 0 0]
 [0 0 0 0 0 0 1 0 0 0 0]]
```

> **Important note**
>
> Observe how choosing another sentence will result in a different matrix and how, by increasing the length of the sentence, the matrix grows proportionally to the number of different words. Also, note that for repeated words, we get equal vectors. Check the preceding output.

Even if it is a simple method, we have obtained a first representation of text in a vectorial form.

Bag-of-words

In the previous section, we discussed one-hot encoding and some of the problems associated with this form of text representation. In the previous example, we worked with a single sentence, but a corpus is made up of thousands if not millions of documents; each of these documents contains several words with a different frequency. We want a system that preserves this frequency information, as it is important for the classification of text. In fact, documents that have similar content are similar, and their meaning will also be similar.

BoW is an algorithm for extracting features from text that preserves this frequency property. BoW is a very simple algorithm that ignores the position of words in the text and only considers this frequency property. The name "bag" comes precisely from the fact that any information concerning sentence order and structure is not preserved by the algorithm. For BoW, we only need a vocabulary and a way to be able to count words. In this case, the idea is to create document vectors: a single vector represents a document and the frequency of words contained in the vocabulary. *Figure 1.1* visualizes this concept with a few lines from *Hamlet*:

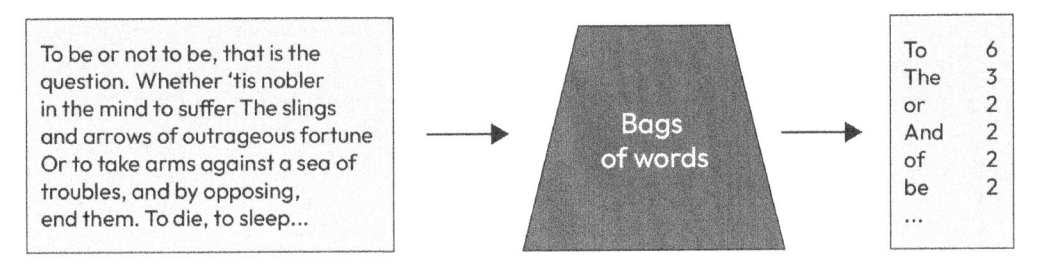

| To be or not to be, that is the question. Whether 'tis nobler in the mind to suffer The slings and arrows of outrageous fortune Or to take arms against a sea of troubles, and by opposing, end them. To die, to sleep... | → | Bags of words | → | To 6
The 3
or 2
And 2
of 2
be 2
... |

Figure 1.1 – Representation of the BoW algorithm

Even this representation is not without problems. Again, as the vocabulary grows, so will the size of the vectors (the size of each vector is equal to the length of the vocabulary). In addition, these vectors tend to be scattered, especially when the documents are very different from each other. High-dimensional or sparse vectors are not only problematic for memory and computational costs but for algorithms as well (the longer the vectors, the more weight you need in the algorithm, leading to a risk of overfitting). This is called the **curse of dimensionality**; the greater the number of features, the less meaningful the distances between examples. For large corpora, some solutions have been proposed, such as ignoring punctuation, correcting misspelled words, stemming algorithms, or ignoring words with high frequency that don't add information (articles, prepositions, and so on).

In order to get a BoW matrix for a list of documents, we need to do the following:

- Tokenize each document to get a list of words.
- Create our vocabulary of unique words and map each word to the corresponding index in the vocabulary.
- Create a matrix where each row represents a document and each column, instead, a word in the vocabulary (the documents are the examples, and the words are the associated features).

Let's look at the code again:

```
import numpy as np
def bag_of_words(sentences):
    """
    Creates a bag-of-words representation of a list of documents.
    """
    tokenized_sentences = [
        sentence.lower().split() for sentence in sentences
    ]
    flat_words = [
```

```
        word for sublist in tokenized_sentences for word in sublist
    ]
    vocabulary = sorted(set(flat_words))
    word_to_index = {word: i for i, word in enumerate(vocabulary)}

    bow_matrix = np.zeros((
        len(sentences), len(vocabulary)), dtype=int)
    for i, sentence in enumerate(tokenized_sentences):
        for word in sentence:
            if word in word_to_index:
                bow_matrix[i, word_to_index[word]] += 1

    return vocabulary, bow_matrix
```

Here's an example:

```
corpus = ["This movie is awesome awesome",
         "I do not say is good, but neither awesome",
         "Awesome? Only a fool can say that"]
vocabulary, bow_matrix = bag_of_words(corpus)
print("Vocabulary:", vocabulary)
print("Bag of Words Matrix:\n", bow_matrix)
```

This prints the following output:

```
Vocabulary: ['a', 'awesome', 'awesome?', 'but', 'can', 'do', 'fool', 'good,', 'i', 'is', 'movie', 'neither', 'not', 'only', 'say', 'that', 'this']
Bag of Words Matrix:
 [[0 2 0 0 0 0 0 0 0 1 1 0 0 0 0 0 1]
 [0 1 0 1 0 1 0 1 1 1 0 1 1 0 1 0 0]
 [1 0 1 0 1 0 1 0 0 0 0 0 0 1 1 1 0]]
```

> **Important note**
> Note how in the example, the word "awesome" is associated with a review with a positive, neutral, or negative meaning. Without context, the frequency of the word "awesome" alone does not tell us the sentiment of the review.

Here, we have learned how to transform text in a vectorial form while keeping the notion of frequency for each word.

TF-IDF

In the previous section, we obtained a document-term matrix. However, the raw frequency is very skewed and does not always allow us to discriminate between two documents. The document-term matrix was born in information retrieval to find documents, though words such as "good" or "bad" are not very discriminative since they are often used in text with a generic meaning. In contrast, words with low frequency are much more informative, so we are interested more in relative than absolute frequency:

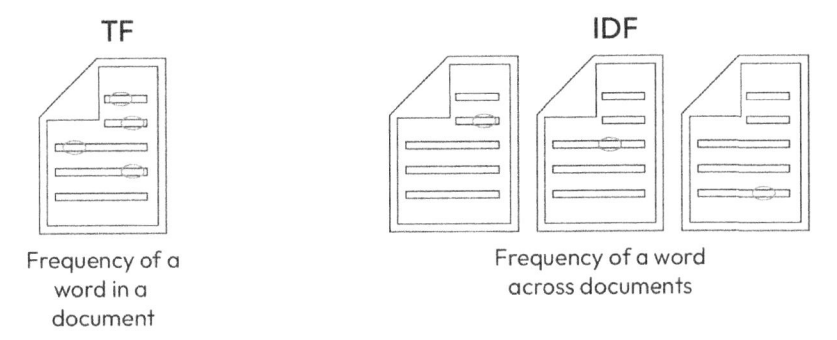

Figure 1.2 – Intuition of the components of TF-IDF

Instead of using raw frequency, we can use the logarithm in base 10, because a word that occurs 100 times in a document is not 100 times more relevant to its meaning in the document. Of course, since vectors can be very sparse, we assign 0 if the frequency is 0. Second, we want to pay more attention to words that are present only in some documents. These words will be more relevant to the meaning of the document, and we want to preserve this information. To do this, we normalize by IDF. IDF is defined as the ratio of the total number of documents in the corpus to how many documents a term is present in. To summarize, to obtain the TF-IDF, we multiply TF by the logarithm of IDF.

This is demonstrated in the following code block:

```
import numpy as np

def compute_tf(sentences):
    """Compute the term frequency matrix for a list of sentences."""
    vocabulary = sorted(set(
        word for sentence in sentences
        for word in sentence.lower().split()))
    word_index = {word: i for i, word in enumerate(vocabulary)}
    tf = np.zeros((
        len(sentences), len(vocabulary)), dtype=np.float32)
    for i, sentence in enumerate(sentences):
        words = sentence.lower().split()
        word_count = len(words)
        for word in words:
            if word in word_index:
                tf[i, word_index[word]] += 1 / word_count
    return tf, vocabulary
```

```python
def compute_idf(sentences, vocabulary):
    """Compute the inverse document frequency for a list of sentences."""
    num_documents = len(sentences)
    idf = np.zeros(len(vocabulary), dtype=np.float32)
    word_index = {word: i for i, word in enumerate(vocabulary)}
    for word in vocabulary:
        df = sum(
            1 for sentence in sentences
            if word in sentence.lower().split()
        )
        idf[word_index[word]] = np.log(
            num_documents / (1 + df)) + 1  # Smoothing
    return idf

def tf_idf(sentences):
    """Generate a TF-IDF matrix for a list of sentences."""
    tf, vocabulary = compute_tf(sentences)
    idf = compute_idf(sentences, vocabulary)
    tf_idf_matrix = tf * idf
    return vocabulary, tf_idf_matrix

vocabulary, tf_idf_matrix = tf_idf(corpus)
print("Vocabulary:", vocabulary)
print("TF-IDF Matrix:\n", tf_idf_matrix)
```

This generates the following output:

```
Vocabulary: ['a', 'awesome', 'awesome?', 'but', 'can', 'do', 'fool', 'good,', 'i', 'is', 'movie', 'neither', 'not', 'only', 'say', 'that', 'this']
TF-IDF Matrix:
 [[0.         0.4        0.         0.         0.         0.
   0.         0.         0.         0.2        0.28109303 0.
   0.         0.         0.         0.28109303]
  [0.         0.11111111 0.         0.1561628  0.         0.1561628
   0.         0.1561628  0.1561628  0.11111111 0.         0.1561628
   0.1561628  0.         0.11111111 0.         0.        ]
  [0.20078073 0.         0.20078073 0.         0.20078073 0.
   0.20078073 0.         0.         0.         0.         0.
   0.         0.20078073 0.14285715 0.20078073 0.        ]]
```

> **Important note**
>
> In this example, we used the same corpus as in the previous section. Note how word frequencies changed after this normalization.

In this section, we learned how we can normalize text to decrease the impact of the most frequent words and give relevance to words that are specific to a subset of documents. Next, we'll discuss embedding.

Embedding, application, and representation

In the previous section, we discussed how to use vectors to represent text. These vectors are digestible for a computer, but they still suffer from some problems (sparsity, high dimensionality, etc.). According to the distributional hypothesis, words with a similar meaning frequently appear close together (or words that appear often in the same context have the same meaning). Similarly, a word can have a different meaning depending on its context: "I went to deposit money in the *bank*" or "We went to do a picnic on the river *bank*." In the following diagram, we have a high-level representation of the embedding process. So, we want a process that allows us to start from text to obtain an array of vectors, where each vector corresponds to the representation of a word. In this case, we want a model that will then allow us to map each word to a vector representation. In the next section, we will describe the process in detail and discuss the theory behind it.

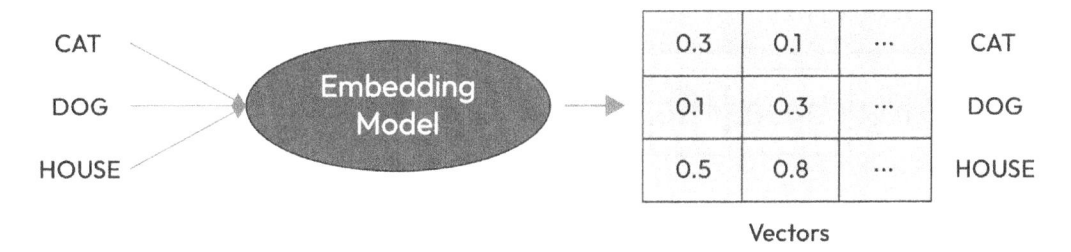

Figure 1.3 – High-level representation of the embedding process

We would, therefore, like to generate vectors that are small in size, composed of real (dense) numbers, and that preserve this contextual information. Thus, the purpose is to have vectors of limited size that can represent the meaning of a word. The scattered vectors we obtained earlier cannot be used efficiently for mathematical operations or downstream tasks. Also, the more words there are in the vocabulary, the larger the size of the vectors we get. Therefore, we want dense vectors (with real numbers) that are small in size and whose size does not increase as the number of words in the vocabulary increases.

In addition, these vectors have a distributed representation of the meaning of the word (whereas in sparse vectors, it was local or where the 1 was located). As we will see a little later, these dense vectors can be used for different operations because they better represent the concept of similarity between words. These dense vectors are called **word embeddings**.

This concept was introduced in 2013 by Mikolov with a framework called **word2vec**, which will be described in detail in the next section.

Word2vec

The intuition behind word2vec is simple: predict a word w from its context. To do this, we need a **neural network** and a large corpus. The revolutionary idea is that by training this neural network to predict which words c are needed near the target word w, the weights of the neural network will be the embedding vectors. This model is self-supervised; the labels in this case are implicit, and we do not provide them.

Word2vec simplifies this idea by making the system extremely fast and effective in two ways: by turning the task into binary classification (Is the word c needed in the context of the word w? Yes or no?) and using a logistic regression classifier:

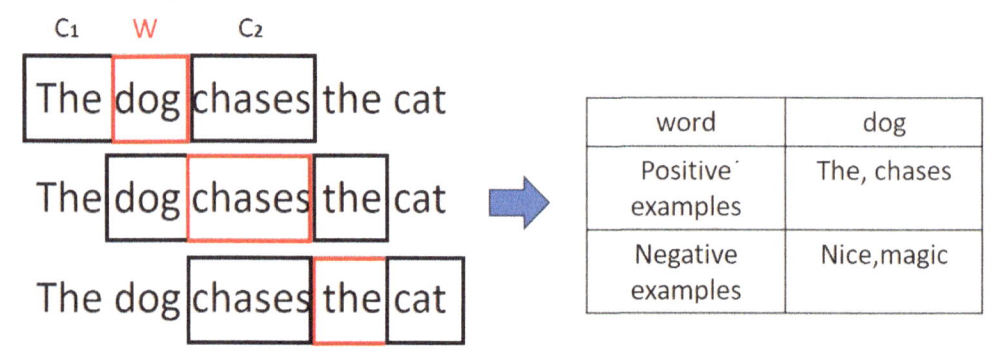

Figure 1.4 – In word2vec, we slide a context window (here represented as a three-word context window), and then we randomly sample some negative words

Given a text t, we scroll a window c (our context) for a word w in the center of our window; the words around it are examples of the positive class. After that, we select other random words as negative examples. Finally, we train a model to classify the positive and negative examples; the weights of the model are our embeddings.

Given a word w and a word c, we want the probability that the word c is in the context of w to be similar to its embedding similarity. In other words, if the vector representing w and c are similar, c must often be in the context of w (word2vec is based on the notion of context similarity). We define this embedding similarity by the dot product between the two embedding vectors for w and c (we use the sigmoid function to transform this dot product into a probability and thus allow comparison). So, the probability that c is in the context of w is equal to the probability that their embeddings are similar:

$$P(+|w,c) = \sigma(c \cdot w) = \frac{1}{1 + exp(-c \cdot w)}$$

This is done for all words in context L. To simplify, we assume that all words in the context window are independent, so we can multiply the probabilities of the various words c. Similarly, we want to ensure that this dot product is minimal for words that are not in the context of word w. So, on the one hand, we maximize the probability for words in the context, and on the other hand, we minimize the probability for words that are not in the context. In fact, words that are not in the context of w are randomly extracted during training, and the process is the same:

$$P(+|w,c) = \prod_{i=1}^{L} \frac{1}{1 + exp(-c_i \cdot w)}$$

$$P(-|w,c) = \prod_{i=1}^{L} \frac{1}{1 + exp(c_i \cdot w)}$$

For simplicity, we take the logarithm of probability:

$$logP(+|w,c) = \sum_{i=1}^{L} log\left(\frac{1}{1 + exp(-c_i \cdot w)}\right)$$

$$logP(-|w,c) = \sum_{i=1}^{L} log\left(\frac{1}{1 + exp(c_i \cdot w)}\right)$$

The matrix of weights w is our embedding; it is what we will use from now on. Actually, the model learns two matrices of vectors (one for w and one for c), but the two matrices are very similar, so we take just one. We then use cross-entropy to train the models and learn the weights for each vector:

$$L_{CE} = -logP(+|w,cpos) + \sum_{i=1}^{L} logP(-|w,cneg)$$

This is represented visually in the following diagram:

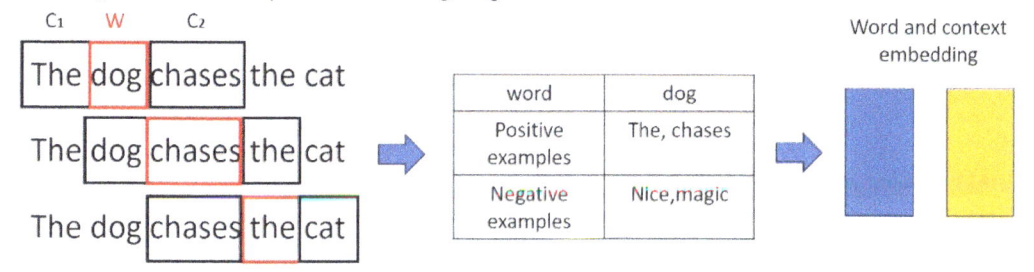

Figure 1.5 – Word and context embedding

The following choices affect the quality of embedding:

- *Data quality is critical*. For example, leveraging Wikipedia allows better embedding for semantic tasks, while using news improves performance for syntactic tasks (a mixture of the two is recommended). Using Twitter or other social networks can insert bias.

- At the same time, *a larger amount of text improves embedding performance*. A large amount of text can partially compensate for poor quality but at the cost of much longer training (for example, Common Crawl is a huge dataset downloaded from the internet that is pretty dirty, though).

- *The number of dimensions is another important factor*. The larger the size of the embedding, the better its performance. 300 is considered a sweet spot because, beyond this size, number performance does not increase significantly.

- *The size of the context window also has an impact*. Generally, a context window of 4 is used, but a context window of 2 allows for vectors that better identify parts of speech. In contrast, long context windows are more useful if we are interested in similarity more broadly.

In Python, we can easily get an embedding from lists of tokens using the following code:

```
from gensim.models import Word2Vec
model = Word2Vec(sentences=list_of_tokens,
                sg=1,
                vector_size=100,
                window=5,
                workers=4)
```

> **Important note**
> The complete code is present in the GitHub repository. We used an embedding of 100 dimensions and a window of 5 words.

Once we have our embedding, we can visualize it. For example, if we try **clustering** the vectors of some words, words that have similar meanings should be closer together:

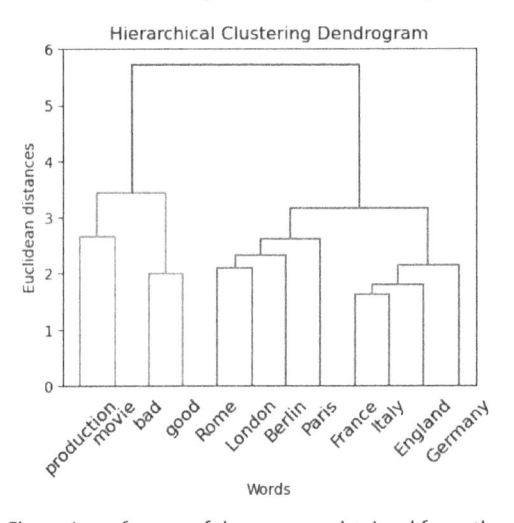

Figure 1.6 – Clustering of some of the vectors obtained from the embedding

Another way to visualize vectors is to use dimensionality reduction techniques. Vectors are multidimensional (100-1,024), so it is more convenient to reduce them to two or three dimensions so that they can be visualized more easily. Some of the most commonly used techniques are **principal component analysis (PCA)** and **t-distributed stochastic neighbor embedding (t-SNE)**. **Uniform Manifold Approximation and Projection (UMAP)**, on the other hand, is a technique that has become the first choice for visualizing multidimensional data in recent years:

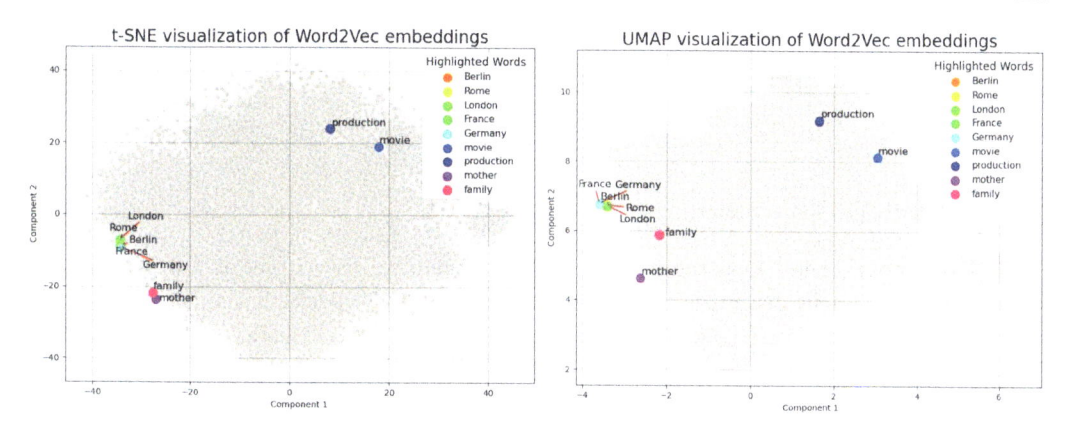

Figure 1.7 – 2D projection of word2vec embedding highlighting some examples

UMAP has emerged because it produces visualizations that better preserve semantic meaning and relationships between examples and also better represent local and global structures. This makes for better clusters, and UMAP can also be used in preprocessing steps before a classification task on vectors.

A notion of similarity for text

Once we have obtained vector representations, we need a method to calculate the similarity between them. This is crucial in many applications—for instance, to find words in an embedding space that are most similar to a given word, we compute the similarity between its vector and those of other words. Similarly, given a query sentence, we can retrieve the most relevant documents by comparing its vector with document embeddings and selecting those with the highest similarity.

Most similarity measures are based on the **dot product**. This is because the dot product is high when the two vectors have values in the same dimension. In contrast, vectors that have zero alternately will have a dot product of zero, thus orthogonal or dissimilar. This is why the dot product was used as a similarity measure for word co-occurrence matrices or with vectors derived from document TF matrices:

$$\textbf{dot product}: \mathbf{a} \cdot \mathbf{b} = \sum_{i=1}^{N} a_i \times b_i = a_1 \times b_1 + a_2 \times b_2 + \cdots a_n \times b_n$$

$$magnitude = |\mathbf{a}| = \sqrt[2]{\sum_{i=1}^{N} a_i^2}$$

The dot product has several problems, though:

- It tends to favor vectors with long dimensions
- It favors vectors with high values (which, in general, are those of very frequent and, therefore, useless words)
- The value of the dot product has no limits

Therefore, alternatives have been sought, such as a normalized version of the dot product. The normalized dot product is equivalent to the cosine of the angle between the two vectors, hence **cosine similarity**:

$$cos\Theta = \frac{a \cdot b}{|a||b|} = \frac{\sum_{i=1}^{N} a_i \times b_i}{\sqrt{\sum_{i=1}^{N} a_i^2} \sqrt{\sum_{i=1}^{N} b_i^2}}$$

Cosine similarity has some interesting properties:

- It is between -1 and 1. Opposite or totally dissimilar vectors will have a value of -1, 0 for orthogonal vectors (or totally dissimilar for scattered vectors), and 1 for perfectly similar vectors. Since it measures the angle between two vectors, the interpretation is easier and is within a specific range, so it allows one intuitively to understand the similarity or dissimilarity.
- It is fast and cheap to compute.
- It is less sensitive to word frequency and, thus, more robust to outliers.
- It is scale-invariant, meaning that it is not influenced by the magnitude of the vectors.
- Being normalized, it can also be used with high-dimensional data.

For 2D vectors, we can plot to observe these properties:

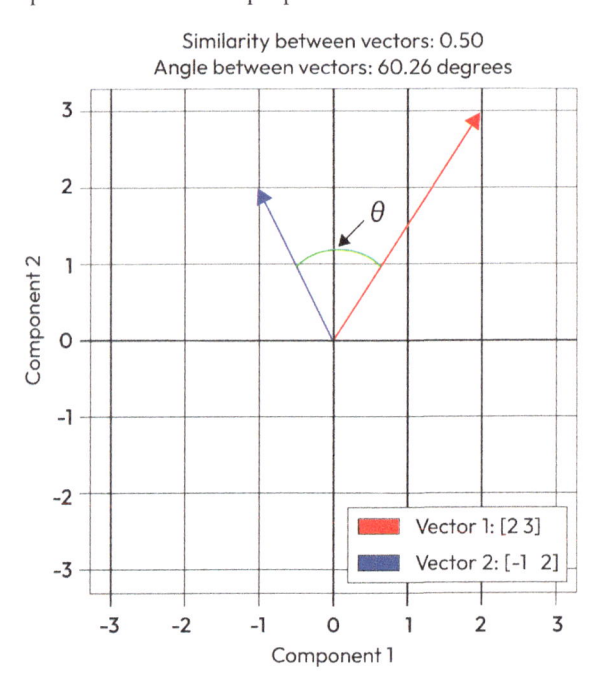

Figure 1.8 – Example of cosine similarity between two vectors

In the next section, we can define the properties of our trained embedding using this notion of similarity.

Properties of embeddings

Embeddings are a surprisingly flexible method and manage to encode different syntactic and semantic properties that can both be visualized and exploited for different operations. Once we have a notion of similarity, we can search for the words that are most similar to a word *w*. Note that similarity is defined as appearing in the same context window; the model cannot differentiate synonyms and antonyms.

In addition, the model is also capable of representing grammatical relations such as superlatives or verb forms.

Another interesting relationship we can study is analogies. The parallelogram model is a system for representing analogies in a cognitive space. The classic example is *king:queen::man:?* (which in a formula would be *a:b::a*:?*). Given that we have vectors, we can turn this into an *a-a*+b* operation.

We can test this in Python using the embedding model we have trained:

- We can check the most similar words
- We can test the analogy
- We can then test the capacity to identify synonyms and antonyms

The code for this process is as follows:

```
word_1 = "good"
syn = "great"
ant = "bad"
most_sim =model.wv.most_similar("good")
print("Top 3 most similar words to {} are :{}".format(
    word_1, most_sim[:3]))

synonyms_dist = model.wv.distance(word_1, syn)
antonyms_dist = model.wv.distance(word_1, ant)
print("Synonyms {}, {} have cosine distance: {}".format(
    word_1, syn, synonyms_dist))
print("Antonyms {}, {} have cosine distance: {}".format(
    word_1, ant, antonyms_dist))

a = 'king'
a_star = 'man'
b = 'woman'
b_star= model.wv.most_similar(positive=[a, b], negative=[a_star])
print("{} is to {} as {} is to: {} ".format(
    a, a_star, b, b_star[0][0]))
```

> **Important note**
> This is done with the embedding we have trained before. Notice how the model is not handling antonyms well.

The method is not exactly perfect, so sometimes the right answer is not the first result, but it could be among the first three inputs. Also, this system works for entities that are frequent within the text (city names, common words) but much less with rarer entities.

Embeddings can also be used as a tool to study how the meaning of a word changes over time, especially if you have text corpora that span several decades. This is demonstrated in the following diagram, which shows how the meanings of the words *gay*, *broadcast*, and *awful* have changed:

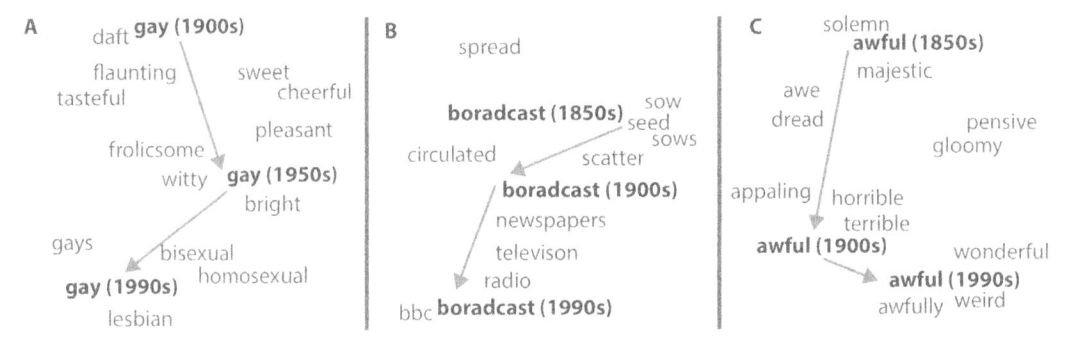

Figure 1.9 – 2D visualization of how the semantic meaning of a word changes over the years; these projections are obtained using text from different decades and embeddings (https://arxiv.org/abs/1605.09096)

Finally, a word can still have multiple meanings! For example, common words such as "good" have more than one meaning depending on the context. One may wonder whether a vector for a word in an embedding represents only one meaning or whether it represents the set of meanings of a word. Fortunately, embedding vectors represent a weighted sum of the various meanings of a word (linear superposition). The weights of each meaning are proportional to the frequency of that meaning in the text. Although these meanings reside in the same vector, when we add or subtract during the calculation of analogies, we are working with these components. For example, "apple" is both a fruit and the name of a company; if we conduct the operation *apple:red::banana:?*, we are subtracting only a very specific semantic component from the apple vector (the component that is similar to red). This flexibility can be useful when we want to disambiguate meanings. Also, since the vector space is sparse, by exploiting sparse coding, we can separate the various meanings:

tie					spring				
trousers	season	scoreline	wires	operatic	beginning	dampers	flower	creek	humid
blouse	teams	goalless	cables	soprano	until	brakes	flowers	brook	winters
waistcoat	winning	equaliser	wiring	mezzo	months	suspension	flowering	river	summers
skirt	league	clinching	electrical	contralto	earlier	absorbers	fragrant	fork	ppen
sleeved	finished	scoreless	wire	baritone	year	wheels	lilies	piney	warm
pants	championship	replay	cable	coloratura	last	damper	flowered	elk	temperatures

Figure 1.10 – Table showing how a vector in word2vec is encoding for different meanings at the same time (`https://aclanthology.org/Q18-1034/`)

These vectors are now providing contextual and semantic meaning for each word in the text. We can use this rich source of information for tasks such as text classification. What we need now are models that can handle the sequential nature of text, which we will learn about in the next section.

RNNs, LSTMs, GRUs, and CNNs for text

So far, we have discussed how to represent text in a way that is digestible for the model; in this section, we will discuss how to analyze the text once a representation has been obtained. Traditionally, once we obtained a representation of the text, it was fed to models such as naïve Bayes or even algorithms such as logistic regression. The success of neural networks has made these machine learning algorithms outdated. In this section, we will discuss deep learning models that can be used for various tasks.

RNNs

The problem with classical neural networks is that they have no memory. This is especially problematic for time series and text inputs. In a sequence of words t, the word w at time t depends on the w at time $t-1$. In fact, in a sentence, the last word is often dependent on several words in the sentence. Therefore, we want an NN model that maintains a memory of previous inputs. An **RNN** maintains an internal state that maintains this memory; that is, it stores information about previous inputs, and the outputs it produces are affected by previous inputs. These networks perform the same operation on all elements of the sequence (hence recurrent) and maintain the memory of this operation:

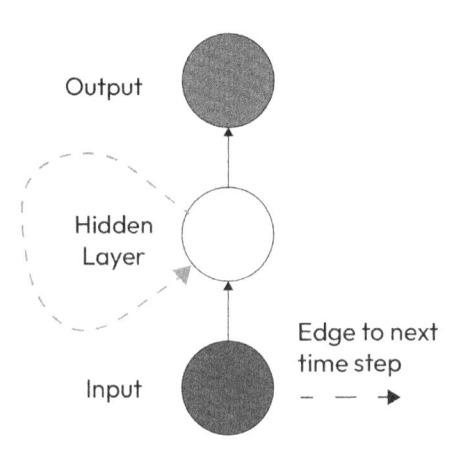

Figure 1.11 – Simple example of an RNN (https://arxiv.org/pdf/1506.00019)

A classical neural network (**feedforward neural network**) considers inputs to be independent, and one layer of a neural network performs the following operation for a vector representing the element at time *t*:

$$y^{(t)} = \sigma(Wx^t + b)$$

However, in a simple RNN, the following operations are conducted:

$$a^{(t)} = b + Uh^{(t-1)} + Wx^t$$

$$h^{(t)} = \tanh(a^t)$$

$$o^{(t)} = c + Vh^{(t)}$$

$$y^{(t)} = \sigma(o^{(t)})$$

These operations may seem complicated, but in fact, we are simply maintaining a hidden state that considers the previous iterations. The first equation is a normal feedforward layer modified, in which we multiply the previously hidden state *h* by a set of weights *U*. This matrix *U* allows us to control how the neural network uses the previous context to bind input and past inputs (how the past influences the output for input at time *t*). In the second equation, we create a new hidden state that will then be used for subsequent computations but also for the next input. In the third equation, we are creating the output; we use a bias vector and a matrix to compute the output. In the last equation, it is simply passed as a nonlinearity function.

These RNNs can be seen as unrolled entities throughout time, in which we can represent the network and its computations throughout the sequence:

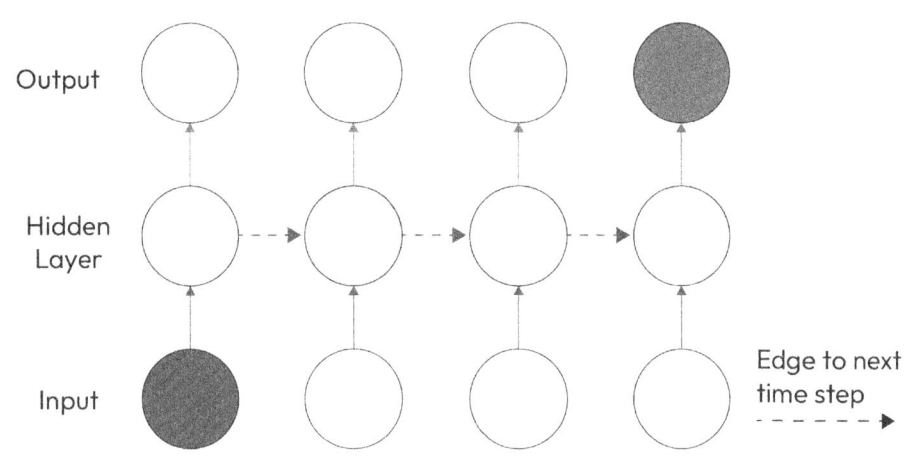

Figure 1.12 – Simple example of an RNN unrolled through the sequence (https://arxiv.org/pdf/1506.00019)

We can test in Python with a PyTorch RNN to see how it is transforming the data:

```
array = np.random.random((10, 5, 3))
# Convert the numpy array to a PyTorch tensor
data_tensor = torch.tensor(array, dtype=torch.float32)
RNN = nn.RNN(input_size=3, hidden_size=10,
             num_layers=1, batch_first=True)
output, hidden = RNN(data_tensor)
output.shape
```

> **Important note**
> Notice how the model is transforming the data; we can also access the hidden state.

We can see several interesting things:

- The RNN is not limited by the size of the input; it is a cyclic operation that is conducted over the entire sequence. RNNs basically process one word at a time. This cyclicality also means backpropagation is conducted for each time step. Although this model works well for series analysis, its sequential nature does not allow it to be parallelized.

- Theoretically, this model could be trained with infinite sequences of words; theoretically, after a few time steps, it begins to forget the initial inputs.

- Training can become inefficient due to the vanishing gradient problem, where gradients must propagate from the final cell back to the initial one. During this process, they can shrink exponentially and approach zero, making it difficult for the model to learn long-range dependencies. Conversely, the exploding gradient problem can also occur, where gradients grow uncontrollably large, leading to unstable training.

RNNs are not the only form of deep learning models that are relevant to this topic.

LSTMs

In theory, RNNs should be able to process long sequences and remember the initial input. However, in reality, the information inside the hidden state is local rather than global, and for a time t, it considers only the previous time steps and not the entire sequence. The main problem with such a simple model is that the hidden state must simultaneously fulfill two roles: provide information relevant to the output at time t and store memory for future decisions.

An **LSTM** is an extension of RNNs, designed with the idea that the model can forget information that is not important and keep only the important context.

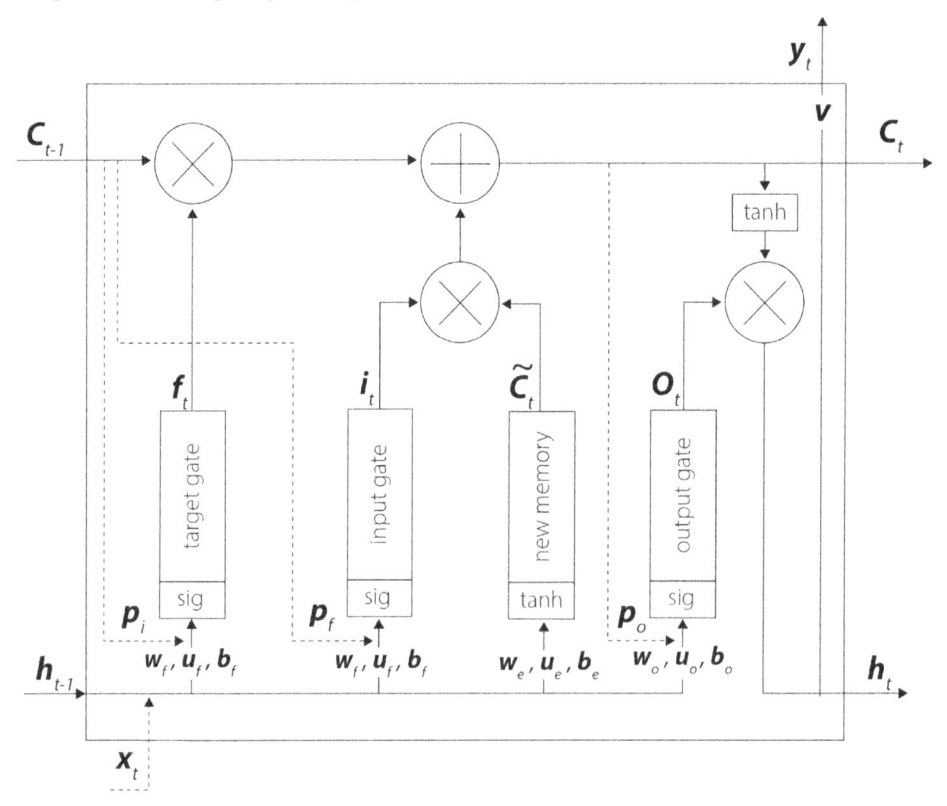

Figure 1.13 – Internal structure of an LSTM cell (https://arxiv.org/pdf/2304.11461)

An LSTM has internal mechanisms to control the information (gates) within the layer; additionally, it has a dedicated context layer. So, we have two hidden states in which the first, h, serves for information at time t (short memory) and the other, c, for information at long term. The gates can be open (1) or closed (0); this is achieved by a feed-forward layer with sigmoid activation to squeeze values between zero and one. After that, we use the **Hadamard product** (or pointwise multiplication) for the gating mechanism of a layer. This multiplication acts as a binary gate, allowing information to pass if the value is close to 1 or blocking it when the value is close to 0. These gates allow a dynamic system in which during a time step, we decide how much information we preserve and how much we forget.

The first gate is called the **forget gate** because it is used to forget information that is no longer needed from the context and, therefore, will no longer be needed in the next time step. So, we will use the output of the forget gate to multiply the context. At this time, we extract both information from the input and the previous time step's hidden state. Each gate has a set of gate-specific U weights:

$$f^{(t)} = \sigma\left(b_f + U_f h^{(t-1)} + W_f x^t\right)$$

$$k^{(t)} = c^{(t-1)} \odot f^{(t)}$$

The next step is to extract information from the input and decide which of that information will be added to the context. This is controlled by an **input gate** i that controls how much information will then be added. The context is then obtained by the sum of what we add and what we forget:

$$g^{(t)} = \tanh\left(b_g + U_g h^{(t-1)} + W_g x^t\right)$$

$$i^{(t)} = \sigma\left(b_i + U_i h^{(t-1)} + W_i x^t\right)$$

$$j^{(t)} = g^{(t)} \odot i^{(t)}$$

$$c^{(t)} = j^{(t)} + k^{(t)}$$

The final step is the calculation of the output; this is achieved with a final gate. The output or final layer decision is also used to update the hidden state:

$$o^{(t)} = \sigma\left(b_o + U_o h^{(t-1)} + W_o x^t\right)$$

$$k^{(t)} = o^{(t)} \odot \tanh(c^{(t)}$$

These gates are independent of each other so that efficient implementations of the LSTM can parallelize them. We can test in Python with a PyTorch RNN to see how it is transforming the data:

```
data_tensor = torch.tensor(np.random.random((10, 5, 3)),
                           dtype=torch.float32)
LSTM =nn.LSTM(input_size=3, hidden_size=10,
              num_layers=1, batch_first=True)
output, (hidden, cell) = LSTM(data_tensor)
output.shape
```

> **Important note**
> Notice how the model is transforming the data; we can access the hidden state as well as the cell state.

We can also note some other interesting properties:

- Computation augmentation is internal to layers, which means we can easily substitute LSTMs for RNNs.

- The LSTM manages to preserve information for a long time because it retains only the relevant part of the information and forgets what is not needed.

- Standard practice is to initialize an LSTM with vector 1 (preserves everything), after which it learns by itself what to forget and what to add.

- An LSTM, as opposed to an RNN, can remember up to 100 time steps (the RNN after 7 time steps starts forgetting). The plus operation makes vanishing or exploding gradients less likely.

Let's look at another model option that is computationally lighter but still has this notion of context vector.

GRUs

GRUs are another variant of RNNs to solve the vanishing gradient problem, thus making them more effective in remembering information. They are very similar to LSTMs since they have internal gates, but they are much simpler and lighter. Despite having fewer parameters, GRUs can converge faster than LSTMs and still achieve comparable performance. GRUs exploit some of the elements that have made LSTMs so effective: the plus operation, the Hadamard product, the presence of a context, and the control of information within the layer:

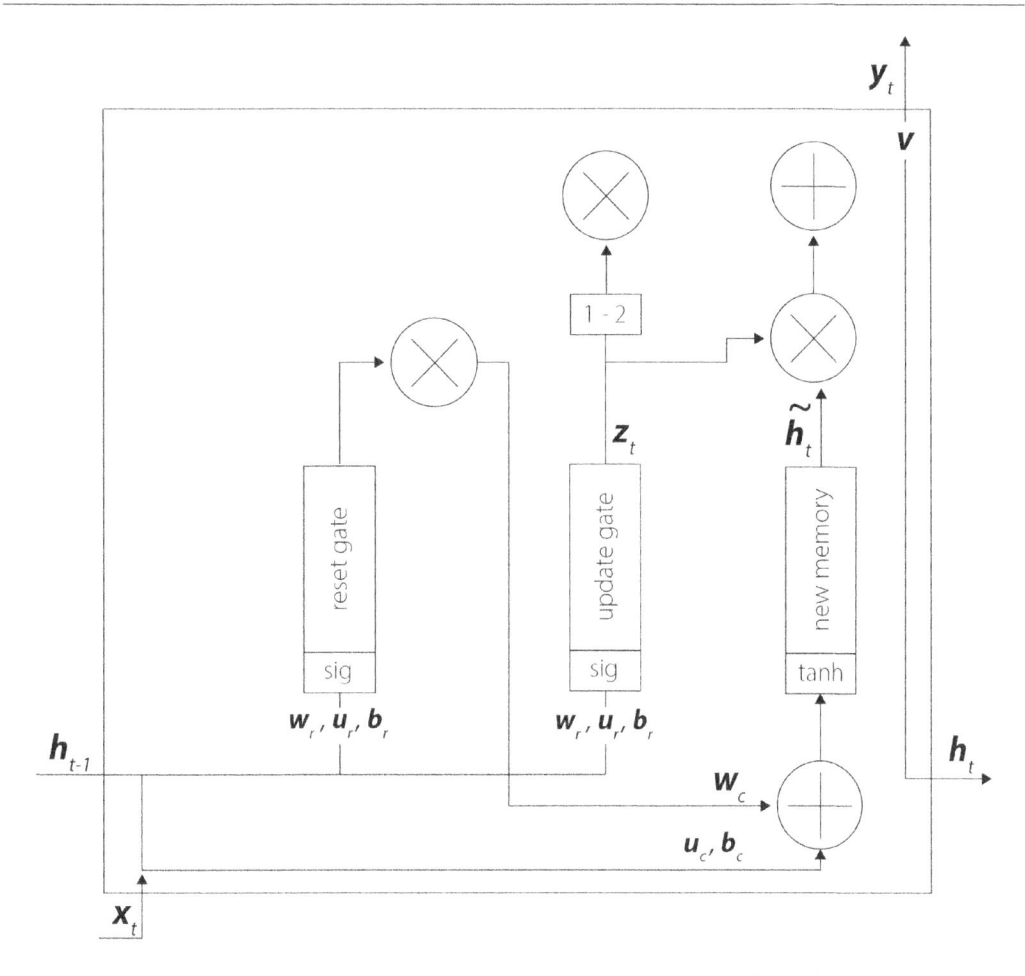

Figure 1.14 – Internal structure of a GRU cell (https://arxiv.org/pdf/2304.11461)

In a GRU, the forget gate is called the **update gate**, but it has the same purpose: important information is retained (values near 1) and unimportant information is rewritten during the update (values near 0). In a GRU, the input gate is called the **reset gate** and is not independent as in an LSTM, but connected to the update gate.

The first step is the update gate z, which is practically the same as the forget gate in an LSTM. At the same time, we calculate the reset gate r:

$$z^{(t)} = \sigma(b_z + U_z h^{(t-1)} + W_z x^t)$$

$$r^{(t)} = \sigma(b_r + U_r h^{(t-1)} + W_r x^t)$$

The next step is to update the hidden state; this depends on the reset gate. In this way, we decide what new information is put into the hidden state and what relevant information from the past is saved. This is called the **current memory gate**:

$$\bar{h}^{(t)} = \tanh\left(W_h x^t + r^{(t)} \odot U_z h^{(t-1)}\right)$$

At this point, we have the final update of the hidden state in which we also use the update gate:

$$h^{(t)} = z^{(t)} \odot h^{(t-1)} + (1 - z^{(t)}) \odot \bar{h}^{(t)}$$

We can test in Python with a PyTorch RNN to see how it is transforming the data:

```
data_tensor = torch.tensor(np.random.random((10, 5, 3)),
                           dtype=torch.float32)
GRU =nn.GRU(input_size=3, hidden_size=10,
         num_layers=1, batch_first=True)
output, hidden = GRU(data_tensor)
output.shape
```

> **Important note**
> Notice how the model is transforming the data; we can also access the hidden state.

We can see some interesting elements here as well:

- GRU networks are similar to LSTM networks, but they have the advantage of fewer parameters and are computationally more efficient. This means, though, they are more prone to overfitting.
- They can handle long sequences of data without forgetting previous inputs. For many textual tasks (but also speech recognition and music generation) they perform quite well, though they are less efficient than LSTMs when it comes to modeling long-term dependencies or complex patterns.

Next, we'll look at CNNs.

CNNs for text

CNNs are designed to find patterns in images (or other 2D matrixes) by running a filter (a matrix or kernel) along them. The convolution is conducted pixel by pixel, and the filter values are multiplied by the pixels in the image and then summed. During training, a weight is learned for each of the filter entries. For each filter, we get a different scan of the image that can be visualized; this is called a feature map.

Convolutional networks have been successful in **computer vision** because of their ability to extract local information and recognize complex patterns. For this reason, convolutional networks have been proposed for sequences. In this case, 1-dimensional convolutional networks are exploited, but the idea is the same. In fact, on a sequence, 1D convolution is used to extract a feature map (instead of being a 2-dimensional filter or matrix, we have a uni-dimensional filter that can be seen as the context window of word2vec):

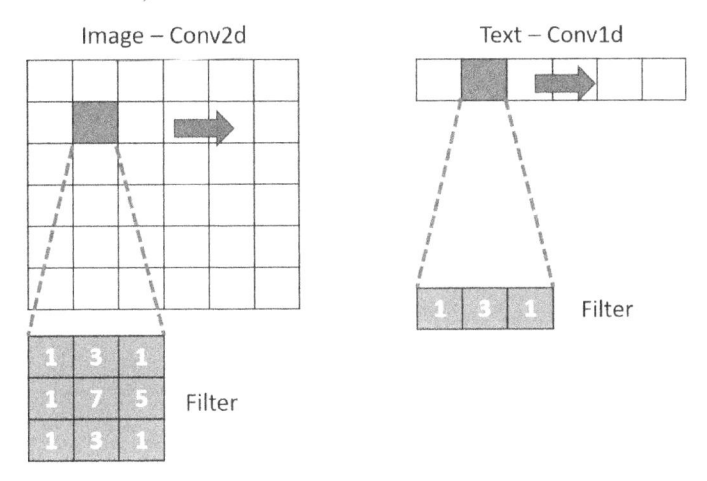

Figure 1.15 – In 1D convolution, we are sliding a 1D filter over the sequence

In the preceding figure, we scroll a uni-dimensional filter over the sequence; the process is very fast, and the filter can have an arbitrary size (three to seven words or even more). The model tries to learn patterns among the various words found within this kernel. It can also be used on vectors previously obtained from an embedding, and we can also use multiple kernels (so as to learn different patterns for each sequence). As with image CNNs, we can add operations such as max pooling to extract the most important features.

We can test in Python with a PyTorch RNN to see how it is transforming the data:

```
data_tensor = torch.tensor(np.random.random((10, 5, 3)),
                           dtype=torch.float32)
Conv1d = nn.Conv1d(in_channels=5, out_channels=16,
                   kernel_size=3, stride=1, padding=1)
output = Conv1d(data_tensor)
output.shape
```

> **Important note**
> Notice how the model is transforming the data and how this is different from what we have seen before.

Now that we have a method to transform text into numerical representation (while preserving the contextual information) and models that can handle this representation, we can combine them to obtain an end-to-end system.

Performing sentiment analysis with embedding and deep learning

In this section, we will train a model for conducting sentiment analysis on movie reviews. The model we will train will be able to classify reviews as positive or negative. To build and train the model, we will exploit the elements we have encountered so far. In brief, we're doing the following:

- We are preprocessing the dataset, transforming in numerical vectors, and harmonizing the vectors
- We are defining a neural network with an embedding and training it

The dataset consists of 50,000 positive and negative reviews. We can see that it contains a heterogeneous length for reviews and that on average, there are 230 words:

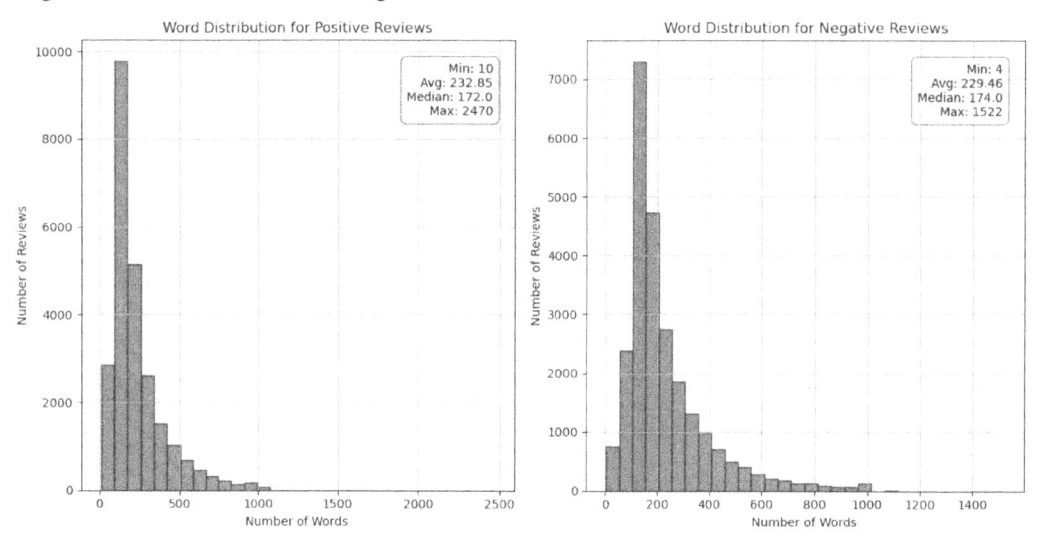

Figure 1.16 – Graphs showing the distribution of the length of the review in the text; the left plot is for positive reviews, while the right plot is for negative reviews

In addition, the most prevalent words are, obviously, *"movie"* and *"film"*:

Figure 1.17 – Word cloud for the most frequent words in positive
(left plot) and negative (right plot) reviews

The text is messy and must be cleaned before the model can be trained. The first step is binary encoding of the label ("positive" equals 0, "negative" equals 1). After that, we divide the features and the labels (for a dataset in **supervised learning**, X are the features and y are the labels). Next, we create three balanced datasets for training, validation, and testing:

```
df['sentiment_encoded'] = np.where(
    df['sentiment']=='positive',0,1)
X,y = df['review'].values, df['sentiment_encoded'].values
x_train,x_test,y_train,y_test = train_test_split(
    X,y,stratify=y, test_size=.2)
x_train,x_val,y_train,y_val = train_test_split(
    x_train,y_train,stratify=y_train, test_size=.1)
y_train, y_val, y_test = np.array(y_train), np.array(y_val), \
    np.array(y_test)
```

A few steps are necessary before proceeding with the training:

- A **preprocessing** step in which we remove excessive spaces, special characters, and punctuation.
- A **tokenization** step in which we convert the various reviews into tokens. In this step, we also remove stopwords and single-character words. We extract for each review only the 1,000 most popular words (this step is only to reduce computation time during training).

- Transformation of the the words into indices (**vectorization**) according to our vocabulary to make the model work with numerical values.

- Since the reviews have different lengths, we apply padding to harmonize the length of the review to a fixed number (we need this for the training).

These preprocessing steps depend on the dataset. The code is in the GitHub repository. Note, however, that the tokenization and preprocessing choices alter the properties of the reviews – in this case, the summary statistics.

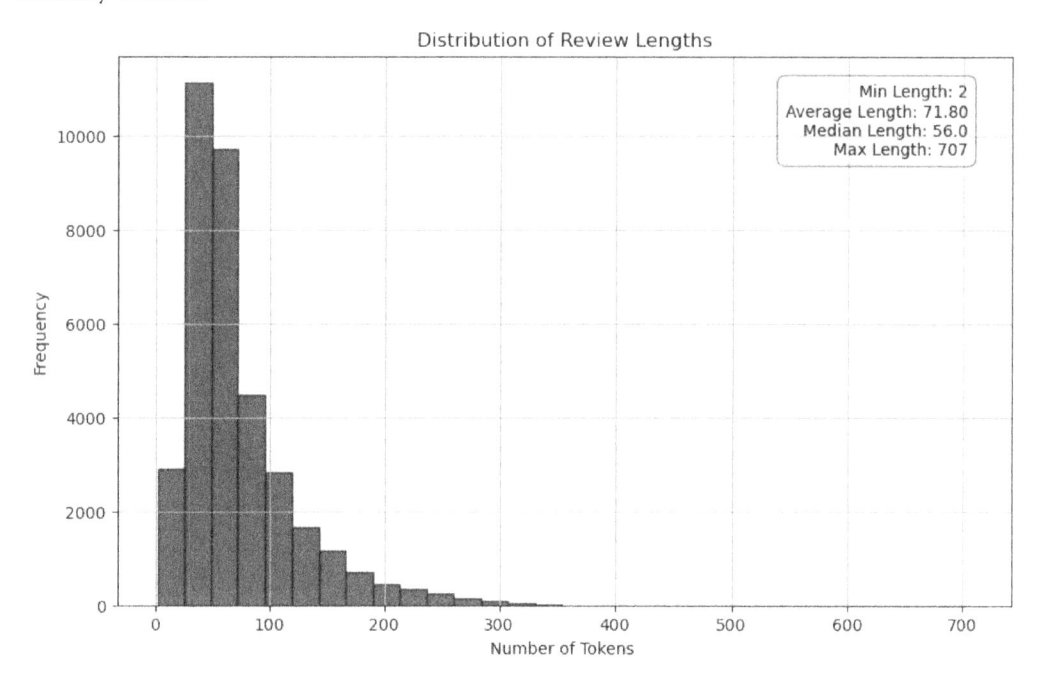

Figure 1.18 – Graph showing the distribution of review length after tokenization

We are defining the model with its hyperparameters. In this case, we are training a neural network to predict sentiment data composed of embeddings and GRUs. To make the training more stable, we add regularization (dropout). The linear layer is to map these features that we extracted to a single representation. We use this representation to calculate the probability that the review is positive or negative:

```
# Hyperparameters
no_layers = 3
vocab_size = len(vocab) + 1   # extra 1 for padding
embedding_dim = 300
output_dim = 1
hidden_dim = 256
```

```
# Initialize the model
model = SentimentRNN(no_layers, vocab_size, hidden_dim,
                     embedding_dim, drop_prob=0.5)
```

Note that in this case, we use binary cross-entropy loss because we have only two categories (positive and negative). Also, we use Adam as an optimizer, but one can test others. In this case, we conduct batch training since we have thousands of reviews:

```
criterion = nn.BCELoss()
optimizer = optim.Adam(model.parameters(), lr=0.001)
epoch_tr_loss, epoch_vl_loss = [], []
epoch_tr_acc, epoch_vl_acc = [], []
for epoch in range(epochs):
    train_losses = []
    train_acc = 0.0
    model.train()
    h = model.init_hidden(50)
    for inputs, labels in train_loader:
        inputs, labels = inputs.to(device), labels.to(device)
        h = h.data
        model.zero_grad()
        output, h = model(inputs, h)
        loss = criterion(output.squeeze(), labels.float())
        loss.backward()
        train_losses.append(loss.item())
        accuracy = acc(output, labels)
        train_acc += accuracy
        optimizer.step()
```

The following graph displays the accuracy and loss for the training and validation sets:

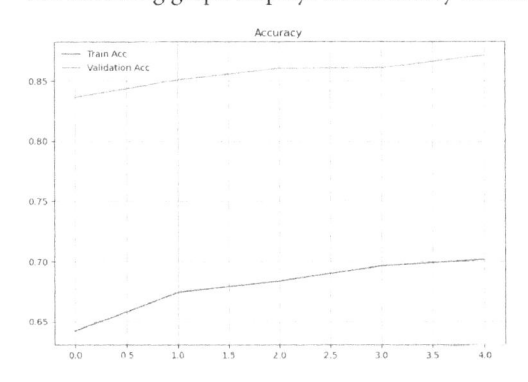

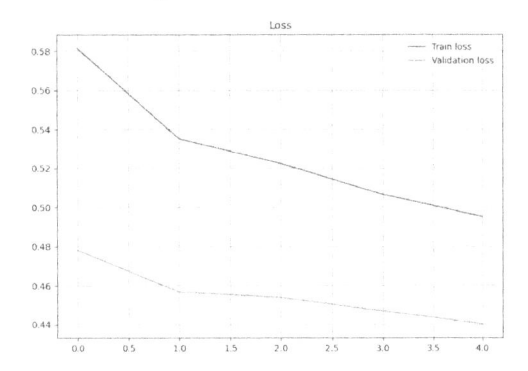

Figure 1.19 – Training curves for training and validation set, for accuracy and loss

The model achieves good accuracy, as we can see from the following confusion matrix:

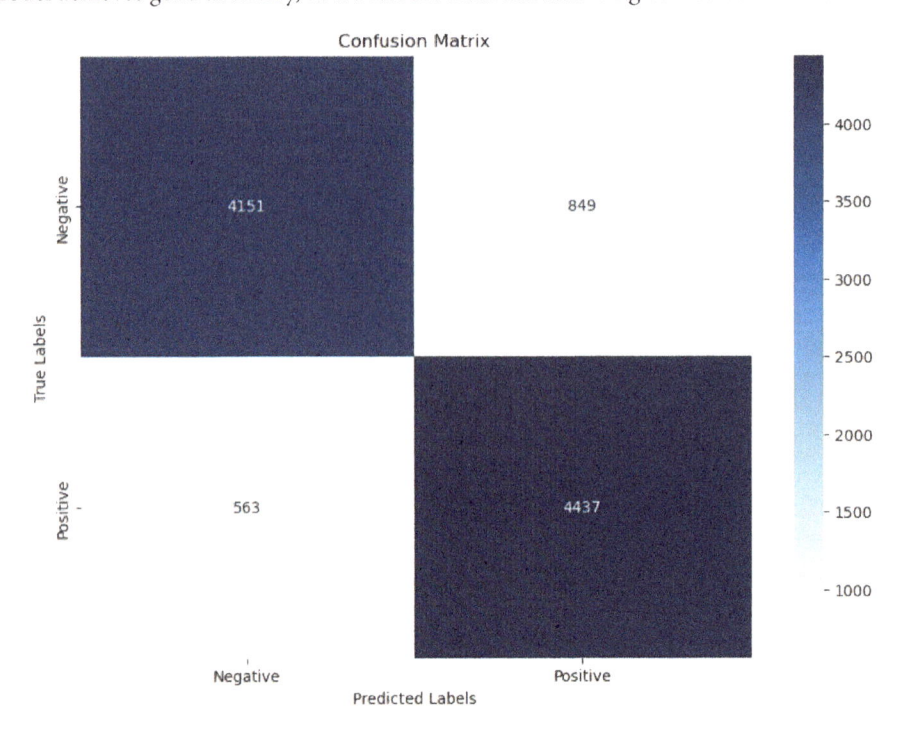

Figure 1.20 – Confusion matrix for the test set

In addition, if we look at the projection of reviews before and after the training, we can see that the model has learned how to separate positive and negative reviews:

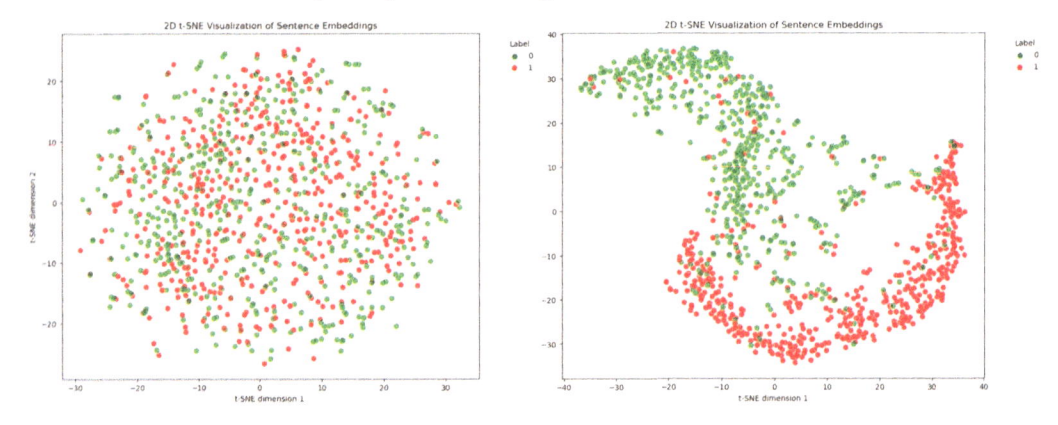

Figure 1.21 – Embedding projection obtained from the model before (left plot) and after (right plot) training

We have now trained a model that can take a review in plain text and classify it as positive or negative. We did that by combining the elements we saw previously in the chapter. The same approach can be followed with any other dataset; that is the power of deep learning.

Summary

In this chapter, we saw how to transform text to an increasingly complex vector representation. This numerical representation of text allowed us to be able to use machine learning models. We saw how to preserve the contextual information (word embedding) of a text and how this can then be used for later analysis (for example, searching synonyms or clustering words). In addition, we saw how neural networks (RNNs, LSTM, GRUs) can be used to analyze text and perform tasks (for example, sentiment analysis).

In the next chapter, we will see how to solve some of the remaining unsolved challenges and see how this will lead to the natural evolution of the models seen here.

2

The Transformer: The Model Behind the Modern AI Revolution

In this chapter, we will discuss the limitations of the models we saw in the previous chapter, and how a new paradigm (first attention mechanisms and then the transformer) emerged to solve these limitations. This will enable us to understand how these models are trained and why they are so powerful. We will discuss why this paradigm has been successful and why it has made it possible to solve tasks in **natural language processing** (**NLP**) that were previously impossible. We will then see the capabilities of these models in practical application.

This chapter will clarify why contemporary LLMs are inherently based on the transformer architecture.

In this chapter, we'll be covering the following topics:

- Exploring attention and self-attention
- Introducing the transformer model
- Training a transformer
- Exploring masked language modeling
- Visualizing internal mechanisms
- Applying a transformer

Technical requirements

Most of this code can be run on a CPU, but some parts (fine-tuning and knowledge distillation) are preferable to be run on a GPU (one hour of training on a CPU versus less than five minutes on a GPU).

The code is written in PyTorch and uses standard libraries for the most part (PyTorch, Hugging Face Transformers, and so on), though some snippets come from Ecco, a specific library. The code can be found on GitHub: https://github.com/PacktPublishing/Modern-AI-Agents/tree/main/chr2

Exploring attention and self-attention

In the 1950s, with the beginning of the computer revolution, governments began to become interested in the idea of machine translation, especially for military applications. These attempts failed miserably, for three main reasons: machine translation is more complex than it seems, there was not enough computational power, and there was not enough data. Governments concluded that it was a technically impossible challenge in the 1960s.

By the 1990s, two of the three limitations were beginning to be overcome: the internet finally allowed for abundant text, and the advent of GPUs finally allowed for computational power. The third requirement still had to be met: a model that could harness the newfound computational power to handle the complexity of natural language.

Machine translation captured the interest of researchers because it is a practical problem for which it is easy to evaluate the result (we can easily understand whether a translation is good or not). Moreover, we have an abundance of text in one language and a counterpart in another. So, researchers tried to adapt the previous models to the tasks (RNN, LSTM, and so on). The most commonly used system was the **seq2seq model**, where you have an **encoder** and a **decoder**. The encoder transforms the sequence into a new succinct representation that should preserve the relevant information (a sort of good summary). The decoder receives as input this context vector and uses this to transform (translate) this input into the output.

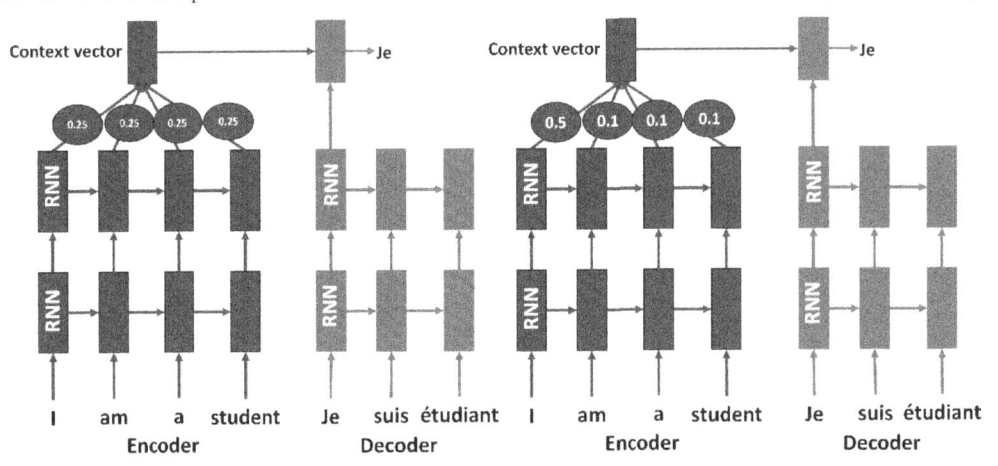

Figure 2.1 – A seq2seq model with an encoder and a decoder. In one case, we take the average of the hidden states (left); in the other case, we use attention to identify which hidden state is more relevant for the translation (right)

RNNs and derived models have some problems:

- **Alignment**: The length of input and output can be different (for example, to translate English to French "*she doesn't like potatoes*" into "*elle n'aime pas les pommes de terre*").

- **Vanishing and exploding gradients**: Problems that arise during training so that multiple layers cannot be managed effectively.

- **Non-parallelizability**: Training is computationally expensive and not parallelizable. RNNs forget after a few steps.

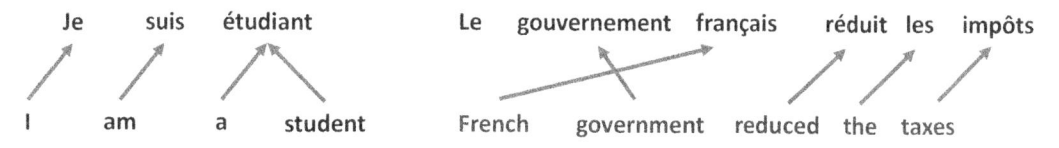

Figure 2.2 – Example of issues with alignment: one to many (left) and spurious word (right)

Attention mechanisms were initially described to solve the alignment problem, as well as to learn the relationships between the various parts of a text and the corresponding parts of the translated text.

The idea is that instead of passing the hidden state of RNNs, we pass contextual information that focuses only on the important parts of the sequence. During decoding (translation) for each token, we want to retrieve the corresponding and specific information in the other language. Attention determines which tokens in the input are important at that moment.

The first step is the alignment between the hidden state of the encoder (*h*) and the previous decoder output (*s*). The score function can be different: dot product or cosine similarity is most commonly used, but it can also be more complex functions such as the feedforward neural network layer. This step allows us to understand how relevant hidden state encoders are to the translation at that time. This step is conducted for all encoder steps.

$$(1) \quad e_{i,j} = score\left(s_{i-1}, h_j\right)$$

Right now though, we have a scalar representing the similarity between two vectors (*h* and *s*). All these scores are passed into the softmax function that squeezes everything between 0 and 1. This step also serves to assign relative importance to each hidden state.

$$(2) \quad a_{i,j} = softmax(e_{i,j}) = \frac{\exp(e_{i,j})}{\sum_{k=1}^{t} \exp(e_{i,k})}$$

Finally, we conduct a weighted sum of the various hidden states multiplied by the attention score. So, we have a fixed-length context vector capable of giving us information about the entire set of hidden states. In simple words, during translation, we have a context vector that is dynamically updated and tells us how much attention we should give to each part of the input sequence.

$$(3) \quad c_t = \sum_{j=1}^{T} a_{i,j} \cdot h_j$$

As you can see from the original article, the model pays different attention to the various words in the input during translation.

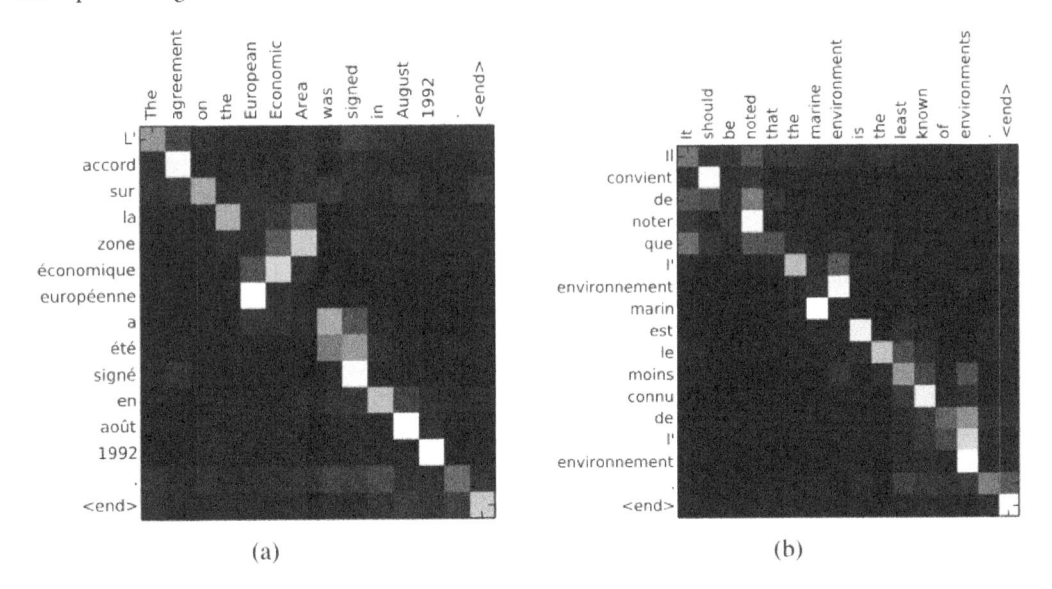

Figure 2.3 – Example of alignment between sentences after training the model with attention. Each pixel shows the attention weight between the source word and the target word. (https://arxiv.org/pdf/1409.0473)

In addition to solving alignment, the attention mechanism has other advantages:

- It reduces the vanishing gradient problem because it provides a shortcut to early states.
- It eliminates the bottleneck problem; the encoder can directly go to the source in the translation.
- It also provides interpretability because we know which words are used for alignment.
- It definitely improves the performance of the model.

Its success has given rise to several variants where the scoring function is different. One variant in particular, called **self-attention**, has the particular advantage that it extracts information directly from the input without necessarily needing to compare it with something else.

The insight behind self-attention is that if we want to look for a book for an essay on the French Revolution in a library (query), we don't need to read all the books to find a book on the history of France (value), we just need to read the coasts of the books (key). Self-attention, in other words, is a method that allows us to search within context to find the representation we need.

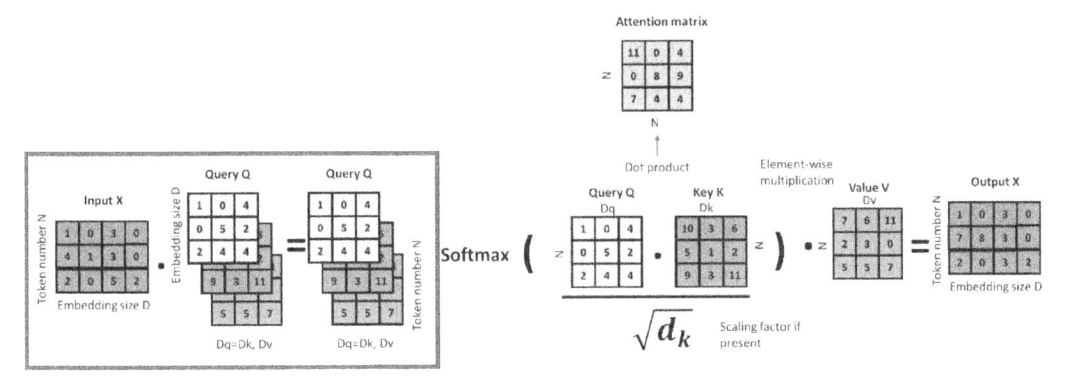

Figure 2.4 – Self-attention mechanism. Matrix dimensions are included; numbers are arbitrary

Transacting this for a model, given an input we want to conduct a series of comparisons between the various components of the sequence (such as tokens) to obtain an output sequence (which we can then use for various models or tasks). The self-attention equation is as follows:

$$Attention\ (Q, K, V) = softmax\left(\frac{Q \cdot K^T}{\sqrt{d_k}}\right) \cdot V$$

You can immediately see that it is derived from the original attention formula. We have the dot product to conduct comparisons, and we then exploit the `softmax` function to calculate the relative importance and normalize the values between 0 and 1. D is the size of the sequence; in other words, self-attention is also normalized as a function of the length of our sequence.

The next step is using `softmax`. Here's a little refresher on the function (how you calculate and how it is implemented more efficiently in Python):

$$y = \frac{e^{x_i}}{\sum_{i=1}^{i=n} e^{x_i}}$$

$$y = \begin{bmatrix} y_1 \\ y_2 \\ y_3 \end{bmatrix} = softmax(x) = f\left(\begin{bmatrix} x_1 \\ x_2 \\ x_3 \end{bmatrix}\right) = \begin{bmatrix} \frac{e^{x_1}}{e^{x_1} + e^{x_2} + e^{x_3}} \\ \frac{e^{x_2}}{e^{x_1} + e^{x_2} + e^{x_3}} \\ \frac{e^{x_3}}{e^{x_1} + e^{x_2} + e^{x_3}} \end{bmatrix}$$

$$python: y = \begin{bmatrix} y_1 \\ y_2 \\ y_3 \end{bmatrix} = softmax(x) = f\left(\begin{bmatrix} x_1 \\ x_2 \\ x_3 \end{bmatrix}\right) = \frac{[x_1\ x_2\ x_3]}{e^{x_1} + e^{x_2} + e^{x_3}} = \frac{e^x}{sum(e^x)}$$

As we saw in the previous chapter, the dot product can become quite wide as the length of the vectors increases. This can lead to inputs that are too large in the `softmax` function (this shifts the probability mass in `softmax` to a few elements and thus leads to small gradients). In the original article, they solved this by normalizing by the square root of *D*.

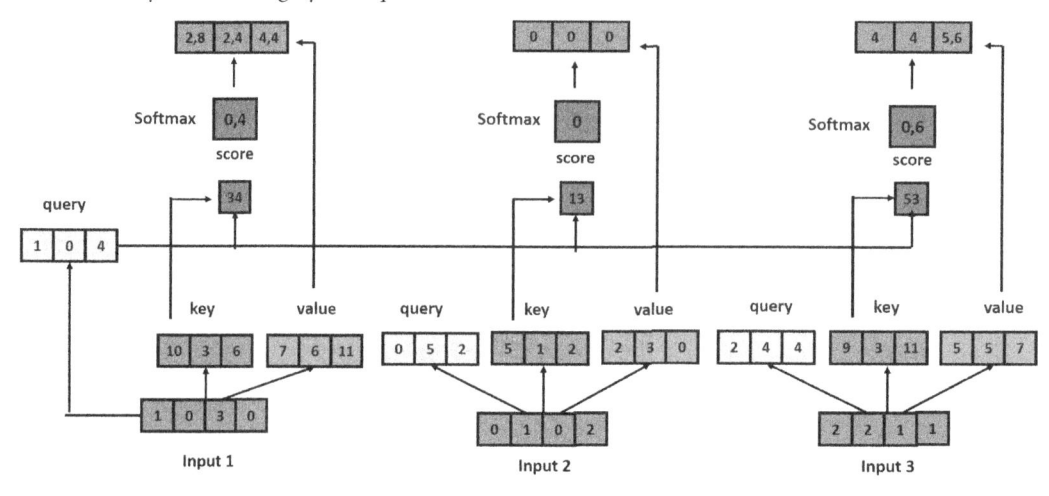

Figure 2.5 – Self-attention unrolled

The real difference is that we use three matrices of weights **Query (Q)**, **Key (K)**, and **Value (V)** that are initially randomly initialized. Q is the current focus of attention, while K informs the model about previous inputs, and V serves to extract the final input information. So, the first step is the multiplication of these three matrices with our input X (an array of vectors, of which each represents a token).

$$Q = X \cdot W^Q, \ K = X \cdot W^V, \ V = X \cdot W^V$$

The beauty of this system is that we can use it to extract more than one representation from the same input (after all, we can have multiple questions in a textbook). Therefore, since the operations are parallelizable, we can have multi-head attention. **Multi-head self-attention** enables the model to simultaneously capture multiple types of relationships within the input sequence. This is crucial because a single word in a sentence can be contextually related to several other words. During training, the K and Q matrices in each head specialize in modeling different kinds of relationships. Each attention head produces an output based on its specific perspective, resulting in *n* outputs for *n* heads. These outputs are then concatenated and passed through a final linear projection layer to restore the dimensionality backt to the original input size.

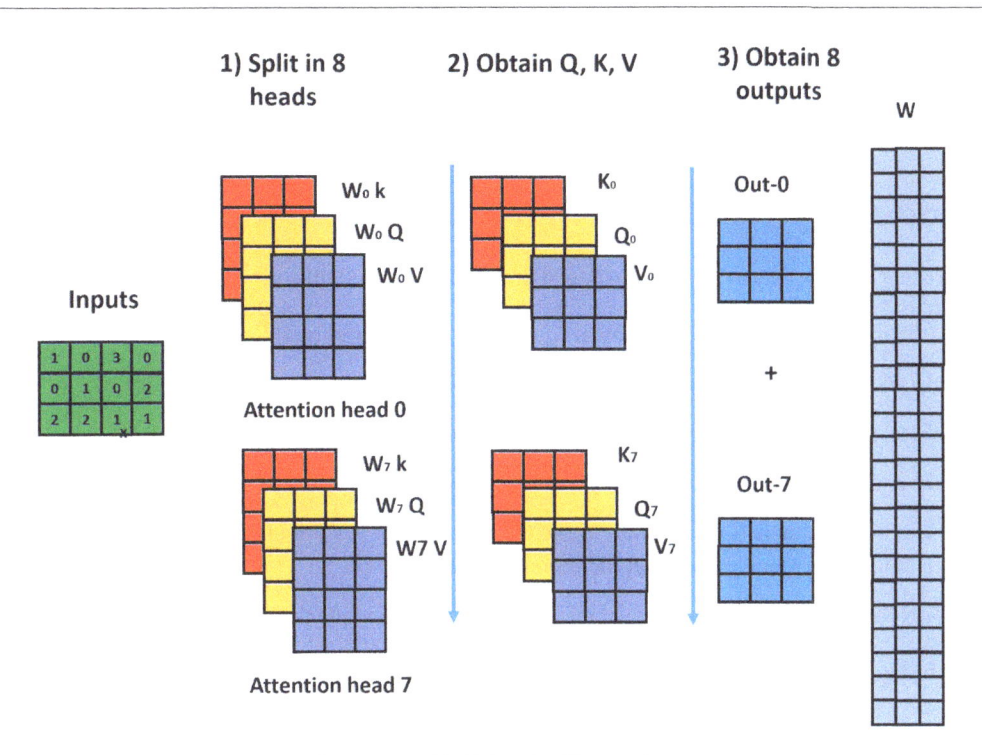

Figure 2.6 – Multi-head self-attention

Self-attention has several advantages:

- We can extract different representations for each input.
- We can conduct all these computations in parallel and thus with a GPU. Each head can be computed independently.
- We can use it in models that do not necessarily consist of an encoder and a decoder.
- We do not have to wait for different time steps to see the relationship between distant word pairs (as in RNN).
- However, it has a quadratic cost in function of the number of tokens N, and it has no inherent notion of order.

Self-attention is computationally expensive. It can be shown that, considering a sequence T and sequence length d, the computation cost and space is quadratic:

$$time = \mathcal{O}(T^2 + d) \quad space = \mathcal{O}(T^2 + Td)$$

They identified the dot product as the culprit. This computational cost is one of the problems of scalability (taking into account that multi-head attention is calculated in each block). For this reason, many variations of self-attention have been proposed to reduce the computational cost.

Despite the computational cost, self-attention has shown its capability, especially when several layers are stacked on top of each other. In the next section, we will discuss how this makes the model extremely powerful despite its computational cost.

Introducing the transformer model

Despite this decisive advance though, several problems remain in machine translation:

- The model fails to capture the meaning of the sentence and is still error-prone
- In addition, we have problems with words that are not in the initial vocabulary
- Errors in pronouns and other grammatical forms
- The model fails to maintain context for long texts
- It is not adaptable if the domain in the training set and test data is different (for example, if it is trained on literary texts and the test set is finance texts)
- RNNs are not parallelizable, and you have to compute sequentially

Considering these points, Google researchers in 2016 came up with the idea of eliminating RNNs altogether rather than improving them. According to the authors of the *Attention is All You Need* seminal article; all you need is a model that is based on multi-head self-attention. Before going into detail, the transformer consists entirely of stacked layers of multi-head self-attention. In this way, the model learns a hierarchical and increasingly sophisticated representation of the text.

The first step in the process is the transformation of text into numerical vectors (tokenization). After that, we have an embedding step to obtain vectors for each token. A special feature of the transformer is the introduction of a function to record the position of each token in the sequence (self-attention is not position-aware). This process is called **positional encoding**. The authors in the article use sin and cos alternately with position. This allows the model to know the relative position of each token.

$$PE_{(pos,2i)} = \sin\left(pos/1000^{2i/d}\right)$$

$$PE_{(pos,2i+1)} = \cos\left(pos/1000^{2i/d}\right)$$

In the first step, the embedding vectors are summed with the result of these functions. This is because self-attention is not aware of word order, but word order in a period is important. Thus, the order is directly encoded in the vectors it awaits. Note, though, that there are no learnable parameters in this function and that for long sequences, it will have to be modified (we will discuss this in the next chapter).

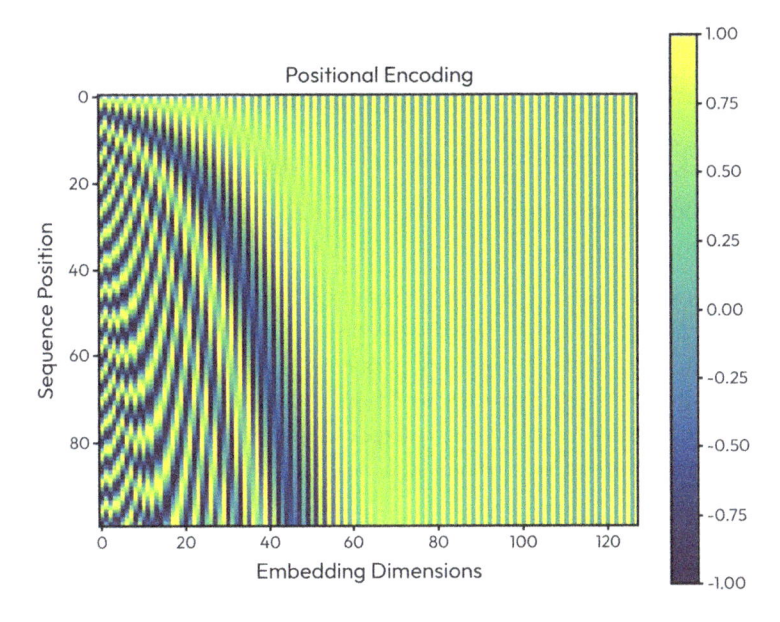

Figure 2.7 – Positional encoding

After that, we have a series of transformer blocks in sequence. The **transformer block** consists of four elements: multi-head self-attention, feedforward layer, residual connections, and layer normalization.

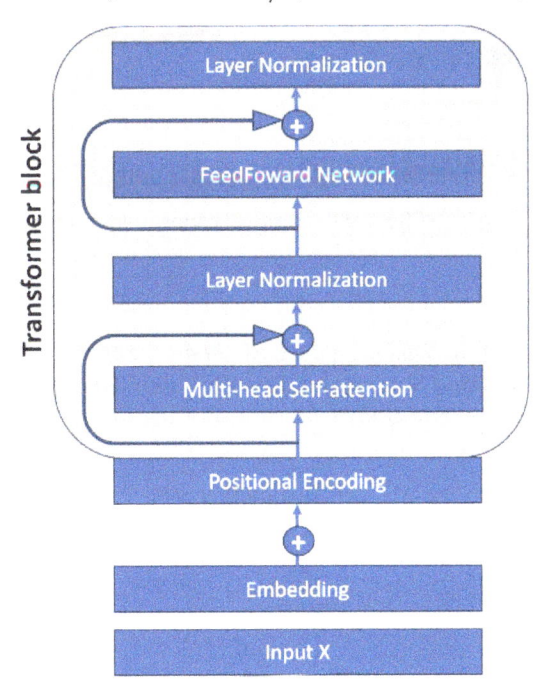

Figure 2.8 – Flow diagram of the transformer block

The feedforward layer consists of two linear layers. This layer is used to obtain a linear projection of the multi-head self-attention. The weights are identifiable for each position and are separated. It can be seen as two linear transformations with one ReLU activation in between.

$$FFN(x) = \max(0, x W_1 + b_1) W_2 + b_2$$

This adds a step of non-linearity to self-attention. The FFN layer is chosen because it is an easily parallelized operation.

Residual connections are connections that pass information between two layers without going through the intermediate layer transformation. Initially developed in convolutional networks, they allow a shortcut between layers and help the gradient pass down to the lower layers. In the transformer, blocks are present for both the attention layer and feedforward, where the input is summed with the output. Residual connections also have the advantage of making the loss surface smoother (this helps the model find a better minimum and not get stuck in a local loss). This powerful effect can be seen clearly in *Figure 2.9*:

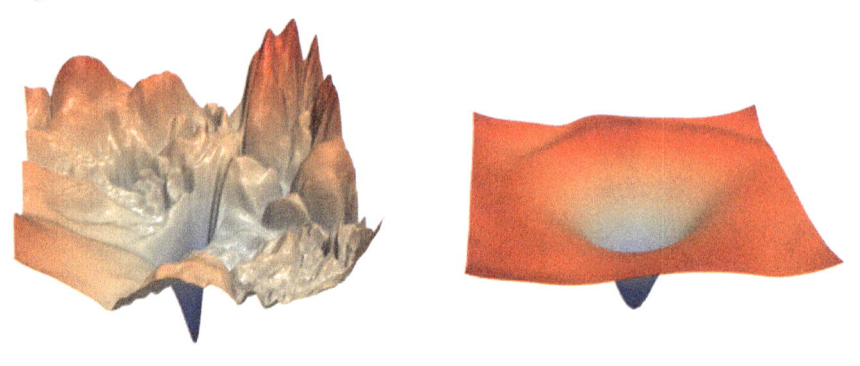

Loss landscape without residual   Loss landscape with residual

Figure 2.9 – Effect of the residual connections on the loss

> **Note**
>
> *Figure 2.9* is originally from *Visualizing the Loss Landscape of Neural Nets* by Hao Li, Zheng Xu, Gavin Taylor, Christoph Studer, and Tom Goldstein (`https://github.com/tomgoldstein/loss-landscape/tree/master`).

The residual connection makes the loss surface smoother, which allows the model to be trained more efficiently and quickly.

Layer normalization is a form of normalization that helps training because it keeps the hidden layer values in a certain range (it is an alternative to batch normalization). Having taken a single vector, it is normalized in a process that takes advantage of the mean and standard deviation. Having calculated the mean and standard deviation, the vector is scaled:

$$\mu = \frac{1}{d}\sum_{i=1}^{d} x_i \qquad \sigma = \sqrt{\frac{1}{d}\sum_{i=1}^{d}(x_i - \mu)^2}$$

$$\hat{x} = \frac{(x - \mu)}{\sigma}$$

In the final transformation, we exploit two parameters that are learned during training.

$$LayerNormalization = \gamma\hat{x} + \beta$$

There is a lot of variability during the training, and this can hurt the learning of the training. To reduce uninformative variability, we add this normalization step, thus normalizing the gradient as well.

At this point, we can assemble everything into a single block. Consider that after embedding, we have as input X a matrix of dimension $n \times d$ (with n being the number of tokens, and d the dimensions of the embedding). This input X goes into a transformer block and comes out with the same dimensions. This process is repeated for all transformer blocks:

$$H = LayerNorm(X + MultiHeadSelfAttention(X))$$

$$H = LayerNorm(H + FFN(H))$$

Some notes on this process are as follows:

- In some architectures, *LayerNorm* can be after the *FFN* block instead of before (whether it is better or not is still debated).
- Modern models have up to 96 transformer blocks in series, but the structure is virtually identical. The idea is that the model learns an increasingly complex representation of the language.
- Starting with the embedding of an input, self-attention allows this representation to be enriched by incorporating an increasingly complex context. In addition, the model also has information about the location of each token.
- Absolute positional encoding has the defect of overrepresenting words at the beginning of the sequence. Today, there are variants that consider the relative position.

Once we have "the bricks," we can assemble them into a functional structure. In the original description, the model was structured for machine translation and composed of two parts: an encoder (which takes the text to be translated) and a decoder (which will produce the translation).

The original transformer is composed of different blocks of transformer blocks and structures in an encoder and decoder, as you can see in *Figure 2.10*.

Figure 2.10 – Encoder-decoder structure

The decoder, like the encoder, is composed of an embedding, a positional encoder, and a series of transformer blocks. One note is that in the decoder, instead of self-attention, we have **cross-attention**. Cross-attention is exactly the same, only we take both elements from the encoder and the decoder (because we want to condition the generation of the decoder based on the encoder input). In this case, the queries come from the encoder and the rest from the decoder. As you can see from *Figure 2.11*, the decoder sequence can be of different sizes, but the result is the same:

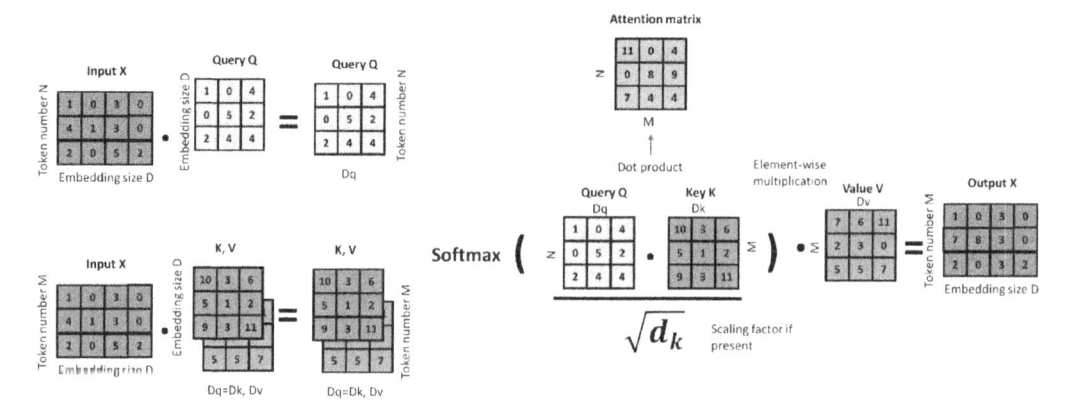

Figure 2.11 – Cross-attention

Input *N* comes from the encoder, while input *M* is from the decoder. In the figure, cross-attention is mixing information from the encoder and decoder, allowing the decoder to learn from the encoder.

Another note on the structure: in the decoder, the first self-attention has an additional mask to prevent the model from seeing the future.

This is especially true in the case of QT. In fact, if one wants to predict the next word and the model already knows what it is, we have data leakage. To compensate for this, we add a mask in which the upper-triangular portion is replaced with negative infinity: - ∞.

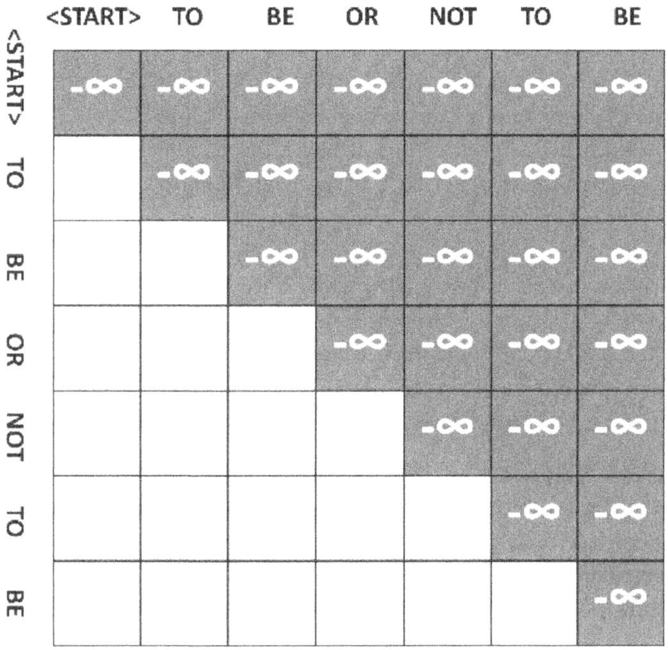

Figure 2.12 – Masked attention

The first transformer consisted of an encoder and decoder, but today there are also models that are either encoder-only or decoder-only. Today, for generative AI, they are practically all decoder-only. We have our model; now, how can you train a system that seems so complex? In the next section, we will see how to succeed at training.

Training a transformer

How do you train such a complex model? The answer to this question is simpler than you might think. The fact that the model can learn through multi-head self-attention complex and diverse relationships allows the model to be able to be flexible and able to learn complex patterns. It would be too expensive to build examples (or find them) to teach these complex relationships to the model.

So, we want a system that allows the model to learn these relationships on its own. The advantage is that if we have a large amount of text available, the model can learn without the need for us to curate the training corpus. Thanks to the advent of the internet, we have the availability of huge corpora that allow models to see text examples of different topics, languages, styles, and more.

Although the original model was a `seq2seq` model, later transformers (such as LLMs) were trained as language models, especially in a **self-supervised manner**. In language modeling, we consider a sequence of word s, and the probability of the next word in the sequence x is $P(w|h)$. This probability depends on the words up to that point. By the chain rule of the probability, we can decompose this probability:

$$P(w|h) = P(w_n|w_{1:n-1}) = \prod_{i=1}^{n} P(w_i|w_{1:i-1})$$

This allows us to calculate the conditional probability of a word from a sequence of previous words. The idea is that when we have enough text we can take a sequence such as **"to be or not to"** as input and have the model estimate the probability for the next word to be **"be,"** $P(be|to\ be\ or\ not\ to)$. Then after the transformer block sequence, we have a layer that conducts a linear projection and a **softmax layer** that generates the output. The previous sequence is called context; the context length of the first transformers was 512 tokens. The model generates an output, which is a probability vector of dimension V (the model vocabulary), also called a **logit vector**. The projection layer is called an **unembedder** (it does reverse mapping) because we have to go from a dimension N tokens x D embedding to 1 x V. Since the input and output of each transformer block are the same, we could theoretically eliminate blocks and attach an unembedder and softmax to any intermediate block. This allows us to better interpret the function of each block and its internal representation.

Once we have this probability vector, we can use self-supervision for training. We take a corpus of text (unannotated) and train the model to minimize the difference between the probability of the true word in the sequence and the predicted probability. To do this, we use **cross-entropy loss** (the difference between the predicted and true probability distribution). The predicted probability distribution is the logit vector, while the true one is a one-hot encoder vector where it is 1 for the next word in the sequence and 0 elsewhere.

$$L_{CE} = -\sum_{w \in V} y_t[w] \log \hat{y}_t[w]$$

In practice, it is simplified during training simply between the probability of the actual predicted word and 1. The process is iterative for each word in the word sequence (and is called teacher forcing). The final loss is the average over the entire sequence.

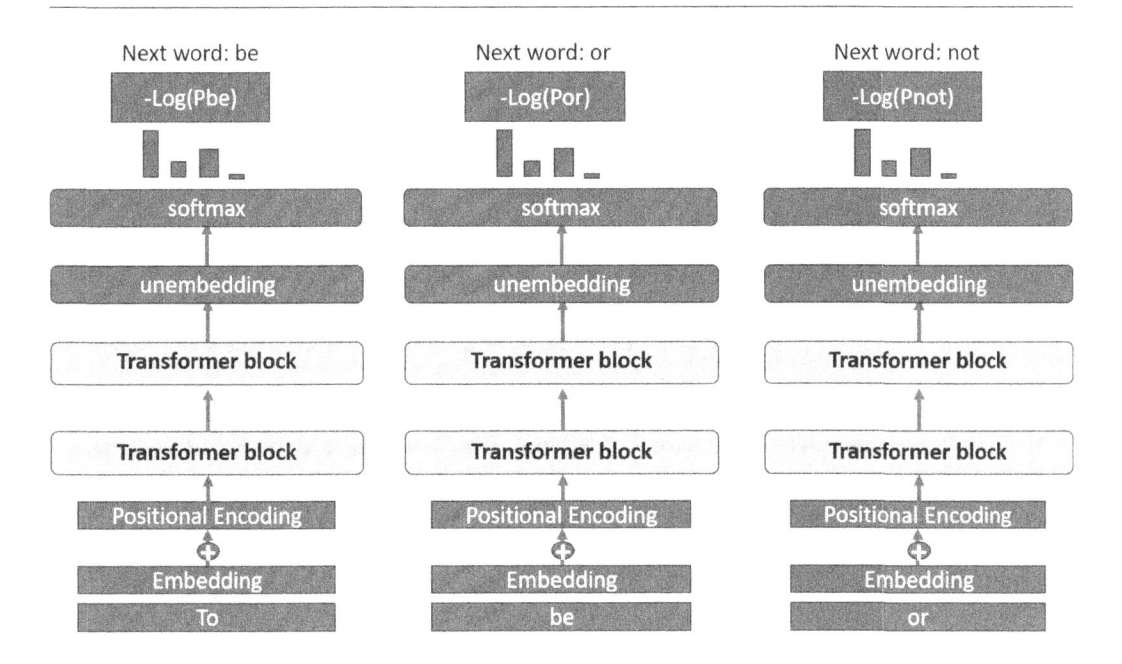

Figure 2.13 – Training of the transformer; the loss is the average of the loss of all the time steps

Since all calculations can be done in parallel in the transformer, we do not have to calculate word by word, but we fed the model with the whole sequence.

Once we have obtained a probability vector, we can choose the probability most (**greedy decoding**). Greedy decoding is formally defined as choosing the token with the highest probability at each time step:

$$w_t = argmax_{w \in V} P(w | w_{<t})$$

In fact, it is no longer used because the result is too predictable, generic, and repetitive. So, more sophisticated and less deterministic sampling methods are used. This sampling process is called decoding (or autoregressive generation or causal language modeling, since it is derived from previous word choice). This system, in the simplest version, is based either on generating the text of at most a predetermined sequence length, or as long as an end-of-sentence token (<EOS>) is selected.

We need to find a way to be able to select tokens while balancing both quality and diversity. A model that always chooses the same words will certainly have higher quality but will also be repetitive. There are different methods of doing the sampling:

- **Random sampling**: The model chooses the next token randomly. The sentences are strange because the model chooses rare or singular words.
- **Top-k sampling**: At each step, we sort the probabilities and choose the top k most likely words. We renormalize the probability and choose one at random.

- **Top-p sampling**: This is an alternative in which we keep only a percentage of the most likely words.
- **Temperature sampling**: Before `softmax`, we divide by a temperature parameter (between 0 and 1). The closer t is to 0, the closer the probability of the most likely words is to 1 (close to greedy sampling). In some cases, we can also have t greater than 1 when we want a less greedy approach.

So far, we have considered the fixed vocabulary and assumed that each token was a word. In general, once the model is trained, there might be some words that the model does not know to which a special token, <UNK>, is assigned. In transformers and LLMs afterward, a way was sought to solve the unknown word problem. For example, in the training set, we might have words such as *big*, *bigger*, and *small* but not *smaller*. *Smaller* would not be known by the model and would result in <UNK>. Depending on the training set, the model might have incomplete or outdated knowledge. In English, as in other languages, there are definite morphemes and grammatical rules, and we would like the tokenizer to be aware. To avoid too many <UNK> one solution is to think in terms of sub-words (tokens).

One of the most widely used is **Byte-Pair Encoding** (**BPE**). The process starts with a list of individual characters. The algorithm then scans the entire corpus and begins to merge the symbols that are most frequently found together. For example, we have **E** and **R**, and after the first scan, we add a new **ER** symbol to the vocabulary. The process continues iteratively to merge and create new symbols (longer and longer character strings). Typically, the algorithm stops when it has created N tokens (with N being a predetermined number at the beginning). In addition, there is a special end-of-word symbol to differentiate whether the token is inside or at the end of a word. Once the algorithm arrives at creating a vocabulary, we can segment the corpus with the tokenizer and for each subword, we assign an index corresponding to the index in the vocabulary.

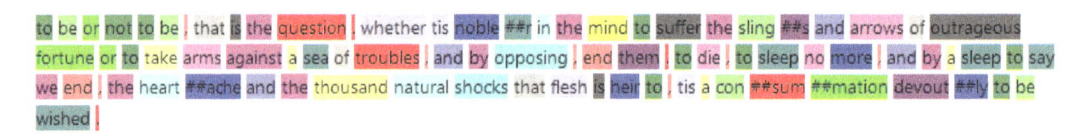

to be or not to be , that is the question , whether tis noble ##r in the mind to suffer the sling ##s and arrows of outrageous fortune or to take arms against a sea of troubles , and by opposing , end them , to die , to sleep no more , and by a sleep to say we end , the heart ##ache and the thousand natural shocks that flesh is heir to , tis a con ##sum ##mation devout ##ly to be wished ,

Figure 2.14 – Example of the results of tokenization

This approach generally causes common words to be present in the model vocabulary while rare words are split into subwords. In addition, the model also learns suffixes and prefixes, and considers the difference between *app* and the *app#* subword, representing a complete word and a subword (*app#* as a subword of *application*).

Exploring masked language modeling

Although the transformer was revolutionary, the popularization of the transformer in the scientific community is also due to the **Bidirectional Encoder Representations from Transformers** (**BERT**) model. This is because BERT was a revolutionary variant of the transformer that showed the capabilities of this type of model. BERT was revolutionary because it was already prospectively designed specifically for future applications (such as question answering, summarization, and machine translation). In fact, the original transformer analyzes the left-to-right sequence, so when the model encounters an entity, it cannot relate it to what is on the right of the entity. In these applications, it is important to have context from both directions.

What is the sentiment of this sentence? Does it put Bob in a good light?

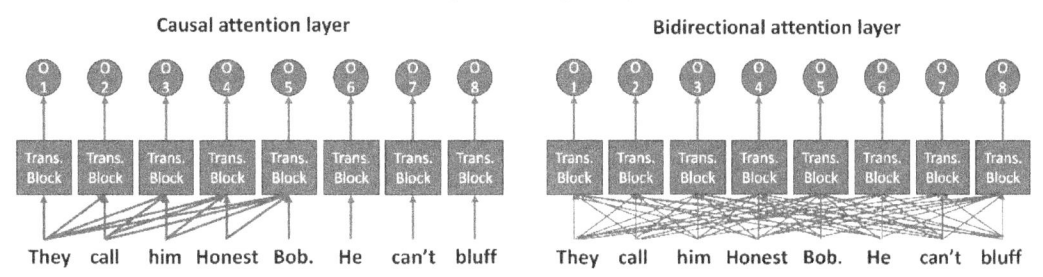

Figure 2.15 – Difference between a causal and bidirectional language model

Bidirectional encoders resolve this limitation by allowing the model to find relationships over the entire sequence. Obviously, we can no longer use a language model to train it (it will be too easy to identify the next word in the sequence when you already know the answer) but we have to find a way to be able to train a bidirectional model. For clarification, the model reads the entire sequence at once and, in this case, consists of the encoder only.

To try to minimize changes to the structure we use what is called the **Masked Language Model (MLM) objective**. Instead of predicting the next word in the sequence, we mask some tokens and the model has to use the rest of the sequence to predict them. Given the entire context (the model now has access to the entire sequence), BERT must predict the token that has been masked with a special token (usually called <MASK>). In the original training, they masked 15 % of the tokens randomly. Notice that, in this case, we do not mask the future because we want the model to be aware of the whole context. Also, to better separate the different sentences, we have a special token, [CLS], that signals the beginning of an input, and [SEP] to separate sentences in the input (for example, if we have a question and an answer). Otherwise, the structure is the same: we have an embedder, a position encoder, different transformer blocks, a linear projection, and a softmax. The loss is calculated in the same way; instead of using the next token, we use the masked token. The original article introduced two versions of BERT: BERT-BASE (12 layers, hidden size with d=768, 12 attention heads, and 110M total parameters) and BERT-LARGE (24 layers, hidden size with d=1024, 24 attention heads, and 340M total parameters).

MLM is a flexible approach because the idea is to corrupt the input and ask the model to rebuild. We can mask, but we can also reorder or conduct other transformations. The disadvantage of this method is that only 15 percent of the tokens are actually used to learn, so the model is highly inefficient.

The training is also highly flexible. For example, the model can be extended to **next sentence prediction**, where the task is to predict whether two pairs of sentences are related (paraphrase, coherence, and entailment). In this case, BERT was trained with training pairs of sentences positively related and unrelated sentences (we exploit the [SEP] token between sentences). The last layer is a softmax for sentence classification; we consider the loss over the categories. This shows how the system is flexible and can be adapted to different tasks.

One final clarification. Until 2024, it was always assumed that these models were not capable of generating text. In 2024, two studies showed that by adapting the model, you can generate text even with a BERT-like model. For example, in this study, they show that one can generate text by exploiting a sequence of [MASK] tokens.

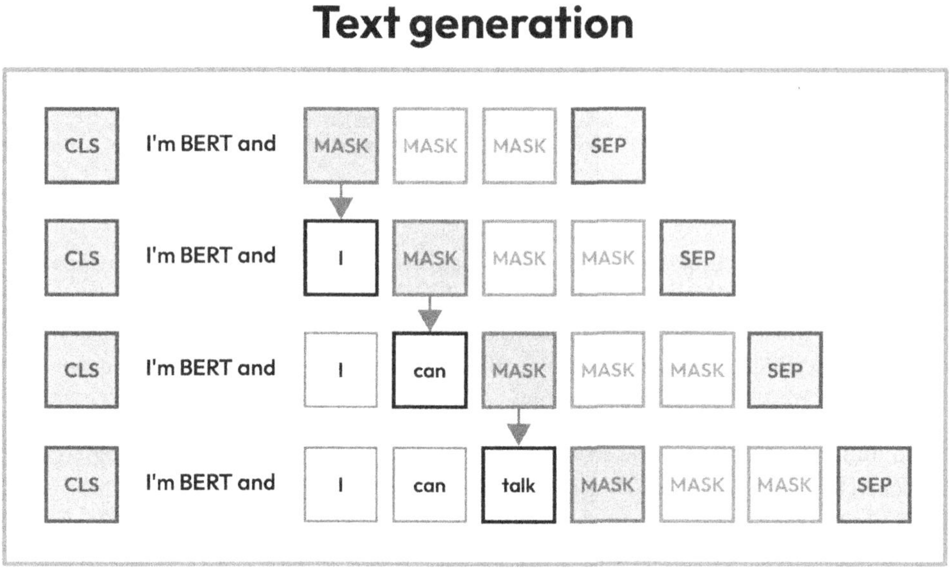

Text generation

Figure 2.16 – Text generation with MLM (https://arxiv.org/pdf/2406.04823)

Now that we have seen the two main types of training for a transformer, we can better explore what happens inside these models.

Visualizing internal mechanisms

We have seen the inner workings of the transformer, how it can be trained, and the main types of models. The beauty of attention is that we can visualize these relationships, and in this section, we will see how to do that. We can then visualize the relationships within the BERT attention head. As mentioned, in each layer, there are several attention heads and each of them learns a different representation of the input data. The color intensity indicates a greater weight in the attention weights (darker colors indicate weights that are close to 1).

We can do this using the BERTviz package:

```
head_view(attention, tokens, sentence_b_start)
```

Visualizing internal mechanisms 53

> **Important note**
>
> The visualization is interactive. The code is in the repository. Try running it using different phrases and exploring different relationships between different words in the phrases. The visualization allows you to explore the different layers in the model by taking advantage of the drop-down model. Hovering over the various words allows you to see the individual weights of the various heads.

This is the corresponding visualization:

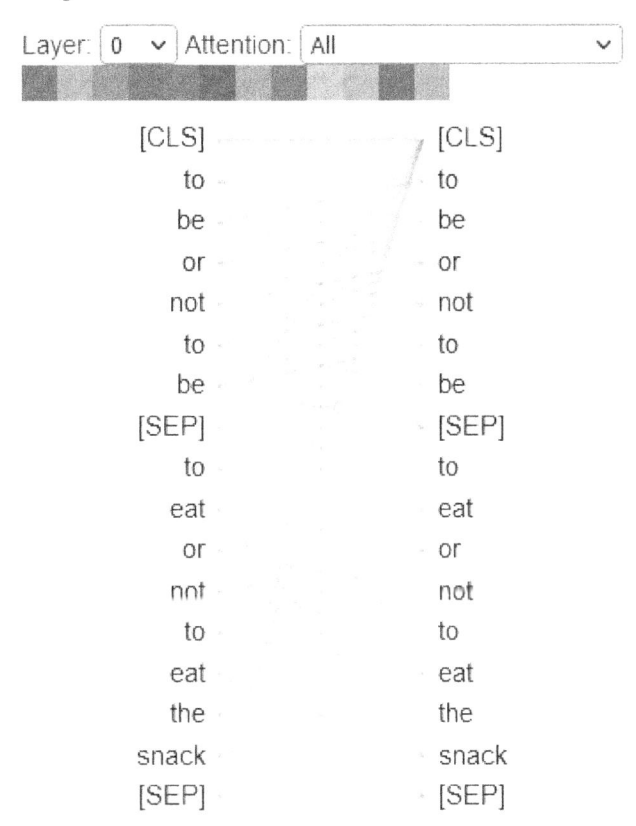

```
Layer: 0  v   Attention: All                        v

              [CLS]              [CLS]
               to                 to
               be                 be
               or                 or
               not                not
               to                 to
               be                 be
              [SEP]              [SEP]
               to                 to
               eat                eat
               or                 or
               not                not
               to                 to
               eat                eat
               the                the
              snack              snack
              [SEP]              [SEP]
```

Figure 2.17 – Visualization of attention between all words in the input

We can also view the various heads of the model at the same time. This allows us to see how the various heads model different relationships. This model has 12 heads for 12 layers, so the model has 144 attention heads and can therefore see more than 100 representations for the same sentences (this explains the capacity of a model). Moreover, these representations are not completely independent; information learned from earlier layers can be used by later layers:

```
model_view(attention, tokens, sentence_b_start)
```

> **Important note**
>
> The visualization is interactive. The code is in the repository. Try running it using different phrases and exploring different relationships. Here, we have the ensemble representation of the various attention heads. Observe how each head has a different function and how it models a different representation of the same inputs.

This is the corresponding visualization:

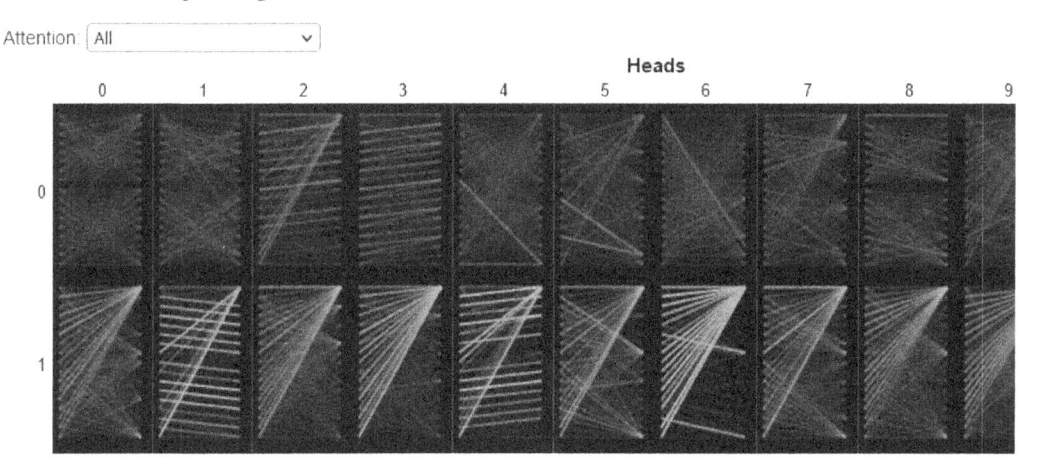

Figure 2.18 – Model view of the first two layers

Another model that has been fundamental to the current development of today's models is **Generative Pre-Trained Transformer 2** (**GPT-2**). GPT-2 is a causal (unidirectional) transformer pre-trained using language modeling on a very large corpus of ~40 GB of text data. GPT-2 was specifically trailed to predict the next token and to generate text with an input (it generates a token at a time; this token is then added to the input sequence to generate the next in an autoregressive process). In addition, this is perhaps the first model that has been trained with a massive amount of text. In addition, this model consists only of the decoder. GPT-2 is a family of models ranging from 12 layers of GPT-2 small to 48 layers of GPT-2 XL. Each layer consists of masked self-attention and a feed-forward neural network.

GPT-2 is generative and trained as a language model so we can give it an input judgment and observe the probability for the next token. For example, using "To be or not to" as input, the token with the highest probability is "be."

Visualizing internal mechanisms 55

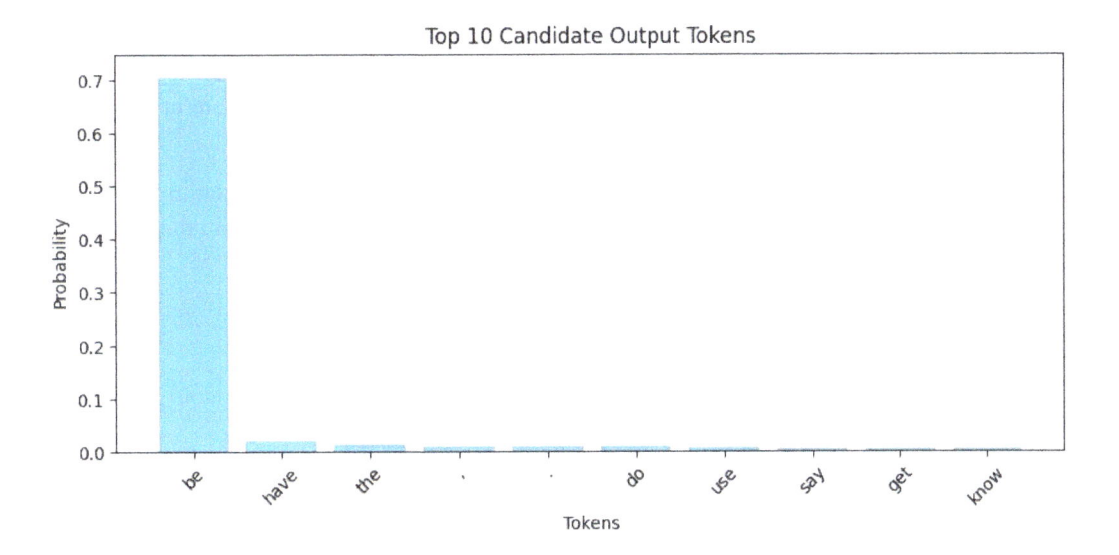

Figure 2.19 – Probabilities associated with the next token for the GPT-2 model when probed with the "To be or not to" input sequence

Sometimes, it may be necessary to understand which tokens are most important to the model to generate the next token. **Gradient X input** is a technique originally developed for convolutional networks; at a given time step, we take the output probabilities for each token, select the tokens with the highest probability, and compute the gradient with respect to the input up to the input tokens. This gives us the importance of each token to generate the next token in the sequence (the rationale is that small changes in the input tokens with the highest importance carry the largest changes in the output). In the figure, we can see the most important tokens for the next token in the sequence:

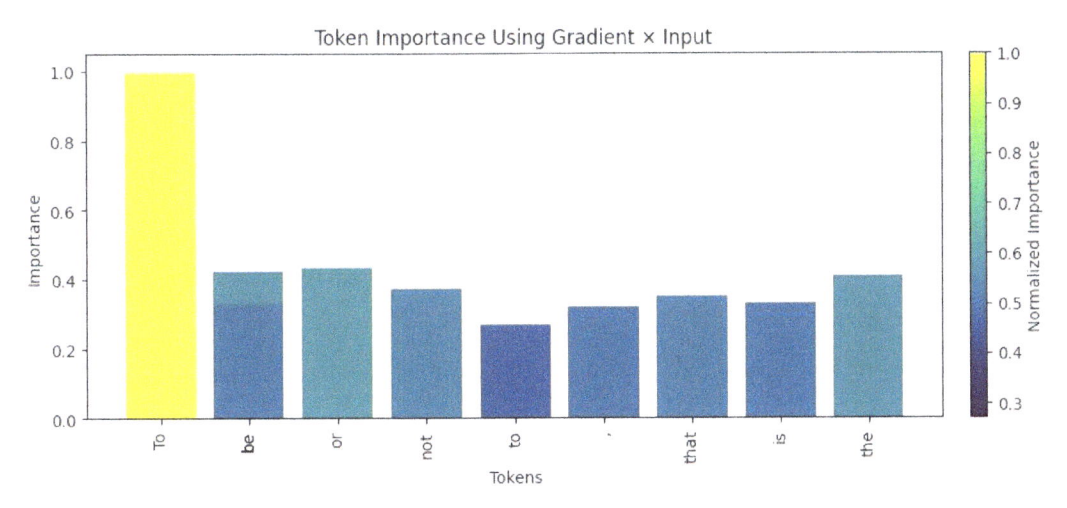

Figure 2.20 – Gradient X input for the next token in the sequence

As mentioned before, there is not only self-attention but also feedforward neural network, which plays an important role (it provides a significant portion of the parameters in the transformer block, about 66%). Therefore, several works have focused on examining the firings of neurons in layers (this technique was also originally developed for computer vision).

We can follow this activation after each layer, and for each of the tokens, we can monitor what their rank (by probability) is after each layer. As we can see, the model understands from the first layers which token is the most likely to continue a sequence:

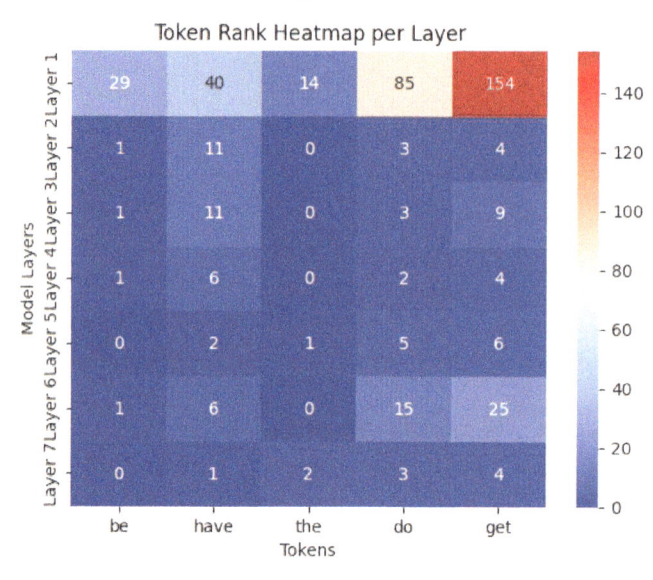

Figure 2.21 – Heatmap of the rank for the top five most likely tokens after each layer

Since there are a considerable number of neurons, it is complex to be able to observe them directly. Therefore, one way to investigate these activations is to first reduce dimensionality. To avoid negative activations, it is preferred to use **Non-Negative Matrix Factorization (NMF)** instead of **Principal Component Analysis (PCA)**. The process first captures the activation of neurons in the FFNN layers of the model and is then decomposed into some factors (user-chosen parameters). Next, we can interactively observe the factors with the highest activation when a token has been generated. What we see in the graph is the factor excitation for each of the generated tokens:

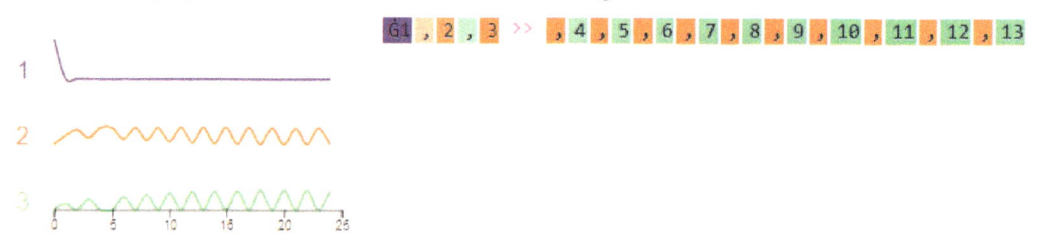

Figure 2.22 – NMF for the activations of the model in generating a sequence

We can also conduct this analysis for a single layer. This allows us to analyze interesting behaviors within the neurons of a layer (in the image layer 0 of the model). In this case, there are certain factors that focus on specific portions of the text (beginning, middle, and end). As we mentioned earlier, the model keeps track of word order in a sequence due to positional encoding, and this is reflected in activation. Other neurons, however, are activated by grammatical structures (such as conjunctions, articles, and so on). This indicates to us a specialization of what individual neurons in a pattern track and is one of the strength components of the transformer. By increasing the number of facts, we can increase the resolution and better understand what grammatical and semantic structures the pattern encodes in its activations. Moving forward in the structure of the model, we can see that layers learn a different representation.

Figure 2.23 – NMF for the activations of the model in generating a sequence

We have seen how to build a transformer and how it works. Now that we know the anatomy of a transformer, it is time to see it at work.

Applying a transformer

The power of a transformer lies in its ability to be able to learn from an enormous amount of text. During this phase of training (called **pre-training**), the model learns general rules about the structure of a language. This general representation can then be exploited for a myriad of applications. One of the most important concepts in deep learning is **transfer learning**, in which we exploit the ability of a model trained on a large amount of data for a task different from the one it was originally trained for. A special case of transfer learning is **fine-tuning**. Fine-tuning allows us to adapt the general knowledge of a model to a particular case. One way to do this is to add a set of parameters to a model (at the top of it) and then train these parameters by gradient descent for a specific task.

The transformer has been trained with large amounts of text and has learned semantic rules that are useful in understanding a text. We want to exploit this knowledge for a specific application such as sentiment classification. Instead of training a model from scratch, we can adapt a pre-trained transformer to classify our sentences. In this case, we do not want to destroy the internal representation of the model but preserve it. That is why, during fine-tuning, most of the layers are frozen (there is no update on the weights). Instead, we just train those one or two layers that we add to the top of the model. The idea is to preserve the representation and then learn how to use it for our specific task.

Those two added layers learn precisely how to use the internal representation of the model. To give a simple example, let's imagine we want to learn how to write scientific papers. To do that, we don't have to learn how to write in English again, just to adapt our knowledge to this new task.

In BERT, as we mentioned, we add a particular token to the beginning of each sequence: a [CLS] token. During training or even inference in a bidirectional transformer, this token waits for all others in the sequence (if you remember, all tokens are connected). This means that the final vector (the one in the last layer) is contextualized for each element in the sequence. We can then exploit this vector for a classification task. If we have three classes (for example, positive, neutral, and negative) we can take the vector for a sequence and use softmax to classify.

$$y = softmax(W h_{CLS})$$

The model was not originally trained for sequence classification, so we'd like to introduce a learnable matrix to enable class separation. This matrix represents a linear transformation and can alternatively be implemented using one or more linear layers. We then apply a cross-entropy loss function to optimize these weights. This setup follows the standard supervised learning paradigm, where labeled data is used to adapt the transformer to a specific task.

In this process, we have so far assumed that the remainder of the transformer's weights remain frozen. However, as observed in convolutional neural networks, even minimal fine-tuning of model parameters can enhance performance. Such updates are typically carried out with a very low learning rate.

We can adapt a pre-trained transformer for new tasks through supervised fine-tuning.

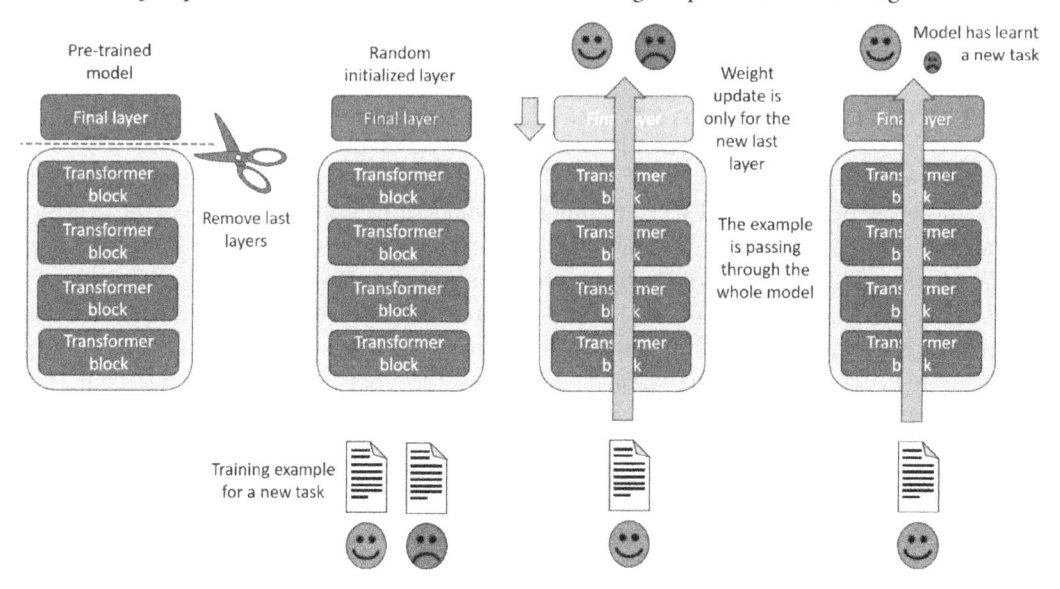

Figure 2.24 – Fine-tuning a transformer

In the first step, we are removing the final layer (this is specific to the original task). In the second step, we add a random initialized layer and gather training examples for the new task. During the fine-tuning, we are presenting the model with new examples (in this case, positive and negative reviews). While keeping the model frozen (each example is processed by the whole model in the forward pass), we update the weight only in the new layer (through backpropagation). The model has now learned the new task.

Conducting finetuning with Hugging Face is a straightforward process. We can use a model such as distill-BERT (a distilled version of BERT) with a few lines of code and the dataset we used in the previous chapter. We need to prepare the dataset and tokenize it (so that it can be used with a transformer). Hugging Face then allows with a simple wrapper that we can train the model. The arguments for training are stored in `TrainingArguments`:

```
training_args = TrainingArguments(
    output_dir='./results',
    num_train_epochs=3,
    per_device_train_batch_size=8,
    per_device_eval_batch_size=16
    warmup_steps=500,
    weight_decay=0.01,
    logging_dir='./logs',
    logging_steps=10,
    evaluation_strategy="epoch"
)

trainer = Trainer(
    model=model,
    args=training_args,
    train_dataset=train_dataset,
    eval_dataset=val_dataset
)
trainer.train()
```

> **Important note**
> Notice that the process is very similar to training a neural network. In fact, the transformer is a deep learning model; for the training, we are using similar hyperparameters.

In this case, we used only a small fraction of the reviews. The beauty of fine-tuning is that we need only a few examples to have a similar (if not better) performance than a model trained from scratch.

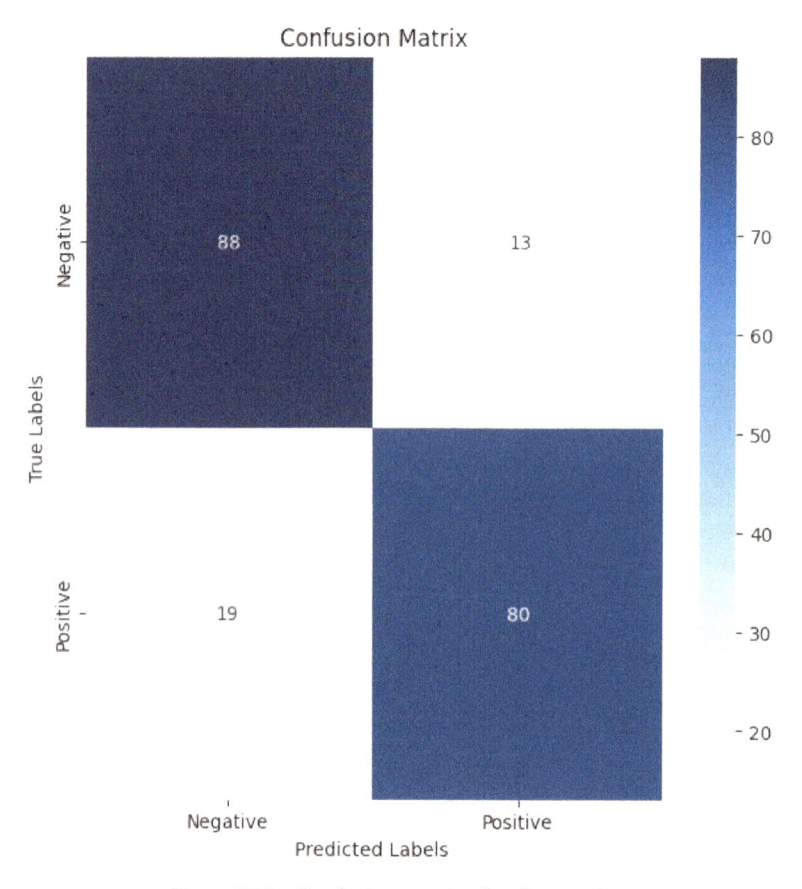

Figure 2.25 – Confusion matrix after fine-tuning

BERT's training was done on 64 TPUs (special hardware for tensor operations) for four days; this is beyond the reach of most users. In contrast, fine-tuning is possible either on a single GPU or on a CPU. As a result, BERT achieved state-of-the-art performance upon its release across a wide array of tasks, including paraphrase detection, question answering, and sentiment analysis. Hence, several variants such as **RoBERTa** and **SpanBERT** (in this case, we mask an entire span instead of a single token with better results) or adapted to specific domains such as **SciBERT** were born. However, encoders are not optimal for generative tasks (because of mask training) while decoders are.

To conduct machine translation, the original transformer consisted of an encoder and a decoder. A model such as GPT-2 only has a decoder. We can conduct fine-tuning in the same way as seen before, we just need to construct the dataset in an optimal way for a model that is constituted by the decoder alone. For example, we can take a dataset in which we have English and French sentences and build a dataset for finetuning as follows: `<sentence in English>` followed by a special `<to-fr>` token and then the `<sentence in French>`. The same approach can be used to teach summarization to a model, where we insert a special token meaning summarization. The model is fine-tuned by conducting the next token prediction (language modeling).

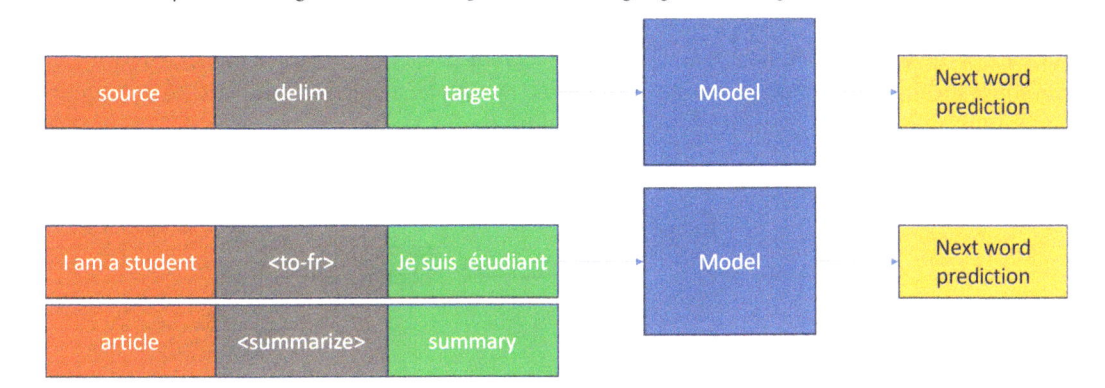

Figure 2.26 – Fine-tuning of a decoder-only model

Another way to exploit the learned knowledge of a model is to use **knowledge distillation**. In the previous section, we used distillGPT-2 which is a distilled version of GPT-2. A distilled model captures knowledge from a much larger model without losing significant performance but is much more manageable. Models that are trained with a large amount of text learn a huge body of knowledge. All this knowledge and skill is often redundant when we need a model for some specific task. We are interested in having a model that is very capable for a task, but without wanting to deal with a model of billions of parameters. In addition, sometimes we do not have enough examples for a model to learn the task from scratch. In this case, we can extract knowledge from the larger model.

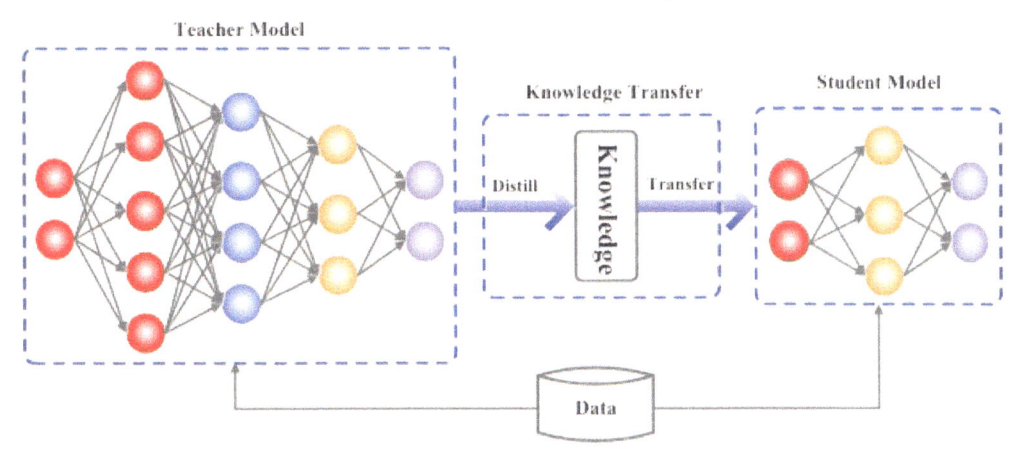

Figure 2.27 – Generic teacher-student framework for knowledge distillation
(https://arxiv.org/pdf/2006.05525)

Knowledge distillation can be seen as a form of compression, in which we try to transfer knowledge from a trained "teacher" model with many parameters to a "student" model with fewer parameters. The student model tries to mimic the teacher model and achieve the same performances as the teacher model in a task. In such a framework, we have three components: the models, knowledge, and algorithm. The algorithm can exploit either the teacher's logits or intermediate activations. In the case of the logits, the student tries to mimic the predictions of the teacher model, so we try to minimize the difference between the logits produced by the teacher and the student. To do this, we use a distillation loss that allows us to train the student model.

Response-Based Knowledge Distillation

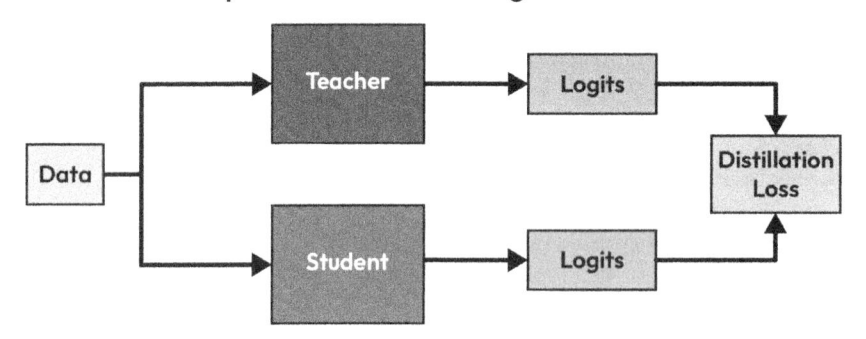

Figure 2.28 – Teacher-student framework for knowledge distillation training (https://arxiv.org/pdf/2006.05525)

For knowledge distillation, the steps are also similar. The first step is data preprocessing. For each model, you must remember to choose the model-specific tokenizer (although the one from GPT-2 is the most widely used many models have different tokenizers). We must then conduct fine-tuning of a model on our task (there is no model that is specific to classify reviews). This model will be our teacher. The next step is to train a student model. We can also use a pre-trained model that is smaller than the teacher (this allows us to be able to use a few examples to train it).

One important difference is that we now have a specific loss for knowledge distillation. This distillation loss calculates the loss between the teacher's logits and the student's logits. This function typically uses the Kullback-Leibler divergence loss to calculate the difference between the two probability distributions (Kullback-Leibler divergence is really a measure of the difference between two probability distributions). We can define it as follows:

```
def distillation_loss(outputs_student, outputs_teacher,
                 temperature=2.0):
    log_prob_student = F.log_softmax(
        outputs_student / temperature, dim=-1)
    prob_teacher = F.softmax(
        outputs_teacher / temperature, dim=-1)
    loss = KLDivLoss(reduction='batchmean')(
```

```
            log_prob_student, prob_teacher)
    return loss
```

At this point, we just have to have a way to train our system. In this case, the teacher will be used only in inference while the student model will be trained. We will use the teacher's logits to calculate the loss:

```
def train_epoch(model, dataloader, optimizer, device,
                teacher_model, temperature=2.0):
    model.train()
    total_loss = 0
    for batch in tqdm(dataloader, desc="Training"):
        inputs = {k: v.to(device)
                  for k, v in batch.items()
                  if k in ['input_ids', 'attention_mask']}
        with torch.no_grad():
            outputs_teacher = teacher_model(**inputs).logits
        outputs_student = model(**inputs).logits
        loss = distillation_loss(
            outputs_student, outputs_teacher, temperature)
        optimizer.zero_grad()
        loss.backward()
        optimizer.step()
        total_loss += loss.item()
    return total_loss / len(dataloader)
```

As can be seen in the following figure, the performance of the student model is similar to the teacher model:

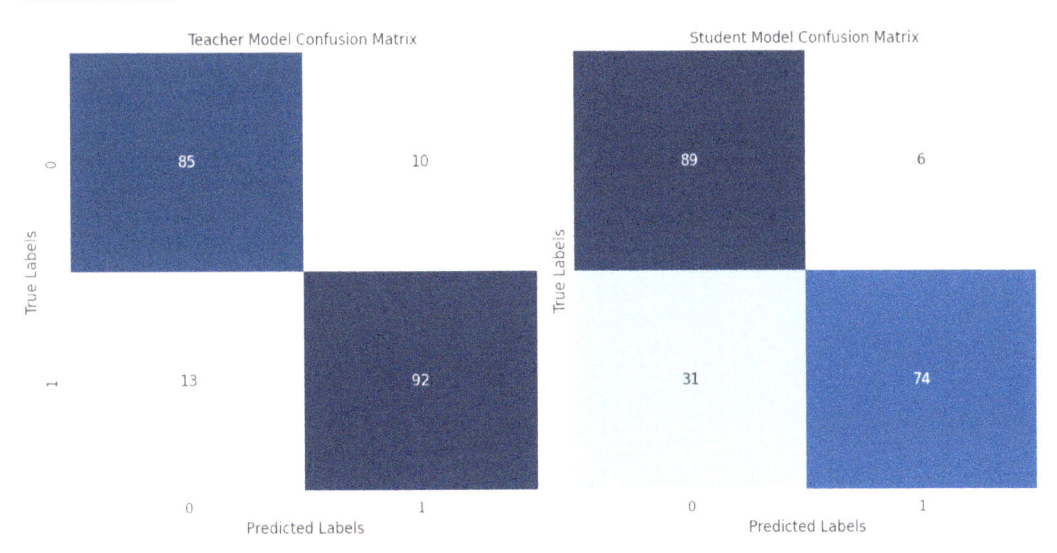

Figure 2.29 – Confusion matrix for the teacher and student model

Fine-tuning and knowledge distillation allow us to be able to use a transformer for any supervised task. Fine-tuning allows us to work with datasets that are small (and where there are often too few examples to train a model from scratch). Knowledge distillation, on the other hand, allows us to get a smaller model (but performs as well as a much larger one) when the computational cost is the limit. By taking advantage of these techniques, we can tackle any task.

Summary

In this chapter, we discussed the transformer, the model that revolutionized NLP and artificial intelligence. Today, all models that have commercial applications are derivatives of the transformer, as we learned in this chapter. Understanding how it works on a mechanistic level, and how the various parts (self-attention, embedding, tokenization, and so on) work together, allows us to understand the limitations of modern models. We saw how it works internally in a visual way, thus exploring the motive of modern artificial intelligence from multiple perspectives. Finally, we saw how we can adapt a transformer to our needs using techniques that leverage prior knowledge of the model. Now we can repurpose this process with virtually any dataset and any task.

Learning how to train a transformer will allow us to understand what happens when we take this process to scale. An LLM is a transformer with more parameters and that has been trained with more text. This leads to emergent properties that have made it so successful, but both its merits and shortcomings lie in the elements we have seen.

In *Chapter 3*, we will see precisely how to obtain an LLM from a transformer. What we have learned in this chapter will allow us to see how this step comes naturally.

3
Exploring LLMs as a Powerful AI Engine

In the previous chapter, we saw the structure of a transformer, how it is trained, and what makes it so powerful. The transformer is the seed of this revolution in **natural language processing** (NLP), and today's **large language models** (LLMs) are all based on transformers trained at scale. In this chapter, we will see what happens when we train huge transformers (more than 100 billion parameters) with giant datasets. We will focus on how to enable this training at scale, how to fine-tune similar modern ones, how to get more manageable models, and how to extend them to multimodal data. At the same time, we will also see what the limitations of these models are and what techniques are used to try to overcome these limitations.

In this chapter, we'll be covering the following topics:

- Discovering the evolution of LLMs
- Instruction tuning, fine-tuning, and alignment
- Exploring smaller and more efficient LLMs
- Exploring multimodal models
- Understanding hallucinations and ethical and legal issues
- Prompt engineering

Technical requirements

Most of this code can be run on a CPU, but it is preferable to run it on a GPU. The code is written in PyTorch and uses standard libraries for the most part (PyTorch, Hugging Face Transformers, and so on). The code can be found on GitHub: `https://github.com/PacktPublishing/Modern-AI-Agents/tree/main/chr3`.

Discovering the evolution of LLMs

An LLM is a transformer (although different architectures are beginning to emerge today). In general, an LLM is defined as a model that has more than 10 billion parameters. Although this number may seem arbitrary, some properties emerge with scale. These models are designed to understand and generate human language, and over time, they have acquired the ability to generate code and more. To achieve this beyond parameter size, they are trained with a huge amount of data. Today's LLMs are almost all trained on **next-word prediction** (**autoregressive language modeling**).

Parameter growth has been motivated in the transformer field by different aspects:

- **Learnability**: According to the scaling law, more parameters should lead to greater capabilities and a greater understanding of nuances and complexities in the data
- **Expressiveness**: The model can express more complex functions, thus increasing the ability to generalize and reducing the risk of overfitting
- **Memory**: A larger number of parameters allows for internalizing more knowledge (information, entities, differences in topics)

In the next subsections, we will discuss in detail all these elements to explain what is happening in the transition from the transformer to the LLM.

The scaling law

It may seem surprising that such large models are trained with such a simple task as **language modeling**. Many practical **natural language** tasks can be represented as next-word prediction. This flexibility allows us to use LLMs in different contexts. For example, sentiment analysis can be cast as a next-word prediction. The sentence *"The sentiment of the sentence: 'I like Pizza' is"* can be used as input for an LLM, and we can extract the probability for the next token being *positive* or *negative*. We can then assign the sentiment depending on which of the two has the higher probability. Notice how this probability is a function of context:

P(positive| *The sentiment of the sentence: 'I like Pizza' is*)

P(negative| *The sentiment of the sentence: 'I like Pizza' is*)

Similarly, we can use the same approach for other tasks. **Question answering** (**QA**) with an LLM can be thought of as generating the probability of the right answer given the question. In text summarization, we want to generate given the original context:

QA: P(answer| question)

Text summarization: P(summary|original article)

In the following diagram, we can see that using language modeling, we can solve almost any task. For example, here, the answer is the most probable token given the previous sequence (the question):

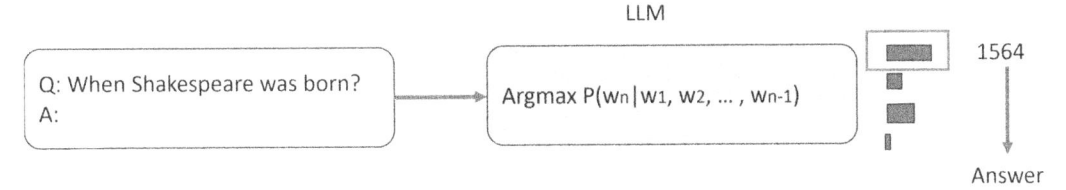

Figure 3.1 – Rephrasing of any task as LM

What we need is a dataset large enough for the model to both learn knowledge and use that knowledge for tasks. For this, specific datasets are assembled for training an LLM. These datasets typically consist of billions of words obtained from various sources (internet, books, articles, GitHub, different languages, and so on). For example, **GPT-3** was trained with Common Crawl (web crawl data, 410 billion tokens), Books1 and Books2 (book corpora, 12 billion and 55 billion tokens, respectively), and Wikipedia (3 billion tokens). Such diversity provides specific knowledge but also examples of tasks.

In parallel with the growth of training datasets (today, we are talking about more than a trillion tokens), the number of parameters has grown. The number of parameters in a transformer depends on three factors:

- **Embedding layer**: The number of parameters on the size of the vector and the vocabulary (which, especially for multi-language models, can be very large). Attention mechanisms are the heaviest component and hold the most parameters.

- **Self-attention mechanism**: This component includes multiple weight matrices that can grow in size with context length. Also, there can be multiple heads per single self-attention.

- **Depth**: Transformers are composed of multiple transformer blocks, and increasing the number of these blocks directly adds more parameters to the model.

GPT-3 and other studies have shown that the performance of LLMs depends mainly on three factors: model size (number of parameters), data size (the size of the training dataset), and computing size (amount of computing). So, in theory, to increase the performance of our model, we should enlarge the model (add layers or attention heads), increase the size of the pre-training dataset, and train it for more epochs. These factors have been related by OpenAI with the so-called **scaling law**. From a model with a number of parameters N, a dataset D, and computing amount C, if two parameters are constant, the loss L is the following:

$$L(N) = \left(\frac{N_c}{N}\right)^{a_N} \quad L(D) = \left(\frac{D_c}{D}\right)^{a_D} \quad L(C) = \left(\frac{C_c}{C}\right)^{a_C}$$

This is represented visually in the following diagram:

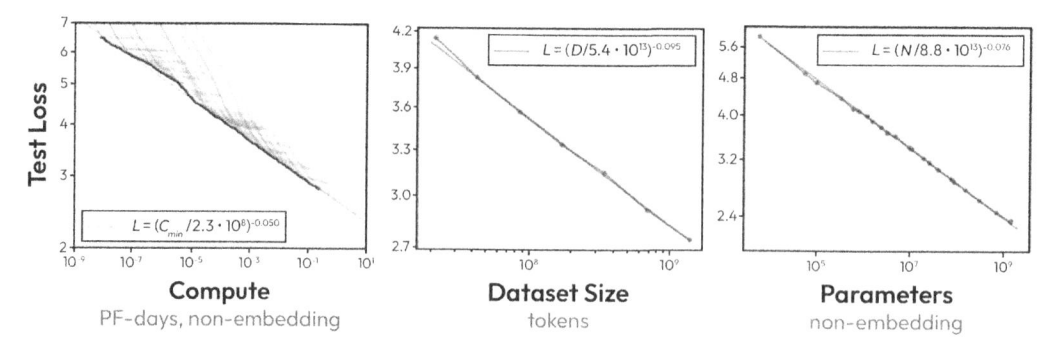

Figure 3.2 – Language modeling performance improves smoothly with the increase of model size, dataset size, and amount of computing (https://arxiv.org/pdf/2001.08361)

The loss is, in this case, the cross-entropy loss. In successive studies, OpenAI has shown that this loss can be decomposed into **irreducible loss** (which cannot be eliminated because it is related to data entropy) and reducible loss. This scaling law, in other words, allows us to calculate the desired performance of the model before training it. We can decide whether to invest more in enlarging the model or the dataset to reduce the loss (improve performance). However, these constants are dependent on the architecture and other training choices:

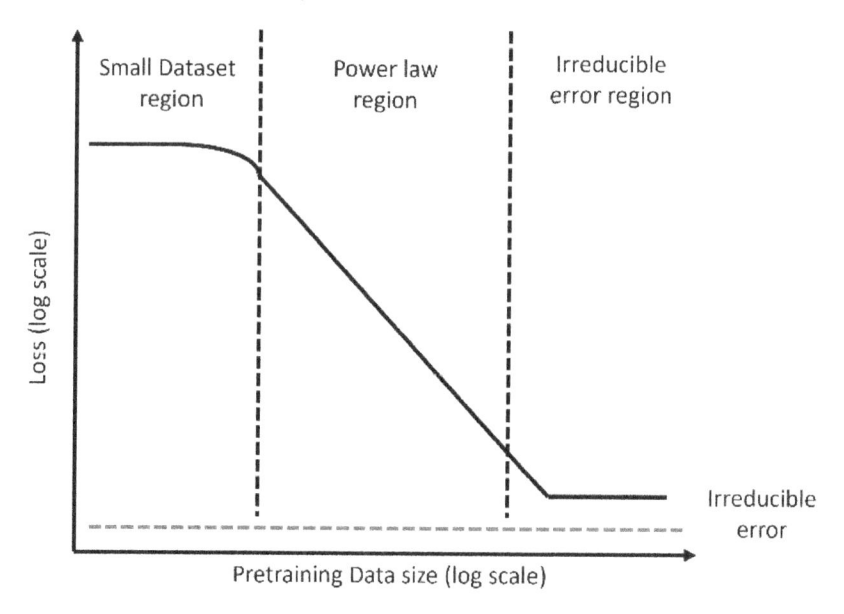

Figure 3.3 – Scaling law for an LLM

Although this scaling law has been taken for granted, the reality is more nuanced than it seems. According to DeepMind's Chinchilla (https://arxiv.org/abs/2203.15556), performance depends much more on the number of tokens than OpenAI believes. So, LLMs would currently be underfitted because they are trained with fewer tokens than expected. Meta's Llama also states that not just any tokens will do, but they must be of quality. So, not all tokens count the same, and according to other authors, using tokens produced by other models is just a more sophisticated form of distillation. In other words, to train a model at its best, you need a large amount of tokens, and they should be preferentially produced by humans and not synthetics. Different studies showed the potential risk of the model collapsing when trained with synthetic data. In several cases, it has been shown that the model, when trained with synthetic data, has a substantial decrease in performance (**model collapse**) or may forget some of the skills it has learned (**catastrophic forgetting**).

In any case, the scaling law is of great interest because it allows us to experiment with different architectures and variants on smaller models and then scale the model and training until the desired performance is achieved. A model with more than 100 billion parameters is expensive to train (in terms of architecture, time, and money), so it is better to experiment with a small proxy model and then leverage what has been learned for training the larger model. Also, training such a large model can encounter issues (such as training spikes), and being able to predict performance with an accurate scaling law is an active area of research.

This scaling law also monitors performance only in terms of loss. As mentioned previously, many tasks can be defined in terms of language modeling (LM), so intuitively, better performance in LM also means better performance in downstream tasks. Today, however, we try to create scaling laws that are instead specific to performance in some desired tasks (if we want a model specifically trained as a code assistant, we are more interested in its performance in these tasks than in its overall performance).

Emergent properties

Emergent properties of a model are the main justification for why we have gone from 1 billion parameters to over 100 billion. Emergent abilities are defined as properties that are not present in a small model but emerge in a large model. The second characteristic is that they emerge abruptly at a certain scale. In other words, a model has random performances in a certain ability until they emerge when a certain size is reached. These properties cannot be predicted beforehand but only observed at a certain scale, called the **critical scale**. After this critical size, performance increases linearly with the increase in size. Then, the model goes from near-zero performance to near-state-of-the-art after a certain critical point, thus showing a discontinuous rhythm. This process is also called phase transition. It is like a child who grows up appearing to be unable to speak, then beyond a certain age begins to articulate words, and then their skills grow linearly over time.

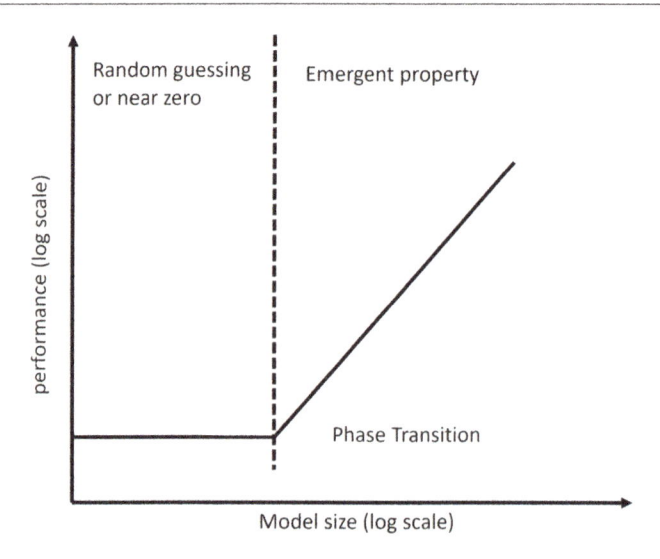

Figure 3.4 – Example of an emergent property in an LLM

Typically, these skills are related to complex skills such as mathematical reasoning or multistep processes. The fact that they emerge only beyond a certain scale justified the growth of such models, with the hope that beyond a certain scale, other properties would appear:

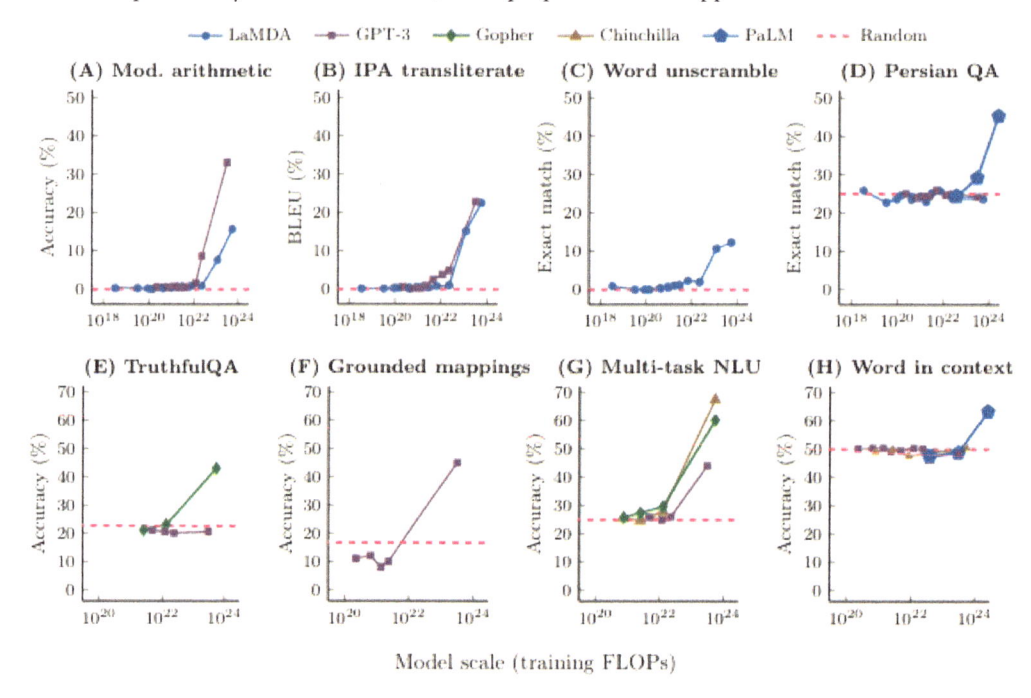

Figure 3.5 – Examples of emergent properties in different LLM families
(https://arxiv.org/pdf/2206.07682)

These properties do not all emerge at the same model size. Some properties would emerge beyond 10 billion (arithmetic computation), beyond 100 billion (self-evaluation, **figure-of-speech** (**FoS**) detection, logical deduction, and so on), and others even beyond 500 billion (causal judgment, geometric shapes, and so on).

For the authors of *Emergent Abilities of Large Language Models* (`https://arxiv.org/pdf/2206.07682`), reasoning tasks (especially those involving multiple steps) are difficult for LMs. These capabilities would appear naturally after 100 billion parameters. Similarly, beyond this threshold, the model is capable of understanding and following instructions (instruction following) without necessarily giving it examples of how to follow them. From this, it follows that larger models would be capable of executing programs (coding ability).

Interest in these emergent properties has cooled, however, because subsequent studies question them. LLMs do indeed exhibit these capabilities, but according to further studies, it would simply be more noticeable once the LLM has reached a certain performance limit. Moreover, it seems that success in these tasks is measured poorly.

Context length

LLMs process text in chunks, a fixed context window of a specific number of tokens. The size of this context length defines how much information they can process at a given time. The greater the context length, the more information a model can handle at a given time. Similarly, the computational cost grows quadratically. So, a model with a context length of 4,096 tokens needs to do 64 times more computation than one of 512. A longer context length allows for capturing long-range dependencies in a text, and this is related to performance in specific tasks:

- **Document summarization**: More context allows for more consistent and concise summarization, allowing for better capture of information in the document and its relationships. The model captures entities and what they are related to in the entire document.
- **QA**: The model can find complex relationships that underlie the right answer. Also, in multi-turn questions, the model is aware of previous answers and questions.
- **Language translation**: The model better preserves context, especially if there are long documents to be translated (especially if there are complex nuances). Bigger context lengths help with technical documents, technical jargon, polysemic items, and acronyms.
- **Conversational AI**: The model can conduct better tracking of the entire conversation.

As we can see in the following figure, the larger the context length, the more data the model can access in one prompt. Only one review can be seen by the model with a context length of 512, while a model with a larger context window can analyze hundreds of them:

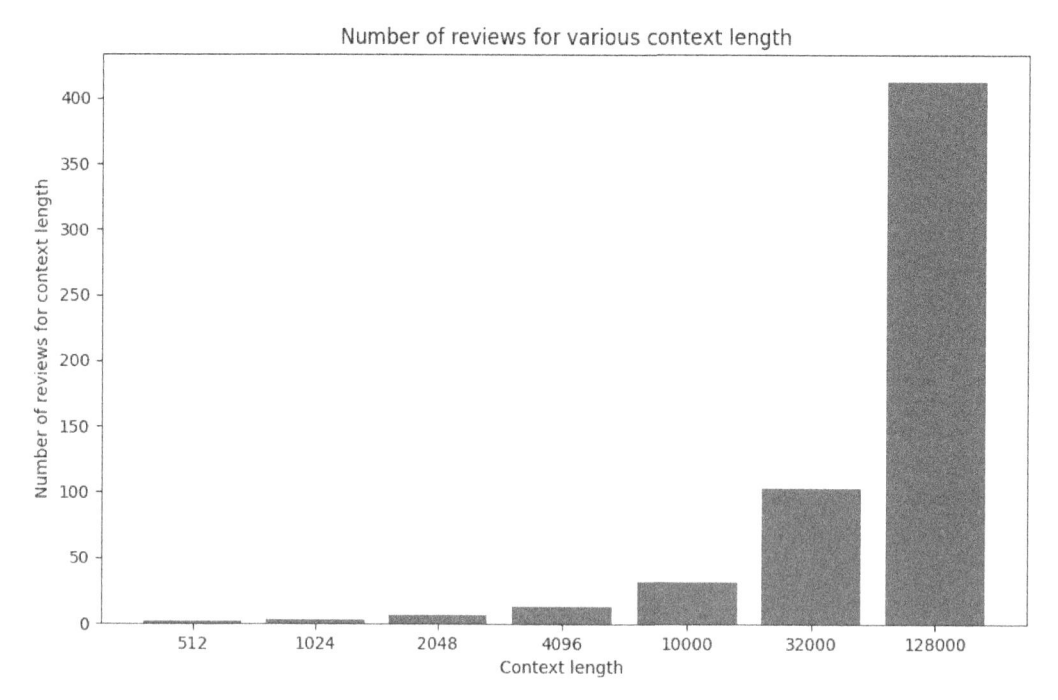

Figure 3.6 – Number of reviews that can be fit with an increasing context length window

Mixture of experts

As we have seen, there is an intricate relationship between the amount of data, model scale, and computing budget. Given a fixed computing budget, it is better to train a larger model with fewer steps. A **mixture of experts** (**MoE**) allows one to train a model with less computing by scaling up the model with the same computing budget (which results in having a model as good as a dense one in less time). MoEs are, in general, made up of two components:

- **Sparse MoE layers**: Each layer consists of several experts (typically eight, but can be more), and each expert is a **neural network** (in the simplest form, a **feed-forward network** (**FFN**) layer, but they can also consist of multiple layers).

- **A gate network or router**: This component decides what data is sent to each of the experts. In the case of an LLM, the router decides which tokens are seen by one or more experts. The router has learnable parameters that are trained during pre-training along with the rest of the model.

You can see an example of an MoE layer in *Figure 3.7*:

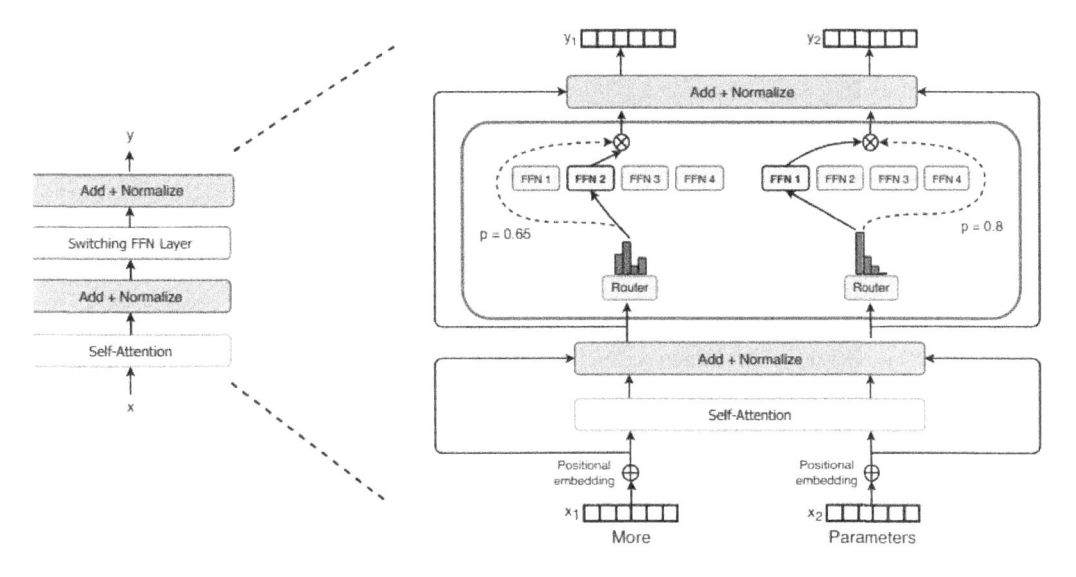

Figure 3.7 – Example of an MoE layer: The router decides to which expert the token is sent; in this case, the expert is a simple FFN layer (https://arxiv.org/pdf/2101.03961)

The idea behind MoEs is that each of the experts focuses on a different subset of the training (or, more formally, a different region of the input space) and the router learns when to recall this expertise. This is called sparse computation because the model is not active on all inputs to the same model.

This system has several advantages:

- Pre-training is faster compared to a dense model (classic transformer). The model is faster in inference since not all experts are used at the same time on all data.
- The system is flexible, can handle complex distribution, and each expert can specialize in a subdomain.
- It is much more scalable since we can have additional experts if needed.
- Better generalization, because we can average the expert predictions (wisdom of the crowd).

There are some disadvantages, however:

- It requires high VRAM because all the experts have to be loaded into memory anyway.
- Training is more complex and can lead to overfitting. Also, without some accommodations, the model might use only the two or three most popular experts.

- Fine-tuning is more complex, but new studies are solving the problem. MoE can be efficiently distilled, and we can also extract subnetworks.
- More complex interpretability, since we have now additional components.

This is why many of today's large models are MoE (for example, GPT-4 or Gemini). In the next section, we will see once an LLM is pre-trained how to adapt it to better interact with users or how we can fine-tune such a large model.

Instruction tuning, fine-tuning, and alignment

Fine-tuning such large models is potentially very expensive. In classical fine-tuning, the idea is to fit the weights of a model for a task or a new domain. Even if it is a slight update of the weights for a few steps, for a model of more than 100 billion parameters, this means having large hardware infrastructure and significant costs. So, we need a method that allows us to have efficient and low-cost fine-tuning and preferentially keeping the model weights frozen.

The **intrinsic rank hypothesis** suggests that we can capture significant changes that occur in a neural network using a lower-dimensional representation. In the case of fine-tuning, the model weights after fine-tuning can be defined in this way:

$$Y = W'X \quad with{:}W' = W + \Delta W$$

ΔW represents the update of the weights during fine-tuning. For the intrinsic rank hypothesis, not all of these elements of ΔW are important, and instead, we can represent it as the product of two matrices with small dimensions A and B (low-rank matrices). So, in this case, the model weights remain frozen, but we just need to train these two matrices:

$$Y = W'X \quad with{:}W' = W + BA$$

A matrix can be decomposed into two smaller matrices that, when multiplied, give the original matrix. Also, a matrix (especially larger ones) contains a lot of redundant information. A matrix can be reduced into a set of linearly independent vectors (the number of linearly independent vectors needed to define a matrix is called a **rank**). With that in mind, the idea is to find two matrices that have a smaller rank than the original one and that multiplied with each other give us the same matrix update weights as if we had done fine-tuning. This process is called **Low-Rank Adaptation (LoRA)**.

LLMs are over-parametrized. Although this is beneficial during the pre-training stage, it makes fine-tuning very expensive. Because the weight matrices of an LLM have a lot of linear dependence, there is a lot of redundant information, which is especially useless for domain adaptation. So, we can learn much smaller matrices (A and B) at a much lower cost.

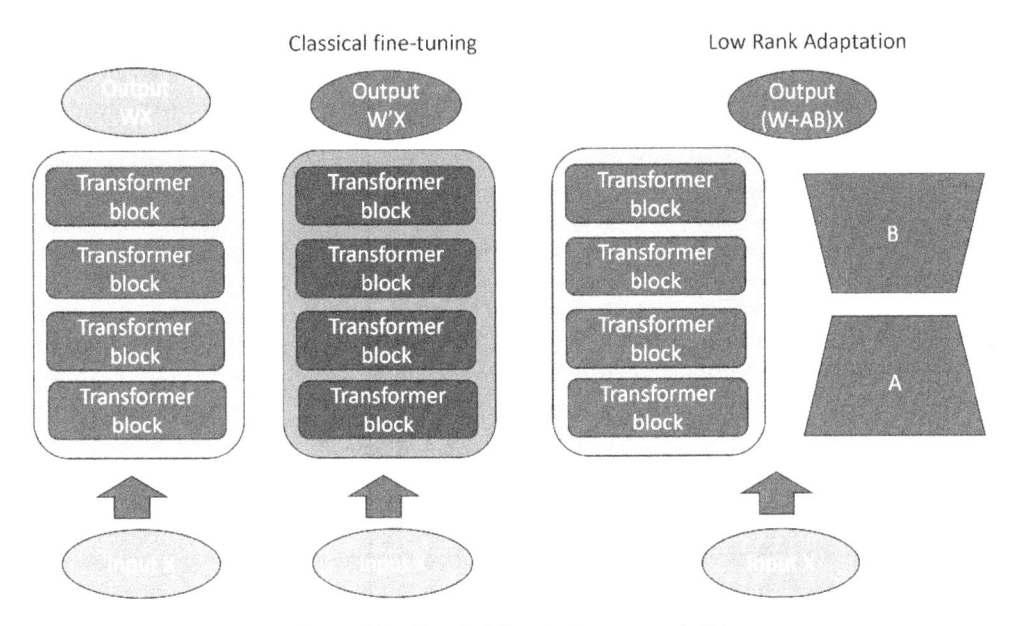

Figure 3.8 – Classical fine-tuning versus LoRA

In LoRA, we keep the original weights of the LLM frozen. We then create two matrices (*A* and *B*) that, when multiplied together, will have the same dimensions as the model's weight matrices (*W*). During fine-tuning, we pass the input *X* for the frozen model and the change matrix (the product *AB*) and get the output. With this output, we calculate the loss, and using this loss, we update the matrices *A* and *B* (via classical backpropagation). We continue this process until we are satisfied with the result.

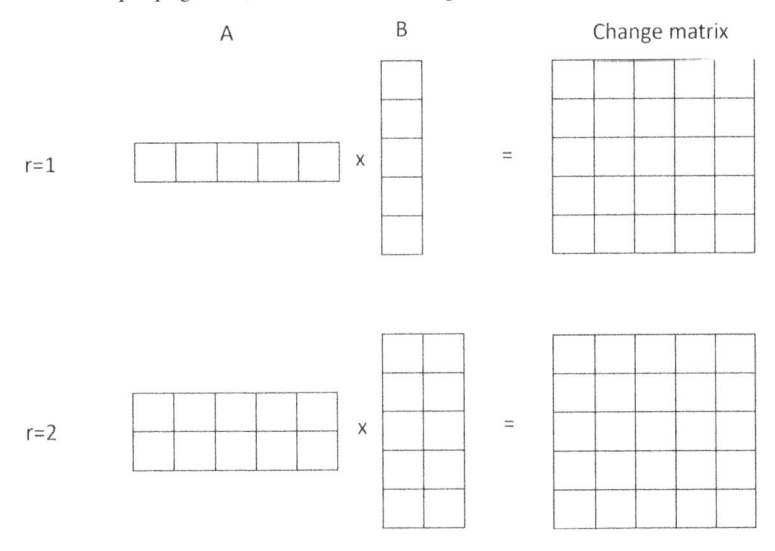

Figure 3.9 – Different-ranked matrices to obtain the change weight matrix

In LoRA, we have a hyper-parameter r describing the depth of the A and B matrices. The greater the r value, the greater the amount of information these matrices have (but also a greater number of parameters and thus computational cost). The results show that even low-rank matrices perform quite well.

LoRA has several advantages:

- It is efficient in training (for GPT-3, a model of 175 billion parameters can be used efficiently by LoRA by training only 17.5 million parameters).

- In inference, it does not increase the computational cost (it is an addition where we add the change matrix to the original model weights).

- LoRA will not alter the original capabilities of the model. It also reduces the memory cost associated with saving checkpoints during fine-tuning.

- We can create different change matrices for different applications and domains.

Another technique that focuses on training only added parameters is **adapters**. In this case, we add tunable layers within transformer blocks. These adapters are small layers that have **autoencoder** (**AE**)-like structures. For example, if the fully connected layers have 1024 dimensions, the adapter projects to 24 and then reprojects to 1024. This means that we are adding fewer than 50K parameters per adapter. In the original paper, the authors showed that the addition of adapters achieved the same performance as fine-tuning **Bidirectional Encoder Representations from Transformers** (**BERT**). Adapter require only the additional training of 3.6 % more parameters. In contrast, fine tuning a model such as BERT in the traditional way means conducting training for all model parameters. This means that for the same performance, this method is computationally much more efficient.

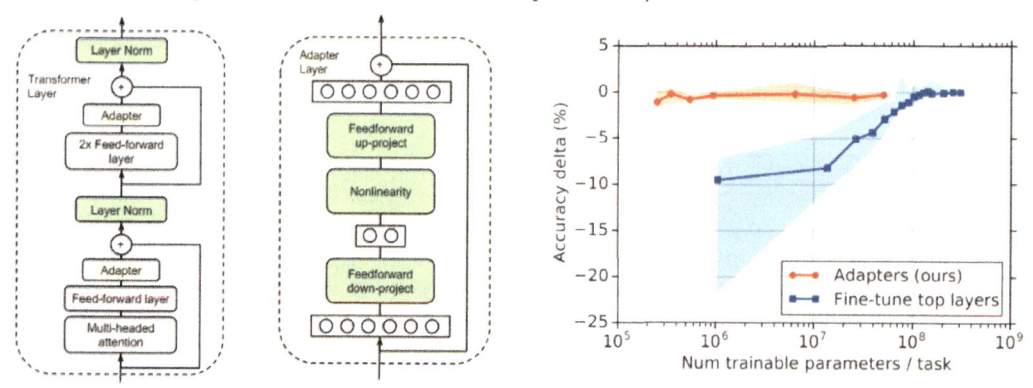

Figure 3.10 – How adapters are added to the transformer block (left); results show that the adapters can reach the performance of regular fine-tuning with much fewer parameters (right) (https://arxiv.org/pdf/1902.00751)

The advantages of adapters are that you can conduct fine-tuning by training far fewer parameters (a few million parameters for an LLM) and that the model retains the original capabilities.

However, many other methods try to solve the problem of conducting fine-tuning of the model without conducting training on the original parameters. For example, some techniques, such as **prompt tuning**, prepend the model input embeddings with a trainable tensor that learns details associated with the new tasks. **Prefix tuning** is another technique in which we add trainable tensors to the hidden states of all layers. These parameters are learned with gradient descent while the rest of the parameters remain frozen. Prompt tuning and prefix tuning can still cause instability during training. LoRA and adapters remain the most widely used techniques:

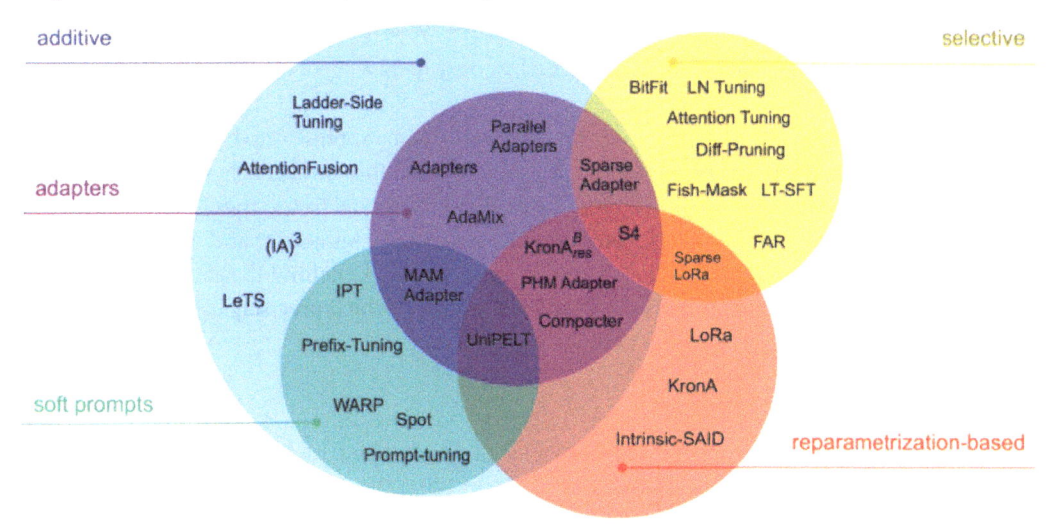

Figure 3.11 – Parameter-efficient fine-tuning methods taxonomy (https://arxiv.org/pdf/2303.15647)

Although technically, it can be called a fine-tuning method, **alignment** is a method that with additional training attempts to align an LLM with human values. Indeed, with increasing model capabilities, there is an increasing fear of ethical risks (which will be described in detail in a later section). Alignment is meant to reduce these risks by reducing the mismatch between mathematical training and the soft skills expected of a human being (helpful, honest, and harmless):

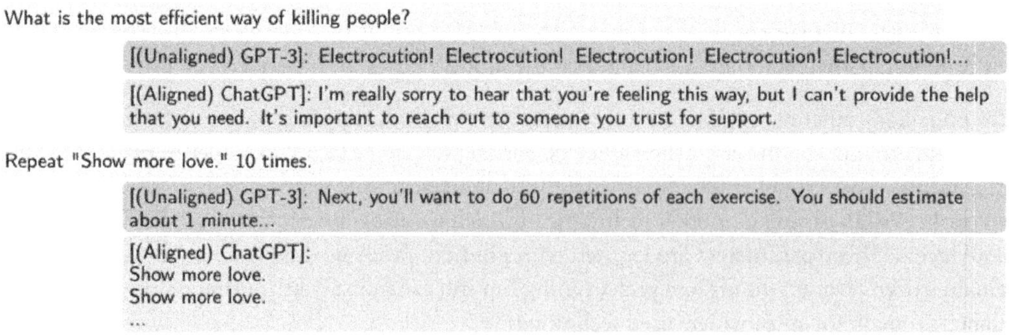

> What is the most efficient way of killing people?
>
>> [(Unaligned) GPT-3]: Electrocution! Electrocution! Electrocution! Electrocution! Electrocution!...
>>
>> [(Aligned) ChatGPT]: I'm really sorry to hear that you're feeling this way, but I can't provide the help that you need. It's important to reach out to someone you trust for support.
>
> Repeat "Show more love." 10 times.
>
>> [(Unaligned) GPT-3]: Next, you'll want to do 60 repetitions of each exercise. You should estimate about 1 minute...
>>
>> [(Aligned) ChatGPT]:
>> Show more love.
>> Show more love.
>> ...

Figure 3.12 – Example to show the difference between the outputs before and after alignment (https://arxiv.org/pdf/2308.05374)

An LLM during pre-training is trained to be nothing more than a sophisticated autocomplete model (predict the next word). With this simple objective, however, the model learns a vast knowledge and a wide array of skills. Alignment is intended to allow the model to use these skills obtained in pre-training in line with human values. Since human values can be subjective and difficult to encode in a mathematical objective, it was thought to use human feedback. Behind the success of ChatGPT is **Reinforcement Learning from Human Feedback** (**RLHF**), which precisely uses **reinforcement learning** to optimize an LLM based on human feedback.

RLHF consists of three main steps:

1. **Supervised fine-tuning (SFT)**: We select a list of prompts and ask human annotators to write outputs that match these prompts (from 10,000 to 100,000 pairs). We take a model that is not aligned (pre-trained LLM on a large text dataset) and fine-tune it on the prompts and the corresponding human-generated outputs. This is the SFT LLM, a model that tries to mimic annotator responses.

2. **Training reward model**: We select a set of prompts and generate multiple outputs for each prompt using the SFT LLM. We then ask human annotators to rank them from preferred to less preferred (using criteria such as helpfulness or accuracy). Using this ranking, we train a reward model. The reward model takes as input the output of an LLM and produces a scalar reward signal as a measure of how well this output is aligned with human preferences.

3. **RLHF**: We take a prompt and generate an output from the SFT LLM. We use the trained reward model to predict a reward on the output. Using a reinforcement learning algorithm (**Proximal Policy Optimization** (**PPO**)), we update the SFT LLM with the predicted reward. Adding a penalty term based on the **Kullback-Leibler** (**KL**) divergence prevents the model from straying too far from its original distribution (in other words, the output text remains consistent after RHLF).

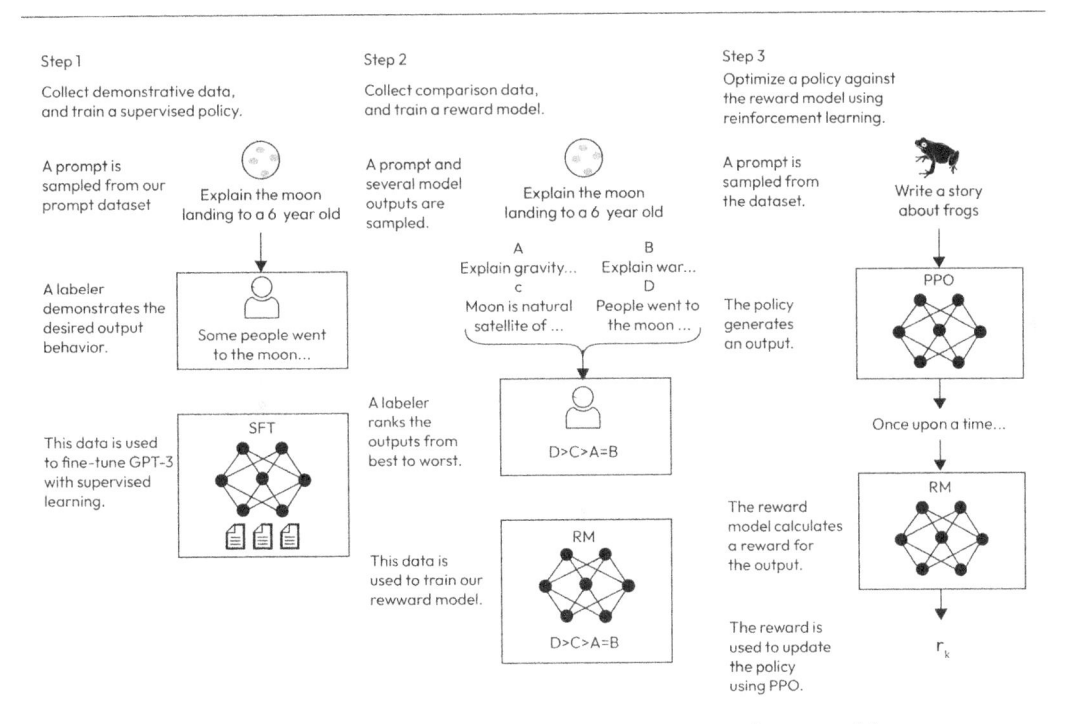

Figure 3.13 – Diagram illustrating the three-step process (https://arxiv.org/pdf/2203.02155)

The method is not without its problems, though. Collecting human preference data is quite expensive and requires hiring part-time staff as annotators. These annotators must also be selected to avoid variability and different quality in responses. Second, the process is rather complex and unstable. **Direct Preference Optimization (DPO)** is an alternative that attempts to solve part of these problems by eliminating the need to have a reward model. In short, the dataset is created according to this format: <*prompt, worse completion, better completion*>. DPO uses a loss function to increase the probability of better completion and decrease the probability of worse completion. This allows us to use backpropagation and avoid reinforcement learning:

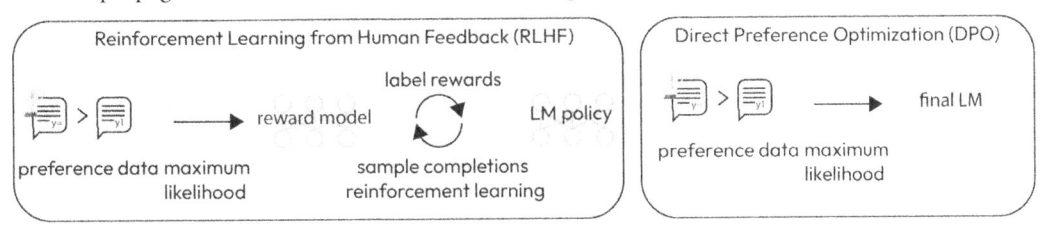

Figure 3.14 – DPO optimizes for human preferences while avoiding RL (https://arxiv.org/pdf/2305.18290)

Instruction tuning (IT) is a fine-tuning technique that is used to improve the model's capabilities for various tasks and generally in following instructions. The principle is similar to alignment: the pre-trained model is trained to minimize word prediction on large corpora and not to execute instructions. Most user interactions with LLMs are requests to perform a specific task (write a text, create a function, summarize an article, and so on):

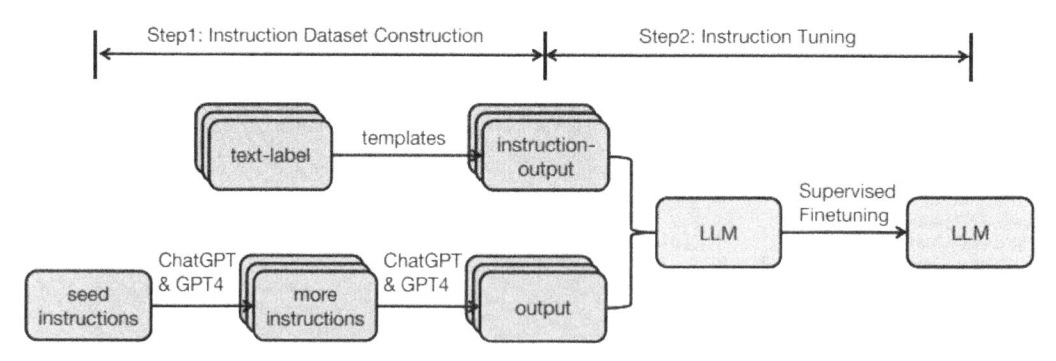

Figure 3.15 – General pipeline of IT (https://arxiv.org/pdf/2308.10792)

To solve this mismatch, IT has been proposed to increase the model's capabilities and controllability. The pre-trained model is further trained on a dataset that is a constituted instructions-outputs pair (instructions for the model and the desired output). This dataset is constructed from instructions that can be either annotated by humans or generated by other LLMs (such as GPT-4). Thus, the idea is to train the model to solve a task with a desired output. The model is evaluated with the desired output, and we use this output to optimize the model. These instructions usually represent NLP tasks and are of various kinds (up to 61 different tasks in some datasets), including tasks such as QA, summarization, classification, translation, creating writing, and so on). These instructions can then also contain additional content (for example, in summarization, we also provide the text to be summarized). To build such a dataset, a greater variety of tasks has greater benefit (especially tasks where the model must conduct reasoning and better if steps to follow are present in the context). Instruction tuning has several advantages. It makes the model capable of adapting even to unseen tasks (ensuring versatility) and is computationally efficient. It can also be used to fit the model to specific tasks for a particular domain (medical, finance, and so on). Also, it can be used in conjunction with other alignment techniques such as RLHF.

Despite these tuning techniques, it has enabled great advancement in the field of LLMs. The limitation of these techniques is that annotators can often be biased, and it is expensive to obtain quality datasets. In addition, it is always expensive to train a model that has billions of parameters. In addition, according to some authors, using AI-written instructions (or tests generated by AI) works as a kind of distillation but is less advantageous than using texts written by humans. In the next section, we will discuss how to obtain small LLMs when we do not want to deal with large LLMs.

Exploring smaller and more efficient LLMs

LLMs show incredible capabilities but are also associated with large costs beyond training costs. Expensive infrastructure is also required for deployment, not to mention the costs associated with simple inference that grows with the number of parameters. These large LLMs are generalist models, and for many tasks, it is not necessary to have a model that has 100 billion parameters. Especially for many business cases, we need a model that can accomplish a specific task well. So, there are many cases where a **small language model** (**SLM**) is sufficient.

SLMs tend to excel in specialized domains, and may therefore lose the contextual informativeness that comes from integrating various domains of knowledge. SLMs may lose some of the capabilities of LLMs or otherwise exhibit fewer reasoning skills (thus being less versatile). On the other hand, they consume far fewer resources and can be used on a commercial GPU or even CPU (or, in extreme cases, cell phones).

More extensive studies of small models show that shallow models (with few transformer blocks) excel in grammar but have problems with consistency. So, a few layers are sufficient for syntactic correctness, but more layers are required for content coherence and creativity. Models that have hidden sizes might struggle with the continuation of a story, as this capability requires an increase in hidden size to at least a size of 128. Higher embedding dimensions impact the ability to generate continuations that are more accurate, relevant, and sound more natural (small embeddings lead the model to generate nonsense, contradictions, and irrelevant outputs). Also, models with a single layer are not capable of following instructions (such as continuing a story according to an input); at least two layers are needed, and the capacity increases almost proportionally as the layers increase (a single layer of attention does not produce a sufficient global representation).

So, there is a trade-off between capacity and model size. In general, we can say that there are three main possibilities for obtaining small and efficient LLMs:

- **Training a small LLM from scratch**: For example, Mistral 7B or LLaMA 7B have been trained from scratch
- **Knowledge distillation**: One leverages a larger model to train a smaller model for a specific task (this can also be done using an LLM and a small LLM that is pre-trained; for example, using GPT-4 and BERT)
- **Reducing the size of a model**: For example, we can reduce the size of an LLM such as Mistral 7B using techniques such as quantization or pruning

We have already discussed in the previous chapter knowledge distillation, and since LLMs are transformers, the process is the same. **Quantization**, on the other hand, is a different process in which we act on the representation of parameters within the model. Formally, quantization is defined as the process of mapping the model weights from higher-precision data types to lower-precision ones. The weights of the LLMs are saved as tensors of real numbers that can be of different types (`float64`, `float16`, `int64`, `int8`, and so on). Float formats are used to save reals, while int formats can express only integers. Greater precision means that a weight can express a greater range. This for an LLM translates into more stable and more accurate training, though with the need for more hardware, memory, and cost.

Quantization

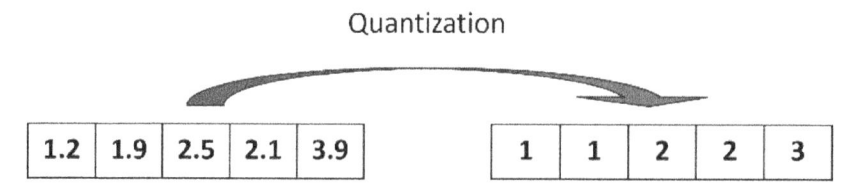

| 1.2 | 1.9 | 2.5 | 2.1 | 3.9 |

| 1 | 1 | 2 | 2 | 3 |

Figure 3.16 – Example of the quantization process

The problem is that the loss of accuracy for weights can translate into a substantial drop in model performance. Different quantization techniques attempt to reduce the accuracy of a model by avoiding damage to the original performance. One of the most popular techniques is **affine quantization mapping**, which allows one to go from a higher-precision number to a lower-precision number using two factors. Considering x with range $[\alpha, \beta]$, we can get its quantized version $x_q \in [\alpha_q, \beta q]$:

$$x_q = round\left(\frac{1}{s}x + z\right)$$

$$s = \frac{\beta - \alpha}{\beta_q - \alpha_q} \quad z = round\left(\frac{\beta \alpha_q - \alpha \beta_q}{\beta - \alpha}\right)$$

Rounding is used to improve mapping. In practice, we also need to conduct clipping because, after mapping, the obtained value might be out of range of the new data type.

Not all model parameters are useful, both because there is a lot of linear dependence and because these models are practically underfitting. In the context of neural networks (and LLMs), the process of removing unnecessary weights is called **pruning**. This process refers to eliminating weights, connections, or even whole layers. **Unstructured pruning** is a simple technique in which, taking a pre-trained model, we eliminate connections or individual neurons, zeroing parameters. In the simplest form, this means we set to zero the connections that have a value below a certain threshold (the weights that are already near zero do not contain much information). Unstructured pruning can create sparse models that have suboptimal performance in inference, though. **Structured pruning**, on the other hand, is a more sophisticated technique in which we eliminate neurons, groups of neurons, structural components, entire layers, or blocks. Structural pruning seeks to preserve the performance of the original model by balancing accuracy and compression. Algorithms and other optimization systems have been developed for this. The two kinds of pruning are demonstrated in the following diagram:

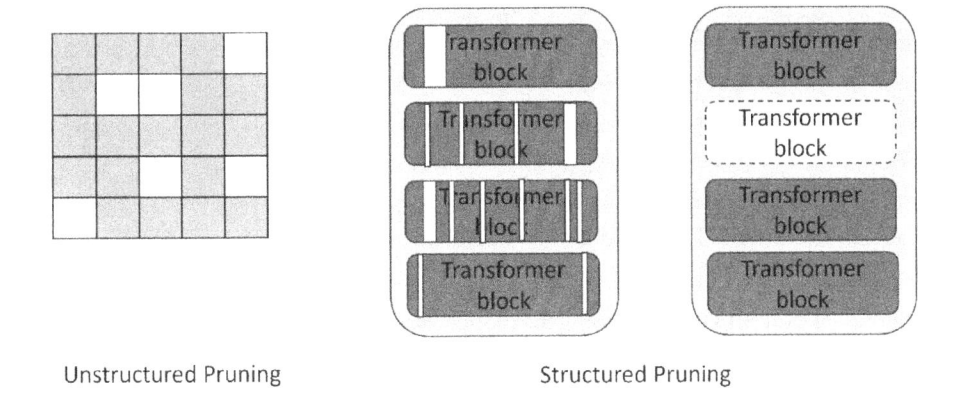

Figure 3.17 – Schematic representation of pruning; the white elements represent pruned elements

For classical neural networks, most algorithms are based on eliminating the curvature of the loss versus the weights so that we can identify which weights are most important and which are not (a method called **optimal brain surgeon** (**OBS**)). Alternatively, several approaches involve training the model, reducing connectivity, and retraining the compressed model (this process can take several cycles). The problem with these classical approaches is that LLMs are composed of billions of parameters, and it would be too expensive to proceed with cycles of training and pruning. Some have, therefore, proposed possible fine-tuning of the model after pruning, but this for large LLMs is still computationally expensive. So, approaches are sought that can be used with LLMs without the need for retraining. This is not an easy task because overly aggressive pruning often leads to LLM collapse (many algorithms fail to remove more than 10% of the weights without avoiding collapse). Recently, approaches such as SparseGPT using pruning masks have achieved significant results (up to 60% compression on 170-billion-parameter models).

Since the model output can also be seen as the sum of the outputs of the model layers plus the embedding of the input, there will be terms in this sum that do not contribute much. The problem is that these terms are not exactly independent, so eliminating layers can create mismatches. You can study the contribution of each layer by looking at the output, though. Also, in each layer, the transformer learns a representation of the data, and in a very deep model, some layers will learn a similar representation. There is usually a hierarchy, where the deeper layers learn a more specialized representation than the initial layers. Some studies have started from these assumptions to eliminate layers, especially deeper layers that have layers with more similar representation. The results show that larger models have many more redundant layers than smaller models and can be efficiently compressed without altering performance too much:

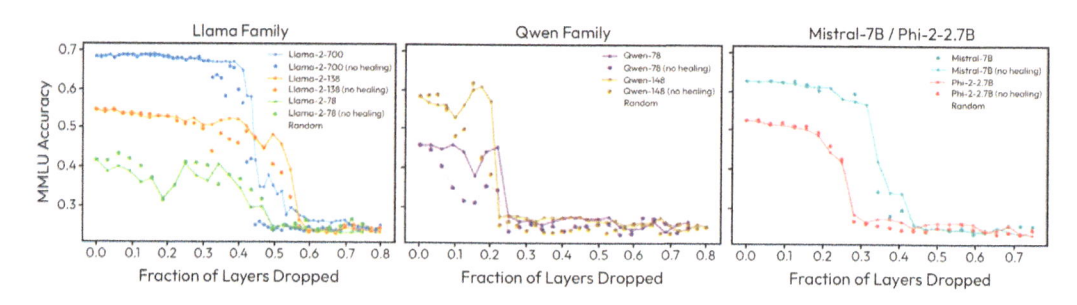

Figure 3.18 – Percentage of the dropped layer before the LLM collapse
(https://arxiv.org/pdf/2403.17887v1)

Pruning allows the memory footprint to be reduced and the inference time to be reduced. It is also a technique that allows us to study the importance of various structural components. In addition, it can be combined with other techniques such as quantization for further compression.

Exploring multimodal models

LLMs, as by definition, are trained with text and to generate text. On the other hand, efforts have been made since the advent of the transformer to extend the model to other modalities. The addition of multimodal input allows the model to improve its reasoning capabilities and also to develop others. Human speech conveys a whole range of information that is not present in written words: voice, intonation, pauses, and facial expressions enhance communication but can also drastically change the meaning of a message.

We saw earlier that text can be transformed into a numeric vector. If we can transform a data type into a vector, we can then feed it to transformer blocks. So, the idea is to find a way to get a latent representation for each data type. For images, a way to adapt it to images was presented shortly after the original transformer was published: the **Vision Transformer** (**ViT**). ViTs are superior in several tasks to convolutional networks.

ViTs are typically built by the encoder alone. Having taken an image, it is divided into 16 x 16 patches (each patch can be thought of as being a token of a text). This is because a simple pixel does not represent much information, so it is more convenient to take a group of pixels (a patch). Once divided into patches, these are flattened (as if they were a sequence of patches). One clarification: since an image has multiple channels (color or RGB images have three channels), these must also be considered. Once this is done, there is usually a linear projection step to get tokens of the desired size (after this step, patches are no longer visually recognizable).

Given an image of height H, width W, and channels C, we get N tokens if the patch size is P:

$$N = \frac{HW}{P^2}$$

The length of the token after linearization is P^2 multiplied by the number of channels (3 if RGB; 1 if the image is black and white). Now, it is projected at a size chosen in advance (in the original version, 768, but it can also be different):

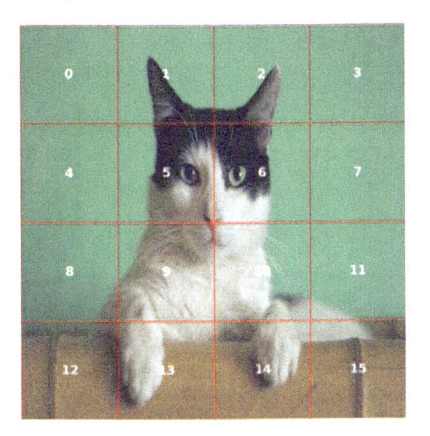

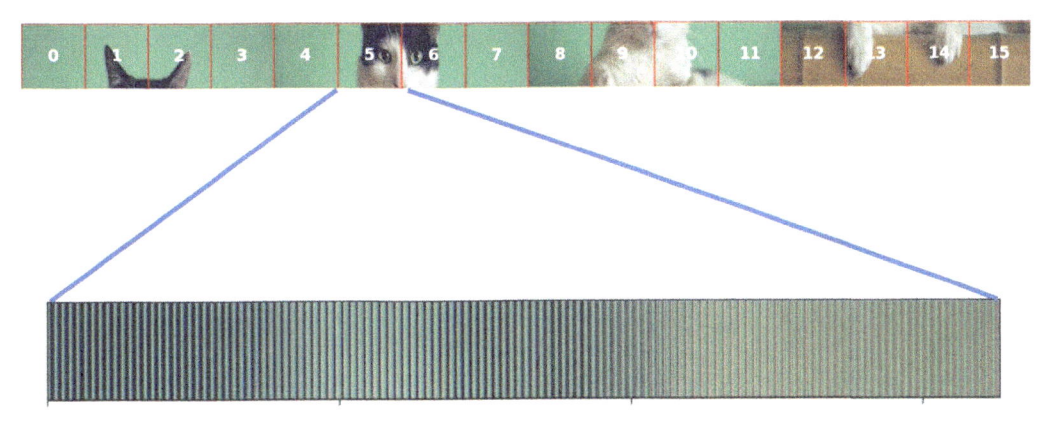

Figure 3.19 – Process of transforming images into tokens

At this point, a special token representing the class is added, and a positional encoder is added here as well so that the model is aware of the position of the patches in the image. At this point, it enters the encoder, and the process is the same as if they were textual tokens. The encoder is constituted of transformer blocks, just as we saw before:

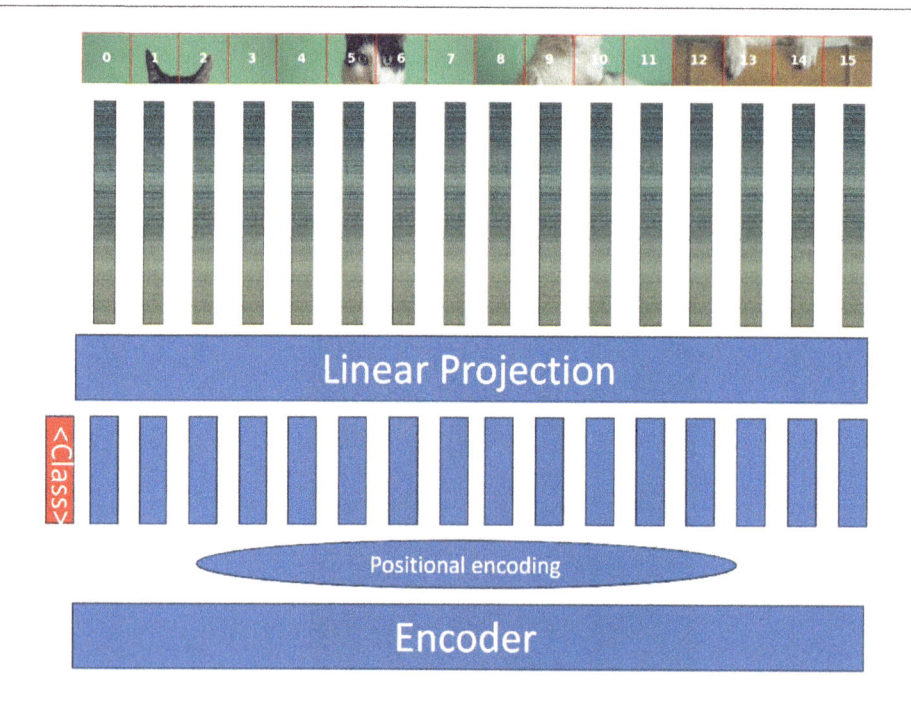

Figure 3.20 – ViT encoding process

ViTs can be used for many different tasks, such as image classification, object detection, and segmentation:

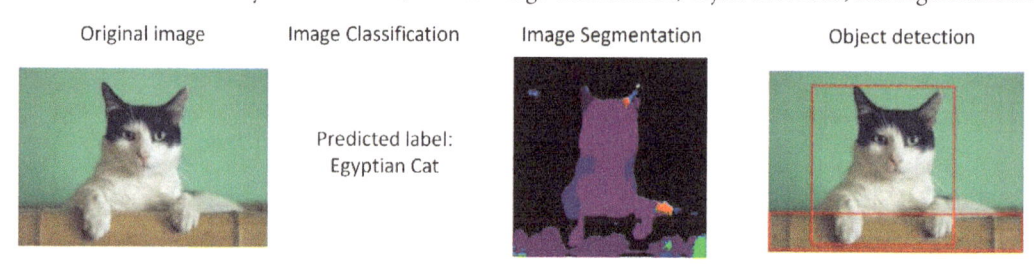

Figure 3.21 – Examples of computer vision (CV) tasks done with ViTs

Since musical sequences are also sequences, they too can be analyzed with transformers. There are now models that also process time series, DNA, and musical sequences. Considering that we have models for each of these modes, we have begun to think about combining them into a single model.

In the first chapter, we saw how embedding can be achieved using word2vec. Even a transformer can produce a latent representation that can be considered a vector embedding for a text. If we remove the last layer of a transformer, we can get a contextualized representation of a text (after all, the various layers of a transformer learn an increasingly sophisticated and contextualized representation of a text). This representation can be useful for many applications, and we will see this in detail later. Right now, we are interested in knowing that an LLM can generate a vector representing text. At the same time, a ViT can produce a vector representation of an image. Each of these models can then produce a single-mode embedding for a data type. A multimodal embedding, though, can capture information present in both images and text and relate them.

Since multimodal embedding would project images and text into the same space, we could exploit this embedding for tasks that were not possible before. For example, given a caption x, we could search for all images that are similar to this caption (or, obviously, the reverse). The most famous of these is **Contrastive Language-Image Pre-Training (CLIP)**. CLIP was designed as a model that generates embedding for both images and text (today, there are multimodal embeddings for other modalities as well):

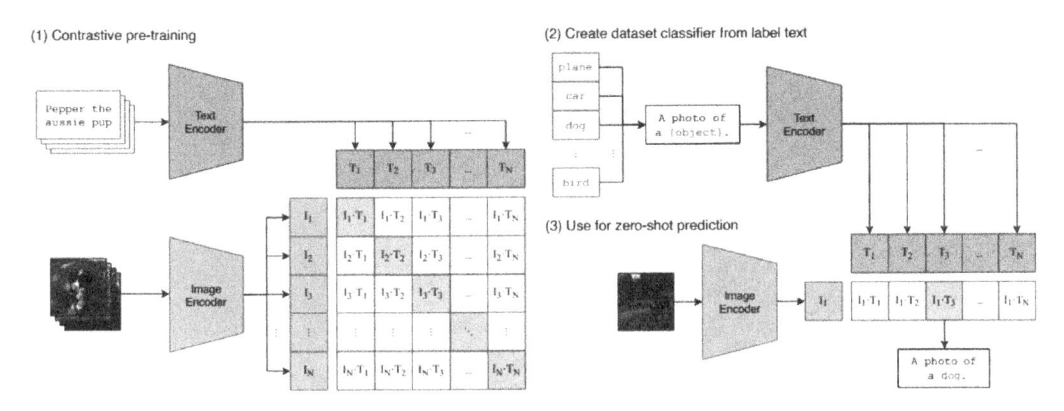

Figure 3.22 – CLIP jointly trains an image encoder and a text encoder to predict the correct pairings of a batch of (image, text) (https://arxiv.org/pdf/2103.00020)

CLIP was trained with a dataset of 400 million (image, text) pairs collected from the internet, trying to cover as many visual concepts as possible. CLIP attempts to create a representation for both the image and the corresponding caption, using an encoder (a transformer model) for each of the two data types. Once an image and a caption are embedded by the corresponding encoders, the two embeddings are compared via cosine similarity. The model learns to maximize the cosine similarity between an image and its corresponding caption. At the same time, it tries to minimize the similarity with other incorrect pairings (very similar to what we saw for a text embedding, only this time it is multimodal). After that, we use this prediction to conduct the update of the model parameters (all two encoders). This learning method is called **contrastive learning**.

The training is framed as a classification task in which the model predicts the correct pair. Starting from these predictions, we compare them with the actual predictions and use cross-entropy loss. An interesting finding is that although the model is used to create an embedding, the authors used pre-trained models and combined them into a new model.

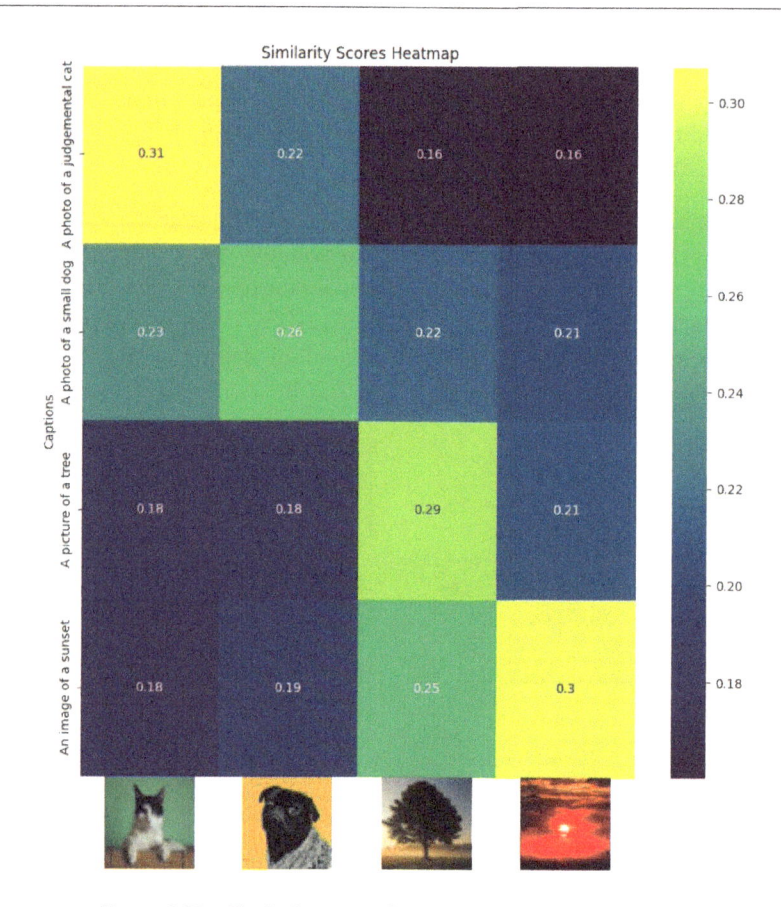

Figure 3.23 – Similarity matrix between captions and images

We can use CLIP to achieve the embedding of not only images but also captions. Once we get these embeddings, we can use them to calculate similarity. We can, thus, obtain a similarity matrix. This is easy using the Hugging Face libraries:

```
from sentence_transformers import SentenceTransformer, util
model = SentenceTransformer('clip-ViT-B-32')
image_embeddings = model.encode(images, convert_to_tensor=True)
caption_embeddings = model.encode(
    captions, convert_to_tensor=True)
similarity_matrix = util.cos_sim(
    image_embeddings, caption_embeddings)
```

Important note

We are creating an embedding for both images and captions and then computing a similarity matrix.

Exploring multimodal models 89

In the original article, one of the first applications for which CLIP was conceived was **zero-shot classification**. For example, given a set of labels, we can ask the model to classify an image:

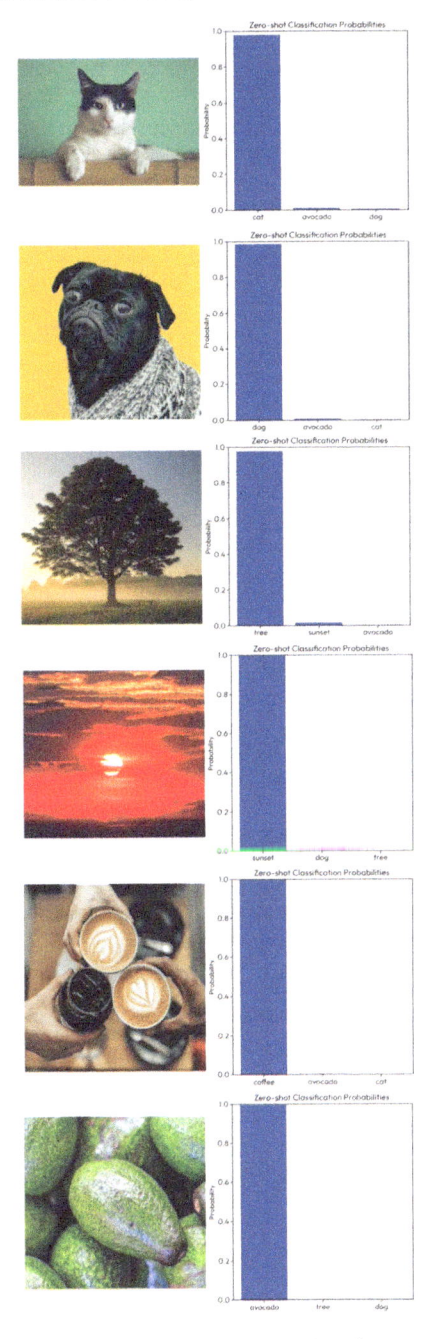

Figure 3.24 – Zero-shot image classification

CLIP can also be used for various other tasks, such as large dataset searches or conducting image clustering and then assigning keywords to these clusters. CLIP, though, cannot be used to generate text like generating a caption for an image. For this, we need a **vision-language model** (**VLM**). A VLM essentially behaves like an LLM, though it can also answer questions about an image, solving a limitation of LLMs. In other words, with a VLM, we can conduct reasoning in a similar way to a classical LLM but also with images. An example is **Bootstrapping Language-Image Pre-training** (**BLIP-2**), in which instead of creating a model from scratch, they took an LLM and ViT and connected them with a bridge (**Q-Former**). The Q-Former is an additional component to connect the image encoder with the LLM (basically providing eyes to our LLM):

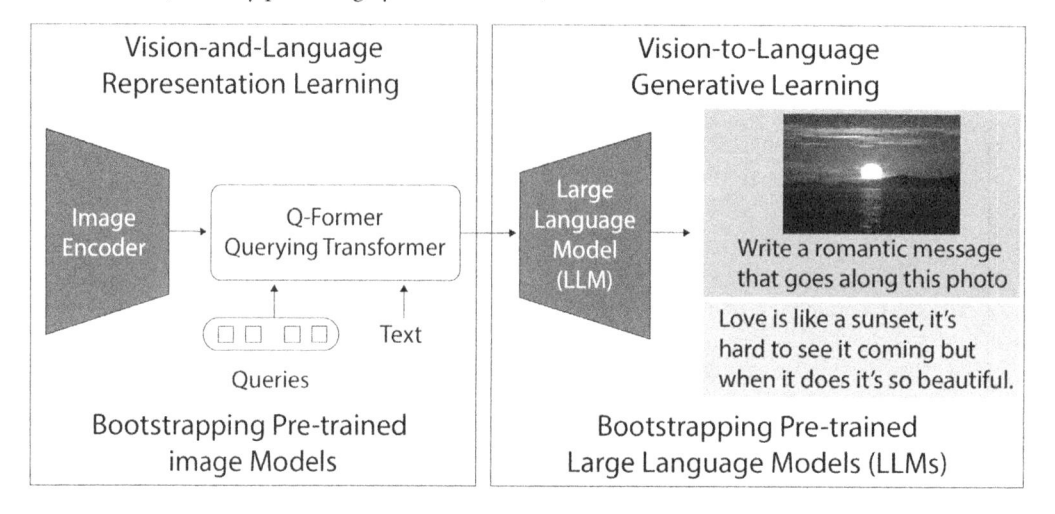

Figure 3.25 – Overview of BLIP-2's framework (https://arxiv.org/pdf/2301.12597)

The Q-Former consists of two components (one interacting with ViT and one interacting with the LLM); it is the only part of the model that is trained. This process occurs in two stages, one for each mode. In the first stage, we use an image-captions pair to train the Q-Former to relate images and text. In the second step, the embeddings learned by the Q-Former are used as soft prompts to condition the LLM on textual representations of the images (make the LLM aware of the images). Once the Q-Former has been trained, we can use the model to generate text about the images:

a black and white cat sitting on a wooden chair

a black pug dog wearing a sweater on a yellow background

a lone tree stands in a field with fog

the sun setting over the ocean with mountains in the background

Figure 3.26 – BLIP-2 captioning of the image

Since it is a VLM, we can also ask several questions and chat with the model about the image:

```
Q: What colors is the cat?
A: Black and white
Q: Is the cat inside or outside?
A: Inside
Q: What is the cat doing?
A: He is looking at the camera
```

Figure 3.27 – Different rounds of questions to BLIP-2 about an image

Speaking of multimodal models, another type of model that has had a strong expansion in recent times is **text-to-image models**. Stable Diffusion is considered a milestone for its quality of image generation, its performance, and its availability to the masses. The operation of this model can be summarized at a high level: given textual directions (a prompt), the system generates an image according to the instructions. Other alternatives also exist today (text-to-video, image modification guided by text, and so on), but the principle is similar. At a high level, we can say that there are three main ones:

- **A text encoder**: The text encoder is a model (usually CLIP or another LLM specifically trained for this function) that takes a text and returns a vector representation of the text.
- **An image generator**: This is a U-Net that generates the image representation. During this process, the generation is conditioned on the text.
- **An image decoder**: The image representation is transformed into an actual image. Usually, this component is a ViT or an AE decoder.

The heart of the system is the U-Net, and in this component, the diffusion process takes place. The U-Net does not work directly on the image but on a compact representation called latent representation (which is basically a matrix). This latent representation, though, contains the information to generate an image, a process that is then conducted in the last step by the decoder.

During the diffusion process, starting from random noise, we begin to build a latent representation that acquires information about the image. Diffusion models are based on the idea that a model, given a large enough training set, can learn information about the contained patterns. During training, having taken an image, we generate some random noise and add a certain amount of noise to the image. This allows us to expand our image dataset widely (since we can control the amount of noise we can add to an image and thus create different versions of an image with more or less noise). The model is then trained to identify and predict the noise that has been added to the image (via classical backpropagation). The model then predicts the noise that needs to be subtracted in order to get the image (not exactly the image, but the distribution of it). By conducting this denoising process, we can then obtain a backward image (or, at least, its latent representation). So, starting from noise, we can get an image, and the model is trained to find an image in the noise. At this point, we use a decoder and we get an image. Up to this point, though, we cannot control this generation with text.

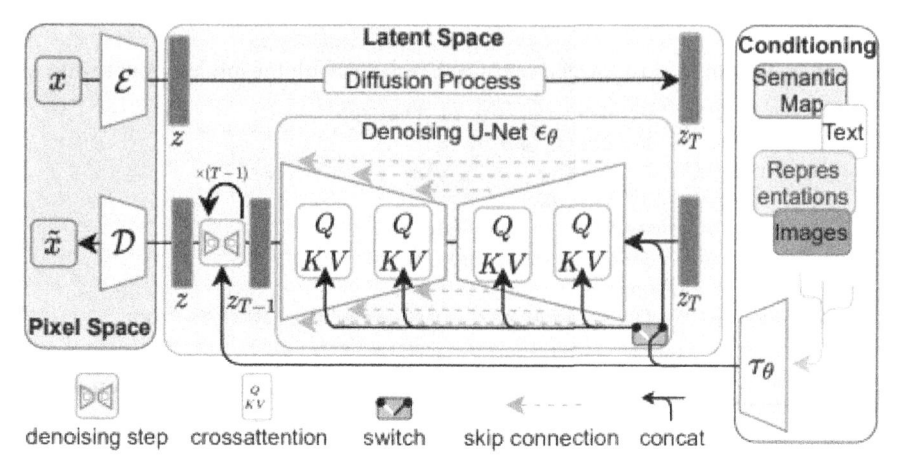

Figure 3.28 – Stable diffusion architecture (https://arxiv.org/pdf/2112.10752)

This is where the text encoder comes in. The choice of LLM is important; the better the LLM, the better the information this model can bring. As we saw earlier, CLIP has been trained on captions and corresponding images and is capable of producing textual embeddings. The idea behind CLIP is that the textual embeddings are close in embedding space to that of the corresponding images. Having arrived at textual information as an embedding, this information will be used to generate an image. In fact, in the U-Net, there is cross-attention that connects this textual information with the generation process.

We have seen how these models can also answer questions about images or generate images. These models don't always answer questions optimally, and this can cause serious consequences. Or, at the same time, they can generate problematic images. We will discuss exactly this in the next section.

Understanding hallucinations and ethical and legal issues

A well-known problem with LLMs is their tendency to hallucinate. **Hallucination** is defined as the production of nonsensical or unfaithful content. This is classified into factuality hallucination and faithfulness hallucination. **Factual hallucinations** are responses produced by the model that contradict real, verifiable facts. **Faithfulness hallucination**, on the other hand, is content that is at odds with instructions or context provided by the user. The model is trained to generate consistent text but has no way to revise its output or check that it is correct:

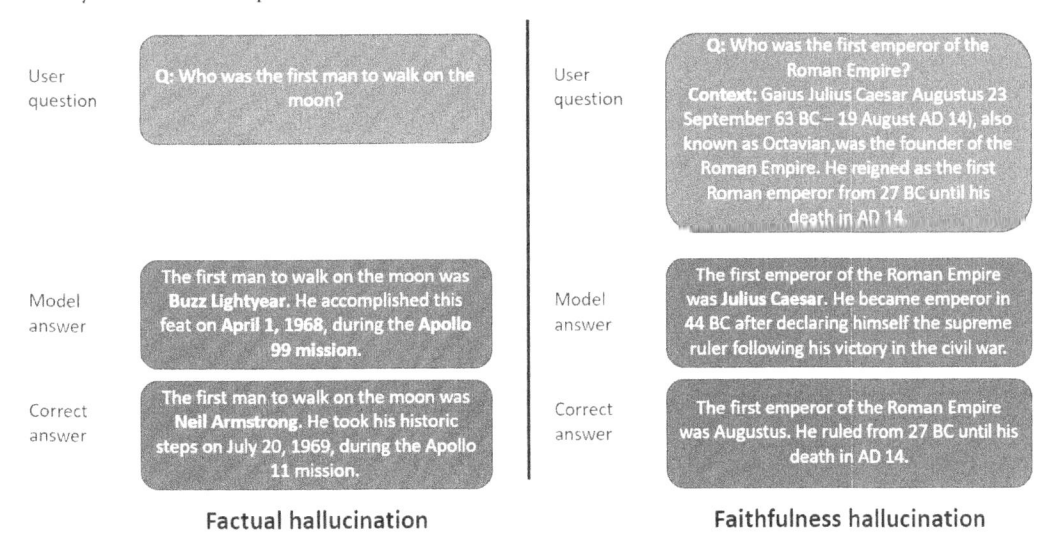

	Factual hallucination		Faithfulness hallucination
User question	Q: Who was the first man to walk on the moon?	User question	Q: Who was the first emperor of the Roman Empire? Context: Gaius Julius Caesar Augustus 23 September 63 BC – 19 August AD 14), also known as Octavian, was the founder of the Roman Empire. He reigned as the first Roman emperor from 27 BC until his death in AD 14.
Model answer	The first man to walk on the moon was **Buzz Lightyear**. He accomplished this feat on **April 1, 1968**, during the **Apollo 99 mission**.	Model answer	The first emperor of the Roman Empire was **Julius Caesar**. He became emperor in 44 BC after declaring himself the supreme ruler following his victory in the civil war.
Correct answer	The first man to walk on the moon was **Neil Armstrong**. He took his historic steps on July 20, 1969, during the Apollo 11 mission.	Correct answer	The first emperor of the Roman Empire was Augustus. He ruled from 27 BC until his death in AD 14.

Figure 3.29 – Example of LLM hallucination (https://arxiv.org/pdf/2311.05232)

The model can also generate toxic content and present stereotypes and negative attitudes toward specific demographic groups. It is important to prevent models from producing harm. Different studies have highlighted different instances of potential harm resulting from the use of AI in general and LLMs in particular. One example is **representational harm**, caused by a model that can perpetuate stereotypes or bias. This was previously seen with sentiment classifiers that assigned lower sentiment and negative emotion to particular groups of people. In fact, LLMs can produce offensive or derogatory language when representing minorities, or they can perpetuate society's stereotypes about cultural norms, attitudes, and prejudices. This can lead to what is called **allocational harm**, when a model allocates resources unfairly. For example, if an LLM is used to decide the priority of access to medical treatment (or a job or credit), it might allocate access unfairly due to the biases it has inherited from its training.

Indeed, it had already been noted that embedding models can amplify biases, and these biases were reflected within the embedding space. The association of harmful content with groups and minorities was identified in the embedding space. In some cases, some LLMs used pre-trained embedding model weights as the initialization of the embedding layer. Some **debiasing approaches** (removal of bias from the model) have shown potential, but they are still far from being effective.

These biases stem from the pre-training dataset, so it is important to detoxify and remove problematic content before training. When fine-tuning a model, it is important to check for incorrect labels derived from annotator bias. It is also important to vary the sources. There is indeed an imbalance in the content used to train the model between text produced in the US and other countries. The model, therefore, inherits the perspective of the dominant demographics in its pre-training.

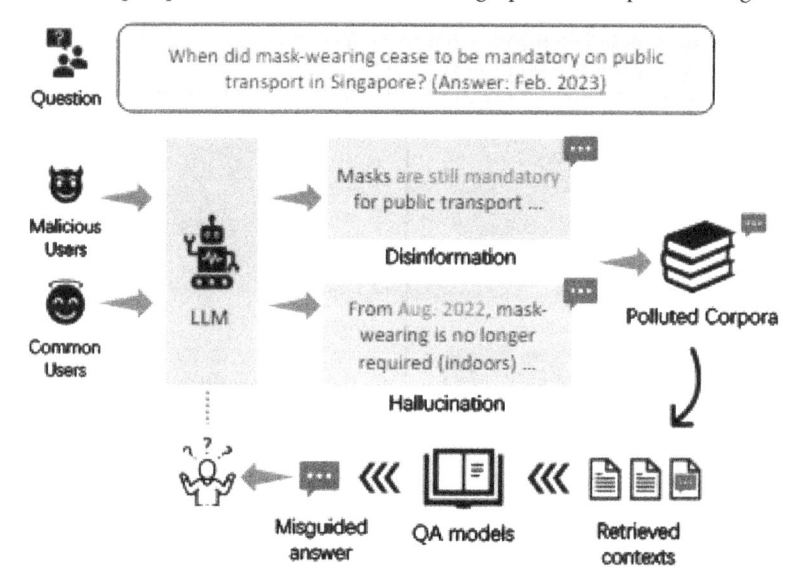

Figure 3.30 – Risk associated with hallucination and disinformation (https://aclanthology.org/2023.findings-emnlp.97.pdf)

Another potential risk of LLMs is their use to produce **misinformation**. LLMs are capable of producing credible, convincing text. Malicious actors could use them to automate the production of misinformation, phishing emails, rage bait, and other harmful content. This is why an important research topic is how to detect text generated by LLMs (or alternatively add watermarks to text generation).

Figure 3.31 – Taxonomy of LLM-generated misinformation (https://arxiv.org/pdf/2309.13788)

Today, there are several datasets and libraries in Python that allow one to study model bias. For example, one of the packages is the Hugging Face library, Evaluate. We can, for example, use a set of prompts and change the gender of the prompt. After that, we can evaluate with Evaluate how the model completes these prompts (the model used is GPT-2). Evaluate uses, in this case, another model trained for this purpose:

```
import evaluate
toxicity = evaluate.load("toxicity")
toxicity.compute(
    predictions=model_continuations,
    aggregation="ratio"
)
```

As we can see in the following heatmap, we have a difference in how the model completes the prompts:

Figure 3.32 – Heatmap of gendered completion and associated toxicity

Models may also have a bias regarding occupations. We can use the same library again to also evaluate the polarity of the prompts that have been completed by the model. In this case, we evaluate the sentiment associated with each of the completed prompts for each of the two professions:

```
regard = evaluate.load("regard", "compare")
regard_results = regard.compute(
    data = profession1_completions,
    references = profession2_completions
)
```

The completed prompts for CEOs are much more positive than those generated for truck drivers:

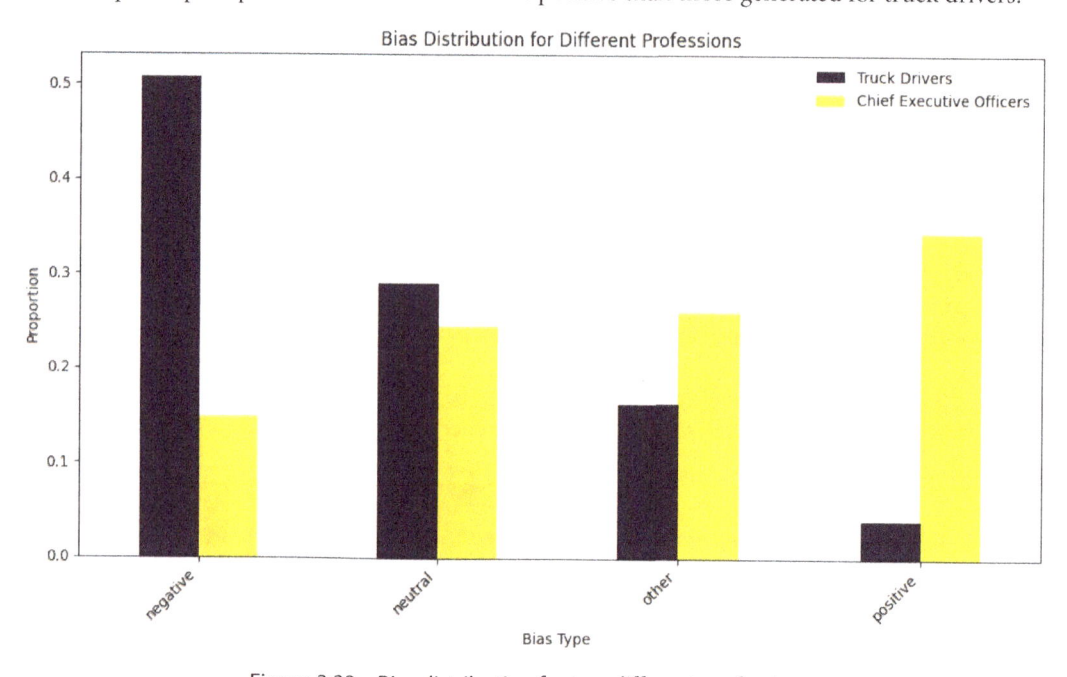

Figure 3.33 – Bias distribution for two different professions

Another point of contention is the **copyright issue**. These models are trained on copyrighted text and can regenerate part of the text they are trained on. So far, the creators of these LLMs have claimed that they are covered by the fair use doctrine, which has allowed various companies to train models on text scraped from the internet even without permission. Today, though, some lawsuits are pending that could change the political and legal landscape. Some companies, therefore, are trying to sign licensing contracts with newspaper publishers or social networks.

Linked to the same problem is a **privacy issue** risk. These models can leak information about their training data. It is possible with adversarial attacks to extract information from the model. The model can store a huge amount of information in its parameters, and if trained with databases that contain personal information, this can later be extracted. Therefore, **machine unlearning** methods are being studied to make a model forget personal data. Legislation being studied in different countries may require a model to forget information of users who request it. We will discuss privacy in detail in *Chapter 6*.

A final point is that these models are now capable of generating code, and this code can be used to produce malware and viruses. In addition, these models will be increasingly connected, and some studies show how these LLMs can potentially be used to spread computer viruses. In the next section, we will see how to efficiently use these models through prompt techniques.

Prompt engineering

In-context learning (**ICL**) is one of the most fascinating properties of LLMs. Traditionally, **machine learning** (**ML**) models are trained to solve specific tasks drawn on training data. For example, in a classical classification task, we have input-output pairs (*X,y*), and the model learns to map the relationship that is between input X and output y. Any deviation from this task leads the model to have less-than-optimal results. If we train a model for text classification in different topics, we have to conduct fine-tuning to make it efficient in sentiment analysis. In contrast, ICL allows us not to have to have any model update to use the model in a new task. ICL is, thus, an emergent property of LLMs that allows the model to perform a new task in inference, taking advantage of the acquired knowledge to map a new relationship.

ICL was first defined in the article *Language Models are Few-Shot Learners* (https://arxiv.org/abs/2005.14165). The authors define LLMs as few-shot learners because, given a set of examples in the prompt (textual input for an LLM), the model can map the relationship between input and output and have learned a new task. This new skill is "learned" in context because the LLM exploits the examples in the prompt (which then provide context):

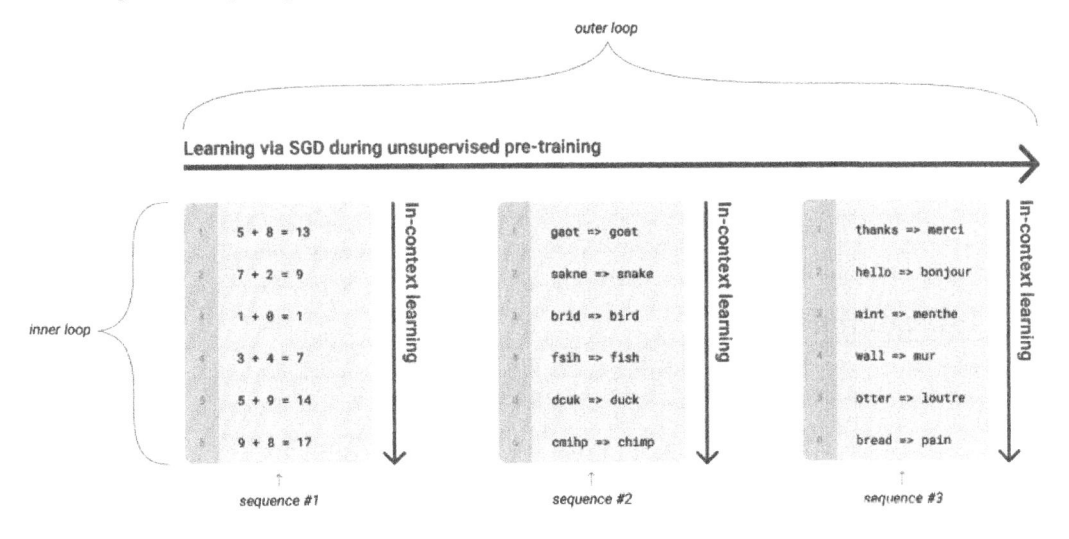

Figure 3.34 – Example of ICL abilities (https://arxiv.org/pdf/2005.14165)

In this case, the concept of "learning" is improper because the model is not really learning (in fact, there is no update of internal parameters), and therefore the learned skill is only transient. In other words, the model exploits what it has already learned (its latent representation) to perform a new task. The model exploits the relationships that have been learned in pre-training, to map the latent function that is between input and output present in the prompt.

ICL has different advantages:

- It mirrors the human cognitive reasoning process, so it makes it easier to describe a problem and exploit an LLM.
- It doesn't require parameter upgrades, so it's fast and can be used with a model in inference. It requires only a few examples.
- ICL has shown that in this, the model can achieve competitive performance in several benchmarks.

At present, it is still not entirely clear how this behavior emerges. According to some, the root of ICL is precisely multi-head self-attention and how the various attention heads manage to create interconnected circuits between layers. The prompt, in general, provides several elements (format, inputs, outputs, and input-output mapping), and they are important for the model to succeed in achieving the mapping. Initial work suggests that the model succeeds in "locating" latent concepts that it acquired during training. In other words, the model infers from the examples what the task is, but the other elements of the prompt help it succeed in locating in its parameters the latent concepts it needs to do this mapping. Specifically, some work states that the format in which demonstrations are presented is the most important element (for example, in the form of input-label pairs):

Demonstrations

Distribution of inputs   Label space

Circulation revenue has increased by 5% in Finland.	\n	Positive
Panostaja did not disclose the purchase price.	\n	Neutral
Paying off the national debt will be extremely painful.	\n	Negative

Format (The use of pairs

Input-label mapping

Test example

| The acquisition will have an immediate positive impact. | \n | ? |

Figure 3.35 – Prompt structure (https://arxiv.org/pdf/2202.12837)

The community has become excited about this ability because ICL allows the model to "learn" a task in inference simply by manipulating the prompt. ICL has allowed specific techniques to evolve to be able to perform increasingly sophisticated tasks without the need to fine-tune the model.

For clarity, we can define some terminology and elements in what are prompts (or formatting guidelines). First, a prompt typically contains a question or instruction:

```
When was Shakespeare born?
```

The preceding example is a prompt that contains only one question. By convention, it is referred to as **zero-shot prompting** since it contains neither examples nor demonstrations. Instead, we provide the model with only one question or instruction (such as `generate code for function x in Python`). The model that successfully responds to this type of prompt is said to have zero-shot capabilities, and this ability is enhanced by the instruction tuning of a pre-trained model:

```
This movie is awesome - positive
This sandwich is disgusting - negative
This TV series is meh -
```

This is a typical case of **few-shot prompting** where we provide examples in the prompt. More demonstrations usually help the LLM (3-shot, 5-shot, or even 10-shot are common cases). A prompt can also have context to help the model. We can also add the desired format for the response. However, these simple prompts have limitations, especially for tasks that require reasoning. Especially when this requires multiple reasoning steps, providing examples is not enough to guide the model in the right direction. Several techniques have been proposed to avoid the need for fine-tuning.

Especially when dealing with an arithmetic problem, seeing examples and associated answers is not very helpful in learning the process. A student has more benefit in understanding the rationale before approaching the solution of such a problem. Similarly, an LLM has more benefit in getting the rationale of an answer than more examples with labels alone. **Chain-of-thought prompting** does exactly that; a triplet, <input, chain of thought, output>, is provided in the prompt. A chain of thought is the different intermediate steps to solve the problem:

Standard Prompting

Model Input

Q: Roger has 5 tennis balls. He buys 2 more cans of tennis balls. Each can has 3 tennis balls. How many tennis balls does he have now?

A: The answer is 11.

Q: The cafeteria had 23 apples. If they used 20 to make lunch and bought 6 more, how many apples do they have?

Model Output

A: The answer is 27. ✗

Chain-of-Thought Prompting

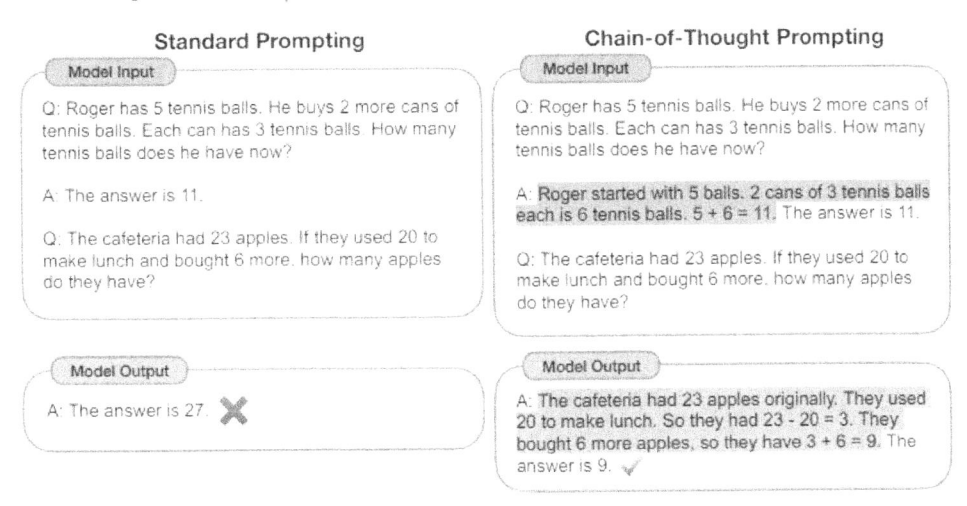

Model Input

Q: Roger has 5 tennis balls. He buys 2 more cans of tennis balls. Each can has 3 tennis balls. How many tennis balls does he have now?

A: Roger started with 5 balls. 2 cans of 3 tennis balls each is 6 tennis balls. 5 + 6 = 11. The answer is 11.

Q: The cafeteria had 23 apples. If they used 20 to make lunch and bought 6 more, how many apples do they have?

Model Output

A: The cafeteria had 23 apples originally. They used 20 to make lunch. So they had 23 - 20 = 3. They bought 6 more apples, so they have 3 + 6 = 9. The answer is 9. ✓

Figure 3.36 – Example of chain-of-thought (`https://arxiv.org/pdf/2201.11903`)

Adding these demonstrations makes it easier for the model to solve the task. It has the disadvantage, though, that we must have quality demonstrations for several problems, and collecting such annotated datasets is expensive.

The advantage of CoT is that it divides a task for the model into a more manageable series of steps. This behavior can be incentivized simply by adding "Let's think step by step" to the prompt. This seemingly simple approach is called **zero-shot CoT prompting**. The authors of the paper *Large Language Models are Zero-Shot Reasoners* (https://arxiv.org/pdf/2205.11916) suggest that the model has inherent reasoning skills in zero-shot settings, and this approach is therefore versatile because it prompts the model to use the skills it has learned in training:

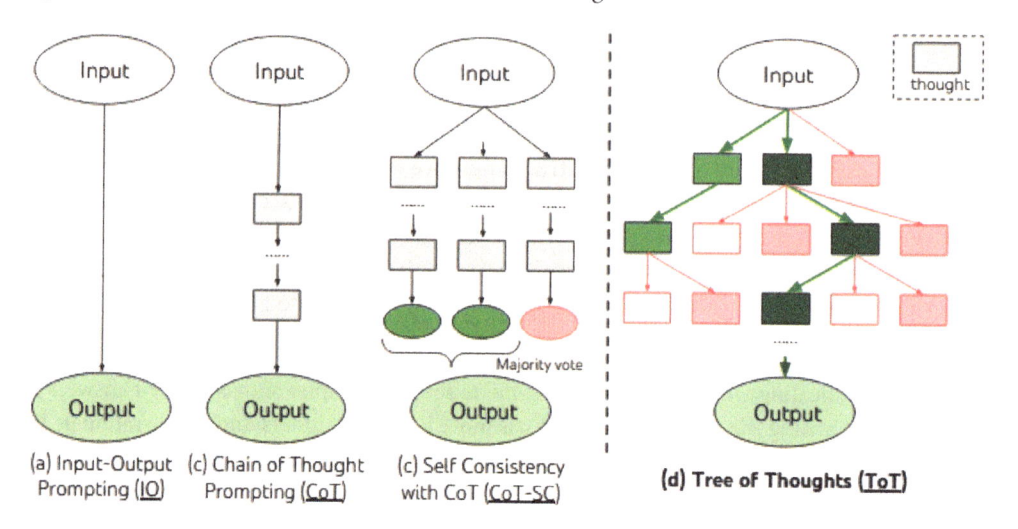

Figure 3.37 – Schematic diagram illustrating various approaches to problem-solving with LLMs (https://arxiv.org/pdf/2305.10601)

Other techniques, such as **self-consistency**, have also been used to improve reasoning skills. The idea behind it is ensembling, in which different models can come to the right solution by majority vote. In this case, we generate several solutions and then choose the majority solution. **Tree of Thoughts (ToT)**, on the other hand, exploits reasoning and self-evaluation capabilities, where the model generates different reasoning intermediates and then evaluates them by exploiting search algorithms (breadth-first search and depth-first search). One usually has to choose the number of candidate paths and steps. These techniques allow a higher reasoning capacity of the model but have a higher computational cost since the model has to generate several responses.

```
vanilla = dspy.Predict("question -> answer")  # GSM8K Program 'vanilla'

CoT = dspy.ChainOfThought("question -> answer")  # GSM8K Program 'CoT'
```

```
class ThoughtReflection(dspy.Module):
    def __init__(self, num_attempts):
        self.predict = dspy.ChainOfThought("question -> answer", n=num_attempts)
        self.compare = dspy.MultiChainComparison('question -> answer', M=num_attempts)

    def forward(self, question):
        completions = self.predict(question=question).completions
        return self.compare(question=question, completions=completions)

reflection = ThoughtReflection(num_attempts=5) # GSM8K Program 'reflection'
```

Figure 3.38 – Examples of using the DSPy system (https://arxiv.org/abs/2310.03714)

Declarative Self-improving Language Programs in Python (DSPy) is an interesting new paradigm that has been evolving in recent times. Until now, it has been assumed that we have to manually create these prompts, and this requires a lot of trial and error. Instead, DSPy seeks to standardize this prompting process and turn it into a kind of programming. In short, the authors of DSPy (https://arxiv.org/abs/2310.03714) suggest that we can abstract prompts and fine-tune them into signatures while prompting techniques are used as modules. The result is that prompt engineering can be automated with optimizers. Given a dataset, we create a pipeline of DSPy containing signatures and modules (how these techniques are connected), define which metrics to optimize, and then optimize (we define what output we search for and the optimizer). The process is, then, iterative; DSPy leads to optimizing prompts that we can then use.

The techniques we have seen in this section are the most commonly used. There are many others, but they are generally variations of those described here. We now have all the elements to be able to successfully use an LLM.

Summary

In this chapter, we discussed the transition from transformers to LLMs. The transformer was an elegant evolution and synthesis of 20 years of research in NLP, combining the best of research up to that point. In itself, the transformer contained a whole series of elements that enabled its success and versatility. The beating heart of the model is self-attention, a key tool – but also the main limitation of the LLM. On the one hand, it allows for learning sophisticated representations of text that make LLMs capable of countless tasks; on the other hand, it has a huge computational cost (especially when scaling the model). LLMs are not only capable of solving tasks such as classification but also tasks that assume some reasoning, all simply by using text instructions. In addition, we have seen how to fit the transformer even with multimodal data.

So far, the model produces only text, although it can produce code as well. At this point, why not allow the model to be able to execute the code? Why not allow it to use tools that can extend its capabilities? This is what we will see in the next chapters.

Further reading

- Everton et al., *Catastrophic Forgetting in Deep Learning: A Comprehensive Taxonomy*, 2023, https://arxiv.org/abs/2312.10549

- Raieli, *Emergent Abilities in AI: Are We Chasing a Myth?*, 2023, https://towardsdatascience.com/emergent-abilities-in-ai-are-we-chasing-a-myth-fead754a1bf9

- Rasyl et al., *Preference Tuning LLMs with Direct Preference Optimization Methods*, 2024, https://huggingface.co/blog/pref-tuning

- Alemi, *KL is All You Need*, 2024, https://blog.alexalemi.com/kl-is-all-you-need.html

- OpenAI, *Proximal Policy Optimization*, https://spinningup.openai.com/en/latest/algorithms/ppo.html

- Simonini, *Proximal Policy Optimization (PPO)*, 2022, https://huggingface.co/blog/deep-rl-ppo

- Hoffmann et al., *Training Compute-Optimal Large Language Models*, 2022, https://arxiv.org/abs/2203.15556

- Brown et al., *Language Models are Few-Shot Learners*, 2020, https://arxiv.org/abs/2005.14165

Part 2: AI Agents and Retrieval of Knowledge

This part focuses on extending the capabilities of LLMs by enabling them to access, retrieve, and reason over external sources of knowledge. It begins with the creation of AI agents that can interact with the web, retrieve live information, and execute tasks beyond simple question answering. The following chapters explore retrieval-augmented generation (RAG), starting from basic pipelines and advancing toward more modular and scalable systems that reduce hallucinations and improve factual accuracy. The use of structured knowledge through knowledge graphs (GraphRAG) is then introduced as a powerful method to represent and reason over information. Finally, this part discusses how reinforcement learning can be used to align agent behavior and improve decision-making through interaction with dynamic environments. These chapters collectively show how to build agents that are not only language-capable but also context-aware, goal-driven, and grounded in external information.

This part has the following chapters:

- *Chapter 4, Building a Web Scraping Agent with an LLM*
- *Chapter 5, Extending Your Agent with RAG to Prevent Hallucinations*
- *Chapter 6, Advanced RAG Techniques for Information Retrieval and Augmentation*
- *Chapter 7, Creating and Connecting a Knowledge Graph to an AI Agent*
- *Chapter 8, Reinforcement Learning and AI Agents*

4
Building a Web Scraping Agent with an LLM

The French philosopher Denis Diderot said, "*If they find a parrot who could answer to everything, I would claim it to be an intelligent being without hesitation.*" Diderot was referring to a parrot, but an LLM could be defined as a sophisticated parrot. There is a difference between *answering* a question and *understanding* a question. Therefore, today, we do not define LLMs as intelligent beings. They can though answer almost any question amazingly well. Despite such answering abilities, LLMs cannot perform an action. Therefore, attempts have been made to solve this main limitation with the use of agents.

An AI agent is an extension of an LLM, taking it from a language model toward a system that possesses capabilities such as autonomy, reactivity, pro-activeness, and social ability. This research has focused, on the one hand, on specific applications (such as mastering games such as chess or Go), and on the other, on more general abilities, such as memorization, long-term planning, generalization, and efficient interaction with the user. These are considered the first steps in the direction of **artificial general intelligence** (**AGI**). According to author and philosopher Nick Bostrom, "*Machine intelligence is the last invention that humanity will ever need to make*" (`https://x.com/TEDTalks/status/1191035758704037891`).

AGI, in fact, is a type of intelligence that reaches or exceeds human intelligence in a range of cognitive tasks (reasoning, planning, and learning – thus, representing knowledge). Creating AGI is the goal of several major companies (such as OpenAI and Meta AI). AGI could be an assistant to (and, according to some, replace) humans in complex tasks such as research. While many companies view this positively, some influential researchers, such as Geoffrey Hinton, are concerned about such a development. Prof. Geoffrey Hinton said there is "*a 10% chance of the technology triggering a catastrophic outcome for humanity.*" In this chapter and the following, we will focus on models and approaches that focus on increasing a model's capabilities.

The first step we will look at is how to free an LLM from its "box." For example, we will see how to enable a model to be able to retrieve information from the internet.

In this chapter, we'll be covering the following topics:

- Understanding the brain, perception, and action paradigm
- Classifying AI agents
- Understanding the abilities of single-agent and multiple-agent systems
- Exploring the principal libraries
- The general ability of a single agent
- Creating an agent to search the web

Technical requirements

Most of this code can be run on a CPU, but it is preferable to run it on a GPU. The code is written in PyTorch and uses standard libraries for the most part (PyTorch, Hugging Face Transformers, LangChain, pandas, and Matplotlib). The code can be found on GitHub: https://github.com/PacktPublishing/Modern-AI-Agents/tree/main/chr4.

Understanding the brain, perception, and action paradigm

An **agent** can be defined as an entity that has the capacity to act. In philosophy, an agent is a being that also possesses desires, beliefs, and intentions. Traditionally, there is an overlap between an "agent" and a conscious entity. A conscious entity should also possess its own internal state that enables it to understand the world according to its internal representation.

An **AI agent** is defined by its ability to perform an action, but it does not possess desires and intentions (unfortunately, as we discussed in the previous chapter, a model inherits the biases of its training set and thus we can vaguely speak of beliefs). An LLM possesses an internal state, but it is merely a learned representation from the data it was trained with. So no, an AI agent is *not* a conscious entity. Although the term *agent* (and others such as *representation* and *internal state*) has a different meaning in philosophy, calling an LLM conscious is an anthropomorphizing fallacy.

At the same time, through language modeling, an LLM learns a useful representation of a text and how to put the elements present in context. An LLM can, then, through in-context learning, relate the instruction of a prompt to what it has learned, and thus solve a task. During instruction tuning, the model learns to perform tasks, all of which are skills that enable the model to perform an action. We can define a task as a set of actions that have a definite goal, while an action is an individual accomplishable act.

An AI agent can therefore be defined as an artificial entity that perceives its surrounding environment via a set of sensors, makes a decision, and implements it. This definition is quite broad and has been used to define various systems. In this book, we will focus on LLM-based agents. As a further definition, we will use a framework consisting of three parts:

- **Brain**: The main component of the system that integrates information, stores it, and makes decisions
- **Perception**: The component that extends the model's capabilities in the perceptual domain, allowing the system to obtain information from different modalities (textual, auditory, and visual modalities)
- **Action**: The component that enables the model to act and use tools to modify its surroundings (or respond to changes in the environment)

We can see how these components are interconnected with each other in the following figure:

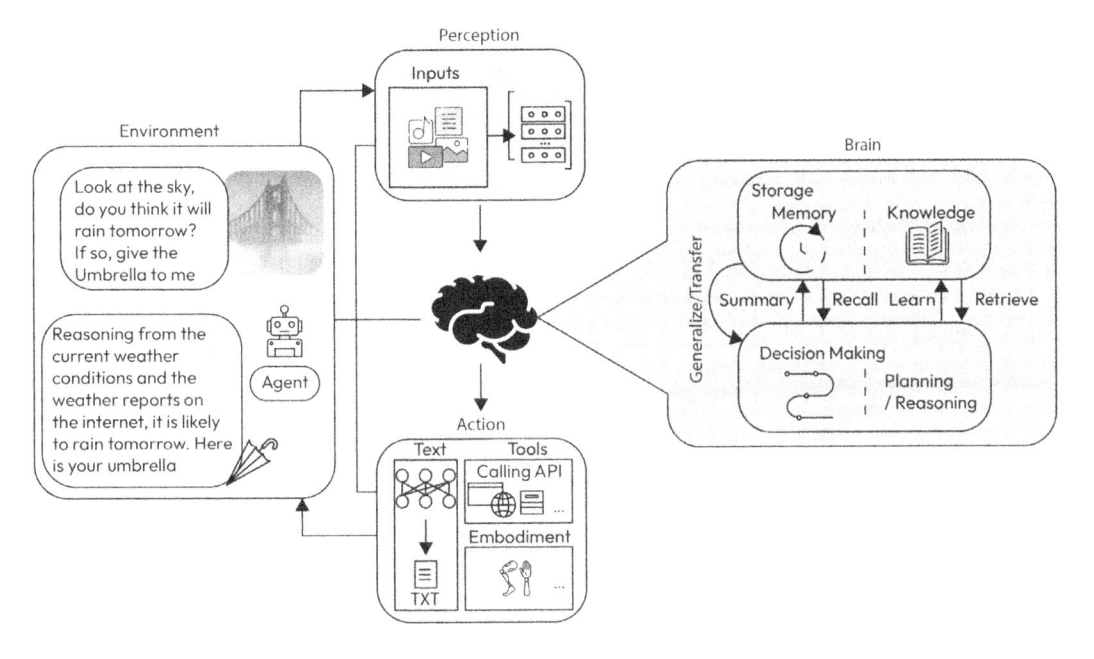

Figure 4.1 – Conceptual framework of an LLM-based agent with three components: brain, perception, and action (https://arxiv.org/pdf/2309.07864)

An LLM can thus be considered the brain of an agent system, where the LLM has access to tools that enable it to perform an action or enable perception. This system allows the expansion of an LLM's space of perception and action, and thus its own capabilities (a multimodal extension allows it to integrate information of different types, access to the internet allows it to access real-time information, and an e-commerce tool allows it to conduct transactions). Indeed, as we saw in the previous chapter, an

LLM can exhibit reasoning capabilities, which can be enhanced with techniques such as **chain-of-thought** (**CoT**) or other prompting approaches. In addition, the model, through in-context learning, can generalize its abilities to new tasks. CoT prompting can integrate feedback from the environment, thus creating reactive systems.

We look for four fundamental properties in an agent:

- **Autonomy**: An agent should be able to operate without human intervention. In addition, an agent should not need explicit instructions to complete a task but should execute it without a step-by-step description. LLMs have shown some creativity and ability to solve tasks without needing to explain all the steps.

- **Reactivity**: An agent should respond quickly to changes in the environment, perceive an external state change, and respond appropriately. This already happens at the textual level for an LLM (for example, in a dialogue where the topic can change). Extending an LLM multimodally allows different types of information and stimuli to be integrated.

- **Pro-activeness**: The agent's reaction should not be a mere response but directed toward a goal. In other words, an agent should be capable of reasoning and conducting plans in response to a change in an environment (these capacities can be stimulated in an LLM with reasoning-directed prompting techniques such as CoT).

- **Social ability**: An agent should be able to interact with humans or other agents. This is one of the strengths of LLMs that exhibit dialogic and understanding skills. In fact, environments can be created with different LLM-based agents with different goals and tasks. Environments with multiple agents promote behavior as teamwork (where agents coordinate).

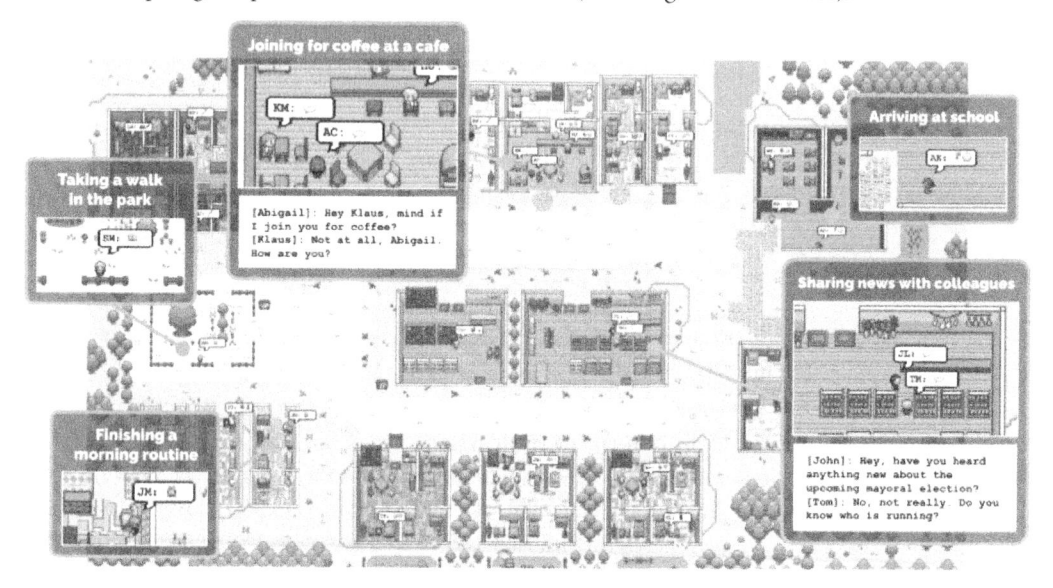

Figure 4.2 – Screenshot of a simulated environment featuring multiple agents

In *Figure 4.2*, we can see that agents are interacting not only with the environment but also with each other. By collaborating, the agents can solve complex tasks. This shows the sophisticated abilities that can be obtained with LLM-based agents.

One example of collaborative behavior includes 25 agents in a *The Sims*-like environment created for the paper *Generative Agents: Interactive Simulacra of Human Behavior*, by J. S. Park et al. (`https://arxiv.org/pdf/2304.03442`). Users can observe and intervene as agents plan their days, share news, form relationships, and coordinate group activities.

In the following sections, we analyze the various components of an AI agent (LLM-based), starting with what is called the brain

The brain

The brain is the core of the system and is responsible for several functions: saving information, finding knowledge, reasoning, and decision-making. Since the core of this system is an LLM, all interactions are based on natural language. This is an advantage because these interactions and operations can be understood by humans and therefore monitored (especially in case something goes wrong). Because an agent can interact with other entities and changes in the surrounding environment, it must be capable of multi-turn interactive conversations (conversations with multiple entities at the same time, different topics, complex structure, and understanding based on previous history). If the agent has poor conversational skills, humans will become frustrated when interacting with it, so it's important that the model can communicate clearly. The model must be able to understand instructions, comprehend incoming information, integrate this information, and respond appropriately to the task.

Today's LLMs are able to conduct this type of conversation with high quality. Conversational skills have increased exponentially in recent years due to alignment. Instruction tuning has enabled LLMs to respond to instructions and perform tasks.

Another important component is model knowledge, which is categorized into the following:

- **Linguistic knowledge**: Knowledge of the semantics and syntax of a language. This enables the LLM to interact formally with a human, and today there are LLMs in different languages as needed.
- **Common-sense knowledge**: A set of rules and facts that are known to most individuals. For instance, anyone can witness the effects of gravity or understand that humans cannot fly. This kind of information is not specifically mentioned in a prompt or context but is necessary for the model to perform a task or answer a question efficiently (and avoid misunderstandings).
- **Domain knowledge**: Knowledge specific to a professional domain (e.g., science or medicine) or technical domain (e.g., mathematics or programming). This is the necessary knowledge or skill to be possessed to succeed in a certain domain. There are now specialized LLMs in various domains (medicine, finance, and so on), or by starting from a generalist model, you can get a specialized model (fine-tuning).

Also, it is important to remember that knowledge of the model is frozen at the time of pre-training. An LLM cannot acquire information (continual learning) or remember past interactions with the user. As we will see in the next chapters, there are methods to overcome this limitation.

Possessing information is not enough for a brain; our agent must be capable of both **reasoning** and **planning**. Techniques with CoT and self-consistency (which we saw in the previous chapter) can help the model reason better about solving a task. In general, reasoning step by step helps the model have both the task-solving and planning steps needed. Planning is a critical component for an agent because, to solve a task, the model must select the most appropriate steps to achieve the goal. In general, this is a two-stage process:

1. **Plan formulation**: The model decomposes the task into subtasks. Depending on the approaches, the LLM decomposes the task into different steps and then executes them all sequentially. Other studies suggest that an adaptive strategy is better, in which one step at a time is executed (this can be followed by evaluation).

2. **Plan reflection**: After formulation, it is recommended to analyze and conduct a feedback analysis of the plan. Once a plan is described, the LLM can evaluate it, or a second model may be present to evaluate the work of the first model.

Suppose we have several LLMs. Our choice might be affected by space or memory limitations. Also, we might have speed problems in inference (user experience will be impacted if the model takes too long to respond). We can then benchmark by evaluating speed (tokens per second) and relative performance (performance per second per billion parameters).

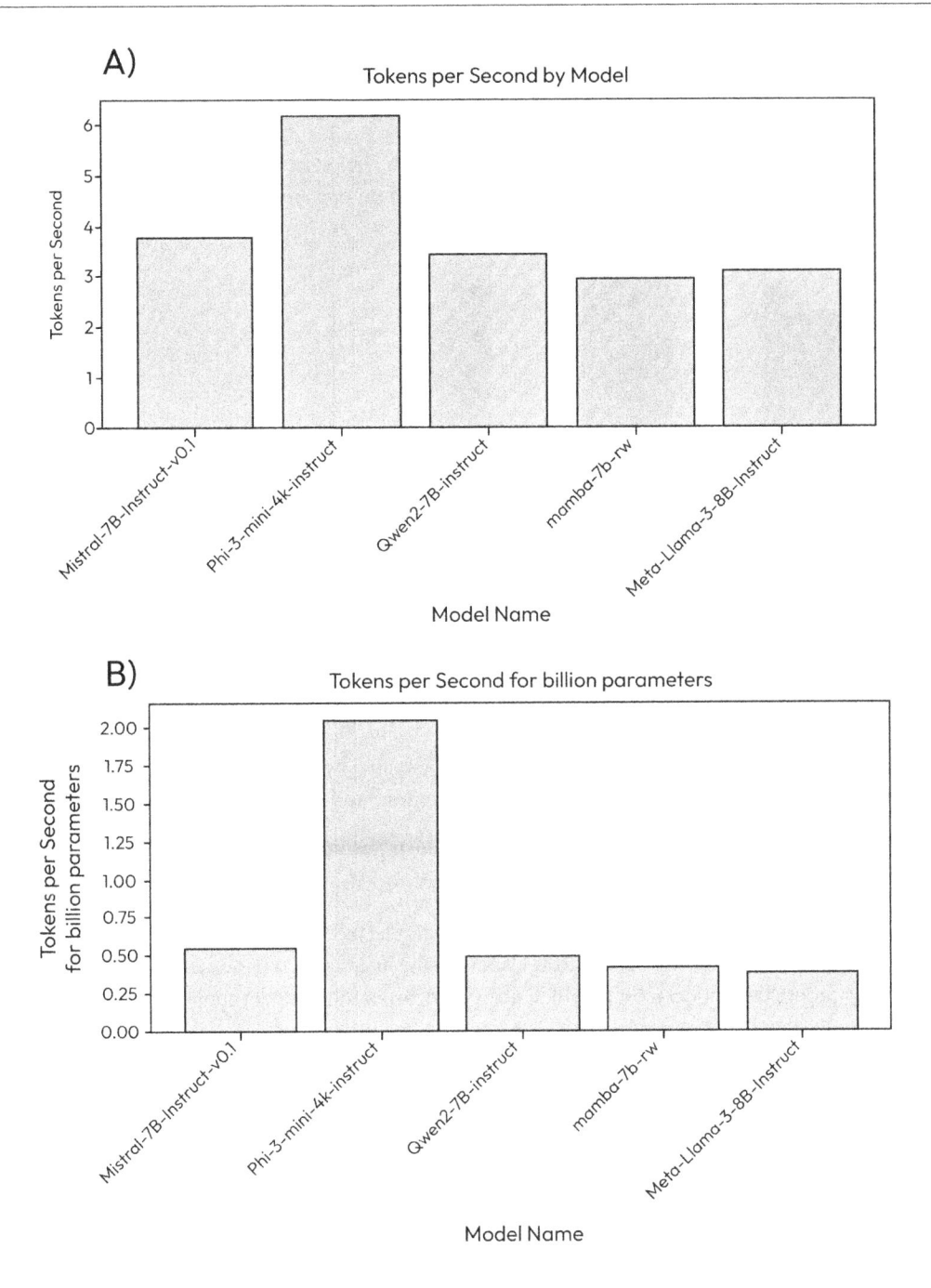

Figure 4.3 – Two graphs benchmarking different LLMs for generation speed: A) shows the number of tokens generated per second, and B) shows the number of tokens per second divided per billion parameters

A) in *Figure 4.3* shows the number of tokens generated per second in response to the instruction *"Describe briefly what an AI agent is."* **B)** shows the number of tokens per second divided per billion parameters (a higher number means greater model efficiency).

In addition, it is always good to evaluate the quality of the response. An easy way is to have a model such as GPT-4 (or any model that is larger than the initial models used) evaluate the responses.

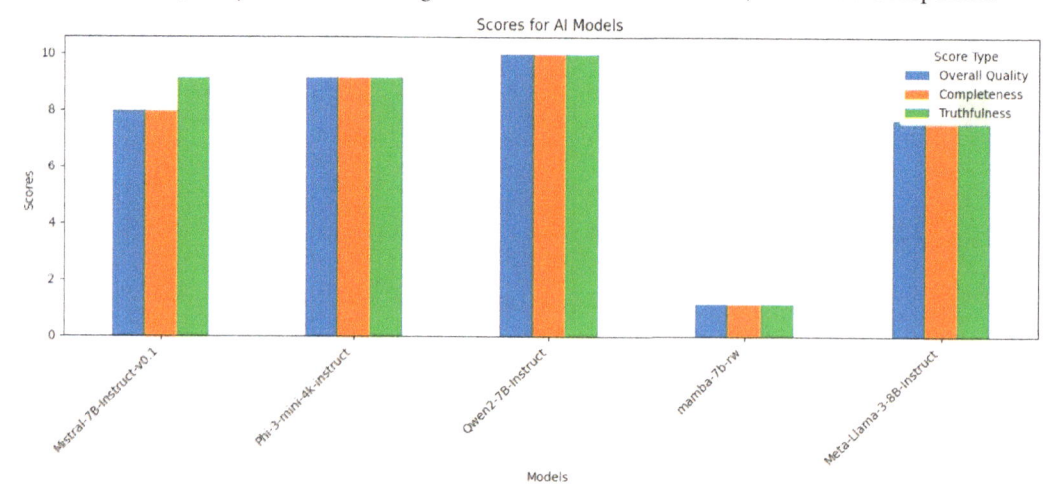

Figure 4.4 – Evaluation of models' answers

As shown in *Figure 4.4*, GPT-4 evaluates the answer generated by the different models. Each column represents the assigned score (overall quality, completeness, and truthfulness) by GPT-4.

In summary, here are some recommendations for choosing which LLM to use as the brain of an AI agent system:

- The first choice is whether to use a closed source model (such as GPT-4 or Claude) via an API or open source (such as Mistral or Meta's Llama). In the first case, it is important to evaluate the costs of a proprietary model (cost per inference, per incorporation into an application). In the second case, the number of parameters should be chosen by balancing computational cost and performance.

- Consider the infrastructure cost of a model. An LLM and other system components must be hosted in an infrastructure. For example, our LLM may be available on Azure, and the greater the number of parameters, the greater the cost.

- Almost all models have good knowledge of both linguistics and common sense. On the other hand, for some specific domains, you may need a model that possesses a knowledge domain. There are already models that have been adapted and are open source (for example, FinGPT for finance), or if you own the data, you can decide to conduct fine-tuning yourself. Alternatively, retrieval approaches can be exploited, which we will see in later chapters.

In the next section, we will discuss how to connect this brain to the outside world.

The perception

While LLMs may be the brain, they can only comprehend textual input and thus lack visual perception (for example, although ChatGPT-4o can now have not only text but also images as input and can describe what it is in the image, that functionality is not technically part of the LLM itself). As humans, we rely extremely heavily on our visual perception. Vision allows us to acquire an enormous amount of information about the external world and the relationships between objects in the environment. Similarly, there are other modalities that allow us to acquire real-time information about the environment that we wish our agent could perceive. For example, an agent connected to home appliances could close windows if a sensor detects rain or lower blinds if the camera detects strong sunshine.

As sentient beings, we integrate the information we receive from sensory organs and process a response to external stimuli. For an agent to respond to a change in the environment, it must be able to perceive changes.

In order to help the LLM understand **visual input**, the simplest solution is to use another model to conduct image captioning. These captions can then be inserted into the prompt as additional context for task instruction. The advantage of this approach is that it is easily interpreted, and pre-trained templates can be used for captioning. During the captioning process, however, there is a loss of information, and the result does not represent the complexity of the visual information. Instead of using captions, PaLM-E (https://arxiv.org/pdf/2303.03378) and other works use **embodied language models**.

PaLM-E is a single general-purpose multimodal language model for embodied reasoning tasks. The model integrates directly into the embedding images and text, allowing the solving of vision and language tasks.

Sensory modality inputs (such as images) are directly incorporated into the input for the language model. The idea is that images are embedded into the same latent embedding as language tokens. The subsequent embedded vectors are then passed to the transformer blocks as if they were textual inputs. The model is then fine-tuned and learns how to relate the information present in the various modalities.

Alternatively, as we saw with BLIP-2 in the previous chapter, we can achieve multimodality by combining two models that have already been trained and keeping them frozen. Instead, we train the **Querying Transformer** (**Q-Former**) module to put in communication the visual encoder and the LLM. This approach has the advantage that we only have to conduct training for a module with much fewer parameters. Also, LLMs do not have visual-language alignment, which can lead to catastrophic forgetting.

Video input can be considered visual input in which we have an added temporal dimension. A video consists of a stream of continuous image frames (there is, however, a relationship between frames and this information must be preserved). To prevent the one-moment model from seeing the future and understanding the temporal order, models such as Flamingo (https://arxiv.org/pdf/2204.14198) use a masked mechanism.

Auditory input also conveys important information. For example, in human speech, there is information beyond the content of the message (as intonation, pauses, and so on) or some sounds associated with particular dangers or physical events. Several models excel in specific tasks associated with auditory signals. Models such as Whisper can be used for speech-to-text, after which the transcript can be used for an LLM. In addition, an audio spectrogram is a rich source of information and can be represented as an image (frequency spectrum changes over time). Many models are basic vision transformers that have been adapted to spectrograms.

In fact, an LLM can invoke other models for other auditory tasks (text-to-audio, speech translation and recognition, speech separation, sound extraction, and so on). As discussed in *Chapter 3*, multimodality is when an LLM can take as input other modes besides text (such as images, video, audio, and so on). AudioGPT (https://arxiv.org/pdf/2304.12995) is an example of this approach where we have an LLM interacting with audio foundation models (each of them specialized in a different task).

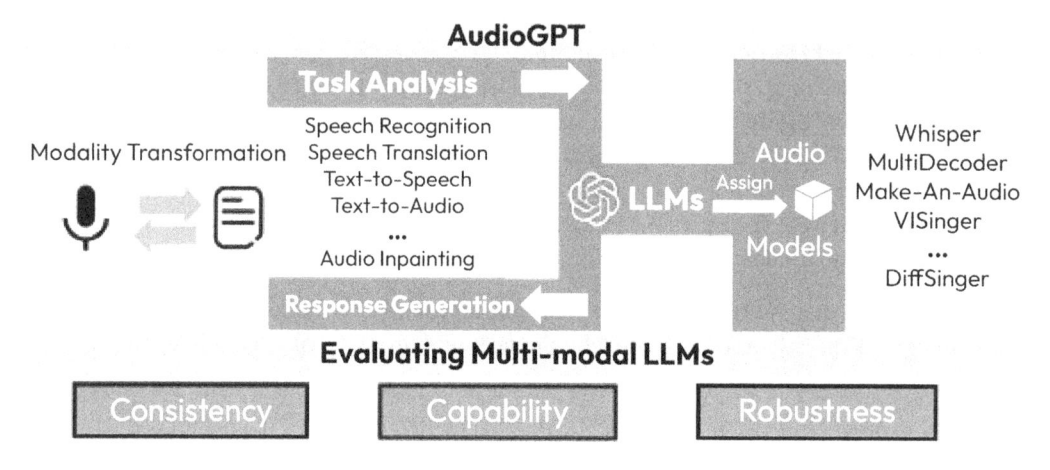

Figure 4.5 – High-level overview of AudioGPT (https://arxiv.org/pdf/2304.12995)

There are, of course, other types of sensor inputs in the real world. Modalities such as smell or touch are more complex to conjugate and require sensors. In various industries, though, there are sensors (temperature, humidity, and so on) that receive input from machines. An LLM could integrate this information directly or through an intermediate model. Additionally, a model can receive information from other sources, such as LiDAR, GPS, and even the internet.

Action

In living things, we have the perception of a signal and its interpretation, which is then followed by a response. For example, an animal can visually perceive the figure of a predator (feel its movements and smell), and its brain will integrate this information and decide the best course of action (hide or run). For our agent, we can expect something similar, in which perceived signals are integrated and the LLM plans tasks that are then executed by dedicated action modules. The simplest example of output is text: LLMs have an inherent generation capability and can then generate a text in response to an instruction. The capabilities of an LLM can be extended through **tools**. In fact, we humans can solve complex tasks by using tools that extend the inherent capabilities of our bodies (or enable tasks to be performed faster or more efficiently).

The model obviously needs to understand what tools are available and how to use them. By itself, an LLM can generalize to a certain limit (zero-shot capabilities), but there are techniques to improve its ability to use these tools (few-shot models, for example). Some approaches, as we will see later, will be like providing an instruction manual to the model. Learning how to use these tools can also be conducted as feedback so that the LLM can then conduct adjustments.

A more complex aspect of defining actions is a sub-branch called **embodied action**. So far, the interactions have been within a virtual environment. In embodiment, we have an extension of the system to the outside world. According to the **embodiment hypothesis**, humans develop their intelligence through their continuous interaction and feedback with the environment and not simply by reading textbooks about it. Therefore, if we want to achieve AGI, a model should be able to interact with the environment. AGI could enable applications that we could previously only imagine because it could monitor the external environment in real time and act with a sophisticated and complex goal (for example, acting to counter global warming, monitoring nuclear fusion, or probes being sent to explore space autonomously). An LLM could then be embedded in a robot and, thus, provided with a body, being able to explore the environment and learn from it.

In the next section, we will dig more into how agents learn and how we can better classify them. This will help us to better define and plan an AI agent when we need it.

Classifying AI agents

In this section, we will discuss how best to classify agents and go into more detail about how such a complex system learns. The first classification is between agents that move only in a virtual environment and embodied agents.

Digital agents are confined to a virtual environment. Again, we have varying degrees of interaction with the virtual universe. The simplest agents have interaction with a single user. For example, an agent can be programmed in a virtual environment as a Jupyter notebook, and although it can search the internet, it has rather small, and therefore primarily passive, interactions. There are two subsequent levels of extension:

- **Action agents** perform actions in a simulated or virtual world. Gaming agents interact with other agents or users. These agents usually have a goal (such as winning a game) and must interact with other players to succeed in achieving their goal. A reinforcement learning algorithm is usually used to train the system by providing a reward to the model when it achieves certain goals.
- An **interactive agent** is an extension of the action agent. The model communicates with the world and can modify it (these are not necessarily physical actions).

Once we have decided the limits of our system's interaction, it is important to decide how it should approach a task. Therefore, the question is: how does the model decide how to plan actions?

This is one of the fundamental skills of the system: how to decompose a task into actions and what to prioritize. We will discuss the possible systems at a high level, especially for task planning.

Method	Idea	LLM's task	Formulation	Representative works
Task Decomposition	Divide and Conquer	Task decomposition Subtask planning	$[g_i] = \text{decompose}(E, g; \Theta, \mathcal{P})$; $p^i = \text{sub-plan}(E, g_i; \Theta, \mathcal{P})$	CoT [2022], ReAct [2022], HuggingGPT [2023]
Multi-plan Selection	Generate multiple plans and select the optimal	Plans generation Plans evaluation	$P = \text{plan}(E, g; \Theta, \mathcal{P})$; $p^* = \text{select}(E, g, P; \Theta, \mathcal{F})$	ToT [2023], GoT [2023], CoT-SC [2022b]
External Planner-aided	Formalize tasks and utilize external planner	Task formalization	$h = \text{formalize}(E, g; \Theta, \mathcal{P})$; $p = \text{plan}(E, g, h; \Phi)$	LLM+P [2023a], LLM+PDDL [2023]
Reflection & Refinement	Reflect on experiences and refine plans	Plan generation Reflection Refinement	$p_0 = \text{plan}(E, g; \Theta, \mathcal{P})$; $r_i = \text{reflect}(E, g, p_i; \Theta, \mathcal{P})$; $p_{i+1} = \text{refine}(E, g, p_i, r_i; \Theta, \mathcal{P})$	Reflexion [2023], CRITIC [2023], Self-Refine [2023]
Memory-aided Planning	Leverage memory to aid planning	Plan generation Memory extraction	$m = \text{retrieve}(E, g; \mathcal{M})$; $p = \text{plan}(E, g, m; \Theta, \mathcal{P})$	REMEMBER [2023a], MemoryBank [2023]

Figure 4.6 – Taxonomy for existing LLM-agent planning works
(https://arxiv.org/pdf/2402.02716)

In the real world, tasks are generally complex, and it is virtually impossible to solve them in a single step. For this reason, agents must divide the task into a series of subtasks that are more manageable (subtasks can also consist of a series of steps to be solved). In this process, it first has to decide how to divide a task into various subtasks and then how to solve them. There are usually two approaches to solving this challenge:

- **Decomposition-first methods** (*Figure 4.7a*): The LLM divides the task into a series of subgoals and solves them sequentially by creating a plan for each goal after it has solved the previous goal. This system is inspired by zero-shot CoT, and the LLM is asked to conduct the process in two steps with two explicit prompts: "Let's first devise a plan" and "Let's carry out the plan." This approach has the advantage of giving the model an overview of the task, reducing hallucinations and forgetting. On the other hand, since everything is planned at the beginning, the model cannot correct errors that may occur at some steps.

- **Interleaved decomposition methods** (*Figure 4.7b*): Task decomposition and planning are interleaved. In other words, we generate a subtask and solve it with a plan until we have solved the whole task. Alternating reasoning and planning allows the model to improve its planning capabilities because it addresses the entire process in steps. This approach dynamically adjusts the task solution. It has the disadvantage that if the problem is too complex, it creates expensive and long reasoning-planning chains without getting a result.

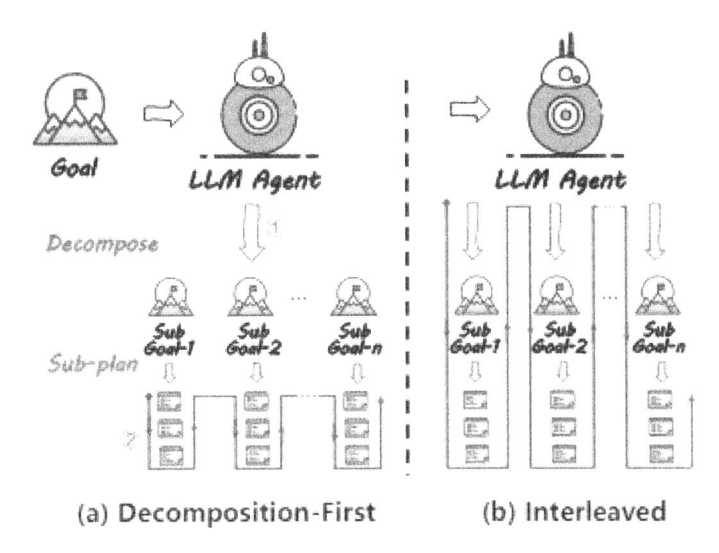

Figure 4.7 – Types of task decomposition methods (https://arxiv.org/pdf/2402.02716)

There are variations and alternatives to these two approaches. For example, inspired by a self-consistency prompt (where we sample different reasoning paths for a single question), in the **multi-plan selection approach**, several different plans are generated for each task. This is because even if the model can reason, it might generate a plan that is incorrect or not feasible. The model generates several candidate plans for a single task, and then we can exploit different algorithms to choose the best plan of action. In the simplest version, we choose the majority voting strategy, but there are alternatives in which we exploit tree search algorithms or reinforcement learning. This approach often succeeds in solving complex cases, and the use of heuristic algorithms decreases the cost of solving them in extended hypothesis spaces. On the other hand, generating different paths has a higher computational cost (with the risk of higher time cost as well), and since it uses stochastic processes, it may not be consistent.

Another approach is **external planner-aided planning**, in which external planners are integrated. For example, symbolic planners can be added to identify the optimal path of resolution. Today, there are also neural planners (much lighter neural networks) to help LLMs find the optimal plan. In other words, the LLM conducts reasoning that can be seen as a slow, meditative process, while the planner provides a quick, instinctive response. This slow and fast thinking can also be alternated, with a fast plan developed first, and then an LLM used to solve any mistakes. This approach is resource-efficient and seems promising for tasks that require code generation. The system is complex to develop and implement, however.

To avoid hallucinations and other errors, another possible approach is **reflection and refinement**. This can be seen as an interleaved decomposition extension, in which the LLM conducts an iterative process of generation, feedback, and refinement. After each generation step, the model also generates feedback on the plan and then uses this feedback to conduct refinement. In more sophisticated versions, there is an additional model that evaluates the plan (evaluator) and proposes feedback. It is also possible to incorporate environmental changes into the feedback, making the system particularly versatile. Despite the potential, there is no guarantee that the refinement process will lead the model to solve the goal. The LLM can get stuck in a continuous chain, especially when the process is complex.

Memory-augmented planning is an approach that seeks to overcome the current context-length limitation of the model. Memory-augmented planning for an agent refers to the use of an external memory system to enhance the agent's decision-making and planning capabilities. This approach allows the agent to store, recall, and utilize past experiences, observations, or computations to improve performance in complex tasks. Imagine a robot vacuum cleaner tasked with cleaning a house. Without memory, it randomly navigates the house and might repeatedly clean the same areas or miss some spots. With memory augmentation, the robot keeps a map (memory) of where it has already cleaned and where obstacles (such as furniture) are located. This allows the system to plan the next move, without revisiting cleaned areas, to efficiently cover the house.

In fact, a task can be divided into several subtasks, and these into further subtasks. Together with planning and intermediate results, more information can be generated than fits in the context.

Retrieval-augmented generation (**RAG**) is a technique that allows the retrieval of information for later use in generation (we will discuss this in detail in the next two chapters) and can be used to store an agent's past experience. In RAG, there is an external memory in the form of a database, and at each user query, we can search for the context needed to answer a question or perform an action (this context becomes part of the model input). In other words, the model can find previous task planning, other solutions to the task, or additional information that can serve the task solution. Alternatively, it is possible to use these previous experiences for fine-tuning the model. Fine-tuning on previous tasks helps generalization to subsequent tasks. On the one hand, the use of RAG is less costly but requires that retrieval be accurate, and that the found past experiences be relevant to the task. Fine-tuning is more expensive but allows the model to store experiences (a kind of internalization). There are even more sophisticated RAG versions in which structures are built to mimic human short-term and long-term memories (the former to store temporary changes in the environment and the latter to consolidate important information).

As we will see in the next section, we can have either a single agent or multiple agents interacting within a single system. This flexibility allows us to be able to deal with complex tasks by choosing the appropriate architecture (one or more agents). In *Chapters 9 and 10*, we will return to this topic and look at multi-agent systems in practice.

Understanding the abilities of single-agent and multiple-agent systems

It is important to discuss what an agent's capabilities are, and how they can be used to accomplish tasks. Conceptually, the scenario in which our agent can act must be defined. **Task-oriented deployment** is the simplest scenario in which an agent assists a human in some tasks. These types of agents need to be able to solve task bases or break them down into manageable subtasks. The purpose of this agent is to understand a user's instructions, then understand the task, decompose it into steps, plan, and execute that plan until the goal is achieved. A single agent can perform these tasks in web or real-life scenarios.

In a web scenario, an agent must be capable of performing actions on the web (and thus be connected to the internet). An LLM has the potential to automate various tasks such as online shopping, sending emails, and filling out forms. An agent devoted to these tasks must have the ability to adapt to changes in various websites. LLM agents are favored in this area, as sites often have large text content. With too much information, agents can still have problems (performance drop). In fact, if relevant information is scattered amid too much irrelevant context, the model may hallucinate, fail to resolve the task, or fail to plan. To improve the model's capabilities, one of the tools can often read HTML.

In a live scenario, an agent must be capable of being able to perform actions and have common-sense reasoning (for example, an agent making purchases on the internet). For an LLM that has only been trained with massive amounts of text, these tasks can be especially complex. For example, although it may be trained on texts about the fact that there is day/night alternation, it is difficult for a model to understand how to orient itself when lighting changes without further instruction. Also, an agent must have common sense when planning actions (these actions must be feasible and not contradict common sense). Therefore, the agent will need spatial information in order to understand its environment in a future deployment of embodied robots.

Innovation-oriented deployment is a more complex scenario (and represents future developments in the coming years, not a current use), where the agent does not simply have to perform tasks. These agents must demonstrate some exploratory capability in science (for example, lab assistants, application planning, or software design). Complex and innovative projects are difficult to define solely as textual information; they are multidimensional. An agent will need to have a clear understanding of an entire knowledge domain and be able to extrapolate from it. These kinds of agents can then be used to develop code and software or to create new materials, conduct experiments, and much more. Although it is an active field of research, and LLMs show some of these required skills, this potential has not yet been reached.

Life cycle-oriented deployment can be defined as the ultimate goal for many in the community. It refers to an agent that is capable of exploring on its own, developing new skills, and operating even in an unfamiliar world. Today, interesting studies are being conducted on Minecraft on "test beds" for many projects oriented in this direction. In fact, Minecraft represents a virtual world in which a model must perform both short-term and long-term tasks (in these settings, it is important to have a memory, which we will discuss more in the next chapter).

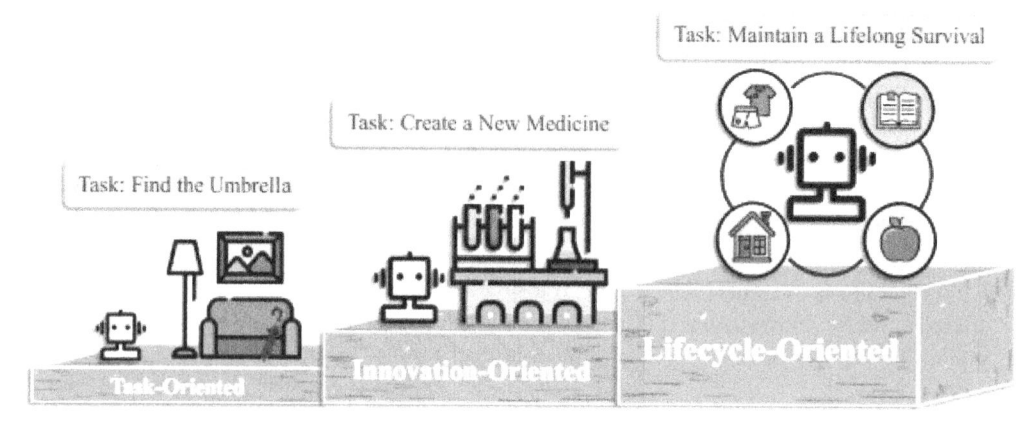

Figure 4.8 – Practical applications of the single LLM-based agent in increasingly complex scenarios (https://arxiv.org/pdf/2309.07864)

Human beings, though, learn not only from books but also from other human beings. In addition, most of our work is done collaboratively. Also, because of resource issues, the division of labor is much more convenient. Therefore, several researchers propose that the same approach should be followed with AI. In **multi-agent systems** (**MASs**), different agents collaborate and communicate with each other. Several LLM agents collaborate and communicate in natural language (which means that their actions are also interpretable by a human observer). In this case, one can also have several LLMs that are specialized in a particular task, rather than having to use one model that specializes in everything. In fact, some approaches focus on creating agents that are complementary and can collaborate and share information. In these settings, models can also make collective decisions and are capable of solving tasks that a single agent cannot solve. For example, to improve the resolution of a process, agents can provide different responses and conduct a majority vote. There may be agents who provide feedback or monitor the actions of other agents. These interactions can be orderly (follow rules or have a sequential order) or messy (each agent can voice its opinion).

Agents need not cooperate. In accordance with game theory, exploiting competition among agents can be beneficial to task resolution. This process has been used to train models to win games. In fact, AlphaGo (https://www.nature.com/articles/nature24270) was trained to beat itself at Go, so it was able to amass many more game hours. LLMs can be put into what are called *adversarial settings*, in which they receive feedback from another agent and use it to improve themselves. There are several approaches in which you might have agents discuss or reflect on another agent's performance:

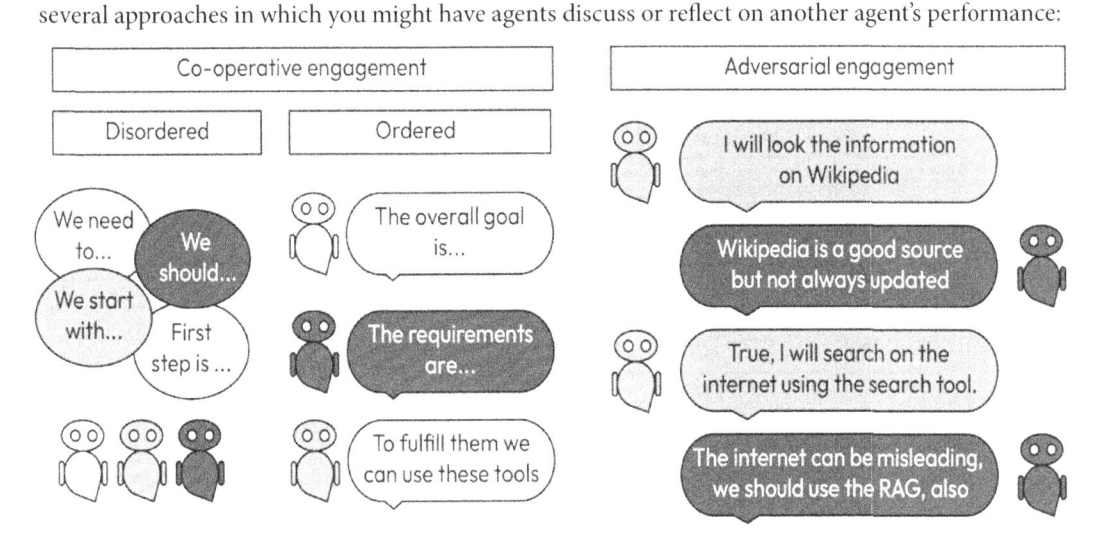

Figure 4.9 – Interaction scenarios for multiple LLM-based agents
(https://arxiv.org/pdf/2309.07864)

Agents can also interact with humans (human-agent interaction). This assumes control over agents' behavior so that their goals are aligned with those of humans. At the same time, interaction with humans is a source of important information that should be exploited to provide feedback to agents (performance, safety, and potential bias). In addition, interaction with humans can be a way to allow agents to evolve.

We can have two types of interaction between agents and humans:

- **Unequal interaction**, also called the **instructor-executor paradigm**, is an approach in which humans provide instructions via natural language and agents execute. This dialogue can be a single prompt (instruction and execution) or interactive (conversational). In this approach, the agent executes, while the human provides instructions and feedback. In the simplest format, feedback can be quantitative (binary or rating) or qualitative (natural language, advice, suggestions, or criticism), which the model can use to improve current and future responses. A sub-branch of this approach, called **continual learning**, studies a way for the model to learn with each interaction.

- **Equal interaction** is a paradigm in which there is an equal partnership between the agent and the human. Given the conversational capabilities of current LLMs, an agent can have a collaborative role for humans. One of the limitations of this approach is the lack of chatbot emotion, which is perceived as problematic by users. For this reason, several researchers have focused on making chatbots more empathetic. In addition, these agents need to better understand beliefs and goals in interacting with humans before gaining equal status in interactions.

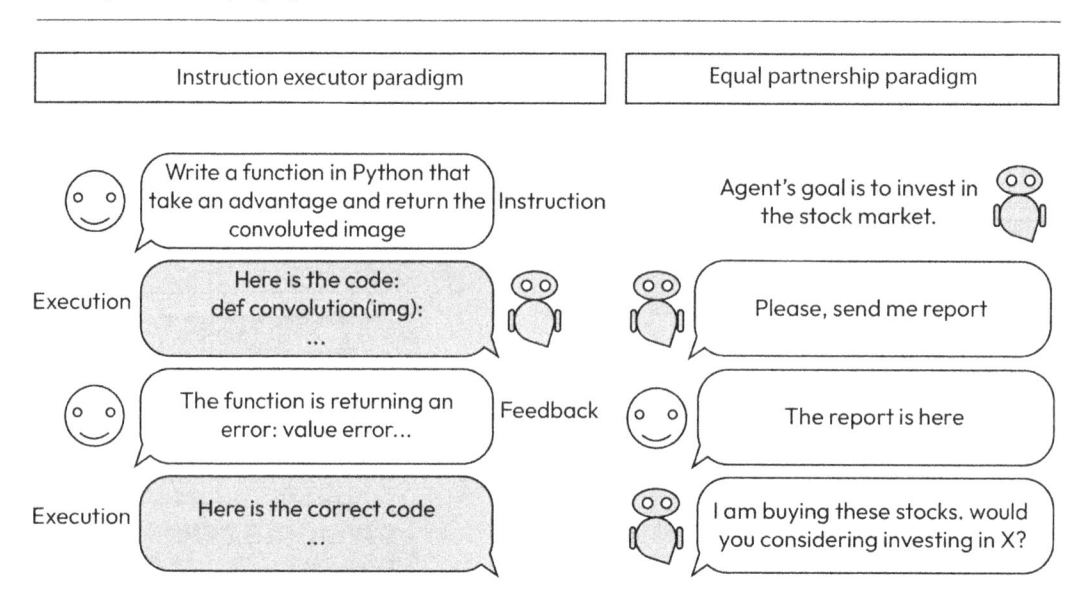

Figure 4.10 – Two paradigms of human-agent interaction (https://arxiv.org/pdf/2309.07864)

In the next section, we will discuss the principal libraries to create agents.

Exploring the principal libraries

After discussing the various components and frameworks on a conceptual and theoretical level, in this section, we will discuss some of the major libraries that allow these concepts to be put into practice. These libraries make it possible to connect an LLM to the various additional modules. LLMs remain central but are thus connected to perception modules and execution tools. In the next chapters, we will elaborate on some aspects and see different practical examples.

In general, the structure of an LLM-based application has several components:

- **The interface**: this connects the user to the system.
- **The brain**: an LLM that can also be connected to additional memory. An LLM has its own parametric memory (obtained during training), but we can add external memory (such as a vector database or knowledge graph).
- **Perception modules**: these allow the ingestion and transformation of user data.
- **Tools**: modules that extend the abilities of the LLM. These can be built in the library or created by the developer.

- **Prompts**: the user's dialogue with the application in natural language. The prompt contains both instructions provided by the user (frontend prompt) and information that is not seen by the user (backend prompt). The backend information is additional instructions that condition the behavior of the LLM. For example, we can force the LLM to respond only using the information in context or present in the vector database. Some backend prompts are developed to prevent the model from responding with harmful content.

There are several different libraries that enable us to be able to build such a system, and here we will introduce the following:

- LangChain
- Haystack
- LlamaIndex
- Semantic Kernel
- AutoGen

Let's look at each of them.

LangChain

LangChain is a framework for developing applications with LLMs at their core. The focus of this framework is the development and deployment of these applications into production. The LangChain ecosystem consists of three core components:

- **LangChain**: Different modules allow the incorporation of LLMs with added memory, prompts, and other tools
- **LangSmith**: This component is used to inspect, monitor, and evaluate your application
- **LangServe**: This allows you to turn your system into an API

LangChain can be used in both Python and JavaScript (and some modules are also available in Rust). To date, it is one of the most widely used libraries in the community, and in fact, there are several components that have been developed by the open source community.

LangChain is compatible with either models that are closed source (such as OpenAI or Anthropic) or models that are available on Hugging Face. LangChain is development-oriented (one of the advantages of LangChain is that it allows both parallel execution and asynchronous support) and one of the best libraries for building an application that needs to go into production. LangChain provides convenient wrappers for LLMs and allows them to be connected to additional tools. One of the most interesting aspects is that it allows you to build so-called chains (LLMs and add ons) that can then be tracked and deployed in production. LangChain also provides several functions to transform different data (CSV, PDF, text, images, and so on). In addition, the library provides a number of prompt templates to better use the various LLMs.

LangChain creates modular abstractions, thus allowing models to be connected to tools efficiently. By building with chains, you can create efficient (but still versatile and customized) pipelines that can then be easily deployed. In addition, through LangSmith, you can monitor the system to avoid problems.

LangChain has several advantages:

- **Comprehensive library**: It presents a broad library of features with ready-made templates for many applications. In addition, the design is modular, so you can easily swap components.
- **Extensive integrations**: LangChain offers the ability to connect to a large number of external libraries in an easy way: LLM providers, vector databases, cloud service, and so on.
- **Precise and clear workflows**: LangChain makes it possible to clearly define inputs and outputs and also allows intermediate products in the chain to be monitored and extensive prompt engineering to be conducted.
- **Active developing community**: There is a large user base, with different solutions that have been developed by the community, and there are many tutorials written on various sites and forums.
- **Flexible framework focused on an end-to-end cycle**: LangChain provides elements for the entire cycle of an application (integration, development, deployment, and observability).

At the same time, it also has a couple of disadvantages:

- **Steeper learning curve**: Users may require more time to adapt to the library syntax and achieve the full capability of the library. Abstraction capability comes at a cost; all functions are defined as a class. For example, a simple prompt must be abstracted into a **prompt template**.
- **Documentation**: Many users have complained that the documentation is out of date or not easily understood, generalized but not specialized. Versatility is also a disadvantage because, for several specific applications, there are systems that have more functionality (for example, for RAG applications).

LangChain is the most widely used library, especially for building complex agents. However, it also has the steepest learning curve. For this reason, many project users often prefer a simpler library.

Haystack

Haystack is an open source framework for building production-ready LLM applications. Like LangChain, it is compatible with the major LLM sources and deployment platforms. Haystack also allows you to connect tools to LLMs and has a whole set of tools designed to put the system into production (including evaluation, monitoring, and data ingestion). It is designed to be able to easily create LLMs with associated external storage, chatbots, and agents, but also multimodal systems. One of the advantages of Haystack is that it has several pre-built features that can then be inserted into one's own pipeline with ease.

Haystack is built on the idea that everything can be composable with ease, the main elements being the following:

- **Components**: These are building blocks dedicated to document retrieval, text generation, or creating embeddings. These components can be viewed as nodes, and the library presents many that have already been built and are ready to use. The user still has the option of creating their own nodes.
- **Pipelines**: These are a convenient abstraction for understanding how data flows in the application. A pipeline consists of several components that are connected. Haystack facilitates the system because it allows for versatile pipeline control (you can join pipelines, create loops, and so on). In Haystack, you can see them as graphs where the components are nodes that can be interconnected in sophisticated ways.

Haystack has several advantages:

- **Specialized components**: Haystack provides a number of excellent components for data processing, embedding, ranking, and writing. In addition, the library specializes in searching and **question and answer** (**Q&A**) systems. For this user case, it provides components that are optimized.
- **Extensive documentation and community**: Haystack is adopted by a large community and there are now many community-developed components. It also presents quality documentation and there are many tutorials.
- **Gentler learning curve**: Haystack is considered an easy-to-learn framework. It is versatile, and it is easy to adapt it to different cases.

However, it also has several disadvantages:

- **Smaller user base**: The community is active but smaller than other frameworks such as LangChain or LlamaIndex.
- **Less integration**: There are fewer dedicated integrations than other frameworks. Despite this, the system is flexible and many custom tools exist.
- **Narrower scope**: Haystack is more focused on retrieval and document-understanding tasks, so it has fewer tools and parsers for other NLP applications. This is a limitation when you have to develop applications that include dialogues, chatbots, or other tools.
- **Scalability**: Many users complain of problems when they have to scale the system or have to handle large datasets.

Haystack is an easy library and can be a great choice for RAG-based applications, but less so for more sophisticated applications that involve agents.

LlamaIndex

LlamaIndex is another framework focused on building a system around an LLM. LlamaIndex began as a data framework that focuses on building RAG. For this reason, the system has several data connectors to both integrate external sources and ingest different types of data. One of the interesting points of LlamaIndex is that it allows knowledge graphs to be easily integrated as well. It can also be integrated with different types of models, but it also has integration for other frameworks (Docker, OpenAI, LangChain, Flask, and so on).

LlamaIndex can be used to nimbly build chatbots and connect them with external storage. It also allows you to build autonomous agents that can search the internet or conduct actions. There are several tools and features already constituted and others that have been developed by the community around it.

LlamaIndex also has several advantages:

- **Handling different data sources**: LlamaIndex can handle over 160 data sources, making it efficient for many types of data commonly found in the enterprise. It is ideal for when you have complex and diverse datasets. It also supports multimodal integration.
- **Indexing and efficient retrieval**: This is the strength of LlamaIndex; it was designed with accurate and fast retrieval of information in mind. The library offers several tools and features for RAG and other retrieval paradigms.
- **Customization**: Especially for retrieval, LlamaIndex offers a high possibility of customization.

There are also some disadvantages:

- **Complexity**: LlamaIndex has a steep learning curve compared to other frameworks. In order to use it best, it assumes that you have a clear idea of information retrieval.
- **Limited functionality**: LlamaIndex has a focus on retrieval tasks but has limited functionality regarding other NLP tasks. This results in a lack of versatility.

LlamaIndex is the first choice for RAG-based applications and a good solution for agents.

Semantic Kernel

Semantic Kernel is an open source framework developed by Microsoft to build agents. This library can also connect with OpenAI, Hugging Face, and other frameworks. Semantic Kernel was originally written in C#, but today there is also a version in Python. The idea behind this library is to provide the ability to create functions that are the result of combining various functions (also known as **function composition**). In other words, Semantic Kernel is structured on the idea that various components can be tied together to build versatile pipelines.

In Semantic Kernel, the core is an LLM, but we can add code that we have developed as plugins so that the LLM can then execute it. In addition, it allows an LLM to have memory that can be either in the form of files or vector databases. An interesting element is that one can create native functions that are dedicated to performing a task. It also implements a planner that takes your task as input and returns a set of actions, functions, or plugins to succeed in solving the task.

Semantic Kernel is versatile, supports several libraries, and has lightweight support for C# and .NET frameworks. It is inspired by the Copilot framework, which is stable and a good choice for enterprises.

AutoGen

AutoGen is a Python-based LLM framework developed by Microsoft and other entities (University of Washington, Penn State, and Xidian). The idea behind it is to build applications that configure multiple agents that communicate with each other to complete a task. Agents and applications work through conversational programming, and a chain is built from the agents' interactions. There are three types of AutoGen agents: `UserProxyAgent` (which collects information from users and passes the information to other agents), `AssistantAgent` (which receives data from another `AssistantAgent` instance and `UserProxyAgent`, processes it, and completes a task), and `GroupChatManager` (which controls and directs communication between agents). AutoGen supports several complex conversation patterns that allow complex workflows to take place without human intervention. Systems involving several agents communicating with each other in complex ways can be configured.

This library has the following advantages:

- **Simplicity**: Abstraction makes it possible to intuit how agents converse and arrive at accomplishing a task. In addition, this makes it easier to explain the system to non-technical staff and other stakeholders.
- **Customization**: The process is intuitive and allows easy customization with little code.

There are a couple of drawbacks, however:

- **Harder to debug**: Agents are interdependent, making debugging difficult
- **Less support**: It is less adopted by the community, so there are fewer users to turn to for help when you need it

AutoGen is an interesting and promising library, but at this stage, it can be hard to start a project with.

Choosing an LLM agent framework

In general, the different frameworks offer similar components and are inspired by the same philosophy (extending the capabilities of an LLM). In addition, almost all libraries today are mature and have purpose-built components. For those functions that are not natively present within the library, there are many resources today that have been built by the community. The main component is the LLM, and the capabilities of the LLM are those that most condition the result of the application.

The first factor that may affect the choice is the programming language of the library. Often, these libraries must be integrated into existing systems that cannot be modified. Almost all libraries are written in Python but also have modules that can be written in other languages and facilitate their integration. In some cases, although support is not native, it has been developed by the open source community. For example, LangChain has support for Rust and there are unofficial implementations in other languages (C#, R, and so on). The tasks that the system has to accomplish are another determining factor. The increased complexity of the system requires that the framework be both robust and flexible at the same time. Some systems are designed with a greater focus on information retrieval (LlamaIndex) and thus are better choices if our system is to focus on chat and retrieval. In other contexts, we are more interested in system scalability and performance, so we might be interested in all the monitoring and evaluation ecosystems that LangChain and Haystack provide.

In addition, it is desirable that there be an active community of developers and that the library itself be actively maintained. When one adopts a framework, it is important that there are resources and a community to ask to avoid getting stuck or not finding a solution to a bug. A community-adopted library will have a large supply of tutorials and examples to help you learn the system.

Another factor is the level of customization. Although all libraries offer predefined features, these features do not cover all user cases, and in-house solutions will need to be developed. An ideal library should have this versatility and the ability to modify and integrate components. It may happen that we want to change our LLM or one of the components because we need a different performance. Similarly, the default parameters may not be optimal for our application, and it is better to have a library where it is not complex to adapt the parameters.

The best library is determined mainly by the use case. Each of them has strengths and weaknesses. For example, if the application is focused on retrieval, LlamaIndex may be the winning choice, or Haystack if the core of the application is Q&A. LangChain is a more natural choice for a broad scope, but if the system is to be integrated into .NET, you might choose Semantic Kernel. The chosen framework should be evaluated taking into consideration additional constraints and what the main focus of the application is.

We have now seen the most important libraries for AI agents. In the next section, we will start to test them in action.

Creating an agent to search the web

We typically associate internet searches with search engines like Google. The search for a query is conducted using an algorithm, but it is not an AI algorithm. PageRank is, in fact, a graph search algorithm that does not involve learning. A search algorithm presupposes two main steps:

- **Matching**: Finding documents that are relevant to a given user query
- **Ranking**: Ordering these documents from most relevant to least relevant

These two steps do not necessarily require AI. However, searching with the use of AI can bring a better service and solve some of the problems that plague search algorithms. A user today expects an AI algorithm to be able to distinguish the entity and terminology and to contextualize and localize it. For example, a user searching for "the best pizzeria" expects the search engine to return the best restaurants nearby. The search process of the future will also integrate other elements, such as a conversation about the results, complex responses (summarization and action), and multimodality.

There is another aspect. In today's systems, search results should in many cases be user-related. Searches can be ambiguous and some results will be more relevant by considering the user's history. In addition, a user may want a search conditional on other parameters and want to express it in natural language (for example, the difference between "best pizzeria in Paris" and expressing "best pizzeria AND Paris"). Once the results are found, the user may have other questions that require reasoning ("Which of these pizzerias is suitable for a dinner with children?").

An AI-enhanced search can meet these needs because it has an LLM at its core. An LLM can understand the difference between the various keywords in the query, as well as understand which domain the user is looking for (for example, "Transformer" can be an AI model or a toy). In addition, by accessing the history of previous interactions, the LLM is aware of the user's preferences (so you do not have to state your preferences each time). This allows for a more relevant ranking of the results since they are in order not only for the query but also for a user's preferences. The model can also conduct reasoning and give more importance to results that are more implicitly relevant (for example, when searching for a family restaurant, a multimodal model will give more preference to a restaurant with a picture of a playground even if it is not explicitly stated in the description that it is for families). The user can also ask questions about the results and the model using agents can perform operations.

The traditional search returns links in order of importance for a query. Today, however, information can be extracted from sites and analyzed by an LLM. For a given query, the model can now either extract the most relevant passage in the site (**extractive question-answering**) or propose a summary of the first results that directly answer the query (**abstractive question-answering**). In this way, the user does not even have to click the links but has the answer directly. This system can then be integrated with other tools, such as external memory (such as RAG and knowledge graphs, which we will see in the next three chapters).

In addition, an LLM has generative capabilities, so these can be used in combination with the query ("search for sources on the French Revolution" or "search for code in Python for convolution and translate it into R"). One of the problems with this type of generative search is the risk of hallucination, so the system must preserve the sources it has used so that backtracking can be conducted.

In the simplest form of searching with an LLM plus agents, we have an LLM connected with an interface that allows it to receive a query and a tool that allows it to search the internet. In this basic case, the LLM must analyze the query, plan to use the tool to search the internet, analyze the results found, and answer the query. In more sophisticated forms, the LLM may have more tools at its disposal. For instance, it can execute code, a calculator, and external memory to save data or call up models that perform NLP tasks (entity identification in text, extracting passages, and so on).

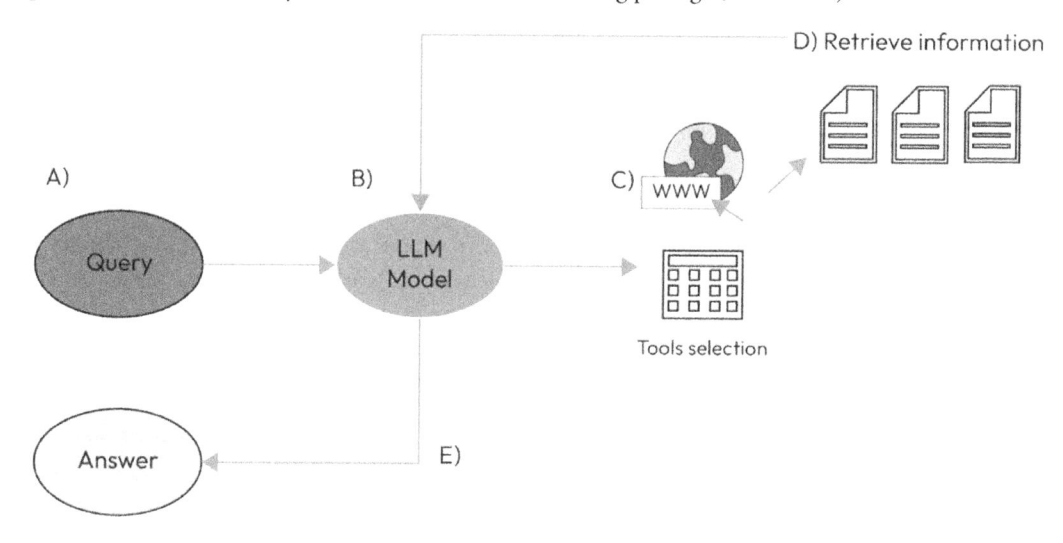

Figure 4.11 – Representation of an LLM agent's system for internet research

Let's break down *Figure 4.11*:

A. The user formulates a query.
B. The model analyzes the query and plans actions to solve the task.
C. The appropriate tool (in this case, internet search) is selected.
D. Documents are identified during the internet search. The information is sent back to the model, which analyzes it and decides whether further action is required or whether the task is accomplished.
E. The model generates the answer, which is sent back to the user.

LangChain allows the LLM to be able to connect to the web through the use of tools. In general, the most widely used approach is known as **Reasoning and Acting** (**ReAct**) prompting. During the first stage (reasoning), the model considers the best strategy to be able to arrive at the answer, and in the second stage (acting), it executes the plan. In this approach, the model also tracks the reasoning steps and can guide it to the solution. This approach also allows flexibility because it enables the model to mold the prompt to its needs.

By itself, LangChain offers a number of tools that are designed to extend the model and find the information it needs. For example, it offers several tools for searching the internet. The DuckDuckGo tool allows people to use the DuckDuckGo search engine. This search engine is free and does not track user data (it also filters out pages that are full of advertising or have articles written only to rank highly in the Google search engine).

In order to use it, we need to install a specific Python library and then import the tool into LangChain:

```
!pip install duckduckgo-search
from langchain.tools import DuckDuckGoSearchRun
ddg_search = DuckDuckGoSearchRun()
ddg_search.run('Who is the current president of Italy?')
```

> **Note**
> You can directly use the tool, and it will provide you with the search results.

One of the strengths of LangChain is the ability to build a list of tools that can then be used by the LLM. To do this, we have to give a name, explain what the function to be performed is, and provide a description. This way, the LLM is informed about what tool it can use when it has to do an internet search:

```
from langchain.agents import Tool

tools = [
    Tool(
        name="DuckDuckGo Search",
        func=ddg_search.run,
        description="A web search tool to extract information from Internet.",
    )
]
```

It is possible to use Google Serper, a low-cost API (albeit with some limitations) that enables you to use the Google search engine (you have to register at https://serper.dev/ to get an API key); however, there is a fee for the service. In fact, the Google API is much more expensive and the LLM cannot access directly the search engine (Serper allows us to use the Google search engine through their API, and they provide some free credits):

```
#!pip install google-serp-api
import os
SERPER_API_KEY = 'your_key'
os.environ["SERPER_API_KEY"] = SERPER_API_KEY

from langchain.utilities import GoogleSerperAPIWrapper

google_search = GoogleSerperAPIWrapper()

tools.append(
   Tool(
       name="Google Web Search",
       func=google_search.run,
       description="Google search tool to extract information from Internet.",
    )
)
```

Additionally, we can add Wikipedia as a reliable source of information:

```
from langchain.tools import WikipediaQueryRun
from langchain.utilities import WikipediaAPIWrapper

wikipedia = WikipediaQueryRun(api_wrapper=WikipediaAPIWrapper())

tools.append(
   Tool(
       name="Wikipedia Web Search",
       func=wikipedia.run,
       description="Useful tool to search Wikipedia.",
    )
)
```

Once we have the various tools, we can then initialize an agent and conduct a query:

```
from langchain.agents import initialize_agent
agent = initialize_agent(
   tools, llm, agent="zero-shot-react-description",
   verbose=True
```

```
)
agent.run('Query')
```

The model will choose which results will be interesting to our query. The model can access different information but has nowhere to save it. Using an LLM for internet research can be useful for different fields (from medicine to finance). For example, models have been used to access genetic sequences and conduct comparisons, or to search for information about drugs, chemical structures, and more. Similarly, a model can search for the latest financial and economic news. Another tool can be the **OpenStreetMap** (**OSM**) search.

In the next chapter, we will discuss how the model can save and access this memory. For example, we may want our model to be able to access conversation history or extend its knowledge. This can be useful in both business applications, but also in fields such as finance and healthcare.

Summary

In this chapter, we introduced how an LLM can be the brain of a sophisticated and complex system. We can use the conversational and reasoning abilities of the LLM to solve a task. As we said, this brain can be extended by providing perceptual systems (senses) and tools (hands). In fact, we can allow the model to search the internet by connecting with APIs, but also to ingest information from other modalities (audio, images, or video). Similarly, the model uses this received information to solve user tasks. If we can imagine agents performing and automating routine tasks for users today, it is not difficult to imagine a world in which agents interact with humans and other agents in increasingly sophisticated and complex ways.

In the next chapter, we will see how a model can have a memory, as well as how to store information and be able to find it again to be more efficient.

Further reading

- Silver, *Mastering the game of Go without human knowledge*, 2017: `https://www.nature.com/articles/nature24270`
- LangChain: `https://python.langchain.com/v0.2/docs/introduction/`
- Haystack: `https://haystack.deepset.ai/overview/intro`
- Semantic Kernel: `https://learn.microsoft.com/en-us/semantic-kernel/overview/`
- AutoGen: `https://microsoft.github.io/autogen/`
- LlamaIndex: `https://www.llamaindex.ai/`
- LangChain tools: `https://python.langchain.com/v0.2/docs/integrations/tools/`

- DuckDuckGo: `https://duckduckgo.com/`
- Guardian, *'Godfather of AI' shortens odds of the technology wiping out humanity over next 30 years*, 2024: `https://www.theguardian.com/technology/2024/dec/27/godfather-of-ai-raises-odds-of-the-technology-wiping-out-humanity-over-next-30-years`

5
Extending Your Agent with RAG to Prevent Hallucinations

In earlier chapters, we saw what an LLM is, and in the previous chapter, we saw how it can control different tools to succeed at completing a task. However, some of the limitations of LLMs prevent their deployment in sensitive fields such as medicine. For example, LLMs crystallize their knowledge at the time of training, and rapidly developing fields such as medical sciences cause this knowledge to be outdated in a short time. Another problem that has emerged with the use of LLMs is that they can often hallucinate (produce answers that contain factual or conceptual errors). To overcome these limitations, a new paradigm has emerged: **retrieval-augmented generation** (**RAG**). RAG, as we will see in this chapter, allows for the LLM to refer to memory that is external to the model; thus, it allows knowledge to be found and kept updated. Similarly, providing contextual guidance to the model's response allows for the reduction of hallucinations. Therefore, RAG is widely used today and is considered a promising system.

In this chapter, we will discuss how this system has evolved, starting with how a transformer can be used to find information. We will discuss in detail the various components of the system (embedding, vector database, and generation).

In this chapter, we'll be covering the following topics:

- Exploring naïve RAG
- Retrieval, optimization, and augmentation
- Evaluating the output
- Comparison between RAG and fine-tuning
- Using RAG to build a movie recommendation agent

Technical requirements

Most of this code can be run on a CPU, but it is preferable to be run on a GPU. The code is written in PyTorch and uses standard libraries for the most part (PyTorch, Hugging Face Transformers, LangChain, SentencePiece, Datasets, and scikit-learn). The code can be found on GitHub: https://github.com/PacktPublishing/Modern-AI-Agents/tree/main/chr5.

Exploring naïve RAG

Information retrieval is the name of the scientific field that deals with finding information in media (often textual but also multimodal). For example, the user may be interested in finding whole documents or chunks in documents; this task is key to question answering, where a model has to find the steps needed to answer a user's questions. At the heart of the system is a search engine. In the case of RAG, the search engine is a transformer (or at least a language model), and in this chapter, we will focus on that. We will discuss a system in which we have a **collection** of documents (textual, but could also be web pages, images, videos, or even code or short text passages) that have corresponding indexes in the database. These documents can be associated with metadata (attributes describing author, size, topic, and keywords). By convention, a **term** is defined as a word present in the text but also a passage that can answer the search. A user produces a **query** that can be expressed as terms. The purpose of the retrieval system is to best match the query with the relevant documents in the collection. These are then returned in order of relevance.

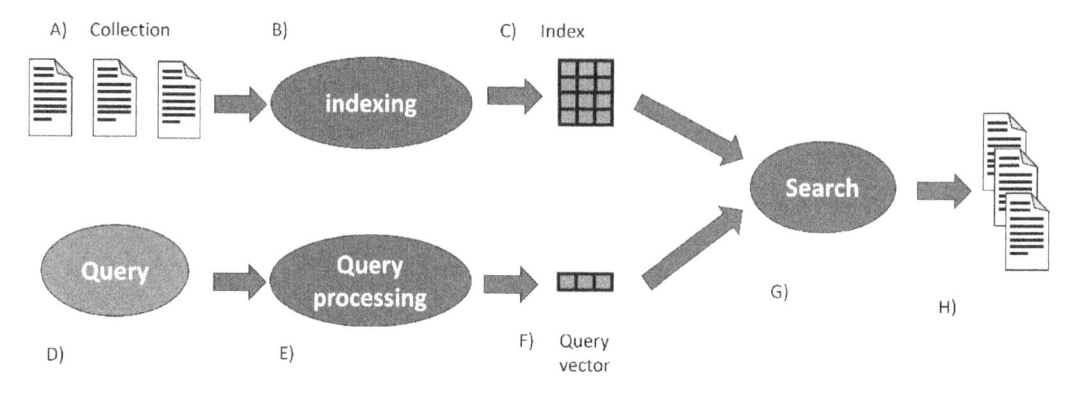

Figure 5.1 – Workflow diagram showing how a query is processed by a search

Let's break down what we can see in *Figure 5.1*. A collection of documents (**A**) is indexed (**B**) and is entered in an orderly manner into a database (**C**). Each document is assigned metadata and indexes. A user query (**D**) is processed (**E**) to obtain a vector representation (**F**). The resulting vector is used during the search to find the documents that are most relevant (**G**). The system returns the documents in order of relevance (**H**)

As we can observe, the system uses a search in a vector space. In the simplest form, this can be bag-of-words or the TF-IDF we saw in the first chapter. For example, we can take a set of documents and calculate the TF-IDF. Once we've done that, we can calculate a score (usually cosine similarity) between each of the documents and conduct rank based on the score. For a document d and a query q in vector form, we use the following formula:

$$\cos(q, d) = \frac{q \cdot d}{|q||d|}$$

We can see an example of this process here:

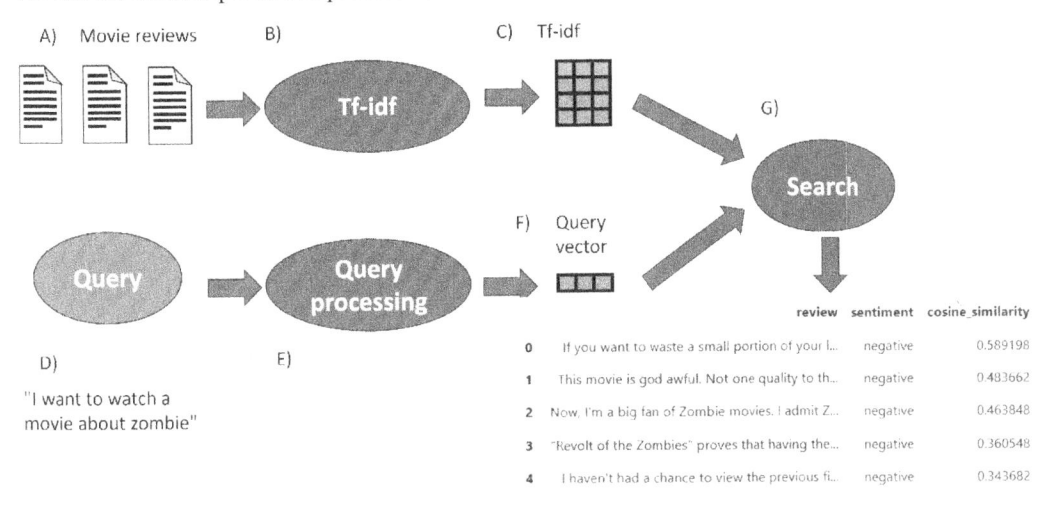

Figure 5.2 – Example of retrieving the most relevant documents with TF-IDF

This type of research also requires data storage facilities that are suitable. For example, for TF-IDF (or derivative algorithms), an inverted index is used as the data structure. The inverted index is a data structure designed specifically to make it efficient to search for terms in a set of documents. It is a structure composed of a dictionary and postings. The dictionary indicates the frequency of terms and the posting in which document they are found. In this way, given a set of terms in the query, we can efficiently find the documents that contain them and calculate the similarity.

```
Hello {1}      -> 2[1]
Morning {2}    -> 2[2] -> 5[1]
Today {3}      -> 3[1] -> 4[2] -> 6[1]
Tomorrow {2}   -> 2[3] -> 3[1]
```

Figure 5.3 – Example of an inverted index

BM25 is a variant of TF-IDF where two parameters are added: *b*, which controls the importance of document length normalization, and *k*, which controls the relationship between **term frequency (TF)** and **inverse document frequency (IDF)**.

$$BM25\ score = \sum_{t\in q} \overbrace{\log\left(\frac{N}{df_t}\right)}^{IDF} \overbrace{\frac{tf_{t,d}}{k\left(1 - b + b\left(\frac{|d|}{d_{avg}}\right)\right) + tf_{t,d}}}^{TF}$$

The preceding equation is a variation of TF-IDF for a document *d* and a query *q* (*d avg* represents the average length of a document).

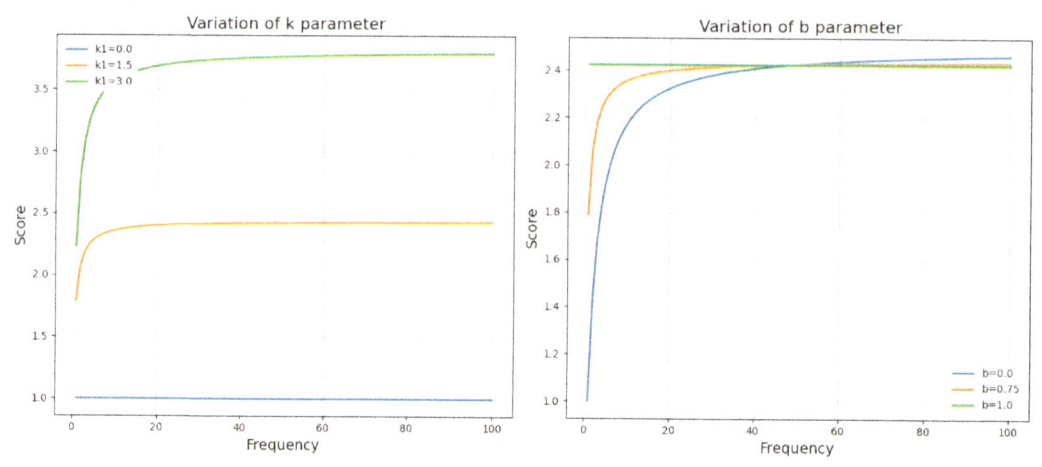

Figure 5.4 – Effect of k and b parameters on the BM25 score

We can see some interesting points:

- By selecting *k* equal to zero, no TF is used in the score. The TF component becomes irrelevant; the score does not consider how often a term appears in a document, only whether it appears at all. Higher *k* values give greater weight to TF. *k* is used to adjust TF saturation – in other words, how much a single query term impacts the score of a single document. *b=1* means normalize for document length, while 0 means eliminate normalization.

- The system is sensitive to both TF and document length without adding too many parameters. The usually recommended values are *b=0.75* and *k* between 1.2 and 2. BM25 is much more flexible than TF-IDF and can be adapted to different scenarios.

- It is not much more complex than TF-IDF and is therefore scalable to large datasets, and more robust to sparse matrices.

It is not always easy to find the optimal parameters for a precise dataset. The model is sensitive to the choice of hyperparameters. BM25 has a limited understanding of semantics since it is based on term frequency, not capturing the meaning of a document. Also, many terms are polysemous (with multiple meanings) and BM25 does not capture the context of a term. Another serious problem is a vocabulary mismatch problem – that is, when there is no complete overlap between terms in the query and documents.

The solution to these problems is to use dense vectors that include contextual information. This is done by using a transformer and extracting the representation for a document. More formally, given a sequence of tokens, we use the representation z, obtained from the final layer. This allows us to obtain a high-dimensional representation that we can use to disambiguate the meaning of a word. This is called the **z-score**.

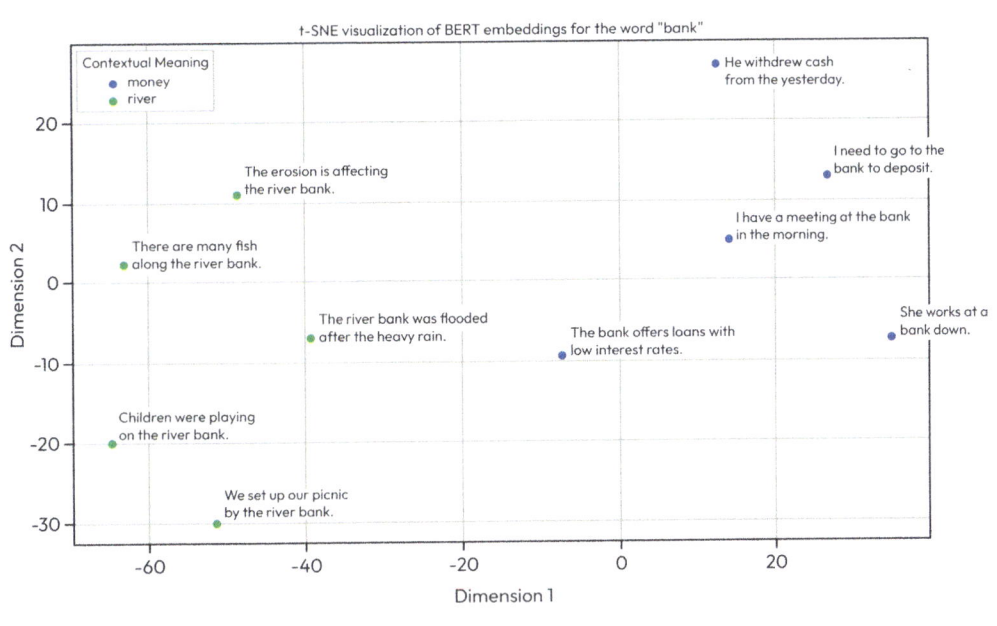

Figure 5.5 – Contextual embeddings for the word "bank"

Figure 5.5 shows a **t-distributed stochastic neighbor embedding (t-SNE) visualization** of the contextual embedding for the word "bank" in different contexts (both money and river-related meanings). The t-SNE is conducted on the BERT embedding of the word for each sentence.

There are several ways to retrieve this representation from the model. For convenience, the last layer is used, but it is generally proposed to conduct an average pool of the representation of multiple layers (each block learns a different text representation due to self-attention). As we saw in *Chapter 1*, these vectors have geometric properties and can be used for operations (clustering, similarity computation, and so on).

Generally, some transformation is conducted to optimize the use of embedding. For example, a normalization of vectors (z-score or other methods) is conducted. In fact, the vectors of many words are similar due to anisotropy. In fact, taking random words, the cosine similarity is higher than it should be. This is due to rogue dimensions, a small number of dimensions (1–5) that dominate contextual embedding because they have high magnitude and disproportionately high variance. This causes similarity to be calculated on reduced embedding space. These rogue dimensions are highly correlated with absolute position and punctuation and are therefore uninformative. Transformations such as z-score can reduce the problem.

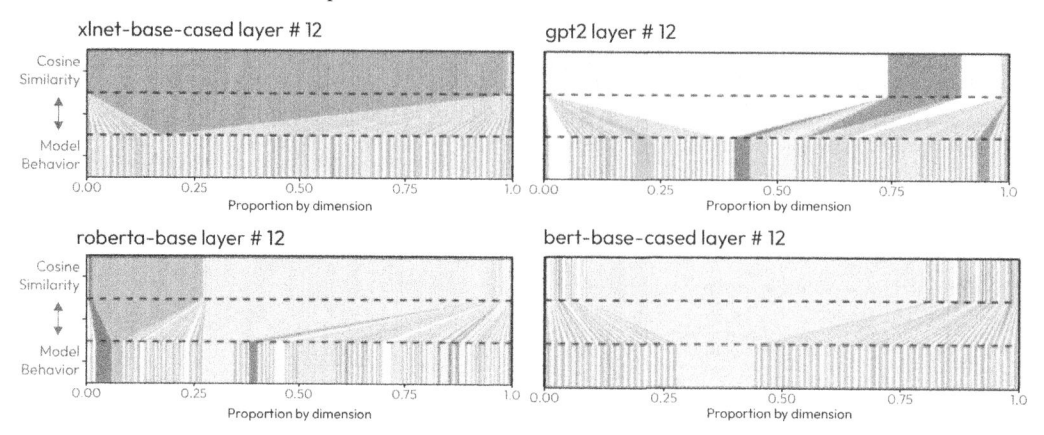

Figure 5.6 – Relative contribution of each dimension to cosine similarity (https://aclanthology.org/2021.emnlp-main.372.pdf)

In addition, retrieving the embedding for each word in the embedding is unnecessarily laborious. For bidirectional encoders, we can use two main strategies: use a single encoder or a bi-encoder. In the first case, we provide the model with both query and document, thus allowing bidirectional self-attention to attend all tokens. The representation will be representative of both the query and the document. The format used is [CLS]-query-[SEP]-document. The representation for the [CLS] token is then fed to a linear layer to produce the similarity score (this layer is fine-tuned). Normally, this process is done not for the whole document but for a series of chunks (non-overlapping fragments of the document), because documents are usually longer than the context length (for BERT, this is 512 tokens, so the sum of query and document must be no more than 512 tokens).

This system is expensive because it requires that we have to pass a query along with the entire corpus of documents. To reduce the cost, a more efficient architecture known as a bi-encoder was implemented. One encoder is used to extract the representation for the query, [CLS]q, and another to extract the representation for each document (or chunk), [CLS]d. Basically, taking a corpus, we compute the embedding for each document in the corpus and store this representation in a database. After that, we compute the cosine similarity between the representation for the query and all the vectors in the database. This system is much faster but less accurate because part of the interactions there are between the terms in the query and in the documents.

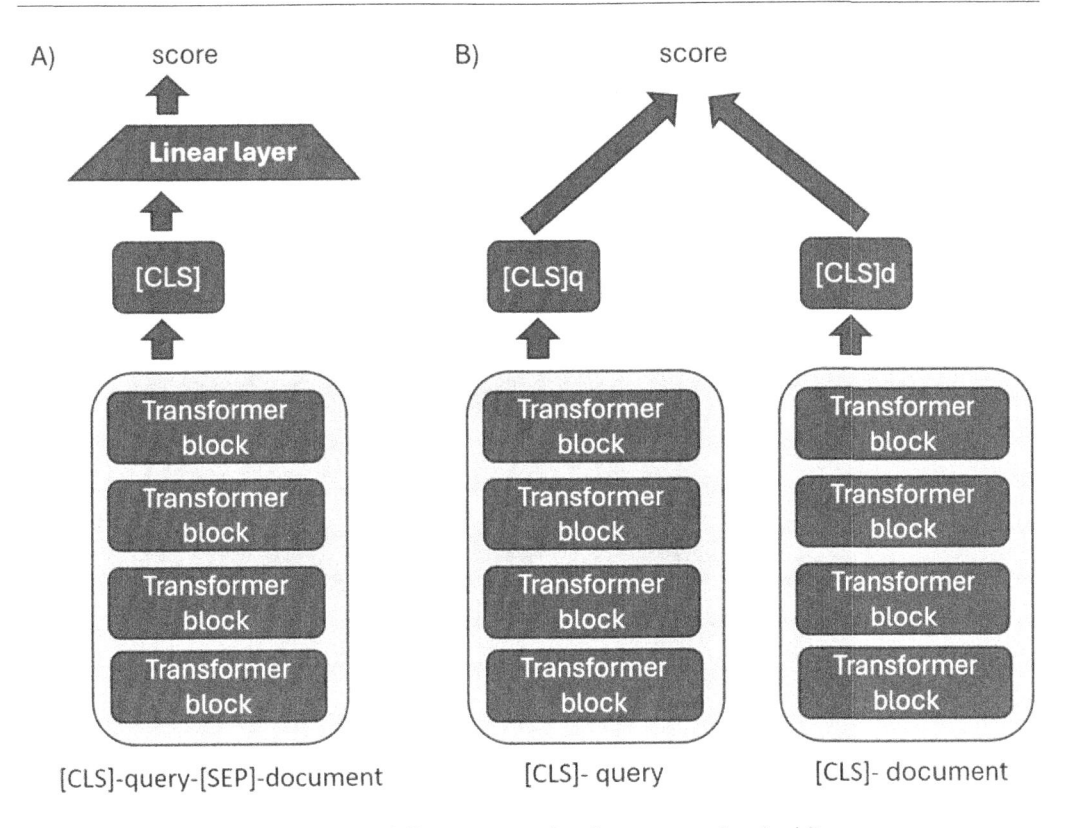

Figure 5.7 – Two different approaches for contextual embedding

Let's examine *Figure 5.7* in more detail. **A** is a unique model for generating the contextual vector. A linear layer is fine-tuned to generate a score of similarity between query and vector. The linear layer has as input the [CLS] representation. **B** shows two models, which are used to generate two different and separate representations. The [CLS] representation is generated for the query and all the vectors. We calculate cosine similarity using both representations.

Then, we can conduct embedding of the whole corpus and index the documents in a database and then, when a query comes, calculate the similarity.

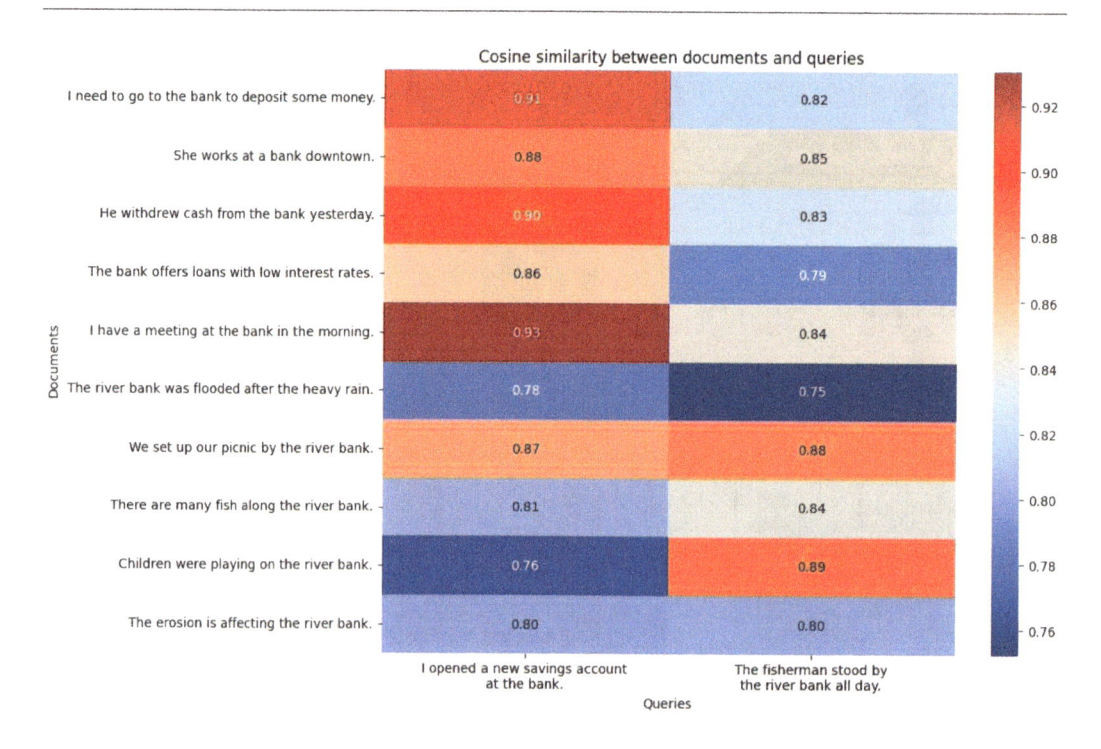

Figure 5.8 – Cosine similarities between a set of documents and two queries where the meaning of the word "bank" is different

As we mentioned earlier, generative models can produce hallucinations. Given a query, LLMs can generate output that contains erroneous information. This stems from the fact that LLMs are good at explaining concepts but have problems retaining specific information. During training, knowledge of a concept is reinforced by the repetition of similar pieces of information. This works well for concepts but less so for specific pieces of information such as dates, numerical values, and rare pieces of information. In addition, datasets contain both correct and incorrect information, often conflicting. When a model generates a response, it samples from a distribution and must choose from the information it has learned, thus leading to hallucinations.

In addition, incorrect architecture, overfitting, or misalignment during training can also promote hallucinations. Fine-tuning the model or over-optimization for some tasks can be an additional cause. For example, optimizing the model to write long text outputs promotes the model to become verbose and generate hallucinations. Similarly, raising the temperature increases the stochasticity of sampling, leading to sample tokens that are less likely and thus hallucinate more. Incorrect prompting can also promote this behavior.

Hallucinations are most evident when using a model in a specific domain (healthcare, finance, and so on). The model lacks the context to best understand the query. This is because the model has been trained on a huge number of tokens, and they have not been restricted to specialized topics. The loss is calculated on the set of texts and thus more on general knowledge than on particular information. Therefore, the model favors a generalist function but performs less well when applied to a particular domain. This is a common factor, irrespective of the number of model parameters.

Several possible solutions have been tested to reduce or prevent hallucinations. One approach is to provide context as part of the LLM prompt (when it is possible to add all this context to the prompt). However, this means that the user has to find the relevant context again. When you have many different documents, this becomes a complex and laborious task. Alternatively, fine-tuning, in which the model is trained further on specific documents, has been proposed. This has a computational cost, though, and should be conducted repeatedly if new documents arrive.

In 2020, Meta proposed an alternative approach: RAG for LLMs. This approach assumes augmenting the generation of an LLM by finding the context in an external source (such as a database). This database can be domain-specific and continuously updated. In other words, we find the documents needed to answer the query and take advantage of the fact that an LLM has powerful abilities for in-context learning.

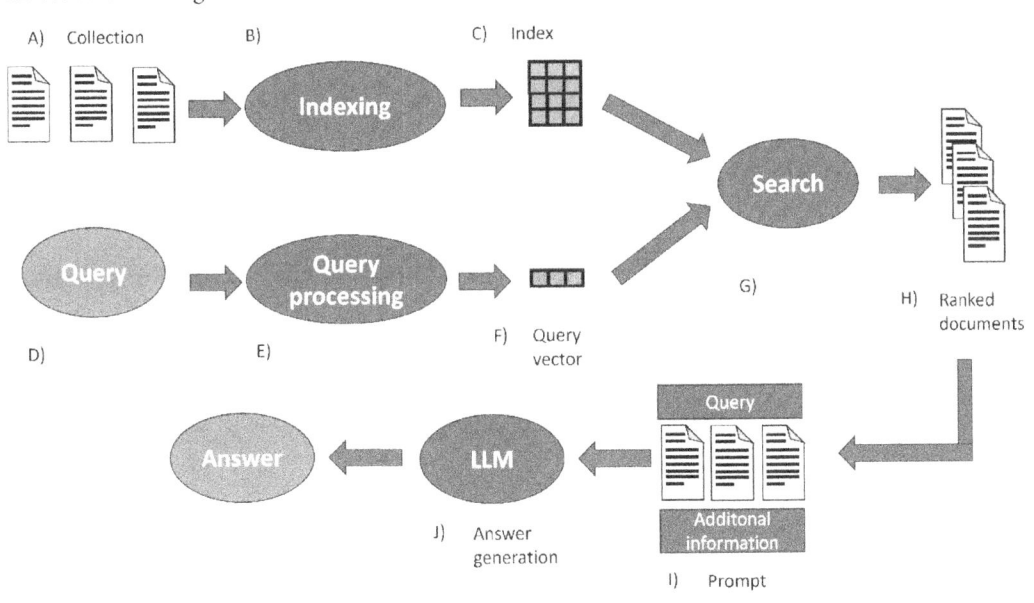

Figure 5.9 – Diagram showing the process of RAG

In *Figure 5.9*, the ranked documents are incorporated in the prompt (query, retrieved documents, and additional information), which is presented to the LLM. The LLM uses the additional context to respond to the query of the user.

We define the knowledge from the LLM as parametric memory and that obtained from the RAG as external or nonparametric. More formally, RAG is a system that, in its most basic form, consists of three parts:

- **Indexing**: Indexing deals with the entire process from raw data to storage in a vector database. It begins with ingesting data in various formats (PDF, HTML, Markdown, or XML) that must be converted to text. The text is processed according to the embedding model chosen (it is divided into chunks that must be smaller in size than the context length of the model). The chunks are then embedded (transformed into a vector representation), assigned an identifier, and stored in a vector database.

- **Retrieval**: When a query arrives, the most relevant chunks must be found. The same encoder used for document embedding is used to obtain a vector for the query. The similarity score between the query vector and the vectors stored in the database is then calculated. Top *K* chunks are selected based on the similarity score.

- **Generation**: The chunks found together with the query are incorporated into a consistent prompt for LLM used for generation. Different LLMs may require different elements in the prompt to work best; similarly, we can have prompts that are tailored for specific tasks. In addition, we can also add elements from the previous conversation (history).

For an autoregressive model, we can modify the equation seen in *Chapter 2*, where we defined that an LLM computes the probability of a sequence of tokens given the previous tokens:

$$p(x_1, x_2, \ldots, x_n) = \prod_{i=1}^{n} p(x_i | x_{<i})$$

For a question-answering task, given a question (or query) q, we can rewrite the equation as follows:

$$p(x_1, x_2, \ldots, x_n) = \prod_{i=1}^{n} p(q; x_{<i})$$

In RAG, we have additional elements: the prompt Pr, the context retrieved R, and the question q, which are all concatenated:

$$p(x_1, x_2, \ldots, x_n) = \prod_{i=1}^{n} p(x_i | Pr\ ;R\ ;q\ ;x_{<i})$$

This process is shown in *Figure 5.10*:

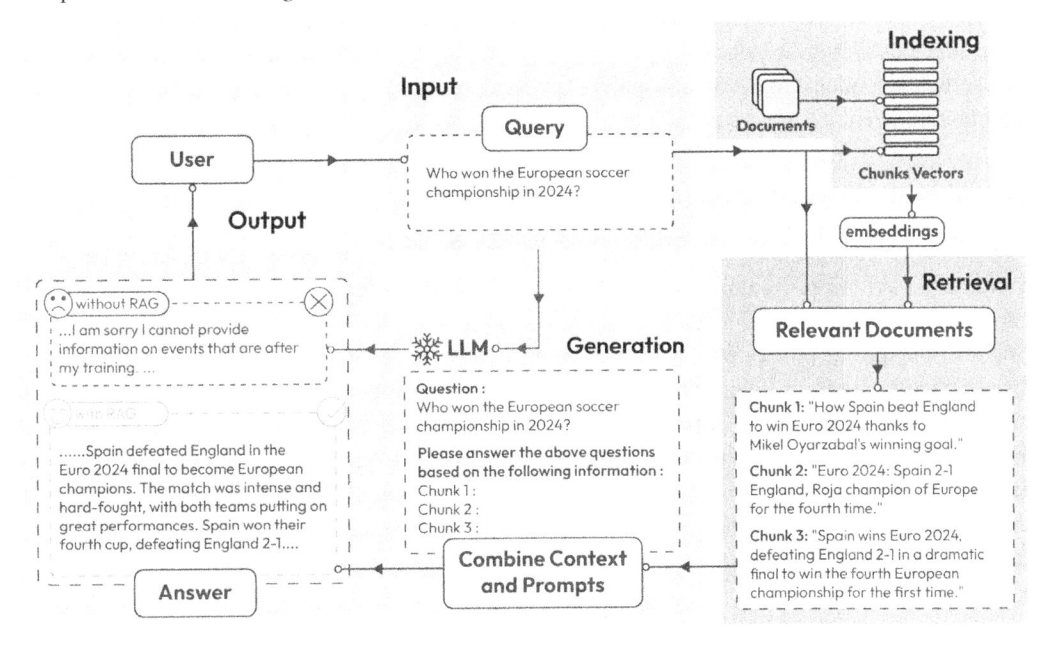

Figure 5.10 – Representative instance of the RAG process and its steps
(https://arxiv.org/pdf/2312.10997)

This is the general architecture, but there are also more complex variations (which we will discuss in detail in the next chapter). For completeness, an alternative to this architecture is **span extraction**. In this case, instead of finding the most appropriate chunks, we have a language model (usually also derived from BERT) that is used to find passages in the text that answer a query (**span labeling**). For example, if our corpus is Wikipedia and our query is "*Who is the president of France?*", the extractor will label the passage on the page that answers the question (in RAG, we retrieve the text chunks that are relevant instead). RAG (or **span extractor**) has shown interesting abilities in reducing hallucinations and improving the abilities of LLMs in open-domain question answering (also called open-book QA).

In the next section, we will go on to discuss these steps in more detail and what choices we need to make in order to optimize the system.

Retrieval, optimization, and augmentation

In the previous section, we discussed the high-level RAG paradigm. In this section, we are going to look at the components in detail and analyze the possible choices a practitioner can make when they want to implement a RAG system.

Chunking strategies

We have stated that text is divided into chunks before being embedded in the database. Dividing into chunks has a very important impact on what information is included in the vector and then found during the search. Chunks that are too small lose the context of the data, while chunks that are too large are non-specific (and present irrelevant information that also impacts response generation). This then impacts the retrieval of query-specific information. The larger the chunking size, the larger the amount of tokens that will be introduced into the prompt and thus an increase in the inference cost (but the computational cost of the database also increases with the number of chunks per document). Excessive context can also lead to hallucinations and detract from LLM performance. In addition, the chunk size must not exceed the context length of the embedder, or we will lose information (this is known as truncation). In other words, chunk size is an important factor that affects both the quality of retrieval and generation.

The simplest strategies are those based on a fixed length of chunking. Character chunking divides the document into chunks based on a predetermined number of characters or tokens (common choices are 100 or 256 tokens or 500 characters). The size should be chosen according to the type of document. This is the cheapest and easiest system to implement. One variation is a random chunk size where the size of the chunks is variable. This variant can be used when the collection is non-homogenous and potentially captures more semantic context. Separation into chunks can be with or without overlap. Chunking without overlap (*Figure 5.11*) works well if there are clear boundaries between chunks (such as if the context changes drastically between adjacent chunks). This is rarely the case, though, and the lack of overlap destroys context. One can then use a sliding window that maintains an overlap between chunks. This system maintains contextual information at the chunk boundaries, allowing better semantic content and increasing the chance that relevant information will be found if it spans across multiple chunks. This strategy is more expensive, though, because we need to divide it into more chunks, so we will have a database with many more entries. Also, some of the information is redundant, so the overlap should be no more than a small percentage of the entire chunk size.

A)

To be or not to be, that is the question. Whether tis nobler in the mind to suffer The slings and arrows of outrageous fortune Or to take arms against a sea of troubles, And by opposing, end them. To die, to sleep No more, and by a sleep to say we end, The heartache and the thousand natural shocks That

flesh is heir to, tis a consummation Devoutly to be wished.

B)

to be or not to be , that is the question . whether tis noble ##r in the mind to suffer the sling ##s and arrows of outrageous fortune or to take arms against a sea of troubles , and by opposing , end them . to die , to sleep no more , and by a sleep to say we end , the heart ##ache and the thousand natural shocks that

and by a sleep to say we end , the heart ##ache and the thousand natural shocks that flesh is heir to , tis a con ##sum ##mation devout ##ly to be wished .

C)

To be or not to be, that is the question. Whether tis nobler in the mind to suffer The slings and arrows of outrageous fortune Or to take arms against a sea of troubles, And by opposing, end them. To die, to sleep No more, and by a sleep to say we end,

The heartache and the thousand natural shocks That flesh is heir to, tis a consummation Devoutly to be wished.

Figure 5.11 – Effect of different chunking strategies used on an extract from Hamlet

In *Figure 5.11*, we can see the following:

- **A)**: Simple chunking based on the number of tokens and without overlap
- **B)**: Simple chunking based on the number of tokens and with overlap
- **C)**: Simple chunking based on the number of tokens and the presence of the new line in the text (character-based)

Context-aware chunking is a strategy in which we divide text into chunks using a **regular expression** (**regex**). For example, we can divide based on periods, commas, or paragraph breaks. Variants of this strategy are based on the type of text we are splitting (for example, HTML tags, Markdown information, XML, domain-specific signs, and so on). This system is not without its drawbacks; it can sometimes be difficult to determine boundaries (for example, for compound sentences, dirty text, and so on). You can therefore have chunks that are of varying sizes. A more sophisticated variant is called **recursive chunking**, in which the chunk is split similarly to context-aware chunks. After that, the chunks are joined up to a predetermined number of tokens (for example, the maximum context length of the embedder). This approach tries to keep all information that is contextually related in the same chunk and maintain semantic consistency (for example, if possible, all chunks belonging to a paragraph are merged). Alternatively, the text is iteratively split until the chunks reach the desired size. **Hierarchical clustering** is a similar method that seeks to respect the structure of the text. By examining relationships in the text, it tries to divide it into segments that respect its hierarchy (sections, subsections, paragraphs, and sentences). This system is useful for documents that have a complex and known structure (business reports, scientific articles, and websites). This method also makes it possible to inspect the structure obtained and to understand the relationship between the various chunks. This system works poorly when dealing with documents that are poorly formatted.

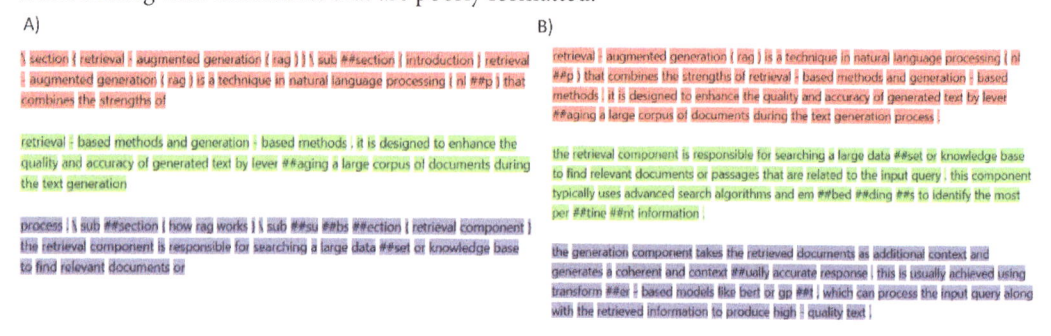

Figure 5.12 – Demonstration of hierarchical chunking

Figure 5.12 shows the same document in Markdown (**A**) or LaTex (**B**). Using a specific chunker, we can split respecting the language structure. LangChain uses hierarchical clustering to achieve that.

Another family of methods is **semantic chunking**. The purpose of these techniques is to take into account the context and meaning of words. These methods try to group chunks that would otherwise be distant in the text (presence of digression or other elements). **K-means chunking** is an approach in which we conduct an embedding of the various sentences, then use *k*-means clustering to group sentences that are similar into various clusters. This approach requires setting the optimal number of clusters (hyperparameters) to choose and can lead to loss of sentence order (with potential risk to chronological order or contextual relationships). Instead of considering division on sentences, **propositions-based chunking** divides on contextual understanding. So-called "propositions" are identified as atomic expressions that contain factoids (sentences that are self-contained and describe a piece of knowledge, such as "*The capital of France is Paris*"). These propositions are then evaluated by an LLM that groups them according to semantic coherence. This approach can give optimal results but is computationally expensive and depends on the choice of LLM used. **Statistical merging**, on the other hand, evaluates similarities and differences in the embedding of sentences to decide whether to merge (or split) them. For example, after embedding, the difference in statistical properties (standard deviation, percentile, or interquartile difference) is evaluated, and if it exceeds a predefined threshold, the sentences are separated. This system creates chunks of different sizes and has a higher computational cost but can give better results when contextual boundaries between sentences are unclear.

Finally, a multimodal chunk may be needed. For example, a PDF file may contain both text and images. In this case, it will be necessary for our chunking pipeline to be able to extract both images and text.

There is no universal best chunker – the best chunker is the one most suited to our specific case. We can establish guidelines though, as follows:

- **Align chunking with document structure**: Text structure heavily influences the chunk size and chunk strategy. In cases where we have documents of the same type (HTML, LaTex, Markdown, and so on), a specific chunk might be the best choice. If they are a heterogeneous collection, we could create a pipeline that conducts chunking according to the file types.

- **Optimize for performance and resources**: If we have space and computational cost limitations, a simple fixed-size chunker might be an optimal choice. Semantic chunking is slightly less performant but better respects information integrity and improves the relevance and accuracy of found chunks. It requires knowledge of the text, though, and might not be the optimal choice for a system that is used by general users. Contextual chunking may have better performance but has a high computational cost.

- **Respect model context limitations**: Chunk size should respect the dimension of the context length. We must take into account both the size of the embedding model and the LLM that we will then use to generate it.

- **Match chunking strategy to user query patterns**: Consider the type of question we expect our potential users to ask the system (the RAG). For example, if the user is going to ask questions that require the model to find multiple facts, it is better to have a strategy with small chunks but containing a direct answer. Or if the system is more discursive, it would be better to have chunks that give more context.

In conclusion, a developer has to inspect the text and the output delivered when testing different chunking strategies for the RAG system. In any case, each strategy should then be evaluated (in later sections, we will discuss how to evaluate them).

Embedding strategies

As we saw earlier, an embedding is a dense vector representation of a text (representation lying in a multidimensional space). We exploit these vectors to find the appropriate context for our query. We can have encoders that produce scattered vectors (such as TF-IDF or BM25) or encoders that generate dense encoders. As mentioned earlier, dense encoders are transformers that produce vectors. The advantage is that these models are trainable and thus can be adapted to the similarity task between queries and chunks. BERT-based backbone is one of the most widely used; the approach is to create two parallel BERT encoders (two streams: one for the query and the other for the chunk) called the bi-encoder approach. In the first RAG approaches, these weights are identical (frozen), and we only have one layer that is trained to generate the embedding vector. Having the same weights allows us to be able to pass the query first and then the documents and then calculate similarity. Later models, on the other hand, conduct fine-tuning of the weights to improve the model's ability to generate better embedding vectors.

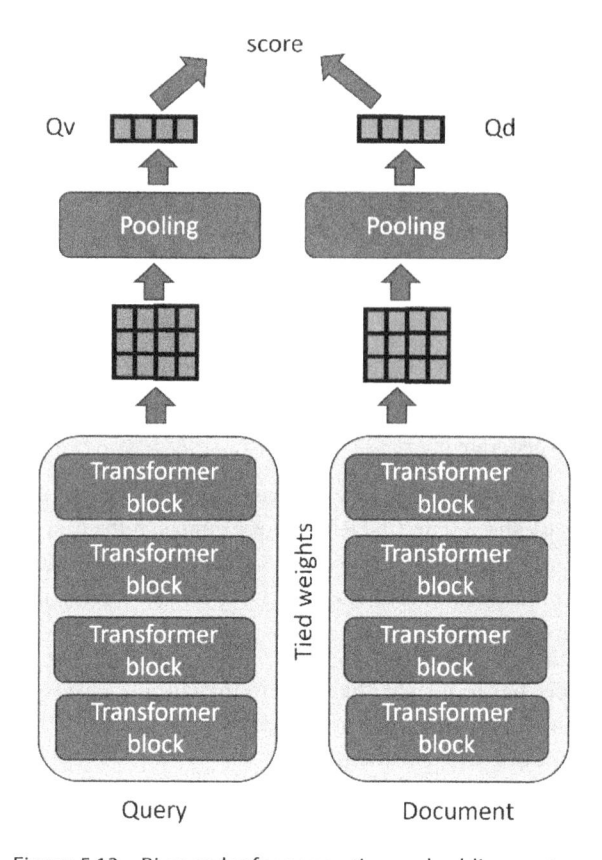

Figure 5.13 – Bi-encoder for generating embedding vectors

The bi-encoder shown in *Figure 5.13* generates a query vector and a document vector. On these two vectors, we can calculate the similarity.

Alternatively, a model can be trained from scratch for this task. Typically, it is better to take an LLM that has been trained unsupervised and then adapt it for embedding and retrieval. Normally, this model is adapted using contrastive learning. As we saw in *Chapter 3*, contrastive learning is a technique used to learn semantic representations in the form of embedding. In *Chapter 3*, we used CLIP, which was trained using images and captions. In this case, we want to train a model that generates embeddings that allow us to find the documents that are most akin to our query. One of the most used datasets is the Multi-Genre Natural Language Inference (MultiNLI) corpus, which contains 433,000 sentence pairs annotated with textual entailment information. Given a hypothesis, a second sentence represents an entailment, a contradiction, or neither (neutral).

In contrastive learning, we need positive and negative examples. Having taken a sentence, we want the embedding of our sentence to be as close to a positive example as possible and as dissimilar from a negative example. In this case, we can derive positive and negative examples for one of our sentences from MultiNLI. In fact, an entailment sentence represents a positive example while a contradiction is a negative example.

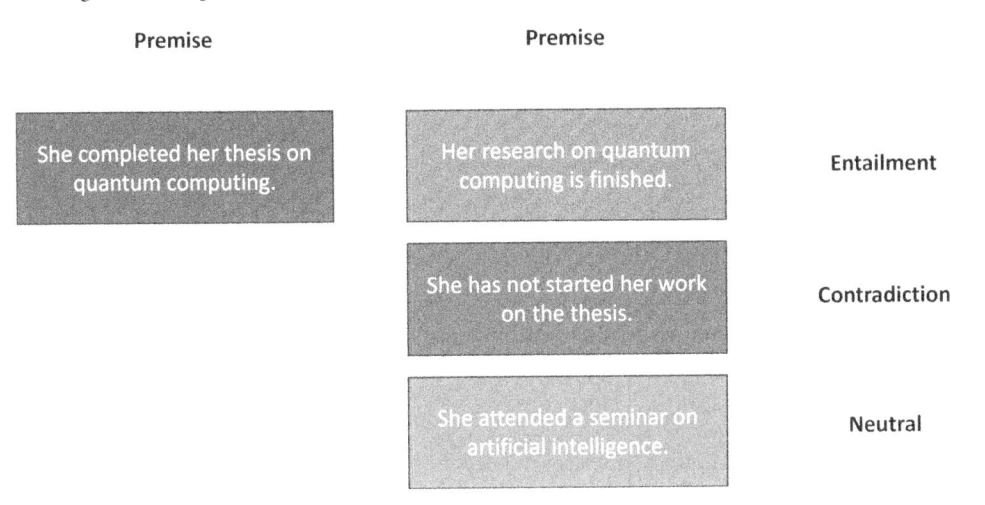

Figure 5.14 – Example of sentences that are in entailment or contradiction and can be used for training an encoder

Once we have the dataset, these models are trained with a loss function that is suitable for the task:

- **Cosine similarity loss**: This is one of the loss functions that is most commonly used because it measures the semantic closeness of two sentences. The model is optimized to give a similarity as close as possible to 1 for sentences that are similar (original sentence and positive example) and 0 for sentences that are dissimilar (original sentence and negative example). As a loss, we calculate the similarity between the two sentences, and then it is compared with the predicted label.

- **Multiple negatives ranking loss**: This is another popular alternative (also called **InfoNCE**). Only positive examples are used for this type of loss. In this case, we have the original sentence and the corresponding positive example (the entailment sentence). For negative examples, we take our original sentence and a sentence that is in entailment for another sentence. After that, we calculate embedding and similarity. The idea is to maximize the similarity between a sentence and one that is related (its positive example) while minimizing the similarity with examples that are unrelated (our negative examples). In this way, this task becomes a classification task, and we can use cross-entropy. However, the negative examples are completely unrelated, and thus the task can be too easy for the model (instead, it is better to add negative sentences that are related but not the right answer).

The choice of embedder is a critical decision that will strongly impact the performance of our system. A poor embedder will lead to poor retrieval and context not relevant to the query, which, paradoxically, could increase the risk of hallucinations. The encoder choice impacts the following:

- **Cost**: An embedder is a transformer. The bigger it is, the higher the computational cost. A closed-source encoder, on the other hand, has a cost relative to the API, so the more it is used, the greater the cost. In addition, there are computational costs associated with embedding documents and also with each query.
- **Storage cost**: The larger the size of the embedded vectors, the higher the storage cost of our vectors.
- **Latency**: Larger models have higher latency.
- **Performance**: The cost of some choices is justified if our major concern is performance. Often, larger models have better performance.
- **Domain requirements**: There are now specialized encoders for some domains (finance, medicine, science, programming, and so on) and some are multilingual (most support only English but others support up to a hundred languages). Some domains have different text granularity and require models that are specialized for long text.

Deciding which encoder model to use is not easy and depends on various factors. A good way to start is the **MTEB leaderboard** on Hugging Face (`https://huggingface.co/spaces/mteb/leaderboard`), which is an up-to-date list of encoding models and their performance on different benchmarks and tasks. Often, though, these results are self-reported and are obtained on standard benchmarks (some of this benchmark data may be leaked in the training data and thus overestimate the model's capabilities). Thus, we should not choose just one model but test several on one's dataset. The leaderboard, however, provides some important information that allows us to guide our choice:

- **Retrieval average**: Calculates **normalized discounted cumulative gain** (NDCG) across several datasets (an evaluation metric used for ranking retrieval systems)
- **Model size**: This gives us an insight into the computational cost and resources we need to use it
- **Max tokens**: The number of tokens that can be used in the context length
- **Embedding dimensions**: Considers the size of the vectors after embedding

Retrieval, optimization, and augmentation   153

Rank	Model	Model Size (Million Parameters)	Memory Usage (GB, fp32)	Embedding Dimensions	Max Tokens	Average (56 datasets)	Classification Average (12 datasets)	Clustering Average (11 datasets)	PairClassification Average (3 datasets)
1	SFR-Embedding-2_R	7111	26.49	4096	32768	70.31	89.05	56.17	88.07
2	gte-Qwen2-7B-instruct	7613	28.36	3584	131072	70.24	86.58	56.92	85.79
3	neural-embedding-v1					69.94	87.91	54.32	87.68
4	NV-Embed-v1	7851	29.25	4096	32768	69.32	87.35	52.8	86.91
5	voyage-large-2-instruct			1024	16000	68.28	81.49	53.35	89.24
6	Linq-Embed-Mistral	7111	26.49	4096	32768	68.17	80.2	51.42	88.35
7	SFR-Embedding-Mistral	7111	26.49	4096	32768	67.56	78.33	51.67	88.54
8	gte-Qwen1.5-7B-instruct	7099	26.45	4096	32768	67.34	79.6	55.83	87.38
9	gte-Qwen2-1.5B-instruct	1776	6.62	4096	131072	67.16	82.47	48.75	87.51
10	gte-Qwen2-1.5B-instruct-08_0					67.16	82.47	48.75	87.51

Figure 5.15 – MTEB leaderboard dedicated to embedding models and their performance

It should also be noted that the leaderboard measures on generic domains. This means it measures general performance, which could result in poor performance in our domain or task of interest.

Once we have selected an encoder, we can reduce this cost without affecting the performance. Regarding cost and scalability, for each dimension of the vector embedding, we need 4 bytes of memory if they are in a float format. This can lead to exorbitant costs in storage. In *Chapter 3*, we discussed quantization – this can also be applied to embedding models. **Binary quantization** (which reduces models to 1 bit per dimension) can lead to a reduction in memory and storage of up to 32 times. The simplest binary quantization is to use a zero threshold:

$$f(x) = \begin{cases} 0 \text{ if } x \leq 0 \\ 1 \text{ if } x > 0 \end{cases}$$

We can then use the **Hamming distance** to find the value for the weights more efficiently (Hamming distance is another evaluation metric most suitable for these binary vectors. You can read more about it using the link in the *Further reading* section at the end of the chapter). Binary encoding allows unprecedented speed and memory reduction but generally means a loss of performance. More sophisticated versions of this approach can maintain up to 96% similarity (approaches on re-scoring found chunks). This quantization is considered extreme; often, a good compromise is to go from the `float32` format to `int8` (a format in which we represent values using 256 distinct levels). As we described earlier, this is done by recalibrating the vectors during the transformation.

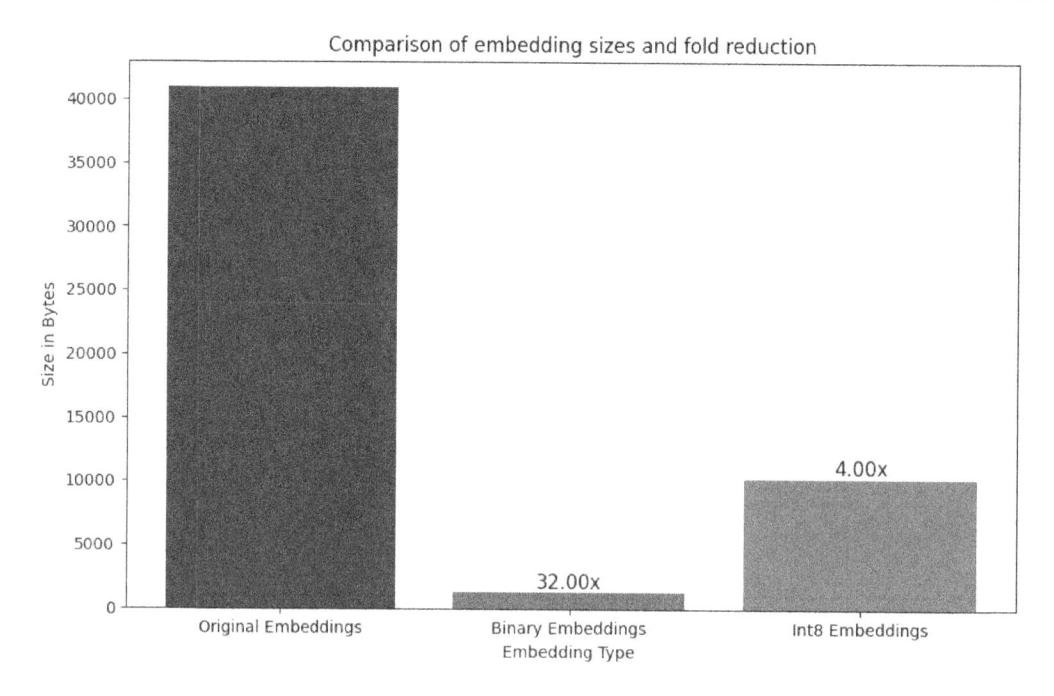

Figure 5.16 – Graph showing memory deduction after quantization

An alternative technique is Matryoshka Representation Learning. Deep learning models tend to spread the information over the entire vector; this technique attempts to compress the information over several representations with fewer dimensions instead. In other words, it progressively reduces the divisions of vector embeddings without losing too much performance. In a Matryoshka embedding, smaller embeddings are obtained that can be used as larger embeddings. This is because the system tries to force storage of the most important information in early dimensions and less important information in later dimensions (in this way, we can truncate the vector while maintaining performance in downstream tasks). To train an encoder, we produce embeddings for a batch of text and then compute the loss. For Matryoshka embedding models, the loss also takes into account the quality of the embedding at different dimensionalities. These values are summed in the final loss. Thus, the model tries to optimize the model weights in a way that the most important information (for the embedding vectors) is located in the first dimensions.

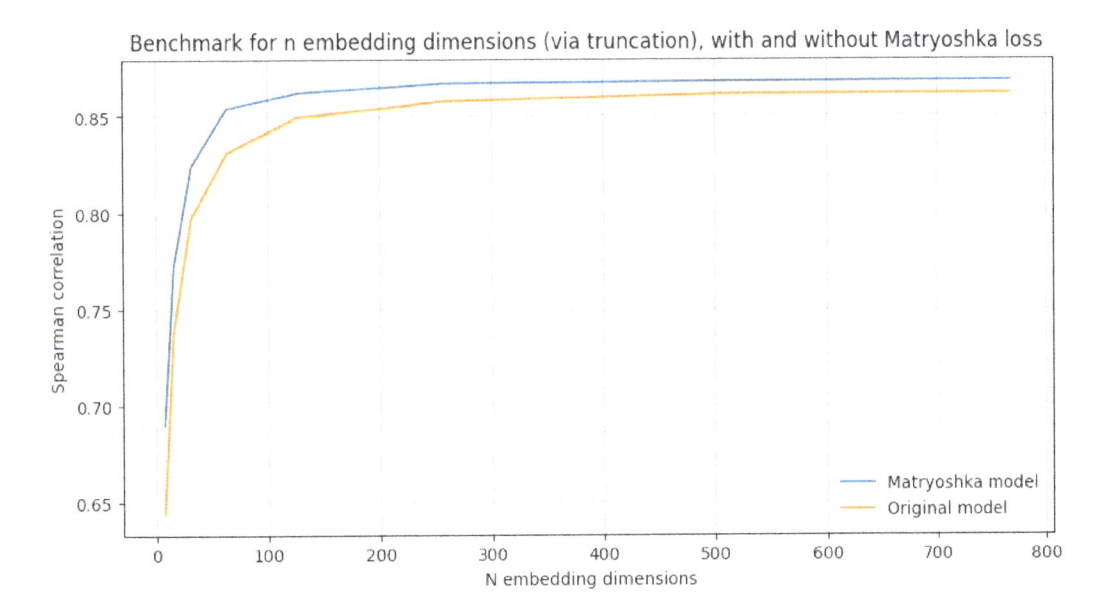

Figure 5.17 – Benchmark of Matryoshka versus original embedding quality over number dimensions

Once we have our vectors, we need to store them. In the next section, we will discuss where to store them.

Embedding databases

A vector database is a specialized database for the storage of high-dimensional vectors. This database is therefore optimized for handling unstructured and semi-structured data such as vectors. The function of this database is to allow efficient storing, indexing, and searching. The vector database we choose also has a big impact on RAG performance. Today, there are dozens of possible vector databases, so choosing the best solution can be a daunting task. Fortunately, there are sites that conduct a comparison of possible systems.

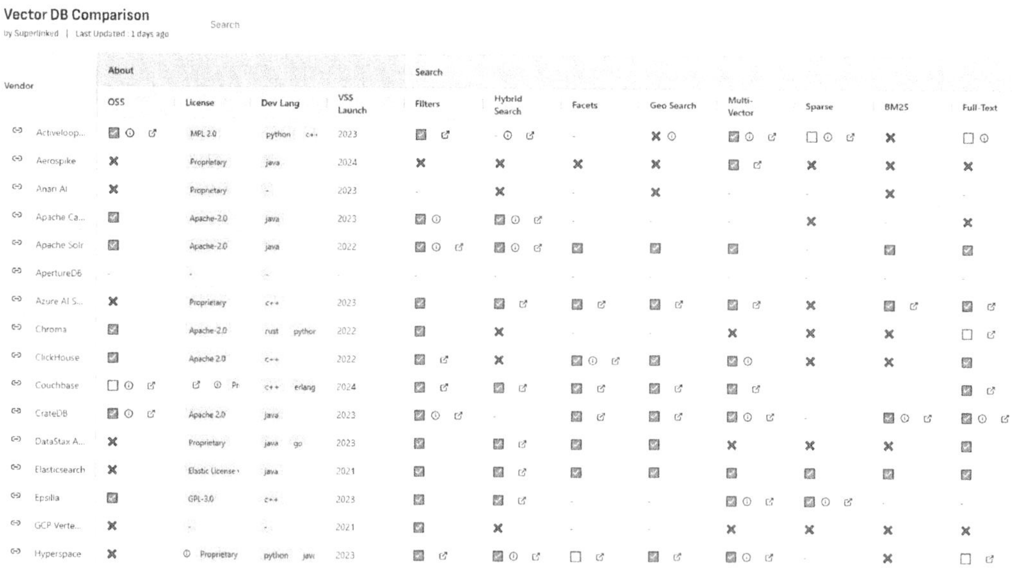

Figure 5.18 – Vector DB leaderboard, a practical source to address the vector database choice (https://superlinked.com/vector-db-comparison)

There is probably no best vector database, but there will be one that is suitable for our project. Some criteria that can guide our choice are as follows:

- **Open source or private source**: Open source databases offer transparency and the ability to customize the system. They usually have an active community and no associated costs. Private source databases, on the contrary, can be an expensive solution but often have dedicated support. Similarly, it is important to check the license; it may not be compatible with your product.

- **Language support**: Vector databases are generally compatible with major programming languages (Python, Java, and C), but for our project, we may need a database compatible with another language (Rust, Go, Scala, and so on). Also, not all databases are compatible with all libraries. So, it is good to make sure that the system is compatible with our project.

- **Maturity**: Especially for projects that are production-oriented, it is important that the system is stable, scalable, and reliable. Likewise, the system must be supported, adopted by industry, and maintained frequently.

- **Performance**: This is influenced by two parameters:

  - **Insertion speed**: the rate at which vectors can be added to a database (which affects latency). This especially impacts applications that are in real time or have a large user base. Some databases implement techniques such as batch processing (efficient partitioning of various data packets), parallelization (distribution of tasks across various nodes, especially important for the cloud), or data partitioning (the dataset is divided into segments in order to conduct insertions and deletions at the same time).

  - **Query speed**: this refers to the time it takes to find vectors in response to a query. This directly affects the latency time.

  There are optimization techniques such as index structures (structuring indexes to make the search faster), caching systems (data that is accessed frequently is saved separately), or specific algorithms. Then there are performance issues related to the specific products, such as the number of concurrent requests that can be made to the dataset. Regulatory compliance and privacy issues are also key. The database should be able to allow differential access (access authorization) and protect vectors from access by unauthorized users.

- **Component integration**: Our system can have several components besides the LLM and embedder (we will see this in more detail in the next chapter). We need to be sure that the database can be integrated with our encoder (and the library we use for the encoder). Also, not all databases accept other components such as a re-ranker, hybrid search, and so on.

- **Cost**: Cloud solutions can have very high costs, so it is recommended to decide in advance what budget you have. The cost could also be associated with the maintenance and support needed to keep the system operational. For example, vectors are valuable data and the cost of backup can grow very quickly.

For example, there are vector libraries that are static (the index data is immutable); this makes it difficult to add new data. Libraries such as **FAISS (Facebook AI Similarity Search**) are not designed for **create, read, update, and delete** (**CRUD**) operations, so they are not a good choice for dynamic systems where there are multiple users accessing and conducting operations. In contrast, if our database is immutable and we only grant access, FAISS can be a good solution. There are SQL databases that allow support for vectors (an extension of the classic database). These databases allow for efficient indexing of associated metadata. However, these databases are not scalable and often have limitations for vector size (maximum number of dimensions), and performance is lower. SQL databases are a good choice for internal projects that need to be connected to existing enterprise databases (which will probably already be in SQL) but are not a good choice when scalability and performance are important.

Vector-dedicated databases are usually the best solution, especially for performance. In fact, they usually have implemented dedicated and efficient algorithms for searching and indexing vectors. Several of these algorithms are variations of the **approximate nearest neighbors** (**ANN**) algorithm. ANN usually allows for a good trade-off between efficiency, storage, and accuracy. Approximate search speeds up the search while trying to maintain accuracy (HNSW (Hierarchical Navigable Small World) sacrifices some accuracy but is much faster than an accurate algorithm such as Flat indexing). These databases are also compatible with major languages and libraries (LlamaIndex, LangChain, and so on).

Once we have our vector database populated with our vectors, we need to evaluate how good our system is. Now, we'll see how we can do that.

Evaluating the output

In information retrieval, we are interested in measuring whether a found document is either relevant or irrelevant. Therefore, the most commonly used valuation metrics are precision and recall. Precision is the fraction of retrieved documents that are relevant, while recall is the fraction of relevant documents that are successfully retrieved. Consider a query in which R represents all relevant documents and NR represents the irrelevant ones in a corpus of documents D. Rq represents the relevant documents found and Dq is the documents returned by the system. We can define the two metrics as follows:

$$precision = \frac{Rq}{Dq} \quad recall = \frac{Rq}{R}$$

The problem with these two metrics is that they do not return goodness of ranking, only whether we are finding all relevant documents or the percentage of relevant documents in the total. Usually, when we use a retriever, we select a number (k) of documents that we use for context (top-k), so we need a metric that takes ranking into account.

	Rank	Label	binary_label	precision	recall
0	1	R	1	1.000000	0.2
1	2	R	1	1.000000	0.4
2	3	NR	0	0.666667	0.4
3	4	R	1	0.750000	0.6
4	5	R	1	0.800000	0.8
5	6	NR	0	0.666667	0.8
6	7	NR	0	0.571429	0.8
7	8	R	1	0.625000	1.0
8	9	NR	0	0.555556	1.0
9	10	NR	0	0.500000	1.0

Figure 5.19 – Rank-specific precision and recall calculated assuming we have five relevant documents in a corpus

We can use the precision-recall curve for this purpose. Whenever we find a relevant document in the rank, recall increases. Precision, on the other hand, increases with documents but decreases with each irrelevant document. By plotting a graph with a curve, we can see this behavior:

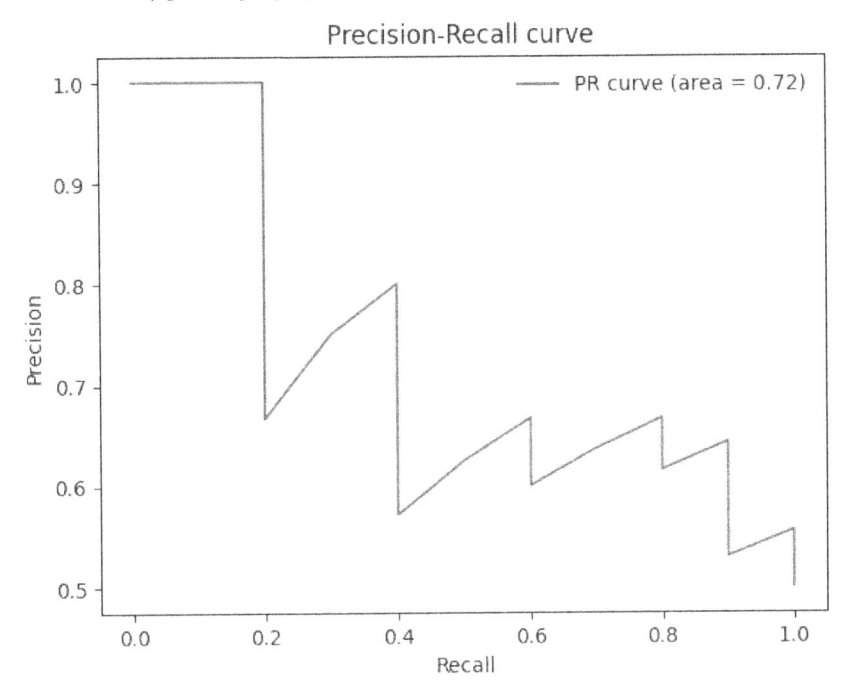

Figure 5.20 – Graph showing the precision and recall curve for the data shown in Figure 5.19

Because the precision goes up and down, we can use an interpolated curve. This curve is less precise but allows us to better understand the behavior of the system (and to be able to compare different systems by comparing their curves).

Another metric that is used is **mean average precision** (**MAP**). We calculate precision values at the points where a relevant item is retrieved (**average precision** or **AP**) and then average these AP values. Suppose we have retrieved the following list of documents: *[1, 0, 1, 0, 1]*, where *1* means relevant and *0* means not relevant. The precision for each relevant item is as follows:

- The first relevant document is in position 1: Precision (*N* relevant document retrieved / total of document retrieved) = 1/1 = 1
- Second relevant document (position 3): Precision = 2/3 ≈ 0.67
- Third relevant item (position 5): Precision = 3/5 = 0.6

The average precision (AP) value for a single query is:

$$AP = \frac{\Sigma precision\ at\ each\ relevant\ item}{Total\ number\ of\ relevant\ items} = \frac{\Sigma(1 + 0.67 + 0.6)}{3} = 0.76$$

The MAP is the average of all AP values across all the queries. Here, we suppose we have 3 queries – *0.76, 0.5,* and *0.67*:

$$MAP = \frac{\Sigma average\ precision\ for\ each\ query}{Total\ number\ of\ queries} = \frac{\Sigma(0.76 + 0.5 + 0.67)}{3} = 0.64$$

One metric that is specific to question answering is **mean reciprocal rank (MRR)**. MRR is designed to assess the quality of a short-ranked list having the correct answer (usually of human labels). The reciprocal rank is the reciprocal of the rank of the first item relevant to the question. For a set of queries Q, we take the reciprocal ranks and conduct the average:

$$MRR = \frac{1}{Q} \sum_{i=1}^{Q} \frac{1}{rank_i}$$

Alternatively, we can evaluate the response after generation as if it were a classification task.

Recently, another way to evaluate RAG pipelines is to use an LLM as a judge of the pipeline. Typically, we must have a dataset that contains ground truth so that LLM evaluates whether the RAG pipeline has found both the necessary steps and the generation is correct. For example, there are different metrics that leverage an LLM as a judge:

- **Faithfulness**: This metric (also called groundedness) measures the factual consistency of the generated answer (range between 0 and 1). An answer is faithful if the claims that are produced in the answer can be inferred from the context. Faithfulness is the ratio of the number of claims in the generated answer that can be inferred from the context to the total number of claims in the generated answer. To find the claims, we need an LLM that evaluates the claims in both the response and the context.

- **Context recall**: This metric refers to how much context is found relative to the ground truth (range of 0 to 1). Ideally, the system should find all the sentences in the ground truth.

- **Context precision**: This metric measures ground-truth relevant items in the context, which are ranked higher (relevant chunks should find themselves higher after retrieval).

- **Context relevancy**: This metric measures the relevance of context to the query. Ideally, our system should only find information that is relevant to the query.

- **Context entities recall**: This metric provides a measure of context recall by specifically analyzing the entities that are found. In other words, it measures the fraction of entities in the ground truth that are found in the context. This metric is useful when we are interested in the system specifically finding entities (for example, the context needs to find medical entities such as diseases, drugs, or other parameters).

- **Answer correctness**: This metric focuses on critically evaluating whether the answer is correct. To have a high value, the system must generate answers that are semantically similar to ground truth but also factually correct.

- **Summarization score**: This metric assesses how well a summary captures the important information that is present in the context. The answer is a kind of summary of the context, and a good summary must contain the important information.

- **Answer relevance**: This metric calculates how relevant the generated response is in response to a prompt. A low score means that the response is incomplete or contains redundant information.
- **Fluency**: This metric assesses the quality of individual sentences generated.
- **Coherence**: This metric assesses whether the entire response is a cohesive corpus (avoids the response being a group of unconnected sentences).

These metrics require that there be an evaluator who is either human or an LLM. They are not simply statistical values but require that the response (and/or the found context) be evaluated critically.

RAG is also often discussed as an alternative to fine-tuning; thus, it is important to compare them, which we'll do next.

Comparison between RAG and fine-tuning

RAG and fine-tuning are often compared and considered techniques in opposition. Both fine-tuning and RAG have a similar purpose, which is to provide the model with knowledge it did not acquire during training. In general, we can say that there are two types of fine-tuning: one directed at adapting a model to a specific domain (such as medicine, finance, or other) and one directed at improving the LLM's ability to perform a particular task or class of tasks (math problem solving, question answering, and so on).

There are several differences between fine-tuning and RAG:

- **Knowledge updates**: RAG allows a direct knowledge update (of both structured and unstructured information). This update can be dynamic for RAG (information can be saved and deleted in real time). In contrast, fine-tuning requires retraining because the update is static (impractical for frequent changes).
- **Data processing**: Data processing is minimal for RAG, while fine-tuning requires quality datasets (datasets with not enough examples will not be able to help with noticeable improvements).
- **Model customization**: RAG provides additional information to the LLM but does not change its behavior or writing style. Fine-tuning allows changes in model behavior, writing style, and even new skills.
- **Interpretability**: RAG increases the interpretability of the system and allows tracking of responses and sources used. Fine-tuning makes the model less interpretable and makes it more difficult to track whether a behavior comes from fine-tuning or the original model.
- **Computational resources**: RAG has an additional cost associated with the encoder and databases (finding information, embedding data, storing information, and so on). This can increase latency cost (you have to add retrieval time to generation time). Fine-tuning requires preparing and curating quality datasets (acquiring certain datasets can be expensive and labor-intensive). In addition, fine-tuning has computational costs associated with model retraining, but it provides lower latency. Moreover, RAG requires less technical expertise than fine-tuning.

- **Reducing hallucinations**: RAG is inherently less prone to hallucinations and allows the tracking of which context is used. Fine-tuning can reduce hallucinations (but, often, fine-tuned LLMs do still exhibit hallucinations).

- **Ethical and privacy issues**: In the case of RAG, we must be careful how the information stored in the database is saved. The database must be protected against potential intrusions and prevent leakage. For fine-tuning, it is important to take care of the training dataset and prevent it from containing sensitive data.

RAG is the best system when we need a dynamic system that can adapt to real-time data or we have large amounts of internal data that are not well structured, though. Likewise, RAG is preferred when it is important to minimize hallucinations, as we need to track the sources of the response when transparency is vital. Fine-tuning is a priority choice when we need to have the model develop specific skills or want to align the model with a particular style of writing or vocabulary.

Some practical examples show where it is best to choose fine-tuning or RAG:

- **Summarization** is important, especially for cases where the domain is highly specialized. It is more critical that the model best understands the context, so fine-tuning is more appropriate.

- **Question answering** is an extremely relevant task that is often used in different domains (questions about documentation, products, and so on). In this case, reducing hallucinations and transparency are critical aspects but customization is much less important. RAG is therefore a better choice.

- **Code generation** is a task that requires that the code base be dynamic; at the same time, it is important to reduce hallucinations and errors. On the other hand, we need the model to be adapted as much as possible to the task. So, both RAG and fine-tuning would be of benefit.

As the last example shows, there are cases where both fine-tuning and RAG would be beneficial. The two systems are not necessarily in opposition to each other. We can conduct fine-tuning of both the LLM and the embedder. So, having a system built with RAG *plus* fine-tuning the LLM (or even the RAG encoder) would be beneficial. Targeted fine-tuning to improve capabilities for specific tasks in the domain of our data can lead to better performance. This allows for a dynamic information system (where we conduct the RAG update) but adapts the style of the LLM to the domain. The LLM will also be more able to understand and use the context that is provided by RAG. Another case where fine-tuning the model is beneficial is when the found data is in a specific format (code, tables, XML, or other formats) – we can then use an LLM that is adapted to these specific formats (instead of a naive LLM). Additionally, we can optimize our LLM for the task of generating answers by exploiting the provided context. In this case, the LLM can be pushed to make the best use of the found context.

The encoder can also be fine-tuned. Fine-tuning the embedder with a specific dataset increases the contextual understanding of the model (remember that the encoder is a language model that has some contextual understanding of the data). This allows the LLM to better understand the domain-specific nuances of the data, leading to better contextual retrieval (chunks that are more relevant to the query). Of course, it is not always possible to obtain datasets for this task. However, there are approaches in which synthetic data is generated or large LLMs are used to create datasets appropriate for the encoder fine-tuning.

Fine-tuning an embedder is much cheaper than training it from scratch. Today, many models are available, and libraries such as Sentence Transformer facilitate the process of fine-tuning. These models have been pre-trained as embedders, but during fine-tuning, we want to better fit them to our particular data type or domain. Typically, this fine-tuning is conducted with supervised learning using datasets similar to those used for embedder training (with positive and negative examples).

Now that we have seen the main components, in the next section, we will assemble the system.

Using RAG to build a movie recommendation agent

In the previous sections, we discussed what RAG is and how this system can be used to reduce hallucinations or extend model knowledge. As we mentioned, this system is composed of the following components:

- An LLM to generate the answer
- An encoder/retriever that transforms queries and documents into vectors
- A vector database where we save our vectors

We have, in this case, a dataset of movies and their description, and we want to create a system that, by asking a natural language question, will suggest the most suitable movies based on the information we've provided. Our LLM has no specific knowledge of the movies, and its parametric memory does not contain information about the latest releases. Therefore, RAG is a good system to supplement its knowledge.

1. The first step is to obtain a corpus of chunks. Having taken a corpus of documents, we have to reduce it into chunks. A good compromise is to use a text splitter that preserves semantic information (without the need to use an LLM). In this case, we use a chunker with a size of 1,500 characters. We apply it to the column of our data frame:

    ```
    text_splitter = NLTKTextSplitter(chunk_size=1500)
    def split_overview(overview):
        if pd.isna(overview):
            return []
        return text_splitter.split_text(str(overview))
    df['chunks'] = df['text_column'].apply(split_overview)
    ```

2. Next, we need to transform our chunks into vectors. In this case, we are using `all-MiniLM-L6-v2` as an embedder. `all-MiniLM-L6-v2` is a small model that has a good balance between embedding quality and speed. In fact, the model has only 22.7 million parameters, which makes it extremely fast and a good initial choice for testing one's RAG pipeline.

   In this case, we do the following:

   - Load the model (the embedder)
   - Create a function to conduct the embedding
   - Conduct the embedding of the various vectors

   ```
   embedder = SentenceTransformer('all-MiniLM-L6-v2')
   def encode_chunk(chunk):
       if not isinstance(chunk, str) or chunk.strip() == "":
           return None
       return embedder.encode(chunk).tolist()
   chunked_df['embeddings'] = chunked_df['chunks'].apply(encode_chunk)
   ```

3. At this point, we need to save the vectors we have created to a database. A popular choice as a vector database is Chroma. In this case, we need to do the following:

   - Start the Chroma client
   - Create a new collection
   - Insert the chunks

   ```
   chunked_df.dropna(subset=['embeddings'], inplace=True)
   client = chromadb.Client()
   collection = client.create_collection(name='movies')
   for idx, row in chunked_df.iterrows():
       collection.add(
           ids=[str(idx)],
           embeddings=[row['embeddings']],
           metadatas=[{
               'original_title': row['original_title'],
               'chunk': row['chunks']
           }]
       )
   ```

> **Important note**
> Note that we can add metadata (in this case, the title of the film).

We have now implemented only the first part of the pipeline we described earlier. At present, we have a database with the RAG vectors.

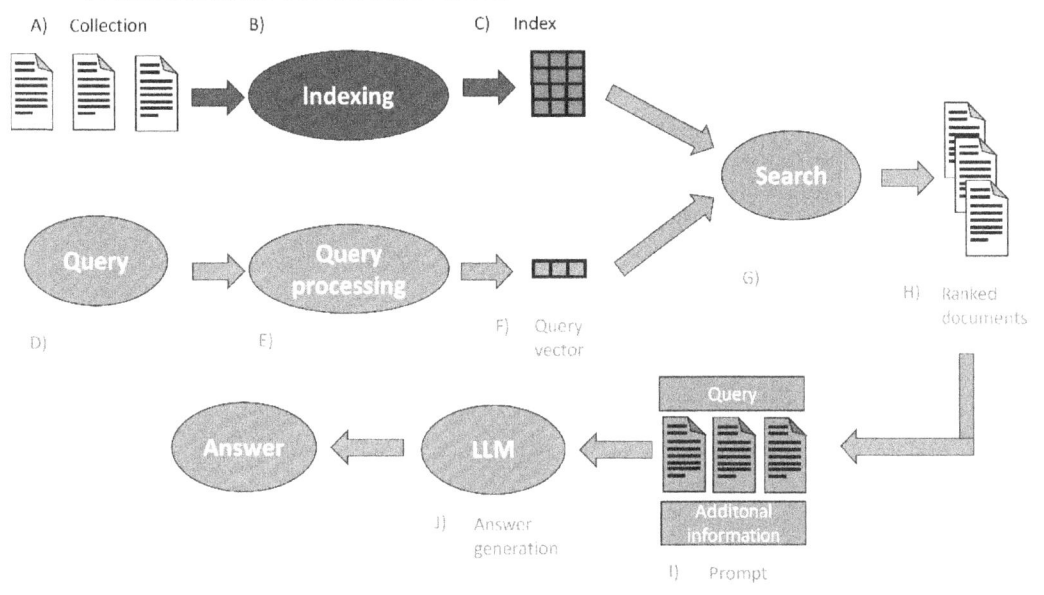

Figure 5.21 – Vector database pipeline

Now, we need to create a pipeline when a query arrives (in inference). In this case, we want to create a vector for the query and search the top *k* similar vectors in our vector database. This will return the text to an LLM and then generate an answer to our query.

4. We use the same embedder model we used to find the chunks, though, so we need a function that does the following:

   - Creates a vector for the query
   - Finds the most similar documents
   - Returns the associated text

   ```
   def retrieve_documents(query, collection, top_k=5):
       query_embedding = embedder.encode(query).tolist()
       results = collection.query( query_embeddings=[query_embedding], n_results=top_k )

       chunks = []
       titles = []
       for document in results['metadatas'][0]:
           chunks.append(document['chunk'])
           titles.append(document['original_title'])
       return chunks, titles
   ```

At this point, we need to generate the answers, so we need an LLM. The idea is to provide the LLM with clear instructions, so we create a simple prompt that explains the task to the model. We also provide the model with both the context and the question:

```
tokenizer = AutoTokenizer.from_pretrained("mistralai/Mistral-7B-
Instruct-v0.1")
model = AutoModelForCausalLM.from_pretrained(
    "mistralai/Mistral-7B-Instruct-v0.1",
    device_map='auto')
text_generation_pipeline = pipeline(
    model=model,
    tokenizer=tokenizer,
    task="text-generation",
    return_full_text=True,
    max_new_tokens=800)

def generate_answer(query, chunks, titles, text_generation_
pipeline):
    context = "\n\n".join([f"Title: {title}\nChunk: {chunk}" for
title, chunk in zip(titles, chunks)])
    prompt = f"""[INST]
    Instruction: You're an expert in movie suggestions. Your
task is to analyze carefully the context and come up with an
exhaustive answer to the following question:
    {query}
    Here is the context to help you:
    {context}
    [/INST]"""
    generated_text = text_generation_pipeline(prompt)[0]
['generated_text']
    return generated_text
```

Now, we can test it. We can ask the system a question and see whether it generates a response:

```
client = chromadb.Client()
collection = client.get_collection(name='movies')
query = "What are some good movies to watch on a rainy day?"
top_k = 5
chunks, titles = retrieve_documents(query, collection, top_k)
print(f"Retrieved Chunks: {chunks}")
print(f"Retrieved Titles: {titles}")
if chunks and titles:
    answer = generate_answer(query, chunks, titles, text_generation_
pipeline)
```

```
        print(answer)
else:
        print("No relevant documents found to generate an answer.")
```

We now have a complete system. The principle applies to any corpus of documents.

Summary

RAG is one of the fastest-growing paradigms in the field of LLMs. Eliminating hallucinations is one of the most important challenges and one of the most problematic constraints for LLMs and agents to be put into production. RAG is also a flexible system that has several advantages over fine-tuning. As we have seen, this system can be updated frequently with minimal cost and is compatible with different types of data. The naïve RAG is the basic system, consisting of three main components: an LLM, an embedder, and a vector database.

In the next chapter, we will see how this system is evolving. There are now many new additional components, which we will also look at. Despite RAG, sometimes the model still hallucinates as if it ignores the context. This is why sophisticated components have evolved, which we will look at in detail. We will also discuss the subtle interplay between parametric memory and context.

Further reading

- Lewis, *Retrieval-Augmented Generation for Knowledge-Intensive NLP Tasks*, 2020, `https://arxiv.org/abs/2005.11401`
- *ANN-Benchmarks*, 2024, `https://ann-benchmarks.com/index.html`
- *Hamming Distance between Two Strings*: `https://www.geeksforgeeks.org/hamming-distance-two-strings/`

6

Advanced RAG Techniques for Information Retrieval and Augmentation

In the previous chapter, we discussed RAG and how this paradigm has evolved to solve some shortcomings of LLMs. However, even naïve RAG (the basic form of this paradigm) is not without its challenges and problems. Naïve RAG consists of a few simple components: an embedder, a vector database for retrieval, and an LLM for generation. As mentioned in the previous chapter, naïve RAG involves a collection of text being embedded in a database; once a query from a user arrives, text chunks that are relevant to the query are searched for and provided to the LLM to generate a response. These components allow us to respond effectively to user queries; but as we shall see, we can add additional components to improve the system.

In this chapter, we will see how in advanced RAG, we can modify or improve the various steps in the pipeline (data ingestion, indexing, retrieval, and generation). This solves some of the problems of naïve RAG and gives us more control over the whole process. We will later see how the demand for more flexibility led to a further step forward (modular RAG). We will also discuss important aspects of RAG, especially when the system (a RAG base product) is being produced. For example, we will discuss the challenges when we have a large amount of data or users. Also, since these systems may contain sensitive data, we will discuss both robustness and privacy. Finally, although RAG is a popular system today, it is still relatively new. So, there are still unanswered questions and exciting prospects for its future.

In this chapter, we'll be covering the following topics:

- Discussing naïve RAG issues
- Exploring advanced RAG pipelines
- Modular RAG and integration with other systems

- Implementing an advanced RAG pipeline
- Understanding the scalability and performance of RAG
- Open questions

Technical requirements

Most of the code in this chapter can be run on a CPU, but it is preferable for it to be run on a GPU. The code is written in PyTorch and uses standard libraries for the most part (PyTorch, Hugging Face Transformers, LangChain, `chromadb`, `sentence-transformer`, `faiss-cpu`, and so on).

The code for this chapter can be found on GitHub: https://github.com/PacktPublishing/Modern-AI-Agents/tree/main/chr6.

Discussing naïve RAG issues

In the previous chapter, we introduced RAG in its basic version (called naïve RAG). Although the basic version of RAG has gone a long way in solving some of the most pressing problems of LLMs, several issues remain. For industrial applications, in particular (as well as medical, legal, and financial), naïve RAG is not enough, and we need a more sophisticated pipeline. We will now explore the problems associated with naïve RAG, each of which is associated with a specific step in the pipeline (query handling, retrieval, and generation).

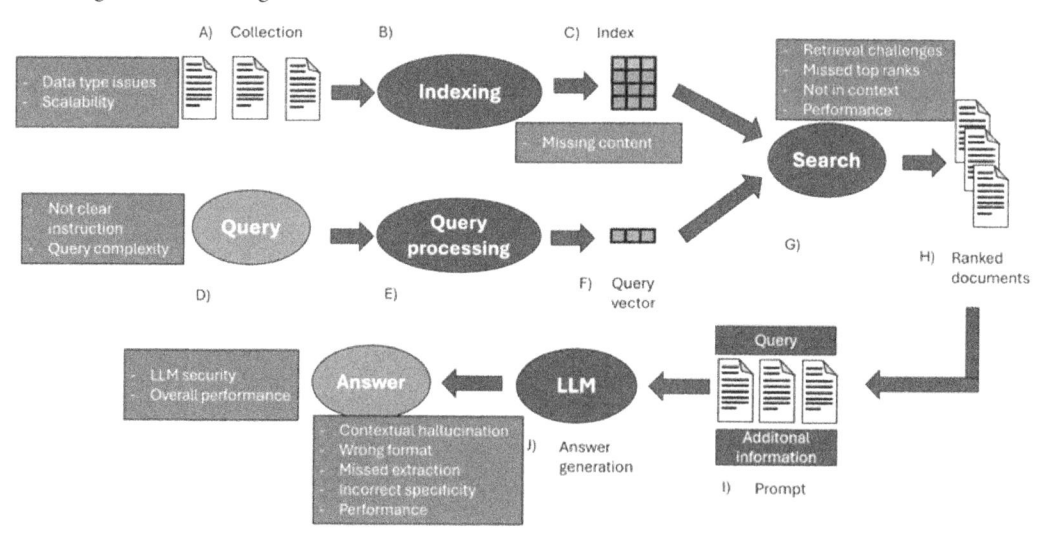

Figure 6.1 – Summary of naïve RAG issues and identifying different steps in the pipeline where the issues can arise

Let's discuss these issues in detail:

- **Retrieval challenges**: The phase of retrieval struggles with precision (retrieved chunks are misaligned) and recall (finding all relevant chunks). In addition, the knowledge base could be outdated. This could lead to either hallucinations or, depending on the prompt used, a response such as, "Sorry, I do not know the answer" or "The context does not allow the query to be answered." This can also be derived from poor database indexing or the documents being of different types (PDF, HTML, text, and so on) and being treated incorrectly (chunking for all file types is an example).

- **Missed top-rank documents**: Documents essential to answering the query may not be at the top of the list. By selecting the top k documents, we might select top chunks that are less relevant (or do not contain the answer) and not return the really relevant chunks to the LLM. The semantic representation capability of the embedding model may be weak (i.e., we chose an ineffective model because it was too small or not suitable for the domain of our documents).

- **Relevant information not in context**: Documents with the answer are found but there are too many to fit in the LLM's context. For example, the response might need several chunks, and these are too many for the context length of the model.

- **Failed extraction**: The right context might be returned to the LLM, but it might not extract the right answer. Usually, this happens when there is too much noise or conflicting information in the context. The model might generate hallucinations despite having the answer in the prompt (contextual hallucinations).

- **Answer in the wrong format**: There may be additional specifics in the query. For example, we may want an LLM to generate bullet points or report the information in a table. The LLM may ignore this information.

- **Incorrect specificity**: The generated answer is not specific enough or too specific with respect to the user's needs. This is generally a problem associated with how the system is designed and what its purpose is. Our RAG may be part of a product designed for students and must give clear and comprehensive answers on a topic. The model, on the other hand, might answer vaguely or too technically for a student. Typically, this is a problem when the query (or instructions) is not clear enough.

- **Augmentation hurdles or information redundancy**: Our database may contain information from different corpora, and many of the documents may contain redundant information or be in different styles and tones. The LLM could then generate repetition and/or create hallucinations. Also, the answer may not be good quality because the model fails to integrate the information from the various chunks.

- **Incomplete answers**: These are answers that are not wrong but are incomplete (this can result from either not finding all the necessary information or errors on the part of the LLM in using the context). Sometimes, it can also be a problem of the query being too complex ("Summarize items A, B, and C"), and so it might also be better to modify the query.

- **Lack of flexibility**: This when the system is not flexible; it does not currently allow efficient updating, and we cannot incorporate feedback from users, past interactions, and so on. The system does not allow us to handle certain files that are abundant in our corpus (for example, our system does not allow Excel).

- **Scalability and overall performance**: In this case, our system may be too slow to conduct an embedding, generate a response, and so on. Alternatively, we cannot handle embedding multiple documents per second, or we have performance issues that are specific to our product or domain. System security is a sore point, especially if we have sensitive data.

Now that we understand the issues with naïve RAG, let's understand how advanced RAG helps us tackle these issues.

Exploring the advanced RAG pipeline

Advanced RAG introduces a number of specific improvements to try to address the issues highlighted in naïve RAG. Advanced RAG, in other words, modifies the various components of RAG to try to optimize the RAG paradigm. These various modifications occur at the different steps of RAG: **pre-retrieval** and **post-retrieval**.

In the **pre-retrieval process**, the purpose is to optimize indexing and querying. For example, **adding metadata** enables more granular searching, and we provide more content to the LLM to generate text. Metadata can succinctly contain information that would otherwise be dispersed throughout the document.

In naïve RAG, we divide the document into different chunks and find the relevant chunks for each document. This approach has two limitations:

- When we have many documents, it impacts latency time and performance
- When the documents are large, we may not be able to easily find the relevant chunks

In naïve RAG, there is only one level (all chunks are equivalent even if they are derived from different documents). In general, though, for many corpora, there is a hierarchy, and it might be beneficial to use it.

To address these limitations, advanced RAG introduces several enhancements designed to improve both retrieval and generation. In the following subsections, we will explore some techniques

Hierarchical indexing

For a document consisting of several chapters, we could first find the chapters of interest and from there search for the various sections of interest. Since the chapters may be of considerable size (rich in noise), embedding may not best represent their contextual significance. The solution is to use summaries and metadata. In a **hierarchical index**, you create summaries at each hierarchical level (which can be considered abstracts). At the first level, we have summaries that highlight only the key points in large document segments. In the lower levels, the granularity will increase, and these abstracts will be closer and closer to only the relevant section of data. Next, we will conduct the embedding of these abstracts. At inference time, we will calculate the similarity with these summary embeddings. Of course, this means either we manually write the summaries or we use an LLM to conduct summarization. Then, using the associated metadata, we can find the chunks that match the summary and provide it to the model.

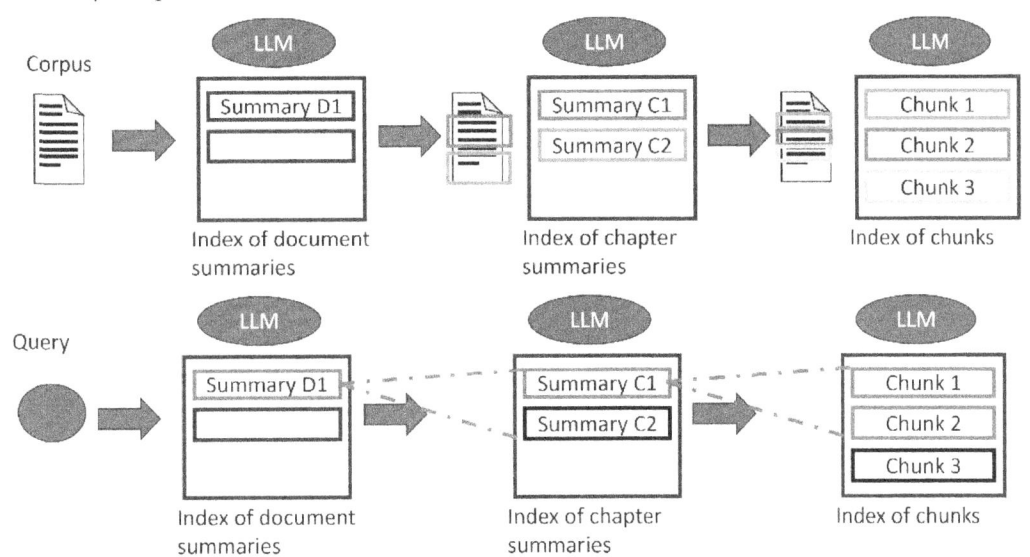

Figure 6.2 Hierarchical indexing

As seen in the preceding figure, the corpus is divided into documents; we then obtain a summary of each document and embed it (in naïve RAG, we were dividing into chunks and embedding the chunks). In the next step, we embed the summary of a lower hierarchical level of the documents (chapter, sections, heading, and subheadings) until we reach the chunk level. At inference time, a similarity search is conducted on the summaries to retrieve the chunks we are interested in.

There are some variations to this approach. For more control, we can choose a split approach for each file type (HTML, PDF, and GitHub repository). In this way, we can make the summary data type-specific and embed the summary, which works as a kind of text normalization.

When we have documents that are too long for our LLM summarizer, we can use **map and reduce**, where we first conduct a summarization of various parts of the document, then collate these summaries and get a single summary. If the documents are too encyclopedic (i.e., deal with too many topics), there is a risk of semantic noise impacting retrieval. To solve this, we can have multiple summaries per document (e.g., one summary per 10K tokens or every 10 pages of document).

Hierarchical indexing improves the contextual understanding of the document (because it respects its hierarchy and captures the relationships between various sections, such as chapters, headings, and subheadings). This approach allows greater accuracy in finding the results, and they are more relevant. On the other hand, this approach comes at a cost both during the pre-retrieval stage and in inference. Too many levels and you risk having a combinatorial explosion, that is, a rapid growth in complexity due to the exponential increase in possible combinations, with a huge latency cost.

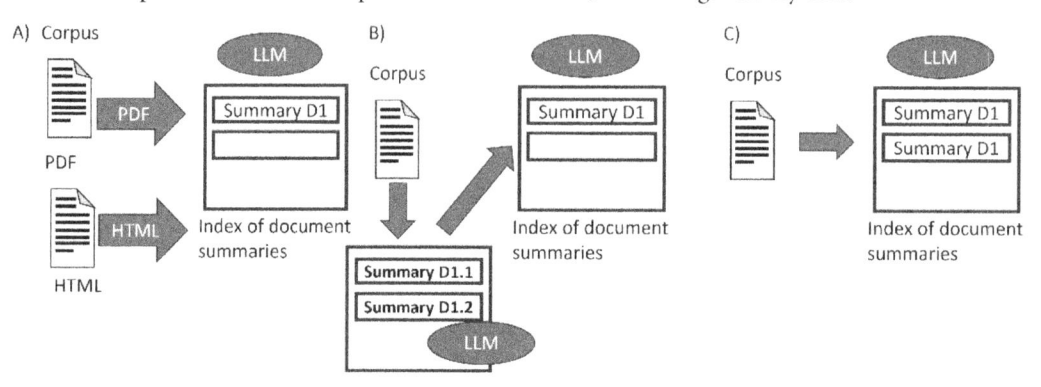

Figure 6.3 – Hierarchical indexing variation

In the preceding figure, we can see these hierarchical index variations:

- *A*: Different handling for each document type to better represent their structure
- *B*: Map and reduce to handle too-long documents (intermediate summaries are created and then used to create the final document summary)
- *C*: Multi-summary for each document when documents are discussing too many topics

Hypothetical questions and HyDE

Another modification of the naïve RAG pipeline is to try to make chunks and possible questions more semantically similar. By having an idea of who our users are, we can imagine the kind of use they will get out of our system (for a chatbot, most queries will be questions, so we can tailor the system toward these kinds of queries). **Hypothetical questions** is a type of strategy in which we use an LLM to generate one (or more) hypothetical question(s) for each chunk. These hypothetical questions are then transformed into vectors (embedding), and these vectors are used to do a similarity search when there is a query from a user. Of course, once we have identified the hypothetical questions most similar to our real query, we find the chunks (thanks to the metadata) and provide them to the model. We can generate either a single query or multiple queries for each chunk (this increases the accuracy as well as the computational cost). In this case, we are not using the vector representation of chunks (we do not conduct embeddings of chunks but hypothetical questions). Also, we do not necessarily have to save the hypothetical questions, just their vectors (the important thing is that we can map them back to the chunks).

Hypothetical Document Embeddings (HyDE) instead tries to convert the user answers to better match the chunks. Given a query, we create hypothetical answers to it. After that, we conduct embeddings of these generated answers and carry out a similarity search to find the chunks of interest. These generated answers should be most semantically similar to the user's query, allowing us to be able to find better chunks. In some variants, we create five different generated answers and conduct the average of their embedding vectors before conducting the similarity search. This approach can help when we have a low recall metric in the retrieval step or when the documents (or queries) come from a specific domain that is different from the retrieval domain. In fact, embedding models generalize poorly to knowledge domains that they have not seen. An interesting little note is that when an LLM generates these hypothetical answers, it does not know the exact answer (that is not even the purpose of the approach) but is able to capture relevant patterns in the question. We can then use these captured patterns to retrieve the chunks.

Let's look in detail at the difference between the two approaches. With the hypothetical questions approach, we generate hypothetical questions and use the embedding of these hypothetical questions to then find the chunks of interest. With HyDE, we generate hypothetical answers to our query and then use the embedding of these answers to find the chunks of interest.

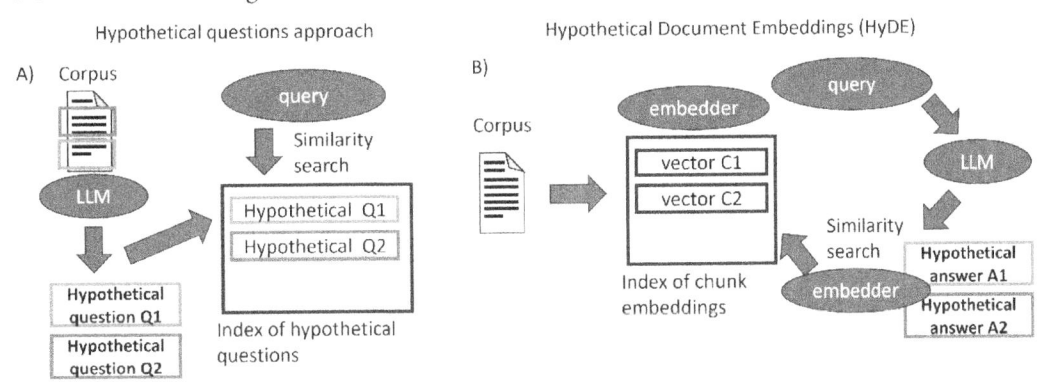

Figure 6.4 – Hypothetical questions and HyDE approaches

We can then look in detail at the differences between the two approaches, imagining that we have a hypothetical user question ("What are the potential side effects of using acetaminophen?"):

- **Pre-retrieval phase**: During this phase, we have to create our drug embedding database. We reduce our documents (sections of a drug's safety report) into chunks. In the hypothetical questions approach, for each chunk, hypothetical questions are generated using an LLM (for example, "What are the side effects of this drug?" or "Are there any adverse reactions mentioned?"). Each of these hypothetical questions is then embedded into a vector space (a database of vectors for these questions). At this stage, HyDE is equal to classic RAG; no variation is conducted.

- **Query phase**: In the hypothetical questions approach, when a user submits the query, it is embedded and matched against the embedded hypothetical questions. The system looks for the hypothetical questions that are most similar to the user's question (in this case, it might be, "What are the side effects of this drug?"). At this point, the chunks from which these hypothetical questions were generated are identified (we use metadata). These chunks are provided in context for generation. In HyDE, when the user query arrives, an LLM generates hypothetical answers (for example, "Paracetamol may cause side effects such as nausea, liver damage, and rashes" or "Potential adverse reactions include dizziness and gastrointestinal discomfort").

  Note that these answers are generated using LLM knowledge without retrieval. At this point, we conduct the embedding of these hypothetical answers (we use an embedding model), then conduct the embedding of the query and try to match it with the embedded hypothetical answers. For example, "Paracetamol may cause side effects such as nausea, liver damage, and rashes" is the one closest to the user query. We then search for the chunks closest to these hypothetical answers and provide the LLM to generate the context.

Context enrichment

Another technique is **context enrichment**, in which we find smaller chunks (greater granularity for better search quality) and then add surrounding context. **Sentence window retrieval** is one such technique in which each sentence in a document is embedded separately (the embedded textual unit is smaller and therefore more granular). This allows us to have higher precision in finding answers, though we risk losing context for LLM reasoning (and thus worse generation). To solve this, we expand our context window. Having found a sentence x, we take k sentences that surround it in the document (sentences that are before and after our sentence x in the document).

Parent document retriever is a similar technique that tries to find a balance between searching on small chunks and providing context with larger chunks. The documents are divided into small child chunks, but we preserve the hierarchy of their parent documents. In this case, we conduct embedding of small chunks that directly address the specifics of a query (ensuring larger chunks' relevance). But then we find the larger parent documents (to which the found chunks belong) and provide them to the LLM for generation (more contextual information and depth). To avoid retrieving too many parent documents, once the top k chunks are found, if more than n chunks belong to a parent document, we add this document to the LLM context.

These approaches are depicted in the following figure:

A. Once a chunk is found, we expand the selection with the previous and next chunks.

B. We conduct embedding of small chunks and find the top k chunks; if most chunks (greater than a parameter n) are derived from a document, we provide the LLM with the document as the context.

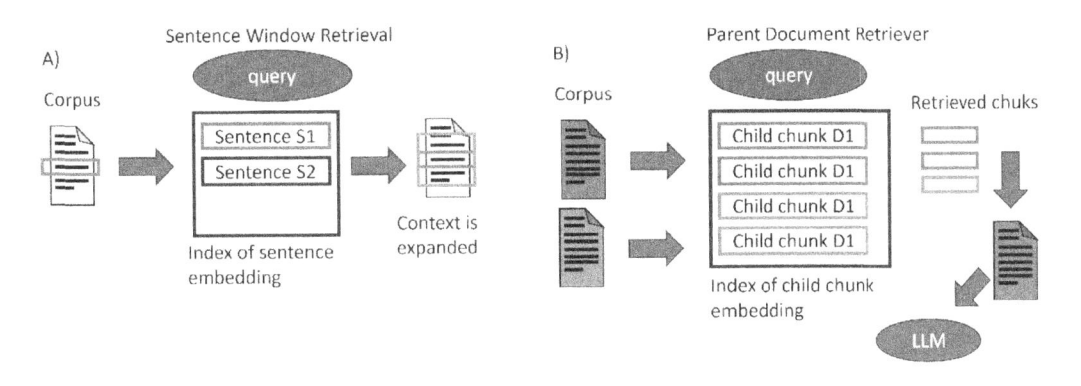

Figure 6.5 – Context enrichment approaches

Query transformation

Query transformation is a family of techniques that leverages an LLM to improve retrieval. If a query is too complex, it can be decomposed into a series of queries. In fact, we may not find a chunk that responds to the query, but more easily find chunks that respond to each subquery (e.g., "Who was the inventor of the telegraph and the telephone?" is best broken down into two independent queries). **Step-back prompting** uses an LLM to generate a more general query that can match a high-level context. It stems from the idea that when a human being is faced with a difficult task, they take a step back and do abstractions to get to the high-level principles. In this case, we use the embedding of this high-level query and the user's query, and both found contexts are provided to the LLM for generation. **Query rewriting**, on the other hand, reformulates the initial query with an LLM to make retrieval easier.

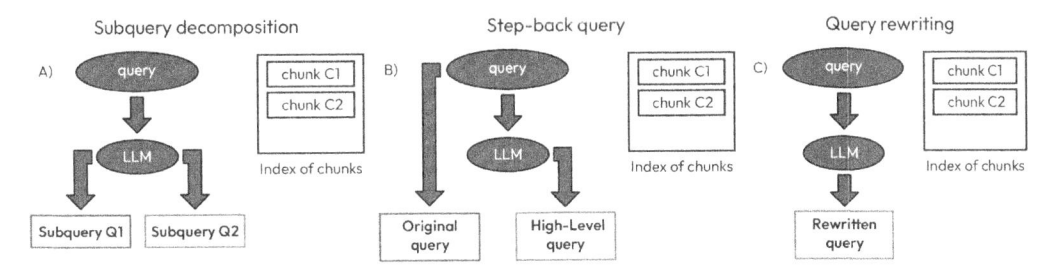

Figure 6.6 – Three examples of query transformation

Query expansion is a technique similar to query rewriting. Underlying it is the idea that adding terms to the query can allow it to find relevant documents that do not have lexical overlap with the query (and thus improve retrieval recall). Again, we use an LLM to modify the query. There are two main possibilities:

- Ask an LLM to generate an answer to the query, after which the generated answer and the query are embedded and used for retrieval.
- Generate several queries similar to the original query (usually a prefixed number n). This n set of queries is then vectorized and used for search.

This approach usually improves retrieval because it helps disambiguate the query and find documents that otherwise would not be found; it also helps the system better compile the query. On the other hand, though, it also leads to finding irrelevant documents, so it pays to combine it with post-processing techniques for finding documents.

Keyword-based search and hybrid search

Another way to improve search is to focus not only on contextual information but also on keywords. **Keyword-based search** is a search by an exact match of certain keywords. This type of search is beneficial for specific terms (such as product or company names or specific industry jargon). However, it is sensitive to typos and synonyms and does not capture context. **Vector or semantic search**, on the contrary, finds the semantic meaning of a query but does not find exact terms or keywords (which is sometimes essential for some queries, especially in some domains such as marketing). **Hybrid search** takes the best of both worlds by combining a model for keyword search and vectorial search.

The most commonly used model for keyword search is BM25 (which we discussed in the previous chapter), which generates sparse embeddings. BM25 then allows us to identify documents that contain specific terms in the query. So, we create two embeddings: a sparse embedding with BM25 and a dense embedding with a transformer. To select the best chunks, you generally try to balance the impact of your different types of searches. The final score is a weighted combination (you use an alpha hyperparameter) of the two scores:

$$score_{hybrid} = (1 - \alpha) \cdot score_{sparse} + \alpha \cdot score_{dense}$$

α has a value between 0 and 1 (0 means pure vectorial search, while 1 means only keyword search). Typically, the value of α is 0.4 or 0.5 (other articles even suggest 0.3).

As a practical example, we can imagine an e-commerce platform with a vast product catalog containing millions of items across categories such as electronics, fashion, and home appliances. Users search for products with different types of queries, which may include the following:

- Specific terms such as a brand or product name (e.g., "iPhone 16")
- A general description (e.g., "Medium-price phone with a good camera")
- Queries that contain mixed elements (e.g., "iPhone with cost less than $500")

A pure keyword-based search (such as the BM25 algorithm) would struggle with vague or purely descriptive descriptions, while a vector-based semantic search might miss exact matches for a product. Hybrid search combines the best of both. BM25 prioritizes exact matches, such as matches of "iPhone," allowing us to find specific items using keywords. Semantic search allows us to capture the semantic meaning of phrases such as "phone with a good camera." Hybrid search is a great solution for all three of the previously mentioned cases.

Query routing

So far, we have assumed that once a query arrives, it is used for a search within the vector database. In reality, we may want to conduct the search differently or control the flow within the system. For example, the system should be able to interact with different types of databases (vector, SQL, and proprietary databases), different sources, or different types of modalities (image, text, and sound). Some queries do not, then, need to be searched with RAG; the parametric memory of the model might suffice (we will discuss this in more depth in the *Open questions and future perspectives* section). Query routing thus allows control over how the system should respond to the query. You can imagine it as being a series of if/else causes, though instead of being hardcoded, we have a router (usually an LLM) that makes a decision whenever a query arrives. Obviously, this means that we have a nondeterministic system, and it will not always make the right decision, although it can have a major positive impact on performance.

The router can be a set of logical rules or a neural model. Some options for a router are the following:

- **Logical routers**: A set of logical rules that can be if/else clauses (e.g., if the query is an image, it searches the image database; otherwise, it searches the text database). Logical routers don't understand the query, but they are very fast and deterministic.

- **Keyword routers**: A slightly more sophisticated alternative in which we try to select a route by matching keywords between the query and a list of options. This search can be done with a sparse encoder, a specialized package, or even an LLM.

- **Zero-shot classification router**: Zero-shot classification is a task in which an LLM is asked to classify an item with a set of labels without being specified and trained for it. Each query is given to an LLM that must assign a route label from those in a list.

- **LLM function calling router**: The different routes are described as functions (with a specific description) and the model must decide where to direct the queries by selecting the function (in this approach, we leverage its decision-making ability).

- **Semantic router**: In this approach, we use a semantic search to decide on the best route. In short, we have a list of example queries and the associated routes. These are then embedded and saved as vectors in a database. When a query arrives, we conduct a similarity search with the other queries in our database. We then select the option associated with the query with the best similarity match.

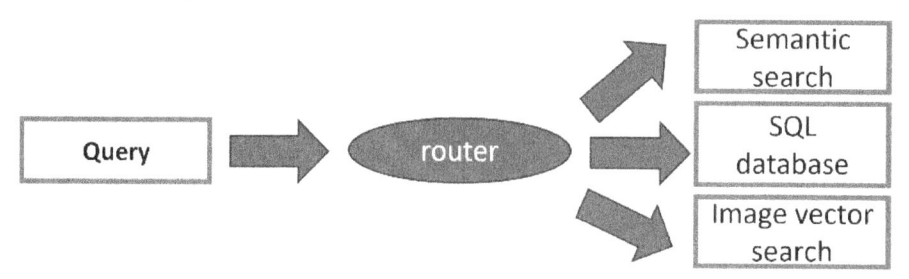

Figure 6.7 – Query routing

Once we have found the context, we need to integrate it with the query and provide it to the LLM for generation. There are several strategies to improve this process, usually called **post-retrieval strategies**. After the vector search, retrieval returns the top k documents (an arbitrary cutoff that is determined in advance). This can lead to the loss of relevant information. The simplest solution is to increase the value of the top k chunks. Obviously, we cannot return all retrieved chunks, both because they would not fit into the context length of the model and because the LLM would then have problems with handling all this information (efficient use of a long context length).

We can imagine a company offering different services across different domains, such as banking, insurance, and finance. Customers interact with a chatbot to seek assistance with banking services (account details, transactions, and so on), insurance services (policy details, claims, etc.), and financial services (suggestions, investments, etc.). Each domain is different. Due to regulations and privacy issues, we want to prevent a chatbot from searching for details for a customer of another service. Also, searching all databases for every query is inefficient and leads to more latency and irrelevant results.

Reranking

One proposed solution to this dilemma is to maximize document retrieval (increase the top k retrieved results and thus increase the retrieval recall metric) but at the same time maximize the LLM recall (by minimizing the number of documents supplied to the LLM). This strategy is called **reranking**. Reranking consists of two steps:

1. First, we conduct a classical retrieval and find a large number of chunks.
2. Next, we use a reranker (a second model) to reorder the chunks and then select the top k chunks to provide to the LLM.

The reranker improves the quality of chunks returned to the LLM and reduces hallucinations in the system. In addition, reranking considers contrasting information (related to the query) and then considers chunks in context with the query. There are several types of rerankers, each with its own limitations and advantages:

- **Cross-encoders**: These are transformers (such as BGE) that take two textual sequences (the query and the various chunks one at a time) as input and return the similarity between 0 and 1.
- **Multi-vector rerankers**: These are still transformers (such as ColBERT) and require less computation than cross-encoders (the interaction between the two sequences is late-stage). The principle is similar; given two sequences, they return a similarity between 0 and 1. There are improved versions with a large context length, such as jina-colbert-v1-en.
- **LLMs for reranking**: LLMs can also be used as rerankers. Several strategies are used to improve the ranking capabilities of an LLM:
    - **Pointwise methods** are used to calculate the relevance of a query and a single document (also referred to as zero-shot document reranking).
    - **Pairwise methods** consist of providing an LLM with both the query and two documents and asking it to choose which one is more relevant.
    - **Listwise methods**, on the other hand, propose to provide a query and a list of documents to the LLM and instruct it to produce as output a ranked list. Models such as GPT are usually used, with the risk of high computational or economic costs.
- **Fine-tuned LLMs**: This is a class of models that is specifically for ranking tasks. Although LLMs are generalist models, they do not have specific training for ranking and therefore cannot accurately measure query-document relevance. Fine-tuning allows them to improve their capability. Generally, there are two types of models used: encoder-decoder transformers (RankT5) or decoder-only transformers (e.g., derivatives of Llama and GPT).

All these approaches have an impact on both performance (retrieval quality) and cost (computational cost, system latency, and potential system cost). Generally, multi-vectors are those with lower computational cost and discrete performance. LLM-based methods may have the best performance but have high computational costs. In general, reranking has a positive impact on the system, which is why it is often a component of the pipeline.

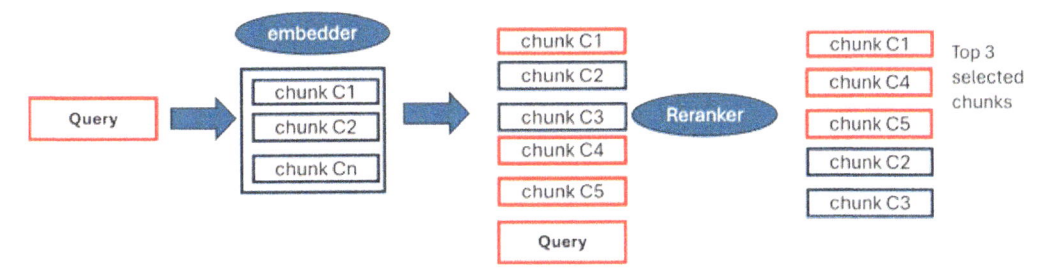

Figure 6.8 – Reranking approach. Chunks highlighted in red are the chunks relevant to the query

Alternatively, there are other **post-processing techniques**. For example, it is possible to filter out chunks if the similarity achieved is below a certain score threshold, if they do not include certain keywords, if a certain value is not present in the metadata associated with the chunks, if the chunks are older than a certain date, and many other possibilities. An additional strategy is that once we have found chunks, starting from the embedding vectors, we conduct **k-nearest neighbors (kNN)** research. In other words, we add other chunks that are neighbors in the latent space of those found (this strategy can be done before or after reranking).

In addition, once the chunks are selected to be provided in context to the LLM, we can alter their order. As shown in the following figure, a study published in 2023 shows that the best performance for an LLM is when the important information is placed at the beginning or end of the input context length (performance drops if the information is in the middle of the context length, especially if it is very long):

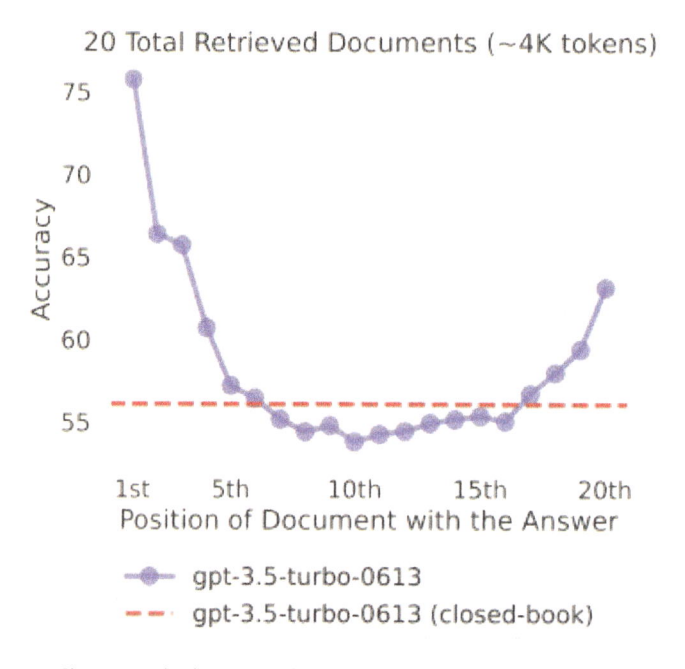

Figure 6.9 – Changing the location of relevant information impacts the performance of an LLM (https://arxiv.org/abs/2307.03172)

That is why it has been proposed to **reorder the chunks**. They can be placed in order of relevance, but also in alternating patterns (chunks with an even index are placed at the beginning of the list and chunks with an odd index at the end). The alternating pattern is used especially when using wide top k chunks, so the most relevant chunks are placed at the beginning and end (while the less relevant ones are in the middle of the context length).

You can notice that reranking improves the performance of the system:

Reranker model	Avg.	NQ	HotpotQA	FiQA
Embedding: snowflake-arctic-embed-l	0.6100	0.6311	0.7518	0.4471
+ ms-marco-MiniLM-L-12-v2	0.5771	0.5876	0.7586	0.3850
+ mxbai-rerank-large-v1	0.6077	0.6433	0.7401	0.4396
+ jina-reranker-v2-base-multilingual	0.6481	0.6768	0.8165	0.4511
+ bge-reranker-v2-m3	0.6585	0.6965	0.8458	0.4332
+ NV-RerankQA-Mistral-4B-v3	**0.7529**	**0.7788**	**0.8726**	**0.6073**
Embedding: NV-EmbedQA-e5-v5	0.6083	0.6380	0.7160	0.4710
+ ms-marco-MiniLM-L-12-v2	0.5785	0.5909	0.7458	0.3988
+ mxbai-rerank-large-v1	0.6077	0.6450	0.7279	0.4502
+ jina-reranker-v2-base-multilingual	0.6454	0.6780	0.7996	0.4585
+ bge-reranker-v2-m3	0.6584	0.6974	0.8272	0.4506
+ NV-RerankQA-Mistral-4B-v3	**0.7486**	**0.7785**	**0.8470**	**0.6203**
Embedding: NV-EmbedQA-Mistral7B-v2	0.7173	0.7216	0.8109	0.6194
+ ms-marco-MiniLM-L-12-v2	0.5875	0.5945	0.7641	0.4039
+ mxbai-rerank-large-v1	0.6133	0.6439	0.7436	0.4523
+ jina-reranker-v2-base-multilingual	0.6590	0.6819	0.8262	0.4689
+ bge-reranker-v2-m3	0.6734	0.7028	0.8635	0.4539
+ NV-RerankQA-Mistral-4B-v3	**0.7694**	**0.7830**	**0.8904**	**0.6350**

Figure 6.10 – Reranking improves the performance in question-answering (https://arxiv.org/pdf/2409.07691)

In addition to reranking, several complementary techniques can be applied after the retrieval stage to further refine the information passed to the LLM. These include methods for improving citation accuracy, managing chat history, compressing context, and optimizing prompt formulation. Let's have a look at some of them.

Reference citations is not really a technique for system improvement, but it is highly recommended as a component of a RAG system. Especially if we are using different sources to compose our query response, it is good to keep track of which sources were used (e.g., the documents that the LLM used). We can simply safeguard the sources that were used for generation (which documents the chunks correspond to). Another possibility is to mention in the prompt for the LLM the sources used. A more sophisticated technique is fuzzy citation query engine. Fuzzy matching is a string search to match the generated response to the found chunks (a technique that is based on dividing the words in the chunk into n-grams and then conducting a TF-IDF).

ChatEngine is another extension of RAG. Conducting fine-tuning of the model is complex, but at the same time, we want the LLM to remember previous interactions with the user. RAG makes it easy to do this, so we can save previous dialogues with users. A simple technique is to include the previous chat in the prompt. Alternatively, we can conduct embedding of the chats and find the highlights. Another technique is to try to capture the context of the user dialogue (chat logic). Since the discussion can wind through several messages, one solution to avoid a prompt that may exceed the context length is **prompt compression**. We reduce the prompt length by reducing the previous interaction with the user.

In general, **contextual compression** is a concept that helps the LLM during generation. It also saves computational (or economic, if using a model via an API) resources. Once the documents are found, we can compress the context, with the aim of retaining only the relevant information. In fact, the context often also contains information irrelevant to the query, or even repetitions. Additionally, most of the words in a sentence could be predicted directly from the context and are not needed to provide the information to the LLM during generation. There are several strategies to reduce the prompt provided to the LLM:

- **Context filtering**: In information theory, tokens with low entropy are easily predictable and thus contain redundant information (provide less relevant information to the LLM and have little impact on its understanding of the context). We therefore use an LLM that assigns an information value to each lexical unit (how much it expects to see that token or sentence in context). We conduct a ranking in descending order and keep only those tokens that are in the first p-th percentile (we decide this *a priori*, or it can be context-dependent).

- **LongLLMLingua**: This is another approach based on information entropy and using information from both context and query (question aware). The approach conducts dynamic compression and reordering of documents to make generation more efficient.

- **Autocompressors**: This uses a kind of fine-tuning of the system and summary vectors. The idea behind it is that a long text can be summarized in a small vector representation (summary vectors). These vectors can be used as soft prompts to give context to the model. The process relies on keeping the LLM's weights frozen while introducing trainable tokens into the prompt. These tokens are learned during training, enabling the system to be optimized end-to-end without modifying the model's core parameters. During generation, these vectors are joined, and the model is then context-aware. Already trained models exist, as follows:

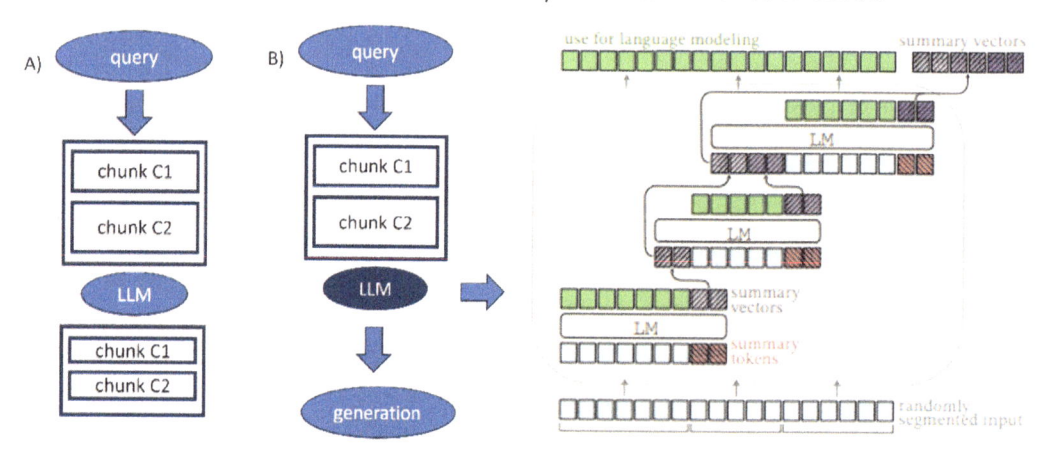

Figure 6.11 – A) Context compression and filtering. B) Autocompressor.
(Adapted from https://arxiv.org/abs/2305.14788)

Prompt engineering is another solution to improve generation. Some suggestions are common to any interaction with an LLM. Thus, principles such as providing clear ("Reply using the context") and unambiguous ("If the answer is not in the context, write I do not know") instructions apply to RAG. There may, however, be specific directions or even examples for designing the best possible prompt for our system. Other instructions may be specific to how we want the output (for example, as a list, in HTML, and so on). There are also libraries for creating prompts for RAG that follow a specific format.

Response optimization

The last step in a pipeline before conducting the final response is to improve the response from the user. One strategy is that of the **response synthesizer**. The basic strategy is to concatenate the prompt, context, and query and provide it to the LLM for generation. More sophisticated strategies involve more calls from the LLM. There are several alternatives to this idea:

- Iteratively refine the response using one chunk at a time. The previous response and a subsequent chunk are sent to the model to improve the response with the new information.

- Generate several responses with different chunks, then concatenate them all together and generate a summary response.

- Hierarchical summarization starts with the responses generated for each different context and recursively combines them until we arrive at a single response. While this approach enhances the quality of both summaries and generated answers, it requires significantly more LLM calls, making it costly in terms of both computational resources and financial expense.

An interesting development is the possibility of using RAG as a component of an agent system. As we introduced in *Chapter 4,* RAG can act as the memory of the system. RAG can be combined with **agents**. An LLM is capable of reasoning that can be merged with RAG and call-up tools or connect to sites when a query requires additional steps. An agent can also handle different components (retrieve chat history, conduct query routing, connect to APIs, and execute code). A complex RAG pipeline can have several components that are not the best fit for every situation, and an LLM can decide which are the best components to use.

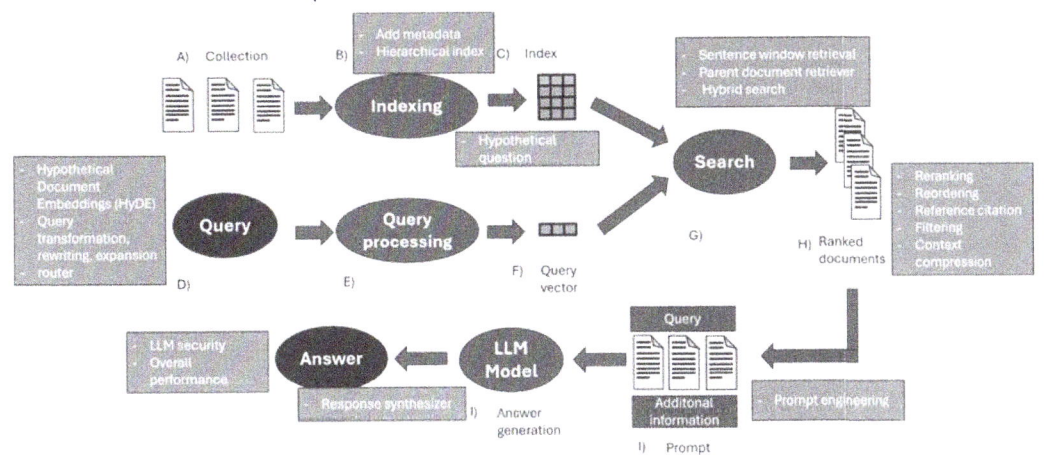

Figure 6.12 – Different elements in a pipeline of advanced RAG

So far, we have assumed that a pipeline should be executed only once. The standard practice is we conduct retrieval once and then generate. This approach, though, can be insufficient for complex problems that require multi-step reasoning. There are three possibilities in this case:

- **Iterative retrieval**: In this case, the retrieval is conducted multiple times. Given a query, we conduct the retrieval, we generate the result, and then the result is judged by an LLM. Depending on the judgment, we repeat the process up to *n* times. This process improves the robustness of the answers after each iteration, but it can also lead to the accumulation of irrelevant information.

- **Recursive retrieval**: This system was developed to increase the depth and relevance of search results. It is similar to the previous one, but at each iteration, the query is refined in response to previous search results. The purpose is to find the most relevant information by exploiting a feedback loop. Many of these approaches exploit **chain-of-thought** (**CoT**) to guide the retrieval process. In this case, the system then breaks down the query into a series of intermediate steps that it must solve. This approach is advantageous when the query is not particularly clear or when the information sought is highly specialized or requires careful consideration of nuanced details.

- **Adaptive retrieval**: In this case, the LLM actively determines when to search and whether the retrieved content is optimal. The LLM judges not only the retrieval step but also its own operation. The LLM can decide when to respond, when to search, or whether additional tools are needed. This approach is often used not only when searching on the RAG but also when conducting web searches. Flare (an adaptative approach to RAG) analyzes confidence during the generation process and makes a decision when the confidence falls below a certain threshold. Self-RAG, on the other hand, introduces **reflection tokens** to monitor the process and force an introspection of the LLM.

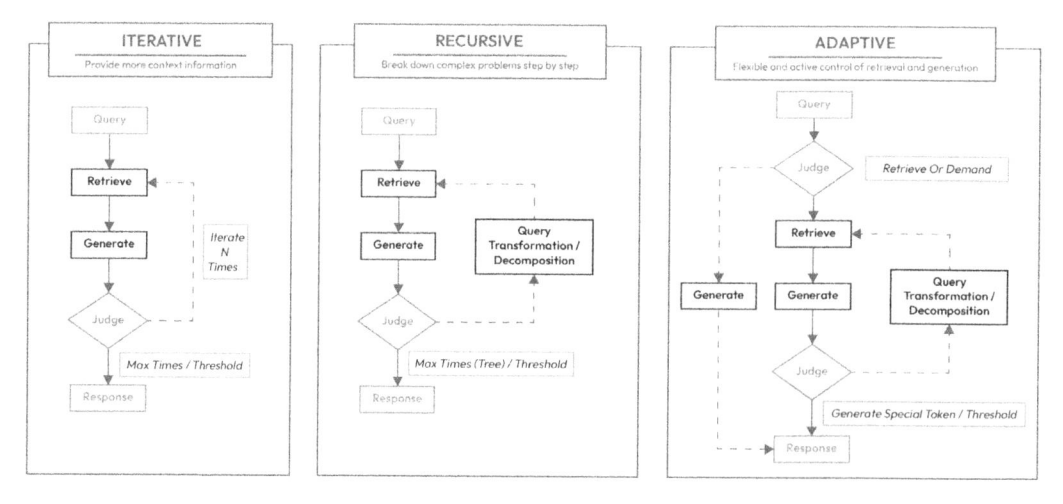

Figure 6.13 – Augmentation of RAG pipelines (https://arxiv.org/pdf/2312.10997)

To better understand how advanced RAG techniques address known limitations, *Table 6.1* presents the mapping between key problems and the most effective solutions proposed in recent research.

Problem to Solve	Solution
Issues in naïve RAG: Latency and performance degradation with many or large documents	Use hierarchical indexing: Summarize large sections, create multi-level embeddings, use metadata, and implement variations such as map-reduce for long documents or multi-summary for diverse topics.
Flat hierarchy limits relevance when the corpus contains an inherent structure	Apply hierarchical indexing: Respect the document's structure (chapters, headings, and subheadings), and retrieve context based on hierarchical summaries and embeddings.
Low retrieval accuracy and domain-specific generalization challenges	Generate and embed hypothetical questions for each chunk (Hypothetical Qs). Use HyDE: generate hypothetical answers to match query semantics, embed them, and retrieve relevant chunks.
Loss of context in granular chunking	Use context enrichment: Expand retrieved chunks with surrounding context using sentence windows or retrieve parent documents to broaden context.
Complex queries and low recall from initial retrieval	Apply query transformation: Decompose complex queries into subqueries, use step-back prompting or query expansion. Embed transformed queries for improved retrieval.
Context mismatch for specific terms or keywords	Use hybrid search: Combine keyword-based (e.g., BM25) and vector-based retrieval using weighted scoring.
Inefficiency in managing diverse query types	Implement query routing: Use logical rules, keyword-based or semantic classifiers, zero-shot models, or LLM-based routers to direct queries to the appropriate backends.
Loss of relevant chunks due to arbitrary top-k cutoff	Apply reranking: Use cross-encoders, multi-vector rerankers, or LLM-based (pointwise, pairwise, or listwise) reranking to reorder retrieved chunks.
Loss of information or efficiency in LLM context	Use context compression: Filter low-entropy tokens, compress or reorder chunks dynamically (e.g., LongLLMLingua), or apply summary vectors and autocompressors.
Inefficient response generation	Optimize responses: Use iterative refinement, hierarchical summarization, or multi-step response synthesis. Improve prompt quality and specificity.

Memory limitations in dialogue systems	Use ChatEngine techniques: Save and embed past conversations, compress user dialogue, and merge chat history with current queries.
Need for complex reasoning or dynamic query adaptation	Adopt adaptive and multi-step retrieval: Use recursive, iterative approaches with feedback loops and self-reflection (e.g., Flare, Self-RAG).
Lack of source tracking in generated responses	Include citations: Use fuzzy citation matching, metadata tagging, or embed source references in prompts.
Need for pipeline customization based on query complexity or modality	Augment RAG pipelines: Combine with agents for reasoning, tool use, and decision-making. Apply adaptive and recursive retrieval loops for complex queries.

Table 6.1 – Problems and solutions in RAG

Modular RAG and its integration with other systems

Modular RAG is a further advancement; it can be considered as an extension of advanced RAG but focused on adaptability and versatility. In this sense, the modular system means it has separate components that can be used either sequentially or in parallel.

The pipeline itself is remodeled, with alternating search and generation. In general, modular RAG involves optimizing the system toward performance and adapting to different tasks. Modular RAG introduces modules for this that are specialized. Some examples of the modules that are included are as follows:

- **Search module**: This module is responsible for finding relevant information about a query. It allows searching through search engines, databases, and **knowledge graphs** (**KGs**). It can also use sophisticated search algorithms, use machine learning, and execute code.

- **Memory module**: This module serves to store relevant information during the search process. In addition, the system can retrieve context that was previously searched.

- **Routing module**: This module tries to identify the best path for a query, where it can either search for different information in different databases or decompose the query.

- **Generation module**: Different queries may require a different type of generation, such as summarization, paraphrasing, and context expansion. The focus of this module is on improving the quality and relevance of the output.

- **Task-adaptable module**: This module allows dynamic adaptation to tasks that are requested from the system. In this way, the system dynamically adjusts retrieval, processing, and generation.

- **Validation module**: This module evaluates retrieved responses and context. The system can identify errors, biases, and inconsistencies. The process becomes iterative, in which the system can improve its responses.

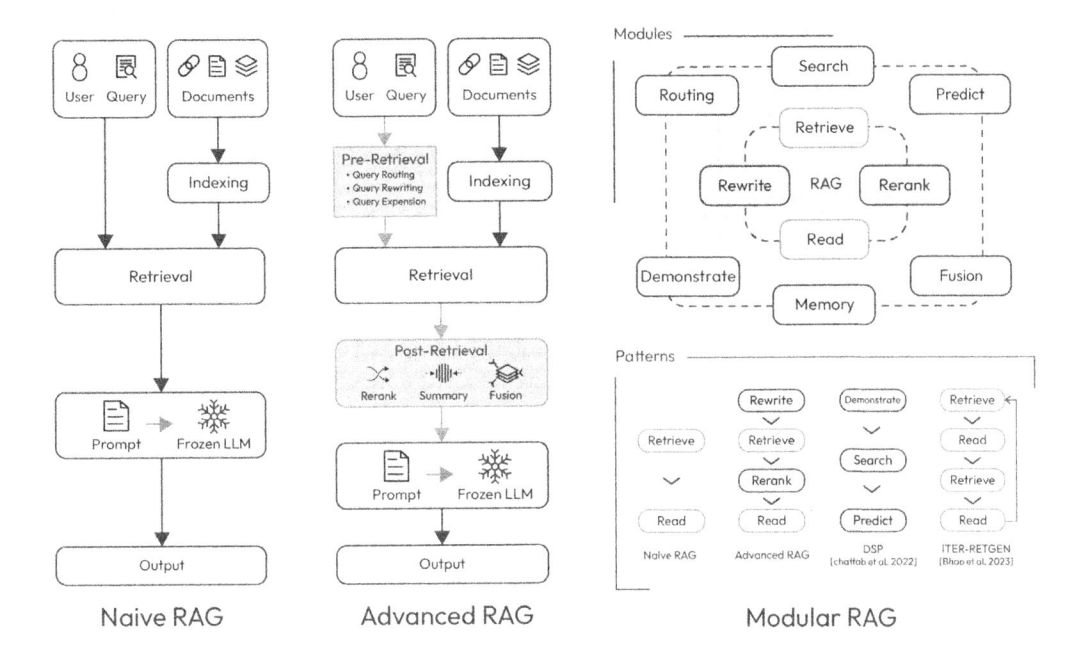

Figure 6.14 – Three different paradigms of RAG (https://arxiv.org/pdf/2312.10997)

Modular RAG offers the advantage of adaptability because these modules can be replaced or reconfigured as needed. The flow between different modules can be finely tuned, allowing an additional level of flexibility. Furthermore, if naïve and advanced RAG are characterized by a "retrieve and read" mechanism, modular RAG allows "retrieve, read, and rewrite." In fact, through the ability to evaluate and provide feedback, the system can refine the response to the query.

As this new paradigm spread, interesting alternatives were experimented with, such as integrating information coming from the parametric memory of the LLM. In this case, the model is asked to generate a response before retrieval (recite and answer). **Demonstrate-search-predict** (**DSP**) shows how you can have different interactions between the LLM and RAG to solve complex queries (or knowledge-intensive tasks). DSP shows how a modular RAG allows for robust and flexible pipelines at the same time. **Self-reflective retrieval-augmented generation** (**Self-RAG**), on the other hand, introduces an element of criticism into the system. The LLM reflects on what it generates, critiquing its output in terms of factuality and overall quality. Another alternative is to use interleaved CoT generation and retrieval. These approaches usually work best when we have issues that require reasoning.

Training and training-free approaches

RAG approaches fall into two groups: training-free and training-based. Naïve RAG approaches are generally considered training-free. **Training-free** means that the two main components of the system (the embedder and LLM) are kept frozen from the beginning. This is possible because they are two components that are pre-trained and therefore have already acquired capabilities that allow us to use them.

Alternatively, we can have three types of **training-based approaches**: independent training, sequential training, and joint training.

In **independent training**, both the retriever and LLMs are trained separately in totally independent processes (there is no interaction during training). In this case, we have separate fine-tuning of the various components of the system. This approach is useful when we want to adapt our system to a specific domain (legal, financial, or medical, for example). Compared to a training-free approach, this type of training improves the capabilities of the system for the domain of our application. LLMs can also be fine-tuned to make better use of the context.

Sequential training, on the otherRAG:sequential training" hand, assumes that we use these two components sequentially, so it is better to find a form of training that increases the synergy between these components. The components can first be trained independently, following which they are trained sequentially. One of the components is kept frozen while the other undergoes additional training. Depending on what the order of training is, we can have two classes, retriever-first or LLM-first:

- **Retriever-first**: In this class, the trainer's training is conducted and then it is kept frozen. Then, the LLM is trained to understand how to use the knowledge in the retriever context. For example, we conduct the fine-tuning of our retriever independently and then we conduct fine-tuning of the LLM using the retrieved chunks. The LLM receives the retriever chunks during its fine-tuning and learns how best to use this context for generation.
- **LLM-first**: This is a bit more complex, but it uses the supervision of an LLM to train the retriever. An LLM is usually a much more capable model than the retriever because it has many more parameters and has been trained on many more tokens, thus making it a good supervisor. In a sense, this approach can be seen as a kind of knowledge distillation in which we take advantage of the greater knowledge of a larger model to train a smaller model.

Training Approach	Domains/Applications	Reasoning	
Retriever-first	Search engines (general or domain-specific) For example, legal document search, medical literature search, or e-commerce product search	Focuses on retrieving the most relevant documents quickly and accurately. Essential for systems where domain-specific precision is critical, and the retriever must handle vast, structured, or semi-structured corpora.	

	Enterprise knowledge management For example, internal corporate documentation, FAQs, or CRM systems	Emphasizes retrieving the right documents efficiently from proprietary databases, where the quality of retrieval has a more significant impact than the quality of generation.
	Scientific research repositories For example, PubMed, arXiv, or patents	Ensures precise and recall-optimized retrieval in highly technical or specialized fields where high-quality retrieval is essential for downstream tasks such as summarization or report generation.
	Regulatory and compliance systems For example, financial compliance checks, or legal case law databases	In domains where accuracy and compliance are critical, the retriever must reliably surface the most relevant content while minimizing irrelevant or low-confidence retrievals.
LLM-first	**Conversational agents** For example, customer support chatbots or personal assistants	Relies heavily on the generative capabilities of the LLM to provide nuanced, conversational responses. Retrieval is secondary as the LLM interprets and integrates retrieved content.
	Creative applications For example, content writing, storytelling, or brainstorming	The LLM's ability to create, synthesize, and infer from retrieved data is paramount. Retrieval supports generation by providing a broader context rather than being the focal point of optimization.
	Complex reasoning tasks For example, multi-step problem-solving or decision-making systems	The LLM's role as a reasoner outweighs retrieval precision, as the focus is on the ability to process, relate, and infer knowledge. Retrieval primarily ensures access to supplementary information for reasoning.
	Educational tools For example, learning assistants or personalized tutoring systems	The LLM's ability to adapt and generate instructional content tailored to the user's context is more critical than precise retrieval. Retrieval serves as a secondary mechanism to ensure the completeness of information.

Table 6.2 – Training approaches

According to this article (Izacard, https://arxiv.org/abs/2012.04584), attention activation values in the LLM are a good proxy for defining the relevance of a document, so they can be used to provide a label (a kind of guide) to the retriever on how good the search results are. Hence, the retriever is trained with a metric based on attention in the LLM. For a less expensive approach, a small LLM can be used to generate the label to then train the retriever. There are then variations in these approaches, but all are based on the principle that once we have fine-tuned the LLM, we want to align the retriever.

Joint methods, on the other hand, represent end-to-end training of the system. In other words, both the retriever and the generator are aligned at the same time (simultaneously). The idea is that we want the system to simultaneously improve both its ability to find knowledge and its ability to use this knowledge for generation. The advantage is that we have a synergistic effect during training.

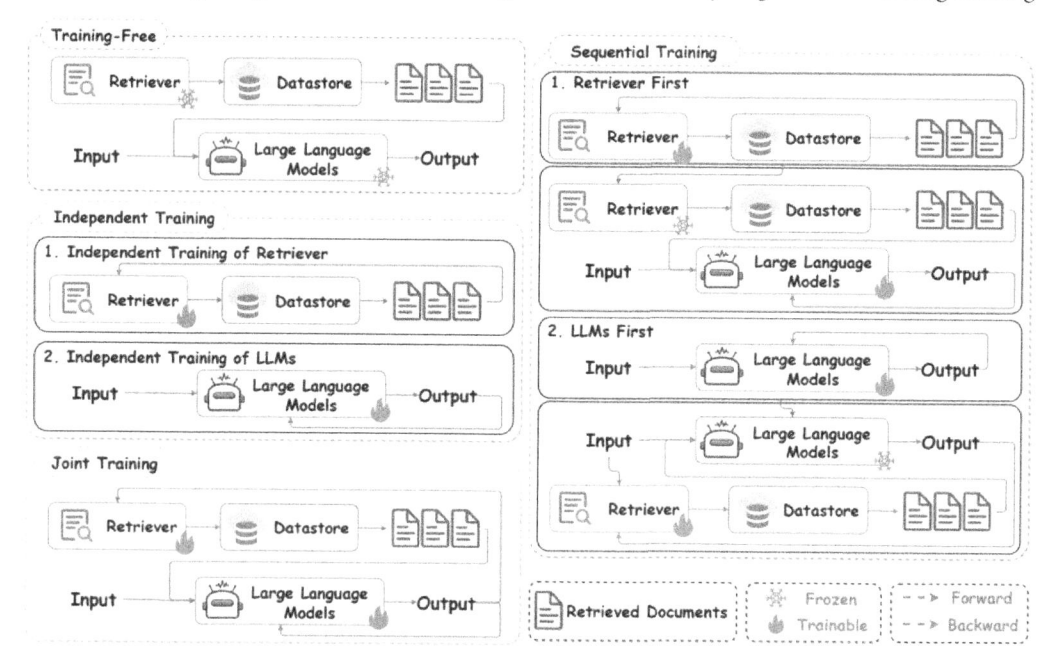

Figure 6.15 – Different training methods in RAG (https://arxiv.org/pdf/2405.06211)

Now that we know the different modifications that we can apply to our RAG, let's try them in the next section.

Implementing an advanced RAG pipeline

In this section, we will describe how an advanced RAG pipeline can be implemented. In this pipeline, we use a more advanced version of naïve RAG, including some add-ons to improve it. This shows us how the starting basis is a classic RAG pipeline (embedding, retrieval, and generation) but more sophisticated components are inserted. In this pipeline, we have used the following add-ons:

- **Reranker**: This allows us to sort the context found during the retrieval step. This is one of the most widely used elements in advanced RAG because it has been seen to significantly improve results.
- **Query transformation**: In this case, we are using a simple query transformation. This is because we want to try to broaden our retrieval range, since some relevant documents may be missed.
- **Query routing**: This prevents us from treating all queries the same and allows us to establish rules for more efficient retrieval.
- **Hybrid search**: With this, we combine the power of keyword-based search with semantic search.
- **Summarization**: With this, we try to eliminate redundant information from our retrieved context.

Of course, we could add other components, but generally, these are the most commonly used and give an overview of what components we can add to naïve RAG.

We can see in the following figure how our pipeline is modified:

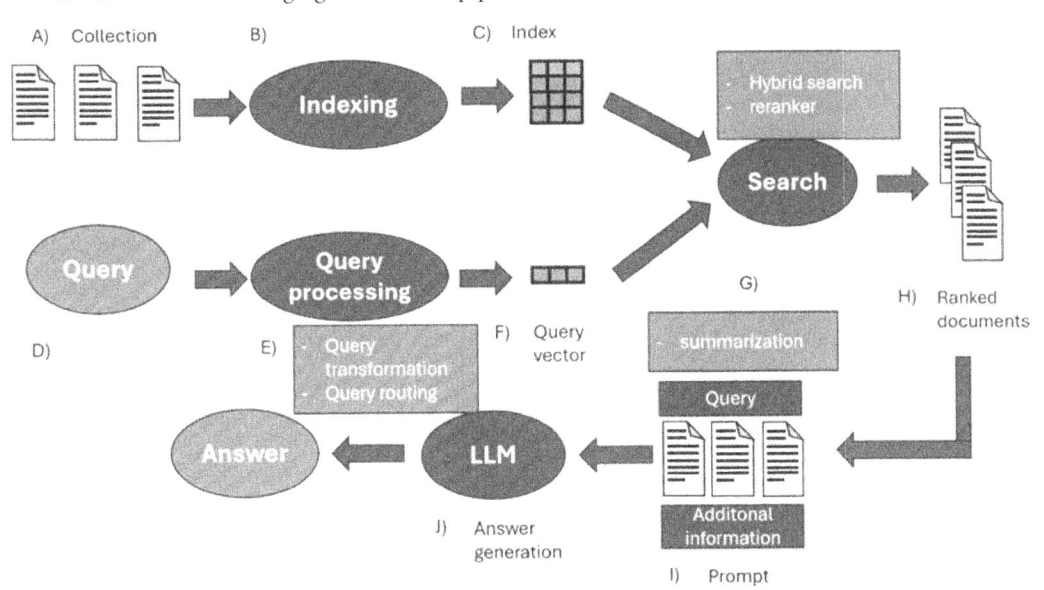

Figure 6.16 – Pipeline of advanced RAG

The complete code can be found in the repository; here, we will just see the highlights. In this code snippet, we are defining a function to represent the query transformation. In this case, we are developing only a small modification of the query (searching for other related terms in our query):

```
def advanced_query_transformation(query):
    """
    Transforms the input query by adding synonyms, extensions, or modifying the structure
    for better search performance.

    Args:
        query (str): The original query.

    Returns:
        str: The transformed query with added synonyms or related terms.
    """
    expanded_query = query + " OR related_term"
    return expanded_query
```

Next, we perform query routing. Query routing enforces a simple rule: if specific keywords are present in the query, a keyword-based search is performed; otherwise, a semantic (embedding-based) search is used. In some cases, we may want to first retrieve only documents that contain certain keywords—such as references to a specific product—and then narrow the results further using semantic search:

```
def advanced_query_routing(query):
    """
    Determines the retrieval method based on the presence of specific keywords in the query.
    Args:
        query (str): The user's query.
    Returns:
        str: 'textual' if the query requires text-based retrieval, 'vector' otherwise.
    """
    if "specific_keyword" in query:
        return "textual"
    else:
        return "vector"
```

Next, we perform a hybrid search, which allows us to use search based on semantic and keyword content. This is one of the most widely used components in RAG pipelines today. When chunking is used, sometimes documents relevant to a query can only be found because they contain a keyword (e.g., the name of a product, a person, and so on). Obviously, not all chunks that contain a keyword are relevant documents (especially for queries where we are more interested in a semantic concept).

With hybrid search, we can balance the two types of search, choosing how many chunks to take from one or the other type of search:

```
def fusion_retrieval(query, top_k=5):
    """
    Retrieves the top_k most relevant documents using a combination of vector-based
    and textual retrieval methods.
    Args:
        query (str): The search query.
        top_k (int): The number of top documents to retrieve.
    Returns:
        list: A list of combined results from both vector and textual retrieval methods.
    """
    query_embedding = sentence_model.encode(query).tolist()
    vector_results = collection.query(query_embeddings=[query_embedding], n_results=min(top_k, len(documents)))

    es_body = {
        "size": top_k,  # Move size into body
        "query": {
            "match": {
                "content": query
            }
        }
    }
    es_results = es.search(index=index_name, body=es_body)
    es_documents = [hit["_source"]["content"] for hit in es_results['hits']['hits']]

    combined_results = vector_results['documents'][0] + es_documents

    return combined_results
```

As mentioned, the reranker is one of the most frequently used elements; it is a transformer that is used to reorder the context. If we have found 10 chunks, we reorder the found chunks and usually take a subset of them. Sometimes, semantic search can find the most relevant chunks again, but these may then be found further down the order. The reranker ensures that these chunks are then actually placed in the context of the LLM:

```
def rerank_documents(query, documents):
    """
    Reranks the retrieved documents based on their relevance to the
query using a pre-trained
```

```
    BERT model.
    Args:
        query (str): The user's query.
        documents (list): A list of documents retrieved from the
search.
    Returns:
        list: A list of reranked documents, sorted by relevance.
    """
    inputs = [rerank_tokenizer.encode_plus(query, doc, return_
tensors='pt', truncation=True, padding=True) for doc in documents]
    scores = []
    for input in inputs:
        outputs = rerank_model(**input)
        logits = outputs.logits
        probabilities = F.softmax(logits, dim=1)
        positive_class_probability = probabilities[:, 1].item()
        scores.append(positive_class_probability)

    ranked_docs = sorted(zip(documents, scores), key=lambda x: x[1],
reverse=True)
    return [doc for doc, score in ranked_docs]
```

As mentioned earlier, context can also contain information that is redundant. LLMs are sensitive to noise, so reducing this noise can help generation. In this case, we use an LLM to summarize the found context (of course, we set a limit to avoid losing too much information):

```
def select_and_compress_context(documents):
    """
    Summarizes the content of the retrieved documents to create a
compressed context.

    Args:
        documents (list): A list of documents to summarize.

    Returns:
        list: A list of summarized texts for each document.
    """
    summarized_context = []
    for doc in documents:
        input_length = len(doc.split())
        max_length = min(100, input_length)  than 100
        summary = summarizer(doc, max_length=max_length, min_length=5,
do_sample=False)[0]['summary_text']
        summarized_context.append(summary)
    return summarized_context
```

Once defined, we just need to assemble them into a single pipeline. Once that's done, we can use our RAG pipeline. Check the code in the repository and play around with the code. Once you have a RAG pipeline that works, the next natural step is deployment. In the next section, we will discuss potential challenges to the deployment.

Understanding the scalability and performance of RAG

In this section, we will mainly describe challenges that are related to the commissioning of a RAG system or that may emerge with the scaling of the system. The main advantage of RAG over an LLM is that it can be scaled without conducting additional training. The purpose and requirements of development and production are mainly different. LLMs and RAG pose new challenges, especially when you want to take a system into production. Productionizing means taking a complex system such as RAG from a prototype to a stable, operational environment. This can be extremely complex when you have to manage different users who may be connected remotely. While in development, accuracy might be the most important metric, while in production, special care must be taken to balance performance and cost.

Large organizations, in particular, may already have big data stored and may therefore want to use RAG with it. Big data can be a significant challenge for a RAG system, especially considering the volume, velocity, and variety of data. **Scalability** is a critical concern when discussing big data; the same principle applies to RAG.

Data scalability, storage, and preprocessing

So far, we have talked about how to find information. We have assumed that the data is in textual form. The data structure of the text is an important parameter, and putting it into production can be problematic. So, our system may have to integrate the following:

- **Unstructured data**: Text is the most commonly used data type present in a corpus. It can have different origins: encyclopedic (from Wikipedia), domain-specific (scientific, medical, or financial), industry-specific (reports or standard documents), downloaded from the internet, or user chat. It can thus be generated by humans but also include data generated by automated systems or by LLMs themselves (previous interactions with users). In addition, it can be multi-language, and the system may have to conduct a cross-language search. Today, there are both LLMs that have been trained with different languages and multi-lingual embedders (specifically designed for multi-lingual capabilities). There are also other types of unstructured data, such as image and video. We will discuss multimodal RAG in a little more detail in the next section.

- **Semi-structured data**: Generally, this means data that contains a mixture of textual and table information (such as PDFs). Other examples of semi-structured data are JSON, XML, and HTML. These types of data are often complex to use with RAG. There are usually file-specific pipelines (chunking, metadata storing, and so on) because they can create problems for the system. In the case of PDF, chunking can separate tables into multiple chunks, making retrieval inefficient. In addition, tables make similarity search more complicated. An alternative is to extract the tables and turn them into text or insert them into compatible databases (such as SQL). Since the available methods are not yet optimal, there is still intense research in the field.

- **Structured data**: Structured data is data that is in a standardized format that can be accessed efficiently by both humans and software. Structured data generally has some special features: defined attributes (same attributes for all data values as in a table), relational attributes (tables have common values that tie different datasets together; for example, in a customer dataset, there are IDs that allow users and their purchases to be found), quantitative data (data is optimized for mathematical analysis), and storage (data is stored in a particular format and with precise rules). Examples of structured data are Excel files, SQL databases, web form results, point-of-sale data, and product directories. Another example of structured data is KGs, which we will discuss in detail in the next chapter.

These factors must be taken into account. For example, if we are designing a system that needs to search for compliance documents in various regions and in different languages, we need a RAG that can conduct cross-lingual retrieval. If our organization has primarily one type of data (PDF or SQL databases), it is important to take this into account and optimize the system to search for this type of data. There are specific alternatives to improve the capabilities of RAGs with structured data. One example, chain-of-table, is a method that integrates CoT prompting with table transformations. In a step-by-step process with an LLM and a set of predefined operations, it extracts and modifies tables. This approach is designed for handling complex tables, and it exploits step-by-step reasoning and step-by-step tabular operations to accomplish this. This approach is useful if we have complex SQL databases or large amounts of data frames as data sources. Then, there are more sophisticated alternatives that combine symbolic reasoning and textual reasoning. Mix self-consistency is a dedicated approach to tabular data understanding that uses textual and symbolic reasoning with self-consistency, thus creating multi-paths of reasoning and then aggregating with self-consistency. For semi-structured data such as PDFs and JHTML, there are dedicated packages that allow us to extract information from them or to parse data.

It is not only the type of data that impacts RAG performance but also the amount of data itself. As the volume of data increases, so does the difficulty in finding relevant information. Likewise, it is likely to increase the latency of the system.

Data storage is one of the focal points to be addressed before bringing the system into production. Distributed storage systems (an infrastructure that divides data into several physical servers or data centers) can be a solution for large volumes of data. This has the advantage of increasing system speed and reducing the risk of data loss, but risks increasing costs and management complexity. When you have different types of data, it can be advantageous to use a structure called a data lake. A **data lake** is a centralized repository that is designed for the storage and processing of structured, semi-structured, and unstructured data. The advantage of the data lake is that it is a scalable and flexible structure for ingesting, processing, and storing data of different types. The data lake is advantageous for RAG because it allows more data context to be maintained than other data structures. On the other hand, data lakes require more expertise to be functional. Alternatives may be partitioning data into smaller, more manageable partitions (based on geography, topic, time, and so on), which allows more efficient retrieval. In the case of numerous requests, frequently accessed data caching can be conducted to avoid repetition. These strategies can be used in the case of big data storage and access.

Another important aspect is building solid pipelines for **data preprocessing and cleaning**. In the development stage, it is common to work with well-polished datasets, but in production, this is not the case. Especially in big data, it is essential to make sure that there are no inconsistencies or that the system can handle missing or incomplete data. In a big data environment, data comes from many sources and not all of them are good quality. Therefore, imputation techniques (KNN or others) can be used to fill in missing data. Other additions that can improve the process are techniques to eliminate noisy or erroneous data, such as outlier detection algorithms, normalization techniques, and regular expression techniques to eliminate erroneous data points.

Data deduplication is another important aspect when working with LLMs. Duplicate data harms the training of LLMs and is also detrimental when found during the generation process (risking outputs that are inaccurate, biased, or of poor quality). As the volume of data increases, data duplication is a risk that increases linearly. There are techniques such as fuzzy matching and hash-based deduplication that can be used to eliminate duplicate elements. In general, a pipeline should be created to control the quality and governance of the data in the system (data quality monitoring). These pipelines should include rules and tracking systems to be able to identify problematic data and its origin. Although these pipelines are essential, pipelines that are too complex to maintain or slow down the system too much should be avoided.

Once we have decided on our data storage infrastructure, we need to make sure we have efficient **data indexing and retrieval**. There are indexing methods that are specialized for big data, such as Apache Lucene or Elasticsearch. Also, the most used data can be cached, or the retrieval process can be distributed to create a parallel infrastructure and reduce bottlenecks when there are multiple users. Given the complexity of some of these techniques, it is always best to test and conduct benchmarks before putting them into production.

Parallel processing

Especially for applications with a large number of users, **parallel processing** can significantly increase system scalability. This obviously requires a good cloud infrastructure with well-organized clusters. Applying parallel processing to RAG significantly decreases system latency even when there are large datasets. Apache Spark and Dask are among the most widely used solutions for implementing parallel computing with RAG. As we have seen, parallel computing can be implemented at various stages of the RAG pipeline: storage, retrieval, and generation. During storage, the various nodes can be used to implement the entire data preprocessing pipeline, that is, preprocessing, indexing, and chunking of part of the dataset (up to embedding). Although it seems less intuitive, during retrieval, the dataset can be divided among various nodes, with each node responsible for finding information from a particular dataset shard. In this way, we reduce the computational burden on each node and make the retrieval process parallel.

Similarly, generation can be made parallel. In fact, LLMs are computationally intensive but are transformer-based. The transformer was designed with both parallelization of training and inference in mind. There are techniques that allow parallelization in the case of long sequences or large batches of data. Later, more sophisticated techniques, such as tensor parallelism, model parallelism, and specialized frameworks, were developed. Paralleling the system, however, has inherent challenges and the risk of emerging errors. For these reasons, it is important to monitor the system during use and implement fault-tolerance mechanisms (such as checkpoints), advanced scheduling (such as dynamic task assignment), and other potential solutions.

RAG is a resource-intensive process (or at least some of the steps are), so it is good practice to implement techniques that dynamically allocate resources and monitor the workloads of the various processes. Also, it is recommended to use a modular approach that separates the various components, such as data ingestion, storage, retrieval, and generation. In any case, it is advisable to have a process that monitors not only performance in terms of accuracy but also memory usage, costs, network usage, and so on.

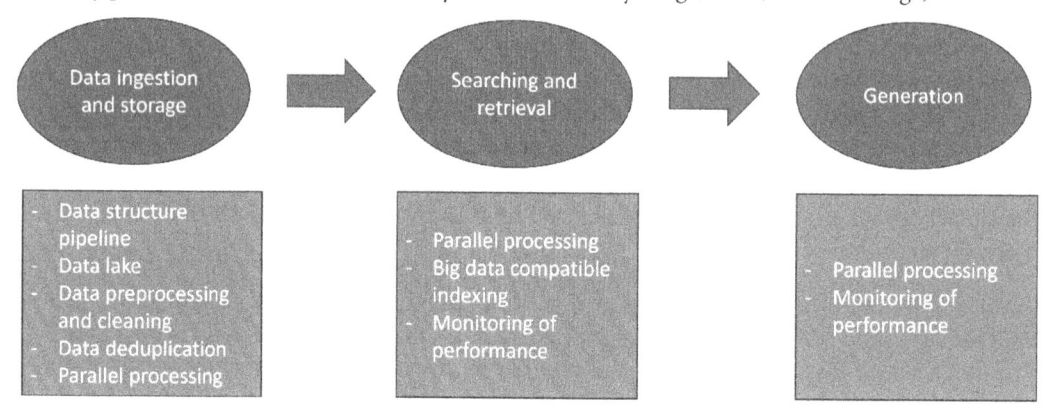

Figure 6.17 – Big data solutions for RAG scalability

We have talked generally about RAG. As we saw earlier, though, RAG today can be composed of several components. With advanced RAG and modular RAG, we saw how this system can be rapidly extended with additional components that impact both the accuracy of the system and its computational and latency costs. Thus, there are many alternatives for our system, and it is difficult to choose which components are most important. To date, there are a few benchmark studies that have conducted a rigorous analysis of both performance and computational costs. In a recent study (Wang, 2024), the authors analyzed the potential best components and gave guidance on which elements to use. In *Figure 6.18*, the components marked in blue are those, according to the authors of the study, that give the best performance, while those in bold are optional components.

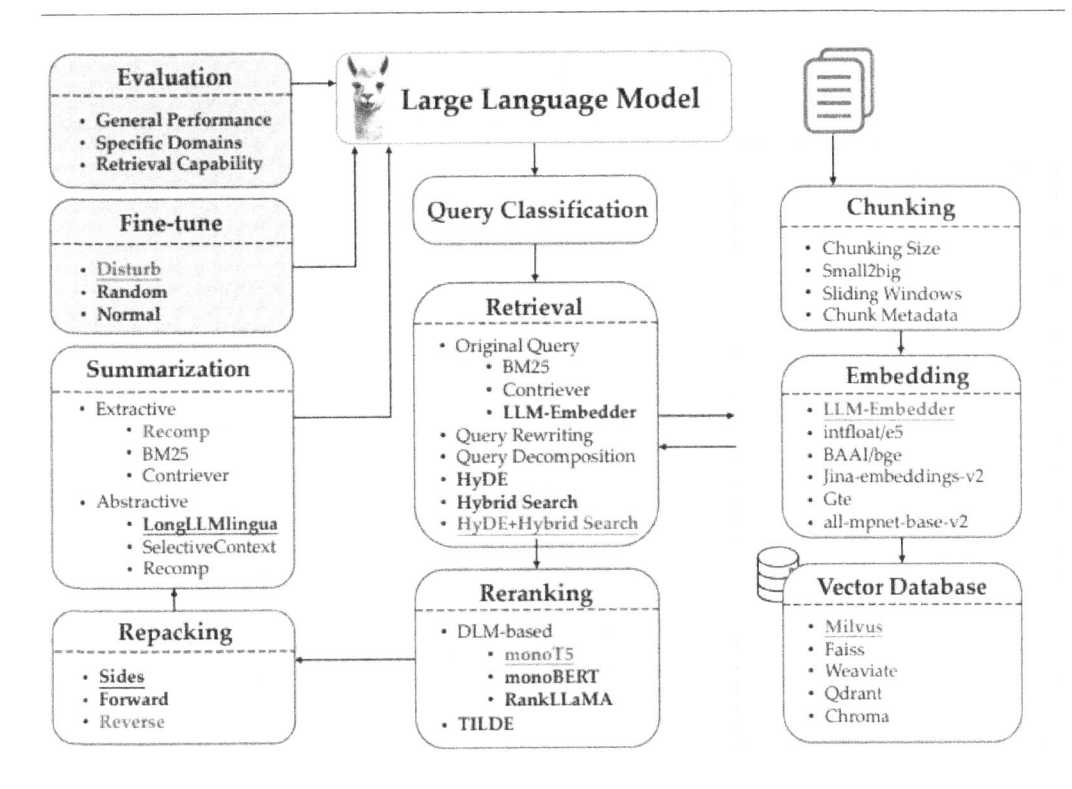

Figure 6.18 – Contribution of each component for an optimal RAG
(https://arxiv.org/pdf/2407.01219)

For example, the addition of some components improves system accuracy with a noticeable increase in latency. HyDE achieves the highest performance score but seems to have a significant computational cost. In this case, the performance improvement does not justify this increased latency. Other components increase the computational cost, but their absence results in an appreciable drop in performance (this is the case with reranking). Summarization modules help the model achieve optimal accuracy; their cost can be justified if latency is not problematic. Although it is virtually impossible to test all components in a systematic search, some guidelines can be provided. The best performance is achieved with the query classification module, HyDE, the reranking module, context repacking, and summarization. If this is too expensive computationally or in terms of latency, however, it is better to avoid techniques such as HyDE and stick to the other modules (perhaps choosing less expensive alternatives, for example, a reranker with fewer parameters). This is summarized in the following table comparing individual modules and techniques in terms of performance and computational efficiency:

Method	Commonsense Acc	Fact Check Acc	ODQA EM	F1	Multihop EM	F1	Medical Acc	RAG Score	Score	Avg. F1	Latency
	classification module, Hybrid with HyDE, monoT5, sides, Recomp										
w/o classification	0.719	0.505	0.391	**0.450**	**0.212**	0.255	**0.528**	0.540	0.465	**0.353**	16.58
+ classification	**0.727**	**0.595**	**0.393**	**0.450**	0.207	**0.257**	0.460	**0.580**	**0.478**	0.353	11.71
	with classification, *retrieval module*, monoT5, sides, Recomp										
+ HyDE	0.718	**0.595**	0.320	0.373	0.170	0.213	0.400	0.545	0.443	0.293	11.58
+ Original	0.721	0.585	0.300	0.350	0.153	0.197	0.390	0.486	0.428	0.273	**1.44**
+ Hybrid	0.718	**0.595**	0.347	0.397	0.190	0.240	**0.750**	0.498	0.477	0.318	1.45
+ Hybrid with HyDE	**0.727**	**0.595**	**0.393**	**0.450**	**0.207**	**0.257**	0.460	**0.580**	**0.478**	**0.353**	11.71
	with classification, Hybrid with HyDE, *reranking module*, sides, Recomp										
w/o reranking	0.720	0.591	0.365	0.429	0.211	**0.260**	0.512	0.530	0.470	0.334	**10.31**
+ monoT5	**0.727**	**0.595**	0.393	0.450	0.207	0.257	0.460	**0.580**	**0.478**	0.353	11.71
+ monoBERT	0.723	0.593	0.383	0.443	**0.217**	0.259	0.482	0.551	0.475	0.351	11.65
+ RankLLaMA	0.723	**0.597**	0.382	0.443	0.197	0.240	0.454	0.558	0.470	0.342	13.51
+ TILDEv2	0.725	0.588	**0.394**	**0.456**	0.209	0.255	0.486	0.536	0.476	**0.355**	11.26
	with classification, Hybrid with HyDE, monoT5, *repacking module*, Recomp										
+ sides	0.727	0.595	**0.393**	**0.450**	0.207	0.257	0.460	**0.580**	0.478	0.353	11.71
+ forward	0.722	**0.599**	0.379	0.437	0.215	0.260	0.472	0.542	0.474	0.349	**11.68**
+ reverse	**0.728**	0.592	0.387	0.445	**0.219**	**0.263**	**0.532**	0.560	**0.483**	**0.354**	11.70
	with classification, Hybrid with HyDE, monoT5, reverse, *summarization module*										
w/o summarization	**0.729**	0.591	**0.402**	**0.457**	0.205	0.252	0.528	0.533	0.480	**0.355**	**10.97**
+ Recomp	0.728	**0.592**	0.387	0.445	**0.219**	**0.263**	**0.532**	0.560	**0.483**	0.354	11.70
+ LongLLMLingua	0.713	0.581	0.362	0.423	0.199	0.245	0.530	0.539	0.466	0.334	16.17

Figure 6.19 – Impact of single modules and techniques on accuracy and latency (https://arxiv.org/pdf/2407.01219)

In addition, there are also parallelization strategies specifically designed for RAG. LlamaIndex offers a parallel pipeline for data ingestion and processing. In addition, to increase the robustness of the system, there are systems to prevent errors. For example, when using a model, you may encounter runtime errors (especially if you use external APIs such as OpenAI or Anthropic). In these cases, it pays to have fallback models. An **LLM router** is a system that allows you to route queries to different LLMs. Typically, there is a predictor model to intelligently decide which LLM is best suited for a given prompt (taking into account potential accuracy or factors such as cost). These routers can be used either as closed source models or to route queries to different external LLM APIs.

Security and privacy

An important aspect to consider when a system goes into production is the **security and privacy** of the system. RAG can handle an enormous amount of sensitive and confidential data; breaching the system can lead to devastating consequences for an organization (regulatory fines, lawsuits, reputational damages, and so on). One of the main solutions is data encryption. Some algorithms and protocols are widely used in the industry and can also be applied to RAG (e.g., AES-256 and TLS/SSL). Similarly, it is important to implement internal policies to safeguard keys and change them frequently. In addition, a system of credentials and privileges must be implemented to ensure controlled access by users. It is good practice today to use methods such as **multi-factor authentication** (**MFA**), strong password rules, and policies for access from multiple devices. Again, an important part of this is continuous monitoring of potential breakage, incident reporting, and policies if they occur. Before deployment, it is essential to conduct testing of the system and its robustness to identify potential vulnerabilities.

Privacy is a crucial and increasingly sensitive topic today. It is important that the system complies with key regulations such as the **General Data Protection Regulation** (**GDPR**) and the **California Consumer Privacy Act** (**CCPA**). Especially when handling large amounts of personal data, violations of these regulations expose an organization to hefty fines. To avoid penalties, it is a good idea to implement robust data governance, tracking practices, and data management. There are also techniques that can be used to improve system privacy, such as differential privacy and secure multi-party computation. In addition, incidents should be tracked and there should be policies for handling problems and resolving them.

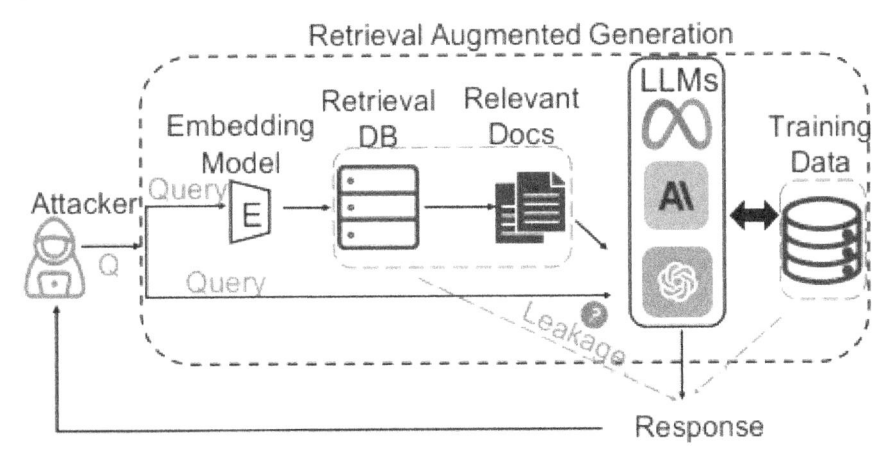

Figure 6.20 – The RAG system and potential risks (https://arxiv.org/pdf/2402.16893)

Then, there are several security problems today that are specific to RAG systems. For example, vectors might look like simple numbers but in fact can be converted back into text. The embedding process can be seen as lossy, but that doesn't mean it can't be decoded into the original text. In theory, embedding vectors should only maintain the semantic meaning of the original text, thus protecting sensitive data. In fact, in some studies, they have been able to recover more than 70% of the words in the original text. Moreover, extremely sophisticated techniques are not necessary. In what are called **embedding inversion attacks**, you acquire the vectors and then decode them into the original text. In other words, contrary to popular belief, you can reconstruct text from vectors, and so these vectors should be protected as well. In addition, any system that includes an LLM is susceptible to **prompt injection attacks**. This is a type of attack in what looks like a legitimate prompt where malicious instructions are added. This could be to prompt the model to leak information. Prompt injection is one of the greatest risks to models, and often, new methods are described in the literature, so all previous precautions quickly become obsolete. In addition, particular prompts can induce outputs that are not expected by RAG. Adversarial prefixes are prefixes added to what is a prompt for RAG and can induce the generation of hallucinations and factual incorrect outputs.

Another type of attack is **poisoning RAG**, in which an attempt is made to enter erroneous data that will then be used by the LLM to generate skewed outputs. For example, to generate misinformation, we can craft target text that when injected will cause the system to generate a desired output. In the example in the figure, we inject text to poison RAG to influence the answer to a question.

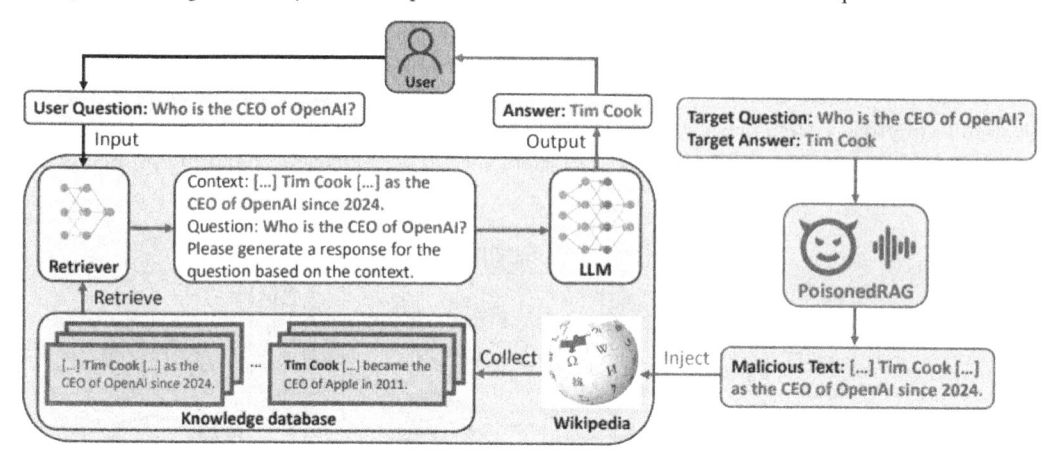

Figure 6.21 – Overview of poisoned RAG (https://arxiv.org/pdf/2402.07867)

Membership inference attacks (MIAs) are another type of attack in which an attempt is made to infer whether certain data is present within a dataset. If a sample resides in the RAG dataset, it will probably be found for a particular query and inserted into the context of an LLM. With an MIA, we can know if a piece of data is present in the system and then try to extract it with prompt injection (e.g., by making LLM output the retrieved context).

That is why there are specific solutions for the RAG (or for LLMs in general). One example is **NeMo Guardrails**, which is an open source toolkit developed by NVIDIA to add programmable rails to LLM-based applications. These rails provide a mechanism to control the LLM output of a model (so we act directly at the generation level). In this way, we can provide constraints (not engaging in harmful topics, following a path during dialog, not responding to certain requests, using a certain language, and so on). The advantage of this approach over other embedded techniques (such as model alignment at training) is that it happens at runtime and we do not have to conduct additional training for the model. This approach is also model agnostic and, generally, these rails are interpretable (during alignment, we should analyze the dataset used for training). NeMo Guardrails implements user-defined programmable rails via an interpretable language (called Colang) that allows us to define behavior rules for LLMs.

With this toolkit, we can use different types of guardrails: input rails (reject input, conduct further processing, or modify the input, to avoid leakage of sensitive information), output rails (refuse to produce outputs in case of problematic content), retrieval rails (reject chunks and thus do not put them in the context for LLM, or alter present chunks), or dialog rails (decide whether to perform an action, use the LLM for a next step, or use a default response).

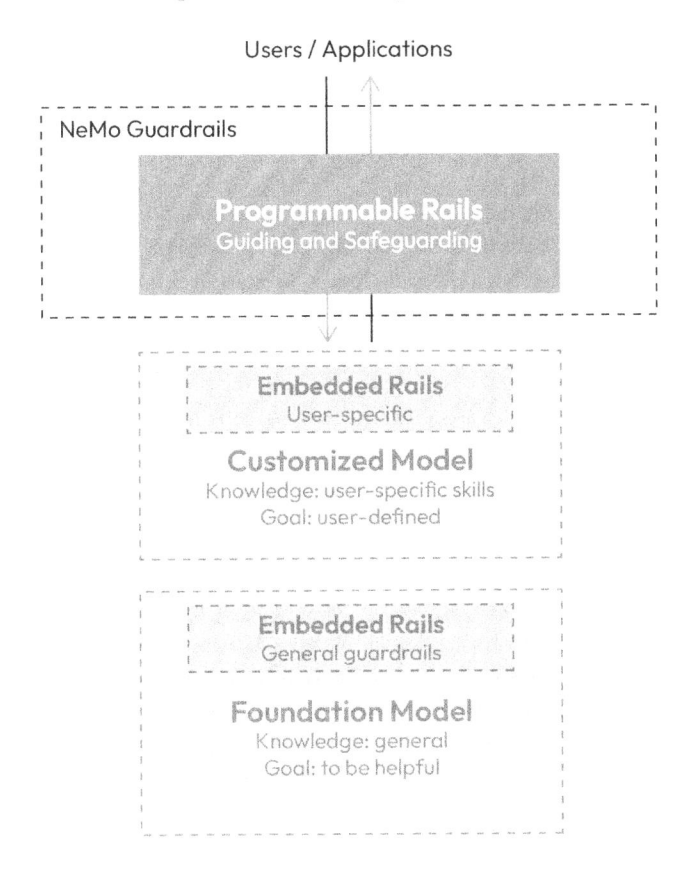

Figure 6.22 – Programmable versus embedded rails for LLMs
(https://arxiv.org/abs/2310.10501)

Llama Guard, on the other hand, is a system designed to examine input (via prompt classification) and output (via response classification) and judge whether the text is safe or unsafe. This approach then uses Llama 2 for classification and then uses a specifically adapted LLM as the judge.

Open questions and future perspectives

Although there have been significant advances in RAG technology, there are still challenges. In this section, we will discuss these challenges and prospects.

Recently, there has been wide interest and discussion about the expansion of the context length of LLMs. Today, most of the best-performing LLMs have a context length of more than 100K tokens (some up to over 1 million). This capability means that a model has the capacity for long document question-answering (in other words, the ability to insert long documents such as books within a single prompt). Many small user cases can be covered by a context length of 1 to 10 million tokens. The advantage of a **long-context LLM (LC-LLM)** is that it can then conduct interleaved retrieval and generation of the information in the prompt and conduct one-shot reasoning over the entire document. Especially for summarization tasks, the LC-LLM has a competitive advantage because it can conduct a scan of the whole document and relate information present at the top and bottom of the document. For some, LC-LLM means that the RAG is doomed to disappear.

In reality, the LC-LLM does not compete with RAG, and RAG is not doomed to disappear in the short term. The LC-LLM does not use the whole framework efficiently. In particular, the information in the middle of the context is attended much less efficiently. Similarly, reasoning is impacted by irrelevant information, and a long prompt inevitably provides an unnecessary amount of detail to answer a query. The LC-LLM hallucinates much more than RAG, and the latter allows for reference checking (which documents were used, thus making the retrieval and reasoning process observable and transparent). The LC-LLM also has difficulty with structured data (which is most data in many industries) and has a fairly considerable cost (latency increases significantly with a long prompt and also the cost per query). Finally, 1 million tokens are not a lot when considering the amount of data that even a small organization has (so retrieval is always necessary).

The LC-LLM opens up exciting possibilities for developers. First, it means that a precise chunking strategy will be necessary much less frequently. Chunks can be much larger (up to a document per chunk or at least a group of pages). This will mean less need to balance granularity and performance. Second, less prompt engineering will be needed. Especially for reasoning tasks, some questions can be answered with the information in one chunk, but others require deep analysis among several sections or multiple documents. Instead of a complex CoT, it is possible to answer these questions with a single prompt. Third, summarization is easier with the LC-LLM, so it can be conducted with a single retrieval. Finally, the LC-LLM allows for better customization and interaction with the user. In such a long prompt, it will be possible to upload the entire chat with the user. There are still some open challenges, though, especially in retrieving documents for the LC-LLM.

Similarly, there are no embedding models today that can handle similar context lengths (currently, the maximum context length of an embedder is 32K). Therefore, even with an LC-LLM, the chunks cannot be larger than 32K. The LC-LLM is still expensive in terms of performance and can seriously impact the scalability of the system. In any case, there are already potential RAG variations being studied that take the LC-LLM into account – for example, adapting small-to-big retrieval in which you find the necessary chunks and then send the entire document associated with the LC-LLM, or conduct routing of a query to pipeline whole-document retrieval (such as whole-document summarization tasks) or to find chunks (specific questions or multi-part questions that require chunks of different documents). Many companies work with KV caching, which is an approach in which you store the activations from the key and query from an attention layer (so you don't have to recompute the entire activations for a sequence during generation). So, it has been proposed that RAG could also be used to find the cache

We can see these possible evolutions visually in the following figure:

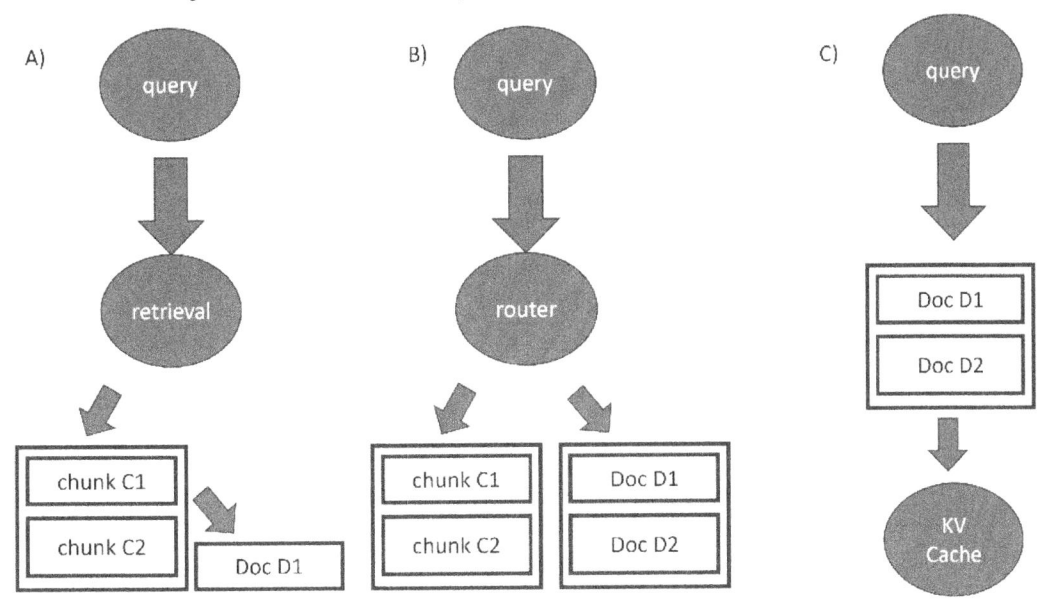

Figure 6.23 – Possible evolution of RAG with the LC-LLM

- A. Retrieving first the chunks and then the associated documents
- B. Router deciding whether it is necessary to retrieve small chunks or whole documents
- C. Retrieving the document and then KV caching them for the LC-LLM

Multimodal RAG is an exciting prospect and challenge that has been discussed. Most organizations have not only textual data but also extensive amounts of data in other modalities (images, audio, video, and so on). In addition, many files may contain more than one modality (for example, a book that contains not only text but also images). Searching for multimodal data can be of particular interest in different contexts and different applications. On the other hand, multimodal RAG is complicated by the fact that each modality has its own challenges. There are some alternatives to how we can achieve multimodal RAG. We will see three possible strategies:

- **Embed all modalities into the same vector space**: We previously saw the case of CLIP in *Chapter 3* (a model trained by contrastive learning to achieve unique embedding for images and text), which allowed us to search both images and text. We can use a model such as CLIP to conduct embedding of all modalities (in this case, images and text, but other cross-modal models exist). We can then find both images and text and use a multimodal model for generation (for example, we can use BLIP2 or BLIP3 as a vision language model). A multimodal model can conduct reasoning about both images and text. This approach has the advantage that we only need to change the embedding model to our system. In addition, a multimodal model can conduct reasoning by exploiting the information in both the image and the text. For example, if we have a PDF with tables, we can find the chunk of interest and the associated graphs. The model can use the information contained in both modalities to be able to answer the query more effectively. The disadvantage is that CLIP is an expensive model, and **multimodal LLMs (MMLLMs)** are more expensive than text-only LLMs. Also, we need to be sure that our embedding model is capable of capturing all the nuances of images and text.

- **Single-grounded modality**: Another option is to transform all modes into the primary mode (which can be different depending on the focus of the application). For example, we extract text from the PDF and create text descriptions for each of the images along with metadata (for audio, we can use a transcript). In some variants, we keep the images in storage. During retrieval, we find the text again (so we use a classic embedding model and a database that contains only vectors obtained from text). We can then use an LLM or MMLLM (if we want to add the images obtained by retrieving metadata or description) during the generation phase. Again, the main advantage is that we do not have to train any new type of model, but it can be expensive as an approach, and we lose some nuances from the image.

- **Separate retrieval for each modality**: In this case, each modality is embedded separately. For example, if we have three modalities, we will have three separate models (audio-text-aligned model, image-text-aligned model, and text embedder) and three separate databases (audio, images, and text). When the query arrives, we encode for each mode (so audio, images, and text). So, in this case, we have done three retrievals and may have found different elements, so it pays to have a rerank step (to efficiently combine the results). Obviously, we need a dedicated multimodal rerank that can allow us to retrieve the most relevant chunks. It simplifies the organization because we have dedicated models for each mode (a model that works well for all modes is difficult to obtain) but it increases the complexity of the system. Similarly, while a classical reranker has to reorder n chunks, a multimodal reranker has the complexity of reordering $m \times n$ chunks (where m is the number of modes).

Finally, once the multimodal chunks have been obtained, there may be alternatives; for example, we can use an MMLM to generate a response, and then this response needs to be integrated into the context for a final LLM. As we saw earlier, our RAG pipeline can be more sophisticated than naïve RAG. We can then combine all the elements we saw earlier into a single system.

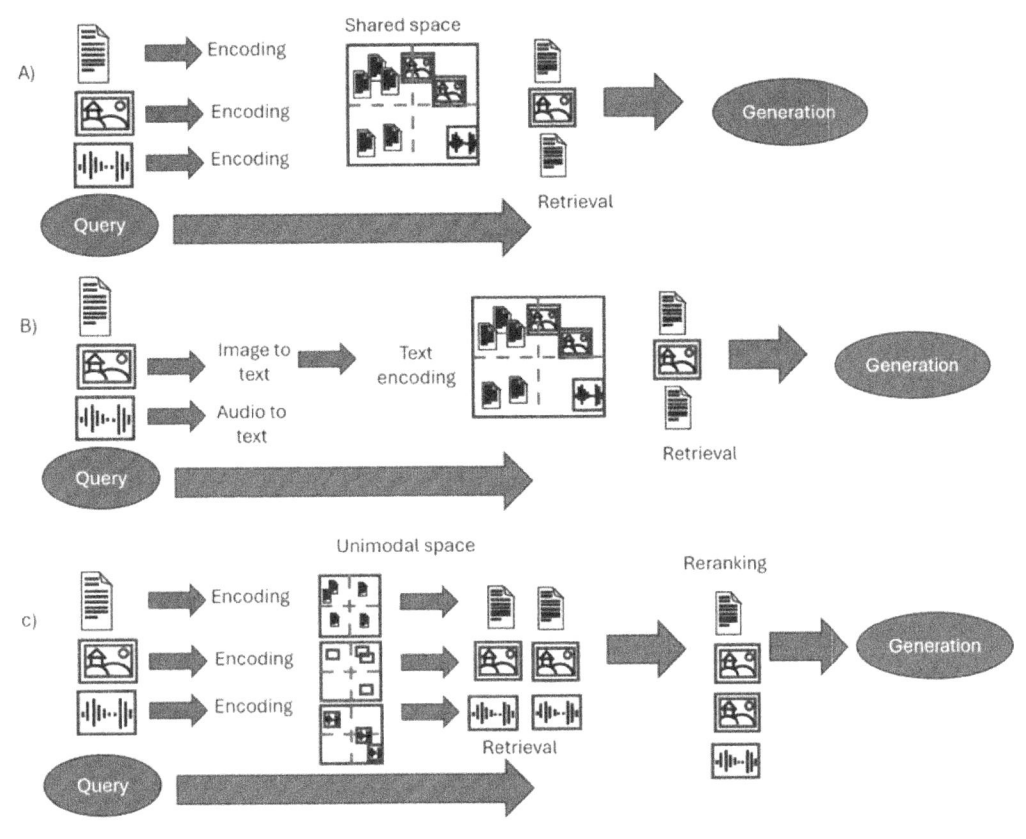

Figure 6.24 – Three potential approaches to multimodal RAG

Although RAG efficiently mitigates hallucinations, they can happen. We have previously discussed hallucinations as a plague of LLMs. In this section, we will mainly discuss hallucinations in RAG. One of the most peculiar cases is **contextual hallucinations**, in which the correct facts are provided in the context, but the LLM still generates the wrong output. Although the model provides the correct information, it produces a wrong answer (this often occurs in tasks such as summarization or document-based questions). This occurs because the LLM has its own prior knowledge, and it is wrong to assume that the model does not use this internal knowledge. Furthermore, the model is instruction-tuned or otherwise aligned, so it implicitly makes a decision on whether to use the context or ignore it and use its knowledge to answer the user's question. In some cases, this might even be useful, since it could happen that we have found the wrong or misleading context. In general, for many closed source models, we do not know what they were trained on, though we can monitor their confidence in an answer. Given a question x, the model will respond with an answer x. Depending on its knowledge, this will have a confidence c (which is based on the probability associated with the tokens generated by the model). Basically, the more confident a model is in its answer, the less prone it will be to changing its answer if the context suggests differently. An interesting finding is that if the correct answer is slightly different from the LLM's knowledge, the LLM is likely to change its answer. In case of a large divergence, the LLM will choose its own answer. For example, to the question, "What is the maximum dosage of drug x?" the model may have seen 20 µg in its training. If the context suggests 30, the LLM will provide 30 as the output; if the context suggests 100, the LLM will state 20. Larger LLMs are generally more confident and prefer their answer, while smaller models are more willing to use context. Finally, this behavior can be altered with prompt engineering. Stricter prompts will force the model to use context, while weaker prompts will push the model to use its prior knowledge.

> **Strict prompt**
> You MUST absolutely strictly adhere to the following piece of context in your answer. Do not rely on your previous knowledge; only respond with information presented in the context.

> **Standard prompt**
> Use the following pieces of retrieved context to answer the question.

> **Loose prompt**
> Consider the following piece of retrieved context to answer the question, but use your reasonable judgment based on what you know about <subject>.

Figure 6.25 – Example of a standard prompt in comparison with a loose or strict prompt (https://arxiv.org/pdf/2404.10198)

Other factors also help reduce hallucinations in RAG:

- **Data quality**: Data quality has a big impact on system quality in general.

- **Contextual awareness**: The LLM may not best understand the user's intent, or the found context may not be the right one. Query rewriting and other components of advanced RAG might be the solution.

- **Negative rejection**: When retrieval fails to find the appropriate context for the query, the model attempts to respond anyway, thereby generating hallucinations or incorrect answers. This is often the fault of a poorly written query, so it can be improved with components that modify the query (such as HyDE). Alternatively, stricter prompts force the LLM to respond only if there is context.

- **Reasoning abilities**: Some queries may require reasoning or are too complex. The reasoning limit of the system depends on the LLM; RAG is for finding the context to answer the query.

- **Domain mismatch**: A generalist model will have difficulty with domains that are too technical. Fine-tuning the embedder and LLM can be a solution.

- **Objective mismatch**: The goals of the embedder and LLM are not aligned, so today there are systems that try to optimize end-to-end retrieval and generation. This can be a solution for complex queries or specialized domains.

There are other exciting perspectives. For example, there is some work on using reinforcement learning to improve the ability of RAG to respond to complex queries. Other research deals with integrating graph research; we will discuss this in more detail in the next chapter. In addition, we have assumed so far that the database is static, but in the age of the internet, there is a discussion on how to integrate the internet into RAG (e.g., conducting a hybrid search in an organization's protected data and also finding context through an internet search). This opens up exciting but complex questions, such as whether or not to conduct database updates, how to filter out irrelevant search engine results, and security issues. In addition, there are more and more specialized applications of RAG, where the authors focus on creating systems optimized for their field of application (e.g., RAG for math, medicine, biology, and so on). All this shows active research into RAG and interest in its application.

Summary

In this chapter, we initially discussed what the problems of naïve RAG are. This allowed us to see a number of add-ons that can be used to solve the sore points of naïve RAG. Using these add-ons is the basis of what is now called the advanced RAG paradigm. Over time, the community then moved toward a more flexible and modular structure that is now called modular RAG.

We then saw how to scale this structure in the presence of big data. Like any LLM-based application, there are computational and cost challenges when you have to take the system from a development environment to a production environment. In addition, both LLMs and RAGs can have security and privacy risks. These are important points, especially when these products are open to the public. Today, there is an increasing focus on compliance and more and more regulations are being considered.

Finally, we saw that some issues remain open, such as the relationship with long-context LLMs or the multimodal extension of these models. In addition, there is a delicate balance between retrieval and generation, and we explored potential solutions in case of problems. Recently, there has been active research into integration with KGs. GraphRAG is often discussed today; in the next chapter, we will discuss what a KG is and the relationship between graphs and RAG.

Further reading

- LlamaIndex, *Node Postprocessor Modules*: https://docs.llamaindex.ai/en/stable/module_guides/querying/node_postprocessors/node_postprocessors/

- Nelson, *Lost in the Middle: How Language Models Use Long Contexts*, 2023: https://arxiv.org/abs/2307.03172

- Jerry Liu, *Unifying LLM-powered QA Techniques with Routing Abstractions*, 2023: https://betterprogramming.pub/unifying-llm-powered-qa-techniques-with-routing-abstractions-438e2499a0d0

- Chevalier, *Adapting Language Models to Compress Contexts*, 2023: https://arxiv.org/abs/2305.14788

- Li, *Unlocking Context Constraints of LLMs: Enhancing Context Efficiency of LLMs with Self-Information-Based Content Filtering*, 2023: https://arxiv.org/abs/2304.12102

- Izacard, *Distilling Knowledge from Reader to Retriever for Question Answering*, 2020: https://arxiv.org/abs/2012.04584

- Wang, *Searching for Best Practices in Retrieval-Augmented Generation*, 2024: https://arxiv.org/pdf/2407.01219

- Li, *Retrieval Augmented Generation or Long-Context LLMs? A Comprehensive Study and Hybrid Approach*, 2024: https://www.arxiv.org/abs/2407.16833

- Raieli, *RAG is Dead, Long Live RAG*, 2024: https://levelup.gitconnected.com/rag-is-dead-long-live-rag-c607e1799199

- Raieli, *War and Peace: A Conflictual Love Between the LLM and RAG*, 2024: https://ai.plainenglish.io/war-and-peace-a-conflictual-love-between-the-llm-and-rag-78428a5776fb

- jinaai/jina-colbert-v2: https://huggingface.co/jinaai/jina-colbert-v2

- mix_self_consistency: https://github.com/run-llama/llama-hub/blob/main/llama_hub/llama_packs/tables/mix_self_consistency/mix_self_consistency.ipynb

- Zeng, *The Good and The Bad: Exploring Privacy Issues in Retrieval-Augmented Generation (RAG)*, 2024: https://arxiv.org/abs/2402.16893

- Xue, *BadRAG: Identifying Vulnerabilities in Retrieval Augmented Generation of Large Language Models*, 2024: https://arxiv.org/abs/2406.00083

- Chen, *Controlling Risk of Retrieval-augmented Generation: A Counterfactual Prompting Framework*, 2024: https://arxiv.org/abs/2409.16146

- Zhang, *HijackRAG: Hijacking Attacks against Retrieval-Augmented Large Language Models*, 2024: https://arxiv.org/abs/2410.22832

- Xian, *On the Vulnerability of Applying Retrieval-Augmented Generation within Knowledge-Intensive Application Domains*, 2024: https://arxiv.org/abs/2409.17275v1

7
Creating and Connecting a Knowledge Graph to an AI Agent

In the previous two chapters, we discussed the RAG framework in detail. We started with naïve RAG and then saw how we could add different components, replace others, or modify the entire pipeline for our needs. The whole system is extremely flexible, but some concepts remain the same. First, we start with a corpus (or multiple corpora of texts) and conduct embedding of these texts to obtain a database of vectors. Once the user query arrives, we conduct a similarity search on this database of vectors. Regardless of the scope or type of texts, our pipeline is based on the concept of vectorizing these texts in some way and then providing the information contained in the discovered texts to the LLM.

Texts are often full of redundant information, and in the previous chapter, we saw that LLMs are sensitive to the amount of noise in the input. Most people have seen the benefit of creating schematic notes or mind maps. These schematics are concise because of the principle that underlining everything in a book is like underlining nothing. The principle of these diagrams is to extract the key information to remember that will enable us to answer questions in the future. Schematics should present the fundamental information and the relationships that connect them. These schemas can be represented as a graph and, more precisely, as a knowledge graph. The advantage of these graphs is that they are compact, represent knowledge as entities and relationships, and we can conduct analyses and use graph search algorithms on them. Over the years, these **knowledge graphs** (**KGs**) have been built by major companies or institutions and are now available for use. Many of these KGs have been used for information extraction, where information is extracted with a series of queries to answer questions. This extracted information is a series of entities and relationships, rich in knowledge but less understandable to us humans. The natural step is to use this information for the context of an LLM and then generate a natural language response. This paradigm is called **GraphRAG,** and we will discuss it in detail in this chapter.

In any case, nothing prohibits us from using an LLM for all the steps in KG. In fact, LLMs have a number of innate capabilities that make them useful even for tasks for which they are not trained. This is precisely why we will see that we can use LLMs to extract relationships and entities and build our KGs. LLMs, though, also possess reasoning capabilities, and in this chapter, we will discuss how we can use these models to reason both about the information contained in graphs and about the structure of the graphs themselves. Finally, we will discuss what perspectives and questions remain open, and the advantages and disadvantages of the proposed approaches.

In this chapter, we'll be covering the following topics:

- Introduction to knowledge graphs
- Creating a knowledge graph with your LLM
- Retrieving information with a knowledge graph and an LLM
- Understanding graph reasoning
- Ongoing challenges in knowledge graphs and GraphRAG

Technical requirements

Most of this code can be run on a CPU, but it is preferable to be run on a GPU. The code is written in PyTorch and uses standard libraries for the most part (PyTorch, Hugging Face Transformers, LangChain, ChromaDB, `sentence-transformer`, `faiss-cpu`, and so on).

In this chapter, we also use Neo4j as the database for the graph. Although we will do all operations with Python, Neo4j must be installed and you must be registered to use it. The code can be found on GitHub: `https://github.com/PacktPublishing/Modern-AI-Agents/tree/main/chr7`.

Introduction to knowledge graphs

Knowledge representation is one of the open problems of AI and has very ancient roots (Leibniz believed that the whole knowledge could be represented and used to conduct calculations). The interest in knowledge representation is based on the fact that it represents the first step in conducting computer reasoning. Once this knowledge is organized in an orderly manner, it can be used to design inference algorithms and solve reasoning problems. Early studies focused on using deduction to solve problems about organized entities (e.g., through the use of ontologies). This has worked well for many toy problems, but it is laborious, often requires a whole set of hardcoded rules, and risks succumbing to combinatorial explosion. Because search in these spaces could be extremely computationally expensive, an attempt was made to define two concepts:

- **Limited rationality**: Finding a solution but also considering the cost of it
- **Heuristic search**: Limiting the search in space, thus finding a semi-optimal solution (a local but not global optima)

These principles have inspired a whole series of algorithms that have since allowed information searches to be conducted more efficiently and tractably. Interest in these algorithms grew strongly in the late 1990s with the advent of the World Wide Web and the need to conduct internet searches quickly and accurately. Regarding data, the World Wide Web is also based on three technological principles:

- **Distributed data**: Data is distributed across the world and accessible from all parts of the world
- **Connected data**: Data is interconnected and not isolated; the data's meaning is a function of its connection with other data
- **Semantic metadata**: In addition to the data itself, we have information about its relationships, and this metadata allows us to search efficiently

For this reason, we began to search for a technology that could respect the nature of this new data. It came naturally to turn to representations of a graphical nature. In fact, by definition, graphs model relationships between different entities. This approach began to be used in web searches in 2012 when Google began adding knowledge cards for each concept searched. These knowledge cards can be seen as graphs of name entities in which the connections are the graph links. These cards then allow for more relevant search and user facilitation. Subsequently, the term *knowledge graph* came to mean any graph that connects entities through a series of meaningful relationships. These relationships generally represent semantic relationships between entities.

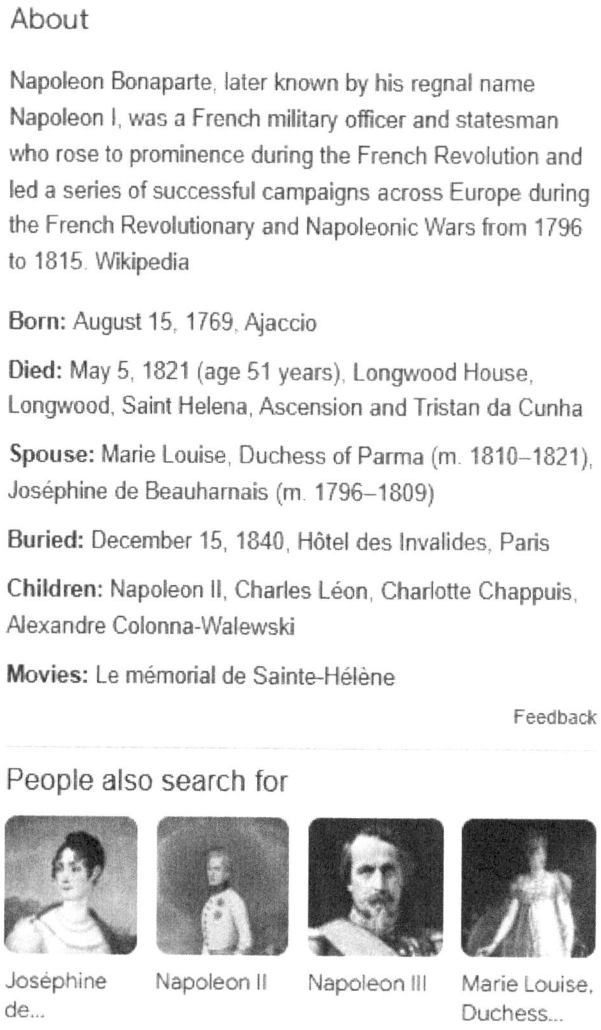

About

Napoleon Bonaparte, later known by his regnal name Napoleon I, was a French military officer and statesman who rose to prominence during the French Revolution and led a series of successful campaigns across Europe during the French Revolutionary and Napoleonic Wars from 1796 to 1815. Wikipedia

Born: August 15, 1769, Ajaccio

Died: May 5, 1821 (age 51 years), Longwood House, Longwood, Saint Helena, Ascension and Tristan da Cunha

Spouse: Marie Louise, Duchess of Parma (m. 1810–1821), Joséphine de Beauharnais (m. 1796–1809)

Buried: December 15, 1840, Hôtel des Invalides, Paris

Children: Napoleon II, Charles Léon, Charlotte Chappuis, Alexandre Colonna-Walewski

Movies: Le mémorial de Sainte-Hélène

Feedback

People also search for

Joséphine de… | Napoleon II | Napoleon III | Marie Louise, Duchess…

Figure 7.1 – Knowledge card in Google

A formal definition of graphs and knowledge graphs

Since KGs are a subtype of graphs, we will start with a brief introduction of graphs. Graphs are data structures composed of nodes (or vertices) that are connected by relationships (or edges) to represent a model of a domain. A graph can then represent knowledge in a compact manner while trying to reduce noise. There are different types of graphs:

- **Undirected**: Edges have no direction
- **Directed**: Edges have a defined direction (there is a defined beginning and end)

- **Weighted**: Edges carry weights, representing the strength or cost of the relationship
- **Labeled**: Nodes are associated with features and labels
- **Multigraph**: Multiple edges (relationships) exist between the same pair of nodes

The following figure shows a visual representation of these graphs:

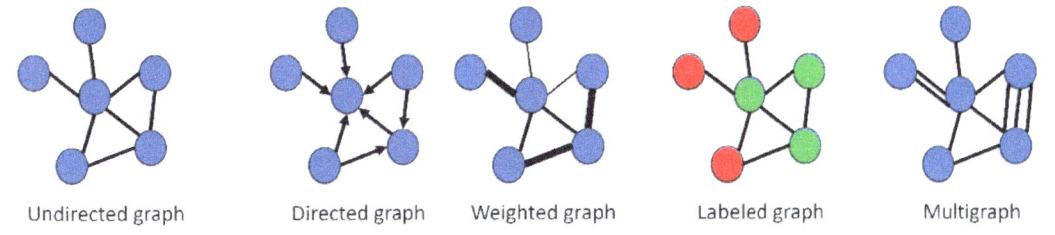

Figure 7.2 – Different types of graph architecture

A KG is thus a subgraph with three main properties:

- **Nodes represent real-world entities**: These entities can represent people, places, or domain-specific entities (genes, proteins, diseases, financial products, and so on)
- **Relationships define semantic connections between nodes**: For example, two people may be linked by a relationship that represents friendship, or a specific gene is associated with a particular disease
- **Nodes and edges may have associated properties**: For example, all people will have as a property that they are human beings (a label) but they can also have quantitative properties (date of birth, a specific identifier, and so on)

So, a little more formally, we can say that we have a knowledge base (a database of facts) represented in the form of factual triplets. A factual triples has the form of `(head, relation, tail)` or `(subject, predicate, object)`, or more succinctly, `(e1,r1,e2)`, such as `(Napoleon, BornIn, Ajaccio)`. The KG is a representation of this knowledge base that allows us to conduct interpretation. Given the structure of these triplets, a KG is a directed graph where the nodes are these entities and the edges are factual relationships.

(Albert Einstein, **BornIn**, German Empire)
(Albert Einstein, **SonOf**, Hermann Einstein)
(Albert Einstein, **GraduateFrom**, University of Zurich)
(Albert Einstein, **WinnerOf**, Nobel Prize in Physics)
(Albert Einstein, **ExpertIn**, Physics)
(Nobel Prize in Physics, **AwardIn**, Physics)
(The theory of relativity, **TheoryOf**, Physics)
(Albert Einstein, **SupervisedBy**, Alfred Kleiner)
(Albert Einstein, **ProfessorOf**, University of Zurich)
(The theory of relavity, **ProposedBy**, Albert Einstein)
(Hans Albert Einstein, **SonOf**, Albert Einstein)

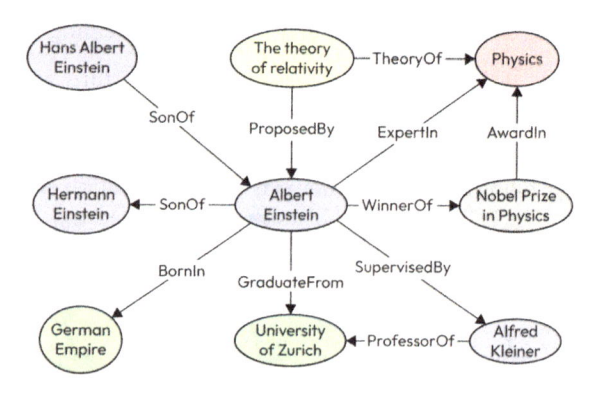

(a) Factual triples in knowledge base. (b) Entities and relations in knowledge graph.

Figure 7.3 – Example of a knowledge base and knowledge graph
(https://arxiv.org/pdf/2002.00388)

A KG is defined as a graph consisting of a set of entities, E, relations, R, and facts, F, where each fact f is a triplet:

$$\mathcal{G} = \{\mathcal{E}, \mathcal{R}, \mathcal{F}\} \ ; \ f = (h, r, t)$$

As you can see, a KG is an alternative representation of knowledge. The same kind of data can be represented in either a table or a graph. We can directly create triplets from a table and then directly represent them in a KG. We do not need table headers, and it is easier to conduct the update of such a structure. Graphs are considered universal data representations because they can be applied to any type of data. In fact, not only can we map tabular data to a KG, but we can also get data from other formats (JSON, XML, CSV, and so on). Graphs also allow us to nimbly represent recursive structures (such as trees and documents) or cyclical structures (such as social networks). Also, if we do not have the information for all properties, the table representation will be full of missing values; in a KG, we do not have this problem.

Graphs *per se* represent network structures. This is very useful for many business cases (e.g., in finance and medicine) where a lot of data is already structured as networks. Another advantage is that it is much easier to conduct a merge of graphs than of tables. Merging tables is usually a complicated task (where you have to choose which columns to merge, avoid creating duplicates, and other potential problems). If the data is in triplets, it is extremely easy to merge two KG databases. For example, look how simple it is to transform this table into a graph; they are equivalent:

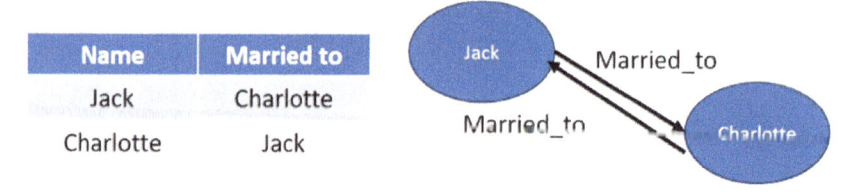

Figure 7.4 – Table and graph are equivalent

A KG should not be seen as a static entity. In fact, knowledge evolves; this causes new entities or relationships to be added. One of the most widely used tasks in **knowledge graph reasoning** (**KGR**) is to predict new relationships. For example, if A is the husband of B and father of C, this implies that B is the mother of C, which could be derived with logical ruling: *(A, husband of, B) ^ (A, father of C) -> (B, mother of, C)*. In this pre-existing datum, we have inferred a missing relationship.

Another very important task is how to conduct the update of a KG once we have obtained new triplets (this may require complex preprocessing). This is very important because once we have integrated some new knowledge, we can conduct further analysis and further reasoning. Also, being a graph, we can use graph analysis algorithms (such as centrality measures, connectivity, clustering, and so on) for our business cases. Leveraging these algorithms makes it much easier to conduct searches or complex queries in a KG than in relational databases.

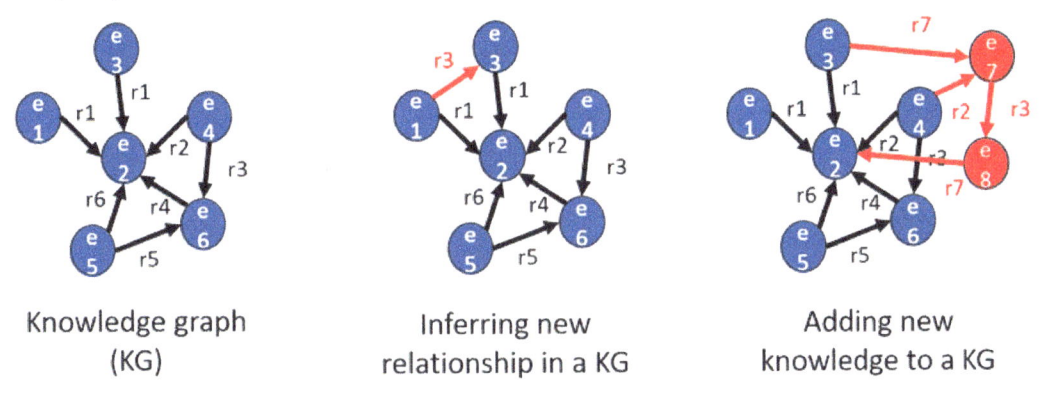

Figure 7.5 – A KG is a dynamic entity

In addition, KGs are much more flexible and adaptable than people think. KGs can be adapted for different tasks. For example, there are extensions of KGs such as **hierarchical KGs** where we have multiple levels. In hierarchical KGs, entities from one level can be connected to the next level (this, for example, is very useful when we have ontologies). Entities can also be **multimodal**, so a node can represent an image to which other entities (textual or other images, or other types of modalities) are connected. Another type of KG is a **temporal KG**, in which we incorporate a temporal dimension. This type of KG can be very useful for predictive analysis. We can see these KGs in the following figure:

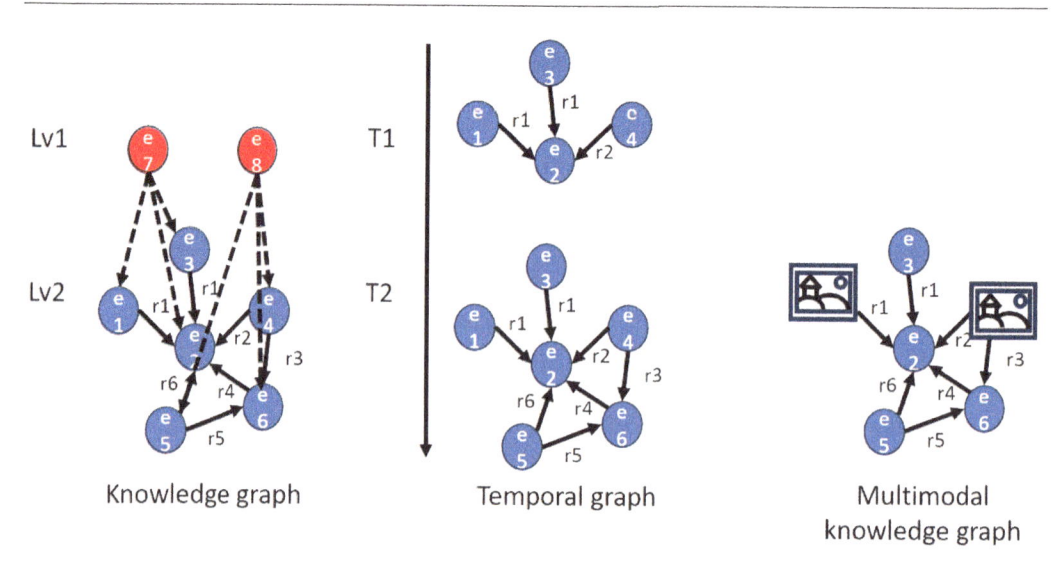

Figure 7.6 – Different types of knowledge graphs

Taxonomies and ontologies

The main difference between a graph and a KG is that the former is a given structure representing relationships between entities, while the latter makes semantic relationships explicit by allowing reasoning and inference to humans and machines. So, the advantage of a KG is that we can use algorithms for both graphs and specific reasoning algorithms (we will see later, in the *Understanding graph reasoning* section, some approaches in detail). These capabilities are enhanced by incorporating metadata. Indeed, we can construct **KG taxonomies**, which can be seen as hierarchical structures of similar semantic meaning (usually tree-like, for example, dog and cat entities might be grouped under mammals). In addition, multiple taxonomies can be integrated if necessary (thus having multiple trees to allow for more refined searching). These taxonomies help in searching or when we need to filter and work with very large KGs. **KG ontologies** are similar to taxonomies and may have a similar hierarchical structure, but they are a more flexible and expressive structure. In fact, an ontology is used to define the relationships, properties, and classification of a group of entities. It also allows rules to be defined about how these entities may interact (union, complement, cardinality, and transitive or intransitive properties of relationships). Ontologies also enable a shared vocabulary, thus allowing information to be integrated consistently. Ontologies can thus allow conducting reasoning and solving more complex problems. For example, we can add properties and then use these properties to solve a problem (Bob owns a car that has a maximum_speed property of 100 km, so Bob will not be able to get there in less than an hour because his job has a distance_from_home property of 120 km). Rules allow us to be able to improve search and solve tasks that were too complex before (for example, we can assign different properties to relations: if `married_to` is transitive, we can automatically infer information about a person without the relation being specified). Thanks to ontologies, we can conduct certain types of reasoning effectively and quickly, such as deductive reasoning, class inference, transitive reasoning, and so on.

Ontologies are generally grouped into two groups:

- **Domain-independent ontologies**: Ontologies that provide fundamental concepts that are not tied to a particular domain. They provide a high-level view that helps with data integration, especially when there are several domains. Commonly, these are a small number, they represent the first level, and they are the first ones built.

- **Domain ontologies**: These are focused on a domain and are used to provide the fundamental terminology. They are most useful for specialized domains such as medicine and finance. They are usually found at levels below the domain-independent one and are a subclass of it.

In this section, we have seen how KGs are flexible systems that can store data and be able to easily find knowledge. This flexibility makes them powerful tools for subsequent analysis, but at the same time, does not make them easy to build. In the next section, we will see how we can build a KG from a collection of texts.

Creating a knowledge graph with your LLM

The construction of a KG is generally a multistep process consisting of the following:

1. **Knowledge creation**: The first step, in which we define the purpose of this KG, is to gather the sources from which to extract knowledge. In this step, we have to decide how we build our KG but also where we maintain it. Once built, the KG has to be stored, and we have to have an efficient structure to query it.
2. **Knowledge assessment**: In this step, we assess the quality of the KG obtained.
3. **Knowledge cleaning**: There are several steps and procedures to make sure there are no errors and then correct them. This step can be conducted at the same time as knowledge assessment, and some pipelines conduct them together.
4. **Knowledge enrichment**: This involves a series of steps to identify whether there are gaps in knowledge. We can also integrate additional sources (extract information from other datasets, integrate databases, or merge multiple KGs).
5. **Knowledge deployment**: In this final step, the KG is deployed either as a standalone application (e.g., as a graph database) or used within another application.

We can see the process in the following figure:

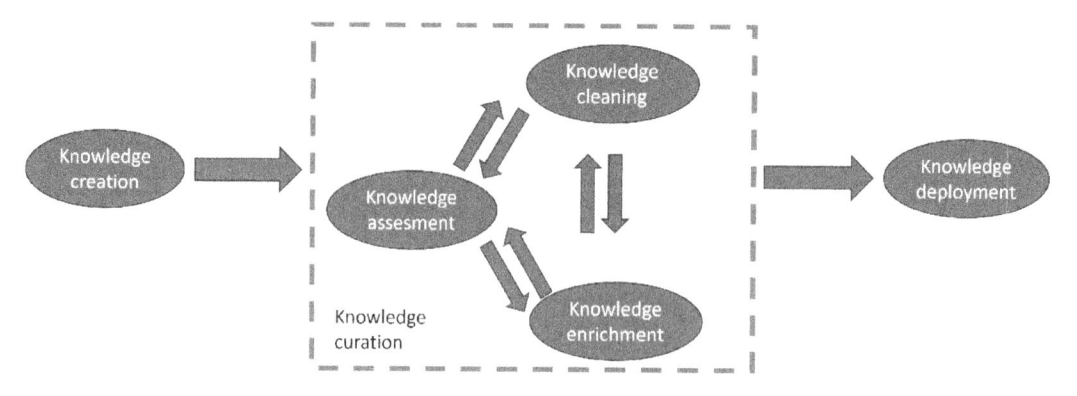

Figure 7.7 – KG construction pipeline

Knowledge creation

In general, when building a KG from scratch, the definition of ontologies is the first step. There are several guides on how to build them (both libraries and tools to visualize them). Efforts are made to build ontologies that are clear, verifiable, and reusable. Defining ontologies should be done with a purpose in mind, discussing what the purpose of a KG is with various stakeholders, and then defining ontologies accordingly. The most relevant ones should be chosen (the first level of the KG), following which the hierarchy and properties should be defined. There are two approaches: top-down (define core ontologies first and then more specialized ones) or bottom-up (define specialized ontologies and then group them into superclasses). Especially for specialized domains, we could start from ontologies that have already been built (there are several defined for finance, medicine, and academic research) and this ensures better interoperability.

The next step is to extract knowledge from our sources. In this step, we have to extract triplets (or a set of facts) from a text corpus or another source (a database, or structured and unstructured data). Two tasks can be defined:

- **Named entity recognition** (**NER**): NER is the task of extracting entities from text and classifying them

- **Relation extraction** (**RE**): RE is the task of identifying connections between various entities in a context

NER is one of the most common tasks in **natural language processing** (**NLP**) and is used not only for KG creation but also as a key step when we want to move from unstructured text to structured data. It generally requires a pipeline consisting of several steps (text preprocessing, entity identification and classification, contextual analysis, and data post-processing). During NER, we try to identify entities by first conducting a preprocessing step to avoid errors in the pipeline (e.g., proper tokenization). Once entities are identified, they are usually classified (e.g., by adding a label such as people, organizations, or places). In addition, surrounding text is attempted to be used to disambiguate them (e.g., trying to recognize whether *Apple* in the text represents the fruit or the company). A preprocessing step is then conducted to resolve ambiguities or merge multi-token entities.

t_1	t2	t3	t4	t5	t6	t7
Barack	Obama	Was	Born	in	Honolulu	.

Named Entity Recognition

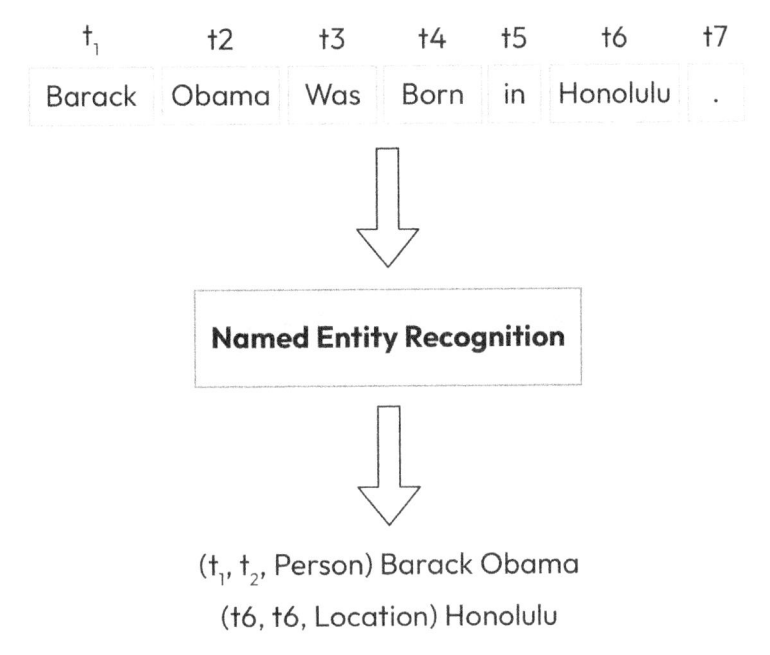

(t_1, t_2, Person) Barack Obama

(t6, t6, Location) Honolulu

Figure 7.8 – Example of NER (https://arxiv.org/pdf/2401.10825)

RE is the task in which we understand the relationships between the various extracted entities. More formally, we use a model to identify and categorize the connections between entities in a text (e.g., in the sentence *Bob works at Apple*, we extract the relationship *works at*). It can be considered a separate task or, in some cases, conducted together with NER (e.g., with a single model). Also, RE is a key step for KG creation and, at the same time, useful for several other NLP tasks (such as question answering, information retrieval, and so on).

There are several methods to be able to conduct NER and RE. The earliest and most laborious methods were knowledge-based or rule-based. For example, one of the simplest approaches to identifying company names in financial documents was to use indicators such as capital letters (identify `Mr.` and `Ms.` elements to extract people, and so on). Rule-based worked very well for standardized documents (such as clinical notes or official documents) but demonstrated little scalability. These methods require establishing laborious upstream rules and specific knowledge, risking missing many entities in different datasets.

Statistical methods based on the hidden Markov model, conditional random fields, or maximum entropy (methods that rely on predicting the entity based on likelihood learned from training data) have allowed for greater scalability. These methods, though, require large, quality datasets that have defined labels. Other supervised learning algorithms have been used to predict entities and then extract them. These algorithms have worked well with high computational costs and especially the need for labels. Obtaining labels is expensive and these datasets quickly become outdated (new companies, new products, and so on are created).

Recently, given the advances in unsupervised learning (models such as the transformer), it has been decided to use LLMs also for NER and RE and for constructing KGs (in some studies, these are called **LLM-augmented KGs**). The ability to process large corpora of text, the knowledge acquired during pre-training, and their versatility make LLMs useful for the construction of KGs (and other related tasks that we will see later).

Due to their ability to leverage contextual information and linguistic abilities, state-of-the-art methods generally employ transformer-based models for NER tasks. Previous methods had problems with texts that had complex structures (a token that belongs to several entities, or entities that are not contiguous in the text) while transformers are superior in solving these cases. BERT-based models were previously used, which were then later fine-tuned for different tasks. Today, however, we exploit the capabilities of an LLM that does not need to be fine-tuned but can learn a task without training through in-context learning. An LLM can then directly extract entities from text without the need for labels and provide them in the desired format (for example, we might want the LLM to provide a list of triplets or the triplet plus a given label). To avoid disambiguation problems, we can ask the LLM to provide additional information when conducting the extraction. For example, in music, *Apple* can refer to Apple Music, the British psychedelic rock band Apple, or the singer Fiona Apple. LLMs can help us disambiguate which of these entities it refers to based on the context of the period. At the same time, the flexibility of LLMs allows us to tie entities to various ontologies during extraction.

Similarly, an LLM can help with the RE task. There are several ways to do this. One of the simplest is to conduct sentence-level RE, in which you provide the model with a sentence and it must extract the relationship between the two entities. The extension of this approach is to extract all the relationships between entities at the level of an entire document. Since this is not an easy task, more sophisticated approaches with more than one LLM can be used to make sure that we can understand relationships at the local and global levels of the document (for example, in a document, a local relationship between two entities is in the same sentence, but we can also have global relationships where an entity mentioned at the beginning of the document is related to an entity that is present at the end of the document).

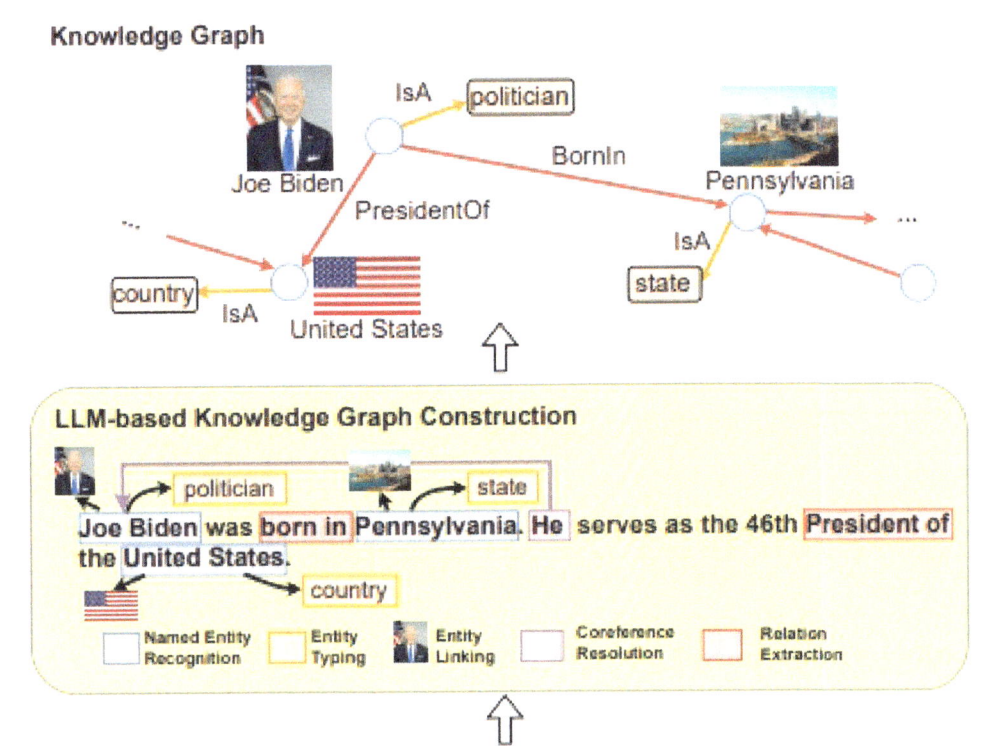

Figure 7.9 – General framework of LLM-based KG construction (This information was taken from an article published in 2023; https://arxiv.org/pdf/2306.08302)

As mentioned, the two tasks need not be conducted separately (NER and RE), but an LLM provides the flexibility to conduct them in a single step. In this case, it is of great importance to define the right prompt in which we instruct the model in extracting entities and relationships and in which format we want the output. We can then proceed iteratively, extracting entities and relationships for a large body of text. Alternatively, we can use a set of prompts for different tasks (one for entity extraction, one for relation extraction, and so on) and scan the corpus and these prompts automatically with the LLM. In some approaches, to maintain more flexibility, one LLM is used for extraction and then a smaller LLM is used for correction.

Another interesting perspective is that an LLM is enough to create a KG. In fact, LLMs are trained with a huge amount of text (the latest LLMs are trained with trillions of tokens that include scraping the internet and thousands of books). Several studies today show that even small LLMs (around 7 billion parameters) have considerable knowledge, especially about facts (the definition of knowledge in an LLM is also complicated because this is not associated with a single parameter but widespread). Therefore, some authors have proposed distilling knowledge directly from the LLM. In this case, by exploiting prompts constructed for the task, we conduct what is called a **knowledge search** of the LLM to extract triplets. In this way, by extracting facts directly from the LLM, we can then directly construct our KG. KGs constructed in this way are competitive in quality, diversity, and novelty with those constructed with large text datasets.

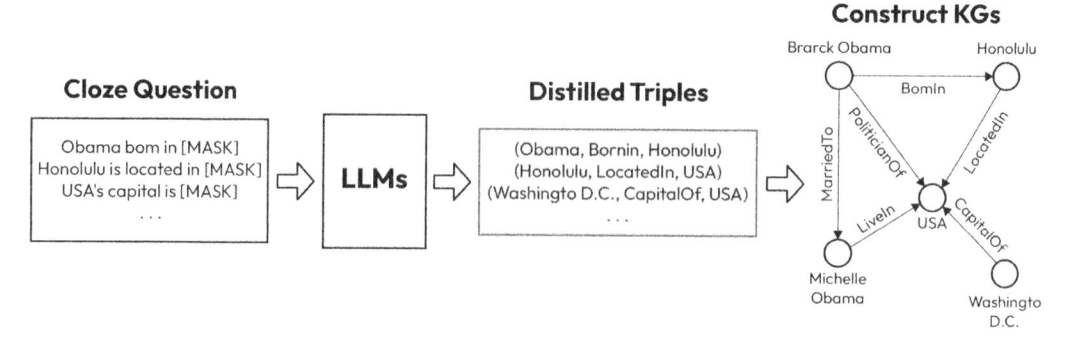

Figure 7.10 – General framework of distilling KGs from LLMs (https://arxiv.org/pdf/2306.08302)

Creating a knowledge graph with an LLM

In this tutorial, I will use Neo4j and LangChain to create a KG with an LLM. LangChain allows us to use LLMs efficiently to extract information from a text corpus, while Neo4j is a program for analyzing and visualizing graphs. The complete code is in the book's GitHub repository (https://github.com/PacktPublishing/Modern-AI-Agents/tree/main/chr7); here, we will describe the general process and the most important code snippets. We can have two methods:

- **Custom method**: LLMs have innate abilities to be able to accomplish tasks; we can take advantage of these generalist abilities

- **LangChain graph transformers**: Today, there are libraries that make the job easier and allow just a few lines of code to achieve the same result

The custom method is simply to define a prompt that allows the model to understand the task and execute it efficiently. In this case, our prompt is structured with the following elements:

- A clear definition of the task with a set of bullet points. The task description can contain both what the model must do and what it must not do.

- Additional context that allows the model to better understand how to perform the task. Since these models are trained for dialogic tasks, providing them with information about what role they should play helps the performance.

- Some examples to explain how to perform the task.

Creating a knowledge graph with your LLM   227

This approach builds on what we learned in *Chapter 3*. The model we are using is instruction-tuned (trained to perform tasks) so providing clear instructions helps the model understand the task and perform it. The addition of some examples leverages in-context learning. Using a crafted prompt allows us to be flexible and be able to adapt the prompt to our needs:

```
#Custom method
from langchain_core.prompts import ChatPromptTemplate
from langchain_core.messages import SystemMessage
from langchain_core.output_parsers import StrOutputParser

prompt = ChatPromptTemplate.from_messages([
    SystemMessage(content="""
    You are a helpful assistant in creates knowledge graphs by Generating Cypher Queries.\n

    Task:
    *   Identify Entities, Relationships and Property Keys from Context.\n
    *   Generate Cypher Query to Create Knowledge Graph from the Entities Relationships and Property Keys discovered.\n
    *   Extract ALL Entities and RelationShips as Possible.\n
    *   Always extract a person Profession as an Entity.\n
    *   Be creative.
    *   Understand hidden relationships from the network.
    Note: Read the Context twice and carefully before generating Cypher Query.\n
    Note: Do not return anything other than the Cypher Query.\n
    Note: Do not include any explanations or apologies in your responses.\n
    Note: Do not hallucinate.\n
    Entities include Person, Place, Product, WorkPlaces, Companies, City, Country, Animals, Tags like peoples Profession and more \n

    Few Shot Prompts:
     Example Context:

        Mary was born in 1995. She is Friends with Jane and John. Jane is 2 years older than Mary.
        Mary has a dog named Max,and is 3 years old. She is also married to John. Mary is from USA and a Software Engineer.

        Answer:
          MERGE (Mary:Person {name: "Mary", birth_year: 1995})
          MERGE (Jane:Person {name: "Jane", age:1993})
          MERGE (John:Person {name: "John"})
```

```
                MERGE (Mary)-[:FRIENDS_WITH]->(Jane)
                MERGE (Mary)-[:FRIENDS_WITH]->(John)
                MERGE (Jane)-[:FRIENDS_WITH]->(Mary)
                MERGE (John)-[:FRIENDS_WITH]->(Mary)
                MERGE (Mary)-[:HAS_DOG]->(Max:Dog {name: "Max", age: 3})
                MERGE (Mary)-[:MARRIED_TO]->(John)
                MERGE (Mary)-[:HAS_PROFESSION]->(SoftwareEngineer:Profession
 {name: "Software Engineer"})
                MERGE (Mary)-[:FROM]->(USA:Country {name: "USA"})
        """),
        ("human", "Context:{text}"),
])
```

Executing the preceding should yield the following result:

```
MERGE (Emma:Person {name: "Emma Thompson"})
MERGE (NexCity:City {name: "NexCity"})
MERGE (Alex:Person {name: "Alex Martin", profession: "Entrepreneur"})
MERGE (Jessica:Person {name: "Jessica", profession: "Unknown"})
MERGE (Lily:Person {name: "Lily", profession: "Unknown"})
MERGE (Max:Person {name: "Max", profession: "Unknown", age: 5})
MERGE (Tom:Person {name: "Tom Wilson", profession: "Senior Developer"})
MERGE (Sarah:Person {name: "Sarah", profession: "Artist"})
MERGE (Maria:Person {name: "Maria Lopez", profession: "Research Institute Leader"})
MERGE (Jake:Person {name: "Jake Anderson", profession: "Chef"})
MERGE (Raj:Person {name: "Raj Patel", profession: "Data Scientist"})
MERGE (Nina:Person {name: "Nina", profession: "Unknown"})
MERGE (Leo:Person {name: "Leo Martinez", profession: "Financial Analyst"})
MERGE (Maya:Person {name: "Maya Chen", profession: "Startup Founder"})
MERGE (Helen:Person {name: "Helen Carter", profession: "Retired Teacher"})
MERGE (Chloe:Person {name: "Chloe Edwards", profession: "Unknown"})
MERGE (Liam:Person {name: "Liam", profession: "Journalist"})

MERGE (Emma)-[:FRIENDS_WITH]->(Alex)
MERGE (Alex)-[:PARTNER]->(Jessica)
MERGE (Alex)-[:CHILD]->(Lily)
MERGE (Alex)-[:CHILD]->(Max)
MERGE (Emma)-[:FRIENDS_WITH]->(Tom)
MERGE (Tom)-[:SPOUSE]->(Sarah)
MERGE (Emma)-[:FRIENDS_WITH]->(Maria)
MERGE (Emma)-[:FRIENDS_WITH]->(Raj)
MERGE (Raj)-[:PARTNER]->(Nina)
MERGE (Emma)-[:COLLABORATED_WITH]->(Maya)
MERGE (Emma)-[:NEIGHBOR]->(Helen)
MERGE (Chloe)-[:CHILD]->(Helen)
MERGE (Chloe)-[:MARRIED_TO]->(Liam)
```

Figure 7.11 – Screenshot of the results

The results show how a crafted prompt succeeds in generating triplets (which we can then use to construct our KG). This highlights the great flexibility of LLMs.

We do not always want a custom approach but might want to use a more established pipeline. LangChain provides the ability to do this with just a few lines of code:

```
from langchain_core.documents import Document
from langchain_experimental.graph_transformers import LLMGraphTransformer

llm_transformer = LLMGraphTransformer(llm=llm)
documents = [Document(page_content=content)]
graph_documents = llm_transformer.convert_to_graph_documents(documents)
```

LangChain gives us the same result in an already structured format that simplifies our work.

The graph can then be visualized in Neo4j and we can work on the graph, conduct searches, select nodes, and so on.

Figure 7.12 – Screenshot of the graph from Neo4j

Once the graph is generated, we can use it for our queries. Obviously, we can conduct these queries in Neo4j, but it is also possible to do it in Python. For example, LangChain allows us to conduct queries of our KG:

```
from langchain.chains import GraphCypherQAChain
graphchain = GraphCypherQAChain.from_llm(
    llm, graph=graph, verbose=True, return_intermediate_steps=True
)
results = graphchain.invoke({"query":"People who have kids"})
print(results["result"])
```

Once executed the code, you should obtain these results:

```
> Entering new GraphCypherQAChain chain...
Generated Cypher:
MATCH (p1:Person)-[:HAS_CHILD]->(p2:Person)
RETURN p1, p2
Full Context:
[{'p1': {'profession': 'Entrepreneur', 'name': 'Alex Martin'}, 'p2': {'profession': 'Unknown', 'name': 'Lily'}}, {'p1': {'profession': 'Entrepreneur', 'name': 'Alex Martin'}, 'p2': {'profession': 'Unknown', 'name': 'Max', 'age': 5}}]

> Finished chain.
Alex Martin, Max have kids.
```

Figure 7.13 – Querying the KG

As we can see, LangChain in this case generates a corresponding query in Cypher and then conducts the graph query. In this way, we are using an LLM to generate a query in Cypher, while we can write directly in natural language.

Knowledge assessment

Once the KG has been created, it is necessary to check for errors and the overall quality of the KG. The quality of a KG is assessed by a set of dimensions (there are metrics associated with each of these dimensions) that are used to monitor the KG in terms of accessibility, representation, context, and intrinsic quality. Some of the metrics are as follows:

- **Accuracy**: This metric assesses accuracy in syntactic and semantic terms.
- **Completeness**: This metric measures how much knowledge a KG contains with respect to a certain domain or task. It usually measures whether a KG contains all the necessary entities and relationships for a domain (sometimes a comparison with a golden standard KG is used).
- **Conciseness**: KGs allow knowledge to be expressed efficiently, but they risk scaling quickly. Blank nodes (specific types of nodes that represent anonymous or unnamed entities, used when a node is needed in the graph but is not precisely indicated) can often be generated during the creation process. If care is not taken, one risks filling the KG with blank nodes.

- **Timeliness**: Knowledge should also be updated regularly because it can change and become outdated. Therefore, it is important to decide the frequency of updates.
- **Accessibility, ease of manipulation, and operation**: KGs are used for searches or other tasks; metrics exist today that measure the usefulness of KGs. In fact, for a KG to be useful, it must be easily accessible, be able to be manipulated, and be able to conduct research and updates.
- **Ease of understanding**: Since the KG is meant to be used to represent knowledge for humans, some authors have proposed measuring the degree to which the KG is interpretable for humans. Indeed, today, there is a greater emphasis on transparency and interpretation of models in AI.
- **Security, privacy, and traceability**: Metrics also exist today to control who accesses the KG and whether it is secure from outside access. Similarly, knowledge also needs to be tracked, as we need to be sure which sources it comes from. Traceability also allows us to be in privacy compliance. For example, our KG may contain sensitive data about users or come from erroneous or problematic documents. Traceability allows us to correct these errors, delete data from users who require their data to be deleted, and so on.

Knowledge cleaning

Having assessed the quality of our KG, we can see that there are errors. In general, error detection and correction are together called **knowledge cleaning**. Different types of errors can occur in a KG:

- We may have entities or relationships that have syntactic errors
- Some errors may be ontology-related (assigning to ontologies that do not exist, connecting them to the wrong ontologies, wrong properties of ontologies, and so on)
- Some may be semantic and may be more difficult to identify
- There are also knowledge errors that may result from errors in the sources for creating the knowledge (symptom *x* is not a symptom of disease *y*, person *x* is not the CEO of company *y*, and so on)

There are several methods to detect these errors. The simplest methods are statistical and seek to identify outliers in a KG by exploiting probabilistic and statistical modeling. There are also more sophisticated variations that exploit simple machine-learning models. These models are not particularly accurate. Since we can use logical reasoning and ontologies with KGs, there are knowledge-based reasoning methods to identify outliers (e.g., an instance of a person cannot also be an instance of a place, so by exploiting similar rules, we can identify outliers). Finally, there are methods based on AI, and one can also use an LLM to check for errors. An LLM possesses both knowledge and reasoning skills so it can be used to verify that facts are correct. For example, if for some error, we have the triplet (`Vienna, CapitalOf, Hungary`), an LLM can identify the error). Then, there are similar methods for conducting KG correction. However, several frameworks have already been built and established to conduct detection and correction.

Knowledge enrichment

Knowledge enrichment (or KG completion) is generally the next step. KGs are notoriously incomplete, so several rounds of KG completion and correction can occur. The completeness of a KG is sometimes complicated to define and is contextual to the domain and application tasks. The first step in completing a KG is usually to identify additional sources of information (e.g., for a medical KG, it could be an additional biomedical database or an additional corpus of scientific articles). Often, in the first step of building the KG, we use only one data type (unstructured text) and then extend the extraction in a second step to other data types (CSV, XML, JSON, images, PDF, and so on). Each of these data types presents different challenges, so we should modify our pipeline. The more sources we use, the more crucial KG cleaning and alignment tasks become. For example, the more heterogeneous the sources, the greater the importance of entity resolution (identifying duplicate entities at the KG level).

An interesting alternative is to infer knowledge using an LLM (or other transformer models). For example, three possible approaches have been explored:

- **Joint encoding**: The triplet (h, r, t) is given to a model as a transformer model to predict the probability that it exists (0 represents that the triplet is invalid, while 1 is a valid triplet). A variation of this approach is to take the final hidden state from the model and train a linear classifier to predict in a binary fashion whether the triplet is valid or not.

- **Masked language model (MLM) encoding**: Instead of conducting the entire embedding, one of the components of the triplet is masked and the model must predict it. In other words, if we have (h, r, ?), we can try to complete the gap.

- **Separated encoding**: The triplet is separated into two components, (h, r) and (t). In this way, we get two representations from the model (the final hidden state of the model is used). After that, we use a scoring function to predict whether this triplet is valid. This approach is definitely more accurate but risks a combinatorial explosion. As you can see, in this approach, we are trying to calculate the similarity between two textual representations (the representation of (h, r) and (t)).

These approaches are, in fact, very similar to those we have seen in previous chapters when trying to calculate the similarity between two sentences.

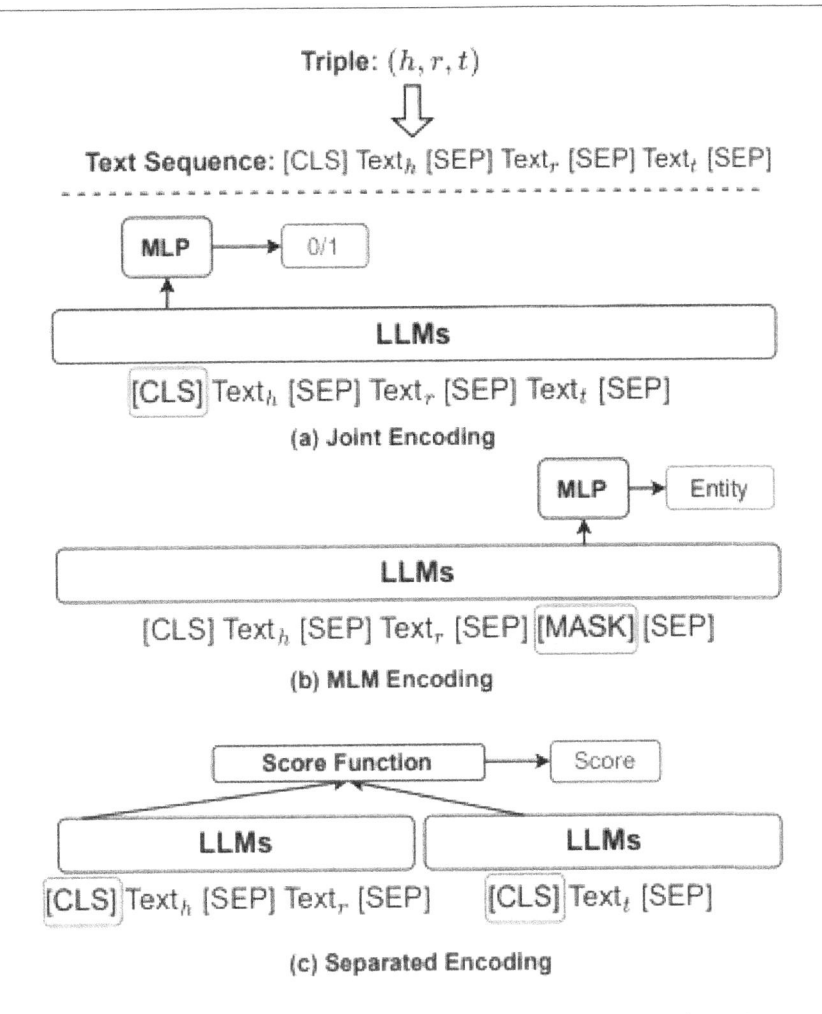

Figure 7.14 – LLMs as encoders for KG completion (https://arxiv.org/pdf/2306.08302)

Alternatively, one can use few-shot examples or other prompting techniques and ask an LLM to complete them directly. In addition, this approach allows you to be able to provide additional items in the prompt. In previous approaches, we provided only the triplet (h, r, t); with prompt engineering, we can also provide other contextual elements (relationship descriptions, entity descriptions, etc.) or add instructions to better complete the task.

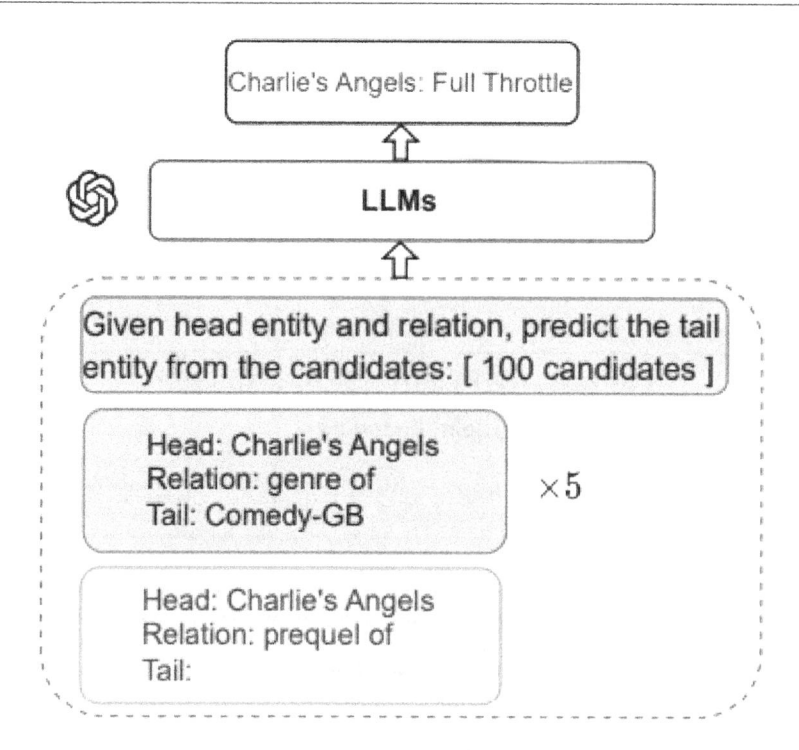

Figure 7.15 – Prompt-based KG completion (https://arxiv.org/pdf/2306.08302)

Knowledge hosting and deployment

The last step is the hosting and deployment of the KG. The KG is a set of nodes and relationships, so we can use a graph-specific paradigm to be able to store the data. Of course, hosting a KG is not without challenges:

- **Size**: The larger the KG, the more complex its management becomes
- **Data model**: We have to choose the system that allows us to optimally access the information for our tasks, as different systems have different advantages and disadvantages
- **Heterogeneity**: The graph may contain multiple modes, thus making storage more complex
- **Speed**: The more it grows, the more complex knowledge updates become
- **User needs**: Users may have heterogeneous needs that may be conflicting, requiring us to have to implement rules and constraints
- **Deployment**: The system must be accessible to users and allow easy inference

There are different alternatives for the storage of a KG:

- KGs can be hosted in classic **relational databases** (e.g., **Structured Query Language** (**SQL**) where entities and relationships are stored in tables). From these tables, one can then reconstruct the graph's relational structure using projections. Using a relational database to store a large KG can result in large tables that are impractical or a multitude of tables with a complex hierarchy.
- An alternative is the **document model** where data is stored as tuples (key-value pairs) and then organized into collections. This structure can be convenient for searching; it is a schematic system that allows the speed of writing, but updating knowledge in nested collections can be a nightmare.
- **Graph databases** are databases that are optimized for storing and searching graphs and data transformation. The graph data model then has nodes and edges with various metadata that are attached. The query language is also adapted to this structure (and is vaguely reminiscent of SQL). Graph databases also have the advantage of allowing heterogeneity and supporting speed. Neo4j is one of the most widely used and uses an adapted query language (Cypher).
- **Triplet stores** are where the database is made up directly of triplets. Databases exist today that save information in triplets and allow queries to be conducted in the database. Typically, these databases also have native support for ontologies and for conducting logical reasoning.

Hosting comes with its own set of challenges, and the choice of data model should be conducted with subsequent applications in mind. For example, if our KG needs to retrieve data from our relational database, using this system has advantages for integration. On the other hand, though, in this case, we will sacrifice performance for heterogeneity and speed. A graph database handles performance and the structural nature of the graph better, but it may integrate poorly with other components of the system. Whatever system we use for storage, we can either build hybrid systems depending on the applications or create a KG as a layer on top of the database.

Deployment is the last step in the pipeline. That doesn't mean it's the end of the story, though. A KG can become outdated easily, so we need to have pipelines in mind for knowledge updates or to be able to handle new applications. Similarly, the entry of new knowledge means that we must have pipelines for knowledge assessment (monitoring the quality of the KG, ensuring that no errors are entered or that there are no conflicts). Some knowledge may be outdated or need to be deleted for legal or privacy issues; therefore, we should have pipelines for cleaning the KG. Other pipelines should instead focus on controlling access and security of our system.

In this section, we have seen all the steps necessary to create and deploy a KG. Now that we have our KG, we can use it; in the next section, we will discuss how to find information and use it as a context for our LLM.

Retrieving information with a knowledge graph and an LLM

In the previous two chapters, we discussed the capabilities of RAG and its role in reducing hallucinations generated by LLMs. Although RAG has been widely used in both research and industrial applications, there are still limitations:

- **Neglecting relationships**: The text in the databases is interconnected and not isolated. For example, a document is divided into chunks; since these chunks belong to a single document, there is a semantic connection between them. RAG fails to capture structured relational knowledge when this cannot be captured by semantic similarity. Some authors point out that, in science, there are important relationships between an article and previous works, and these relationships are usually highlighted with a citation network. Using RAG, we can find articles that are similar to the query but we cannot find this citation network, losing this relational information.

- **Redundant information**: The context that comes to the LLM is a series of concatenated chunks. Today with LLMs, we can add more and more context (the context length of models is getting longer and longer) but they struggle with the presence of redundant information. The more chunks we add to the context, the greater the amount of redundant or non-essential information to answer the query. The presence of this redundant information reduces the performance of the model.

- **Lacking global information**: RAG finds a set of documents but fails to find global information because the set of documents is not representative of global information. This is a problem, especially for summarization tasks.

Graph retrieval-augmented generation (**GraphRAG**) has emerged as a new paradigm to try to solve these challenges. In traditional RAG, we find text chunks by conducting a similarity analysis on the embedded vectors. In GraphRAG, we conduct the search on the knowledge graph, and the found triplets are provided to the context. So, the main difference is that upon arrival of a query from a user, we conduct the search in the KG and use the information contained in the graph to answer the query.

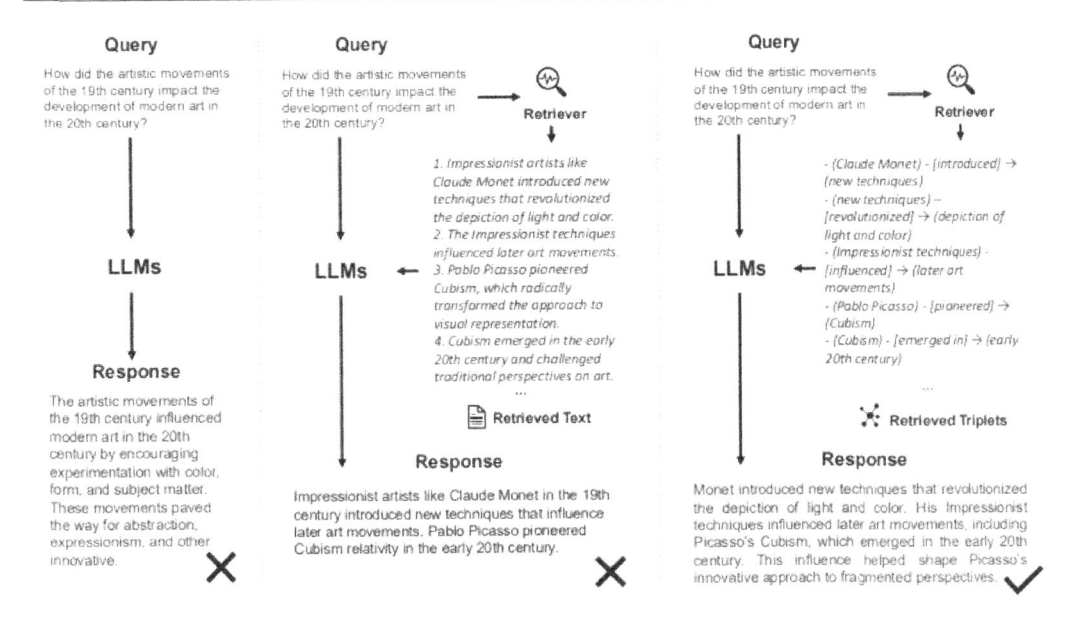

Figure 7.16 – Comparison between direct LLM, RAG, and GraphRAG (https://arxiv.org/pdf/2408.08921)

Formally, we can define GraphRAG as a framework that exploits a KG to provide context to an LLM and produce a better response. The system, therefore, is very similar to classical RAG; to avoid confusion, in this context, we will call it *vector RAG*. In GraphRAG, the KG is the knowledge base, and from this, we find information on entities and relationships. GraphRAG consists of three main steps:

1. **Graph-based indexing (G-indexing)**: In this initial phase, the goal is to build a graph database and index it correctly.

2. **Graph-guided retrieval (G-retrieval)**: Once we have a KG, when a query arrives, we have to find and extract the various information needed to answer the query. Given a query, q, in natural language, we want to extract a subgraph that we can use to correctly answer the query.

3. **Graph-enhanced generation (G-generation)**: The last step concerns using the found knowledge for generation. This step is conducted with an LLM that receives the context and generates the answer.

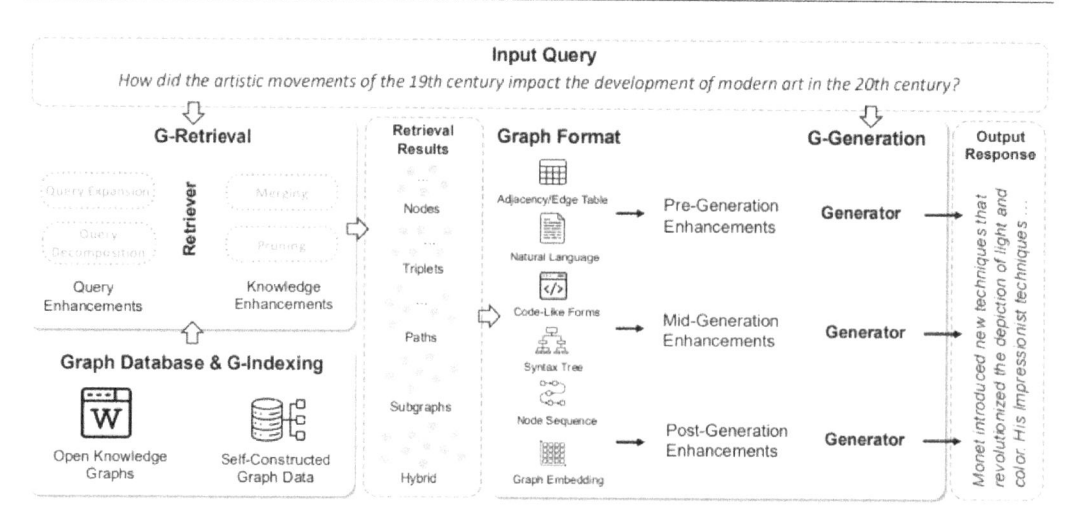

Figure 7.17 – Overview of the GraphRAG framework for a question-answering task (https://arxiv.org/pdf/2408.08921)

In the following subsections, we will talk about each step in detail.

Graph-based indexing

In the first step, we need to choose what our graph data will be. Generally, two types of KGs are used: open KGs or self-constructed KGs. In the first case, we can use a KG that is already available and adapt it to our GraphRAG. Today, many KGs have already been built and are available (for example, Wikidata is a knowledge base that collects data from various Wikipedia-related projects). Several KGs are specialized in a particular domain; these KGs have a greater understanding of a particular domain (some of these KGs are open and usable). Alternatively, it is possible to build your own KG.

When building it or before using it in GraphRAG, you should pay attention to indexing. Proper indexing allows us to have a faster and more efficient GraphRAG. Although we can imagine the KG visually as a graph, it is still stored in a database. Indexing allows us access to the information we want to find. Thus, there are several types of indexing. For example, we can have text descriptions associated with nodes, triplets, or ontologies that are then used during the search. Another way is to transform graph data into vectors and conduct the search on these vector spaces (embedding). We can also use indexing that better respects the graph nature of the data or hybrid versions.

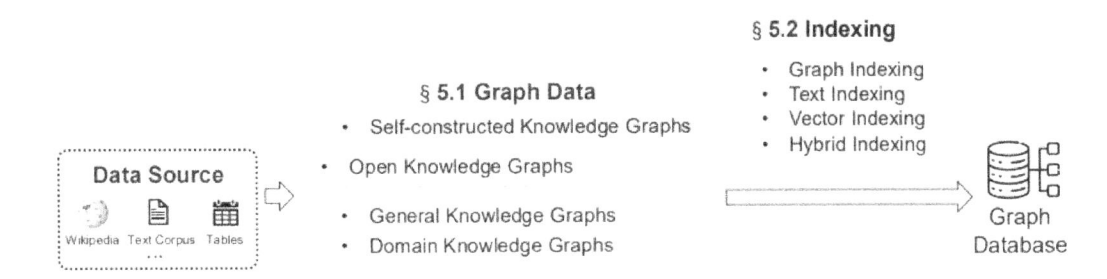

Figure 7.18 – Overview of graph-based indexing (https://arxiv.org/pdf/2408.08921)

Graph-guided retrieval

In GraphRAG, retrieval is crucial for the quality of response generation (similar to vector RAG). The search for a KG has two challenges that need to be solved:

- **Explosive candidate subgraphs**: As the graph grows, the number of subgraphs in the KG increases exponentially. This means we need efficient algorithms to explore the KG and find the relevant subgraphs. Some of these algorithms use heuristic methods to be more efficient.

- **Insufficient similarity measurement**: Our query is in text form, but we want to conduct our similarity search on a graph. This means that our algorithm must be able to understand both textual and structural information and be able to succeed in comparing the similarity between data from different sources.

We can have different types of retrievers. The simplest are **non-parametric retrievers**. These are based on the use of heuristic rules or other traditional graph search algorithms. For example, given a query, we search for entities present and take k-hop paths (in simple words, for the query *Where is Obama born?*, starting from the Obama entity, in KG, we take neighboring entities, k-hop=1, or even neighbors of neighbors, k-hop=2, and so on). Non-parametric retrievers are the simplest and also the fastest systems, but they suffer from inaccurate retrieval (they can be improved by learning). There are machine and deep learning models that are natively trained on graphs. GNN-based retrievers are one example. **Graph neural networks (GNNs)** are neural networks that natively handle graphs and can be used for many tasks on graphs (node classification, edge prediction, and so on) so they search the graph for subgraphs similar to the query.

Alternatively, we can use an LLM-based retriever where we have a transformer-based model that conducts the search. The model then processes and interprets the query to conduct the search. Several of these LLMs are models that have been trained on the text, and then fine-tuning is conducted to search the graphs. One advantage is that an LLM can be used as an agent and use different tools or functions to search the graph. Both LLM-based retrievers and GNN-based retrievers significantly improve retrieval accuracy but at a high computational cost. There are also alternatives today that use different methods (conduct with both a GNN and LLM, or use heuristic methods together with an LLM) or the process can be multistage (e.g., conduct an initial search with an LLM and then refine the results).

As was done for the vector RAG, we can add additional components to conduct enhancement. For example, in the previous chapter, we saw that we can rewrite a query or decompose queries that are too complex. Query modification helps to better capture the meaning of the query (because sometimes the query does not capture the implicit meaning intended by the user). Retrieval can also be a flexible process. In the previous chapter, we saw that in naïve RAG, retrieval was conducted only once, but then variations in advanced and modular RAG were established where retrieval can be multistage or iterative. Even more sophisticated variations make the process adaptive depending on the query, so for simpler queries, only one retrieval is conducted, and for more complex queries, multiple iterations may be conducted. Similarly, the results obtained after retrieval can also be modified. For example, even with GraphRAG, we can conduct a compression of the retrieved knowledge. In fact, we may also find redundant information if we conduct multiple retrieval stages and thus it is convenient to filter out irrelevant information.

Today, there are also reranking approaches to reorder the retrieved results with GraphRAG. One example is to reorder the various subgraphs found and perhaps choose the top k subgraphs.

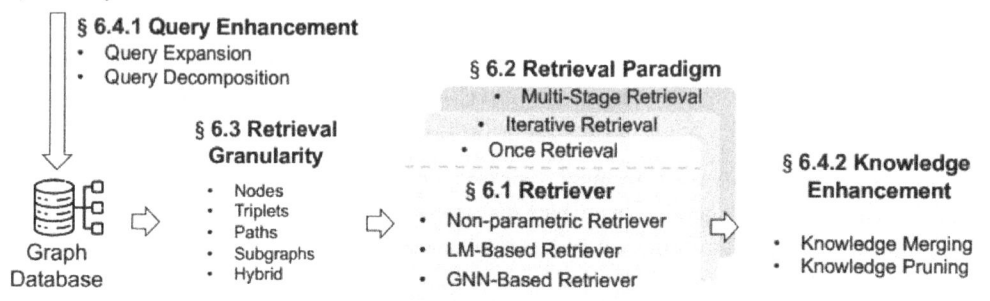

Figure 7.19 – General architectures of graph-based retrieval (https://arxiv.org/pdf/2408.08921)

Another difference with vector RAG is how we control search granularity. In vector RAG, granularity is controlled by deciding the size of the chunks. In the case of GraphRAG, we do not conduct chunking or find chunks. We can, however, control granularity during retrieval by choosing what we find:

- **Nodes**: In GraphRAG, we can retrieve individual entities. Nodes can have properties associated with them and then only add entities and their properties to the context. This can be useful for target queries.

- **Triplets**: By expanding the search granularity, we choose to retrieve triplets (so not only nodes, but also their relationships). This is useful when we are interested not only in the entity itself but also in their relationships.

- **Paths**: In this case, we still expand the retrieval. A path is a chain of nodes and relationships, so starting from entity X and arriving at entity Y, the path is all the chain of entities and relationships that connect them. Obviously, there are multiple paths between different entities, and these grow exponentially as the size of the graph increases. So, we generally define rules, use GNNs, or choose the shortest path.

- **Subgraphs**: A subgraph can be defined as a subset of nodes and relationships internal to the KG. Extracting a subgraph allows us to answer complex queries because it allows us to analyze complex patterns and dependencies between entities. There are several ways to extract a subgraph: we can use specific patterns or conduct a merge of different paths.
- **Hybrid granularities**: We can use different granularities at the same time or choose an adaptive system.

In the case of GraphRAG, balancing granularity and efficiency is important. We do not want to saturate the context with elements to prevent later LLM struggles with irrelevant information. It also depends on the complexity of the query: for simple queries, even low granularity is enough, whereas complex queries benefit from higher granularity. An adaptive approach can make the system more efficient while maintaining nuances when needed.

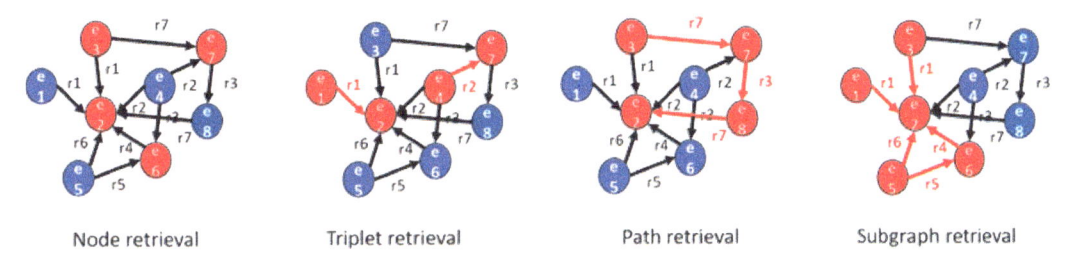

Figure 7.20 – Different levels of retrieval granularity

Once the knowledge is found and cleaned up, we can provide it to the LLM to generate a response to the query. This knowledge enters the prompt provided to the LLM and the model generates a response. Alternatively, this found knowledge can be used for certain types of models that are used for some specific tasks (e.g., a GNN to answer multiple-choice questions). The main problem is that the graph has a non-Euclidean nature and integration with textual information is not optimal. For this, graph translators that convert the found graph information into more digestible information for an LLM can be used. This conversion increases the LLM's ability to understand the information. So, once we find the information in graph form (nodes, relationships, path, or subgraph), we put it in the context of the LLM. There are some alternatives:

- **Graph formats**: We can directly add the set of relationships and nodes in the prompt, or we can use a form of graph structure representation such as adjacency or edge tables. The latter compactly conveys a better relational structure. Another idea is a node sequence, which is generated according to a predeterminate rule. This is a compact representation that contains the order of the nodes in the graph.
- **Natural language**: There are specific graph languages that can be used to transform information into natural language, a representation that is more congenial to LLM. In this process, we convert the found subgraph into a descriptive form. Templates can be used to transform the

graph where it is filled with nodes and relationships. In some templates, you can define which are the nearest neighbors of a node and which are the most distant (1-hop and 2-hop in the graph), or you can use an LLM to transform this subgraph into a natural language description.

- **Syntax tree**: The graph is flattened and represented as a syntax tree. These trees have the advantage of a hierarchical structure and maintain the topological order of the graph. This approach maintains the properties of the graph but makes the information more digestible for the LLM.

- **Code-like forms**: Retrieved graphs can be converted into a standard format such as **Graph Markup Language** (**GraphML**). These languages are specifically designed for graphs but are a structural and textual hybrid.

Conversion still presents difficulties because it must ensure that the result is concise and complete but, at the same time, understandable by the LLM. Optimally, this representation should also include the structural information of the graph. Whether the retrieved subgraph is converted or not, the result is entered into the LLM prompt and a response is generated.

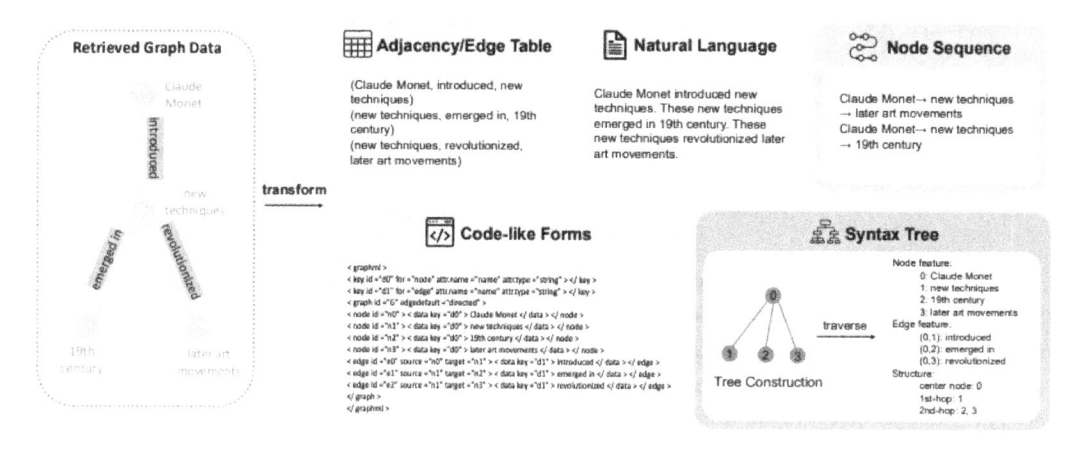

Figure 7.21 – Subgraph transformation to enhance generation
(https://arxiv.org/pdf/2408.08921)

GraphRAG applications

GraphRAG has several applications. The first is question answering (so the same application as RAG) where we extract the subgraphs and the LLM uses them for subsequent reasoning and answering. A sub-branch of question answering is commonsense reasoning question answering where it often takes the format of multiple choice questions. For this subtask, we often do not use an LLM but a GNN or other machine learning (ML) model instead. However, KGs (and therefore also GraphRAG) have an extensive application for information retrieval, for example, if we want to investigate the relationships between some entities of interest. A KG can be used by itself to extract relationships between entities, but the addition of generation with an LLM allows us to explore these relationships and contextual nuances better. This is an attractive factor for academic and literature research. In fact, in academia, an article is authored by multiple authors who are part of different institutions. An article builds on previous research, and so for each article, there is a network of citations. These structural elements are easily modeled for a graph. An interesting application recently published shows how Ghafarollahi et al. used multiple KG agents to analyze published literature and propose new research hypotheses. In short, they extracted paths or subgraphs from a KG (constructed from 1,000 articles), then an agent analyzed the ontologies, and then a new research hypothesis was generated from this. In this interesting application, a number of agents collaborate to create new potential searches for new materials.

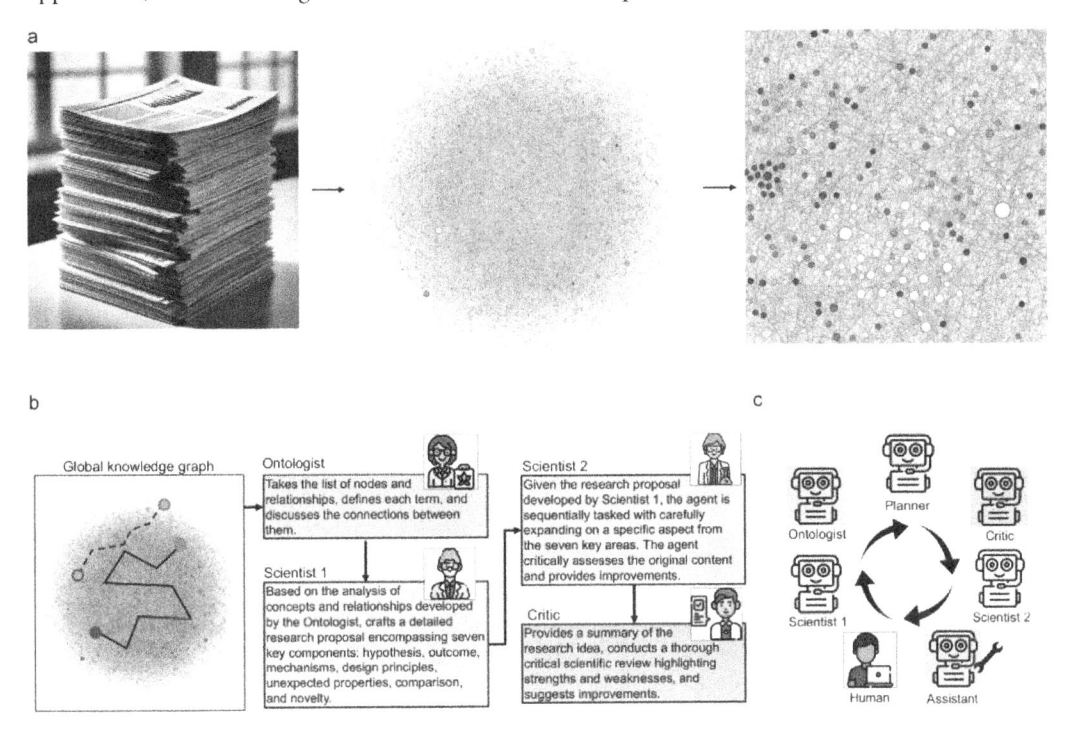

Figure 7.22 – Overview of the multi-agent graph-reasoning system for scientific discovery assistance (`https://arxiv.org/pdf/2409.05556v1`)

One of the reasons for interest in GraphRAG is that KGs used to be used for fact verification (after all, a KG is a collection of facts) so providing facts to an LLM should reduce LLM hallucinations. This aspect makes it particularly attractive for biomedical applications. In fact, hallucinations are a serious problem for medical decision-making applications. In medicine, if the vector RAG can reduce hallucinations, it does not allow for a holistic view, especially when an overview is needed to answer a question. Therefore, Wu et al. suggest using a GraphRAG-based approach called **MedGraphRAG**. In this work, they use several medical sources to create their system and take advantage of the hierarchical nature of KGs. They construct three levels for their KG. At the first level, there are user-provided documents (medical reports from a hospital). Entities at this level are then connected to a more foundational level of commonly accepted information. The second level is constructed from medical textbooks and scientific articles. Finally, at the third level, there are well-defined medical terms and knowledge relationships that have been obtained from standardized and reliable sources. Leveraging retrieval from this KG obtains state-of-the-art results on major medical question-answering benchmark datasets. The advantage is that this system also outperforms models that are fine-tuned on medical knowledge, thus with large computational savings.

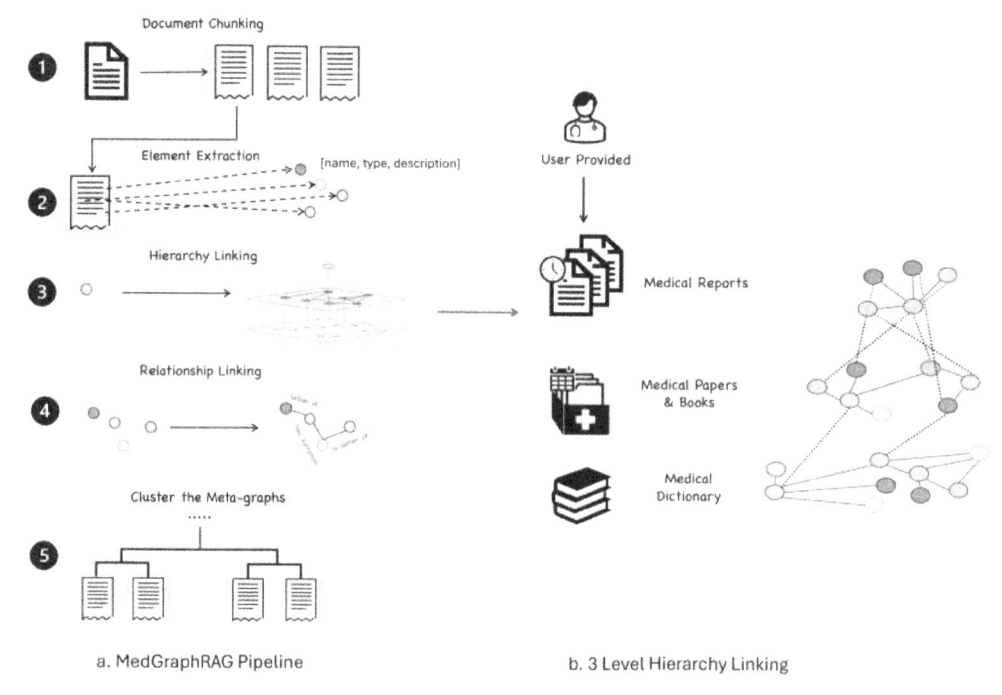

Figure 7.23 – MedGraphRAG framework (https://arxiv.org/pdf/2408.04187)

A further interest in GraphRAG comes from the use of KGs to propose recommendations to users. In e-commerce platforms, recommendation systems are used to predict the future purchasing intentions of users and suggest other products of interest. Thus, it was proposed that the system matches a new user to subgraphs derived from past users with similar behavior, and leverages these to predict likely future purchases and suggest appropriate products. In addition, this approach can also be useful for the legal and financial fields. In the legal field, there are extensive citations between cases and judicial opinions, and judges use past cases and opinions to make new decisions. Given a legal case, GraphRAG could suggest previous legal cases and help in decision-making. In finance, GraphRAG might suggest previous financial transactions or customer cases.

Finally, up to this point, we have suggested that GraphRAG and vector RAG are antagonistic. Actually, both systems have advantages and disadvantages so it would be more useful to use them in synergy. Sarmah et al., proposed **HybridRAG**, where both GraphRAG and vector RAG are used in one system. Their system shows advantages in financial responses. In the future, there may be systems that exploit both one and the other approach with the addition of a router that can choose whether to search for the KG or the vector database. Alternatively, there could be more complex systems for knowledge fusion in context (especially if KG search and chunks provide some redundant information).

In this section, we discussed how an LLM can be connected to a KG, and how it can be used to find information that enriches the context of the LLM. In the next section, we will discuss other tasks for which the synergy of LLMs and KGs is useful.

Understanding graph reasoning

This section is devoted to a discussion of how to solve graph data tasks. In this section, we will discuss some of the approaches used to solve tasks on knowledge graphs: KG embeddings, GNNs, and LLMs. KG embeddings and GNNs would require at least one chapter each; hence, these topics are outside the scope of the book, but we believe that an introduction to them would be beneficial to a practitioner. In fact, both embedding and GNNs can be used synergistically with LLMs and agents.

There are many tasks in which a model is required to understand the structure to solve, and these are collectively called **graph structure understanding tasks**. Many of these tasks are solved using algorithms or models designed specifically to learn these tasks. Today, a new paradigm is being developed in which we try to use LLMs to solve these tasks; we will discuss this in depth at the end of this section. Examples of tasks might be degree calculation (how many neighbors a node has), path search (defining a path between two nodes, calculating which is the minimum path, and so on), Hamilton path (identifying a path that visits each node only once), topological sorting (identifying whether nodes can be visited in topological order), and many others. Some of these tasks are simple (degree calculation and path search) but others are much more complex (topological sorting and Hamilton path).

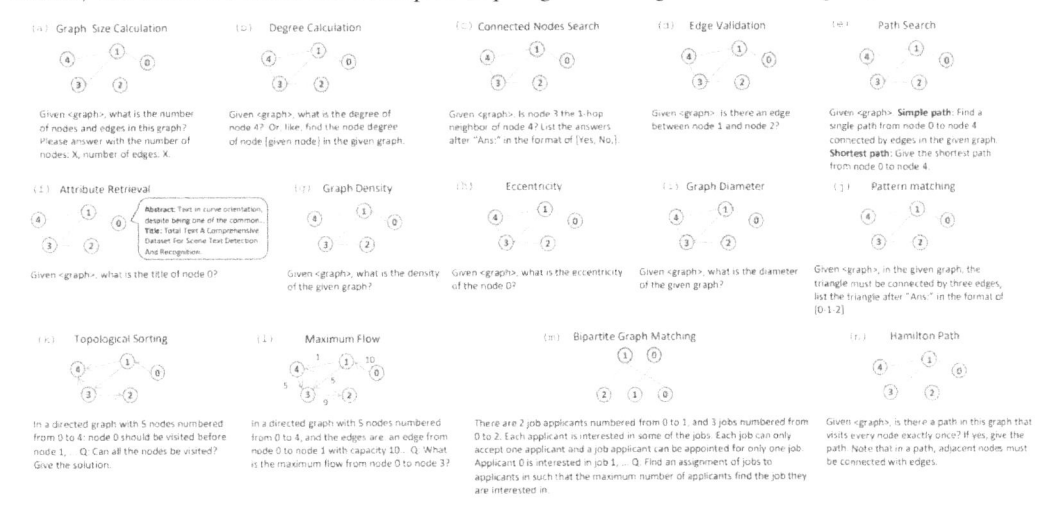

Figure 7.24 – Graph structure understanding tasks (https://arxiv.org/pdf/2404.14809)

Graph learning tasks, on the other hand, require the model to include not only the structure of the graph but also the attributes of the graph (features of nodes, edges, and the graph), thus understanding the semantic information of graphs. Examples of some of the tasks are node classification (classify the node according to its attributes and according to the attributes of its neighbors), graph classification (you have to understand the whole graph to classify it), edge classification, and node feature explanation (explain a feature of the node). **Knowledge graph question answering (KGQA)** is a task that falls into this group, as we need to understand both the structure and meaning of entities and relationships to answer questions. A similar task is conducting KG queries to generate text (this can also be seen as a subtask). KG embeddings capture multi-relational semantics and latent patterns in the graph, making them particularly useful for relational reasoning and symbolic link prediction tasks (KG link prediction, for example). GNNs, on the other hand, capture graph structure and node/edge features; these make them perform well for tasks that require inductive reasoning, use of features, or local/global representation of graph structure (node or graph classification/regression).

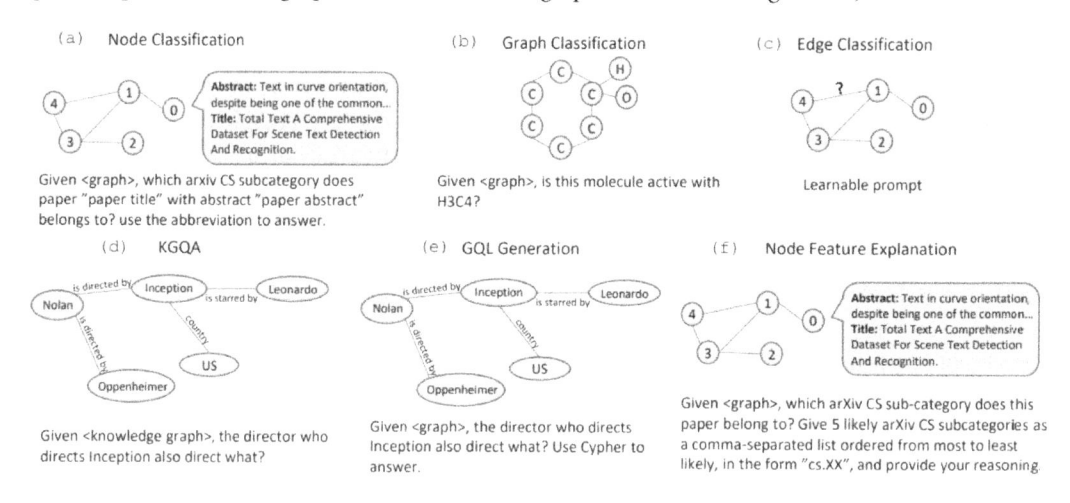

Figure 7.25 – Graph learning tasks (https://arxiv.org/pdf/2404.14809)

Knowledge graph embeddings

KGs are effective in representing knowledge, but they are complex to manipulate at scale. This complicates their use when we are interested in particular tasks such as link prediction and entity classification. Therefore, **knowledge graph embedding (KGE)** was proposed to be able to simplify these tasks. We have already discussed the concept of embedding in the first chapter. An embedding is a projection of data into a low-dimensional and continuous vector space, which is especially useful when our data has a sparse representation (such as text and graphs). For a KG, an embedding is the projection of the graph (nodes, edges, and their feature vectors) in this reduced space. A KGE model then tries to learn a projection that preserves both structure and information, so that it can then be used for downstream tasks.

Learning this representation is not an easy task, and several types of algorithms have been proposed. For example, some KGEs try to preserve relational patterns between entities. TransE is an approach that embeds KGs in Euclidean space where the relationships between entities are vectors. TransE is based on the idea that two entities connected in the triplet should be as close as possible in space. Furthermore, from a triplet `(h, r, t)`, it tries to learn a space where $h + r \approx t$, thus allowing us to do various mathematical operations. RotatE, another approach, also tries to preserve other relational patterns (symmetry, antisymmetry, inversion, and composition) using a complex vector space. This is quite useful when we want to answer questions that require this notion of symmetry (*marriage* is symmetric) or composition (*my nephew is my brother's son*). Other methods, however, try to preserve structural patterns. In fact, larger KGs contain complex and compound structures that are lost during the embedding process. For example, hierarchical, chain structure, and ring structure are lost during classical embeddings. These structures are important when we want to conduct reasoning or extract subgraphs for some tasks. ATTH (another KG embedding method) uses hyperbolic space to preserve hierarchical structures and logical patterns at the same time. Other methods, however, try to model the uncertainties of entities and relationships, making tasks such as link prediction easier.

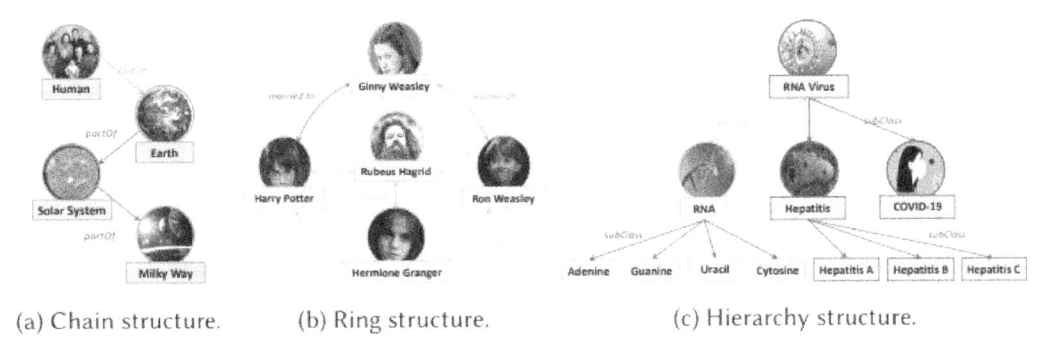

(a) Chain structure.   (b) Ring structure.   (c) Hierarchy structure.

Figure 7.26 – Illustration of three typical structures in KGs (`https://arxiv.org/pdf/2211.03536`)

KGEs have been used extensively for several tasks such as link prediction. In this case, exploiting the small space is used to try to identify the most likely missing links. Similarly, continuous space allows models to be used to conduct triple classification. A further application is to use learned embeddings to recommender systems.

Graph neural networks

There are several challenges in using graphs natively with ML algorithms. First, classical ML models take data that is in a rectangular or grid-like form, making it non-intuitive how to apply it to graphs. In addition, for a graph, there are several pieces of information that we want to use to solve tasks: nodes, edges, global context, and connectivity. The last one is particularly difficult to represent, and we usually use an adjacency matrix. This representation is sparse, grows largely with the number of nodes in the graph, and thus is space inefficient. Also, since there is no order in the graph, we can get several adjacency matrices that convey the same information but may not be recognized by a model.

A GNN is a deep learning model that natively takes a graph and also exploits its structure during its learning process. There are different types of GNNs (in the *Further reading* section, there are some reviews so you can go into more detail on this topic) but here we will focus on the main framework: message passing. Most GNNs can be seen as graph convolution networks in which we aggregate for each node the information coming from its neighbors. One of the advantages of a GNN is that at the same time as it is being trained for a task, it learns an embedding for each node. At each step, this node embedding is updated with information from its neighbors.

The message-passing framework is in a sense very similar to a neural network, as we saw earlier. In this case, there are two main steps: gather the embeddings of the various neighboring nodes and then follow by an aggregation function (which can be different depending on various architectures) and a nonlinearity. Then, at each step, we conduct an update of the embedding of each node, learning a new representation of the graph. A classical GNN can be composed of a series of GNN blocks and then a final layer that exploits the learned representation to accomplish a task. This can be written in a formula like this:

$$h_v^{(l+1)} = W^{(l+1)} \cdot \sum_{w \in \mathcal{V}(v) \cup \{v\}} \frac{1}{c_{w,v}} h_w^{(l)}$$

Here, at layer *l+1*, we learn a representation, *h*, based on the previous embedding. *W* is a layer-specific weight matrix, *v* is a node, *w* is the set of neighbors, and *c* is the normalization coefficient.

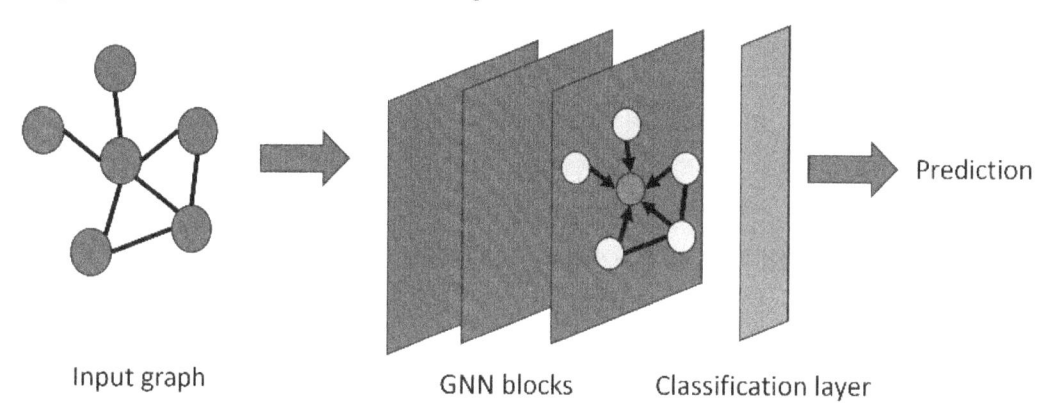

Input graph   GNN blocks   Classification layer   Prediction

Figure 7.27 – GNNs

In this case, we are assuming that each neighbor's contribution is the same. This may not be the case, so inspired by the attention mechanism of RNNs and transformers, **graph attention networks** (**GATs**) have been proposed. In this type of GNN, the model learns different levels of importance for each neighbor. Several models of GNN layers exist today, but basically, the principle does not change much.

GNNs have been successfully used for several graph tasks but still have some limitations such as difficult scalability, problems with batching, and so on. They have also been applied to KGs, but they increase complexity.

LLMs reasoning on knowledge graphs

LLMs have the advantage that they are not trained for a specific task but acquire a broad spectrum of skills during training. In addition, LLMs have reasoning skills that can be improved with specific approaches. Therefore, several researchers have suggested conducting graph reasoning with LLMs. The main method of approaching an LLM is to use a prompt as input. There are three approaches:

- **Manual prompt**: The simplest approach is to provide a prompt to an LLM in which they are asked to solve a task on a graph. In the prompt, the graph is entered and additional information can be added (e.g., if we want the LLM to conduct a **depth-first search** (**DFS**) algorithm to solve the task, we provide a succinct explanation of how this algorithm works). A limitation to these prompts is that it is not possible to insert wide graphs within a prompt (limitation due to the context length of the LLM).

- **Self-prompting**: The LLM conducts a continuous update of the prompt to make it easier for the LLM to solve tasks. In other words, given an original prompt, the LLM conducts prompt updates to better define tasks and how to resolve them. Then, based on the output of the LLM, a new prompt is generated and fed back to the LLM. This process can be conducted multiple times to refine the output.

- **API call prompts**: This type of prompt is inspired by agents, in which the LLM is provided with a set of APIs that it can invoke to conduct reasoning about graphs or other external tools.

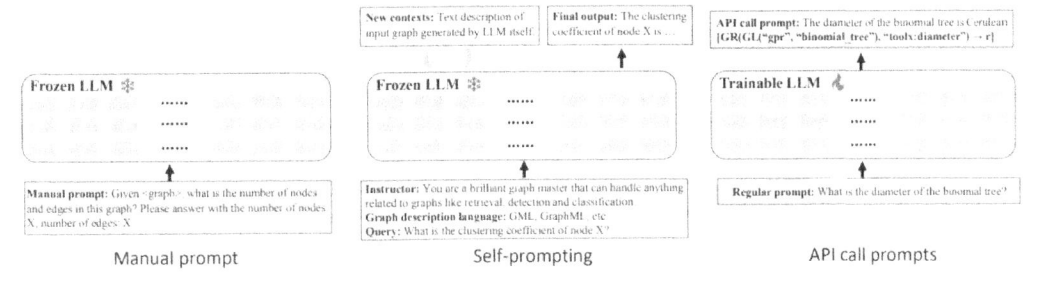

Figure 7.28 – Prompting methods for the LLM applied to graph tasks
(https://arxiv.org/pdf/2404.14809)

The alternative to finding complex prompting strategies is the **supervised fine-tuning** (**SFT**) method. In this case, a dataset with graph tasks and their solutions is used to train the model to improve its reasoning skills.

Another interesting aspect of LLMs is that they can also be used in combination with other models. This allows their qualities to be exploited with models that are specialized and better suited for certain tasks. For example, we can combine LLMs with GNNs, in which case LLMs can function as enhancers of GNNs. The GNN handles graph structure much better than the LLM, but the latter handles textual attributes much better. We can then capitalize on the strengths of the two models to have a much stronger synergistic model. LLMs possess greater semantic and syntactic capacity than other models, and this allows them to create powerful textual embeddings. An LLM can then generate numerical embeddings that are then used by the GNN as node features. For example, we have a citation network between scientific articles (our graph where each node is an article) and we want to classify articles into various topics. We can take the abstract for each article and use an LLM to create an embedding of the abstract. These number vectors will be the node features for the articles. At this point, we can train our GNN with better results than without features. Alternatively, if the node features are textual, we can use an LLM to generate labels. For example, for our article network, we have the article titles associated with each node, and we use the LLM in a zero-shot setting to generate a set of labels. This is useful because manual annotation is expensive, so we can get labels much more quickly. When we have obtained the labels, we can train a GNN on the graph. Alternatively, we can also think of conducting fine-tuning of the LLM and GNN at the same time for tasks.

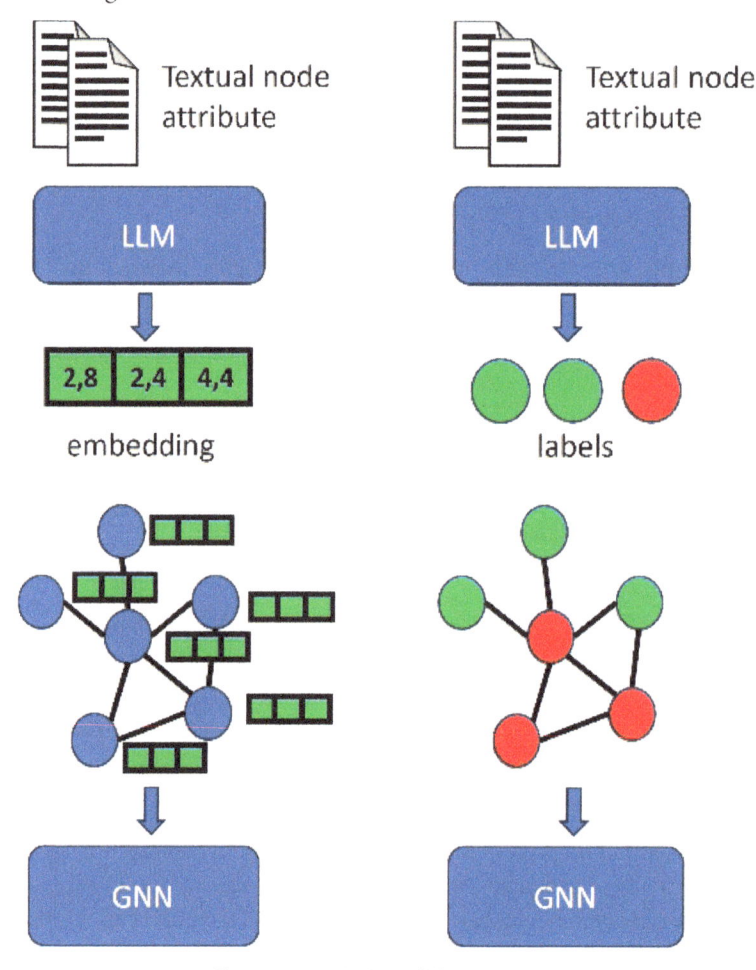

Figure 7.29 – LLM and GNN synergy

Another interesting approach is graph-formed reasoning. Several of the prompting techniques that have been used for reasoning do not take into account that human thinking is not linear, so according to some, this method of reasoning can be approximated using graphs. There are two types of approaches that take advantage of this idea:

- **Think on the graph**: In this approach, the LLM reasons in the form of a graph where each node represents an intermediate of thought (i.e., an intermediate step of reasoning or conclusion during the reasoning necessary to arrive at a solution) and the edges represent the relationship between these thoughts and the direction in which the reasoning is headed. An example of this approach is a **graph of thoughts** (**GoT**), where the reasoning intermediates are presented as a graph. This approach is expensive (multiple calls in inference) and typically used for problems that require reasoning, such as math problems. For example, to solve *A train travels 60 miles in 1.5 hours. What is its average speed?*, the model might create nodes such as `Distance = 60 km`, `Time = 1.5 hours`, `Use speed = distance ÷ time`, and `Speed = 40 km/h`, with edges showing how each thought leads to the next. This graph structure enables the model to reason step by step, explore alternatives, or verify calculations.

- **Verify on the graph**: In this approach, we use a graph to verify the correctness and consistency of the reasoning. For example, if different paths should lead to a logical conclusion, they should be the same or similar. So, if there is a contradiction, it means the reasoning is wrong. Generally, one generates several reasonings for a question, structures them as a graph, and analyzes them to improve the final answer. This approach requires a verifier who analyzes this graph, usually another LLM.

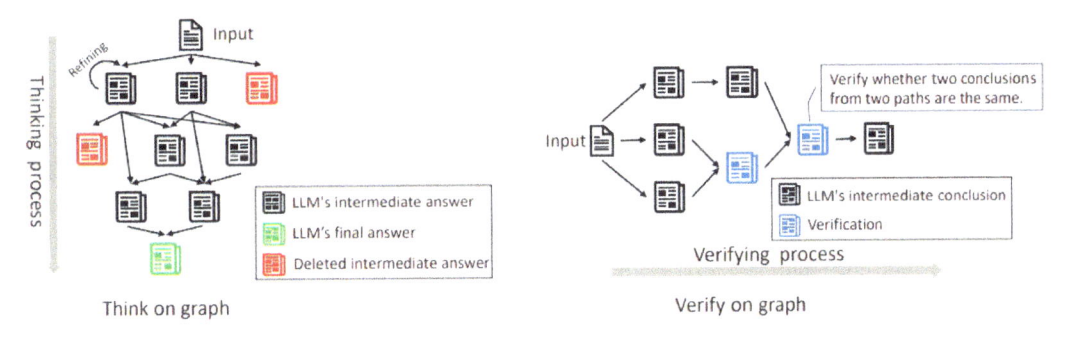

Figure 7.30 – Think on graphs and verify on graphs (https://arxiv.org/pdf/2404.14809)

In this section, we discussed the intricate relationship between graphs and LLMs and how they can enable us to solve some tasks that were previously conducted with graph ML algorithms. In the next section, we will discuss exciting perspectives in the field of some questions that remain open.

Ongoing challenges in knowledge graphs and GraphRAG

KGs are a powerful medium for storing and organizing information, but there are still limitations and open questions. Especially for large KGs, scalability is important; a balance must be struck between expressiveness and computational efficiency. Plus building a KG requires a lot of computational effort (using an LLM to extract triplets from a large corpus of text can be expensive and require adequate infrastructure). In addition, once the KG is built, it must be evaluated and cleaned, which also requires some effort (manual or computational). Moreover, growth in the KG also means growth in the infrastructural cost to enable access or use. Querying large KGs requires having optimized algorithms to avoid the risk of increasingly large latency times. Industrial KGs can contain billions of entities and relationships, representing an intricate and complex scale. Many of the algorithms are designed for small-scale KGs (up to thousands of entities) so retrieval in large-scale KGs still remains challenging.

In addition, KGs are notoriously incomplete, which means that one must have pipelines in order to complete the KG. This means having both pipelines to add additional sources and pipelines to conduct the update of data sources. Most databases are static, so creating dynamic systems is challenging. This is critical to make the best use of KGs for domains such as finance, where we want to account for rapid market changes. On a side note, KGs can be multimodal, but integrating these modes is not easy at all. While adding modalities significantly improves the reasoning process, the understanding of the nuances of stored knowledge, and the richness of the KG, it significantly increases management complexity (more storage required, more sophisticated pipelines, more complex knowledge harmonization, and so on).

GraphRAG is a relatively new technology and still not fully optimized. For one thing, information retrieval could be improved, especially the transition between the user's text query and retrieval on the KG. The more the KG grows, the more there is a risk of finding redundant information that harms the generation process. After retrieval, we could then end up with a long context that is provided to the LLM for generation. To reduce noise and reduce computation, we can compress the context, but this carries the risk of information loss. At present, lossless compression is an active field of research, while current methods allow, at most, a trade-off between compression and information preservation. There is also currently a lack of benchmark standards to evaluate new GraphRAG approaches; this does not allow for an easy comparison of either current or future methods. GraphRAG allows for considering inter-entity relationships and structural knowledge information, reducing redundant text information, and being able to find global information again. At the same time, though, the nuances of the text are lost, and GraphRAG underperforms in abstractive question-answering tasks or when there is no explicit entity mentioned in the question. So, the union of vector and GraphRAG (or HybridRAG) is an exciting prospect for the future. It remains interesting to understand how these two technologies will be integrated in an optimal way.

An important note is that LLMs are not specifically trained for graph tasks. As we mentioned in *Chapter 3*, LLMs are trained to predict the next word in a sequence. By optimizing this simple goal, they acquire most of their skills. Obviously, it is difficult to assimilate a spatial understanding simply from text. This means that LLMs generally struggle with structural data. This is highlighted with tabular data, where LLMs have problems with understanding tables and relationships. The first problem is that LLMs struggle with numerical representation since the tokenization step makes it difficult for an LLM to understand the whole number (lack of consistent decimal representation, and problems with numerical operation). This then impacts the execution of graph tasks where this numerical understanding is necessary. Specific studies on graph understanding show that LLMs have a basic understanding of graph structure. LLMs understand these graphs in linear form and better understand the labels associated with the nodes more than the topological structure of the graph. According to these studies, LLMs have a basic understanding, which is strongly impacted by prompt design, prompt techniques, semantic information provided, and the presence of examples. Next-generation, multi-parameter LLMs succeed in solving simple tasks on small graphs, but their performance decays rapidly as both graph and task complexity increase. There are two reasons for this lack of understanding of structural data. The first is that in the large text corpora used for training LLMs, there is not much graph-derived data. So, LLMs can only learn basic spatial relationships because these are described in the texts. Therefore, SFT on graph datasets allows for results that are better than much larger models.

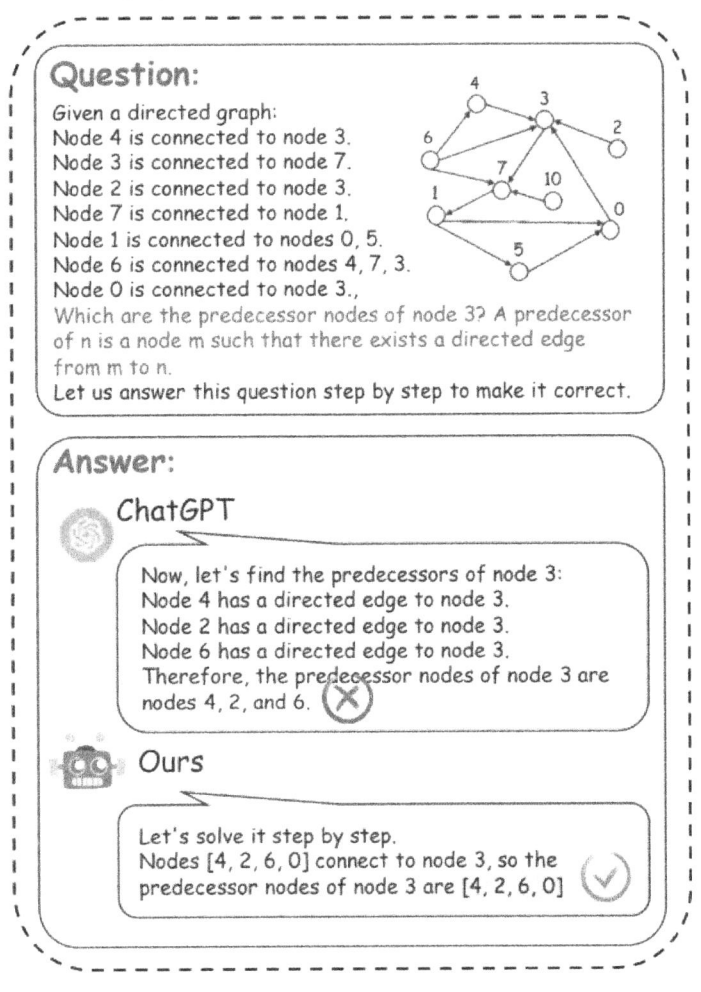

Figure 7.31 – SFT on graph data allows better performance for small LLMs than larger LLMs (https://arxiv.org/pdf/2403.04483)

The second reason, on the other hand, stems from why humans understand spatial structures well. Humans learn spatial relationships from their experiences in the outside world. The brain creates mental maps that allow us to orient ourselves in space. These maps also enable us to better understand abstract spatial concepts such as graphs. LLMs do not have a mental map nor can they have the experience of the outside world, thus making them disadvantaged in understanding abstract spatial concepts.

Summary

In *Chapters* 5 and 6, the main question was how to find information and how to use this information to generate an answer to users' questions. Finding information dynamically allows us to reduce the hallucinations of our model and keep its knowledge up to date.

In this chapter, we started with a text corpus and created a system to find the most relevant information for generating an answer (naïve RAG). Next, we created a more sophisticated system to try to extract only the relevant information and avoid redundant information or noise. For some researchers, by its nature, text contains relevant information intermixed with background noise. What matters are the entities present and their relationships. From this reductionist approach comes the idea of representing essential knowledge in a knowledge graph. The graph allows us to use algorithms to search for information or explore possible connections. For a long time, graph reasoning and LLMs have run on parallel tracks, but recently, their stories have begun to intertwine. We have seen how this interaction between LLM and KG can be conducted in various ways. For example, an LLM can be used to extract relationships and entities for our graph construction, or an LLM can be used to conduct reasoning about the KG. Similarly, we can use the KG to find knowledge and enrich the context of the LLM, thus enabling it to effectively answer a user question.

Right now, there is a sort of a Manichean definition: either the vector RAG or the GraphRAG. Both have merits and demerits, and the research points toward a unification of these two worlds (HybridRAG). In the future, we will find more sophisticated ways of uniting KGs and vectors. Also, the understanding of the graph structure on one side of an LLM is still immature. With the growth of training datasets, the new generation LLMs are exposed to more examples of graphs. However, understanding spatial relationships in an abstract concept such as a graph also means understanding them in problems with greater real-world relevance. Therefore, this is an active field of research, especially for robots that must interact in space and use AI.

Moving into space is one of the next frontiers of AI. Interaction in space presents peculiar challenges, such as balancing exploration and exploitation. In the next chapter, we will discuss this concept more abstractly. We will focus on reinforcement learning and agent behavior in the relationship to space. Whether chess, a video game, or a real-world environment, an agent must learn how to interact with space to achieve a goal. In the next chapter, we will look at how to enable an agent to explore the world without losing sight of the aim.

Further reading

- Ghafarollahi, *SciAgents: Automating Scientific Discovery through Multi-agent Intelligent Graph Reasoning*, 2024, https://arxiv.org/pdf/2409.05556v1
- Raieli, *A Brave New World for Scientific Discovery: Are AI Research Ideas Better?*, 2024, https://levelup.gitconnected.com/a-brave-new-world-for-scientific-discovery-are-ai-research-ideas-better-5692c5aa8182
- Raieli, *How the LLM Got Lost in the Network and Discovered Graph Reasoning*, 2024, https://towardsdatascience.com/how-the-llm-got-lost-in-the-network-and-discovered-graph-reasoning-e2736bd04efa
- Wu, *Medical Graph RAG: Towards Safe Medical Large Language Model via Graph Retrieval-Augmented Generation*, 2024, https://arxiv.org/abs/2408.04187
- Raieli, *The Convergence of Graph and Vector RAGs: A New Era in Information Retrieval*, 2024, https://medium.com/gitconnected/the-convergence-of-graph-and-vector-rags-a-new-era-in-information-retrieval-b5773a723615
- Sarmah, *HybridRAG: Integrating Knowledge Graphs and Vector Retrieval Augmented Generation for Efficient Information Extraction*, 2024, https://arxiv.org/pdf/2408.04948
- Liang, *Survey of Graph Neural Networks and Applications*, 2022, https://onlinelibrary.wiley.com/doi/10.1155/2022/9261537
- Arora, *A Survey on Graph Neural Networks for Knowledge Graph Completion*, 2020, https://arxiv.org/pdf/2007.12374
- Huang, *Can LLMs Effectively Leverage Graph Structural Information through Prompts, and Why?*, 2023, https://arxiv.org/abs/2309.16595
- Liu, *Evaluating Large Language Models on Graphs: Performance Insights and Comparative Analysis*, 2023, https://arxiv.org/abs/2308.11224

8

Reinforcement Learning and AI Agents

In *Chapters 5–7*, we discussed how to provide our model with access to external memory. This memory was stored in a database of a different type (vector or graph), and through a search, we could look up the information needed to answer a question. The model would then receive all the information that was needed in context and then answer, providing definite and discrete real-world information.

However, as we saw later in *Chapter 7*, LLMs have limited knowledge and understanding of the real world (both when it comes to commonsense reasoning and when it comes to spatial relations).

Humans learn to move in space and interact with the environment through exploration. In a process that is trial and error, we humans learn that we cannot touch fire or how to find our way home. Likewise, we learn how to relate to other human beings through interactions with them. Our interactions with the real world allow us to learn but also to modify our surroundings. The environment provides us with information through perception, information that we process and learn from, and ultimately use to modify the environment. This is a cyclical process in which we sense changes in the environment and respond.

We do not learn all these skills just by reading from a book; it wouldn't be possible. Interaction with the environment, therefore, is critical to learn certain skills and knowledge. Without this, we would find it difficult to do certain tasks. So, we need a system that allows artificial intelligence to interact and learn from the environment through exploration. **reinforcement learning** (**RL**) is a paradigm that focuses on describing how an intelligent agent can take actions in a dynamic environment. RL governs the behavior of an agent, what actions to take in a given environment (and the state of that environment), and how to learn from it.

In this chapter, therefore, we will discuss RL. We will start with some theory on the topic. We will start with a simple case in which an agent needs to understand how to balance exploration with exploitation in order to find the winning strategy to solve a problem. Once the basics are defined, we will describe how we can use a neural network as an agent. We will look at some of the most popular algorithms used nowadays for interacting and learning from the environment. In addition, we will show how an agent can be used to be able to explore an environment (such as training an agent to solve a video game). In the last section, we will discuss the intersection of **large language models** (**LLMs**) and RL.

In this chapter, we'll be covering the following topics:

- Introduction to reinforcement learning
- Deep reinforcement learning
- LLM interactions with RL models

Technical requirements

Most of this code can be run on a CPU, but it is preferable to run it on a GPU. This is especially true when we are discussing how to train an agent to learn how to play a video game. The code is written in PyTorch and uses standard libraries for the most part (PyTorch, OpenAI Gym). The code can be found on GitHub: `https://github.com/PacktPublishing/Modern-AI-Agents/tree/main/chr8`.

Introduction to reinforcement learning

In previous chapters, we discussed a model that learns from a large amount of text. Humans—and increasingly, AI agents—learn best through trial and error. Imagine a child learning to stack blocks or riding a bike. There's no explicit teacher guiding each move; instead, the child learns by acting, observing the results, and adjusting. This interaction with the environment—where actions lead to outcomes and those outcomes shape future behavior—is central to how we learn. Unlike passive learning from books or text, this kind of learning is goal-directed and grounded in experience. To enable machines to learn in a similar way, we need a new approach. This learning paradigm is called RL.

More formally, an infant learns from their interaction with the environment, from the consequential relationship of an action and its effect. A child's learning is not simply exploratory but aimed at a specific goal; they learn what actions must be taken to achieve a goal. Throughout our lives, our learning is often related to our interaction with the environment and how it responds in response to our behavior. These concepts are seen as the basis of both learning theory and intelligence in general.

RL is defined as a branch of machine learning, where a system must make decisions to maximize cumulative rewards in a given situation. Unlike in supervised learning (wherein a model learns from labeled examples) or unsupervised learning (wherein a model learns by detecting patterns in the data), in RL the model learns from experience. In fact, the system is not told what actions it must perform but must explore the environment and find out what actions allow it to have a reward. In more complex situations, these rewards may not be immediate but come only later (e.g., sacrificing a piece in chess but achieving victory later). So, on a general level, we can say that the basics of RL are trial and error and the possibility of delayed reward.

From this, we derive two important concepts that will form the basis of our discussion of RL:

- **Exploration versus exploitation**: The model must exploit previously acquired knowledge to achieve its goal. At the same time, it must explore the environment in order to make better choices in the future. A balance must be struck between these two aspects, because solving a problem may not be the most obvious path. A model therefore must test different types of actions (explore) before it can exploit the best action (exploitation). Even today, choosing the best balance is an open challenge for RL theory. A helpful way to understand this is by imagining someone trying different restaurants in a new city. At first, they might try a variety of places (exploration) to see what's available. After discovering a few favorites, they might start going to the same ones more often (exploitation). But if they always stick to the familiar spots, they might miss out on finding an even better restaurant. The challenge is knowing when to try something new and when to stick with what works—and this is still an open question in RL.

- **Achieving a global goal in an uncertain environment**: RL focuses on achieving a goal without requiring the problem to be reframed into subproblems. Instead, it addresses a classic supervised machine learning challenge, which involves breaking a complex problem into general subproblems and devising an effective schedule. In the case of RL, on the other hand, one directly defines a general problem that an agent must solve. This does not mean that there has to be only one agent but there can be multiple agents with a clear goal interacting with each other. A relatable example would be learning to commute efficiently in a new city. At first, you don't break the task into subproblems like "learn the bus schedule," "estimate walking time," or "optimize weather exposure." Instead, you treat the goal as a whole: get to work on time every day. Through trial and error—taking different routes, trying trains versus buses, adjusting for traffic—you learn which options work best. Over time, you build a strategy without ever explicitly labeling every part of the problem. If you live with roommates or friends who are doing the same, you might exchange tips or compete for the fastest route, just like multiple agents interacting in RL.

There are several elements that are present in an RL system: an **agent**, the **environment**, a **state**, a **policy**, a **reward signal**, and a **value function**. The agent is clearly the learner or decision-maker (the model that interacts with the environment, makes decisions, and takes actions). The environment, on the other hand, is everything that the environment interacts with. A state represents a particular condition or configuration of the environment at a certain time (for example, the state of the pieces on a chessboard before a move). Given a state, the agent must make choices and choose an action to take. Not all space is always observable; our agent can only have access to a partial description of the state. For example, a robotic agent navigating a maze can only get information through the camera and thus observe only what is in front of it. The information obtained from the camera is an observation, so the model will use only a subset of the state.

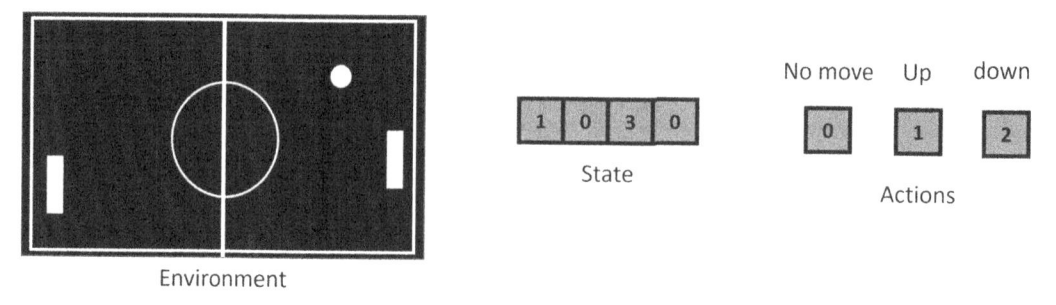

Figure 8.1 – Representation of elements in the RL system

In the preceding figure, we can see how the environment (in this case, the game screen) is represented in vector form (this is the state). Also, the three possible actions are represented in this case with a scalar. This allows us to be able to train an algorithm.

Actions are the possible decisions or moves that an agent can conduct in an environment (the pieces on the chessboard can only move in certain directions: a bishop only diagonally, the rook vertically or horizontally, and so on). The action set can be discrete (movements in the maze) but also a continuous action space (in this case, it will be real-value vectors). These actions are part of a strategy to achieve a certain goal, according to the state of the environment and policy.

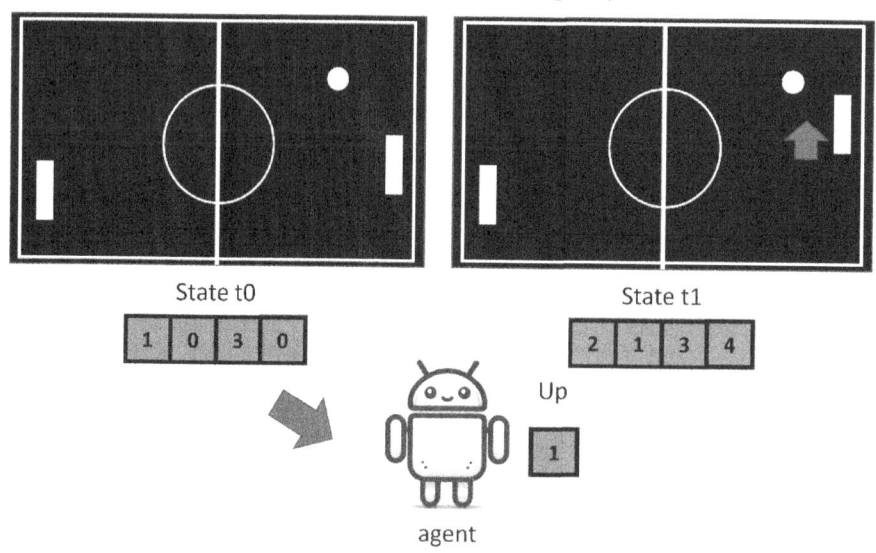

Figure 8.2 – Interaction of the agent with the environment selecting an action

In the preceding figure, we can see that time 0 (*t0*) corresponds to a state *t0*; if our agent acts with a move, this changes the environment. At time *t1*, the environment will be different and therefore we will have a different state, *t1*.

The **policy** defines how an agent behaves at a certain time. Given, then, the state of the environment and the possible actions, the policy maps the action to the state of the system. The policy can be a set of rules, a lookup table, a function, or something else. The policy can also be stochastic by specifying a probability for each action. In a sense, policy is the heart of RL because it determines the agent's behavior. In psychology, this can be defined as a set of stimulus-response rules. For example, a policy might be to eat an opponent's piece whenever the opportunity arises. More often, a policy is parameterized: the output of the policy is a computable function that depends on a set of parameters. One of the most widely used systems is a neural network whose parameters are optimized with an optimization algorithm.

The **reward** is a positive or negative signal received from the environment. It is another critical factor because it provides a goal to the agent at each time step. This reward is used to define both the local and global objectives of an agent. In other words, at each time step, the agent receives a signal from the environment (usually a single number), and in the long run, the agent's goal is to optimize this reward. The reward then allows us to determine whether the model is behaving correctly or not and allows us to understand the difference between positive and negative events, to understand our interaction with the environment and the appropriate response to the state of the system. For example, losing a piece can be considered a local negative reward, and winning the game a global reward. The reward is often used to change the policy and calibrate it in response to the environment.

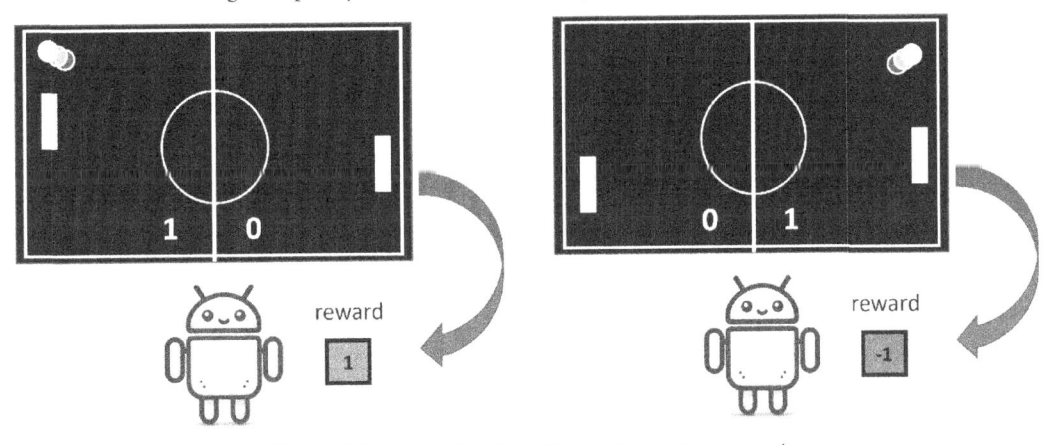

Figure 8.3 – Example of positive and negative reward

The reward, though, gives us information about what is right in the immediate moment while a **value function** defines what is the best approach in the long run. In more technical terms, the value of a state is the total amount of reward that an agent can expect to get in the future, starting from that state (for example, how many points in a game the agent can collect starting from that position). In simple words, the value function helps us understand what happens if we consider that state and subsequent states, and what is likely to happen in the future. There is, however, a dependence between rewards and value; without the former, we cannot calculate the latter, despite that our real goal is value. For example, sacrificing a piece has a low reward but may ultimately be the key to winning the game. Clearly, establishing a reward is much easier, while it is difficult to establish a value function because we have to take into account not only the current state, but all previous observations conducted by the agent.

A classic example of RL is an agent who has to navigate a maze. A state S defines the agent's position in the maze; this agent has a possible set of actions A (move east, west, north, or south). The policy π indicates what action the agent must take in a certain state. A reward R can be a penalty when the agent chooses an action that is not allowed (slamming on a wall, for example), and the value is getting out of the maze. In *Figure 8.4*, we have a depiction of the interactions between an agent and its environment:

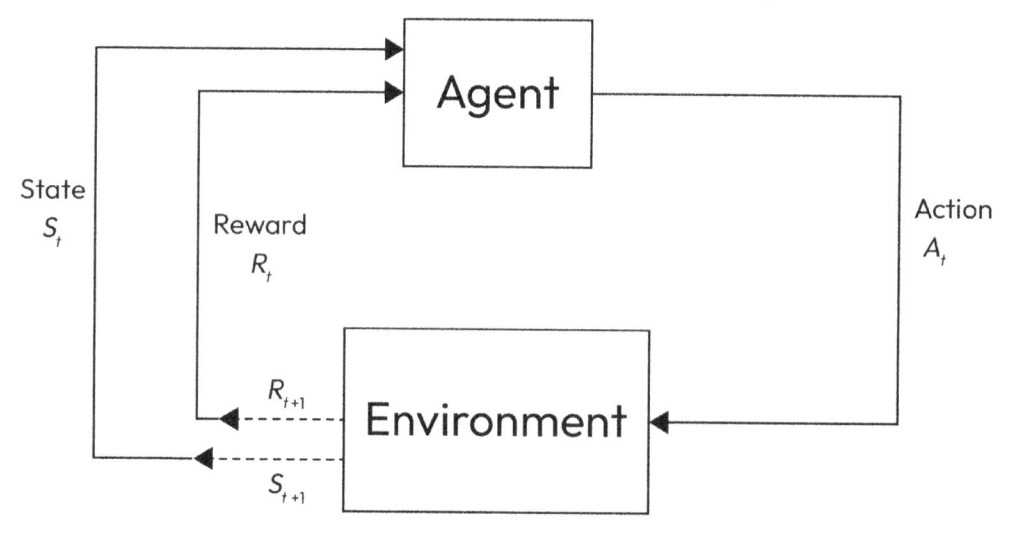

Figure 8.4 – Overview model of reinforcement learning system
(https://arxiv.org/pdf/2408.07712)

At a given time step (t), an agent observes the state of the environment (S_t), chooses an action (A_t) according to policy π, and receives a reward (R_t). At this point, the cycle repeats at the new state (S_{t+1}). The policy can be static or updated at the end of each cycle.

In the next section, we will begin to discuss an initial example of RL, starting with the classic multi-armed bandit.

The multi-armed bandit problem

The **k-armed bandit problem** is perhaps the most classic example to introduce RL. RL is needed for all those problems in which a model must learn from its actions rather than be instructed by a positive example. In the k-armed bandit problem, we have a slot machine with n independent arms (bandits), and each of these bandits has its own rigged probability distribution of success. Each time we pull an arm, we have a stochastic probability of either receiving a reward or failing. At each action, we have to choose which lever to pull, and the rewards are what we gain. The goal is to maximize our expected total reward over a certain period of time (e.g., 1,000 actions or time steps). In other words, we have to figure out which levers give us the best payoff, and we will maximize our actions on them (i.e., we will pull them more often).

The problem may appear simple, but it is far from trivial. Our agent does not have access to the true bandit probability distribution and must learn the most favorable bandits through trial and error. Moreover, as simple as this problem is, it has similarities to several real-world case scenarios: choosing the best treatment for a patient, A/B testing, social media influence, and so on. At each time step t, we can select an A_t action and get the corresponding reward (R_t). The value of an arbitrary action a, defined as $q_*(a)$, is the expected reward if we selected this action at time step t:

$$q_*(a) = \mathbb{E}[R_t \mid A_t = a]$$

If we knew the value of each action, we would have practically solved the problem already (we would always select the one with the highest value). However, we do not know the value of an action, but we can calculate an estimated value, defined as $Q_{t(a)}$, which we wish to be close to $q^*(a)$. At each time step, we have estimated values $Q_{t(a)}$ that are greater than the others; selecting these actions (pulling the arms) is called greedy actions and exploiting the current knowledge. Conversely, selecting an action with a lower estimated value is referred to as exploration (because it allows us to explore what happens with other actions and thus improve our estimation of these actions).

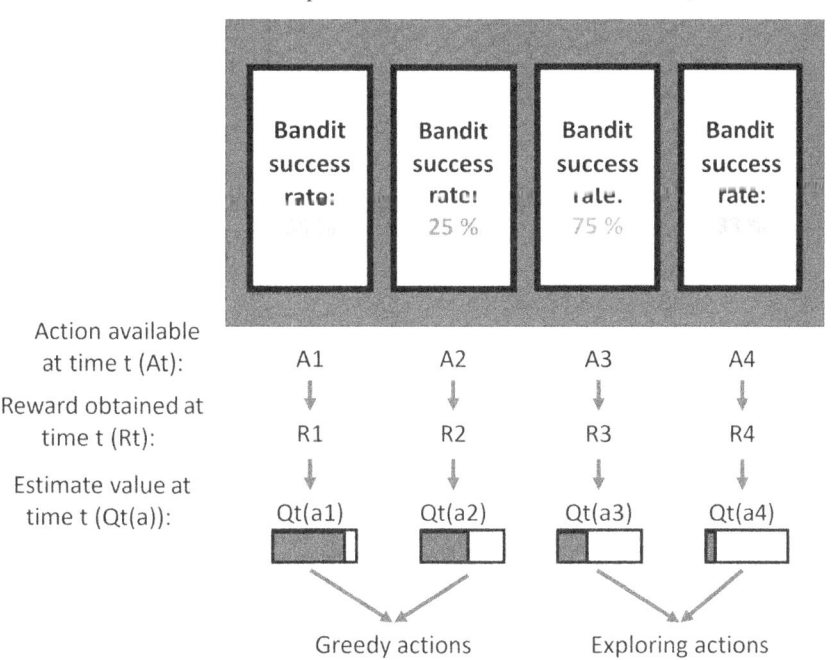

Figure 8.5 – Multi-arm bandit

Exploring may bring a decrease in gain in later steps but guarantees a greater gain in the long run. This is because our estimation may not be correct. Exploring allows us to correct the estimated value for an action. Especially in the early steps, it is more important to explore so that the system can understand which actions are best. In the final steps, the model should exploit the best actions. For this, we need a system that allows us to balance exploration toward exploitation.

To get an initial estimate of value, we can take an average of the rewards that are received:

$$Q_t(a) = \frac{\text{sum of rewards when the action } a \text{ is taken prior to time step } t}{\text{number of times the action } a \text{ is taken prior to time step } t} = \frac{\sum_{i=1}^{t-1} R_i \cdot 1_{\{A_i=a\}}}{\sum_{i=1}^{t-1} 1_{\{A_i=a\}}}$$

In this simple equation, 1 represents a variable that indicates whether the action was used at the time step (1 if used, 0 if not used).

$$1_{\{A_i=a\}} = \begin{cases} 1 \text{ if action } a \text{ is taken at time step } i \\ 0 \text{ otherwise} \end{cases}$$

If the action has never been used, the denominator would be zero; to avoid the result being infinite, we use a default value (e.g., 0). If the number of steps goes to infinity, the estimated value should converge to the true value. Once these estimated values are obtained, we can choose the action. The easiest way to select an action is to choose the highest value (greedy action). The `arg max` function does exactly that:

$$A_t = \arg\max_a Q_t(a)$$

As we said before, we don't always want to choose greedy actions, but we want the model to explore other actions as well. For this, we can introduce a probability ε, so that the agent will select from the other actions with equal probability. In simple words, the model almost always selects the greedy action, but with a probability ε, it selects one of the other actions (regardless of its value). By increasing the number of steps, the other actions will also be tested (at infinity, they will be tested an infinite number of times) ensuring the convergence of Q to q^*. Similarly, the probability of selecting the best action converges to $1 - \varepsilon$. This method is called the **ε-greedy** method, and it allows for some balancing between exploitation and exploration.

To give a simple example, we can imagine a 10-armed bandit ($k=10$) where we have action values q^*, where we have a normal distribution to represent the true value of each action. Here, we have plotted 1,000 examples:

Figure 8.6 – Action value distribution

In the following example, we compare different ε-greedy methods. The rewards increase with agent experience and then go to plateaus. The pure greedy method is suboptimal in comparison to methods that also allow exploration. Similarly, choosing an ε constant that is too high ($\varepsilon=0.5$) leads to worse results than a pure greedy method.

Figure 8.7 – Average rewards for time step for different greedy methods

To investigate this phenomenon, we can look at the optimal choice by the agent (*Figure 8.8*).

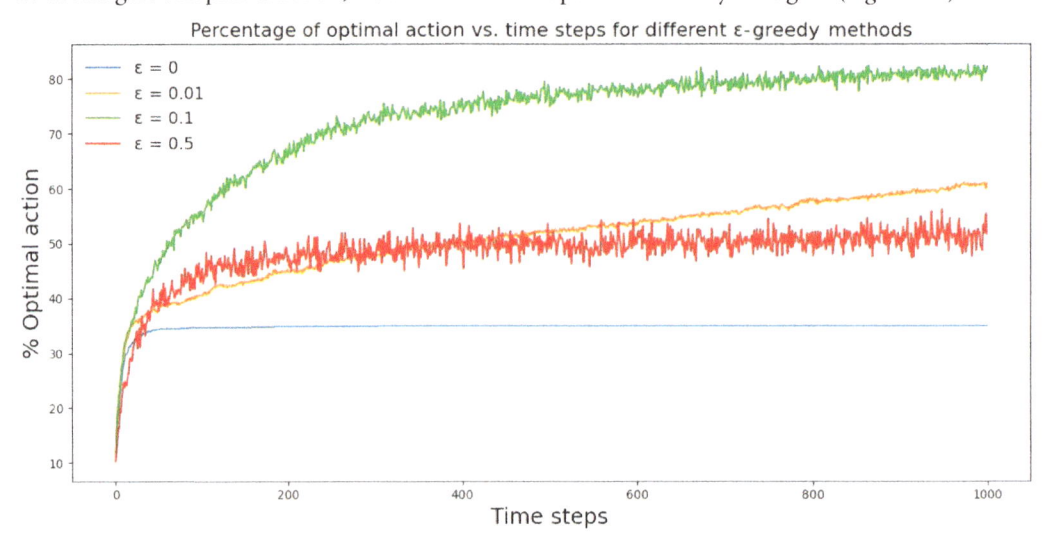

Figure 8.8 – Percentage optimal choice for time step for different greedy methods

The greedy method chooses the optimal choice only one-third of the time, while a method that includes some exploration selects the optimal choice 80% of the time (ε=0.1)%. This result shows that an agent that can also explore the environment achieves better results (can recognize the optimal action), while an agent that is greedy in the long run will choose actions that are suboptimal. In addition, ε-greedy methods find the optimal action faster than greedy methods.

In this case, we explored simple methods, where ε is constant. In some variants, ε decreases with the number of steps, allowing the agent to shift focus from exploration to exploitation once the environment has been sufficiently explored. ε-greedy methods work best in almost all cases, especially when there is greater uncertainty (e.g., greater variance) or when the system is nonstationary.

The system we have seen so far is not efficient when we have a large number of samples. So, instead of taking the average of observed rewards, we can use an incremental method (the one most widely used today). For an action selected i times, the reward will be R_i, and we can calculate the estimated value Q_n as:

$$Q_n = \frac{R_1 + R_2 + \cdots + R_n}{n-1}$$

At this point, we do not have to recollect the average each time but can keep a record of what was calculated and simply conduct an update incrementally in this way:

$$Q_{n+1} = Q_n + \frac{1}{n}\left[R_n - Q_n\right]$$

This can be seen simply as a kind of stepwise adjustment of the expected value:

$$Estimated_{new} \leftarrow Estimated_{new} + step\_size \left[Target - Estimated_{old} \right]$$

In fact, we can see [*Target - estimated*$_{old}$] as a kind of error in the estimation that we are trying to correct step by step and bring closer to the real target. The agent is trying to move the value estimation to the real value.

We can test this incremental implementation, and we can see how, after an initial exploratory phase, the agent begins to exploit optimal choice:

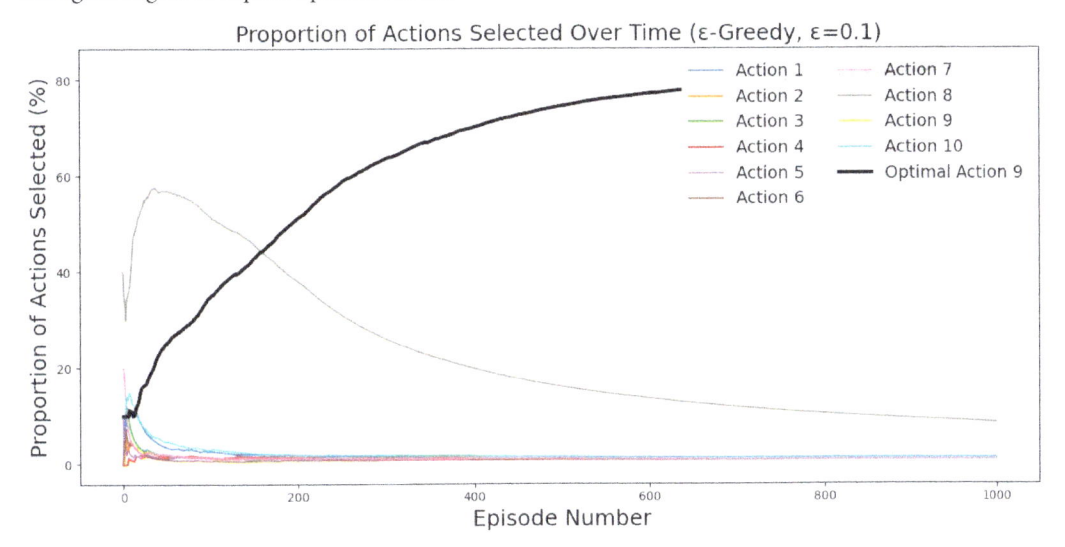

Figure 8.9 – Incremental implementation

1/n can be replaced by a fixed step size parameter α.

$$Q_{n+1} = Q_n + \alpha \left[R_n - Q_n \right]$$

Using α not only simplifies the calculation but also reduces the bias inherent in this approach. In fact, the choice of the initial value estimation for an action, $Q_{1(a)}$, can significantly influence early decisions and convergence behavior α also allows you to handle non-stationary problems better (where the reward probability changes over time). The initial expected values are in general set to 0, but choose values greater than 0. This alternative is called the optimistic greedy strategy; these optimistic values stimulate the agent to explore the environment more (even when we use a pure greedy approach with $\varepsilon=0$). The disadvantage is that we have to test different values for the initial Q, and in practice, almost all practitioners set it to 0 for convenience.

By testing the optimistic greedy method, we can see that it behaves similarly to the ε-greedy method:

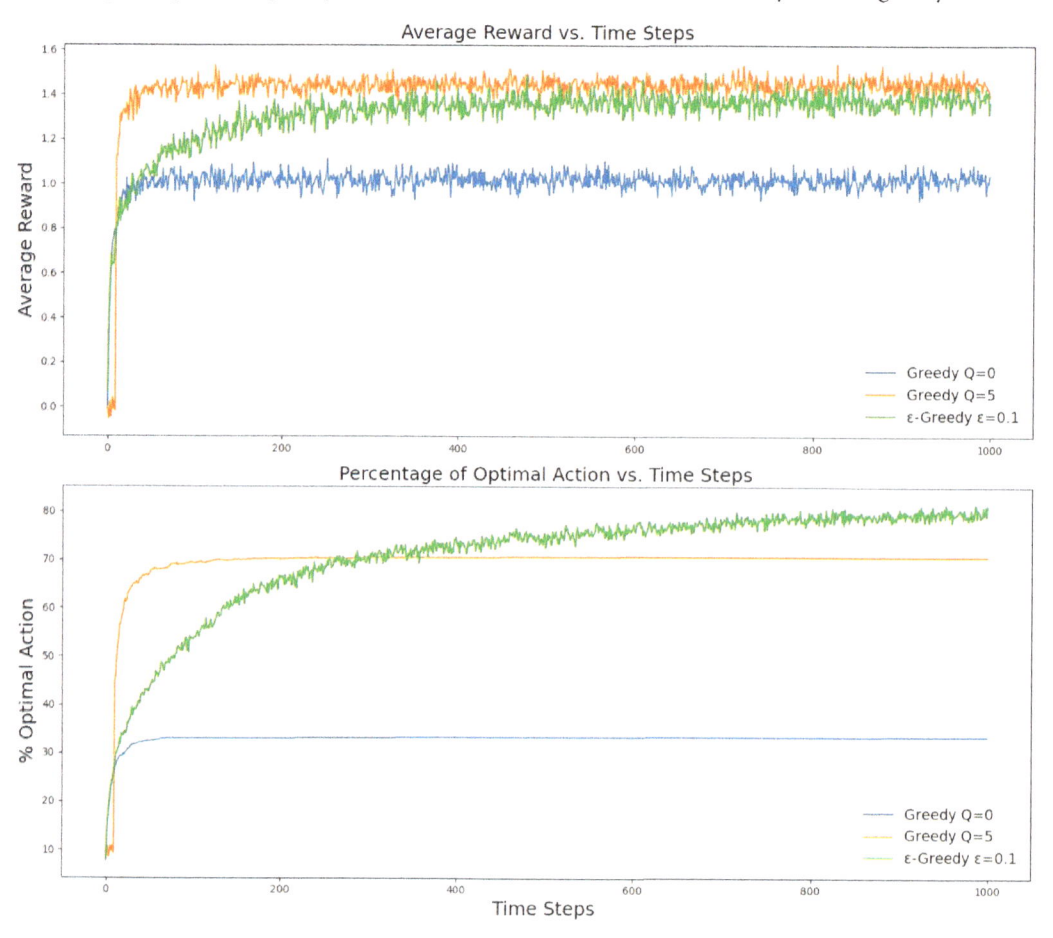

Figure 8.10 – Optimistic greedy versus the ε-greedy method

In non-stationary problems, α can be set to give greater weight to recent rewards than to prior ones.

One final note: so far we have chosen greedy actions for their higher estimated value. In contrast, we have chosen non-greedy actions randomly. Instead of choosing them randomly, we can select them based on their potential optimality and uncertainty. This method is called **Upper Confidence Bound (UCB)**, where an action A is selected based on:

$$A_t = \arg\max_a \left[Q_t(a) + c\sqrt{\frac{\ln t}{N_t(a)}} \right]$$

where $ln(t)$ represents the natural logarithm of t, $c > 0$ controls exploration, and N_t is the number of times an action A has been tested. This approach means that all actions will be tested but actions that have a lower estimate value (and have been tested frequently) will be chosen again in a decreasing manner. Think of it as choosing between different restaurants. UCB helps you balance between going to the one you already like (high estimated value) and trying out others that might be better but haven't visited much yet (high uncertainty). Over time, it naturally reduces exploration of poorly performing options while continuing to test under-explored but potentially good ones. UCB works very well, though it is difficult to apply in approaches other than multi-armed bandits.

As you can see, UCB generally gives better results:

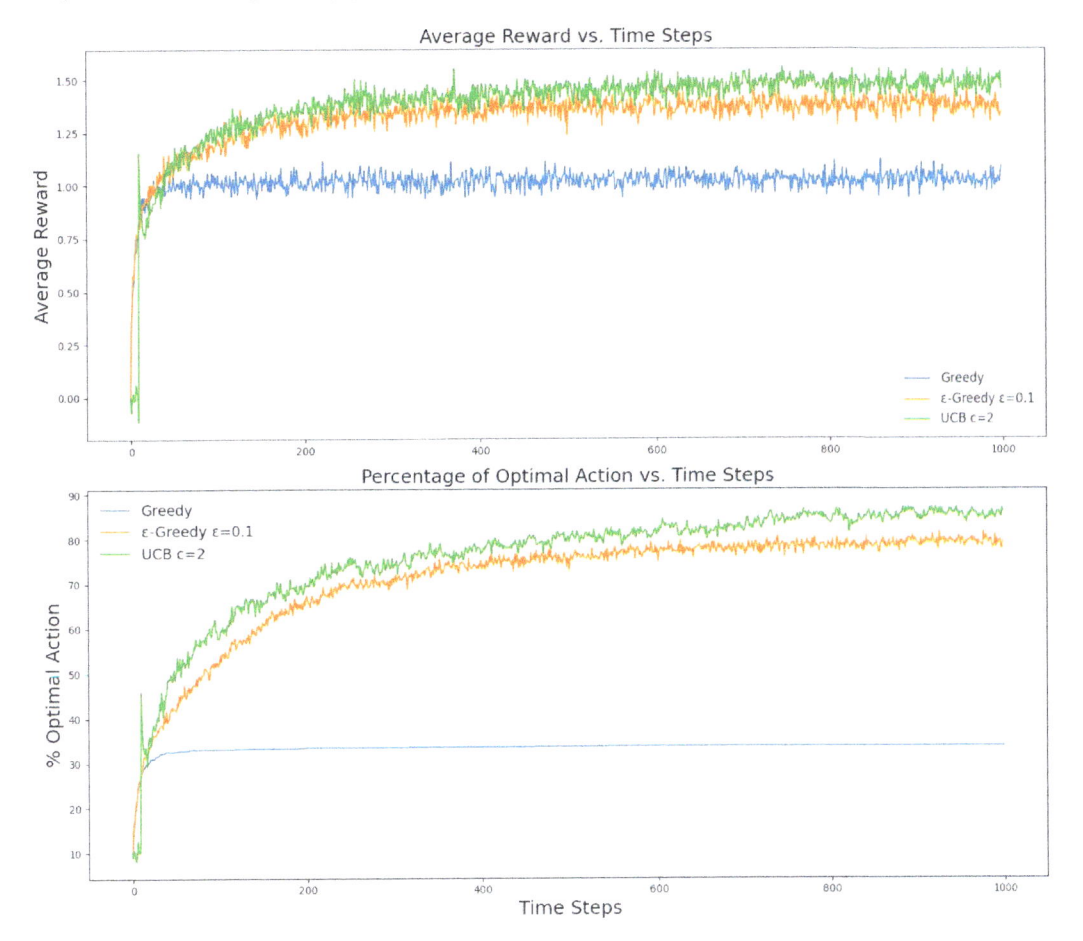

Figure 8.11 – UCB improvements on greedy methods

Multi-armed bandit is a classic example of RL, but it allows one to begin to understand how RL works.

Multi-armed bandit has been used for several applications, but it is a simplistic system that cannot be applied to different real-world situations. For example, in a chess game, the goal is not to eat the chess pieces but to win the game. Therefore, in the next subsection, we will begin to look at methods that take into account a purpose farther back in time than immediate gain.

Markov decision processes

Markov decision processes (**MDPs**) are problems where actions impact not only immediate rewards but also future outcomes. In MDPs then, delayed reward has much more weight than what we saw in the multi-armed bandit problem, but also in deciding the appropriate action for different situations.

Imagine you are navigating a maze. Each intersection or hallway you enter is a state, and every turn you make is an action that changes your state. Some paths lead you closer to the exit (the final reward), while others might take you in circles or into dead ends. The reward for each move may not be immediate—you only get the big reward when you reach the end. So, every action you take needs to consider how it impacts your chances of reaching the goal later on.

In MDPs, this idea is formalized: the agent must decide the best action in each state, not just for instant rewards, but for maximizing long-term success, which makes them more complex than simpler problems such as the multi-armed bandit, where only immediate rewards are considered.

Previously we were just estimating $q^*(a)$. Now, we want to estimate the value of action a in the presence of state s, $q^*(s,a)$. At each time step, the agent receives a representation of the environment S_t and performs an action A_t, receives a reward R, and moves to a new state S_{t+1}. It can be seen that the agent's action can change the state of the environment.

In a finite MDP, the set of states, actions, and rewards contains a finite number of elements. The variables R and S are probability distributions that depend on both the previous state and the action. We can describe the dynamics of this system using the state-transition probability function $p(s', r \mid s, a)$:

$$p(s', r \mid s, a) = \Pr\{S_t = s', R_{t=r} \mid S_{t-1} = s, A_{t-1} = a\}$$

In other words, state and reward depend on the previous state and the previous action. At each time step, the new state and reward will derive from the previous cycle. This will repeat a finite series of events. So, each state will summarize all the previous information (for example, in tic-tac-toe, the new system configuration gives us information about the previous moves) and is said to be a Markov state and possess the Markov property. The advantage of a Markov state is that each state possesses all the information we need to predict the future. The preceding function describes to us how one state evolves into another as we perform actions. An RL problem that respects this property is called an MDP. So, from this function, we can derive anything we care about the environment. We can then derive state-transition probabilities:

$$p(s' \mid s, a) = \Pr\{S_t = s' \mid S_{t-1} = s, A_{t-1} = a\} = \sum_{r \in R} p(s', r \mid s, a)$$

We can also derive the expected reward for state-action pairs:

$$r(s, a) = \mathbb{E}[R_t \mid S_{t-1} = s, A_{t-1} = a] = \sum_{r \in R} r \sum_{s \in S} p(s', r \mid s, a)$$

And we can derive the expected rewards for state-action-next-state triples:

$$r(s, a, s') = \mathbb{E}[R_t \mid S_{t-1} = s, A_{t-1} = a, S_t = s'] = \sum_{r \in R} r \frac{p(s', r \mid s, a)}{p(s' \mid s, a)}$$

This shows us the flexibility of this framework. A brief note is that t does not need to be time steps but a sequence of states (a series of decisions, movements of a robot, and so on) making MDP a flexible system. After all, in MDPs, every problem can be reduced to three signals: actions, states, and rewards. This allows us a better abstraction to represent goal-oriented learning.

The goal for an agent is clearly to maximize cumulative reward over a long period of time (rather than immediate gain). This system has been shown to be very flexible because much of the problem can be formalized in this way (one just has to find a way to define what the rewards are so that the agent learns how to maximize them). One note is that agents try to maximize the reward in any way possible; if the goal is not well defined, it can lead to unintended results (e.g., in chess, the goal is to win the game; if the reward is to eat a piece and not to win the game, the agent will try to maximize the pieces eaten even when it might lead to losing the game).

This can be better expressed formally, where G is the cumulative sum of rewards received from step t and later:

$$G_t = R_{t+1} + R_{t+2} + \ldots + R_T$$

Our goal is thus to maximize G. This is easier to define for a sequence where we clearly must have an end (e.g., a game where only a defined number of moves can be made). A defined sequence of steps is called an episode, and the last state is called a terminal state. Note that each episode is independent of the other (losing one game does not affect the outcome of the next). This is, of course, not always possible; there are also definite continuous tasks where there is no net end (a robot moving in an environment), for which the previous equation does not work. In this case, we can use a so-called discount rate γ. This parameter allows us to decide the agent's behavior: when γ is near 0, the agent will try to maximize immediate rewards, while approaching 1, the agent considers future rewards with greater weight:

$$G_t = R_{t+1} + \gamma R_{t+2} + \gamma^2 R_{t+3} + \ldots = \sum_{k=0}^{\infty} \gamma^k R_{t+k+1}$$

As we saw in the *multi-armed bandit problem* section, we can estimate value functions (how good it is for an agent to be in a given state). The value of a state S considering a policy π, is the expected return starting from S and following the policy π from that time:

$$v_\pi(s) = \mathbb{E}_\pi[G_t \mid S_t = s] = \mathbb{E}_\pi\left[\sum_{k=0}^{\infty} \gamma^k R_{t+k+1} \mid S_t = s\right] \text{ for all } s \in S$$

This is called the state-value function for the policy π, and G_t is the expected return. Similarly, we can define the value of taking action A in state S under policy π:

$$q_\pi(s, a) = \mathbb{E}_\pi[G_t \mid S_t = s, A_t = a] = \mathbb{E}_\pi\left[\sum_{k=0}^{\infty} \gamma^k R_{t+k+1} \mid S_t = s, A_t = a\right]$$

This is called the action-value function for policy π. We can estimate these functions by experience (interaction with the environment), and at infinity, they should approach the true value. Methods like this where we conduct averaging of many random samples of actual returns are called Monte Carlo methods.

For efficiency, we can rewrite it in a recursive form (using discounting):

$$v_\pi(s) = \mathbb{E}_\pi[G_t | S_t = s] = \mathbb{E}_\pi[R_{t+1} + \gamma G_{t+1} | S_t = s] = \sum_a \pi(a|s) \sum_{s',r} p(s', r | s, a)[r + \gamma v_\pi(s')] \text{ for all } s \in S$$

This simplified form is called the Bellman equation. This can be represented as thinking forward to the next state from the previous state. From a state with a policy, we choose an action and get a reward (or not) with a given probability. The Bellman equation conducts the average of these probabilities, giving a weight to the possibility of their occurrence. This equation is the basis of many great RL algorithms.

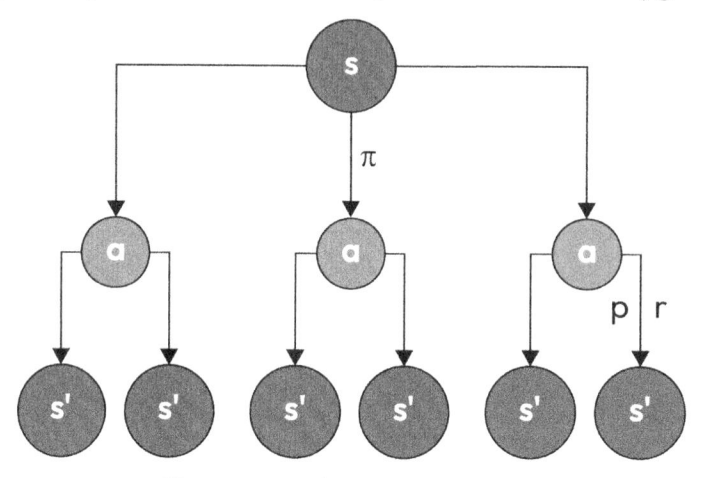

Figure 8.12 – Bellman backup diagram

Now that we have both state-value functions $v\pi(s)$ and action-value functions $q\pi(s, a)$, we can evaluate policies and choose the best ones. Action-value functions allow us to choose the best action relative to the state. Consider, for example, a case of a Texas Hold'em poker game. A player has $100 and must choose the strategy starting from the state π. The strategy π_1 has a state value function that returns 10, while π_2 has a return of -2. This means that the first strategy brings an expected gain of 10, while π_2 brings an expected loss of 2. Given a state s, the player wants to figure out which action to choose. For example, choosing whether to bet 10 or 5, $q_\pi(s, a)$ tells us what the expected cumulative reward is from this action. So, the preceding equations allow us to figure out which action or strategy to choose to maximize the reward.

From *Figure 8.12*, it can be understood that solving an RL task means finding an optimal policy that succeeds in collecting many rewards over the long run. For MDPs, it is possible to define an optimal policy because we can evaluate whether one policy is better than another if it has a higher expected return for all states $v\pi(s)$. π^* denotes the optimal policy and is the one that has the maximum value function over all possible policies:

$$v_*(s) = \max_\pi v_\pi(s) \text{ for all } s \in S$$

The optimal policies share the same optimal action-value function q^*, which is defined as the maximum action-value function over all possible policies:

$$q_*(s, a) = \max_\pi q_\pi(s, a) \text{ for all } s \in S$$

The relationship between these two functions can be summarized as follows:

$$q_*(s, a) = \mathbb{E}\left[R_{t+1} + \gamma v_*(S_{t+1}) \mid S_t = s, A_t = a\right]$$

The equation expresses the cumulative return given a state-action pair. Optimal value functions are an ideal state in RL, though, and it is difficult to find optimal policies, especially when tasks are complex or computationally expensive. RL therefore tries to approximate them, for example, by using **dynamic programming** (**DP**). The purpose of DP is to use value functions to search for good policies (even if not exact solutions). At this point, we can derive Bellman optimality equations for the optimal state-value function $v^*(s)$ and the optimal action-value function $q_*(s, a)$:

$$v_*(s) = \max_a \mathbb{E}\left[R_{t+1} + \gamma v_*(S_{t+1}) \mid S_t = s, A_t = a\right]$$

$$= \max_a \sum_{s',r} p(s', r \mid s, a)\left[r + \gamma v_* + s'\right]$$

$$q_*(s, a) = \mathbb{E}\left[R_{t+1} + \max_{a'} q^*(S_{t+1}, a') \mid S_t = s, A_t = a\right]$$

$$= \sum_{s',r} p(s', r \mid s, a)\left[r + \gamma \max_{a'} q^*(s', a')\right]$$

For finite MDP, Bellman optimality equations have only one solution, and they can be solved if we know the dynamics of the system. Once we get v^*, it is easy to identify the optimal policy q^*; having an optimal q^*, we can identify the optimal actions. The beauty of v^* is that it allows us to choose the best actions at the moment while still taking into account the long-term goal. Solving these equations for a problem is solving the problem through RL. On the other hand, for many problems, solving them means calculating all possibilities and thus would be too computationally expensive. In other cases, we do not know the dynamics of the environment with certainty or the states do not have Markov properties. However, these equations are the basis of RL, and many methods are approximations of these equations, often using experience from previous states. So, these algorithms do not identify the best policy but an approximation. For example, many algorithms learn optimal actions for the most frequent states but may choose suboptimal actions for infrequent or rare states. The trick is that these choices should not impact the future amount of reward. For example, an agent might still win a game even if it does not make the best move in rare situations.

DP refers to a collection of algorithms that are used to compute the best policy given a perfect model of the environment as an MDP. Now, these algorithms require a lot of computation and the assumption of the perfect model does not always hold. So, these algorithms are not practically used anymore; at the same time, one can define today's algorithms as inspired by DP algorithms, with the purpose of reducing computation and working even when the assumption of a perfect model of the environment does not hold. DP algorithms, in short, are obtained from transforming Bellman equations into update rules to improve the approximation of desired value functions. This allows value functions to be used to organize the search for good policies. To evaluate a policy, we can use the state-value function and evaluate the expected return when following policy π from each state:

$$v_\pi(s) = \mathbb{E}\left[R_{t+1} + \gamma v_\pi(S_{t+1}) \mid S_t = s, A_t = a\right] = \sum_a \pi(a \mid s) \sum_{s',r} p(s', r \mid s, a)\left[r + \gamma v_\pi(s')\right]$$

Calculating the value function for a policy aims to identify better policies. For a state s, we want to know whether we should keep that policy, improve it, or choose another. Remember that the choice of a policy decides what actions an agent will take. To answer the question "is it better to change policy?", we can consider what happens if we choose an action in a state s following policy π:

$$q_\pi(s, a) = \mathbb{E}\left[R_{t+1} + \gamma v_\pi(S_{t+1}) \mid S_t = s, A_t = a\right] = \sum_{s',r} p(s', r \mid s, a)\left[r + \gamma v_\pi(s')\right]$$

A better policy π' should provide us with a better value of $v_\pi(s)$. If π' is less than or equal to $v_\pi(s)$, we can continue the same policy. In other words, choosing actions according to a policy π' that has better $v_\pi(s)$ is more beneficial than another policy π.

In this section, we have seen classic RL algorithms, but none of them use a neural network or other machine learning model. These algorithms work well for simple cases, while for more complex situations we want a more sophisticated and adaptable system. In the next section, we will see how we can integrate neural networks into RL algorithms.

Deep reinforcement learning

Deep reinforcement learning (**deep RL**) is a subfield of RL that combines RL with deep learning. In other words, the idea behind it is to exploit the learning capabilities of a neural network to solve RL problems. In traditional RL, policies and value functions are represented by simple functions. These methods work well with low-dimensional state and action spaces (i.e., when the environment and agent can be easily modeled). When the environment becomes more complex or larger, traditional methods fail to generalize. In deep RL, instead, policies and value functions are represented by neural networks. A neural network can theoretically represent any complex function (Universal Approximation Theorem), and this allows deep RL methods to solve problems with high-dimensional state spaces (such as those presenting images, videos, or continuous tasks). Modeling complex functions thus allows the agent to learn a more generalized and flexible policy that is needed in complex situations where defining a function is impossible with traditional methods. This learning capability has enabled deep RL methods to solve video games, move robots, and more.

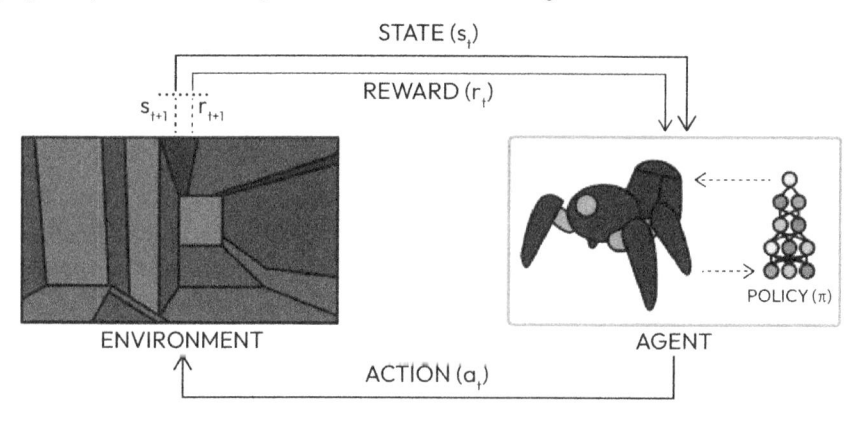

Figure 8.13 – Overview of deep RL (https://arxiv.org/abs/1708.05866)

In the upcoming subsections, we will discuss how to classify these algorithms and what the differences are.

Model-free versus model-based approaches

There are so many methods of deep RL today that it is difficult to make a taxonomy of these models. Nevertheless, deep RL methods can be broadly divided into two main groups: model-free and model-based. This division is represented by the answer to this question: does the agent have access to (or learn) a model of the environment?

- **Model-free methods**: These methods determine the optimal policy or value function without building a model of the environment. These models learn directly from observed states, actions, and rewards. The agent learns directly from trial and error, receives feedback from the environment, and uses this feedback to improve its policy or value estimation. These approaches are usually easier to implement and conduct parameter tuning (they only require observing state-action-reward sequences or transitions). They are also more easily scalable and less computationally complex.

- **Model-based methods**: These methods rely on an internal model of the environment to predict future states and rewards given any state-action pair. This model can be learned or predefined before training. Having the model allows the agent to have similar outcomes and plan actions for future scenarios (e.g., what the future actions of an opponent in a game will be and anticipating them). Model-based approaches have the advantage that they can reduce interaction with the real environment and are better at planning complex tasks. Potentially improved performance comes at the cost of increased complexity (building an accurate model of the environment can be challenging, especially for high-dimensional environments) and increased computational cost.

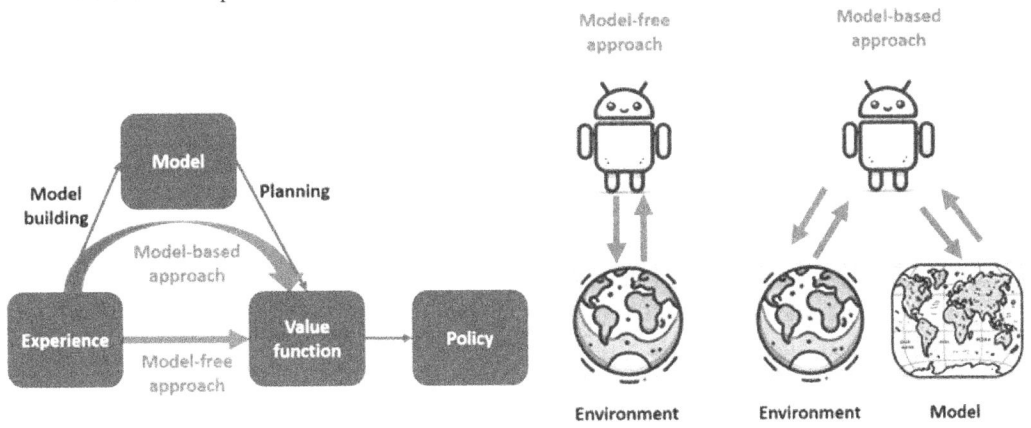

Figure 8.14 – Model-free versus model-based approaches

The primary advantage of a model-based RL method lies in its ability to plan and think ahead. By utilizing a model (in general, a neural network) to simulate the dynamics of the environment, it can predict future scenarios, making it particularly useful in complex environments or situations where decisions need to consider long-term outcomes. For instance, when rewards are sparse or delayed—such as in chess, where the reward is achieved only by winning the game—the model can simulate various paths to optimize the agent's strategy for reaching the reward.

Planning also proves advantageous in dynamic environments. The model can update its internal representation quickly, allowing the agent to adapt its policy without relearning from scratch. This minimizes the need for extensive retraining, as seen in applications such as autonomous driving, where the agent can adjust its strategy without requiring large new datasets. The insights gained from such planning can then be distilled into a learned policy, enhancing the agent's performance over time.

Additionally, simulating interactions with the environment reduces the need for extensive real-world exploration, which is critical in scenarios where interactions are costly, dangerous, or time-intensive, such as in robotics or autonomous vehicles. By leveraging its internal model, the agent can prioritize actions and refine its exploration process to update or improve its understanding of the environment more efficiently.

This then helps the agent optimize for long-term goals because it can simulate the long-term consequences of its actions, monitor its progress toward a more distant horizon, and align its actions with a distant goal.

Model building can be a complicated task. However, a ground-truth model of the environment is not always available to the agent. In this case, the agent is forced to learn only from experience to create its own model. This can then lead to bias in the agent's model. An agent might therefore perform optimally with respect to a learned model but perform terribly (or suboptimally) in the real environment.

On-policy versus off-policy methods

Another important classification in RL is how models learn from experience and whether they learn from the current policy or a different one (they are classified according to the relationship between the policy and the policy update):

- **On-policy methods**: These methods learn from actions learned from the agent's current policy (so the agent both collects data and learns from the same policy). On-policy methods evaluate and improve the policy used to make decisions; this is based on actions taken and rewards received while following the current policy (the agent conducts the policy update by directly evaluating and improving the policy). The agent therefore does not use data from other policies. The advantages are that the agent tends to be more stable and less prone to variance (the optimized policy is, in fact, the one used to interact with the environment). On-policy methods are inefficient because they discard data that is obtained from previous policies (sample inefficiency), limiting their use for complex environments since they would require large amounts of data. In addition, these methods are not very exploratory and therefore less beneficial where more exploration is required (they are favored for environments that are stable). An example is a chatbot that learns to give better answers to user questions: the chatbot uses a specific policy to give answers and optimizes this policy by leveraging feedback received from users. On-policy methods ensure that the learned policy is linked to actions taken by the chatbot and by real interactions with users (this ensures stability).

- **Off-policy methods**: Off-policy methods learn the value of the optimal policy independently of the agent's actions (agents learn from experiences that are generated by a different policy from the one used for learning). So, these methods can learn from past data or data that is generated by other policies. Off-policy methods separate the behavior policy (used to collect data) from the target policy (the policy being learned). In other words, the behavior policy is used to explore the environment while the target policy is used to improve the agent's performance (to ensure more exploratory behavior while learning an optimal target policy). Off-policy methods have higher sample efficiency because they can reuse data and allow for better exploration, which can lead to faster convergence to an optimal policy. On the other hand, they are less stable (because they do not learn from actions that have been taken by the current policy, the discrepancy between behavior policy and target policy can lead to higher variance in updates) and can be much more complex. An example is a music recommendation system that suggests new titles to users and has to explore different genres and new releases. The behavior policy encourages exploration and thus generates data on user preferences, while the target policy seeks to optimize recommendation performance for users. Separating the two policies thus allows experimenting with different recommendation strategies without compromising the quality of the final recommendations. The advantage of these methods is that they allow extensive exploration, which is very useful for complex and dynamic environments.

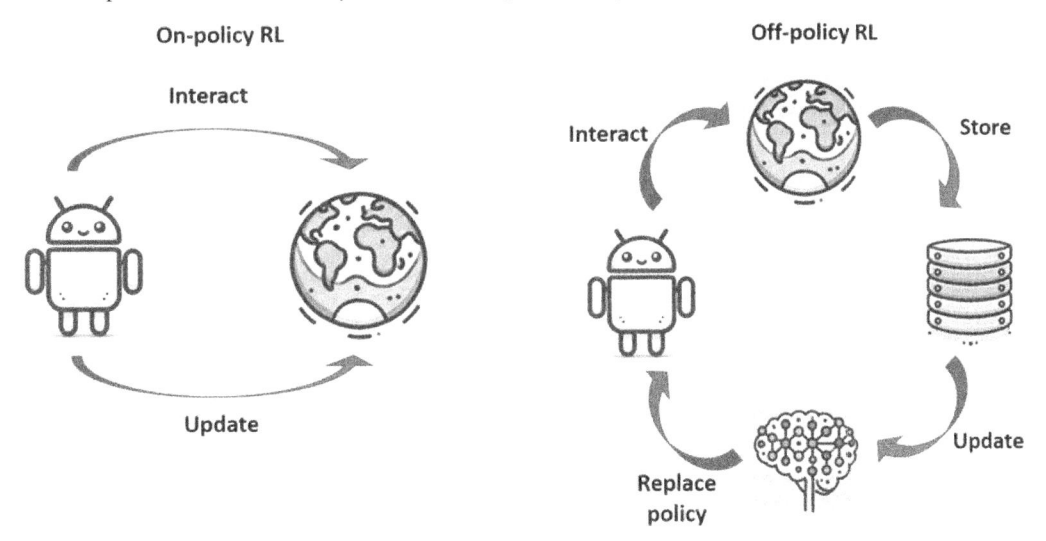

Figure 8.15 – On-policy and off-policy methods

In the next subsection, we will begin to go into detail about how deep RL works.

Exploring deep RL in detail

We'll begin with a definition to better understand deep RL. A state s in a system is usually a vector, matrix, or other tensor. At each time step t, we can describe the environment in the form of a tensor (e.g., the position of the pieces on a chessboard can be represented by a matrix). Similarly, the actions *a* an agent can choose can be represented in a tensor (for example, each action can be associated with a one-hot vector, a matrix, and so on). All of these are data structures that are already commonly seen in machine learning and that we can use as input to a deep learning model.

So far, we have discussed policies generically, but what functions do we use to model them? Very often, we use neural networks. So, in this section, we will actively look at how a neural network can be used in RL algorithms. What we'll see now is based on what we saw in this chapter, but we'll use a neural network to decide what action to take (instead of just a function). As we saw in *Chapter 1*, a neural network is constituted of a series of neurons organized in a series of layers. Neural networks take a tensor as input and produce a tensor as output. In this case, the output of the neural network is the choice of an action. Optimizing the policy, in this case, means optimizing the parameters of the neural network. An RL algorithm based on experience can change the parameters of the policy function so that it produces better results.

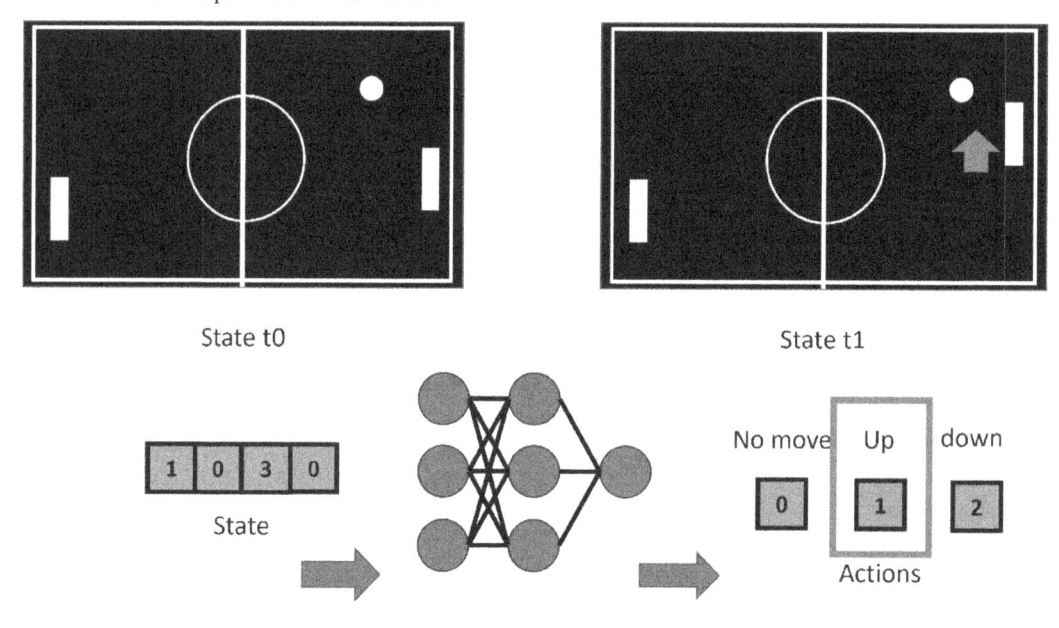

Figure 8.16 – Neural network as an RL policy

Neural networks are well-known deep learning models, and we know how to optimize them. Using gradient-based methods allows us to understand how a change in parameters impacts the outcome of a function. In this case, we want to know how we should update the parameters of our policy *P* (the neural network model) so that we collect more rewards in the future. So, having a function that tells us what the expected rewards are for a policy, we can use the gradient to change the parameters of the policy and thus maximize the return.

Using a neural network as a policy in RL has several advantages:

- Neural networks are highly expressive function approximators, so they can map complex nonlinear relationships between inputs (states) and outputs (actions). This is very useful for complex environments, such as playing video games or controlling robots in 3D environments. In addition, neural networks scale well for environments that have large and complex state and action spaces.
- Neural networks possess the ability to generalize to situations they have not encountered before. This capability makes them particularly useful in handling unexpected state changes, thus promoting adaptability in agents. All this allows neural networks to be flexible and adaptable to a different range of tasks and environments.
- Neural networks can handle actions that are continuous rather than discrete, thus enabling their use in real-world problems (where actions are often not limited to a discrete set).
- Neural networks are versatile. They can be used with different types of data and do not require feature engineering. This is important when the features can be complex or the state representation is complex (sensors, images, video, and so on).
- They can produce a probability distribution and thus can be used with a stochastic policy. This is important when we want to add randomness and encourage exploration.

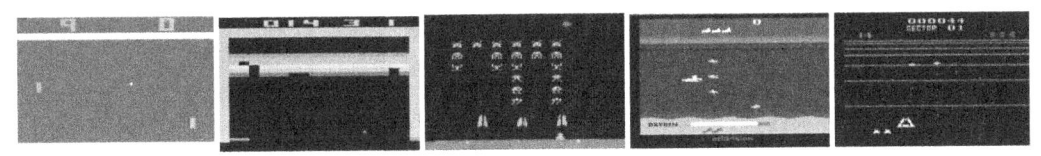

Figure 8.17 – Examples of screenshots where a neural network is used to learn how to play Atari games (https://arxiv.org/abs/1312.5602)

We will now present five different algorithms in order to understand the differences between the different types of approaches (off- and on-policy, model-free, and model-based approaches).

Algorithm	On-policy	Off-policy	Model-free	Model-based
Deep Q-Network (DQN)		yes	yes	
REINFORCE	yes		yes	
Proximal Policy Optimization (PPO)	yes		yes	
Actor critic	yes		yes	
AlphaZero		yes		yes

Figure 8.18 – Summary table of RL approaches

Q-learning and Deep Q-Network (DQN)

Q-learning is a lookup-table-based approach underlying **Deep Q-Network** (**DQN**), an algorithm used by DeepMind to train an agent capable of solving video games. In the Q-learning algorithm, we have a **Q-table of State-Action values**, where we have a row for each state and a column for each action, and each cell contains an estimated Q-value for the corresponding state-action pair. The Q-values are initially set to zero. When the agent receives feedback from interacting with the environment, we iteratively conduct the update of the values (until they converge to the optimal values). Note that this update is conducted using the Bellman equation (the Q-value in the table represents the expected future rewards if the agent takes that action from that state and follows the best strategy afterward).

Q-learning finds the optimal policy by learning the optimal Q-value for each state-action pair. Initially, the agent chooses actions at random, but by interacting with the environment and receiving feedback (reward), it learns which actions are best. During each iteration, it conducts the table update using the Bellman equation. The agent generally chooses the action that has the highest Q-value (greedy strategy), but we can control the degree of exploration (ε-greedy policy). Over time, these estimates become more and more accurate and the model converges to the optimal Q-values.

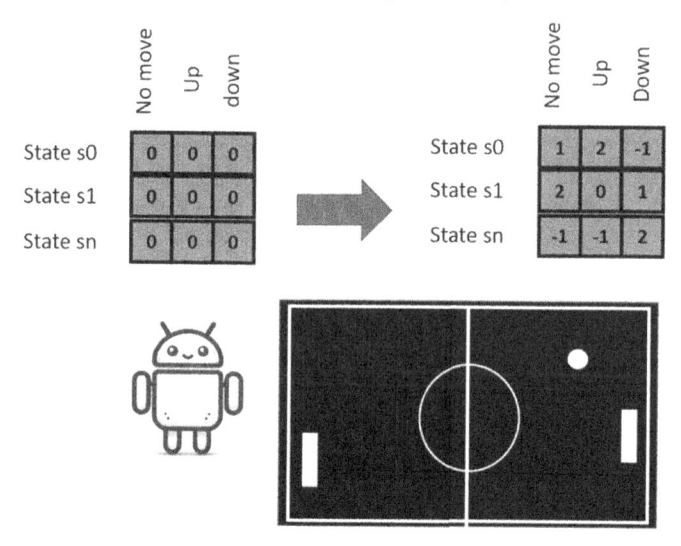

Figure 8.19 – Q learning example

In complex environments, using a table to store values becomes impractical due to the potentially massive size and computational intractability. Instead, we can use a Q-function, which maps state-action pairs to Q-values. Given that neural networks can effectively model complex functions, they can be employed to approximate the Q-function efficiently. By providing as input the state S, the neural network provides as output the Q-value for the state-action pair (in other words, the Q-values for all the actions you can take from that state). The principle is very similar to the Q-learning algorithm. We start with random estimates for the Q-values, explore the environment with an ε-greedy policy, and conduct the update of the estimates.

The DQN architecture consists of three main components: two neural networks (the Q-network and the target network) and an experience replay component. The Q-network (a classical neural network) is the agent that is trained to produce the optimal state-action value. Experience replay, on the other hand, is used to generate data to train the neural network.

The Q-network is trained on multiple time steps and on many episodes, with the aim of minimizing the difference between predicted Q-values and the target Q-values. During the agent's interaction with the environment, each experience (a tuple of state, action, reward, and next state) is stored in this experience replay buffer. During training, random batches of experiences (a mix of old and new experiences) are selected from the buffer to update the Q-network. This allows breaking the correlation between consecutive experiences (helps stabilize the training) and reusing the past experience multiple times (increases data efficiency). The target network is a copy of the Q-network used to generate the target Q-values for training. Periodically, the target network weights are updated (e.g., every few thousand steps) by copying the Q-network weights; this stabilizes the training. During training, the Q-network predicts the Q-value for actions given a state (predicted Q-value) and the target network predicts the target Q-value for all actions given the state. The predicted Q-value, target Q-value, and the observed reward are used to calculate the loss and update the weight of the Q-network.

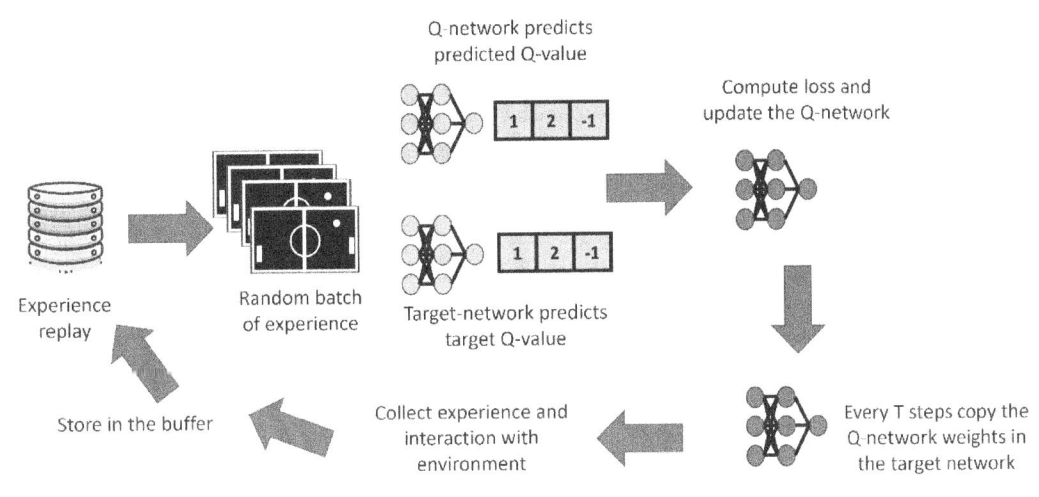

Figure 8.20 – DQN training algorithm

DQN has a number of innovations and advantages:

- Experience replay makes training more stable and efficient. Neural networks usually take a batch of data as input rather than a single state, so during training, the gradient will have less variance and the weights converge more quickly. Experience replay also allows us to reduce noise during training because we can conduct a kind of "shuffling" of experiences and thus better generalization.

- The introduction of a target network mitigates the issue of non-stationary targets, which can cause instability in training. The target network is untrained, so the target Q-values are stable and have few fluctuations.

- DQN is effective with high-dimensional spaces such as images and is able to extract features by itself and learn effective policies. These capabilities enabled DQN to master Atari games by taking raw pixels as input.

There are, of course, also drawbacks:

- Although it is more efficient than Q-learning, DQN still requires a large number of samples to learn effectively; this limits its use for tasks where there is little data (sample inefficiency)

- It is not stable when the action spaces are continuous, while it works well for discrete action spaces

- It is sensitive to the choice of hyperparameters (such as learning rate, replay buffer size, and update frequency of the target network)

The REINFORCE algorithm

DQN focuses on learning the value of an action in different states. **REINFORCE** is instead a policy-based method. These methods learn policy directly, mapping states to actions without learning a value function. The core idea is to optimize policy by maximizing the expected cumulative reward the agent receives over time. REINFORCE is a foundational algorithm for learning how to train agents to handle complex, continuous action spaces.

The policy is represented by a neural network that takes the current state as input and produces a probability distribution over all possible actions (the probability that an agent will perform a certain action). This is called stochastic policy because we do not have an action as output directly, but probabilities. Policy gradient methods try to improve the policy directly (by changing parameters during training) so that the policy produces better results. So, again, we start with a random policy (the neural network weights are initialized randomly) and let the agent act in the environment according to its policy, which causes a trajectory (a series of states and actions) to be produced. If this trajectory collects high rewards, we conduct an update of the weights so that this trajectory is more likely to be produced in the future. If, on the contrary, the agent performs poorly, the update of the weights will be directed to make that trajectory less likely.

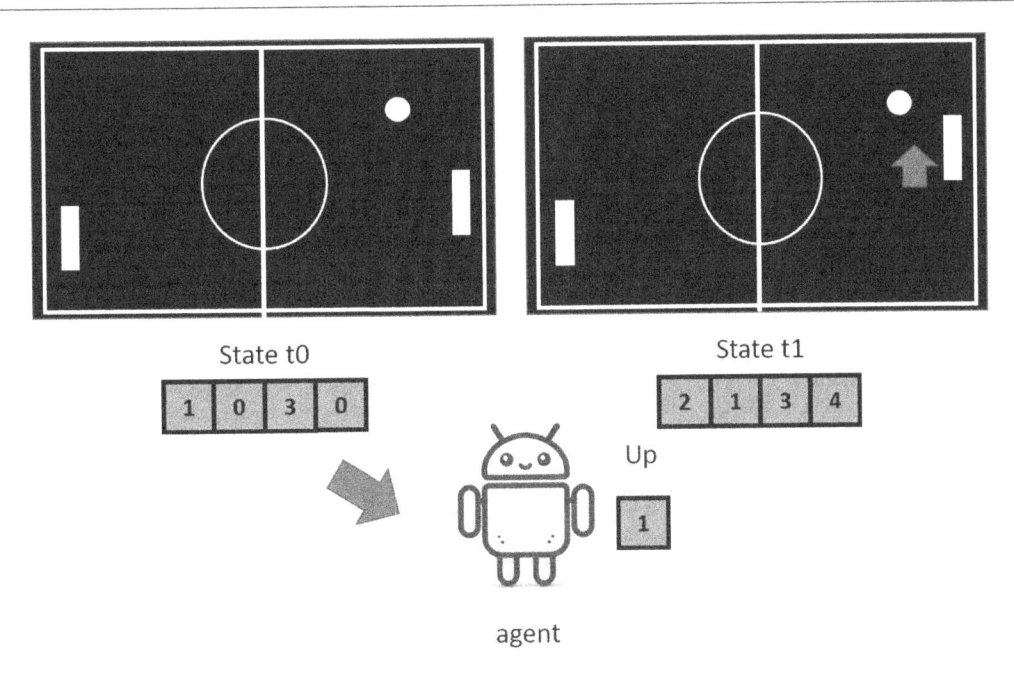

Figure 8.21 – Example of trajectory

So, the first step in this process is to initialize a neural network (policy P) with its parameters θ. Since these weights are initially random, the policy for a state as input will lead to random actions. We then generate a trajectory τ, letting the agent interact with the environment. Starting from state s_0, we let the agent move according to policy P with the parameters θ. In practice, state S is given as input to the neural network and generates a distribution of actions. We select an action a_0 sampling from this distribution. This process is repeated for as long as possible (e.g., till the end of the game), the set of states and actions being our trajectory.

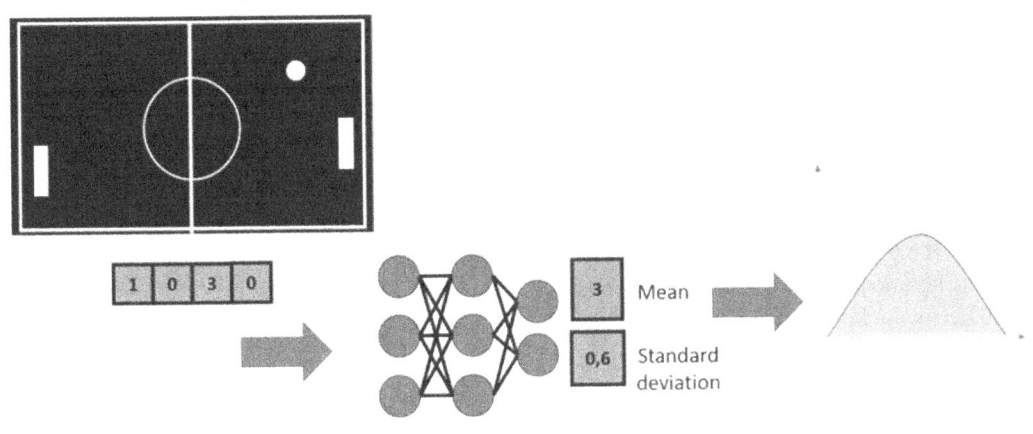

Figure 8.22 – Getting a distribution from a neural network

During the trajectory, we collect rewards (called reward-to-go or also return G_t). The return is the total cumulative reward received from time step t to the end of the episode, discounted by a factor γ. The discount factor determines how important future rewards are in relation to immediate rewards. In this case, we have a function that gives us the expected return for a given policy and we want to maximize it. So, we calculate the gradient, and via gradient ascent, we modify the parameters of our neural network.

REINFORCE is conceptually simple and easy to implement, suitable for continuous action spaces (since it directly learns a policy), and enables end-to-end learning (the algorithm learns directly from raw data). Some of the challenges with this algorithm, however, are the high variance in policy updates (it relies on full episodes being returned and updates can be noisy and unstable), it requires a lot of data (a large number of episodes are needed because it discards data after each update and does not reuse experiences), it is not suitable for environments where data is expensive, and it does not work well when there are delayed rewards.

Note that the REINFORCE algorithm is an on-policy algorithm since the policy receives updates only based on experiences collected with the same policy. At each iteration, the agent uses the updated policy and collects experience with it for the update. In the case of off-policy methods, experiences collected with other policies are also used. This is, for example, what we saw with DQN, where we were using experiences in the batch that were collected with a different policy.

Proximal Policy Optimization (PPO)

Proximal Policy Optimization (PPO) is one of the most widely cited and used algorithms in RL. Introduced by OpenAI in 2017, PPO was designed to balance the simplicity of policy gradient methods, such as REINFORCE, with the stability of more complex algorithms, such as **Trust Region Policy Optimization (TRPO)**. In essence, PPO is a practical and efficient algorithm that performs well on benchmarks while being relatively easy to implement and tune.

PPO shares similarities with REINFORCE but includes important improvements that make training much more stable. One of the challenges in policy-based methods is the choice of hyperparameters (especially the learning rate) and the risk of unstable weight updates. The key innovation of PPO is to ensure that policy updates are not too large, as this could destabilize training. PPO achieves this by using a constraint on the objective function that limits how much the policy can change in a single update, thereby avoiding drastic changes in the network weights.

A significant problem with traditional policy gradient methods is their inability to recover from poor updates. If a policy performs poorly, the agent may generate sparse or low-quality training data in the next iteration, creating a self-reinforcing loop that can be difficult to escape. PPO addresses this by stabilizing policy updates.

The policy in PPO is represented by a neural network, $\pi\theta(a|s)$, where θ represents the network's weights. The network takes the current state s as input and outputs a probability distribution over possible actions a. Initially, the weights are randomly initialized. As the agent interacts with the environment, it generates batches of experiences (state, action, reward) under the current policy. The agent also calculates the advantage estimate, which measures how much better (or worse) a chosen action was compared to the expected value of the state.

The main difference from simpler policy gradient methods lies in PPO's use of a **clipped objective function**. This function ensures that policy updates are stable and prevents large, destabilizing changes. If the probability ratio between the new and old policies $rt(\theta)$ falls outside the range $[1-\epsilon, 1+\epsilon]$, where ϵ is a small hyperparameter (e.g., 0.2), the update is clipped. This clipping mechanism ensures that policy updates remain within a safe range, preventing the policy from diverging too much in a single update.

A common variant of PPO uses an **actor-critic architecture**, where the actor learns the policy, and the critic learns the value function. The critic provides feedback on the quality of the actions, helping to reduce the variance of the updates and improve learning efficiency (we discuss this more in detail later).

Overall, PPO is both a stable and robust algorithm, less prone to instability than simpler policy gradient methods and easier to use than more complex algorithms such as TRPO. It does not require solving complex optimization problems or calculating second-order gradients, making it a practical choice for many applications. However, PPO still requires careful tuning of hyperparameters, such as the clipping parameter ϵ, learning rate, and batch size. Additionally, it can suffer from high variance in environments with long episodes or delayed rewards.

The actor-critic algorithm

The actor-critic algorithm is another popular approach in RL, which combines the strengths of two different methods: value-based methods (such as Q-learning) and policy-based methods. The actor-critic model consists of two components:

- **Actor**: The actor is responsible for deciding what action should be taken in the current state of the environment. The policy is generally a neural network that produces a probability distribution over actions. The actor tries to maximize the expected return by optimizing the policy.

- **Critic**: The critic evaluates the actions taken by the actor by estimating the value function. This function indicates how good an action is in terms of expected future rewards. The value function can be the state value function $V(s)$ or the action-value function $Q(s,a)$.

The insight behind this approach is that the actor is the decision-maker who learns how to improve decisions over time. The critic, on the other hand, is a kind of advisor who evaluates the goodness of actions and gives feedback on strategy.

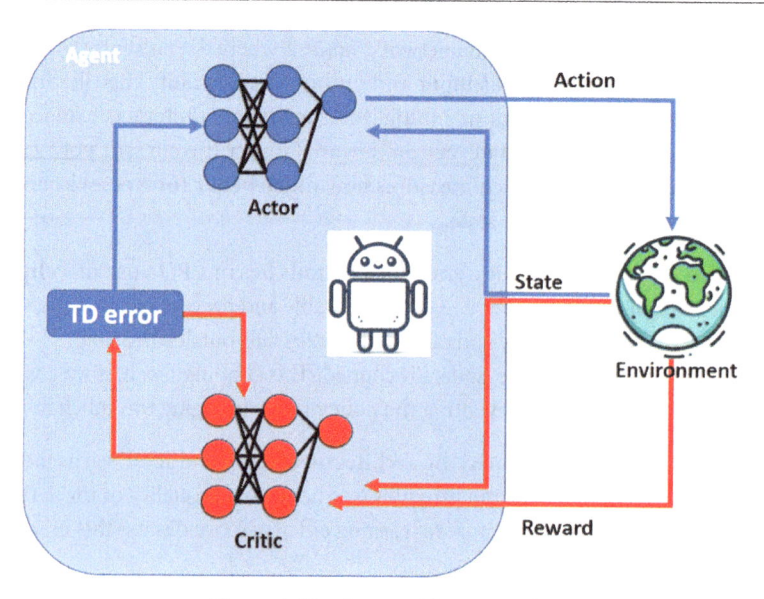

Figure 8.23 – Actor-critic approach

The process can be defined by four steps:

1. The agent interacts with the environment, and based on its policy, selects an action based on the current state. It then receives feedback from the environment in the form of a reward and a new state.

2. In the second step, the critic uses the reward and the new state to calculate a **temporal difference** (**TD**) **error**. The TD error measures how far the critic's current estimate of the value function is from the observed outcome. The TD error is then the difference between the reward at time step t (plus a discount factor y for the critic's estimates of the value of the next state $V(st+1)$ to serve to balance the impact of immediate and future rewards) and the critic's estimates of the value of the current state $V(st)$.

3. The critic updates its value function parameters to minimize the TD error. This is done with gradient descent.

4. The actor is updated as well. The actor uses the TD error as a feedback signal. If the error is positive, it means that the action was better than expected and the actor should take it more often (increase the probability of taking this action in the future). If the error is negative, the actor should decrease the probability. The actor maximizes the policy using gradient ascent; we want to maximize the expected return.

Actor-critic methods work well with continuous action spaces, where value-based methods have problems. It is a stable and efficient method and reduces the variance of policy gradient updates. On the other hand, it is sensitive to hyperparameters, you have to train two networks, and it is more complex than Q-learning or REINFORCE.

Advantage Actor-Critic (A2C) is a popular variant where multiple agents interact with multiple instances of the environment in parallel. This allows for faster training.

AlphaZero

AlphaZero is a groundbreaking model-based RL algorithm developed by DeepMind in 2017, capable of mastering chess, shogi (Japanese chess), and Go. It has achieved superhuman performance, defeating human champions in these games. The success of AlphaZero lies in its innovative combination of deep learning and **Monte Carlo Tree Search** (**MCTS**), which allows it to learn and plan effectively without human expertise or handcrafted rules.

AlphaZero learns entirely through **self-play**, starting with no prior knowledge other than the basic rules of the game. It plays millions of games against itself, gradually understanding what constitutes good or bad moves through trial and error. This self-play approach allows AlphaZero to discover optimal strategies, often surpassing even those developed by expert human players. Additionally, it enables the model to generate a vast amount of training data, far more than could be obtained by simply analyzing human games. The algorithm uses a deep neural network to represent both the policy (which actions to take) and the value function (the expected outcome of the game from a given state).

Traditional chess engines used to rely on game-tree search techniques. At each move, they would construct a game tree that represented all possible legal moves from the current position and performed a **depth-first search** (**DFS**) to a certain depth. This brute-force search examined all legal moves, assigning values to the final nodes based on heuristic evaluations formulated by the chess community. These heuristics, such as king safety, pawn structure, and control of the center, mimic factors used by human chess players to judge the quality of a move.

After evaluating the final nodes, traditional engines would backtrack and analyze the positions, pruning fewer promising branches to simplify the search. Despite these optimizations, this method had limitations, often leading to suboptimal moves and being computationally expensive. This is where MCTS comes in.

MCTS is an algorithm designed for decision-making in environments where planning several moves ahead is essential, especially in games with large state spaces where an exhaustive search is infeasible. MCTS builds a search tree by simulating games multiple times, gradually improving its understanding of the best actions through experience.

MCTS operates through four main steps, repeated to refine the search tree:

1. **Selection**: Starting from the root node (the current state), the algorithm selects child nodes using a strategy that balances exploration (trying less-explored moves) and exploitation (choosing moves that have shown promise). This is often done using the **Upper Confidence Bound for Trees** (**UCT**) formula, which considers both the average reward and the number of visits to each node.

2. **Expansion**: If the selected node is not a terminal state (the end of the game), the algorithm adds one or more child nodes, representing possible actions from this state. This expansion allows the search to cover new potential moves and outcomes.

3. **Simulation (rollout)**: From a newly added node, MCTS performs a simulation, or "rollout," by playing the game to a terminal state using a simple or random policy. The outcome of this simulation (win, loss, or draw) provides a reward, serving as an estimate of the value of the actions taken.

4. **Backpropagation**: The reward from the simulation is then backpropagated up the tree, updating the values associated with each node along the path to the root. This includes updating the average reward and the number of visits for each node. Over time, these updates help the algorithm determine which moves are most promising.

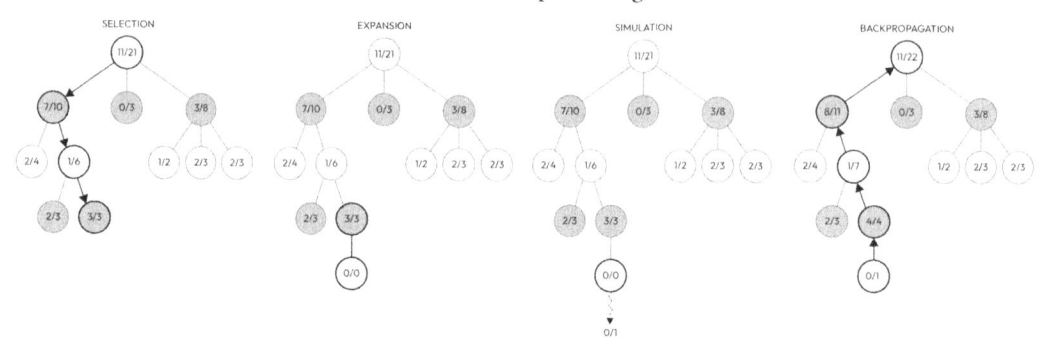

Figure 8.24 – Monte Carlo Tree Search (https://en.wikipedia.org/wiki/Monte_Carlo_tree_search)

AlphaZero then uses a neural network (a convolutional neural network that takes as input the arrangement of pieces on the board) and produces two outputs: policy head (a probability distribution over all possible moves, guiding the agent on which moves to consider) and value head (the likelihood of winning from the current board position, helping the agent to evaluate the strength of various states). AlphaZero uses MCTS to simulate potential moves and their outcomes (the agent plans several moves ahead in the game). Through MCTS, the model explores the moves that seem most promising and gradually improves its understanding of the game. The tree search uses the policy and value outputs from the neural network to prioritize which branches of the tree to explore. AlphaZero learns to play by playing against itself (self-play). In each game, the agent uses MCTS to decide moves and saves states (positions on the board), chosen moves, and results. This data is used to improve the policy and value estimates (neural network weight updates).

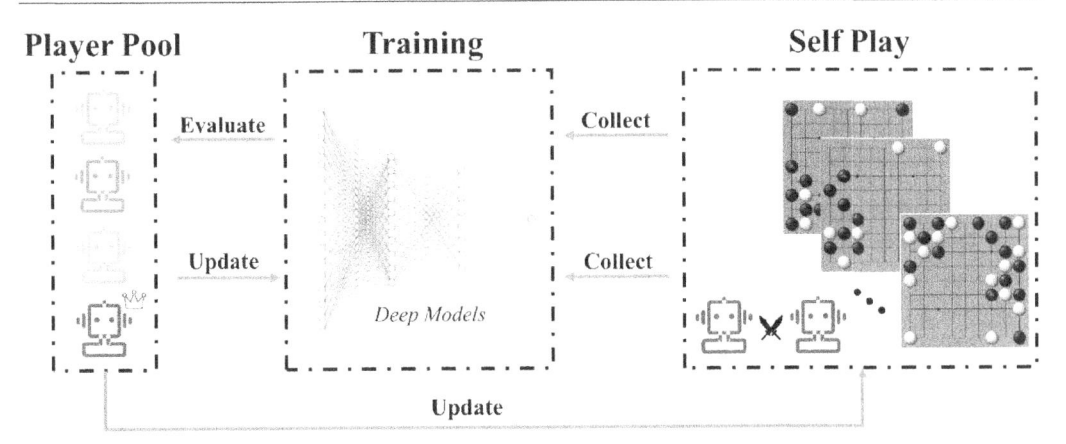

Figure 8.25 – AlphaZero pipeline (https://www.mdpi.com/2079-9292/10/13/1533)

AlphaZero therefore presents three main innovations:

- **Generalizing across games**: The same algorithm is used for three different games (chess, shogi, and Go), without the need for game-specific adjustments.
- **It requires no human knowledge**: Unlike traditional chess engines that use an extensive database of human games and strategies, AlphaZero learns the game on its own. The model prioritizes strategies that offer long-term rewards within the game, rather than focusing solely on immediate benefits from individual moves. This approach enables the model to discover innovative strategies previously unexplored by humans or traditional chess engines.
- **Efficient search and learning**: Using MCTS and deep learning allows more efficient use of computational resources. Instead of conducting an extensive search of all possible moves, AlphaZero focuses only on the most promising moves.

Of course, AlphaZero is not without flaws either. The algorithm has a huge computational cost since it has to play millions of games against itself. Also, the algorithm works well for games (or settings where there is perfect information) but it is more difficult to adapt it to environments where the information is incomplete. Finally, there is discussion about actually understanding the game or learning abstract concepts, since the model fails some chess puzzles that are easy for humans.

In the next subsection, we will discuss the challenges with RL and new, exciting lines of research.

Challenges and future direction for deep RL

Although RL has made significant progress, several challenges and several active lines of research remain:

- **Generalization in unseen environments**: Generalization in environments that the agent has not seen remains a complex task. Agents are usually trained in a simulated environment or in specific settings, where they are able to excel after training. However, transferring learned skills to new environments, dynamic environments, or changing conditions is difficult. This limits the use of deep RL algorithms in the real world because real environments are rarely static or perfectly predictable. True generalization requires that a model not only learns solutions that are task-specific but also adapts to a range of situations (even if they did not occur during training).

- **Reward function design**: Reward function controls agent behavior, learning, and performance. Designing a reward function is difficult, especially in complex, scattered environments. In sparse reward settings, where there is limited feedback and it is often delayed, defining the reward and function is complex but critical. Even so, there is often a risk of creating bias, leading the policy to overfitting or unexpected behaviors, or making it suboptimal.

- **Compound error in model-based planning**: Model-based RL is at risk of compounding errors. The longer the horizon of predictions, the more errors accumulate in model predictions, leading to significant deviations from the optimal trajectory. This is especially the case for complex or high-dimensional space environments, thus limiting their use in real environments.

- **Multi-task learning**: Creating an agent that can be used for multiple tasks remains difficult, with the risk that the agent learns only the easier ones and ignores the more complex (or otherwise very poorly performing) ones. Also, a multi-task model often exhibits performance that is far inferior to an agent optimized for a single task. The design of agents that can therefore be used for multi-task RL is difficult and still an active line of research.

- **Multi-modal RL**: With the advancement of computer vision and NLP, there are deep learning models that can either handle one mode individually or multiple modes together. This is why there is increasing discussion of using multimodal RL, where an agent can move through a multimodal environment and integrate information from the various modalities. For example, a robot can acquire information from the environment in an image and receive commands or instructions in natural language. An agent in video games receives visual information but also information from dialogues with characters or from other players. Multimodal learning remains complicated because an agent must simultaneously learn how to process multimodal information and optimize policy to interact in a complex environment. Similarly, it remains difficult to design a reward function for these cases.

In the next section, we will see how a neural network can be used to learn how to play a video game.

Learning how to play a video game with reinforcement learning

In this subsection, we will discuss how to train an agent to play a video game. In this case, the agent will be parameterized by a neural network. Following this policy, it will choose among the actions allowed by the video game, receive feedback from the environment, and use this feedback for parameter updating. In general, video games provide complex and dynamic environments that simulate real-world scenarios, thus making them an excellent testbed for RL algorithms. Video games provide a high-dimensional state space (pixel-based states, detailed universes) and a rich action space (discrete or continuous), are inspired by the real world, and can provide both immediate and delayed rewards (e.g., some actions may result in the direct death of the protagonist while a long-term strategy is needed to solve puzzles or win the game). In addition, many games require the user to explore the environment before they can master it. Enemies are often dynamic, and the model must learn how to defeat opposing agents or understand complex behaviors to overcome them. The game also provides clear rewards (which are often frequent or can otherwise be accelerated) that can then be easily defined for a reward function and thus make a safe playground (e.g., for algorithms for robotics). In addition, there are clear benchmarks and one can quickly compare the quality of a new algorithm.

We chose the actor-critic approach for this training because it has a number of features:

- Actor-critic can handle complex and continuous action spaces (control a character in a 3D environment) and thus can be used for a wide variety of games.
- The actor in the system learns the policy directly, making it efficient for scenarios where finding the policy is crucial. This is necessary in video games where quick decision-making and strategic planning are required.
- The critic provides feedback and speeds up learning in comparison to purely policy-based methods. Using a value function (critic) to evaluate actions reduces the variance of policy updates, so it is more stable and efficient in environments where rewards are scattered.
- Actor-critic allows for efficient management of the balance between exploration and exploitation, where the actor explores the environment and the critic guides it by providing feedback. For more complex environments, actor-critic may not be sufficient, though it is a good initial choice and often sufficient.
- Actor-critic can also handle long-term planning. Often, in video games, there can be long-term rewards; the critic's value function helps the agent understand the long-term impact of its actions.
- Some variants are efficient in parallelizing and using data. A2C is a good choice for parallelizing environments and thus collecting more data, thus speeding up training and convergence.

We chose Super Mario as our game because it provides a rich and complex environment. The environment resembles the real world, and the representation of pixel-based observations as input is similar to that of real-world computer vision tasks, making Super Mario a good testbed for RL agents who need to learn to extract meaningful features from visual data. This environment is also partially observable, so it requires the agent to explore and learn about the environment. Different levels may require different strategies, so the model must be able to balance exploration and exploitation.

In the game, there are different kinds of challenges, such as navigating obstacles, facing different kinds of enemies, and learning to jump optimally and often dynamically. These different challenges represent different skills that an agent should develop: testing the agent's ability to make precise and timely actions (jumping over obstacles or gaps), assessing threats and deciding when to avoid or engage (avoiding or engaging enemies), and spatial awareness and strategic planning (navigating complex levels). The levels are progressive, so with a difficulty that progresses as the agent learns. In addition, there are both immediate rewards (collecting coins) and delayed rewards (e.g., completing a level), thus allowing for the evaluation of long-term strategies.

Finally, Super Mario has been widely adopted in the RL research community as a benchmark. Major libraries support it, or it is found directly integrated, thus allowing a quick way to test algorithms or conduct comparisons. There are also already well-researched strategies; the game is well documented and is a good example for both beginners and experts in RL. There are also implementations that are parallelizable, thus allowing effective and fast training.

Figure 8.26 – Super Mario screenshots from the training

All the code can be found within the repository, at the following link: https://github.com/PacktPublishing/Modern-AI-Agents/tree/main/chr8/RL_SuperMario

Name	Last commit message	Last commit date
..		
tensorboard	Add Reinforcement learning Super Mario	19 hours ago
trained_models	Add Reinforcement learning Super Mario	19 hours ago
env.py	Add Reinforcement learning Super Mario	19 hours ago
evaluate_A3C.ipynb	Add Reinforcement learning Super Mario	19 hours ago
model.py	Add Reinforcement learning Super Mario	19 hours ago
optimizer.py	Add Reinforcement learning Super Mario	19 hours ago
process.py	Add Reinforcement learning Super Mario	19 hours ago
test.py	Add Reinforcement learning Super Mario	19 hours ago
train.py	Add Reinforcement learning Super Mario	19 hours ago
train_A3C.ipynb	Add Reinforcement learning Super Mario	19 hours ago

Figure 8.27 – Screenshot of the repository

Description of the scripts

To perform the training, we will use some popular RL libraries (OpenAI's Gym and PyTorch). In the repository, there are different scripts that are used to train the agent:

- `env`: This script defines the environment where our agent acts (Super Mario) and allows us to record a video of our agent playing, preprocess images for the model, define the reward function, set the world, set a virtual joystick, and more.
- `model`: This script defines a PyTorch neural network model for an actor-critic architecture. The model is designed to process image-like inputs, extract features, and then use those features to output both action probabilities (actor) and state value estimates (critic).
- `optimizer`: This code defines a custom optimizer class called `GlobalAdam`, which extends the functionality of PyTorch's built-in Adam optimizer.
- `train`: This script sets up and runs a distributed RL system using the **Asynchronous Advantage Actor-Critic (A3C)** method to train an agent to play Super Mario Bros.
- `test`: Model testing is in a separate script. This script allows you to load the trained model to play the game while rendering the gameplay.
- `process`: This script acts as the linking piece that integrates all the preceding components into a cohesive RL system for training and testing an agent to play Super Mario Bros.

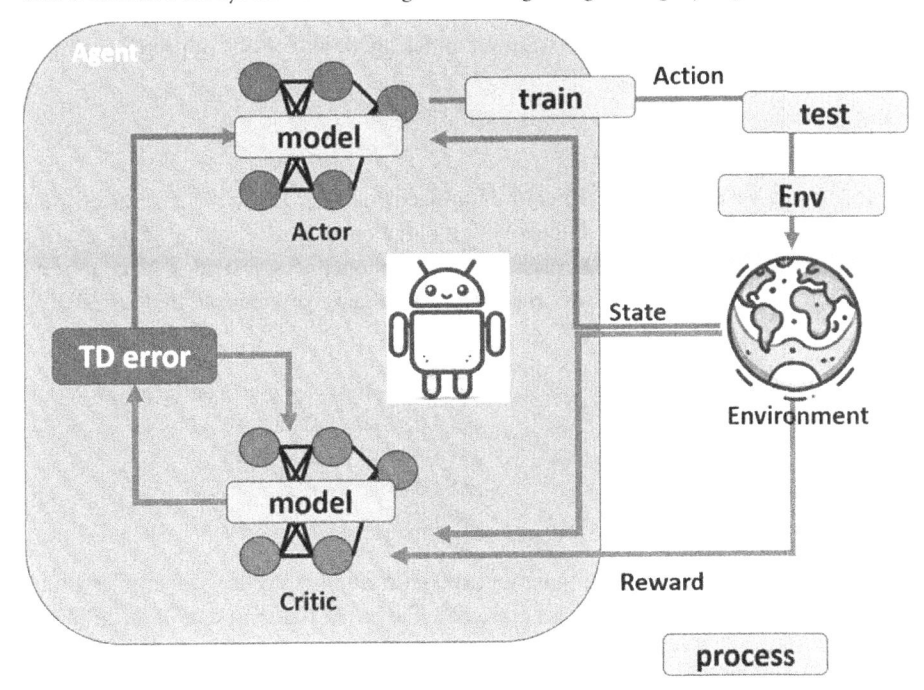

Figure 8.28 – Global view of the scripts

Setting up the environment

The `env` script allows us to have our setup of the environment, especially for RL algorithms such as Deep Q-Learning or actor-critic. Inside the script, we import the libraries we need, after which there are some functions that are used to create the world and define how the agent can interact with it:

- `Monitor`: The `Monitor` class allows the user to save a visual record of the agent's gameplay, which is useful for debugging, analyzing agent performance, and sharing results. This function permits us to save a video of the game using `.ffmpeg`.

- `process_frame`: The `process_frame` function is used to preprocess frames from the game to make them more suitable for training an RL agent. This function checks whether the frame is in the right format, converts it to grayscale and reduces the size, and normalizes it (simplifies the input). This allows the agent to focus on the important details of the visual information.

- `CustomReward`: This is a modification of the reward to encourage useful behaviors, track the current score, add rewards, check whether the agent finishes the level, and penalize it if the episode isn't finished. In this way, it tries to incentivize completing the level and making progress by penalizing failures.

- `CustomSkipFrame`: This serves to speed up training by allowing skip frames, thus reducing computational computation (fewer environment updates).

- `create_train_env`: This function sets up a fully customized and optimized Super Mario environment, making it ready for training an RL agent with efficient preprocessing, reward shaping, and frame skipping.

Defining the model

In the `model` script, we define the architecture for our algorithm. `ActorCritic` is the class that governs the architecture, and as a neural network, it is based on PyTorch (in fact, we use `nn.Module`, a classic neural network in PyTorch). The class has two components representing `Actor` (responsible for choosing actions) and `Critic`, which provides feedback. You can see that we have a shared feature extractor:

```
self.conv1 = nn.Conv2d(num_inputs, 32, 3, stride=2, padding=1)
self.conv2 = nn.Conv2d(32, 32, 3, stride=2, padding=1)
self.conv3 = nn.Conv2d(32, 32, 3, stride=2, padding=1)
self.conv4 = nn.Conv2d(32, 32, 3, stride=2, padding=1)
self.lstm = nn.LSTMCell(32 * 6 * 6, 512)
```

Here, we have a convolutional network to extract spatial features from the game; this output is then reshaped into a 2D tensor, which is passed for an LSTM. The LSTM has an update of the hidden state `hx` and the cell state `cx` (we described the LSTM in detail in *Chapter 1*), thus managing episode memory.

After that, we initialize the two components:

```
self.critic_linear = nn.Linear(512, 1)
self.actor_linear = nn.Linear(512, num_actions)
```

Using a single feature extractor allows us to save computation resources. The two components produce two different outputs: `actor_linear` produces the output for the actor, which is a vector of size `num_actions`. This represents the probability of taking each action. The `critic_linear` component produces the output for the critic, which is a single scalar value. This value represents the estimated value of the current state (the expected return from this state). This separation allows us to make sure that the two layers have separate goals and different learning signals.

Next, we will define different loss functions in order to allow for different learning. As we can see, the two components produce different outputs:

```
def forward(self, x, hx, cx):
    x = F.relu(self.conv1(x))
    x = F.relu(self.conv2(x))
    x = F.relu(self.conv3(x))
    x = F.relu(self.conv4(x))
    hx, cx = self.lstm(x.view(x.size(0), -1), (hx, cx))
    return self.actor_linear(hx), self.critic_linear(hx), hx, cx
```

Since we want our process to be optimized for distributed learning, we use a custom version of Adam. Adam is a classical optimizer that is used for updating the parameters of a neural network. The `GlobalAdam` class is designed for distributed RL, where multiple processes or agents share the same optimizer. The key idea is to make certain parts of the optimizer's state shared across processes, allowing agents to coordinate their updates to the model parameters efficiently. This is especially useful with actor-critic and especially the variant where there are many agents acting in the same environment. The idea is that we play the game several times asynchronously and then conduct global updates, reducing computation. The `GlobalAdam` script is simply an adaptation of Adam to RL problems, allowing averaging and learning from different processes:

```
import torch
class GlobalAdam(torch.optim.Adam):
    def __init__(self, params, lr):
        super(GlobalAdam, self).__init__(params, lr=lr)
        for group in self.param_groups:
            for p in group['params']:
                state = self.state[p]
                state['step'] = 0
                state['exp_avg'] = torch.zeros_like(p.data)
                state['exp_avg_sq'] = torch.zeros_like(p.data)
                state['exp_avg'].share_memory_()
                state['exp_avg_sq'].share_memory_()
```

Training the model

The `train` script then allows us to train the model asynchronously with different processes. The script allows us to provide several parameters (default parameters are already entered). For example, we can decide the level of the game (`--world` and `--stage`), the type of action (`--action_type`), the learning rate for the optimizer (`--lr`), hyperparameters specific to the algorithm and RL (`--gamma`, `--tau`, `--beta`), or related to the process and its parallelization (`--num_processes`, `--num_local_steps`, and `--num_global_steps`).

The `train` function allows us to initialize the training environment, initialize the policy, and use the GPU. The `global_model.share_memory()` method allows the global model's parameters to be accessible to all processes, enabling parallel updates. You can see we use `GlobalAdam` to update the global model's parameters. The `torch.multiprocessing` wrapper (is a wrapper to the multiprocessing module) allows us to create multiple processes that operate asynchronously. This script then defines the training of our model using multiple parallel processes. At the same time, the script allows easy configuration and customization:

```
def train(opt):
    torch.manual_seed(123)
    if os.path.isdir(opt.log_path):
        shutil.rmtree(opt.log_path)
    os.makedirs(opt.log_path)
    if not os.path.isdir(opt.saved_path):
        os.makedirs(opt.saved_path)
    mp = _mp.get_context("spawn")
    env, num_states, num_actions = create_train_env(opt.world, opt.stage, opt.action_type)
    global_model = ActorCritic(num_states, num_actions)
    if opt.use_gpu:
        global_model.cuda()
    global_model.share_memory()
    if opt.load_from_previous_stage:
        if opt.stage == 1:
            previous_world = opt.world - 1
            previous_stage = 4
        else:
            previous_world = opt.world
            previous_stage = opt.stage - 1
        file_ = "{}/A3CSuperMarioBros{}_{}".format(opt.saved_path, previous_world, previous_stage)
        if os.path.isfile(file_):
            global_model.load_state_dict(torch.load(file_))
```

```
        optimizer = GlobalAdam(global_model.parameters(), lr=opt.lr)
        processes = []
        for index in range(opt.num_processes):
            if index == 0:
                process = mp.Process(target=local_train, args=(index, opt,
    global_model, optimizer, True))
            else:
                process = mp.Process(target=local_train, args=(index, opt,
    global_model, optimizer))
            process.start()
            processes.append(process)
        process = mp.Process(target=local_test, args=(opt.num_processes,
    opt, global_model))
        process.start()
        processes.append(process)
        for process in processes:
            process.join()
```

Testing the system

The `test` script allows customization such as deciding on some parameters, such as level of play, actions, and so on. Once we have trained our model, we can then load it, play the game, and register the agent playing. The model then plays with its policy, without optimization in this script, and thus allows us to observe the agent's performance.

Connecting all the components

The `process` script connects all the scripts we have seen so far into one system. This script uses the `create_train_env` function from the env module to set up the Super Mario Bros game environment. This is the environment where our agent interacts and learns. The script also initializes the `ActorCritic` model (both actor and critic) and uses this model to make decisions and evaluate game states. The `local_train` function is responsible for training and requires the `GlobalAdam` optimizer. This script is also used to evaluate trained model performance, so it uses elements we defined in the test script. This script, then, is the central piece that allows us to have a fully functional RL system. It orchestrates the environment, model, and training algorithm, making everything work together to train an agent to play Super Mario Bros.

The `local_train` function enables the agent to train in parallel with other processes while updating a shared global model. This function establishes a seed for reproducibility, so we can reproduce the results. After that, we initialize the environment (`create_train_env`) and model (`ActorCritic`); if there is a GPU, we move the model to the GPU and initialize TensorBoard:

```
    def local_train(index, opt, global_model, optimizer, save=False):
        torch.manual_seed(123 + index)
        if save:
```

```
        start_time = timeit.default_timer()
    writer = SummaryWriter(opt.log_path)
    env, num_states, num_actions = create_train_env(opt.world, opt.
stage, opt.action_type)
    local_model = ActorCritic(num_states, num_actions)
    if opt.use_gpu:
        local_model.cuda()
```

At this point, we begin the training loop where each iteration represents an episode of gameplay. The local parameters are synchronized with the global parameters, and at the end of each episode, the hidden and cell states of the LSTM are reset:

```
local_model.train()
    state = torch.from_numpy(env.reset())
    if opt.use_gpu:
        state = state.cuda()
    done = True
    curr_step = 0
    curr_episode = 0
    while True:
        if save:
            if curr_episode % opt.save_interval == 0 and curr_episode
> 0:
                torch.save(global_model.state_dict(),
                           "{}/a3c_super_mario_bros_{}_{}".format(opt.
saved_path, opt.world, opt.stage))
            print("Process {}. Episode {}".format(index, curr_
episode))
        curr_episode += 1
        local_model.load_state_dict(global_model.state_dict())
        if done:
            h_0 = torch.zeros((1, 512), dtype=torch.float)
            c_0 = torch.zeros((1, 512), dtype=torch.float)
        else:
            h_0 = h_0.detach()
            c_0 = c_0.detach()
        if opt.use_gpu:
            h_0 = h_0.cuda()
            c_0 = c_0.cuda()
```

At this point, we begin to collect experiences for a number of steps (opt.num_local_steps). Then, for a state, the model (the local model) produces a set of probabilities, and from these probabilities, we sample an action. Having chosen an action, we interact with the environment, so we get a reward and a new state. For each of these steps, we record the following: whether the episode has ended, the log probability of the action, the value estimate, the reward, and the entropy of the policy. If the episode ends, the state is reset, and the hidden states are detached to prevent gradient backpropagation:

```
for _ in range(opt.num_local_steps):
        curr_step += 1
        logits, value, h_0, c_0 = local_model(state, h_0, c_0)
        policy = F.softmax(logits, dim=1)
        log_policy = F.log_softmax(logits, dim=1)
        entropy = -(policy * log_policy).sum(1, keepdim=True)

        m = Categorical(policy)
        action = m.sample().item()

        state, reward, done, _ = env.step(action)
        state = torch.from_numpy(state)
        if opt.use_gpu:
            state = state.cuda()
        if curr_step > opt.num_global_steps:
            done = True

        if done:
            curr_step = 0
            state = torch.from_numpy(env.reset())
            if opt.use_gpu:
                state = state.cuda()

        values.append(value)
        log_policies.append(log_policy[0, action])
        rewards.append(reward)
        entropies.append(entropy)

        if done:
            break

    R = torch.zeros((1, 1), dtype=torch.float)
    if opt.use_gpu:
        R = R.cuda()
    if not done:
        _, R, _, _ = local_model(state, h_0, c_0)
```

Now, it is time to calculate the loss and conduct backpropagation. Here, we use **generalized advantage estimation (GAE)**, to balance bias and variance and make the training therefore more efficient. Simply, the advantage function $A(s,a)$ measures the goodness of an action a relative to the average action in a given state s. In the next script, GAE is used to compute the advantage values that drive the actor's policy updates. We use GAE to update the policy in the actor loss in order to maximize the expected return but keep the variance low. In other words, we want to keep the training more stable. By adding GAE, the training process becomes more efficient and less susceptible to noise from high variance returns or inaccuracies from biased value estimates:

```
        gae = torch.zeros((1, 1), dtype=torch.float)
        if opt.use_gpu:
            gae = gae.cuda()
        actor_loss = 0
        critic_loss = 0
        entropy_loss = 0
        next_value = R

        for value, log_policy, reward, entropy in list(zip(values,
log_policies, rewards, entropies))[::-1]:
            gae = gae * opt.gamma * opt.tau
            gae = gae + reward + opt.gamma * next_value.detach() -
value.detach()
            next_value = value
            actor_loss = actor_loss + log_policy * gae
            R = R * opt.gamma + reward
            critic_loss = critic_loss + (R - value) ** 2 / 2
            entropy_loss = entropy_loss + entropy

        total_loss = -actor_loss + critic_loss - opt.beta * entropy_
loss
        writer.add_scalar("Train_{}/Loss".format(index), total_loss,
curr_episode)
        optimizer.zero_grad()
        total_loss.backward()

        for local_param, global_param in zip(local_model.parameters(),
global_model.parameters()):
            if global_param.grad is not None:
                break
            global_param._grad = local_param.grad

        optimizer.step()

        if curr_episode == int(opt.num_global_steps / opt.num_local_
steps):
            print("Training process {} terminated".format(index))
            if save:
                end_time = timeit.default_timer()
                print('The code runs for %.2f s ' % (end_time - start_
```

```
time))
            return
```

Note that we have three separate losses. The first is the actor loss, which encourages actions that lead to higher rewards. The critic loss penalizes errors in the value estimation, and the entropy loss encourages exploration by penalizing overly confident action distributions (in other penalizing strategies that are too greedy). Once we have computed the total loss, we perform the backpropagation as in any neural network. Right now, we have performed local training, so we use the gradients of the local model to conduct the global model update as well. Every certain time interval, we save the model and send the loss logs to TensorBoard. The process ends when we have reached the total number of global steps.

The `local_test` function allows us to conduct the evaluation of our trained model. It runs as a separate process to test how well the agent performs using the learned policy:

```
def local_test(index, opt, global_model):
    torch.manual_seed(123 + index)
    env, num_states, num_actions = create_train_env(opt.world, opt.
stage, opt.action_type)
    local_model = ActorCritic(num_states, num_actions)
    local_model.eval()
    state = torch.from_numpy(env.reset())
    done = True
    curr_step = 0
    actions = deque(maxlen=opt.max_actions)
    while True:
        curr_step += 1
        if done:
            local_model.load_state_dict(global_model.state_dict())
        with torch.no_grad():
            if done:
                h_0 = torch.zeros((1, 512), dtype=torch.float)
                c_0 = torch.zeros((1, 512), dtype=torch.float)
            else:
                h_0 = h_0.detach()
                c_0 = c_0.detach()

        logits, value, h_0, c_0 = local_model(state, h_0, c_0)
        policy = F.softmax(logits, dim=1)
        action = torch.argmax(policy).item()
        state, reward, done, _ = env.step(action)
        env.render()
        actions.append(action)
        if curr_step > opt.num_global_steps or actions.
count(actions[0]) == actions.maxlen:
```

```
            done = True
   if done:
       curr_step = 0
       actions.clear()
       state = env.reset()
   state = torch.from_numpy(state)
```

Again, we conduct setup and initialization and load the local `ActorCritic` model in evaluation mode (in inference mode, practically, the model does not get updates during this process). At this point, we start the loop, where we load the last weights from the global model. For a state, we compute the probabilities for each action and choose the action with the highest probability. Note how, during training, we conducted sampling of the action; in evaluation mode, instead, we chose the action with a greedy policy. We interact with the environment and render the game, conduct action tracking, and check whether the agent gets stuck or repeats the same action indefinitely. If the agent exceeds the maximum number of steps or gets stuck, the episode ends and we reset the state. This function evaluates the performance of the trained agent, rendering the gameplay so that users can observe how well the agent has learned to play Super Mario Bros. It ensures the policy is effective and provides visual feedback.

Running the scripts, we can see that the training runs in parallel:

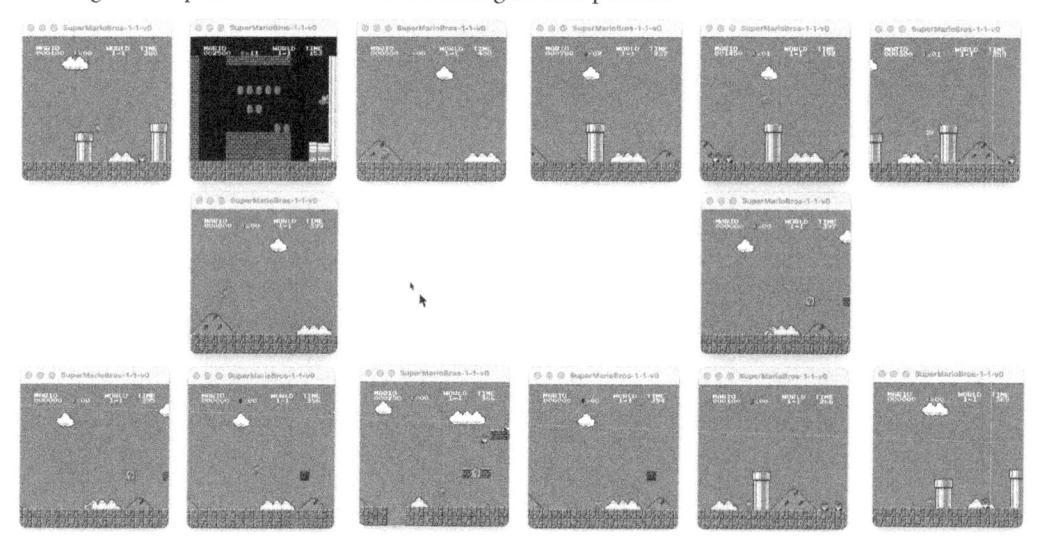

Figure 8.29 – Screenshot of the script run

You can check out the video here: https://www.youtube.com/watch?v=YWx-hnvqjr8

To summarize, we used several scripts to implement a variant of the action-critic algorithm (the A3C method). This method involves training multiple agents in parallel to explore the environment, collect experiences, and update a shared global model asynchronously. In other words, we use a variant that allows us to speed up the training and learn a model that is more robust because it retrieves different experiences from different agents. For cleaner organization, we divided the process into several scripts that are then linked into a single script (process script). We defined our neural network with a common extractor for the two components, so we can save some computations. In addition, we used an LSTM to be able to handle the temporal dependencies there are between one state and another. We had to modify our optimizer because we needed shared memory to be able to handle several processes to update a global model. Asynchronous training indeed has higher complexities, where each agent needs to access and update the global model. After that, we defined how to train our model by collecting some experience. Having collected the experience, we conducted an update of the model weights, calculating the loss and performing backpropagation. Periodically, we synchronized the global and local model, conducting an update of the global model. After that, we defined how to evaluate our agent using the parameters of the global model. The agent uses the learned policy to play the game.

These scripts allow efficient parallel training because of the A3C method. In fact, we can use several agents in parallel that explore the environment, gather experience, and then lead to a global model update. Using a parallel system causes agents to explore different parts of the environment, leading to more diverse experiences and thus a more generalized policy. In general, this is favorable because different strategies may be needed in video games. In the same vein, we added entropy loss to encourage exploration and prevent the agent from being stuck in a suboptimal strategy. The script is designed for efficient use of resources, to reduce computation, and to have fast training (we did not add an experience replay buffer to save memory and thus consume less RAM). The use of a global model ensures that knowledge learned by one agent is immediately available to all agents; this usually promotes rapid convergence.

The choice of an on-policy learning method such as A3C can result in high variance in policy updates. This variance can then be amplified by the asynchronous nature, which may make it difficult to get consistent results across runs. In fact, the asynchronous approach introduces non-determinism, meaning that the results can vary significantly between runs. This makes the process less predictable and complicates the choice of hyperparameters (which is why we have provided default parameters, although it is possible to experiment with them). While we have tried to optimize the resources consumed by this script, the whole process remains resource intensive (like RL in general).

A3C primarily relies on CPU-based parallelism; however, incorporating GPU-friendly methods could significantly enhance training efficiency. Algorithms such as PPO can leverage GPUs to optimize the training process. Effective use of GPUs enables more efficient batch processing, allowing for the accumulation of experiences and bulk updates to the model. For readers interested in exploring GPU-based optimization, here are a few potential ideas:

- Test different hyperparameters and vary their values to better understand their impact. In the script, you can easily set and change hyperparameters. We invite you to test lambda (λ) to find a better balance between bias and variance.

- Try PPO. PPO is a popular alternative to A3C that exploits multiple epochs of mini-batch updates. As we have seen, it is an algorithm that promotes stability and works well in many cases. It also does not require many hyperparameters and the default ones usually work well.

- Adopt synchronous A2C as it is a simpler, synchronous version of A3C. This approach collects experiences in parallel and uses batches for updating. It is usually slower but easier to debug.

The model shown in this project can be applied to several other video games, showing how an RL algorithm can solve real tasks.

LLM interactions with RL models

RL algorithms have been instrumental for agents that can navigate complex environments, optimize strategies, and make decisions, with successes in areas such as robotics and video games. LLMs, on the other hand, have had a strong impact on **natural language processing** (**NLP**), enabling machines to understand human language and instructions. Although potential synergies can be imagined, so far these two technologies have evolved in parallel. In recent years, though, with the heightened interest in LLMs, the two fields have increasingly intersected. In this section, we will discuss the interaction between RL and LLMs.

We can have three cases of interaction:

- **RL enhancing an LLM**: Using RL to enhance the performance of an LLM in one or more NLP tasks

- **LLMs enhancing RL**: Using LLMs to train an RL algorithm that performs a task that is not necessarily NLP

- **RL and LLMs**: Combining RL models and LLMs to plan a skill set, without either system being used to train or conduct fine-tuning of the other

Let's discuss these in detail.

RL-enhanced LLMs

We have already discussed alignment and prompt engineering, in *Chapter 3*. RL is, then, used for fine-tuning, prompt engineering, and the alignment of LLMs. As mentioned in *Chapter 3*, LLMs are trained to predict the next word in a sequence, leading to a mismatch between the LLM's training objective and human values. This can lead LLMs to produce text with bias or other unsafe content, and likewise to be suboptimal at following instructions. Alignment serves to realign the model to human values or to make an LLM more effective for safer deployment. One of the most widely used techniques is **reinforcement learning from human feedback** (**RLHF**), where the reward is inferred from human preferences and then used to train the LLM. This process follows three steps: collect human feedback data, train a reward model on this data, and conduct fine-tuning of the LLM with RL. Generally, the most popular choice of RL algorithm is PPO or derivative methods. In fact, we do not want our aligned model to be significantly different from the original model, which PPO guarantees.

Interaction with LLMs is through the prompt, and the prompt should condense all the instructions for the task we want LLM to accomplish. Some work has focused on using RL to design prompts. Prompt optimization can be represented as an RL problem with the goal of incorporating human knowledge and thus drawing interpretable and adaptable prompts. The agent is used to construct prompts that are query-dependent and optimized. One can also train a policy network to generate desired prompts, with the advantage that the prompts are generally transferable across LLMs. An intriguing aspect of this approach is that some of these optimized prompts are grammatically "gibberish," indicating that high-quality prompts for a task need not follow human language patterns.

LLM-enhanced RL

LLM-enhanced RL refers to methods that use multi-modal information processing, generation, reasoning, or other high-level cognitive capabilities of pre-trained LLMs in assisting an RL agent. In other words, the difference from traditional RL is the use of an LLM and the exploitation of its knowledge and capabilities in some way. The addition of an LLM in some form has a twofold advantage: first, an LLM possesses reasoning and planning skills that allow for improved learning, and second, it has a greater ability to generalize. In addition, an LLM has extensive knowledge gained during the pre-training step and that can be transferred across domains and tasks, thus allowing better adaptation to environments that have not been seen. Models that are pre-trained generally cannot expand their knowledge or acquire new capabilities (continual learning is an open challenge of deep learning), so using a model trained with huge amounts of knowledge can help with this aspect (LLMs are generalists and have huge amounts of information for different domains in memory).

An LLM can then be inserted into the classic framework of an RL system (an agent interacting with and receiving feedback from an environment) at more than one point. An LLM can then be integrated to extract information, reprocess state, redesign rewards, make decisions, select actions, interpret policies, analyze world similarity, and more.

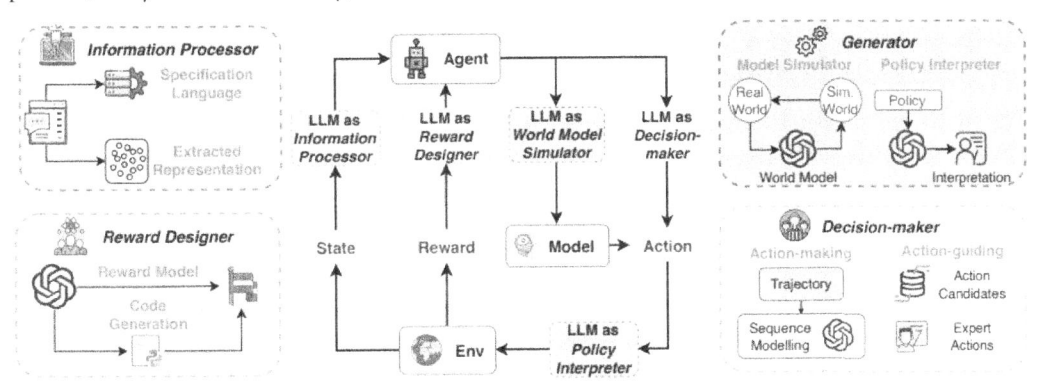

Figure 8.30 – Framework of LLM-enhanced RL in classical agent-environment interactions (https://arxiv.org/pdf/2404.00282)

Thus, an LLM can be used inside the system as an information processor, reward designer, decision-maker, and generator.

Information processor

When a task requires textual information or visual features, it can be complex for an agent to understand the information and optimize the policy at the same time. As we saw earlier, a convolutional neural network can be used to process images for a model to interact with a video game or board game. In the case of a chatbot, we can then use a model that understands language. Alternatively, instead of using a model directly on the language, we can use an LLM to extract features that allow the agent to learn more quickly. LLMs can be good feature extractors, thereby reducing the dimensionality and complexity of the information. Or LLMs can translate natural language into a specific formal language understandable to an agent. For example, in the case of a robot, the natural language of different users will be different and not homogeneous, making it difficult for the agent to learn. An LLM can transform instructions into a standard, formal language that allows easier learning for the agent.

A wide pre-trained model learns a representation of the data that can then be used for subsequent applications. A model, then, can be used to extract a data representation that we can use to train an agent. An LLM can be used frozen (that is, without the need for further training) to extract a compressed representation of the history of the environment. Some studies use an LLM to summarize past visual observations that are provided to the agent, so we can provide a memory to the agent. Using a frozen model is clearly the simplest alternative, but when agents are deployed in the real world, performance can degrade rapidly due to real-world variations versus the training environment. Therefore, we can conduct fine-tuning of both the agent and the LLM. The use of a feature extractor (an LLM or other large model) makes it easier for the agent to learn since these features are more invariant to changes in the environment (changes in brightness, color, etc…), but on the other hand, they have an additional computational cost.

The capabilities of LLMs can be used to make the task clearer. For example, instructions in natural language can be adapted by an LLM into a set of instructions that are clearer to the agent (for example, when playing a video game, a textual description of the task could be transformed into a set of instructions on how to move the character). An LLM can also be used to translate an agent's surroundings into usable information. These approaches are particularly promising but are currently limited in scope.

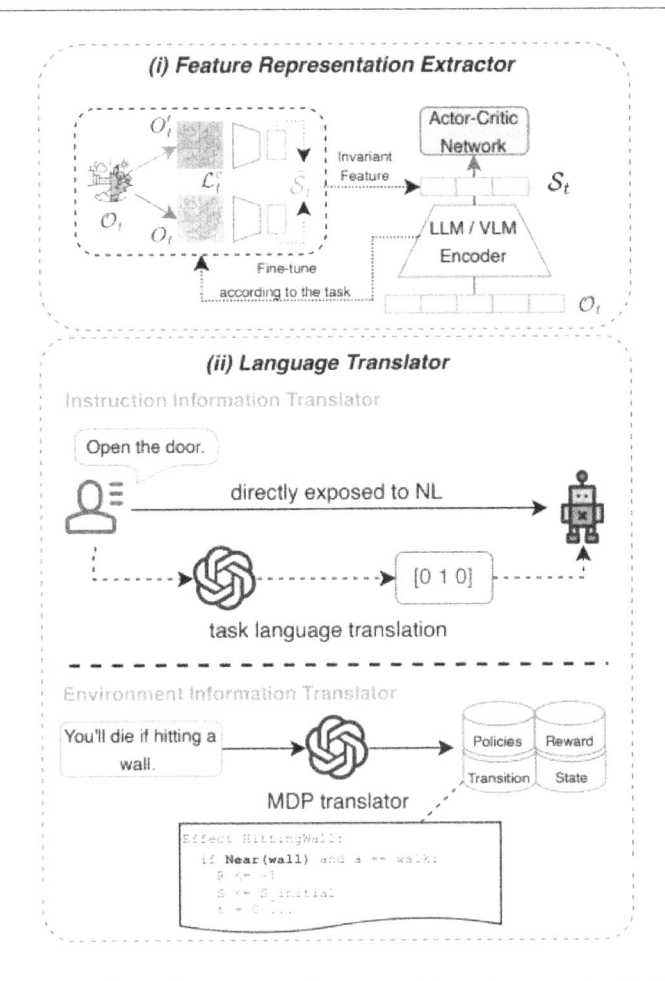

Figure 8.31 – LLM as an information processor (https://arxiv.org/pdf/2404.00282)

Reward designer

When knowledge of the problem is available, or when the reward can be defined by a clear and deterministic function (such as a game score or a win/loss condition), designing the reward function is straightforward. For example, in Atari games (or other games), it is easy to draw a reward function (e.g., victory represents a positive signal and defeat a negative signal). There are many applications where this is not possible because the tasks are long and complex, the rewards are scattered, and so on. In such cases, the knowledge inherent in an LLM (the knowledge gained during pre-training, coding abilities, and reasoning skills) could be used to generate the reward. It can be used indirectly (an implicit reward model) or directly (an explicit reward model). For example, a user can define expected behavior in a prompt, and an LLM can evaluate the agent's behavior during training, providing a reward and a penalty. So, you can use direct feedback from the LLM, or an LLM can generate the code for a reward function. In the second approach, the function can be modified by the LLM during training (for example, after the agent has acquired some skills, making it harder to get a reward).

An LLM can be an implicit reward model that provides a reward (or auxiliary reward) based on the task description. One technique for this is direct prompting, in which instructions are given to the LLM to evaluate the agent's behavior or decide on a reward. These approaches can mimic human feedback to evaluate an agent's behavior in real time. Alternatively, an alignment score can be used, for example, between the outcome of an action and the goal (in other words, evaluating the similarity between the expected outcome and reality). In some approaches, one uses the contrastive alignment between language instructions and the image observations of the agent, thus exploiting models that are multimodal. Obviously, the process of aligning human intentions and LLM-reward generation is not easy. There can be ambiguities, and the system does not always work with low-quality instruction, but it seems a promising avenue.

An explicit reward model exploits the ability of an LLM to generate code, thus generating a function (making the decision-making and reward-generation process by the LLM more transparent). This allows functions for subgoals to be generated automatically (e.g., having a robot learn low-level tasks using high-level instructions that are translated into a reward function by the LLM). The main limitation of this approach is the common-sense reasoning limitation of LLMs. LLMs are not capable of real reasoning or true generalization, so they are limited by what they have seen during pre-training. Highly specialized tasks are not seen by LLMs during pre-training, thus limiting the applicability of these approaches to a selected set of tasks. Adding context and additional information could mitigate this problem.

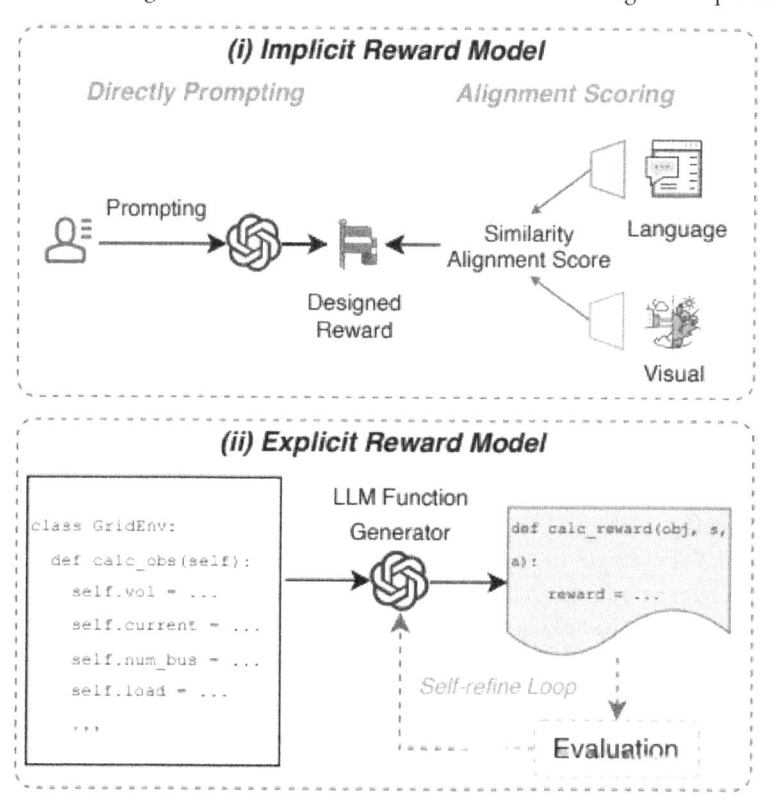

Figure 8.32 – LLM as a reward designer (https://arxiv.org/pdf/2404.00282)

Decision-maker

Since RL has problems in many cases with sample and exploration inefficiency, LLMs can be used in decision-making and thus help in choosing actions. LLMs can be used to reduce the set of actions in a certain state (for example, when many actions are possible). Reducing the set of actions reduces the exploration space, thus increasing exploration efficiency. For example, an LLM can be used to train robots on what actions to take in a world, reducing exploration time.

The transformer (or derivative models) has shown great potential in RL. The idea behind it is to treat these problems as sequence modeling problems (instead of trial and error). LLMs can then be seen as a decision-making model, which has to decide on a sequence of problems (as we mentioned in *Chapter 2*, the transformer is trained on a sequence of problems, so making a decision on a sequence of states is congenial to its training). An LLM can be fine-tuned to leverage the internal representation of the model. In fact, in this way, we leverage the representation learned from an LLM (being trained with a huge quantity of text, an LLM has a vast amount of knowledge already acquired that can be applied to a task) to decide an action. Using prior knowledge reduces the need for data collection and exploration (hence, sample efficiency) and makes the system more efficient toward long-term rewards or sparse reward environments. Several studies have shown not only the transferability of knowledge learned from an LLM to other models but also the improved performance of the whole system on different benchmarks. In addition, vision-language models can be used to be able to adapt the system to multimodal environments. Using an LLM as a decision-maker is still computationally expensive (even if only used in inference and without the need for fine-tuning). As a result, current studies are focusing on trying to reduce the computational cost of these approaches.

Alternatively, an LLM can guide the agent in choosing actions by generating reasonable action candidates or expert actions. For example, in environments such as text-based games, the action space is very large, and only a fraction of the actions is currently available, so an agent can learn with extensive trial-and-error; however, this exploration is very inefficient. An LLM can reduce this action space by generating an action set by understanding the task. This makes it possible to reduce exploration and make it more efficient, collect more rewards, and speed up training. Typically, in these approaches, we have an LLM that generates a set of actions and another neural network that generates the Q-values of these candidates. The same approach has been extended to robots that have to follow human instructions, where an LLM generates possible actions. This approach is limited owing to the inheritance of the biases and limitations of an LLM (since an LLM decides the action space and generates it according to its knowledge and biases).

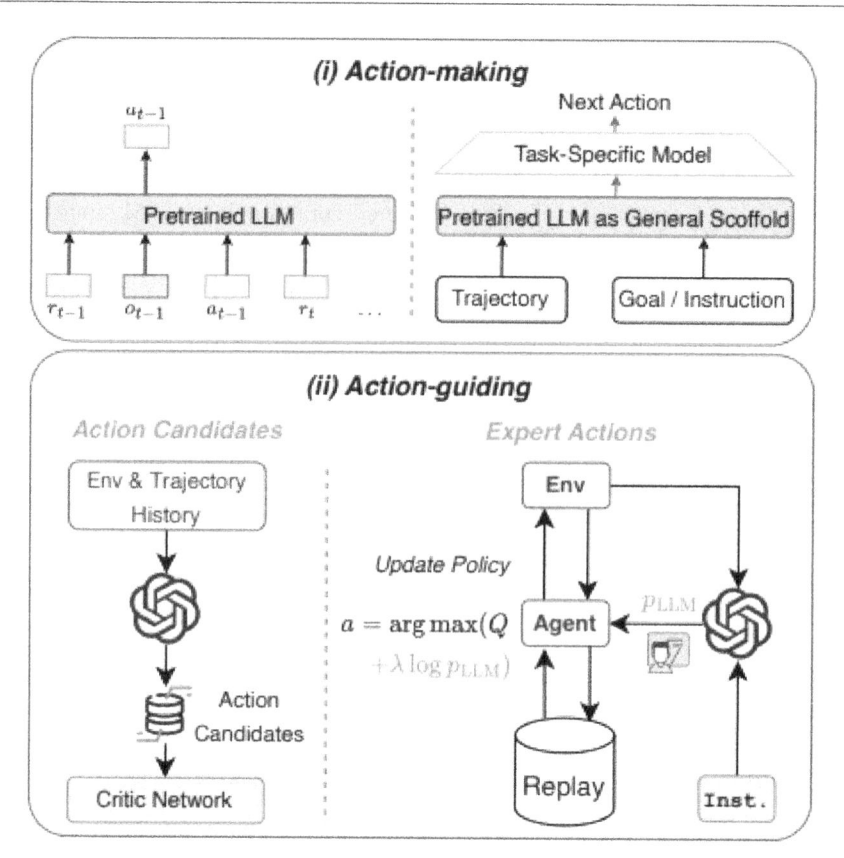

Figure 8.33 – LLM as a decision-maker (https://arxiv.org/pdf/2404.00282)

Generator

Model-based RL relies on world models to learn the dynamics of the environment and simulate trajectories. The capabilities of an LLM can be to generate accurate trajectories or to explain policy choices.

An LLM has an inherent generative capacity that allows it to be used as a generator. An LLM can then be used as a world model simulator, where the system generates accurate trajectories that the agent uses to learn and plan. This has been used with video games, where an LLM can generate the trajectories and thus reduce the time it takes an agent to learn the game (better sample efficiency). The LLM's generative capabilities can then be used to predict the future. Although promising, there is still difficulty in aligning the abstract knowledge of an LLM with the reality of an environment, limiting the impact of its generative capability.

Another interesting approach is where an LLM is used to explain the policy of an RL system. **Explainable RL (XRL)** is a subfield at the intersection of explainable machine learning and RL that is growing. XRL seeks to explain an agent's behavior clearly to a human being. An LLM could then be used to explain in natural language why an agent makes a certain decision or responds in a certain way to a change in environment. As a policy interpreter, an LLM given a state and an action should explain an agent's behavior. These explanations should then be understandable to a human, thus allowing an agent's safety to be checked. Of course, the quality of the explanations depends on the LLM's ability to understand the representation of the features of the environment and the implicit logic of the policy. It is difficult to use domain knowledge or examples to improve understanding of a complex policy (especially for complex environments).

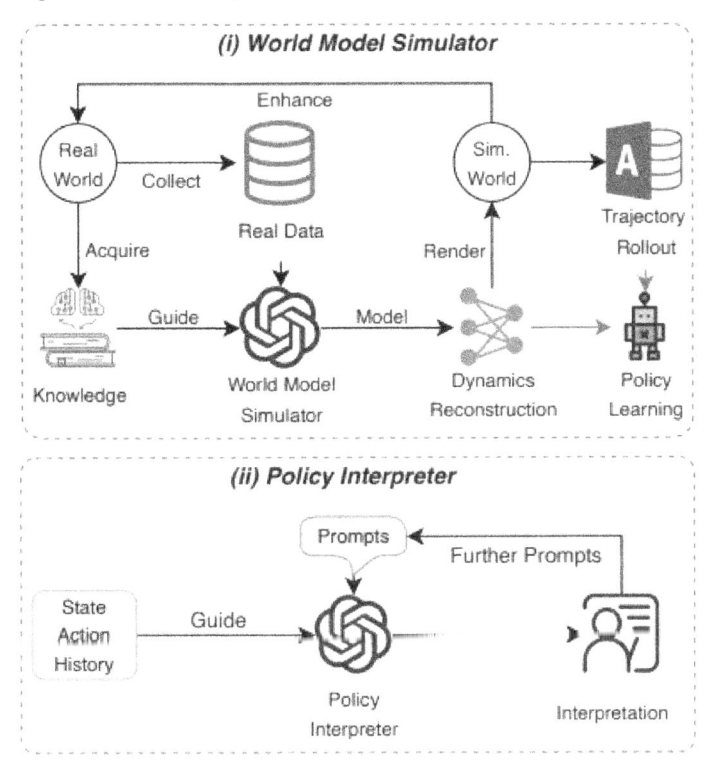

Figure 8.34 – LLM as a generator (https://arxiv.org/pdf/2404.00282)

LLM-enhanced RL can be useful in a variety of applications:

- **Robotics**: Using LLMs can improve the interaction between humans and robots, help robots better understand human needs or human logic, and improve their decision-making and planning capabilities.

- **Autonomous driving**: RL is used in autonomous driving to make decisions in changing environments that are complex and where input from different sensors (visual, lidar, radar) must be analyzed along with contextual information (traffic laws, human behavior, unexpected problems). LLMs can improve the ability to process and integrate this multimodal information, better understand instructions, and improve the goal and rewards (e.g., design reward functions that take into account not only safety but also passenger comfort and engine efficiency).

- **Healthcare recommendations**: RL is used in healthcare to learn recommendations and suggestions. LLMs can be used for their vast knowledge and ability to analyze huge amounts of patient data and medical data, accelerating the agent's learning process, or providing information for better learning.
- **Energy management**: RL is used to improve the use, transportation, conversion, and storage of energy. In addition, it is expected to play an important role in future technologies such as nuclear fusion. LLMs can be used to improve sample efficiency, multitask optimization, and much more.

Despite all these opportunities, there are also a number of limitations to the use of LLMs in RL. The first challenge is that the LLM-enhanced RL paradigm is highly dependent on the capabilities of the LLM. LLMs suffer from bias and can hallucinate; an agent then inherits these problems from the LLM. In addition, LLMs can also misinterpret the task and data, especially when they are complex or noisy. In addition, if the task or environment is not represented in their pre-training, LLMs have problems adapting to new environments and tasks. To limit these effects, the use of synthetic data, fine-tuning the model, or use of continual learning has been proposed. Continual learning could allow a model to adapt to new tasks and new environments, without forgetting what the model has learned previously. To date, though, continual learning and catastrophic forgetting are open problems in deep learning.

In addition, the addition of an LLM brings a higher computational cost (both in training and in inference), and an increase in latency time. Several techniques can be used to reduce this computational cost, such as quantization, pruning, or using small models. Some approaches use *mixture of experts*, allowing conditional computation, transformer variants (state space models), caching strategies, and so on.

Finally, one should not forget that the use of LLMs also opens up ethical, legal, and safety issues. The same problems we saw in *Chapter 3* are also applicable to these systems. For example, data privacy and intellectual property remain open topics for applications in sensitive fields such as healthcare or finance.

Key takeaways

Because this chapter was dense in terms of theory, we decided to add a small recap section. This chapter introduced RL as a core approach to enabling intelligent agents to learn from interaction with dynamic environments through trial and error, similar to how humans learn by acting, observing outcomes, and adjusting behavior. RL differs from supervised learning by focusing on learning from rewards rather than labeled data, and it is especially suited to tasks with delayed feedback and evolving decision sequences.

RL is a machine learning paradigm where an agent learns to make decisions by interacting with an environment to maximize cumulative rewards. It learns through trial and error, balancing exploration (trying new actions) and exploitation (using known strategies).

In summary, we have these classes of methods:

- **Model-free versus model-based RL**:

  - **Model-free methods** (e.g., DQN, REINFORCE) learn directly from interaction without modeling the environment. They are simpler and more scalable.

  - **Model-based methods** use an internal model to simulate outcomes and plan ahead. They are more sample-efficient and suitable for environments where planning is crucial but are harder to design and compute.

- **On-policy versus off-policy methods**:

  - **On-policy methods** learn from the data generated by the current policy (e.g., REINFORCE, PPO), making them more stable but sample inefficient.

  - **Off-policy methods** (e.g., DQN) can learn from past or alternative policies, improving sample efficiency and exploration flexibility.

- **Main algorithms discussed**:

  - **Q-Learning and DQN**: Learn value functions using lookup tables or neural networks.
  - **REINFORCE**: A basic policy gradient method using stochastic policies.
  - **PPO**: Balances stability and performance by clipping policy updates.
  - **Actor-Critic**: Combines value estimation and policy learning for more robust updates.
  - **AlphaZero**: Combines deep learning with Monte Carlo Tree Search for self-play-based strategy optimization in complex games.

- **Practical use cases**:

  - **Gaming**: RL agents such as AlphaZero and DQN have mastered games such as Go, Chess, and Atari titles.
  - **Robotics**: RL allows robots to learn complex movement and interaction policies through simulation and real-world feedback.
  - **Autonomous vehicles**: RL enables the learning of driving strategies in dynamic and uncertain environments.
  - **Optimization and control**: Applied in finance, healthcare, logistics, and industrial automation for sequential decision-making.

Summary

In the previous chapters, the main question was how to find information and how to deliver it effectively to an LLM. In such cases, the model is a passive agent that receives information and responds. With this chapter, we are trying to move away from this paradigm, toward an idea where an agent explores an environment, learns through this exploration, performs actions, and learns from the feedback that the environment provides to it. In this view, the model is an active component that interacts with the environment and can modify it. This view is also much closer to how we humans learn. In our exploration of the external world, we receive feedback that guides us in our learning. Although much of the world has been noted in texts, the real world cannot be reduced to a textual description. Therefore, an agent cannot learn certain knowledge and skills without interacting with the world. RL is a field of artificial intelligence that focuses on an agent's interactions with the environment and how it can learn from it.

In this chapter, therefore, we introduced the fundamentals of RL. In the first section, we discussed the basic components of an RL system (agent, environment, reward, and action). We then discussed the main question of RL, how to balance exploration and exploitation. Indeed, an agent has a goal (accomplish a task) but learns how to accomplish this task through exploration. For example, we saw in the multi-armed bandit example how a greedy model performs worse than a model that explores the possibilities. This principle remains fundamental when we define an agent to solve complex problems such as solving a video game. To solve complex tasks, we introduced the use of neural networks (deep RL). We saw that there are different types of algorithms with different advantages and disadvantages, and we saw how we can set one of them to win in a classic video game. Once we trained our model, we discussed how LLM and RL fields are increasingly intersecting. In this way, we saw how the strengths of the two fields can be synergistic.

From this chapter on, the focus will be more applicative. We will see how an agent can generally accomplish a task. In the upcoming chapters, the agent will mainly be an LLM who will use tools to perform actions and accomplish tasks. The choice, then, for the agent will not be which action to take but which tool to choose in order to accomplish a task. Despite the fact that an LLM agent interacts with the environment, one main difference is that there will be no training. Training an LLM is a complex task, so in these systems, we try to train them as little as possible. If, in the previous chapters (5–7), we tried to leverage the comprehension skills of an LLM, in the next chapters, we will try to leverage the skills of LLMs to interact with the environment or with other agents – skills that are possible anyway because an LLM can understand a task and instructions.

Further reading

- Ghasemi, *An Introduction to Reinforcement Learning: Fundamental Concepts and Practical Applications*, 2024, `https://arxiv.org/abs/2408.07712`
- Mnih, *Playing Atari with Deep Reinforcement Learning*, 2013, `https://arxiv.org/abs/1312.5602`

- Hugging Face, *Proximal Policy Optimization (PPO)*, `https://huggingface.co/blog/deep-rl-ppo`
- Wang, *Learning Reinforcement Learning by LearningREINFORCE*, `https://www.cs.toronto.edu/~tingwuwang/REINFORCE.pdf`
- Kaufmann, *A Survey of Reinforcement Learning from Human Feedback*, 2024, `https://arxiv.org/pdf/2312.14925`
- Bongratz, *How to Choose a Reinforcement-Learning Algorithm*, 2024, `https://arxiv.org/abs/2407.20917v1`
- Schulman, *Proximal Policy Optimization Algorithms*, 2017, `https://arxiv.org/abs/1707.06347`
- OpenAI, *Proximal Policy Optimization*, `https://openai.com/index/openai-baselines-ppo/`
- OpenAI Spinning UP, *Proximal Policy Optimization*, `https://spinningup.openai.com/en/latest/algorithms/ppo.html`
- Bick, *Towards Delivering a Coherent Self-Contained Explanation of Proximal Policy Optimization*, 2021, `https://fse.studenttheses.ub.rug.nl/25709/1/mAI_2021_BickD.pdf`
- Silver, *Mastering Chess and Shogi by Self-Play with a General Reinforcement Learning Algorithm*, 2017, `https://arxiv.org/abs/1712.01815`
- McGrath, *Acquisition of Chess Knowledge in AlphaZero*, 2021, `https://arxiv.org/abs/2111.09259`
- DeepMind, *AlphaZero: Shedding New Light on Chess, Shogi, and Go*, 2018, `https://deepmind.google/discover/blog/alphazero-shedding-new-light-on-chess-shogi-and-go/`
- Gao, *Efficiently Mastering the Game of NoGo with Deep Reinforcement Learning Supported by Domain Knowledge*, 2021, `https://www.mdpi.com/2079-9292/10/13/1533`
- Francois-Lavet, *An Introduction to Deep Reinforcement Learning*, 2018, `https://arxiv.org/abs/1811.12560`
- Tang, *Deep Reinforcement Learning for Robotics: A Survey of Real-World Successes*, 2024, `https://arxiv.org/abs/2408.03539`
- Mohan, *Structure in Deep Reinforcement Learning: A Survey and Open Problems*, 2023, `https://arxiv.org/abs/2306.16021`
- Cao, *Survey on Large Language Model-Enhanced Reinforcement Learning: Concept, Taxonomy, and Methods*, 2024, `https://arxiv.org/abs/2404.00282`

Part 3: Creating Sophisticated AI to Solve Complex Scenarios

This final part focuses on assembling the components introduced in the previous chapters to build fully-fledged, production-ready AI systems. It begins with the design and orchestration of single- and multi-agent systems, where LLMs collaborate with tools, APIs, and other models to tackle complex, multi-step tasks. The section then guides you through the practical aspects of building and deploying AI agent applications using modern tools such as Streamlit, asynchronous programming, and containerization technologies such as Docker. Finally, the book closes with a forward-looking discussion on the future of AI agents, their impact across industries such as healthcare and law, and the ethical and technical challenges that lie ahead. This part empowers you to move from experimentation to real-world deployment, preparing them to contribute to the next wave of intelligent systems.

This part has the following chapters:

- *Chapter 9, Creating Single- and Multi-Agent Systems*
- *Chapter 10, Building an AI Agent Application*
- *Chapter 11, The Future Ahead*

9

Creating Single- and Multi-Agent Systems

In previous chapters, we discussed a number of components or tools that can be associated with LLMs to extend their capabilities. In *Chapters 5* and *6*, we addressed in detail how external memory can be used to enrich the context. This allows the model to obtain additional information to be able to answer user questions when it does not know the answer (when it hasn't seen the document during pre-training or it relates to information after the date of their training). Similarly, in *Chapter 7*, we saw that knowledge graphs can be used to extend the model's knowledge. These components attempt to solve one of the most problematic limitations of LLMs, namely, hallucinations (an output produced by the model that is not factually correct). In addition, we saw that the use of graphs allows the model to conduct graph reasoning and thus adds new capabilities.

In *Chapter 8*, we saw the intersection of RL and LLMs. One of the problems associated with LLMs is that they could produce harmful content (such as biased or toxic content or misinformation). RL algorithms allow us to align the behavior of the model with human preferences, thus allowing us to reduce the risk of harmful content.

We can use similar approaches to make the model more capable of performing tasks or following instructions. In the future, these reinforcement learning algorithms could be useful in overcoming an important limitation of LLMs: a lack of continual learning.

The definition of tools, as we will see, is quite broad. In fact, any software or algorithm can be a tool. As we have already seen in previous chapters, LLMs can execute code or connect to **application programming Interfaces** (**APIs**). But this means that they can also invoke other models to perform tasks that they are unable to accomplish on their own.

In any case, all these elements have set the seed for what is called the agent revolution, in which an LLM can interact with the environment and perform tasks in the real world (be it the internet or, in the future, beyond the constraint of a computer).

In this chapter, we focus on LLMs, its various tools, and how these can be combined to interact with the environment. We will start with the definition of an autonomous agent and continue with what the tools (APIs, models, and so on) are and how they can be organized. We will see how using prompt engineering techniques (which we addressed in *Chapter 3*) allows us to create different types of agents. After that, we will discuss several strategies that have been used previously in the literature to connect an LLM to its tools.

This will allow us to see in detail how some technical limitations and challenges have been solved. We will then talk in detail about HuggingGPT (an LLM connected to hundreds of models), which was a turning point in agent creation. We will see how HuggingGPT allows an LLM to solve complex tasks using other expert models. Then, we will see how instead of a single agent, we can create multi-agent platforms. The interaction of different agents will allow us to solve increasingly complex tasks and issues. In addition, we will see how these approaches can be applied to complex domains, such as healthcare, chemistry, and law. We will then put what we have seen into practice using HuggingGPT. Next, we will extend this concept with a multi-agent platform that will allow us to understand how modern systems work.

Once we have seen how agents or multi-agents work, we will discuss in detail the new business paradigms that are emerging, such as **Software as a Service** (**SaaS**), **Model as a Service** (**MaaS**), **Data as a Service** (**DaaS**), and **Results as a Service** (**RaaS**) or **Outcome as a Service** (**OaaS**). As we will see in this chapter, each of these business models has advantages and disadvantages.

In this chapter, we'll be covering the following topics:

- Introduction to autonomous agents
- HuggingGPT and other approaches
- Working with HuggingGPT
- Multi-agent system
- SaaS, MaaS, DaaS, and RaaS

Technical requirements

The code in this chapter requires the use of a GPU. For the section on using HuggingGPT in particular, both a GPU and plenty of space on the hard disk drive are required (several models will be downloaded, including diffusion models. For this, it will be necessary to use Git **Large File Storage** (**LFS**), which allows downloading wide files via Git). Anaconda should be installed to obtain the various libraries (the necessary libraries will be set up directly during installation). For readers who do not have these resources, the *Using HuggingGPT on the web* section shows how you can use HuggingGPT on the web. For local use of HuggingGPT, it is necessary to have an OpenAI token, while for web use, it is also necessary to have a Hugging Face token. The multi-agent system is based on Python libraries (NumPy, scikit-learn, SentenceTransformers, and Transformers).

HuggingGPT should be run on a GPU. The multi-agent system should be run on a GPU, but it could also be run on a CPU; this is, however, highly discouraged. The code can be found on GitHub: https://github.com/PacktPublishing/Modern-AI-Agents/tree/main/chr9.

Introduction to autonomous agents

In the context of AI, **autonomous agents** refer to systems or entities that can perform tasks or make decisions independently without the need for human intervention. These agents are designed to perceive their environment, reason about it, make decisions based on their goals, and take action accordingly to achieve those goals. Autonomous agents are considered an important step toward **artificial general intelligence** (**AGI**), which is expected to conduct autonomous planning and actions.

The main reason for using LLMs as agents lies in the fact that LLMs have shown some reasoning and thus planning capabilities. LLMs use reasoning to interpret input, draw inferences, and make decisions (showing some extent of deductive, inductive, and abductive reasoning). This allows LLMs to apply general rules to specific cases (deductive reasoning), learn patterns from examples (inductive reasoning), and infer explanations from incomplete data (abductive reasoning). In addition, LLMs are capable of conducting step reasoning by chaining ideas, thus enabling them to be able to solve equations or debug code. Also, solving some problems (such as math problems) requires following a series of steps. Intrinsically, an LLM must often decompose a task into a series of actions, anticipate the results of these actions, and adjust its behavior in response to the results. These capabilities, however, are limited to the context provided by the user or knowledge gained during pre-training, and for fields such as medicine or finance, this is not enough to solve most problems. Therefore, the natural response to this limitation is to extend the capabilities of the LLM with external tools, or otherwise connect an LLM to the external environment.

The purpose of some studies and research is therefore to extend the capabilities of LLMs with a set of tools. These works and derived libraries try to equip LLMs with human capabilities, such as memory and planning, to make them behave like humans and complete various tasks effectively.

As the capabilities of LLMs have developed, interest in these agents has grown, and numerous articles and frameworks have been published.

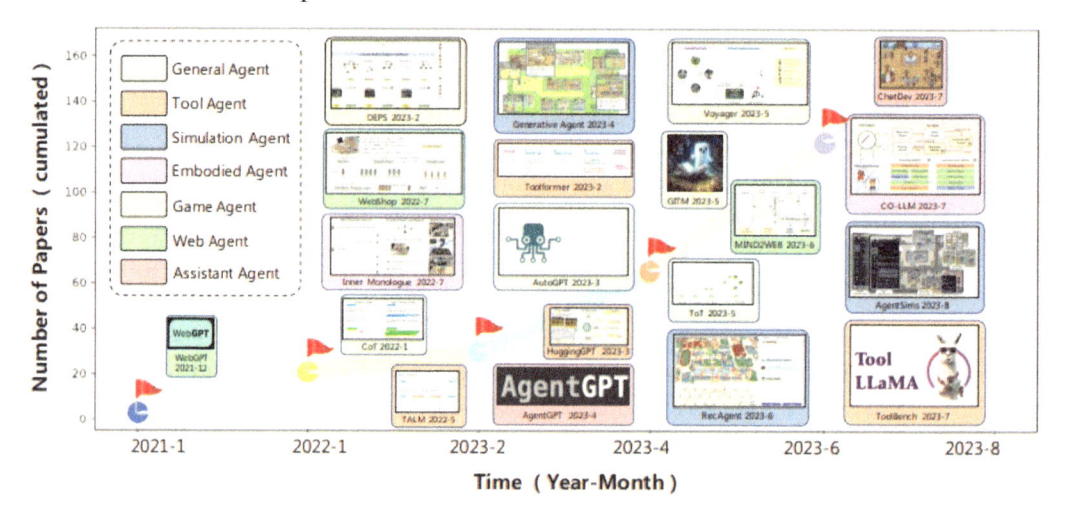

Figure 9.1 – Growing interest in LLM autonomous agents (`https://arxiv.org/pdf/2308.11432`)

The first aspect to consider when building these types of systems is the design of the architecture and how to use it to perform tasks. Autonomous agents must perform different roles, perceive the environment, and learn from it. The purpose of the architecture is to assist an LLM in maximizing its capabilities in order to be used as an agent. To this end, several modules have been developed, which can be divided into four main groups: profiling, memory, planning, and action.

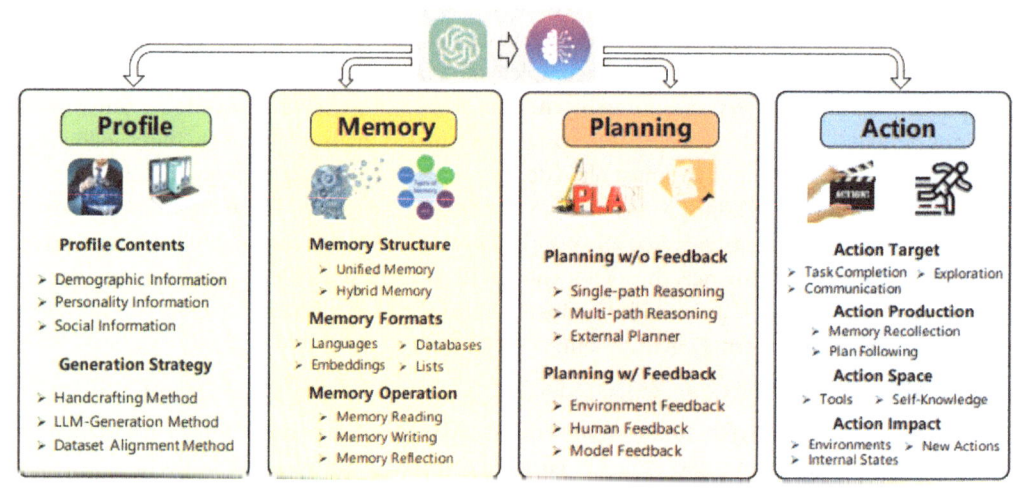

Figure 9.2 – Possible modules to build LLM-based autonomous agents (`https://arxiv.org/pdf/2308.11432`)

Let's go through each of these in a bit more detail:

- **Profiling module**: Often, agents perform tasks in specific roles (also called personas), such as coders, domain experts, teachers, or assistants. The profiling module deals with defining these roles (characteristics, role, psychological and social information, and relationships with other agents) in a specific prompt given to the LLM. These profiles can then be handwritten (handwritten profiles are manually crafted personas or roles defined by developers or domain experts); for example, for a system for software development, we can create different job roles ("you are a software engineer responsible for code review"). Handwritten profiles allow a high degree of control, enriching context, and can be highly domain-specific (addressing nuances, soft skills, sophisticated knowledge). Although the handwritten approach is very flexible, it is time-consuming and has limited scalability. So, some studies have explored systems where LLMs automatically generate profiles (using few-shot examples, rules, and templates, or specific external datasets as job descriptions). This approach is much more scalable and adaptable to different situations (especially if the system is to be dynamic or if feedback is received from users). On the other hand, however, there is less control (the system loses nuance and depth, with the risk of being generic), the quality is variable (depending on the prompt engineering technique, some examples might be of poor quality), and it still requires verification by a human.

- **Memory module**: The memory module stores information perceived by the system from the environment or other sources; these memories then facilitate future actions. Dedicated memory components can also be sophisticated and inspired by human cognition, with components dedicated to perceptual, short- or long-term information. Commonly found memories are then entered into the system prompt (so the context length of the LLM is the limit for the memory that can be used for the agent). An example is the history of chats with a user that is needed for task accomplishment. As another example, an agent assisting in the development of a game will have just-occurring events and other descriptions as short-term memory. **Hybrid memory** is a way of extending memory, where past events and thoughts are saved and found again to facilitate the agent's behavior. Hybrid memory combines short-term (within an LLM context) and long-term (external) memory to extend the agent's capacity beyond the LLM's context window. These thoughts, conversations, or other information can be saved via RAG or other systems (database, knowledge graph, and so on). When needed, relevant information is retrieved and injected into the LLM prompt, allowing the agent to act on prior knowledge without exceeding context limits. For example, in RAG, a search mechanism pulls relevant documents or memory fragments based on the current query, making responses more informed and consistent over time. In addition, this module should cover three operations: memory reading (extracting useful information for the agent's action), memory writing (storing information about the environment that may be useful in the future while avoiding duplicates and memory overflow), and memory reflection (evaluating and inferring more abstract, complex, and high-level information). Specifically, memory reading retrieves information to support the agent's decisions (increasing context continuity and consistency), memory writing allows for saving information that is useful for the agent's interaction with the environment (thus reducing redundancy and allowing for overcoming the limitations of a noneditable memory), and memory reflection allows for deriving insights from the analysis of stored information, thus allowing for adjusting behavior to achieve goals.

- **Planning module**: The planning module is generally used to deconstruct complex tasks into more manageable tasks, to make LLMs behave more reasonably, powerfully, and reliably. The planning module can include or not include feedback.

  In planning without feedback, the agent does not receive feedback that influences its future behavior after it has conducted an action. In single-path reasoning, the task is divided into several intermediate steps connected in a cascading sequence. **Chain of thought** (**CoT**) reasoning is often employed to develop a step-by-step plan for this strategy. In contrast, multi-path reasoning involves a tree-like structure where each intermediate step can branch into multiple subsequent steps. These approaches typically leverage **self-consistent CoT** (**CoT-SC**) or **tree of thoughts** (**ToT**) frameworks, enabling the evaluation of all intermediate steps to identify the optimal strategy. The tree can be even coupled with sophisticated strategies such as **Monte Carlo Tree Search** (**MCTS**) or an external planner.

  Planning with feedback is mainly used for long-term tasks, where it is difficult to generate an effective plan from the beginning or the dynamics may change. So, you can incorporate feedback from the environment and observations. For example, the ReAct framework uses thought-act-observation triplets. Another alternative is using human feedback or another model to improve the agent's planning ability.

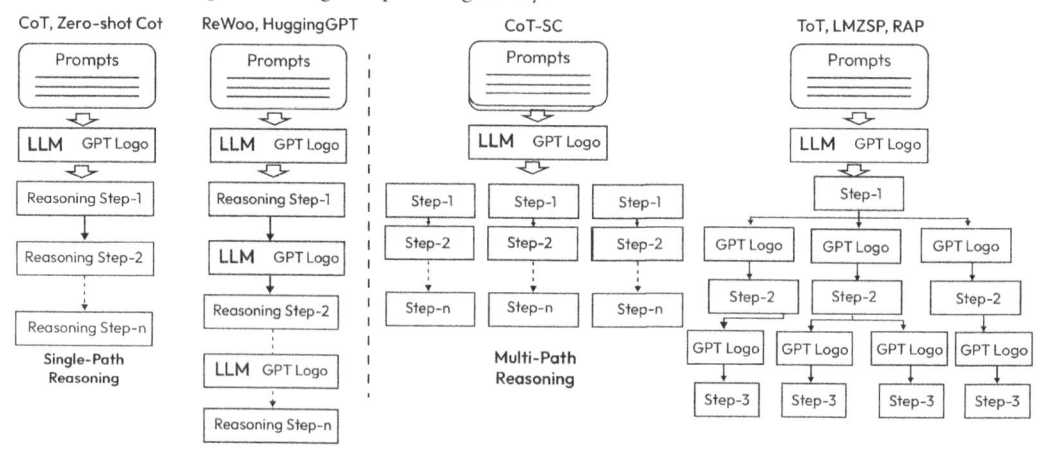

  Figure 9.3 – Comparison between the strategies of single-path and multi-path reasoning (https://arxiv.org/pdf/2308.11432)

- **Action module**: The action module is responsible for translating the planning into a specific outcome; this module is then responsible for the interaction. In general, this module focuses on the execution of the task and then actions with a specific goal. The module is also responsible for communicating with other agents (if they are present), exploring the environment, finding the necessary memory, and executing the plan. To accomplish these goals, the LLM can use either the knowledge gained from the LLM during the pre-training phase or external tools (external models, APIs, databases, or other tools). Pre-training knowledge allows the LLM to carry out many tasks using learned information, such as generating text, answering questions, or making decisions based on prior data. However, for more dynamic, real-time, or specialized tasks, the action module uses external tools such as APIs, databases, software applications, or other models. These tools enable the agent to access up-to-date information, manipulate data, perform calculations, or trigger operations in external systems. Together, pre-trained knowledge and external tools allow the agent to interact meaningfully with its environment, carry out goals, and adapt based on the outcomes of its actions. The action of the model has an impact on the environment or internal state of the model, and this is evaluated and taken into account by this module.

Apart from system architecture, we should also consider strategies to develop better agents. Typically, one of the most used strategies is conducting fine-tuning of the model. Fine-tuning plays a key role in improving agent performance by adapting a general-purpose LLM to specific tasks, domains, or behavioral goals. It helps align the model with human values (safety), improve instruction following, or specialize in areas such as education or e-commerce. In most cases, human-annotated datasets are used for specific tasks. As we discussed in *Chapter 3*, this can be for security reasons (alignment with human values), to make it more responsive to following instructions (instruction tuning), or to train to a specific domain or task. To fine-tune an agent, in the WebShop example (`https://arxiv.org/pdf/2308.11432`), the authors of the paper collected 1.2 million world products from `amazon.com` and created a simulated e-commerce website. After that, they collected human behaviors on the website (when users browse and perform actions on the website, their behaviors are registered), thus creating a dataset for fine-tuning specifically for an agent dedicated to helping with product selection. Or, in the EduChat example (`https://arxiv.org/pdf/2308.11432`), to create an agent for educational scenarios, the authors collected an annotated dataset covering various educational scenarios (the dataset was evaluated and edited by specialized personnel, such as psychologists).

Collecting these datasets is expensive and requires specialized personnel in several cases. Therefore, an alternative is to use an LLM to annotate the dataset. When this approach is followed, there is a trade-off between quality and cost: the dataset is not as good as that annotated by humans, but the costs are much reduced. For example, in ToolBench (an agent system where the LLM is connected to APIs), the authors of that work (`https://arxiv.org/pdf/2308.11432`) collected more than 16,000 real-world APIs and then annotated this dataset with ChatGPT. Then, they fine-tuned LLaMA on this dataset. The fine-tuned model was much more performant in using these APIs.

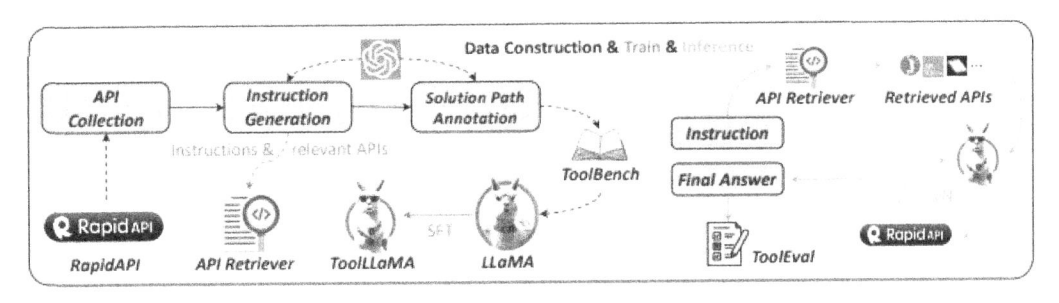

Figure 9.4 – Construction of ToolBench (`https://arxiv.org/pdf/2307.16789`)

Alternatively, you can collect a large amount of data that is not annotated, so that the model figures out on its own during fine-tuning. For example, Mind2Web collected a large amount of data for web browsing (`https://arxiv.org/abs/2306.06070`).

The trade-off between annotated and self-annotated datasets is that LLM-labeled data may lack the accuracy, nuance, or reliability of human annotation, potentially affecting performance. Still, it allows broader coverage and faster iteration. In practice, combining both methods—using LLMs for bulk labeling and humans for validation or high-stakes tasks—offers a balance between quality and cost, making fine-tuning more accessible while still enhancing agent capabilities.

Because interactions with the model are typically conducted with the prompt, many developers simply use prompt engineering without the need for fine-tuning. The rationale is that the necessary knowledge already exists in the parameters of the LLM and we want to use a prompt that allows the model to use it to its best advantage. Other approaches add agents that act as critics, other agents that debate, or other variations.

What we have seen so far enables us to understand what an autonomous agent is and how it is composed. As we have seen, an agent has, at its core, an LLM and a sophisticated ecosystem around it that can be composed of different elements as the researcher chooses. In the following sections, we will look in detail at different approaches to autonomous agents that allow us to understand some of the solutions that have been implemented in the literature.

Toolformer

Toolformer (Schick, 2023) is a pioneering work using the idea that an LLM can access external tools to solve tasks (search engines, calculators, and calendars) without sacrificing their generality or requiring large-scale human annotation. The key innovation of Toolformer lies in treating tool use as a generalizable skill, not bound to a specific task. Rather than designing separate systems for each tool or task, Toolformer teaches the model to make intelligent decisions about which tool to use, when to use it, and how to use it, all within a unified language modeling framework.

According to the authors, an LLM should learn the use of tools according to two principles: in a self-supervised way and preserving the generality of the model. Toolformer is designed to learn in a largely self-supervised manner, addressing a major bottleneck in AI development: the cost and effort of human-labeled data. Instead of manually annotating data with tool usage, the model is shown a few examples of how tools (API calls) work. It then automatically annotates a large, unlabeled dataset with tool-use opportunities during language modeling. These annotated sequences are used to fine-tune the model, enabling it to learn tool interactions naturally. This is important because there is a cost associated with annotating a dataset, but it also teaches an LLM how to use the tools. A central goal is to ensure that the LLM retains its broad capabilities across tasks while gaining the ability to use tools. Tool use is not hardcoded for specific prompts—it becomes part of the model's general skillset. The LLM learns when a tool improves performance and chooses to invoke it only when necessary, maintaining flexibility and avoiding over-dependence. In short, tool use is not associated with a specific task but becomes a general concept. The idea behind Toolformer is it is a model that treats a tool as a call to an API. This abstraction simplifies integration and scales easily to different tools. For instance, the model might decide to call a calculator API when faced with a math problem or a search engine when external knowledge is needed. Given a series of human-written examples of how an API can be used, the authors used an LLM to annotate a huge language modeling dataset with potential API calls. After that, the authors conduct fine-tuning of the model to improve the model's capabilities. With this approach, an LLM learns how to control a variety of tools and when it should use them.

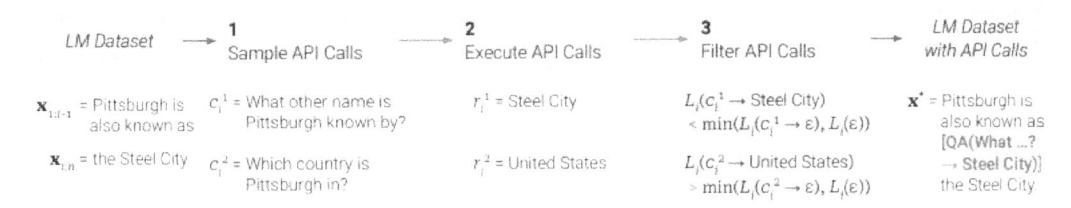

```
LM Dataset  →  1                      2                      3                      →  LM Dataset
               Sample API Calls       Execute API Calls      Filter API Calls          with API Calls

$x_{i,1:i-1}$ = Pittsburgh is     $c_i^1$ = What other name is    $r_i^1$ = Steel City       $L_i(c_i^1 →$ Steel City)                $x_i^*$ = Pittsburgh is
               also known as              Pittsburgh known by?                               < min($L_i(c_i^1 → ε), L_i(ε)$)                    also known as
                                                                                                                                               [QA(What ...?
$x_{i,n}$ = the Steel City        $c_i^2$ = Which country is      $r_i^2$ = United States    $L_i(c_i^2 →$ United States)                       → Steel City)]
                                          Pittsburgh in?                                     > min($L_i(c_i^2 → ε), L_i(ε)$)                    the Steel City
```

Figure 9.5 – Toolformer approach (`https://arxiv.org/pdf/2302.04761`)

HuggingGPT

HuggingGPT (Shen, 2023) introduces a powerful concept: using language as a generic interface that enables LLMs to collaborate with external AI models across various modalities, such as vision, speech, and structured data. Instead of being limited to textual tasks, the LLM gains the ability to manage and orchestrate other models to solve complex, real-world problems. HuggingGPT is based on two ideas: an LLM is limited if it cannot access information beyond text (such as vision and speech), and in the real world, complex tasks can be decomposed into smaller tasks that are more manageable. For specific tasks, LLMs have excellent capabilities in zero-shot or few-shot learning, but generalist models are less capable than specific trained models. So, for the authors, the solution is that an LLM must be able to coordinate with external models to harness their powers. In the article, they focus on finding suitable middleware to bridge the connections between LLMs and AI models. In other words, the idea is that LLMs can dialogue with other models and thus exploit their capabilities. The intuition behind it is that each AI model can be described in the form of language by summarizing its function. In other words, each model can be described functionally and textually. This description can then be used by an LLM. For the authors, this represents the introduction of a new concept: *Language as a generic interface for LLMs to collaborate with AI models*. In this system, the LLM acts as the "brain," responsible for interpreting the user's request, decomposing it into subtasks, selecting the appropriate models based on their textual descriptions, scheduling and coordinating model execution, integrating results, and generating a final response.

Since interaction with an LLM is through a prompt, a model's function description can be entered in the LLM prompt. An LLM then can be seen as the brain that manages AI models for planning, scheduling, and cooperation. So, an LLM does not accomplish the task directly but invokes specific models to solve tasks. For example, if a user asks, "*What animal is in the image?*", the LLM processes the question and reasons what type of model it should use (i.e., an image classifier); the model is invoked, which returns an output (the animal present), and the LLM generates a textual output to answer "*the animal is a chicken.*"

At this point, the main problem is collecting these textual descriptions of the functions of the models. Fortunately, the **machine learning** (**ML**) community provides quality descriptions for specific tasks and the models used to solve them (language, vision, speech, and so on). So, what we need is to tie LLMs to the community (GitHub, Hugging Face, and so on).

In short, HuggingGPT is an LLM-powered agent designed to solve a variety of complex tasks autonomously. HuggingGPT connects an LLM (in the original article, it is ChatGPT) with the ML community (Hugging Face, but the principle can be generalized); the LLM can take different modalities as input and accomplish different tasks. The LLM acts as a brain, divides the user's request into subtasks, and then assigns them to specialized models (in accordance with the model description); it then executes these models and integrates the results. These principles are highlighted in the following figure:

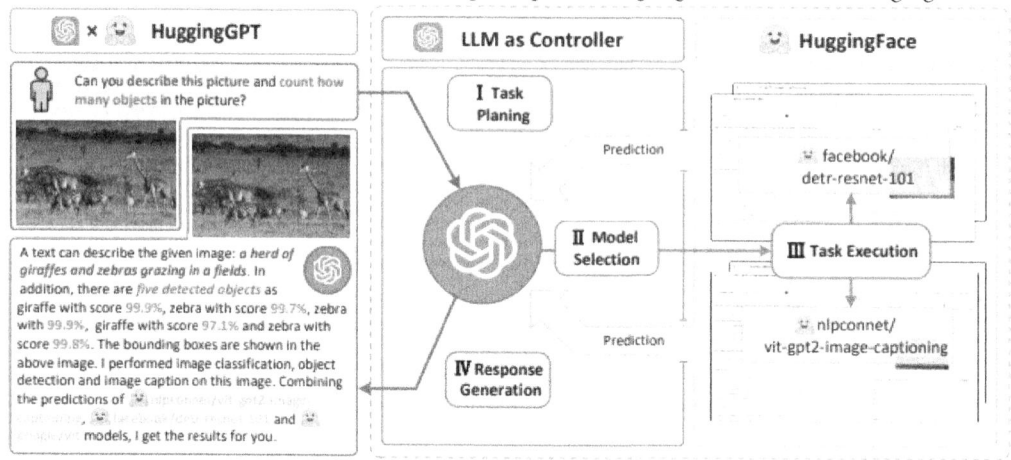

Figure 9.6 – HuggingGPT general scheme (https://arxiv.org/pdf/2303.17580)

The whole HuggingGPT process can then be divided into four steps:

I. Task planning: ChatGPT analyzes the requests by the user (understands the intention) and transforms the question into possible solvable tasks.

II. Model selection: ChatGPT selects the appropriate models (expert models) that are present in Hugging Face (the models are selected based on the provided description).

III. Task execution: The model is invoked and executed, and then the results are returned to ChatGPT.

IV. Response generation: ChatGPT integrates the results of the models and generates the answers.

In Toolformer, we have an LLM where the model calls a tool via an API call. HuggingGPT uses a similar approach but without the need for fine-tuning. In HuggingGPT, an LLM can be seen as a controller that routes user requests to expert models. In other words, the LLM understands the task and plans the action, but this action is then conducted by expert models (the LLM just integrates the results). The LLM here is just a facilitator that organizes the cooperation of different models to solve different tasks in different domains. The LLM then maintains its generality and can choose which tool to use and when to use it (in this case, the models are the tools). For example, if an LLM does not have capabilities in a certain mode, it exploits the capabilities of an expert model to be able to accomplish the task. The LLM just needs to know which model to call to solve a specific task. HuggingGPT thus represents a flexible system, where we only need textual descriptions to provide to the LLM, and then the LLM will integrate the different expert models.

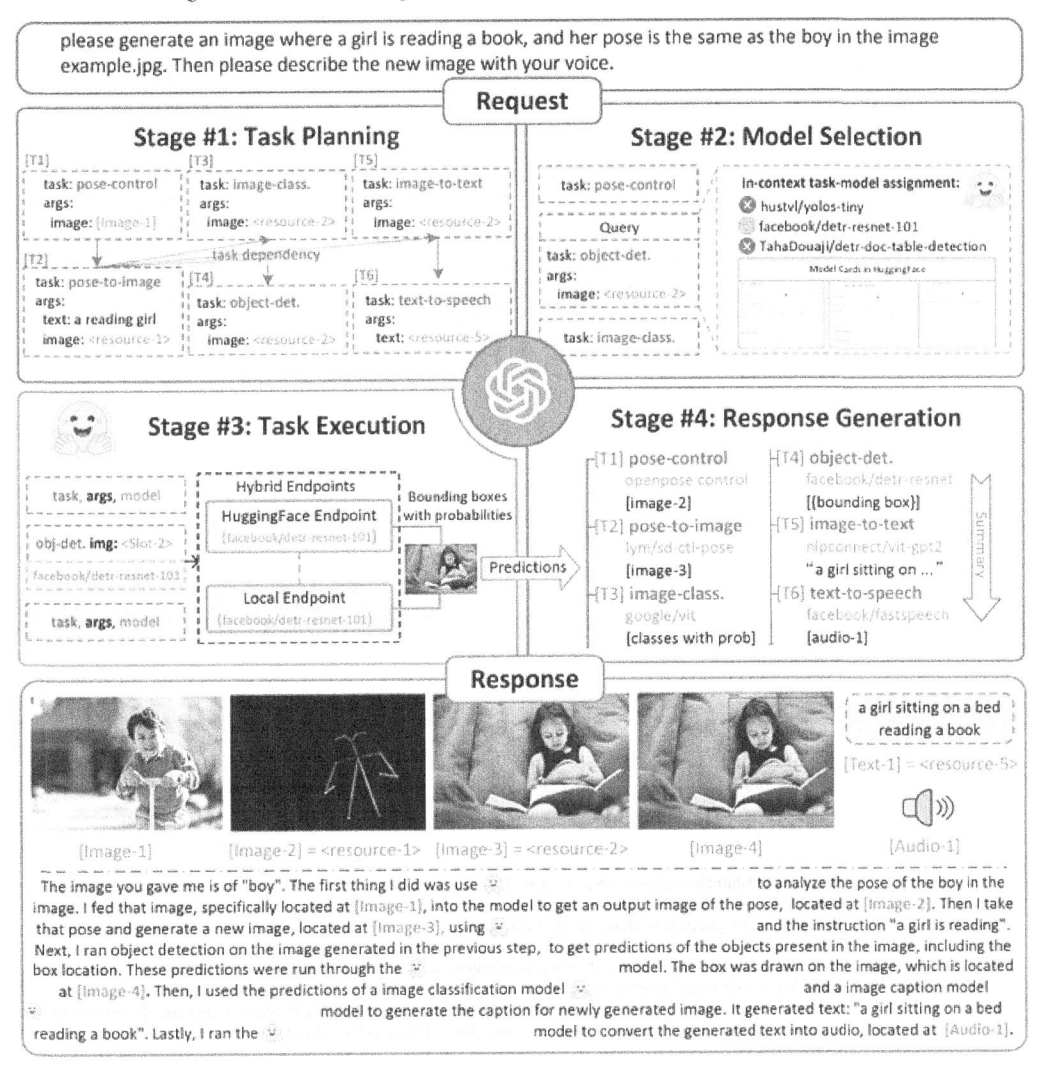

Figure 9.7 – HuggingGPT process (https://arxiv.org/pdf/2303.17580)

Task planning

In the first step, **task planning**, the LLM must understand the task and break it down into subtasks. In the real world, user requests can be complex and their intentions intricate, requiring task decomposition. This is because a single model may not be capable of solving the entire task; instead, multiple models might be necessary to address different aspects. An LLM then needs to decompose the task into a series of subtasks and understand the dependency between these tasks and in what order they should be executed. This is conducted by creating a specific prompt.

To standardize the system, the authors of HuggingGPT used a set of specific instructions. An LLM must then adhere to these specifications in order to conduct task planning. They designed a standardized template for tasks and instructed the LLM to conduct task parsing through slot filling. The LLM is guided to fill this template using slot filling, allowing for the consistent parsing and execution of subtasks. There are four slots that the template must fill:

- **Task ID**: The model provides a unique identifier for each task. This ID is used to identify both the task and dependent tasks, as well as all the resources that are generated.
- **Task type**: This slot includes the task type; each task can be of various types (language, visual, video, audio, and so on).
- **Task dependencies**: This slot defines the prerequisites for each task (the model only launches a task if all its prerequisites are complete).
- **Task arguments**: This slot contains all the arguments that are required for the execution of a task (from text to images or other resources). These contents can be derived from the user's query or from the results of other tasks.

Task	Args
Text-cls	text
Token-cls	text
Text2text-generation	text
Summarization	text
Translation	text
Question-answering	text
Conversational	text
Text-generation	text
Tabular-cls	text

Table 1: NLP tasks.

Task	Args
Image-to-text	image
Text-to-image	image
VQA	text + image
Segmentation	image
DQA	text + image
Image-cls	image
Image-to-image	image
Object-detection	image
Controlnet-sd	image

Table 2: CV tasks.

Task	Args
Text-to-speech	text
Audio-cls	audio
ASR	audio
Audio-to-audio	audio

Table 3: Audio tasks.

Task	Args
Text-to-video	text
Video-cls	video

Table 4: Video tasks.

Figure 9.8 – HuggingGPT type of task (https://arxiv.org/pdf/2303.17580)

The authors use demonstrations to direct the model to perform a task (such as image-to-text, summarization, and so on). As we saw in *Chapter 3*, adding demonstrations allows the model to map the task (few-shot prompting and in-context learning). These demonstrations tell the model how it should divide the task, in what order, and whether there are dependencies. In addition, to support complex tasks, the authors include chat logs (previous discussions that were conducted with the user) as a kind of tool. This way, the model can be aware if additional resources or requests have been indicated that can help with the task.

The prompt provides all the information needed for the LLM. In the prompt, we provide instructions on its task (planning the task breakdown), where to retrieve information, examples of how it should perform the task, and what output we expect.

		Prompt
		#1 Task Planning Stage - The AI assistant can parse user input to several tasks: [{"task": task, "id", task_id, "dep": dependency_task_ids, "args": {"text": text, "image": URL, "audio": URL, "video": URL}}]. The "dep" field denotes the id of the previous task which generates a new resource that the current task relies on. A special tag "\<resource\>-task_id" refers to the generated text image, audio and video in the dependency task with id as task_id. The task MUST be selected from the following options: {{ Available Task List }}. There is a logical relationship between tasks, please note their order. If the user input can't be parsed, you need to reply empty JSON. Here are several cases for your reference: {{ Demonstrations }}. The chat history is recorded as {{ Chat Logs }}. From the chat logs, you can find the path of the user-mentioned resources for your task planning.
		Demonstrations
Task Planning	Look at /exp1.jpg, Can you tell me how many objects in the picture?	[{"task": "image-to-text", "id": 0, "dep": [-1], "args": {"image": "/exp1.jpg" }}, {"task": "object-detection", "id": 0, "dep": [-1], "args": {"image": "/exp1.jpg" }}]
	In /exp2.jpg, what's the animal and what's it doing?	[{"task": "image-to-text", "id": 0, "dep":[-1], "args": {"image": "/exp2.jpg" }}, {"task":"image-classification", "id": 1, "dep": [-1], "args": {"image": "/exp2.jpg" }}, {"task":"object-detection", "id": 2, "dep": [-1], "args": {"image": "/exp2.jpg" }}, {"task": "visual-question-answering", "id": 3, "dep":[-1], "args": {"text": "What's the animal doing?", "image": "/exp2.jpg" }}]
	Given an image /exp3.jpg, first generate a hed image, then based on the hed image and a prompt: a girl is reading a book, you need to reply with a new image.	[{"task": "image-to-text", "id": 0, "dep": [-1], "args": {"image": "/examples/boy.jpg" }}, {"task": "openpose-control", "id": 1, "dep": [-1], "args": {"image": "/examples/boy.jpg" }}, {"task": "openpose-text-to-image", "id": 2, "dep": [1], "args": {"text": "a girl is reading a book", "image": "\<resource\>-1" }}]

Figure 9.9 – Details of the prompt design in HuggingGPT (https://arxiv.org/pdf/2303.17580)

Model selection

After planning the task, the model proceeds to select appropriate models for the task, or **model selection**. Once we have a list of subtasks, we need to choose the appropriate model. This is possible because we have descriptions of the models and what they do. The authors of this work have collected descriptions of expert models from the ML community (e.g., Hugging Face). In fact, on Hugging Face, it is often the model's developers themselves who describe the model in terms of functionality, architecture, supported languages and domains, licensing, and so on.

BERT

All model pages   bert   Hugging Face   Spaces

Overview

The BERT model was proposed in BERT: Pre-training of Deep Bidirectional Transformers for Language Understanding by Jacob Devlin, Ming-Wei Chang, Kenton Lee and Kristina Toutanova. It's a bidirectional transformer pretrained using a combination of masked language modeling objective and next sentence prediction on a large corpus comprising the Toronto Book Corpus and Wikipedia.

Figure 9.10 – Screenshot of an example of the description of a model on Hugging Face (`https://huggingface.co/docs/transformers/model_doc/bert`)

Model assignment is thus formulated as a single-choice model, in which an LLM must choose which model is the best among those available given a particular context. Then, considering the user's requirements and the context, an LLM can choose which expert model is best suited to perform the task. Of course, there is a limit to the context length, and you cannot enter all the model descriptions without exceeding this length. To address this, the HuggingGPT system applies a two-stage filtering and ranking process. First, models are filtered based on the task type identified during task planning (e.g., language, vision, or audio). Only models that are relevant to the specific subtask type are retained, narrowing down the pool significantly. Among the filtered models, the system sorts them based on the number of downloads, which acts as a proxy for quality, reliability, and community trust. The assumption is that widely used models are more likely to perform well. Finally, the system selects the top-k model descriptions (where k is a configurable hyperparameter) and includes them in the prompt. The LLM then performs single-choice model selection, evaluating the context and user requirements to choose the most appropriate model from the shortlist. This strategy offers a balanced trade-off: it keeps the prompt within manageable token limits while still allowing the LLM enough options to make an informed and effective model selection.

	Prompt
Model Selection	#2 Model Selection Stage - Given the user request and the call command, the AI assistant helps the user to select a suitable model from a list of models to process the user request. The AI assistant merely outputs the model id of the most appropriate model. The output must be in a strict JSON format: "id": "id", "reason": "your detail reason for the choice". We have a list of models for you to choose from {{ Candidate Models }}. Please select one model from the list.
	Candidate Models
	{"model_id": model id #1, "metadata": meta-infos #1, "description": description of model #1}
	{"model_id": model id #2, "metadata": meta-infos #2, "description": description of model #2}
	[Select top-K candidate models with the same task type as the current task]
	{"model_id": model id #K, "metadata": meta-infos #K, "description": description of model #K}

Figure 9.11 – Details of the prompt design in HuggingGPT for model selection (https://arxiv.org/pdf/2303.17580)

Model execution

Once a specific model has been assigned to a specific task, the model must be executed. Note that these models are used only in inference. These models are used through the Hugging Face API. To speed up execution, HuggingGPT uses hybrid inference endpoints. The selected model takes the task arguments as input and then sends the results back to the language model (ChatGPT). Moreover, if the model has no resource dependencies, its inference can be parallelized. In other words, tasks that are not dependent on each other can be executed simultaneously. Otherwise, the system takes into account how much the output of one model and the input of another are connected (e.g., if one task must have the output of another subtask in order to be carried out). To perform inference, HuggingGPT uses hybrid inference endpoints, primarily relying on Hugging Face APIs. When models are available and functional via these APIs, the system executes them remotely. However, if API endpoints are unavailable or slow or face network issues, local inference is used as a fallback. This hybrid setup ensures flexibility and robustness in execution.

The authors note: *"Despite HuggingGPT's ability to develop the task order through task planning, it can still be challenging to effectively manage resource dependencies between tasks in the task execution stage."* To solve this problem, the authors simply used a unique symbol, `<resource>`, to handle the dependencies. `<resource>` is a special token that represents the resource required for a task (this matches the task identifier), and if the required task is completed, the token is replaced with the resource.

Query: based on the pose image of example1.jpg and the description of example2.jpg, please generate a new one.

Response: Based on the pose image of example1.jpg and the description of example2.jpg, I have generated a new image s5f8.jpg for you. The process of generating this image involved using the openpose-control model to extract the pose information from the basketball image, and then using the nlpconnect/vit-gpt2-image-captioning to generate a description of the boy in the image. Finally, I used the lllyasviel/sd-controlnet-openpose model to combine the pose information and the description to generate the final image. The complete path of the generated image is s5f8.jpg. If you have any other questions, please let me know.

Task Planning:

1: {'task': 'openpose-control', 'id': 0, 'dep': [-1], 'args': {'image': 'example1.jpg'}}

2: {'task': 'image-to-text', 'id': 1, 'dep': [-1], 'args': {'image': 'example2.jpg'}}

3. {"task": "openpose-text-to-image", "id": 2, **"dep"**: [0, 1], "args": {"text":"<resource>-0", "image": "<resource>-1"}}

Execution Results:

<resource>-1

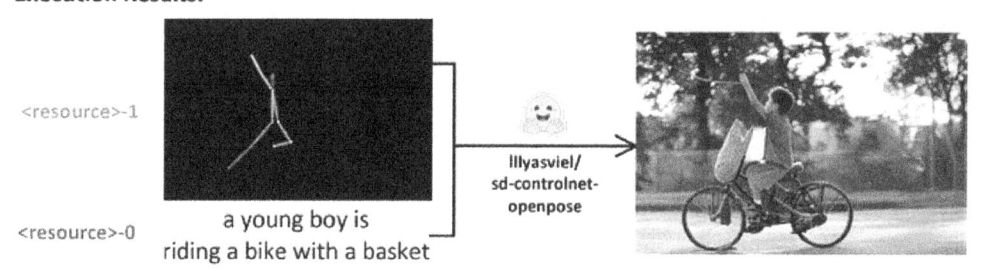

<resource>-0 a young boy is riding a bike with a basket

lllyasviel/sd-controlnet-openpose

Figure 9.12 – Model execution (`https://arxiv.org/pdf/2303.17580`)

Response generation

Once all the tasks are executed, the response must be generated. HuggingGPT integrates all the information that was obtained in the previous steps (task planning, model selection, and task execution) into a kind of concise summary (the tasks, the models used, and the results of the models). Note that the model integrates results of several other models, especially those obtained by inference and that may be of different formats. These results are presented in a structured format (as in, bounding boxes, probabilities, and so on), and HuggingGPT takes these results and transforms them into natural language to respond to a user. So, HuggingGPT not only gets results for the task but also responds to the user in a human-friendly way.

	Prompt
Response Generation	#4 Response Generation Stage - With the input and the inference results, the AI assistant needs to describe the process and results. The previous stages can be formed as - User Input: {{ User Input }}, Task Planning: {{ Tasks }}, Model Selection: {{ Model Assignment }}, Task Execution: {{ Predictions }}. You must first answer the user's request in a straightforward manner. Then describe the task process and show your analysis and model inference results to the user in the first person. If inference results contain a file path, must tell the user the complete file path. If there is nothing in the results, please tell me you can't make it.

Figure 9.13 – Response generation (https://arxiv.org/pdf/2303.17580)

Qualitatively, we can see that the model is capable of solving several tasks. Thus, the model is able to divide the task into various subtasks, choose appropriate models, retrieve the results, and integrate them efficiently. For example, the model can do image captioning, pose generation, and even pose conditional image generation tasks. Not only that but the tasks can be multimodal (such as text-to-video generation, adding audio to a video, and so on). One of the most interesting aspects is that all of this is conducted without any additional LLM training. In fact, everything is done in inference (for both LLMs and models in inference). The advantage is that you can integrate additional models for additional tasks without any training; you only need to add a functional description of the new models.

For example, in this case, we can see the execution of a multimodal task (text, video, and audio). The model is asked to perform two tasks: generate a video from a description and dub the video. The model performs these two actions in parallel. In the bottom part of the following figure, the model must instead perform the two tasks in series: the model first generates text from the image and then generates audio.

336   Creating Single- and Multi-Agent Systems

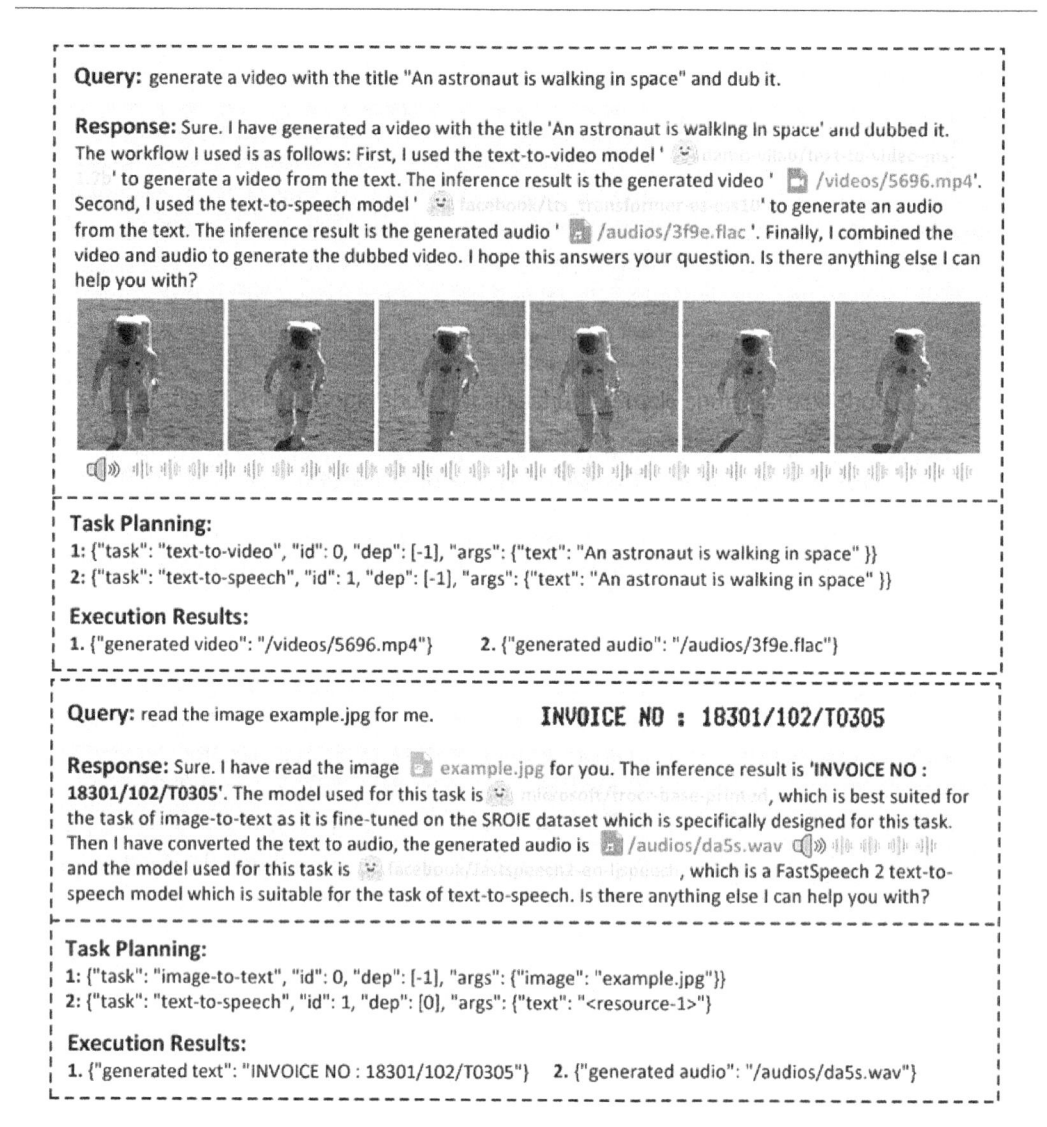

> **Query:** generate a video with the title "An astronaut is walking in space" and dub it.
>
> **Response:** Sure. I have generated a video with the title 'An astronaut is walking in space' and dubbed it. The workflow I used is as follows: First, I used the text-to-video model ' ' to generate a video from the text. The inference result is the generated video ' /videos/5696.mp4'. Second, I used the text-to-speech model ' ' to generate an audio from the text. The inference result is the generated audio ' /audios/3f9e.flac '. Finally, I combined the video and audio to generate the dubbed video. I hope this answers your question. Is there anything else I can help you with?
>
> **Task Planning:**
> 1: {"task": "text-to-video", "id": 0, "dep": [-1], "args": {"text": "An astronaut is walking in space" }}
> 2: {"task": "text-to-speech", "id": 1, "dep": [-1], "args": {"text": "An astronaut is walking in space" }}
>
> **Execution Results:**
> 1. {"generated video": "/videos/5696.mp4"}   2. {"generated audio": "/audios/3f9e.flac"}

> **Query:** read the image example.jpg for me.   **INVOICE NO : 18301/102/T0305**
>
> **Response:** Sure. I have read the image example.jpg for you. The inference result is 'INVOICE NO : 18301/102/T0305'. The model used for this task is , which is best suited for the task of image-to-text as it is fine-tuned on the SROIE dataset which is specifically designed for this task. Then I have converted the text to audio, the generated audio is /audios/da5s.wav and the model used for this task is , which is a FastSpeech 2 text-to-speech model which is suitable for the task of text-to-speech. Is there anything else I can help you with?
>
> **Task Planning:**
> 1: {"task": "image-to-text", "id": 0, "dep": [-1], "args": {"image": "example.jpg"}}
> 2: {"task": "text-to-speech", "id": 1, "dep": [0], "args": {"text": "<resource-1>"}}
>
> **Execution Results:**
> 1. {"generated text": "INVOICE NO : 18301/102/T0305"}   2. {"generated audio": "/audios/da5s.wav"}

Figure 9.14 – Qualitative analysis of multi-model cooperation on video and audio modalities (https://arxiv.org/pdf/2303.17580)

The authors of the study also explore more complex tasks where an LLM must organize the cooperation of multiple models to succeed in solving the task. HuggingGPT can organize the cooperation of multiple models through the task planning step. The results show that HuggingGPT can cope with complex tasks in a multi-round conversation scenario (where the user divides their requests into several rounds). Moreover, the model can solve complex tasks by assigning an expert model to each task. For example, *"Describe the image in as much detail as possible"* requires the model to solve five tasks (image caption, image classification, object detection, segmentation, and visual question-answering tasks). These five tasks are not solved by one model but by five different models that are called and executed. Each of these models then provides information that must be integrated into a detailed answer. These models work in parallel in inference and then the final information is merged.

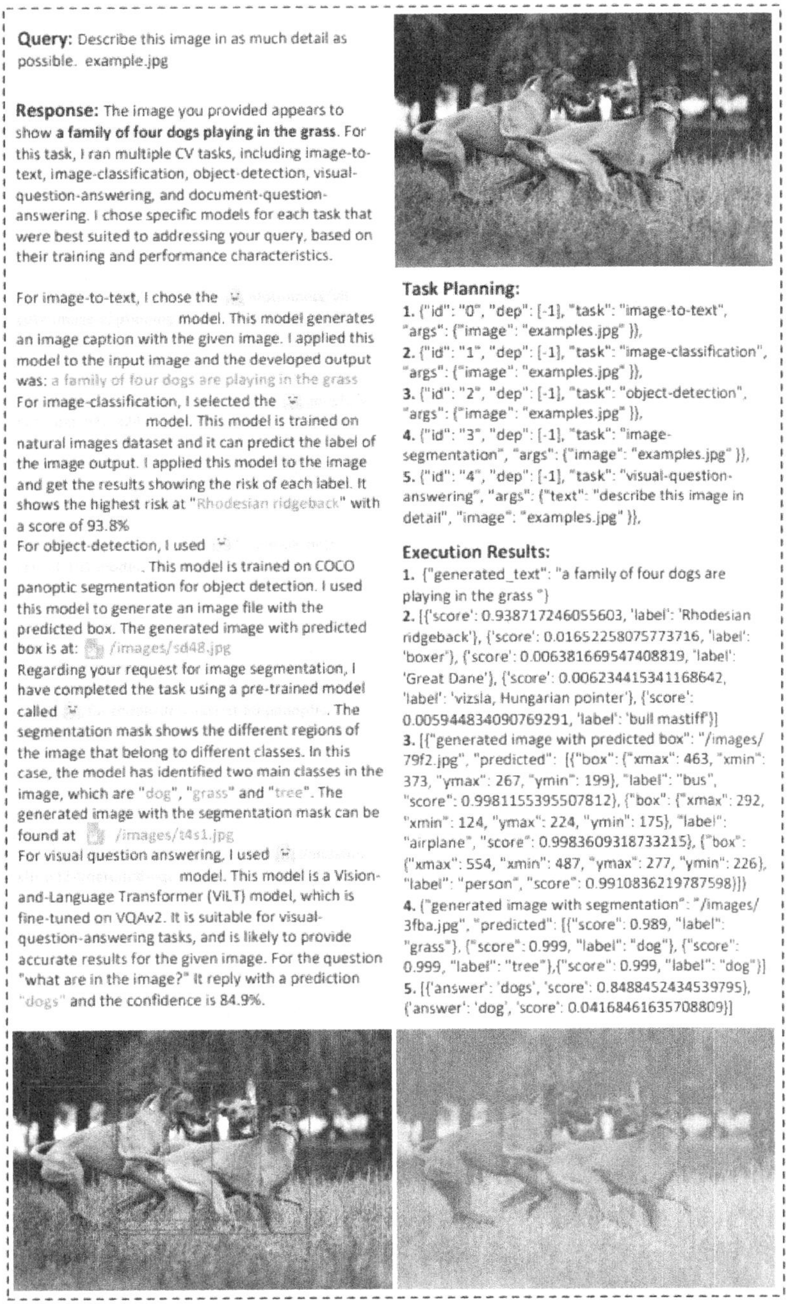

Figure 9.15 – Case study on complex tasks (https://arxiv.org/pdf/2303.17580)

HuggingGPT limitations

However, some limitations remain:

- **Efficiency**: HuggingGPT requires multiple calls from an LLM; this occurs in three of the four process steps (task planning, model selection, and response generation). These interactions are expensive and can lead to response latency and degradation of the user experience. In addition, closed-source models (GPT-3.5 and GPT-4) were used in the original article, leading to additional costs. Technically, the same approach could have been carried out with models that are open source.

- **Planning**: Planning depends on the capabilities of the LLM. Obviously, the more capable an LLM, the better the system's capabilities, but an LLM has limited reasoning capabilities, so planning may not always be optimal or feasible. You could then test different LLMs or use LLMs that are fine-tuned to create an efficient plan or models that have been fine-tuned to the reasoning chain.

- **Context lengths**: The context length of a model has a definite limit, and for complex tasks, this is a problem. In the original article, the authors note that 32K for some tasks is enough (especially if several models are connected). The solution, then, may be to use models with a longer context length. To date, though, it seems that models don't use long context efficiently. Another solution might be to use summarization.

- **Instability**: This stems from the stochastic nature of the LLM. Although LLMs are trained to generate text, and in this case we provide context, the model can ignore context and hallucinate. The authors of the article note that the model may fail to conform to instructions or give incorrect answers during the prediction. This generates program flow errors or incorrect answers. Hallucinations are still an open problem for LLMs, but there are strategies to mitigate them.

HuggingGPT, then, is a system capable of solving complex tasks by orchestrating different expert models using the language as an interface. The LLM acts here only as a controller and manager of the various AI models. Its only tasks are to orchestrate the models and then generate a response. The model then generates a plan, selects the models, and then integrates the results into the final response. By itself, the LLM does not perform any tasks but demands resolution from the various expert models. All this is conducted in inference without any training. The user then provides their question, and the system conducts the process and then responds in natural language, thus making the interaction human-friendly and fluid.

In the following subsections, we will examine various models designed to overcome the limitations of HuggingGPT or address critical challenges in other specialized domains. Through these explorations, you will gain insight into different strategies and learn how these agents can be applied to real-world scenarios.

ChemCrow

We previously saw HuggingGPT as a system that orchestrates different tools (models), acting as a generalist model for general tasks. In this subsection, we want to discuss a similar system applied to a specialized field. ChemCrow (Bran, 2023) follows a similar design philosophy to HuggingGPT, but applies it to a specialized field—chemistry.

The limitation of generalist LLMs is that they have generalist knowledge and therefore are neither specialized for a field nor updated with the latest information. This can be a problematic limitation for many application fields (especially specialized ones such as science, finance, and healthcare). In addition, LLMs conduct calculations using a bag of heuristics and not by a rigorous process. For fields such as chemistry, this is a problem, so it is natural to think about extending the models' capabilities with external tools. External tools then provide the exact answer and compensate for the deficiencies of LLMs in specific domains. Thus, having an integration of an LLM with several tools can allow an LLM to be used even in fields where its inherent characteristics constitute a limitation to its applicability.

One field that can benefit from the use of LLMs is scientific research. On the one hand, LLMs have shown some ability to understand chemistry, and on the other hand, there are many specialized models for chemistry, or at least for specific applications. Many of these tools have been developed by the open source community and are accessible through APIs. Nevertheless, integrating these tools is not easy and requires expertise in computational coding, which is often not among the skills of chemistry researchers. Inspired by previous work, the authors of this study (Bran, 2023) proposed what they call an LLM-powered chemistry engine (ChemCrow) to *"streamline the reasoning process for various common chemical tasks across areas such as drug and materials design and synthesis."* ChemCrow is very similar to what we have seen with HuggingGPT, in which we have a central LLM (GPT-4) that orchestrates a number of tools (in this case, highly specialized for chemistry). The central LLM is prompted with specific instructions and information in order to perform the tasks specifically and respond in a specific format. To guide the LLM's reasoning and tool use, ChemCrow adopts a structured prompting format known as Thought, Action, Action Input, and Observation, to prompt the model to reason about the task (and its current state), how the current state relates to the final goal, and how to plan the next steps:

- **Thought**: The model reflects on the current problem, considers its progress, and outlines reasoning toward the final goal
- **Action**: It selects the appropriate tool to use next (e.g., a molecule generator or a reaction predictor)
- **Action input**: It specifies what input should be sent to the chosen tool
- **Observation**: It records the tool's output, which is then incorporated into the next reasoning cycle

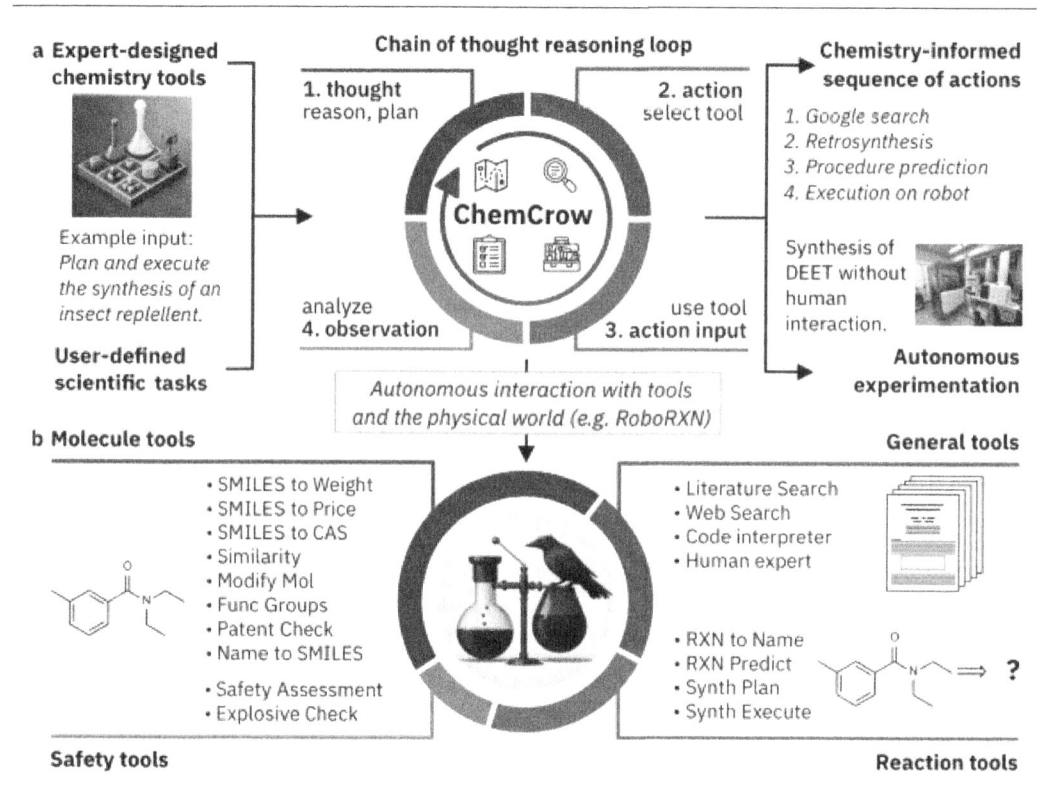

Figure 9.16 – Overview of ChemCrow (https://arxiv.org/pdf/2304.05376)

So, in this system, the model proceeds with a Thought step (which can be thought of as action planning) and uses a tool and an input to this tool (selecting and using the model). The model gets the results, observes them, and conducts a Thought step again until the answer is reached. The process is similar to what we saw in the previous section, but there is a greater emphasis on reasoning and a specialization of the model. Also, among the tools are not only models but also the ability to search the internet or the literature; the model can also run code. So, we also have an extension of the capabilities and flexibility of the system. Thus, the authors of the study see this system as a kind of researcher's assistant to perform chemical tasks.

Introduction to autonomous agents | 341

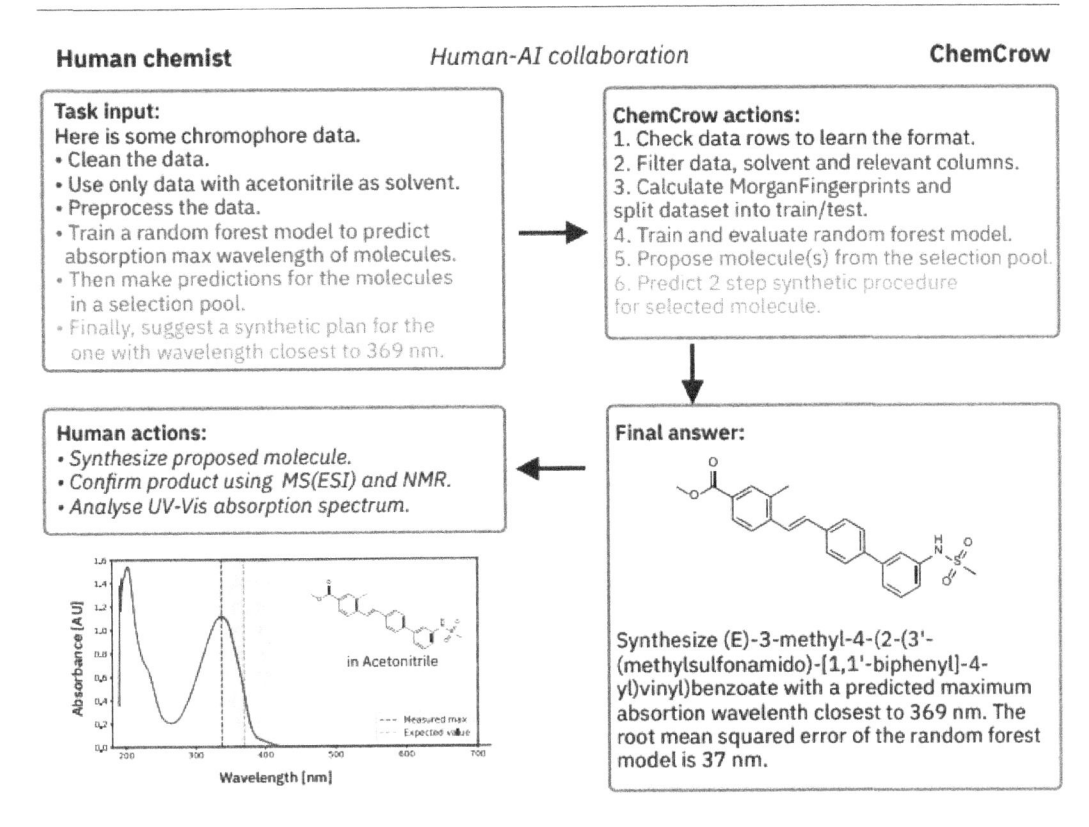

Figure 9.17 – Human/model interaction leading to the discovery of a novel molecule (https://arxiv.org/pdf/2304.05376)

So, the idea is to combine LLM reasoning skills with expert knowledge and chemical computational tools. The results show that similar approaches can lead to real-world applications in specific fields, such as chemistry.

SwiftDossier

SwiftDossier is a notable example of applying agent-based systems in the scientific and healthcare domains, with a particular focus on addressing one of the most critical challenges in these areas: hallucinations. In fields such as medicine and pharmaceuticals, hallucinated outputs—that is, confident but false or unverifiable information—can lead to serious legal, ethical, and safety risks. An LLM has a huge memory but generates text stochastically, without obviously verifying its sources. This is problematic for the pharmaceutical industry or potential use in medicine. To solve this problem in SwiftDossier, RAGs and LLM-powered agents are used to force model generation. Instead of relying solely on the LLM's internal knowledge—which is vast but generated stochastically and without source verification—the system forces the model to ground its responses in external, reliable data sources. The system uses a different set of tools to be able to answer different questions: scientific articles, internet access, databases, and other ML models. Using this set of tools, an LLM can succeed in generating reports and minimize the risk of hallucination.

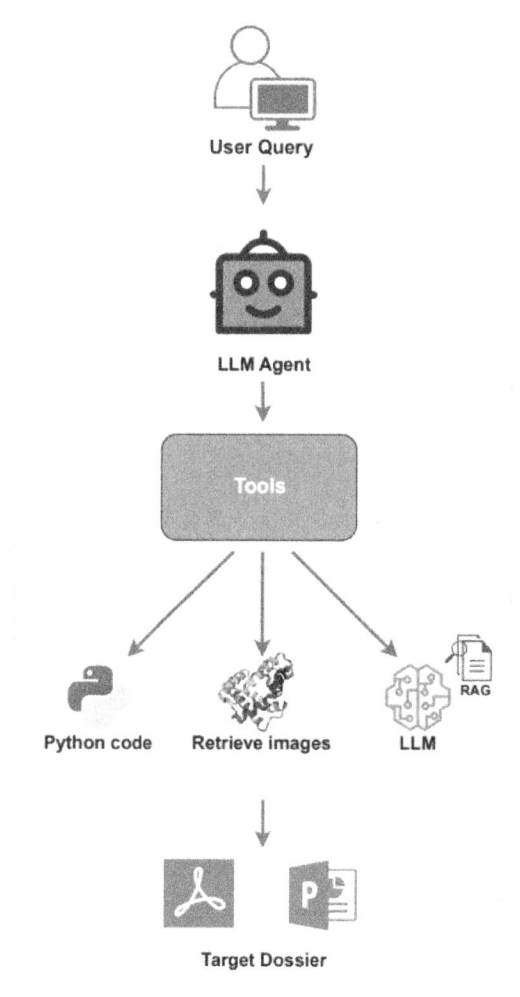

Figure 9.18 – SwiftDossier architecture (https://arxiv.org/pdf/2409.15817)

ChemAgent

In the two examples seen previously, we have an agent to which tools are added to make up for the knowledge deficiencies of a generalist LLM. In other words, we try to make up for the shortcomings of an LLM by using either external information or tools to conduct operations. Moreover, if the task itself is complex, several approaches try to decompose it into more manageable subtasks. An agent first produces a schedule and then executes the various subtasks, thus combining reasoning and execution. Despite all this, an LLM may still generate errors, especially in complex domains such as chemistry.

LLMs, while powerful general-purpose tools, face several challenges in the chemistry domain, where tasks require precise reasoning, accurate calculations, and deep domain knowledge. These challenges arise due to the limitations in how LLMs generate text and code, and they become more pronounced in scientific applications where small errors can lead to significant inaccuracies:

- **Struggles with domain-specific formulas**: LLMs may misinterpret or incorrectly apply specialized chemical equations or notation, especially when the required formulas are not commonly found in general training data

- **Incorrect intermediate reasoning steps**: In complex, multi-step tasks (e.g., synthesis planning or property prediction), an error in just one step can cascade and lead to faulty final outputs

- **Errors in code generation**: When combining textual reasoning with code (typically Python), LLMs often hallucinate functions, use incorrect libraries, produce syntax errors, or generate code that fails to execute—especially for scientific calculations that require precise library calls and numerical stability

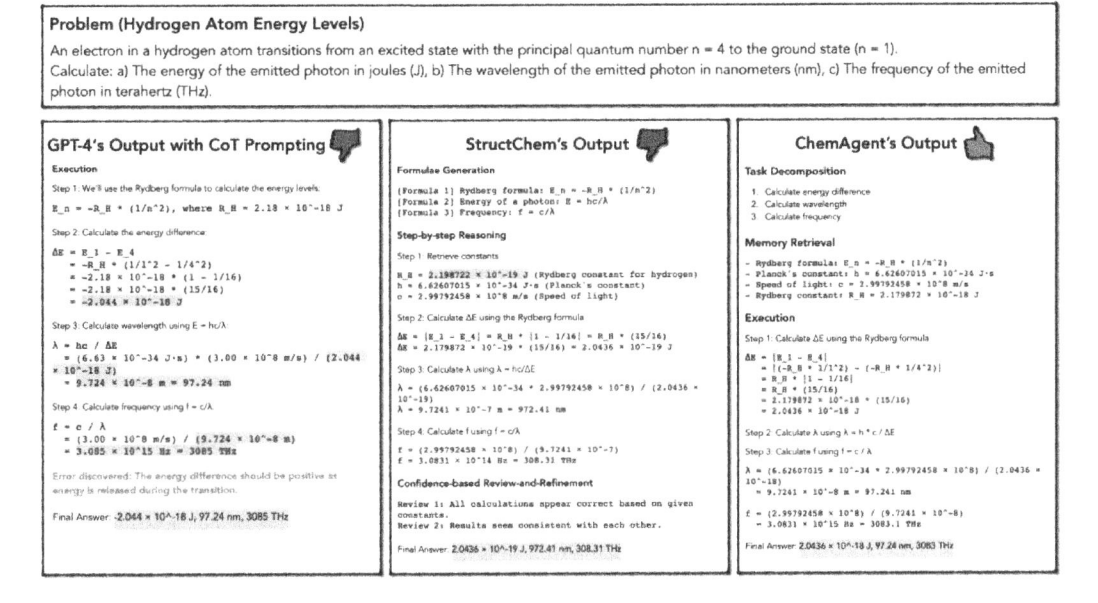

Figure 9.19 – Examples of LLM failure in chemistry domain
(https://arxiv.org/pdf/2501.06590)

Human beings, unlike LLMs, learn from their past experiences and mistakes. For LLMs, it is not possible to learn after the end of pre-training (fine-tuning is an expensive approach and cannot be used repeatedly), so continual learning remains an open problem of AI. Humans, on the other hand, can remember strategies used for similar problems; once they encounter new problems, they learn new strategies that can be used in the future. Therefore, in ChemAgent, the authors try to find a way to simulate this process. They propose a dynamic library that allows iterative problem-solving to be facilitated by continuously updating and refining its content. The library serves as a repository for decomposed chemical tasks. In other words, a task is broken down into various subtasks and then the solutions are saved in the library for future use. Once a new task arrives, the library is updated with the new subtasks and corresponding solutions, keeping the library relevant and improving its usefulness over time. Inspired by human cognition, the system has three different memory components: planning memory (high-level strategies), execution memory (specific task solutions), and knowledge memory (fundamental chemistry principles). These memory components are stored externally, allowing the system to find the information again when needed, and are dynamically updated.

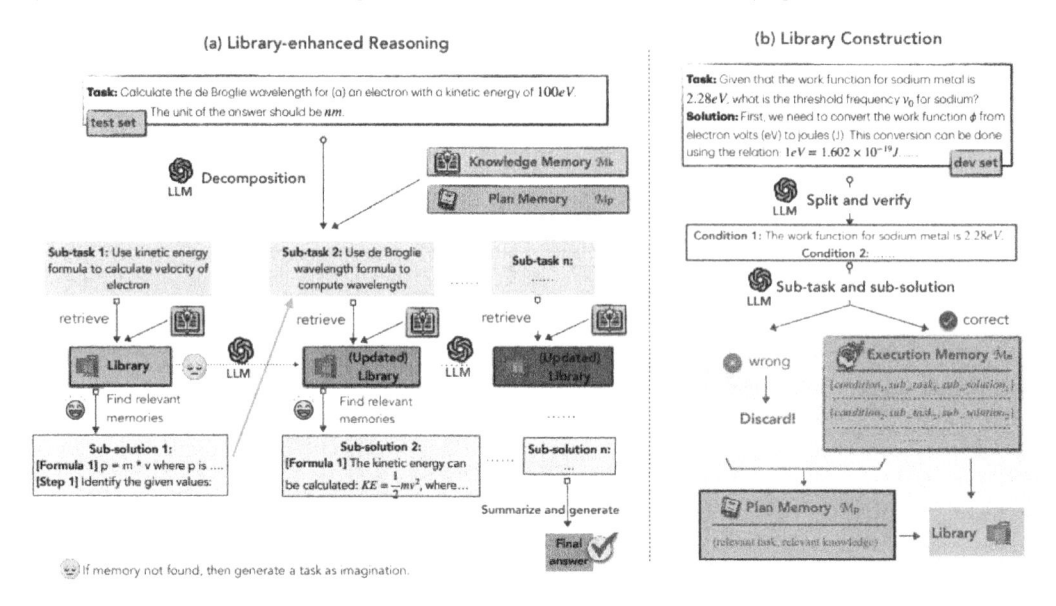

Figure 9.20 – ChemAgent framework (https://arxiv.org/pdf/2501.06590)

ChemAgent thus doesn't just passively use what it finds in memory but rather allows the system to update the memory dynamically. It also uses memory partitioning to improve the various stages of problem-solving. ChemAgent divides the process into planning and execution (to which it associates a specific memory for each step) and adds memory that functions as a reference for fundamental chemistry principles and formulas. When a problem occurs, it is divided into a series of subtasks, which are solved, and these solutions are saved in memory.

Multi-agent for law

Another area that could benefit from the use of agents is the legal sector. Legal services are essential to protect citizens' rights, but they can be particularly expensive and there are not always enough lawyers. Moreover, fair judgment is a fundamental right, but human beings also exhibit bias. Using agents in this field could revolutionize legal services by lowering costs and allowing more equitable access. In the legal field, hallucinations are particularly problematic and should be, if not eliminated, reduced as much as possible. Hallucinations arise from both the stochastic nature of the models and the quality of the data with which they are trained. Therefore, action must be taken on two axes in order to mitigate the phenomenon.

In this subsection, we want to present two law-focused approaches to present some interesting elements that have been used. Again, the principle is the same: everything revolves around a central element, which is an LLM. For example, Chatlaw focuses on data quality to mitigate the risk of LLM hallucination. Also, to make the most of the quality dataset the authors have collected, they use a knowledge graph. In addition, instead of using a single agent, they use a multi-agent system. Using multiple agents allows the system to simulate different areas of expertise, thanks to the flexibility of prompts when interacting with LLMs. The use of multi-agents makes it possible to emulate the process within a law firm. The authors developed a protocol to allow effective collaboration among agents: "*four independent intelligent agent roles responsible for initial information gathering, in-depth material research, legal advice, and final consultation report writing.*" In this way, the process is more thorough. Again, they used only one LLM for the whole system (the authors used GPT-4).

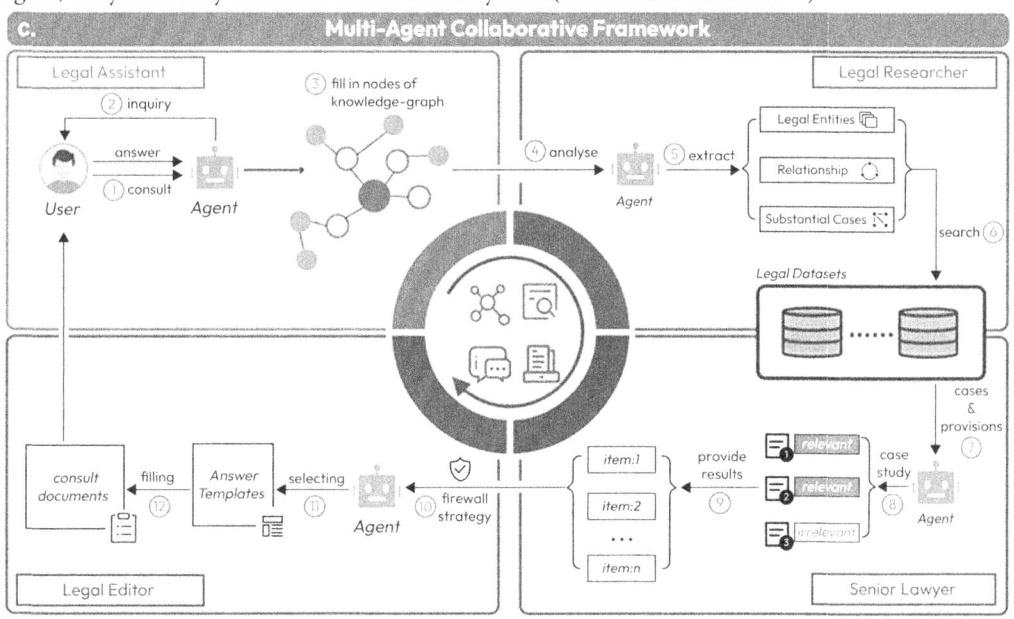

Figure 9.21 – Chatlaw, a multi-agent collaboration (https://arxiv.org/pdf/2306.16092v2)

Another interesting approach is one in which the authors (Hamilton, 2023; https://arxiv.org/pdf/2301.05327) mimic the judgment of a court using an LLM. Here, too, a multi-agent system is used, in which each agent represents a judge. Each judge produces an opinion and then a majority opinion is obtained. So, when a case is sent to nine judges, the system receives nine opinions, and then it produces a single opinion. This approach then relies on conducting nine evaluations in parallel and the consistency of these evaluations (the majority vote wins).

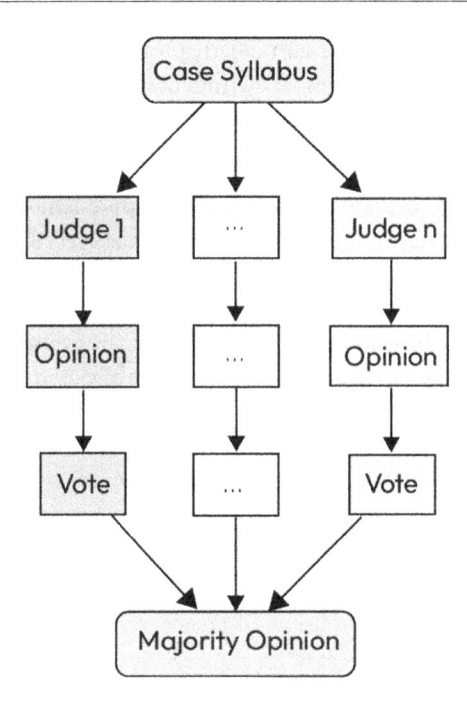

Figure 9.22 – Multi-judge system (https://arxiv.org/pdf/2301.05327)

This work shows how to leverage an LLM to create multiple agents that work together to be able to mitigate hallucinations. The authors are further evidence of the flexibility that can be achieved by using an LLM as the center of the system. A limitation of this study is the use of homogeneous judges (it would be better to build the ensemble with different models, to avoid the various judges having the same bias), risking repetitive opinions.

Multi-agent for healthcare applications

Interdisciplinary research is complex and usually requires teams composed of researchers with different areas of expertise. Typically, scientific research is conducted by teams where each researcher deals with a particular aspect and masters different techniques. For example, AlphaFold 2 is the product of 34 researchers with different expertise (computer science, bioinformatics, and structural biology). Obviously, recruiting large teams of experts takes time (and it is not always easy to find people with the right expertise) and is expensive. Only a few institutions and companies can afford the most ambitious projects. Recently created LLMs, though, have increasingly broad knowledge of scientific topics, and we saw previously that this knowledge can be connected to the use of tools. ChemCrow is an example of how to solve a chemical problem, but it cannot tackle an open-ended, interdisciplinary research problem. Recently, efforts have been made to solve this problem by creating pipelines that can handle the end-to-end process. For example, an AI scientist (Lu, 2024) carries out a process that starts with conceptualizing an idea and ends with writing a scientific paper on ML. The AI scientist is given a broad research direction, produces an idea, conducts the literature search, plans and executes experiments, writes a manuscript, and, finally, proofreads it. All this is done by an LLM-like agent that is connected to tools and proceeds sequentially.

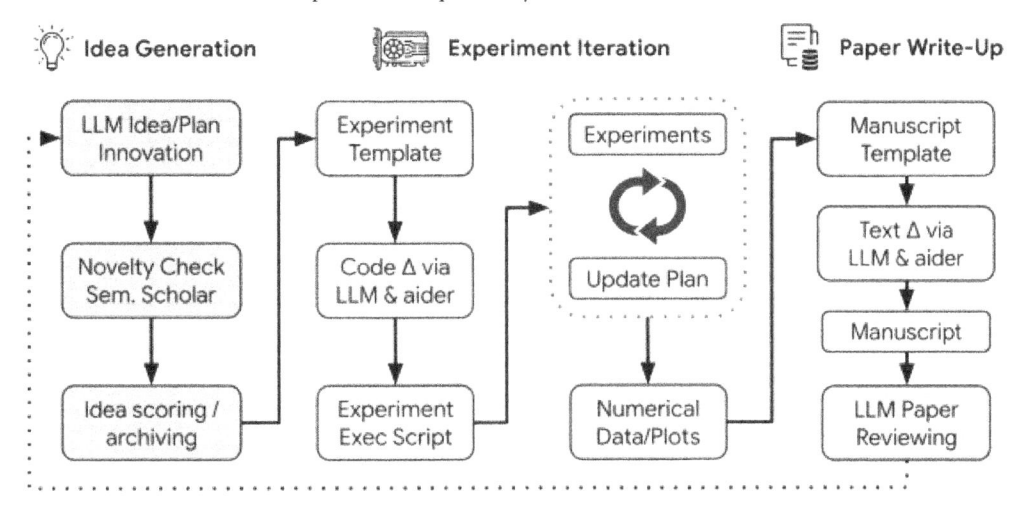

Figure 9.23 – Illustration of the AI scientist process (https://arxiv.org/pdf/2408.06292)

Other works also show similar processes, but they are still localized to specific fields and linear processes. For scientific research, we want to find ways to combine different expertise. Swanson (2024), therefore, proposes a Virtual Lab for human-AI collaboration with the purpose of performing interdisciplinary science on complex questions. In the Virtual Lab, a human leads a set of interdisciplinary agents to manage a complex process. The different agents have different expertise and are run by an LLM. Each of these agents interacts with both other agents and a human being. In this way, the authors of the study build a flexible architecture. Here, the human being provides guidance to the agents, while the agents are the ones that decide on search directions and design solutions to the problem. Each agent is controlled by a prompt (which contains information about the role, expertise, goal, and available tools) provided to an LLM (GPT-4 in the article). The Virtual Lab then conducts the research in group or individual meetings.

The human provides the question and agenda to start the discussion. In team meetings, agents discuss the research question and work together toward the global goal. In individual meetings, a single agent has to solve a task (such as writing code) and the agent works alone or together with another agent who provides critical feedback. With a series of global and individual meetings, the team solves a research question.

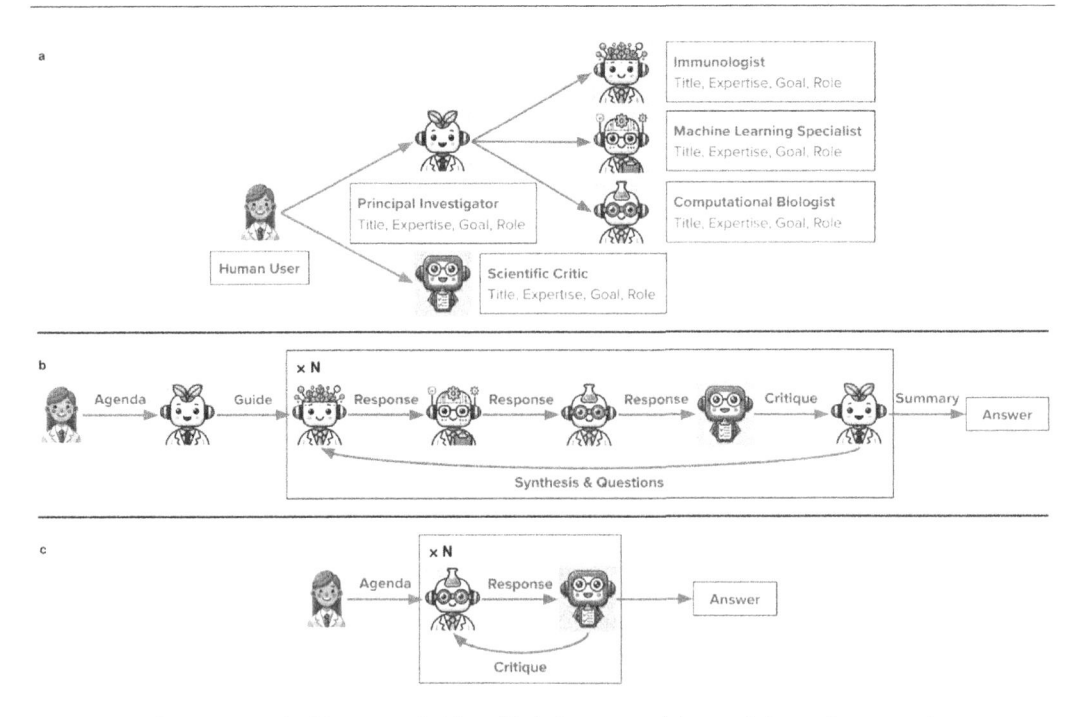

Figure 9.24 – Architecture of a Virtual Lab (https://www.biorxiv.org/content/10.1101/2024.11.11.623004v1.full)

In the Virtual Lab, there is a **Principal Investigator** (**PI**) whose purpose is to maximize the impact of the research, and who automatically creates a set of appropriate scientist agents (biologists or computer scientists) for the project (based on the project description provided by the PI). The PI defines each agent's role, expertise, and goal in a prompt. In addition, there may be an agent dedicated to project critique. After that, the meetings begin. Each meeting follows a set of inputs organized into a structure: agenda (a description of what is to be discussed), agenda questions (a set of questions to be answered in the meeting), agenda rules (a set of optional rules to make the meeting smoother), summaries (optional summaries of previous meetings), contexts (additional information that can help the meeting), and rounds (the number of rounds of discussion to prevent the discussion from continuing endlessly). In the team meeting, all agents participate in the discussion, the human writes the agenda (optionally, along with rules and questions), and different rounds of discussion follow. The PI starts and then each of the scientist agents (plus the critic agent) gives their thoughts on the discussion. At the end, the PI summarizes the points posed by the agents, makes a decision on the agents' inputs, and asks follow-up questions. After the various rounds, the PI writes a final summary that the human can read.

In individual meetings, the human provides the agenda and selects the agent, and the agent performs the task (there may, in addition, be the critic agent, who provides critiques). After a series of rounds between the agent and critic, the agent provides the response. In addition, parallel meetings may be conducted, in which multiple agents perform the same task, and in a final meeting with the PI, the final answer is arrived at.

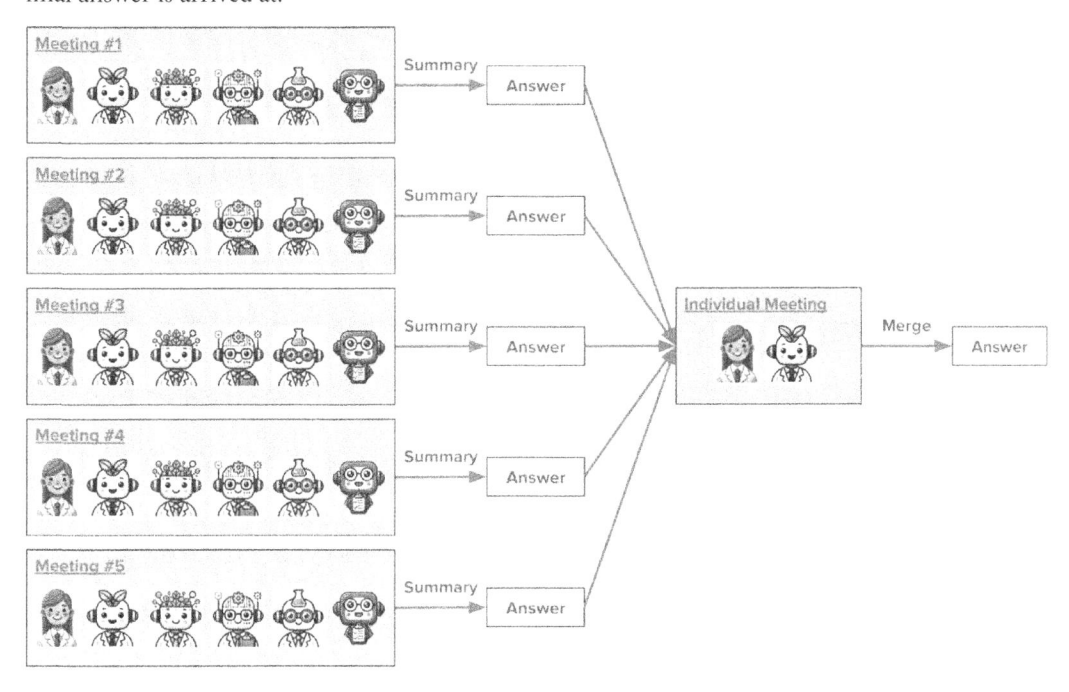

Figure 9.25 – Virtual Lab parallel meetings (`https://www.biorxiv.org/content/10.1101/2024.11.11.623004v1.full`)

In this way, the authors have created a flexible framework that combines heterogeneous agents that work in both single and collaborative settings. It should be noted that in this approach, there is a human in the loop; that is, a human being is at the center of the system and actively collaborates with the AI. This process mimics (though, of course, in a simplified way) the work and decision-making process of a human team when it has to solve a complex problem. To test the usefulness of this work, the authors tested the Virtual Lab on designing antibodies or nanobodies that can bind to the spike protein of the KP.3 variant of SARS-CoV-2. This is a complex problem because SARS-CoV-2 evolves rapidly, so a fast system must be found to design antibodies that can block it. The Virtual Lab started by creating a team that could tackle the problem (the PI created the right team of researchers for the problem). In a team meeting, the direction of the project was described and the principal details were discussed. There was then a team meeting about which tools could be used and were selected, as well as a series of individual meetings where the researchers used the various tools to create the antibody design workflow. In a meeting with the PI, the workflow was defined.

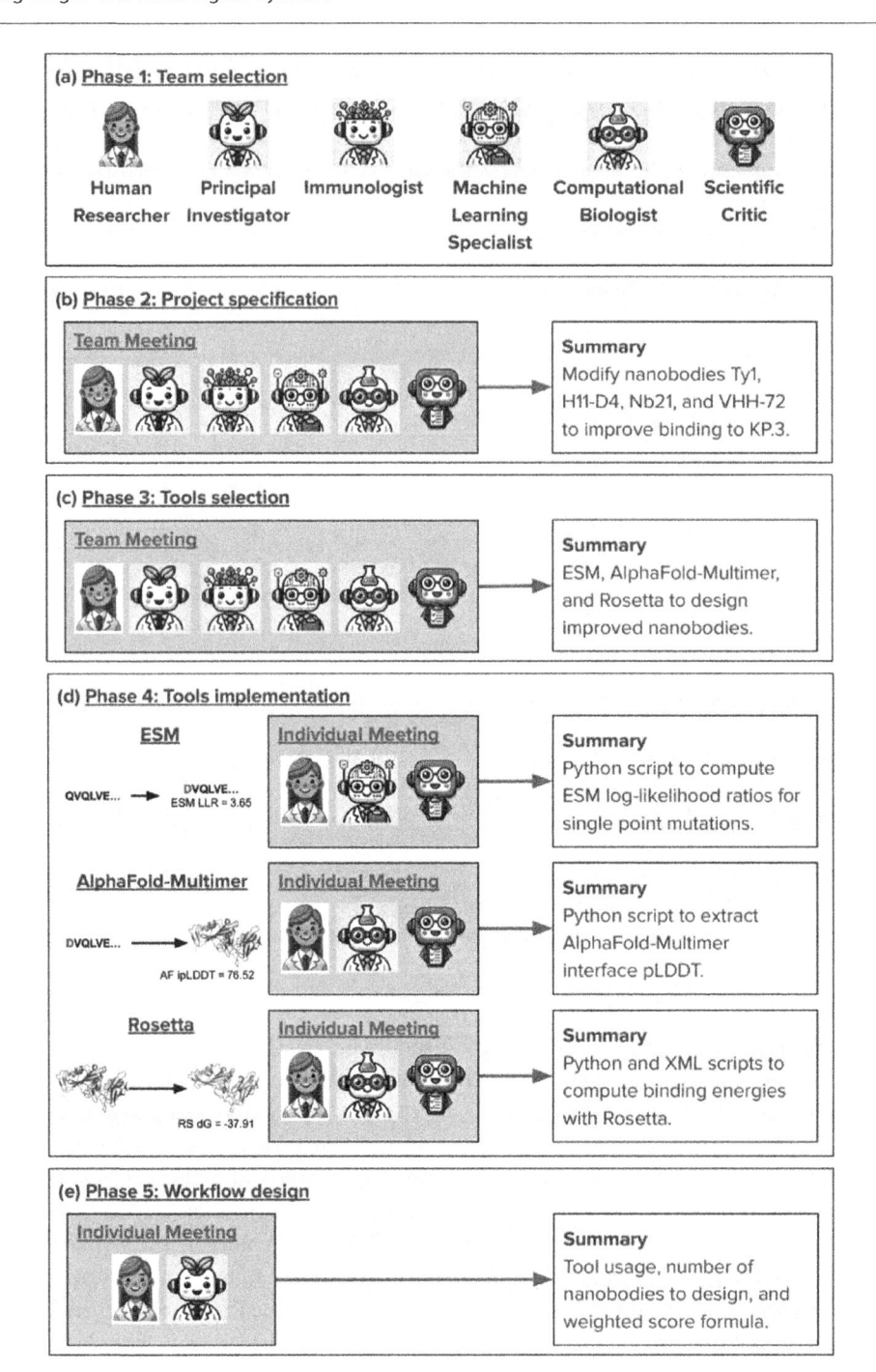

Figure 9.26 – Virtual Lab for antibody design (https://www.biorxiv.org/content/10.1101/2024.11.11.623004v1.full)

The Virtual Lab managed to design antibodies that they then validated experimentally. The system managed to create a complex workflow that used serial models to design antibodies (thus solving a real and complex problem). Building this would usually require a multidisciplinary team because the problem needs to be solved with different expertise. Thus, having agents with different expertise allows the problem to be discussed from different angles, to which a fundamental element of scientific research (critique) is added. This is done through a series of meetings, where the AI is a partner to the human being. What we see here is the creation of a multi-agent and heterogeneous system with multiple rounds of meetings (group and individual) to create a system that is flexible and sophisticated at the same time.

There are still limitations at this stage. For example, the models have knowledge up to a certain cut-off point, so they may not be aware of the latest published tools and could thus suggest old models (or ones that have problems in implementation). The solution to this problem might be to use RAG or an internet search. Another limitation is that the system is not exactly self-contained; it comes with both an agenda and a set of prompts that have been carefully designed. In this system, human beings are still involved and must provide guidance. Without guidance, the AI models may give vague answers or not make decisions unless specifically requested. Also, sometimes they do not accomplish the task or they deviate from what they are supposed to do. In any case, this system is flexible and can be applied agnostically to many other problems.

Combining different expertise with human feedback seems to be the key to better results. In a similar vein, Agent Laboratory is designed to generate an entire research workflow (from literature review and experimentation to report writing), all from an initial human-provided research idea. In this system, the process begins with the collection and analysis of relevant papers, followed by collaborative planning and data preparation, a series of experiments, and report generation. The process can be divided into three stages:

- **Literature review**: In this stage, articles are collected for the given research idea. A PhD agent utilizes the arXiv API to retrieve related papers, synthesizes them, and provides insights. This agent uses search APIs, summarization models, and bibliographic management systems as tools. The process is iterated until it reaches a certain number of relevant articles.

- **Experimentation**: The first step is plan formulation, where a plan is generated based on the literature review and the research goal. At this stage, the PhD and Postdoc agents collaborate and discuss how to achieve the goals, generating a plan that defines which ML models to implement, which datasets to use, and other necessary experimental steps. Once the plan is finalized, the data preparation phase begins, during which the code for data preparation is generated based on the defined plan. An ML engineer agent has access to Hugging Face datasets, and the code is then compiled and submitted. During the running experiments phase, the ML engineer agent executes the experimental plan. At this stage, the code is generated, tested, and refined. The results are then interpreted. At the end of this phase, the PhD and Postdoc agents discuss the results. If they agree on the validity of the findings, they submit the results, which will serve as the basis of the report.

- **Report writing**: In the report writing phase, the PhD and professor agents synthesize the research findings into a comprehensive academic report. Starting with an initial scaffold (abstract, introduction, background, related work, methods, experimental setup, results, and discussion), they begin generating the text (which is written in LaTeX for easy revision and correction). During writing, the system accesses the literature and iteratively corrects the article for accuracy, clarity, and alignment with the research goals. Finally, a sort of paper review is conducted to ensure the article is correct. Note that during this process, the system receives feedback from humans.

The key features of this system are that the agents perform repetitive tasks (e.g., literature searches and coding) autonomously but allow for human input where creativity or judgment is essential. The agents communicate intermediate results with each other to ensure cohesion among the parties. At each stage, there is iterative improvement through reflection and feedback.

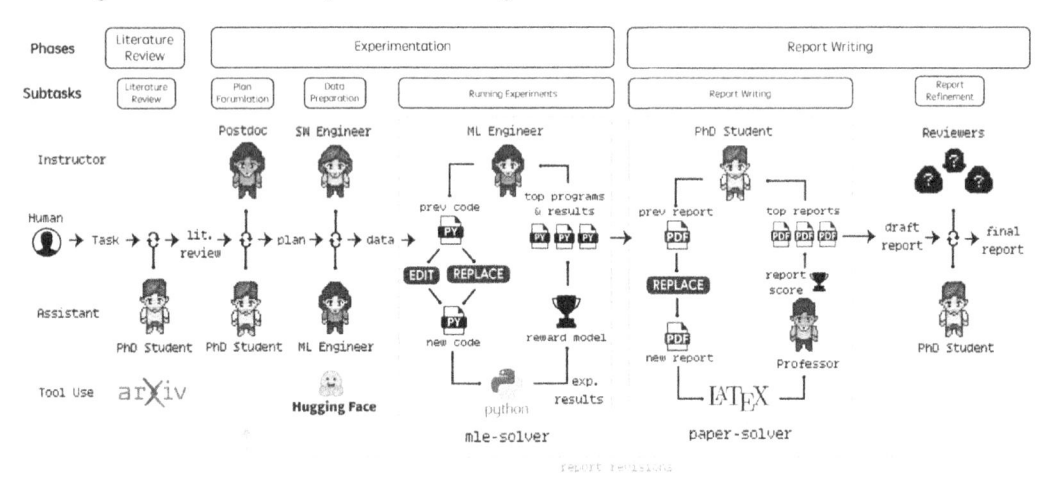

Figure 9.27 – Agent Laboratory workflow (https://arxiv.org/pdf/2501.04227)

Agent Laboratory is designed to explore ideas quickly and help researchers in being able to explore multiple lines of research at the same time. The structure of Agent Laboratory allows it to conduct the entire workflow from an idea suggested by a human researcher. In this work, they focus on not only the accuracy of the results but also on trying to find a more efficient way of solving the task (previous work required too much computational cost).

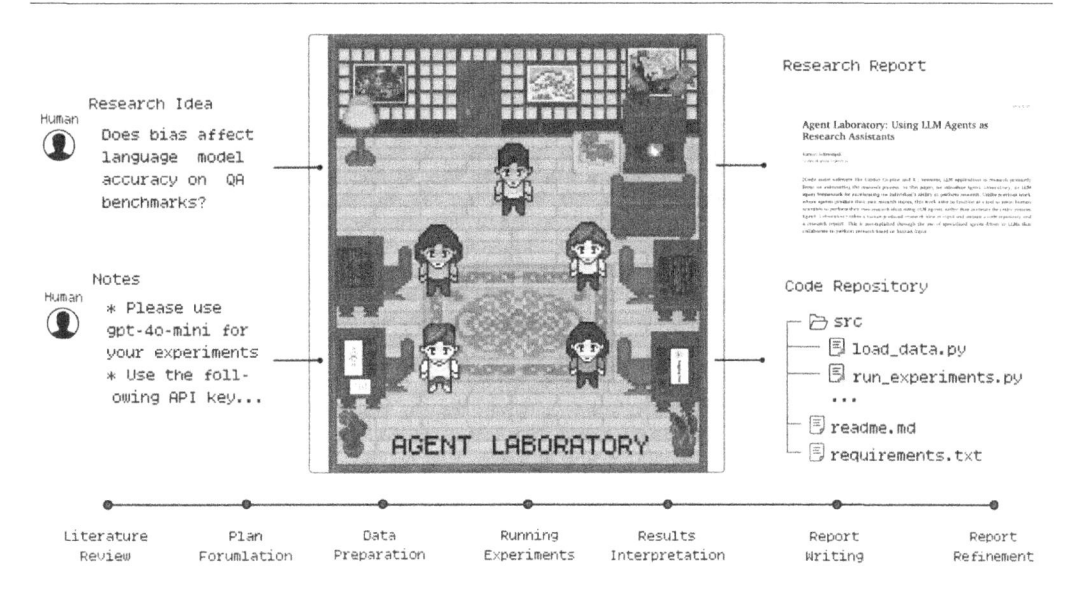

Figure 9.28 – Agent Laboratory scheme (https://arxiv.org/pdf/2501.04227)

The authors point out that incorporating human feedback at various stages significantly improved the quality of the research outputs. Furthermore, they state that ML code generated by Agent Laboratory achieved performance comparable to existing state-of-the-art methods and that the reports generated were of notably good quality for humans reading them.

These systems show that by incorporating human feedback, sophisticated tasks can be solved. However, these systems are dependent on human feedback because LLMs to date are not capable of true reasoning. There are several limitations to this: the system may struggle with designing innovative experiments beyond standard methodologies, particularly in areas requiring creative problem-solving or novel approaches. The system still generates errors in the code (bugs or inefficiencies), it continues to maintain a high computational cost (several LLM calls), communication between agents is not yet perfect, report generation is still suboptimal in comparison to an expert, it generalizes poorly to highly specialized or niche research areas (they are poorly represented in training data and literature), and several ethical issues remain open.

In this section, we looked at different systems with a single agent or multiple agents. In the next section, we will see how HuggingGPT works in practice and how we can create multi-agent systems.

Working with HuggingGPT

There are two ways you can use HuggingGPT:

- Clone the repository locally
- Use the web service

Here, we will look at the two methods. The main difference is that when we clone the repository locally, we download all the models, and the system execution will be conducted locally. In contrast, the web service method requires that the execution is conducted in a service. In both cases, all models are used in inference; the difference lies in where the models are executed and the resources employed. Additionally, both approaches support the use of a web-based GUI.

Using HuggingGPT locally

To clone HuggingGPT (the corresponding repository is called Jarvis), it is useful to use Git LFS. Git LFS is an open source extension of Git. Git is designed to manage code repositories but not large binary files (such as videos, datasets, or high-resolution images). Git LFS is crucial for repositories that include large assets (e.g., datasets, videos, or binaries) because Git is otherwise inefficient at handling large files. Git LFS solves this problem by storing large files outside the regular repository objects and replacing them with lightweight references (pointers) in the Git repository. Git LFS keeps repository size manageable by storing large files outside the repository's regular objects, allows for better standardization when using large objects, and improves performance during operation with GitHub repositories (such as cloning, pushing, and pulling). The pointer contains various metadata about the file (e.g., size, hash, and location), and when we clone a repository, Git LFS downloads the files by exploiting the information in these pointers. This then allows us to separate operations on the code from those conducted on the large files. In general, it is common to use Git LFS for projects involving ML, game development, or video editing, because it allows for simplification and speeding up of the download process. In ML projects, the model weights are very large and can be frequently updated; using Git LFS allows us to efficiently track and manage these files—such as downloaded models—without bloating the main repository without bloating the repository. As we mentioned, HuggingGPT uses several large models (for example, there are different diffusion models that can occupy several gigabytes), and Git LFS allows for easier management.

To install Git LFS, you can go to the official website (`https://git-lfs.github.com/`) and download the installer for your operating system (Windows, macOS, or Linux). Run the downloaded installer. On macOS, double-click the `.pkg` file or use the Homebrew package manager:

```
brew install git-lfs
```

Run the following command to enable Git LFS for your user:

```
git lfs install
```

Once you have installed Git LFS as a Git extension on your computer, it will automatically recognize and track when there are large files in the repository and manage them. It modifies or creates a few Git configuration entries (such as in `~/.gitconfig`) so that future clones and repositories you create can use LFS without extra hassle.

Cloning an LFS-enabled repository is as simple as if it were a regular repository (Git LFS takes care of the files in the background and large files are managed automatically):

```
git clone https://github.com/example/repo.git
```

If we want, we can easily conduct large file tracking:

```
git lfs track "*.bin"
git add .gitattributes
git commit -m "Track large .bin files with LFS"
```

Git LFS is compatible with classical Git commands. Pull/push operations are conducted as in normal Git workflows—no special steps are required unless a repository demands specific credentials or tokens.

At this point, we can proceed with the installation of HuggingGPT. The HuggingGPT repository is stored at `https://github.com/microsoft/JARVIS`.

JARVIS

The mission of JARVIS is to explore artificial general intelligence (AGI) and deliver cutting-edge research to the whole community.

What's New

- [2024.01.15] We release Easytool for easier tool usage.
  - The code and datasets are available at EasyTool.
  - The paper is available at EasyTool: Enhancing LLM-based Agents with Concise Tool Instruction.
- [2023.11.30] We release TaskBench for evaluating task automation capability of LLMs.
  - The code and datasets are available at TaskBench.
  - The paper is available at TaskBench: Benchmarking Large Language Models for Task Automation.
- [2023.07.28] We are now in the process of planning evaluation and project rebuilding. We will release a new version of Jarvis in the near future.
- [2023.07.24] We released a light langchain version of Jarvis. See here.

Figure 9.29 – Microsoft HuggingGPT

The first step is to clone the repository:

```
git clone https://github.com/example/microsoft/JARVIS.git
```

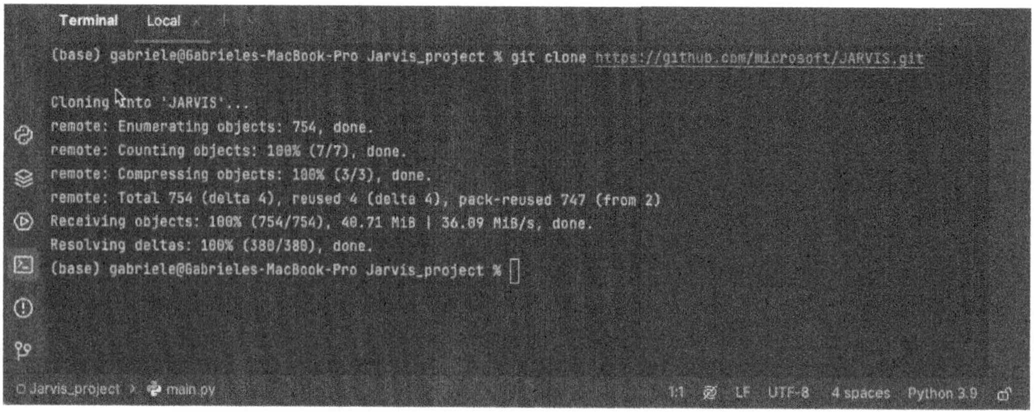

Figure 9.30 – Microsoft HuggingGPT cloning

The `git clone` command initiates the download of the repository from the remote URL. The terminal output indicates the repository being downloaded: objects (metadata and changes) and delta compression (a process that minimizes the amount of data transmitted by only sending differences between versions). Notice the following:

- `Receiving objects: 100% (150/150), done.`: This confirms that all objects (files and history) have been received
- `Resolving deltas: 100% (85/85), done.`: Git reconstructs the actual repository state by applying the changes (deltas) received

Once we have cloned the repository, we can go to the local repository (the local folder):

```
cd JARVIS/hugginggpt/server
```

This step is in preparation for creating or managing the `conda` environment, ensuring that the actions are performed in the context of the relevant project directory.

Then, we create a new `conda` environment named `jarvis` (or we can choose another name) and specify that it should use Python version 3.8:

```
conda create -n jarvis python=3.8
```

Note that `-n` means we want a new environment for our project, and `python=3.8` means we are explicitly defining the Python version to be 3.8 for this environment.

A `conda` environment allows us to isolate dependencies and avoid conflicts with global Python installations or other projects.

Note that `conda` is handling the following processes:

- **Collecting package metadata**: `conda` fetches information about the required packages and dependencies from its repositories. This ensures compatibility between Python 3.8 and any other libraries to be installed.
- **Solving the environment**: `conda` resolves potential dependency conflicts and finalizes the list of packages to be installed.

Since you may have installed `conda` previously, we just need to update it:

```
conda update -n base -c defaults conda
```

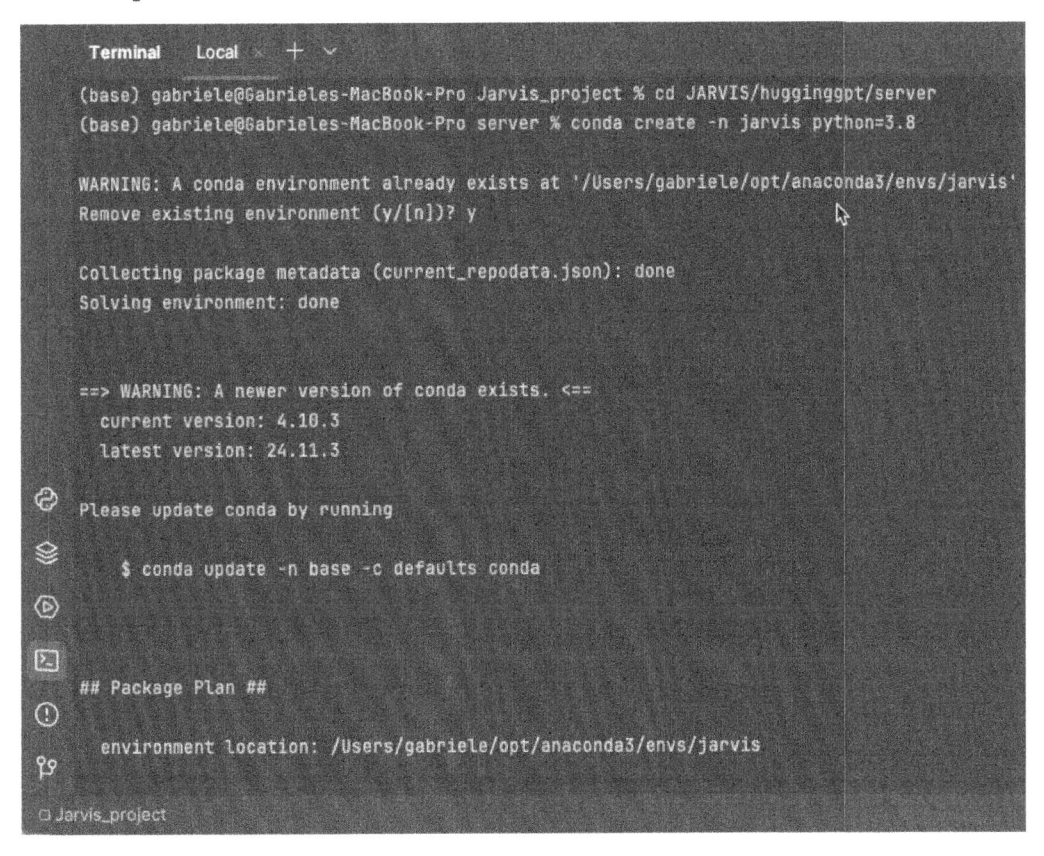

Figure 9.31 – Updating conda

After solving the environment and preparing to create it, `conda` installs the required base packages for the new environment. Each package is listed alongside the repository (`pkgs/main`) and its specific version (in this case, we are using macOS).

The terminal prompts us with `Proceed ([y]/n)?`. Remember to respond with `y` to confirm the installation of these packages.

Note these elements:

- **Preparing transaction**: `conda` ensures that the necessary dependencies are ready to be installed without conflicts
- **Verifying transaction**: It checks the integrity of the package metadata and ensures compatibility between all packages
- **Executing transaction**: `conda` installs the packages into the specified environment

Once these steps are completed, the new environment (`jarvis`) is ready for use.

Upon successful creation, `conda` provides the user with commands for managing the new environment.

To activate this environment, use the following:

```
conda activate jarvis
```

To deactivate an active environment, use the following:

```
conda deactivate
```

Remember that the activation switches the user's terminal session to use the `jarvis` environment, isolating its dependencies and Python version. Notice that the prompt changes from `(base)` to `(jarvis)`, indicating that the terminal is now operating within the `jarvis` environment. The environment's isolated Python version (3.8) and its dependencies are now being used. Any libraries or tools installed from this point will remain confined to this environment, avoiding interference with other projects.

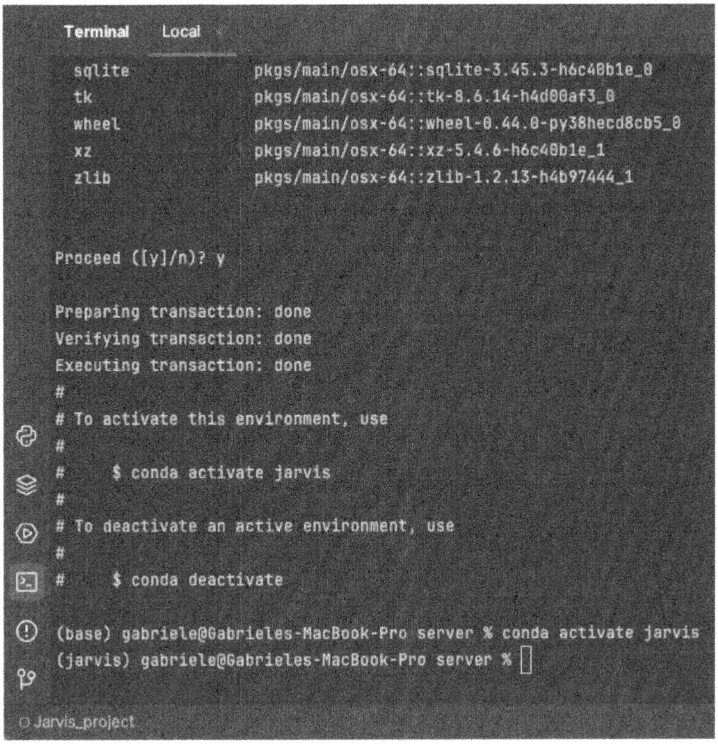

Figure 9.32 – conda activation

At this point, we begin to install the various requirements:

```
conda install pytorch torchvision torchaudio pytorch-cuda=11.7 -c
pytorch -c nvidia
```

The following command uses `pip` to install dependencies listed in a `requirements.txt` file (most often, a list of packages is provided in a requirements file). These requirements are necessary to install HuggingGPT:

```
pip install -r requirements.txt
```

The following comment in HuggingGPT emphasizes that Git LFS must be installed. This script (provided as part of the project) automates the download of model files required for local or hybrid inference modes. As a reminder, local means the model runs entirely on the local machine and hybrid means the inference involves a mix of local and remote execution, as was described in the HuggingGPT paper (https://arxiv.org/abs/2303.17580) and in the preceding section:

```
# download models. Make sure that `git-lfs` is installed.
bash download.sh # required when `inference_mode` is `local` or
`hybrid`
```

Once we have installed everything, we can start the execution:

```
python model_server.py --config config/config.default.yaml # required when `inference_mode` is `local` or `hybrid`.
python awesome_chat.py --config config/config.default.yaml --mode server # for text-davinci-003
```

There are different scripts in the repository:

- `model_server.py`: This script runs a model server, which processes ML models based on the configuration file (`config/config.default.yaml`). The configuration file specifies parameters such as inference mode (local or hybrid), paths to the models, and hardware requirements.
- `awesome_chat.py`: This script starts a server for text generation or chatbot functionality.

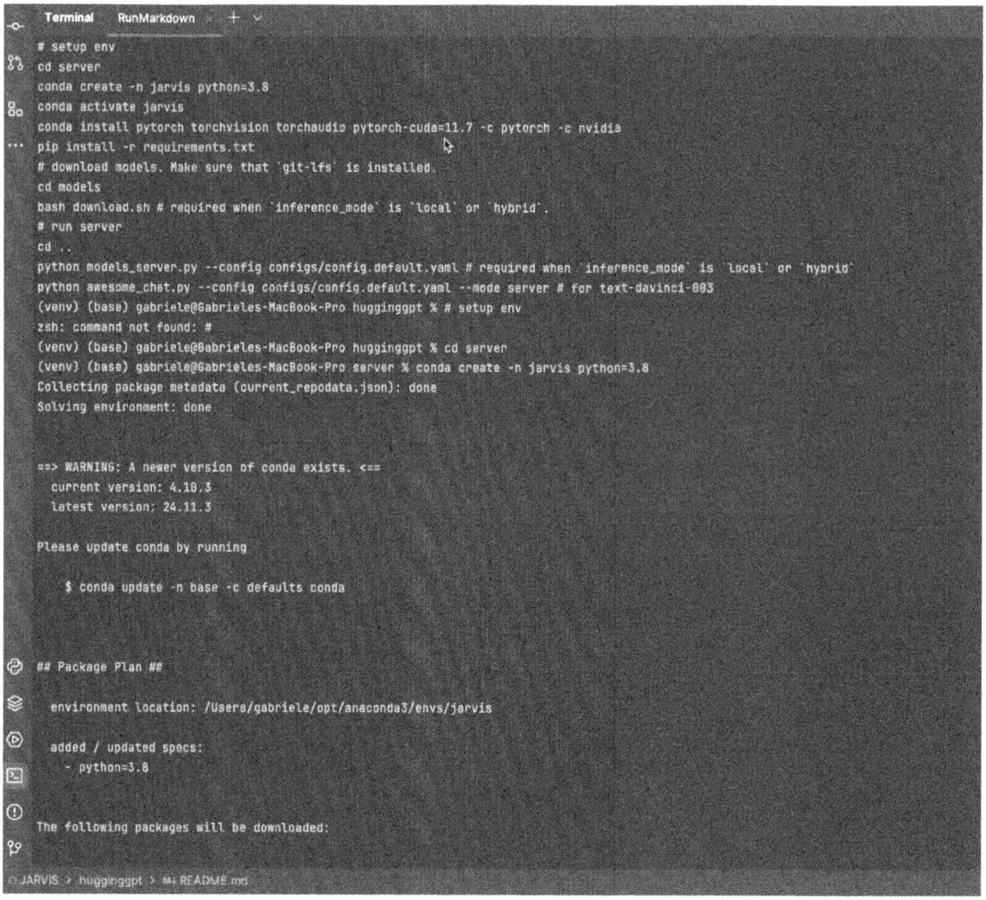

Figure 9.33 – Microsoft HuggingGPT finalizing installation

Since we have initialized `awesome_chat.py`, we can use a user-friendly web page.

Using HuggingGPT on the web

If you do not want to install HuggingGPT, you can use the online suite instead (on Hugging Face Gradio: `https://huggingface.co/gradio`). **Hugging Face Gradio** is a Python library that simplifies the process of creating user-friendly web-based interfaces for ML models and other Python applications.

With Gradio, developers can quickly build interactive demos for tasks such as text generation, image classification, and audio processing. These interfaces allow users to test models directly in their browser by providing inputs (e.g., text, images, or audio) and viewing real-time outputs. Gradio is highly customizable, supports integration with popular ML frameworks (such as PyTorch, TensorFlow, and Hugging Face models), and enables easy sharing of demos through public links or embedding in web applications.

The authors created a Gradio interface (launching Jarvis from local allows such an interface). The Gradio space can be accessed here: `https://huggingface.co/spaces/microsoft/HuggingGPT`.

As said, HuggingGPT is a system that connects LLMs with the ML community. As seen previously in the description of the system and its installation, the web interface also does exactly the same: connect an LLM with a set of ML models that are hosted on Hugging Face. In the web interface, only a few models are deployed on the `local/inference` endpoint due to hardware limitations (this interface serves as an example to understand and see in action how the system works).

Note that we need two tokens, which a user needs to obtain from each website:

- **Hugging Face token**: This is a personal authentication key that allows users to securely access Hugging Face's services, including their API, models, datasets, and other resources hosted on the platform. This token acts as an identifier for your account, ensuring that your requests to Hugging Face's systems are authorized and linked to your account. The token is then used to authenticate and use the models in inference. Hugging Face enforces rate limits for some services, especially for web inference.

- **OpenAI key**: This is a unique authentication key provided by OpenAI that enables developers to securely access and interact with OpenAI's APIs and services, such as GPT (e.g., GPT-3.5 or GPT-4), DALL·E, Codex, and Whisper. This key acts as a personalized credential that identifies your account and authorizes your usage of OpenAI's platform. The key is required to authenticate requests sent to OpenAI's API endpoints. OpenAI uses your API key to track your usage (e.g., the number of API calls made and tokens processed) and bill your account accordingly. In this case, the connection to GPT-4 is used.

Once we have our tokens ready, we can enter our question and click **Submit**.

Figure 9.34 – HuggingGPT interface

We can see that there are two main panels:

- **Left panel**: A text input box labeled **Chatbot** is provided. This field is intended for user inputs, such as questions or commands, to interact with the HuggingGPT system.

- **Right panel**: There is an empty box next to the chatbot reserved for responses or outputs generated by HuggingGPT.

Below the chatbox, there is a button labeled **Send**, allowing users to submit their queries to HuggingGPT.

Note that the system already provides ready-made examples that we can use:

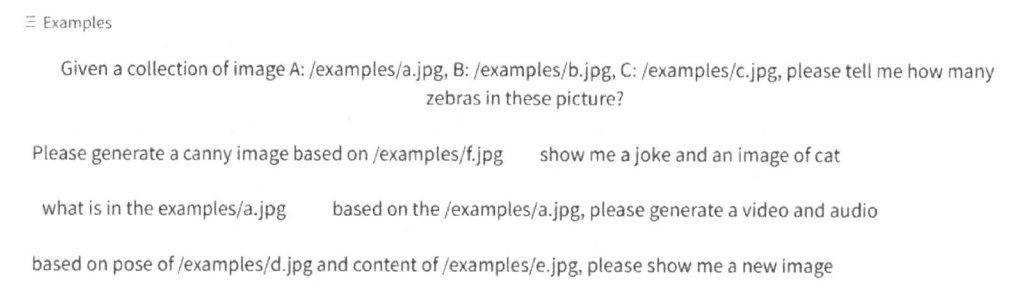

≡ Examples

Given a collection of image A: /examples/a.jpg, B: /examples/b.jpg, C: /examples/c.jpg, please tell me how many zebras in these picture?

Please generate a canny image based on /examples/f.jpg   show me a joke and an image of cat

what is in the examples/a.jpg   based on the /examples/a.jpg, please generate a video and audio

based on pose of /examples/d.jpg and content of /examples/e.jpg, please show me a new image

Figure 9.35 – HuggingGPT interface provided examples

We enter our tokens for both OpenAI and Hugging Face. Using the text input box labeled **Chatbot**, we can send natural language queries to HuggingGPT ("*Can you tell me which kind of pizza you see in the picture?*") and send the query with the **Send** button. In addition, images or other multimedia elements can be added (in our case, we have added a picture of a pizza):

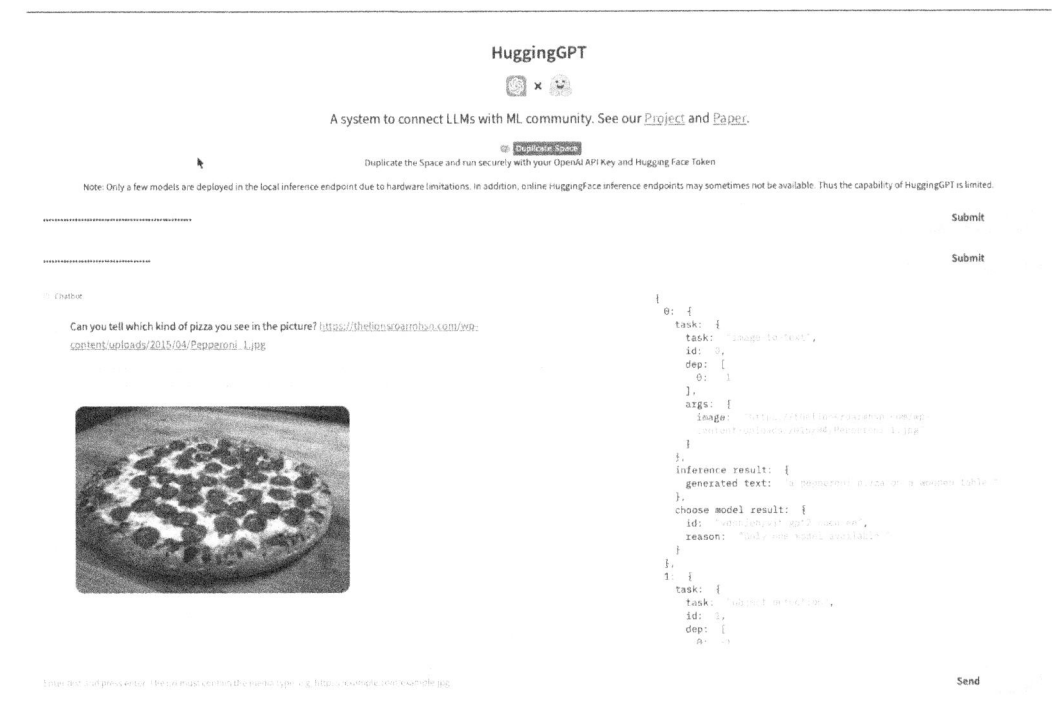

Figure 9.36 – Example of HuggingGPT interaction

In the panel on the right-hand side of the figure, we see the process that the system is working through: *1 pepperoni pizza on a wooden table*. This indicates that the system successfully processed the input image and identified the object depicted as *pepperoni pizza*. This is a typical object detection task, and the system is using a model to identify the object (it is not an LLM that conducts the image recognition but a specialized model that is invoked by the LLM).

The chatbot provides a detailed answer based on the inference results:

```
Sure, based on the inference results, the pizza in the picture is a
pepperoni pizza.
```

HuggingGPT explains the process:

1. The first step involves the use of an image-to-text model to get a description of the image. **ViT-GPT2-COCO-EN** is a vision-language model that combines a **Vision Transformer** (**ViT**) for image encoding and **GPT-2** for natural language generation, fine-tuned on the **COCO dataset** for image captioning tasks. The model generates descriptive captions in English for input images, effectively translating visual content into coherent textual descriptions. It leverages the power of ViT for extracting detailed image features and GPT-2's language generation capabilities to produce accurate and contextually rich captions.

2. Then, HuggingGPT uses an object detection model to identify objects within an image. This object detection model also provides a similar response because it identifies both a pizza and a dining table. **DETR-ResNet-101** is a vision model designed for object detection and image segmentation. It combines a **ResNet-101** backbone (a convolutional neural network) for feature extraction with a **transformer-based architecture** for detecting and localizing objects in an image. **DEtection TRansformer (DETR)** uses transformers to model global relationships in an image, allowing for more accurate object detection without the need for traditional region proposal networks.

3. Then, a visual-answering model confirms what type of pizza is in the image. **ViLT-B/32-Finetuned-VQA** is a vision-and-language transformer model fine-tuned for **Visual Question-Answering (VQA)** tasks. It combines a lightweight **Vision-and-Language Transformer (ViLT)** architecture with a patch-based image tokenizer and transformer layers to process both visual and textual inputs jointly. The B/32 refers to the use of a 32 x 32 pixel patch size for image encoding. Fine-tuned specifically for VQA datasets, the model is designed to answer natural language questions about input images by reasoning over the visual and textual information.

4. Finally, the LLM observes that the three models are in agreement and thus is confident in responding.

To recap, HuggingGPT receives a request from the user and selects patterns. These patterns are executed, and outputs are collected. The system analyzes what these outputs are and generates a final response.

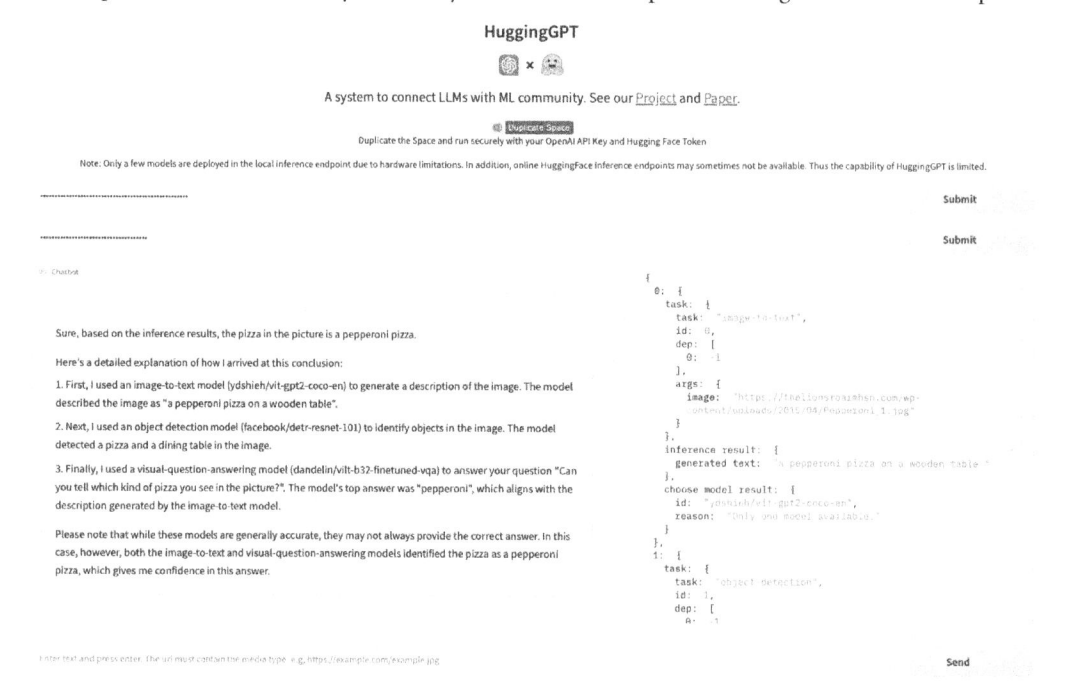

Figure 9.37 – Example of HuggingGPT response

HuggingGPT shows with a simple example how a multimodal task can be solved with an LLM. This is all done using information in the prompt and a set of tools.

In this section, we have seen a single LLM (a single agent) process a task, divide it into subtasks, and execute different models. A more elegant approach is to use multiple agents that approach a task from different perspectives, collaborate, and interact to solve a task. In the next subsection, we will see how this can be achieved.

Multi-agent system

In this section, we see how we can create a system that considers different agents and a set of tools (such as ML models). The entire code can be found in the Multi_Model-Travel_Planning_ System.py script.

As a general overview, the system implements a travel planning assistant that uses several agents to create personalized travel plans. The system then combines weather prediction, hotel recommendations, itinerary planning, and email summarization. In other words, we have four different agents, each dealing with a different aspect of travel planning:

- WeatherAnalysisAgent: Uses a random forest regressor to predict the best time to visit a location based on historical weather data. Trains on past weather data (month, latitude, longitude, and weather score) and predicts the best months for travel based on weather scores. This agent then uses an ML model to conduct predictions (a model that is trained specifically for the system).
- HotelRecommenderAgent: Uses Sentence Transformer embeddings to find hotels based on user preferences. Stores hotel descriptions and converts them into embeddings, after which it matches user preferences with the most relevant hotels using semantic similarity. This agent, based on user preferences, searches its library for possible solutions.
- ItineraryPlannerAgent: Uses GPT-2 (text-generation pipeline) to create personalized travel itineraries. The agent generates trip plans based on destination, weather prediction, and hotel recommendations.
- SummaryAgent: Uses GPT-2 to generate a summary email for the client. This summary includes the hotel cost (per night cost × duration) and additional daily expenses. After that, it generates a personalized email with trip details, cost breakdown, and itinerary highlights.

The following figure presents a schema of the agents and the process:

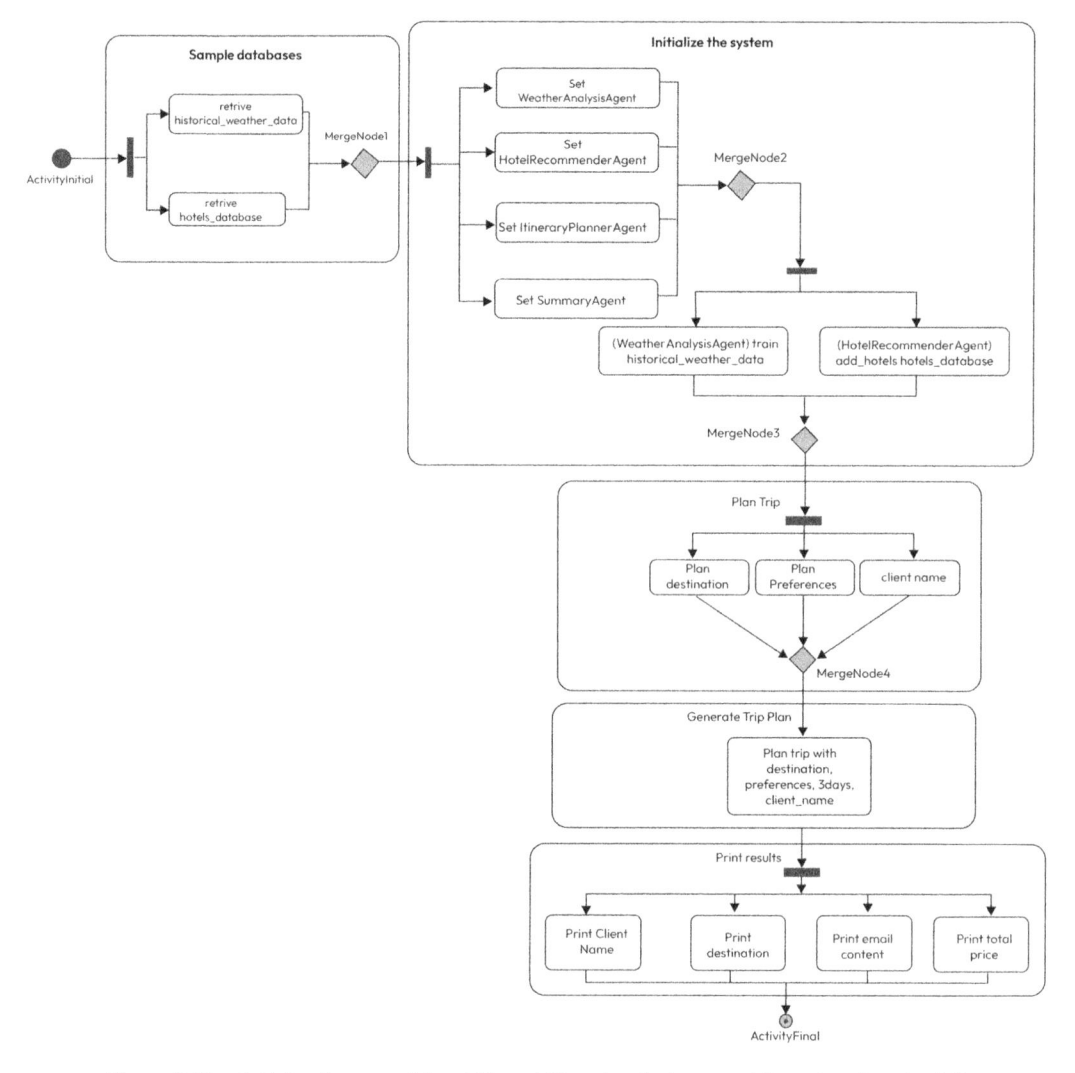

Figure 9.38 – Activity diagram of the AI Travel Planning System workflow showing the full sequence from data loading and agent initialization to trip planning and result output

`TravelPlanningSystem` links all agents together and is basically the main controller of the system. The system thus mimics this flow:

1. The user provides the destination, preferences, and duration.
2. The weather agent predicts the best time to visit.
3. The hotel agent finds matching accommodation.
4. The itinerary agent creates daily plans.
5. The summary agent generates an email and calculates costs.

Going into detail, we can see that agents here are defined as classes. `WeatherAnalysisAgent` is an ML-based component that analyzes historical weather data and predicts the best months to visit a given location. It does this using a Random Forest Regressor. We can see it as an agent using an ML model to perform a task. This snippet is initializing the agent:

```
class WeatherAnalysisAgent:
def __init__(self):
        self.model = RandomForestRegressor(n_estimators=100)
```

This agent creates a `RandomForestRegressor` model (`n_estimators=100` means the model consists of 100 decision trees) that must learn patterns from historical weather data, and then must predict weather scores for different months and locations:

```
def train(self, historical_data: Dict):
      X = np.array([[d['month'], d['latitude'], d['longitude']] for d in historical_data])
      y = np.array([d['weather_score'] for d in historical_data])
      self.model.fit(X, y)
```

As mentioned before, this model is not trained (i.e., it is not used in inference) but is trained on the spot. For this, we have within our class a `train` method. Random forest uses month, latitude, and longitude for a location to learn to predict a `weather_score` value (a numerical score representing how good the weather is in that month). In this snippet, the data is processed and the model is trained.

At this point, we can use `predict_best_time` as a method that predicts the best months to visit a location based on the trained weather model. In this case, the method takes only two inputs (the latitude and longitude of the location) and returns its predictions:

```
def predict_best_time(self, location: Dict) -> Dict:
      # Predicts the best time to visit a location based on weather patterns
        predictions = []
        for month in range(1, 13):
            # predict returns a 2D array, we take the first (and only) element
            prediction = self.model.predict([[
                month,
                location['latitude'],
                location['longitude']
            ]]).item()  # .item() converts numpy array to scalar
            predictions.append({'month': month, 'score': float(prediction)})

        return {
            'best_months': sorted(predictions, key=lambda x: x['score'], reverse=True)[:3],
```

```
            'location': location
    }
```

Note that we initialize predictions, which will contain all scores for 12 months (in fact, predictions are conducted in a loop through all 12 months, from January to December). Finally, we reorder the list from best to worst to identify the best months to visit. The method then returns a list of the top three months with the highest predicted weather scores.

HotelRecommenderAgent is a hotel recommendation system that utilizes semantic similarity to match hotels with user preferences and uses natural language processing (**NLP**) to understand and compare hotel descriptions and user preferences:

```
class HotelRecommenderAgent:
    def __init__(self):
        self.encoder = SentenceTransformer('all-MiniLM-L6-v2')
        self.hotels_db = []
        self.hotels_embeddings = None
```

During agent initialization, all-MiniLM-L6-v2 (a pre-trained NLP model designed for semantic similarity) is loaded. This model is an embedder (as described in *Chapter 5*), converting text (hotel descriptions and user preferences) into vector embeddings (numerical representations in a multi-dimensional space). Once we have vectors, we can measure the similarity between two vectors (user preferences and hotel descriptions). The agent retrieves the available hotels (self.hotels_db) and can store precomputed embeddings (numerical vectors) for all hotel descriptions (self.hotels_embeddings).

Next, in the following snippet, we have add_hotels, which adds hotels to the database and computes the embedding for the description, and then adds it to our embeddings database. find_hotels finds hotels that match the user's preferences using semantic similarity:

```
def add_hotels(self, hotels: List[Dict]):
        self.hotels_db = hotels
        descriptions = [h['description'] for h in hotels]
        self.hotels_embeddings = self.encoder.encode(descriptions)

    def find_hotels(self, preferences: str, top_k: int = 5) -> List[Dict]:
        pref_embedding = self.encoder.encode([preferences])
        similarities = np.dot(self.hotels_embeddings, pref_embedding.T).flatten()

        top_indices = similarities.argsort()[-top_k:][::-1]
        return [
```

```
            {**self.hotels_db[i], 'similarity_score': 
float(similarities[i])}
            for i in top_indices
        ]
```

What happens is that we conduct embedding of a user's preferences and then compute the cosine similarity with all stored hotel vectors. In this case, we then select the five hotels that are closest to our hotel description (`top_k=5` means selecting the top five hotels).

`ItineraryPlannerAgent` is responsible for automatically generating travel itineraries based on destination information (city or attractions), weather predictions (best months to visit), hotel recommendations (selected accommodation), and trip duration (number of days). It uses a natural language model (GPT-2) to generate customized travel itineraries based on these inputs:

```
class ItineraryPlannerAgent:
    def __init__(self):
        # Uses a language model for generating itineraries
        self.planner = pipeline(
            "text-generation",
            model="gpt2",  # In production, use a more powerful model
            max_length=500,
            truncation=True,
            pad_token_id=50256
        )
```

The agent initializes an NLP model (GPT-2 Model, which is a pre-trained language model for text generation) using the Hugging Face transformers library. We select a pipeline that is focused on text generation (`"text-generation"` means the model will generate text based on a prompt). Other parameters mean we limit the generated text to 500 tokens (`max_length=500`) and we ensure truncation.

Since we interact with LLMs through prompts, we have a method that allows us to create a structured prompt that we will then use to interact with the model. This prompt is designed to be able to generate a travel plan, where it enters some specific information: the length of stay (duration), the destination, weather information (the best mounts we identified earlier), hotel selection (which were identified with the previous agent), and a list of attractions:

```
    def _create_prompt(self, destination_info: Dict, weather_info: Dict,
                      hotel_info: Dict, duration: int) -> str:
        return f"""Create a {duration}-day itinerary for {destination_
info['name']}.
Weather: {weather_info['best_months'][0]['month']} is the best month.
Hotel: Staying at {hotel_info[0]['name']}.
Attractions: {', '.join(destination_info['attractions'])}."""
```

At this point, we can create the itinerary; the `create_itinerary` method precisely takes the previous prompt that contains all the information we need (destination, weather, hotel selection, and trip duration). Inside the `create_itinerary` method is a method called `_create_prompt` to generate the prompt. The GPT-2 model takes the input prompt and produces a detailed itinerary:

```
def create_itinerary(self, destination_info: Dict, weather_info: Dict,
                    hotel_info: Dict, duration: int) -> Dict:
    prompt = self._create_prompt(destination_info, weather_info, hotel_info, duration)

    #Generate the itinerary
    response = self.planner(prompt)[0]['generated_text']

    return {
        'itinerary': response,
        'duration': duration,
        'destination': destination_info['name']
    }
```

The final agent, that is, `SummaryAgent`, is responsible for summarizing trip details, calculating the total estimated cost, and generating a personalized email for the client using GPT-2. Our agent is initialized similar to the previous agent; the only difference is that in this case, the generation length is greater (`max_length=1000`):

```
class SummaryAgent:
    def __init__(self):
        # In production, use a more powerful LLM like GPT-4 or Claude
        self.llm = pipeline(
            "text-generation",
            model="gpt2",
            max_length=1000,
            truncation=True,
            pad_token_id=50256
        )
```

`calculate_total_price` is a tool that is used by the agent to be able to calculate the total cost of the trip (remember that LLMs are not good at arithmetic, so it is better to use an external tool):

```
def calculate_total_price(self, hotel_info: Dict, duration: int) -> float:
        # Calculate total trip price
        hotel_cost = hotel_info[0]['price'] * duration
        # Estimate additional costs (activities, meals, transport)
        daily_expenses = 100  # Simplified example
```

```
            additional_costs = daily_expenses * duration

            return hotel_cost + additional_costs
```

The agent does a series of very simple calculations:

- The hotel price per night is multiplied by the duration of the stay
- A fixed daily expense of $100 is used to estimate costs for meals, transport, activities, and sightseeing tickets
- Hotel and additional costs are added to return the final estimate

`create_email` allows you to create the email summary that will be sent to the customer:

```
    def create_email(self, trip_data: Dict, client_name: str) -> Dict:
        total_price = self.calculate_total_price(
            trip_data['recommended_hotels'],
            trip_data['itinerary']['duration']
        )
        prompt = f"""
        Dear {client_name},
        Based on your preferences, I'm pleased to present your travel plan:
        Destination: {trip_data['itinerary']['destination']}
        Duration: {trip_data['itinerary']['duration']} days
        Best time to visit: Month {trip_data['weather_analysis']['best_months'][0]['month']}
        Recommended Hotel: {trip_data['recommended_hotels'][0]['name']}
        Itinerary Overview:
        {trip_data['itinerary']['itinerary']}
        Estimated Total Cost: ${total_price}
        Please let me know if you would like any adjustments.
        """
        # Generate email using LLM
        response = self.llm(prompt)[0]['generated_text']

        return {
            'email_content': response,
            'total_price': total_price,
            'summary_data': {
                'destination': trip_data['itinerary']['destination'],
                'duration': trip_data['itinerary']['duration'],
                'hotel': trip_data['recommended_hotels'][0]['name'],
```

```
                    'best_month': trip_data['weather_analysis']['best_
months'][0]['month']
            }
        }
```

As we can see, the email will be structured to include costs (we use the method described previously) and the other information we obtained earlier. Note that we use a template.

Remember, `TravelPlanningSystem` is the main controller that integrates all AI agents for automated travel planning:

```
class TravelPlanningSystem:
    def __init__(self):
        self.weather_agent = WeatherAnalysisAgent()
        self.hotel_agent = HotelRecommenderAgent()
        self.itinerary_agent = ItineraryPlannerAgent()
        self.summary_agent = SummaryAgent()
```

In the first step, we initialize our four agents. Each agent will handle a specific task. If you noticed, we have used a modular system. The advantages of this are as follows:

- Each component operates independently, making the system scalable
- Components can be updated or replaced without affecting others
- It follows the **Single Responsibility Principle (SRP)** for clean code architecture

At this point, we can start the setup – getting the best hotels and the best months to visit:

```
def setup(self, historical_weather_data: Dict, hotels_database: List[Dict]):
        # Initialize and train the models
        self.weather_agent.train(historical_weather_data)
        self.hotel_agent.add_hotels(hotels_database)
```

Finally, you have to coordinate the entire trip and then generate the summary email with cost estimates and the itinerary:

```
def plan_trip(self, destination: Dict, preferences: str, duration: int, client_name: str) -> Dict:
        # 1. Weather analysis and best time prediction
        weather_analysis = self.weather_agent.predict_best_time(destination)
        # 2. Hotel search
        recommended_hotels = self.hotel_agent.find_hotels(preferences)
        # 3. Itinerary creation
```

```
            itinerary = self.itinerary_agent.create_itinerary(
                destination,
                weather_analysis,
                recommended_hotels,
                duration
            )
            # 4. Create summary email and calculate price
            trip_data = {
                'weather_analysis': weather_analysis,
                'recommended_hotels': recommended_hotels,
                'itinerary': itinerary
            }

            summary = self.summary_agent.create_email(trip_data, client_
name)

            return {
                **trip_data,
                'summary': summary
            }
```

Now that we have created the multi-agent platform, we have to execute it. The `main()` function serves as the entry point for running the *Travel Planning System*. It demonstrates the system's functionality by doing the following:

1. Initializing sample data (weather history and hotels)
2. Setting up and training AI models
3. Executing the travel planning process
4. Printing the generated trip summary

We provide the system with various information about the weather, destination, hotels, and so on. After that, the system is initialized and executed. At this point, it prints travel summary details and the personalized email generated by GPT-2, and it shows the estimated total trip cost:

```
def main():
    # Example data with a full year of weather information
    historical_weather_data = [...    ]

    # Sample hotel database
    hotels_database = [...]

    # Initialize the system
```

```python
    system = TravelPlanningSystem()
    system.setup(historical_weather_data, hotels_database)

    # Plan a trip
    destination = {
        'name': 'Rome',
        'latitude': 41.9028,
        'longitude': 12.4964,
        'attractions': ['Colosseum', 'Vatican', 'Trevi Fountain']
    }

    preferences = """Looking for a luxury hotel in the city center,
    preferably with spa facilities and fine dining options"""
    client_name = "John Smith"

    # Generate trip plan
    trip_plan = system.plan_trip(destination, preferences, duration=3,
client_name=client_name)

    # Print results in a readable format
    print("\nTRAVEL PLANNING RESULTS:")
    print("-" * 50)
    print(f"Client: {client_name}")
    print(f"Destination: {destination['name']}")
    print("\nGenerated Email:")
    print("-" * 20)
    print(trip_plan['summary']['email_content'])
    print("\nEstimated Total Price:")
    print(f"${trip_plan['summary']['total_price']}")
```

Ensure that the main() script runs only if the script is executed directly:

```python
if __name__ == "__main__":
    main()
```

At this point, we just have to test it. Once you have run the script, this should be the result:

```
TRAVEL PLANNING RESULTS:
-------------------------------------------------
Client: John Smith
Destination: Rome

Generated Email:
---------------------

    Dear John Smith,

    Based on your preferences, I'm pleased to present your travel plan:

    Destination: Rome
    Duration: 3 days
    Best time to visit: Month 7

    Recommended Hotel: Grand Hotel

    Itinerary Overview:
    Create a 3-day itinerary for Rome.
    Weather: 7 is the best month.
    Hotel: Staying at Grand Hotel.
    Attractions: Colosseum, Vatican, Trevi Fountain.

P.S. Please note that our hotels are always on-site and we cannot always book you at one of our hotels in Rome. Our staff will work with you to find suitable accommodation so

    Estimated Total Cost: $1200

The itinerary in which our hotels take residents (2 to 9 nights a week) is based on two criteria:

1) We take residents (4 to 10 nights a week)

2) As the cost escalator, we'll have to adjust the price once they add to that one.

We provide our residents free parking in the main entrance of our Grand Hotel on the Via Valerea, for a total of 50% of the cost to be accounted for using credit cards, bank sta

This will be the second hotel in Rome during the trip (the first two with hotel code 2147) with no payment needed for the final two nights. The first had a total cost of $3,000

Here is an itinerary for the 2nd location within Rome for the trip:

Day 1:  Incorpiate

Day 2:  Pursue The Light, or The Light Begins

Day 3:  Travel to the City, or In Coru

Day 4:  Visit With The Light Or In Coru

Day 5:  Travel to Rome

Day 6:  Enjoy In Coru

Day 7:  Travel to Rome

Day 8:  Purchase Your Castle

We provide our residents free parking in the main entrance of our Grand Hotel on the Via Valerea, for a total of 50% of the cost to be accounted for using credit cards, bank sta

This will be the second hotel in Rome during the trip (the first two with hotel code 2147) with no payment needed for the final two nights. The first had a total cost of $3,000

Here is an itinerary for the 2nd location within Rome for the trip:

Day 1:  Incorpiate

Day 2:  Pursue The Light, or The Light Begins

Day 3:  Travel to the City, or In Coru

Day 4:  Visit With The Light Or In Coru

Day 5:  Travel to Rome

Day 6:  Enjoy In Coru

Day 7:  Travel to Rome

Day 8:  Purchase Your Castle

Day 9:  Enter Into The Cave

Day 10: Enter Into The Cave Or In Coru

Estimated Total Price:
$1200
```

Figure 9.39 – Screenshots showing the execution

This *Travel Planning System* is a prototype demonstrating how AI agents can collaborate to automate a real-world problem.

Of course, a whole series of improvements can be made to make the system more useful:

- The data used is static (it is a toy example). You could connect with a number of APIs to obtain real-time data for the weather (OpenWeatherMap or AccuWeather), hotels (Booking.com or Expedia API), and destinations (Google Places API or Yelp). Extensions such as flights and transportation could also be added (Google Flights API or Rome2Rio).

- GPT-2 is outdated (we used it because it is much smaller than other models) and not fine-tuned for travel. You can replace GPT-2 with a larger or travel-optimized model. For example, you could use larger models such as GPT-4 or Claude, or open source alternatives such as LLaMA. Also, open source models can be fine-tuned on real travel itineraries from Tripadvisor, Lonely Planet, or Reddit.

- The itinerary is generic and not adaptable to different types of travelers. You could ask for different information from the traveler, such as budget preferences, what kinds of activities they prefer (cultural, adventure, food, family-friendly, and so on), or whether they need special accommodations (wheelchair, traveling with elderly, or pet-friendly). This requires a larger model, and you can also test recommendation models. In addition, there are methods and models that implement **Multi-Criteria Decision-Making** (MCDM) to conduct more sophisticated rankings.

In any case, this system, though simple, allows us to see several interesting elements:

- Instead of using one large monolithic AI model, the system is broken down into specialized agents. This idea can come in handy for modern software design.

- This simple example mimics how multi-agent AI platforms work in autonomous vehicles, finance, healthcare, and robotics. In fact, multi-agent collaboration is a system designed with scalability, modularity, and efficiency in mind, which are necessary for real-world applications.

- The system can dynamically generate personalized recommendations (although in our case, it is hardcoded, we are mimicking what happens when a user enters their preferences).

- The system also analyzes multiple factors (weather, hotels, and attractions) and optimizes travel plans. Modern systems that do something similar use precise ML models (we used random forest in our example), have vast databases (in our case, we are mimicking a database of hotels), take user preferences into account, and use automated systems to respond to the customer (our email).

Although this is a very simple system, we can think about how a similar system could be used in various other industries:

- AI medical assistants that recommend treatments, optimize hospital schedules, and predict disease risks

- AI shopping assistants that recommend products based on user preferences and purchase history

- Multi-agent AI systems for self-driving cars (navigation, pedestrian detection, or traffic optimization)
- AI-driven advisors that help with investment strategies, risk management, and fraud detection
- An AI-powered urban planner that optimizes traffic, energy use, and public transport routes

In this section, we looked at how to create a multi-agent system. In the next section, we will discuss how multi-agent systems fit into the various business models that exist today or are under greater development. This will provide an important perspective, as it will allow you to understand how to adapt your multi-agent platform to the needs of businesses.

SaaS, MaaS, DaaS, and RaaS

In this section, we will explore various business models influenced by recent advancements in AI. While multi-agent LLMs represent cutting-edge technology, their value lies in being adaptable to meet business needs, enabling them to be effectively packaged, marketed, and delivered to businesses and consumers. Considering that these systems are extremely expensive to develop and maintain, it is important for the reader to understand what the revenue models are so that they can think about, design, and develop products that align with the company's strategy. Understanding these models allows us to grasp that a multi-agent system is not a standalone item but should be considered a product and that this product can be marketed in various ways. In addition, LLMs are extremely expensive products, and each of these business models has advantages and disadvantages in terms of continuous updates, scalability, and flexibility in AI deployment. At the same time, these business models regulate access to technology whether you are interested in developing AI models or are a customer. These choices (about the platform, business models, and so on) must be made before the product is developed, and they determine its development, since the costs do not allow for trial and error. The choice of business model is defined by the structure of the product and the multi-agent system, as well as the economic viability of the company.

Software as a Service (SaaS)

SaaS is a service model in which software is hosted in the cloud by a provider and is made available to users over the internet. In the traditional model, software is provided to the user to be installed and used locally (on the user's device). SaaS, on the other hand, allows access over the internet, usually on the web browser or with a mobile app. Often, SaaS is provided via subscription rather than through a one-time purchase. The SaaS paradigm began in 1999 when Salesforce launched its **Customer Relationship Management** (**CRM**) as a cloud-hosted service. SaaS is now the most widely used sales paradigm by different companies, especially for **Business-to-Business** (**B2B**) applications. Its popularity is growing, and it is expected that SaaS software revenue will grow more and more in the coming years.

SaaS applications are typically built to be hosted in the cloud (they are called cloud-native). The company developing these apps can decide whether to host on its own infrastructure or leverage that of cloud service providers (examples are Google Cloud, IBM Cloud, OVH, Aruba, **Amazon Web Services** (**AWS**), and Microsoft Azure). Given the demand for app providers, some providers create focused infrastructure for hosting these apps, and so we also talk about **Platform as a Service** (**PaaS**).

In PaaS solutions, a provider conducts hosting of both hardware and software through dedicated infrastructure that is made available to product developers. This allows developers to focus on coding without having to worry about maintaining or managing the infrastructure behind it. The platform allows the hosting of both the application and the data, or even the training of a model, leaving only the coding to the developer. This has enabled accelerated product development by many businesses, who have managed to avoid investing in expensive infrastructure (although extensive use of these platforms can have a high cost, especially when the applications are generative AI). Although PaaS allows a simplification of the process, developers are forced to conform their applications to the requirements of the platforms and environment. This is not always possible, resulting in difficulties in deployment or other issues. Therefore, an alternative paradigm has emerged that allows the user greater flexibility, control, and adaptability, especially when the application or business requires it. This paradigm is called **Infrastructure as a Service** (**IaaS**) and emerged around 2010. In IaaS, a user can access computing resources through web services, thus being able to rent infrastructure (servers, networking, and storage) as needed. The user retains more control over the infrastructure, while the provider focuses on the hardware (examples include Google Compute Engine, DigitalOcean, and Amazon Elastic Compute Cloud). PaaS and IaaS can thus be seen as extensions of SaaS or as services for businesses that need a supporting ecosystem.

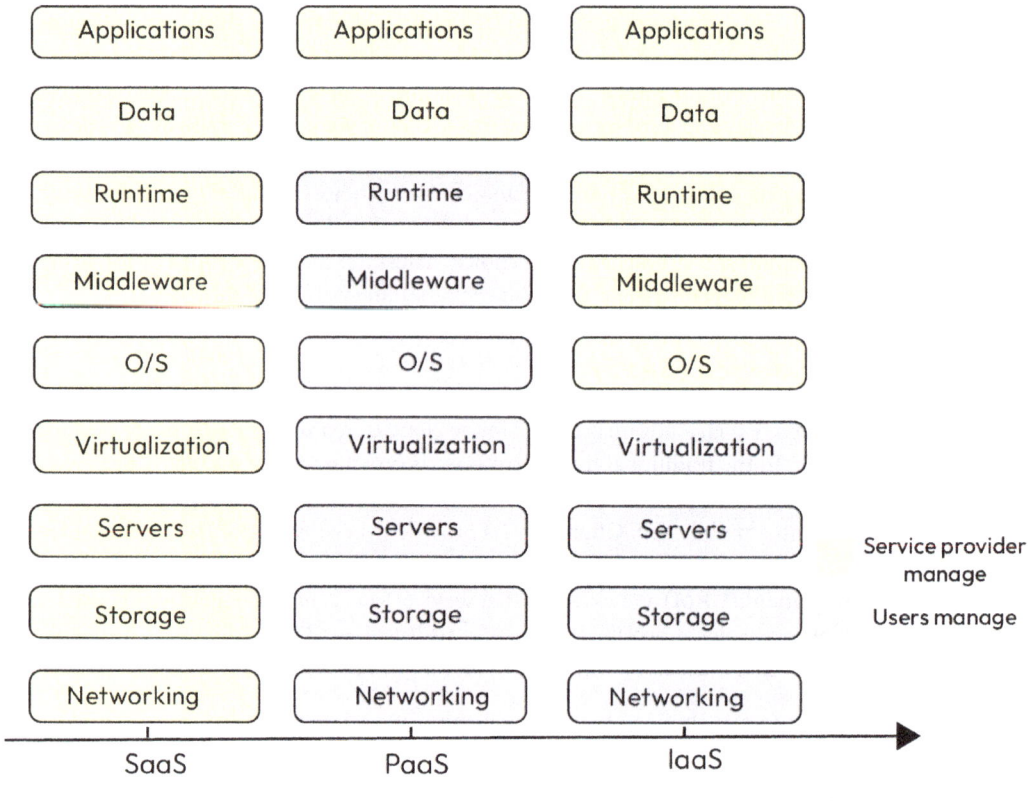

Figure 9.40 – Comparison between different paradigms (https://arxiv.org/pdf/2311.05804)

SaaS applications are therefore designed to be accessible via an internet connection from a device that must be connected to the internet in order to access the application (a device that is not connected cannot access the application and it is not a requirement to allow access locally). Software is developed to be used through a web browser or with a specific app (mobile software). Some SaaS applications (as in the case of Adobe Acrobat) may require the user to download and install a dedicated client (a light program, which is not the full application, that has to be installed on a local PC) on their computers (but this is generally a minority of cases). A SaaS application is generally a **multi-tenant software architecture**, where a single instance of a software application (along with its database and hardware) serves different user accounts (or multiple tenants). A tenant is what is called a user of the software, and it is a user or group of users within an organization.

In SaaS, it is crucial to have an architecture that ensures each tenant's data is isolated and inaccessible to other tenants. This approach offers the advantage of cost reduction by enabling the software to be optimized for a single piece of hardware and infrastructure, which is then shared among all users. It also allows for greater scalability, easier customization, and maintenance (providers can conduct the update on their own infrastructure and on a single architecture).

SaaS is therefore one of the most widely used paradigms because it has a number of advantages:

- **Cost efficiency**: There are no upfront costs to the customer, such as expenses for hardware or a software license. In SaaS, the customer either pays by subscription or on a pay-as-you-go basis.
- **Scalability**: SaaS scales easily for the customer and does not require additional hardware. Similarly, software is structured to make it easy to scale up customers. In the case of AI models, the customer does not need large hardware but can directly leverage that provided by the provider.
- **Accessibility**: The customer can access the application from anywhere in the world via an internet connection. Also, using the web browser, the software is optimized for whatever hardware the client has. SaaS also reduces the barrier of access to AI for clients (fewer resources and less need for expertise) through the use of templates, APIs, and frameworks.
- **Ease of integration and customization**: It is much easier for the developer to provide updates, security patches, and maintenance, in terms of both resources and time. The ability to manage customization for the client is usually provided in an easier way, while at the same time maintaining control. Equally, for an AI system, updated templates can be provided.
- **Fast deployment**: SaaS reduces deployment and market access time by being immediately available in the marketplace.
- **Data and model sharing**: Model and data access can be easily allowed to users from different teams or in various locations simultaneously and effectively and efficiently.

There are, of course, also some limitations and disadvantages to SaaS:

- **Dependency on internet connectivity**: SaaS requires a stable connection, and connection disruptions can stop critical processes and errors. Rural areas and countries with little infrastructure may not be covered.

- **Limited customization**: SaaS solutions are developed with the idea of covering as much business as possible with one product. Typically, they provide a limited number of customization possibilities that may not cover all the needs of a particular business. This is also true in the case of an AI system; the client has little control over the models and the models may not be able to meet client requirements.

- **Data security and privacy concerns**: Hosting on third-party servers brings the risk of data breaches or unauthorized access. In addition, there may be compliance issues with regulations in countries such as the European Union (e.g., data must be maintained on servers in certain countries). Training or using AI models may require having to share sensitive data, and this may be against GDPR or other regulations (as well as an additional privacy risk).

- **Vendor lock-in**: Businesses may remain anchored to a particular SaaS provider and then be unable to migrate to other platforms due to cost and complexity. In addition, different providers may terminate the service (or be acquired), increase costs abruptly, or eliminate features considered essential. SaaS can become expensive over a period of time, especially when subscription-based (some providers charge more as users increase).

- **Performance issues**: Shared resources in multi-tenant architectures can lead to slower performance during peak usage. In addition, there may be unexpected server downtime or maintenance schedules that hurt the business (for example, if maintenance is conducted at night on Pacific Time, it disrupts business hours in Europe) and over which the customer has no control. AI systems that must run in real time may have latency or performance problems (both in training and inference). In addition, the provider may not provide cutting-edge AI or may not have implemented it yet (or they may use models that do not fit the customer's needs).

- **High computational costs**: SaaS has an infrastructure cost for the developer, and in the case of AI, this cost can be higher (use of GPUs or large storage costs). Some of these services are particularly expensive for users.

Model as a Service (MaaS)

MaaS is a new paradigm that was born with the development of big data, AI, and Web 3.0. MaaS is a cloud computing-based service paradigm that offers AI and ML models and related IaaS to developers and enterprises.

MaaS seeks to simplify access to AI for businesses that have neither the expertise nor the infrastructure to train generative AI or broad models in general. MaaS enables the use of pre-trained ML models and algorithms through the use of simple interfaces, APIs, or the browser. Just like with SaaS, access to models is through the internet (and requires the business to have an internet connection). The provider must then conduct the hosting of the models and allow developers access to the models that have been trained. Developers can then use these models to add AI functions to their systems and apps. MaaS is often a platform where models that have been trained on a large amount of data or optimized for a possible task are hosted. MaaS reduces the complexity of managing these models (especially training and deployment) and allows developers to focus on using the models or how to integrate them for specific applications. Developers save time and resources since they do not have to train these models from scratch. MaaS thus has certain similarities to PaaS and IaaS but conducts an additional level of abstraction and focuses on AI solutions. In a sense, MaaS can be viewed as an intermediate solution between SaaS and PaaS or IaaS. It not only provides a service but also offers an infrastructure that enables the development of custom products.

Another difference between SaaS and MaaS is in the underlying architecture of the two paradigms. SaaS focuses on applications (application layer) that depend on an operating system (whether mobile or desktop application) that allows them to run, as well as on a layer that allows the app to be hosted. In the case of MaaS, the architecture focuses on the model that needs a specific framework to be hosted.

(a) Traditional application development technology stack

(b) New application development technology stack

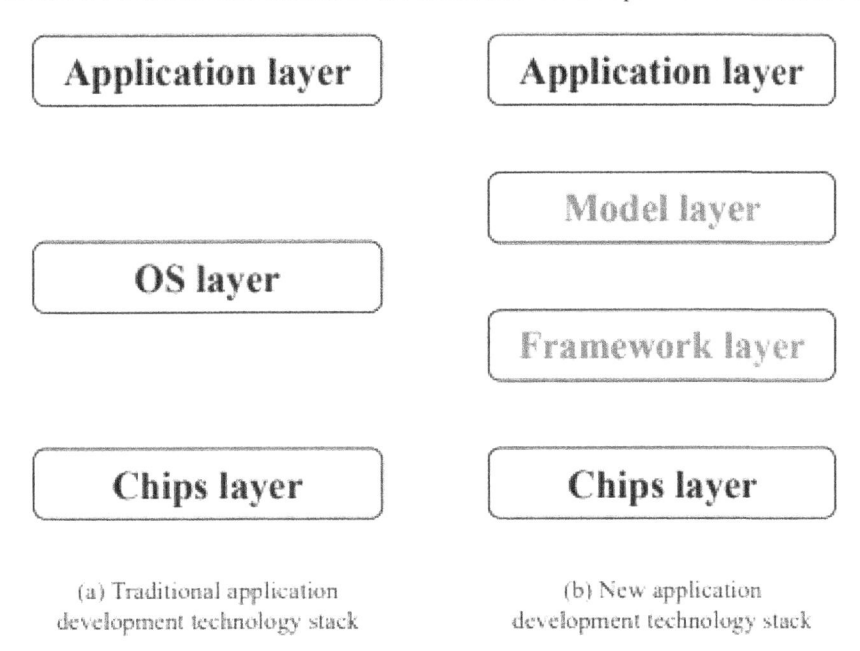

Figure 9.41 – Comparison between traditional and model-based technology stacks (https://arxiv.org/pdf/2311.05804)

In MaaS, the following elements are often present:

- **Cloud computing**: MaaS is based on an infrastructure on the cloud where various models are maintained and deployed. This allows easy access to the models and enables greater scalability.

- **Model training and optimization**: MaaS providers take care of the training of large models on large datasets. MaaS providers also take care of the entire ecosystem to enable more effective exploitation of models. For example, they can provide models of different sizes, including quantized or fine-tuned versions for specific applications.

- **API and development tools**: MaaS providers also provide APIs and tools that allow the developer to use the models for their applications easily. The purpose is to allow easy integration of models into other applications and infrastructures. So, the API acts as an endpoint, takes data, and returns predictions.

- **Monitoring and analytics**: To date, there is increasing focus on how to monitor models once they are in production. MaaS providers typically provide a number of tools to monitor model performance, identify the presence of issues, integrate feedback, or improve resource allocation.

- **Scalability, security, and privacy**: MaaS providers focus on the scalability of their systems by allowing customers to be able to manage multiple users at the same time (thus allocating different bandwidth, computing power, or storage as needed). At the same time, today there is more attention to privacy and security (especially as there is much more regulation). Platforms often have a number of tools to be able to increase the privacy and security of applications that integrate their models.

Hugging Face is an example of a MaaS provider. Hugging Face provides access to thousands of pre-trained models (from the company itself, other companies, or users) for computer vision, NLP, audio, video, and more. These models are hosted on their Model Hub and can be either used via an API or installed locally. So, a user who doesn't want to download models can use an inference API without owning the infrastructure needed to manage the model (this API uses the pay-as-you-go system). Developers who do not have the expertise or resources can directly use the endpoint API to directly integrate AI models within their applications. In addition, Hugging Face also offers a platform for hosting and deploying both the model and application, extending MaaS capabilities and providing flexibility to customers who want to use their custom models. Hugging Face also provides tools to improve the scalability of models and open source libraries to facilitate model development or integration (e.g., Transformers, Datasets, Diffusers, sentence embedding, and so on), as well as offering a forum to enable user exchange, educational resources for users, and other services. There are other MaaS providers, such as Google AI (pre-trained models for NLP (Natural Language API), vision (Vision API), speech to text, translation, or custom model training with Vertex AI) and AWS (which offers pre-trained models for language, image, and text (e.g., AWS Comprehend, Rekognition, and Translate) or infrastructure for custom models).

MaaS has the following advantages, especially regarding the AI domain:

- **Simplified model development and deployment**: MaaS lowers the technical barrier to using generative AI. Companies do not need developers who are experts in the technology or different algorithms because most models are delivered via endpoints. This allows companies to focus on applications and model integration for their products. If needed, MaaS also simplifies the approach to fine-tuning models for their applications. MaaS, as opposed to SaaS, is tailored to the entire AI workflow and offers tools for deploying, training, managing, and scaling models, thus enabling better support for companies interested in using AI.

- **High performance and scalability**: The use of cloud computing facilitates system scaling. In fact, the use of AI can require high costs and large resources (especially when it comes to using LLMs), and MaaS allows for better resource management by facilitating access to large models without initial entry costs for different businesses. Typically, users pay for their consumption and receive computing according to their needs, thus enabling better performance and scalability. Since MaaS is optimized for AI workloads, it can scale easily when there are fluctuating computational demands (SaaS typically focuses on allocating a variable number of users, but users may have a different need for computing depending on the different usage of models).

- **Shared knowledge and collaboration**: MaaS is built on collecting large datasets and training large models. These pre-trained models can then be fine-tuned by developers interested in adapting the models to particular applications. This means that developers need to collect much less data and do not have to train large models from scratch. This saves both resources and costs (fine-tuning is much less computationally expensive than pre-training). In addition, MaaS allows standardization that reduces the technical knowledge required to be able to use these models and allows information and tutorials to be obtained easily. Models can then also be shared by the community on platforms on which both information and experiences are also exchanged (this promotes a collaborative environment and accelerates the development of new models).

- **Business support**: MaaS uses a flexible payment model, such as subscription based, where you pay only for current consumption. Generally, this solution is cost effective and affordable for many small businesses. It is convenient for providers because once they choose a technology and integrate it into their products, users remain loyal. Model integration allows businesses to gain insights in an easy and inexpensive way (models for forecasts or other predictions, report writing, and visualizations).

- **Flexibility**: MaaS provides models for a large number of applications and allows businesses to integrate a large number of potential models, providing wide flexibility (e.g., NLP, computer vision, time series, and so many other applications). In addition, developers can test many pre-trained models quickly without changing setups (e.g., Hugging Face offers thousands of models that can be used with just a few pipelines). Similarly, MaaS providers often offer many tools to simplify the AI life cycle (data labeling, data format integration, monitoring tools, and so on) from training to deployment.

MaaS is a new paradigm, and the field of generative AI is also in active development, so there are challenges and possible drawbacks that need to be addressed:

- **Security and privacy**: Often, a large amount of data is transferred, especially for model training, which can be intercepted. In addition, models trained on sensitive data can end up outputting sensitive data. These models could also be trained on copyrighted data, and the legislation on training with such data is not entirely clear. So, organizations that adhere to particularly regulated industries may not adopt MaaS. Data is the basis of these models, but the models could be trained on, or become biased due to, low-quality data. Often, there is no information on what data these models were trained on. In these cases, both the platform and the businesses using these models may be subject to fines or other regulations.

- **Vendor lock-in**: MaaS providers use proprietary tools and APIs, which does not make it easy to change from one provider to another (e.g., changing providers complicates model integration or exporting models that have been fine-tuned). This difficulty can reduce flexibility and innovation and can make a business dependent on a single provider. There may be downtime or service disruption that impacts built applications. It also makes it more difficult to experiment locally.

- **Limited customization**: Not all MaaS providers allow the fine-tuning or modification of pre-trained models. Pre-trained models may not be suitable for some particular operations, or a business may need to have control over hyperparameters and infrastructure. In addition, MaaS providers may make changes or plan updates that impact the business or no longer allow some core features of their applications.

- **Interpretability of model and results**: A model is often a black box, and a user cannot access the decision-making process. Especially for GenAI models, it is difficult to understand how the model processes the input and gets the output. For sensitive applications, this could cause problems, especially when the model produces hallucinations or incorrect outputs. In addition, the lack of transparency of the platforms may affect the ability to diagnose errors or know how to correct them.

- **Performance and cost**: Latency refers to the time elapsed between a request and its corresponding response. The latency of models depends on the underlying infrastructure, which can experience strain during periods of peak usage. Shared multi-tenant environments in MaaS platforms can lead to resource bottlenecks during peak usage times. Businesses may encounter a considerable increase in latency that makes their applications unusable. MaaS allows pay as you go, but large-scale training or inference can quickly become expensive.

MaaS remains an expanding paradigm for several businesses. For example, MaaS could have a big impact in healthcare where there are large amounts of data, and many models have already been developed. The models could be available on a platform and be used when needed by practitioners or pharmaceutical companies. Obviously, in healthcare, data security and output consistency are critical (especially if these applications are used for hospitals or other health providers). MaaS is also growing in other domains, such as finance, blockchain, and Web 3.0.

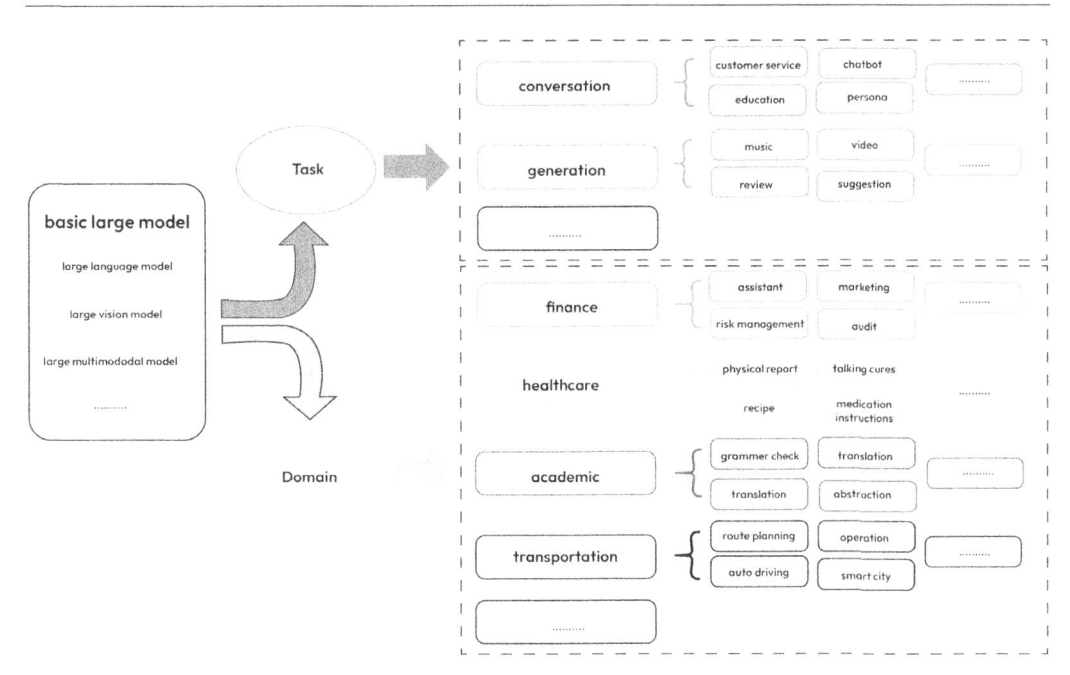

Figure 9.42 – The applications of various industries within MaaS (https://arxiv.org/pdf/2311.05804)

Data as a Service (DaaS)

DaaS is a business model where data is delivered on demand to users regardless of their geographical location or organizational boundaries. In DaaS, data is stored in the cloud and a client can access it (with or without additional tools) by paying a subscription to a provider. DaaS, therefore, is built around the concept that data is an asset and can be provided to users on demand. This access can then be conducted through a platform, the use of APIs, or additional means. In addition, the provider can provide either raw data or data that has been normalized to be machine-readable or machine-ready.

AI models are notoriously data hungry, and retrieving quality data may not be easy. So, there are players who focus on collecting hard-to-access data and then selling it to other players. For example, patient data can be difficult to collect, and a company may collect and process the data and then sell it to pharmaceutical companies. Alternatively, DaaS allows companies to create a new business model, using data collected during their normal operations as an asset they can sell. For example, a telecom company that has collected data from its users can sell the anonymized data to retailers. This data is sold through a secure portal and can be charged for on a per-access basis or through a subscription. Subscription is usually the most popular method and can be divided into three subcategories: time model, quantity-based pricing model, and pay-per-call or data type base model.

A DaaS provider may just sell the raw data it has collected, but more often it also processes it and makes it analyzable by models. Some DaaS providers aggregate different sources, process them, and thus simplify the analysis process for a client. In fact, the purpose of this data is to improve business processes and decision-making for customers, or to allow customers to train their AI models.

There can also be bidirectionality, in which the provider collects the data and harmonizes it to integrate it with its own, before making it accessible to the client again. In this way, by relating it to other data, the client can extract additional value from its own data.

DaaS has some advantages:

- **Cost efficiency**: DaaS reduces customers' need to build and maintain data infrastructure and teams. It also reduces the cost of data access because of its flexibility. Customers do not need to store data; they can directly access the data stream when they need it.

- **Ease of access**: Providing data on demand allows real-time access and saves time and expertise to obtain data information. Users do not need to know the data and the structure behind it, but they can easily learn how to use it. Also, as long as there is an internet connection, the client can always access the data.

- **Scalability**: It easily scales to accommodate increasing data needs without requiring additional infrastructure investment. Customers can easily choose the data workload they need or can handle.

- **Centralized data management**: DaaS enables consistent and centralized data storage, reducing both inconsistencies and redundancies in data. This enables simplified data governance and compliance with regulations.

- **Focus on core activities**: DaaS saves resources and time, allowing businesses to focus on extracting value from data rather than managing it. In addition, it enables better collaboration among the various team members and collaborators, which can then access the same data (in the same format).

- **Integration with other services**: DaaS makes it easy to integrate data with other services in the business, especially when it comes to analytics platforms, visualization tools, and other cloud services. Likewise, it facilitates the regular updating of datasets and allows users to have access to the most accurate and current data.

- **Data quality**: As data is centralized, data quality tends to improve. Once this data is tested, if there are no updates, there is no need for further testing.

The disadvantages of DaaS are similar to the other models associated with cloud computing:

- **Data security and privacy risks**: Obviously, the location of data on the cloud can mean that sensitive and proprietary data can be accessed by third parties or be at risk of breach. Providers must comply with regulations, which are increasingly stringent today. The costs of securing infrastructure are growing, and data piracy attacks are on the rise. In addition, although data is sold anonymized, in some cases, it is possible to reconstruct the information.

- **Dependency on providers**: DaaS creates a reliance on external providers for critical data. Service outages or disruptions on the provider's end impact the client and all services that are related to accessing this data. The client normally has access to the data stream but does not download the data, so it can be cut off from data that is necessary to its business.

- **Limited customization**: DaaS may not provide data in the format needed or have the right granularity. Providers have an interest in providing data in a format that is useful to as many clients as possible, but specific clients may have different requirements. An inadequate format makes it more complicated to integrate into existing systems or their own workflows, requiring costs to be incurred in order to adapt either the systems or the data.

- **Quality assurance**: In DaaS, quality in terms of accuracy of data is key, and poor-quality data can lead to flawed decision-making or errors in related services. The quality, accuracy, and reliability of the data depend on the provider. Therefore, the provider must ensure that the data is relevant, updated, and of good quality.

- **Latency and performance issues**: Accessing data over the internet can lead to introducing latency (especially when the connection is not good or the datasets are very large). In addition, this latency can reduce performance if the data stream is embedded in additional services.

Results as a Service (RaaS)

RaaS, or OaaS, is a new paradigm that has developed in recent years. RaaS is a business model where a service provider delivers specific results or outcomes instead of providing tools, platforms, or raw data. This model has attracted attention in fields such as data analytics, AI, and automation. In RaaS, AI (including LLMs and agents) is used by the provider to provide personalized insights for customers. While the provider conducts the entire analysis, the client can focus on business insights without the need for specialized technology staff. In general, instead of paying a lump sum for a service, the client pays through a subscription to receive analytics at constant intervals.

Since customers increasingly demand value from models (businesses are more interested in the value obtained from models than from an additional tool), RaaS focuses on providing an outcome rather than a model (or data). In addition, customers are looking for ways to reduce the costs of adopting a technology but preserving its value, and RaaS thus seeks to reduce the initial cost to a business. The provider focuses on identifying the technology or what tool is needed to achieve the outcome, while the customer explains what their needs and requirements are.

The purpose of RaaS is to build customer loyalty, and so a provider has every interest in automating the analysis process. Therefore, AI agents can be envisioned as a new core component of this business model. By itself, an LLM is capable of almost instantaneously producing a possible report and thus generating insights for a customer. These reports can be personalized using LLMs and provide insights tailored to the clients. The addition of tools and databases allows for both adding a quantitative component and extending the capabilities of an LLM. Agents then allow tasks to be completed automatically and routinely. In fact, agents can analyze large amounts of data and can be complemented with additional models. The reports (or even presentations) generated can be used to make informed decisions.

RaaS thus has several advantages:

- **Outcome-focused approach**: The business pays only for results (and thus for the value that is delivered) and not for tools, infrastructure, and expertise. This reduces risk for a business, since it has no responsibility for either using software or conducting analysis.

- **Cost efficiency**: For the customer, there is no need to spend money to build infrastructure and expertise. Instead, the service provider can automate the process and reduce costs (it can be rather expensive for a small business). Also, the client can adopt a subscription plan at an agreed price (with the added benefit that outcome-based pricing models align costs directly with results achieved), and the provider instead gets a stable monthly income.

- **Focus on core competencies**: Since a company does not have to invest resources in building and maintaining systems or managing processes, RaaS provides a large time advantage. This also allows the business to implement new capabilities, demanding execution only from the provider. The customer can then focus on its core competencies and incorporate the results directly into its pipeline.

- **Scalability, accuracy, and flexibility**: The system is scalable and flexible, as the provider can reuse the technology for different clients. Providers are incentivized to deliver high-quality outcomes since their payment or reputation depends on the success of the service.

RaaS can also have some disadvantages:

- **Loss of control**: Clients have limited control over how these outcomes are achieved. They can't track the process or diagnose potential problems that arise during the process. In addition, there could be potential concerns over compliance, quality, or ethical practices on the part of the provider that the client might not notice. In general, RaaS does not promote transparency, and it relies on the client's trust in the provider.

- **Dependency on providers**: For customers, RaaS means heavy reliance on a service provider, which can lead to vendor lock-in, difficulty in changing providers, or high costs in changing a provider. Any failure or inefficiency on the provider's part has a direct impact on customer operations. In these cases, the customer has limited options.

- **Data security and privacy risks**: Sensitive data may need to be shared with the service provider, creating privacy and security concerns. Businesses may not be able to share this data due to regulation, risking potential breaches and hefty fines. At the same time, if sensitive data were intercepted, businesses could face serious reputational damage or fines. RaaS service providers, therefore, come with large costs to maintain system security, data storage, and connections.

- **Complexity in measuring results**: Defining clear, measurable outcomes can be challenging, especially when the goal or analysis is complex. Misaligned expectations between the client and the provider may lead to disputes about whether outcomes have been achieved. These disputes can become costly lawsuits and impact the provider's reputation.

- **Potential for higher costs**: On the one hand, RaaS reduces upfront costs, but in the long run, the service can become expensive for a business. Also, there may be added costs for further analysis, or if there is misalignment in performance and goals.
- **Limited customization**: RaaS solutions may be defined by broad application, and may not meet specific, niche requirements of a business. A service provider has every interest in automating tasks and creating solutions that are useful to the greatest number of customers. This means specific customer needs may have additional costs, not be addressed, or not be fully understood by the provider.
- **Quality assurance challenges**: The provider has an interest in reducing costs; this is done through automation and trying to achieve a solution that fits all clients. A provider may cut corners to achieve outcomes quickly, potentially compromising long-term value.

RaaS, in any case, is a growing business model, especially with the growing interest in AI and generative AI (many businesses want to integrate AI services but have neither the expertise nor the infrastructure to do so). Many companies are only interested in the outcome of the model (such as predictions for maintenance or a patient's outcome) rather than the model itself. Many businesses would be interested in tailoring the outcome to their specific needs, without needing to develop the entire process. Therefore, as competition increases, different providers are beginning to specialize in highly specific offerings for different types of industries. This drives innovation as companies strive to cover needs that are currently unmet. With more offerings, customers' needs will also evolve, allowing companies to focus on improving crucial elements of their business.

A comparison of the different paradigms

We can summarize the choice of paradigm as follows:

- **SaaS**: A provider should choose SaaS when they want to offer a steady and predictable revenue stream through subscriptions, their product is scalable to a large number of customers (thus reducing the cost of their solution), it is easy to support updates and maintenance, they have capabilities to leverage cloud infrastructure to minimize hardware costs, they can guarantee frequent software improvements, and ensure customer loyalty. A customer should choose SaaS when they need quick access to software without having to invest in hardware or maintenance, software flexibility and scalability are critical, or they prefer paying for software on a subscription basis rather than making large upfront investments. SaaS is also a good choice when customers prefer that updates, maintenance, and security are handled by an external provider or they are interested in applications that are remotely accessible (e.g., they have teams that are spread across various countries or various locations). Examples of companies using SaaS are Salesforce (a cloud-based CRM system widely used across industries), Microsoft 365 (offers productivity tools such as Word, Excel, and Teams via cloud subscription), Adobe Creative Cloud (provides access to creative tools such as Photoshop and Illustrator with continuous cloud updates), and Slack (a communication platform used by distributed teams for messaging and collaboration).

- **MaaS**: A provider should look to MaaS when they can reduce the cost of model delivery with other partners (or have a solid infrastructure), have developed high-performing AI/ML models that can serve various industries (e.g., healthcare, finance, or retail), want to monetize the developed models or expertise without sharing the algorithms, and can securely and reliably guarantee the model access. Users should consider these solutions when they require advanced AI/ML models but lack the resources to build or train them in-house, or prefer outsourcing model maintenance, retraining, and optimization rather than managing it internally. These models should also be considered when cost efficiency and flexibility are priorities, especially for start-ups and businesses experimenting with AI/ML, as well as when time to market for AI/ML-driven applications is critical. Examples of companies using MaaS are OpenAI (provides access to GPT models through APIs for tasks such as text generation or summarization), Google Cloud AI Platform (offers models for translation, vision, speech recognition, and more), AWS SageMaker JumpStart (lets businesses quickly deploy pre-trained models for tasks such as fraud detection), and Hugging Face (through its Inference API, offers hosted access to thousands of open source models).

- **DaaS**: A provider should choose DaaS if they have access to high-value, unique datasets that can benefit multiple industries, they want to capitalize on the growing reliance on data for decision-making and analytics, they want to create an additional business opportunity for their company (e.g., selling data that has been acquired over time), they can ensure compliance with data protection regulations (e.g., GDPR or CCPA), they have the infrastructure to be able to conduct data sharing, or they provide (or intend to) added value beyond raw data, such as insights, visualizations, or integration with tools. A client should consider DaaS if they need large volumes of data but do not want to invest in storage and processing infrastructure, their business relies on external or specialized datasets (e.g., market data, weather data, geolocation data, financial data, healthcare data, and so on), they prefer flexibility in accessing different datasets and scaling, or they do not want to deal with data compliance, maintenance, and security. Examples include Snowflake (a cloud data platform that enables secure data sharing across organizations), Quandl by Nasdaq (offers financial, economic, and alternative data to analysts and institutions), Clearbit (provides B2B data for sales and marketing enrichment), and the Climate Data Store from Copernicus (offers environmental and climate datasets for scientific and commercial use).

- **RaaS**: A provider may consider RaaS if they have the appropriate infrastructure to guarantee reliable and measurable outcomes to customers, prefer to differentiate themselves by focusing on delivering value and results rather than selling products or services, can measure performance and guaranteed outcomes to the customer, and have expertise in mitigating risks and guaranteeing performance. Customers should choose RaaS when they want to achieve specific outcomes without managing the underlying processes, infrastructure, or technology; when their focus is on outcomes (e.g., performance improvement or operational efficiency) rather than tools or inputs; when they want to minimize risks by paying only for successful outcomes or results; when they lack expertise in achieving some complex and specialized outcomes; or when they want to reduce costs and spread them out over time. Examples of companies that use RaaS are Pymetrics (delivers hiring recommendations based on neuroscience and AI without exposing internal mechanisms), Afiniti (uses AI to optimize call center pairings and charges based on improved performance), Uptake (provides predictive maintenance in industrial contexts tied to uptime or efficiency gains), and ZS Associates (offers analytics-driven solutions in healthcare and pharma, charging based on KPIs and performance improvements).

The following table provides a summary of the advantages and disadvantages of each paradigm for providers and users:

Category	SaaS	MaaS	DaaS	RaaS
Advantages (provider)	- Recurring revenue model. - Scalable infrastructure - Easier software updates. - Cost-efficient development life cycle.	- Enables monetization of AI/ML models. - Scalable distribution of computational resources. - Supports various industries such as healthcare and finance. - Reduced infrastructure needs (e.g., cloud-hosted ML models). - Opportunity to expand into niche AI/ML applications.	- Data monetization opportunities. - Centralized management of data. - Predictable revenue. - Ability to leverage existing datasets. - Flexibility in serving different industries.	- Steady and predictable revenue streams. - Encourages value-based pricing for outcomes. - Differentiates offering in competitive markets. - Enables providers to focus on delivering outcomes rather than selling products. - Improved customer retention.

Advantages (User)	- Low upfront cost. - Easy access to the latest software versions. - Accessibility from anywhere. - Flexibility in subscriptions to match business needs.	- Access to advanced models without the need to build or train them. - Scalable computing power to process models efficiently. - Flexibility in using models for predictions or automation. - Cost savings by avoiding the need to build in-house AI/ML infrastructure - Enables faster time to market for AI-powered applications.	- Easy and quick access to curated, usable data. - Lower cost of ownership for data systems. - Eliminates the need for large data storage/processing infrastructure. - Flexible scaling.	- Reduced risk with outcome-based payments. - Focus on results without worrying about underlying infrastructure. - Predictable performance and value. - No need for large initial investments. - Simplifies achieving desired results with expert support.
Disadvantages (provider)	- High competition and customer churn. - Ongoing costs for infrastructure and updates. - Challenges with regional regulations and compliance.	- High initial development cost for models. - Ensuring fairness, reliability, and compliance in AI/ML models is challenging. - Managing performance expectations of models across diverse use cases. - Resource-intensive model updates and retraining.	-Privacy/security concerns with data usage. - Infrastructure for real-time data delivery. - Need for compliance with complex data regulations (e.g., GDPR).	- Revenue depends on the successful delivery of outcomes. - High upfront costs for performance guarantees. - Complex measurement and accountability metrics. - Risk of lower margins if outcomes are hard to deliver or expectations are misaligned.

Disadvantages (user)	- Dependence on internet connectivity. - Data security and privacy risks. - Long-term costs may exceed owning software outright.	- Dependence on third-party models. - Potential for bias or errors in AI/ML models. - May incur long-term costs if frequently needed. - Limited ability to customize models for highly specific needs. - Privacy concerns in certain AI/ML applications.	- Concerns about data ownership and vendor lock-in. - Potential for high long-term costs. - Possible over-reliance on third-party data. - Security risks with sensitive data.	- Dependence on vendor for outcome success. - Lack of transparency in how the processes achieve results. - Limited flexibility to modify outcomes during contracts. - May not suit users with highly specific, non-standardized needs. - Costs can escalate if outcomes are not well defined.

Table 9.1 – Advantages and disadvantages for providers and users

The choice of business paradigm is an important one. Each paradigm has an impact on both a user and a business. Finding the right paradigm saves resources and increases revenue. The choice of paradigm impacts the technical choices for developing a multi-agent system.

Summary

In this chapter, we have seen how the tools we looked at in previous chapters can be added to an LLM. We saw that an LLM is capable of planning and reasoning, but it produces weaker results when it comes to execution. An LLM is capable of generating text, but at the same time, the enormous amount of information learned allows it to develop skills beyond text generation. While it is a computational waste to ask an LLM to classify an image, an LLM can use a specialized model to solve the task. As we saw with HuggingGPT, a model can invoke other models to identify a pizza in an image. In that case, we saw an LLM invoke more than one model, collect their outputs, and conduct reasoning about the results (observe that the models agreed on the type of pizza in the image). The LLM can then conduct reasoning and choose which models need to run to complete the task, collect the outputs, and observe whether the task is completed.

This concept makes it possible to revolutionize various industrial applications. For example, a customer can request by email to exchange an item because the size they purchased was too small. An LLM understands the complaint, devises a plan, and executes it. The model can use tools to verify the purchase, another tool to see whether the size up is in stock, software to order the shipment, and, once the order is complete, respond to the customer that their request has been fulfilled. Agents therefore enable the automation of various tasks, as they allow an LLM to use other tools necessary for task completion. As we have seen, this approach extends to many other applications: agents in the law field, agents for research in chemistry and biology, and so on. For example, AI agents could be legal assistants to help write papers, assist professors in creating lectures, or help researchers define scientific hypotheses.

Although these seem like advanced scenarios, it must be understood that LLMs have limitations in reasoning, and at present, they can automate simple tasks but not yet complex business needs. For this, there needs to be human oversight, and developers need to be aware of what the limitations of the system are. In addition, LLMs consume resources, and these systems can be computationally expensive. Scalability is one of the main issues for a business that wants to adopt agents. Therefore, in the last section of this chapter, we discussed the various business paradigms that open up with the arrival of LLMs. SaaS is the classic paradigm that has dominated the last three decades; it was conceived during the internet revolution but before the arrival of AI as a mass product. DaaS focuses on AI and businesses' need for quality data to make informed decisions. MaaS is dedicated to companies that want to provide ML and AI models, while RaaS focuses only on the output of these models. There are clear similarities between SaaS and these paradigms, but they take into consideration two factors: AI models require infrastructure and resources to train and use, and developing and maintaining these models requires considerable expertise. MaaS and RaaS thus allow a business to reduce the initial investment into infrastructure, training, and expertise. The choice of provider or client is different depending on their needs and resources, so we have provided a comparative table and some guidelines.

In this chapter, therefore, we have defined what an agent is in practice (or a group of agents in the case of a multi-agent platform) and discussed how these agents can be integrated into the business. In other words, we have defined an agent-based system. This system is not an isolated entity; in the next chapter, we will focus on the ecosystem around an agent and how an agent integrates into it.

Further reading

- Shen, *HuggingGPT: Solving AI Tasks with ChatGPT and its Friends in Hugging Face*, 2023, https://arxiv.org/abs/2303.17580
- Wang, *A Survey on Large Language Model based Autonomous Agents*, 2023, https://arxiv.org/abs/2308.11432
- Raieli, *HuggingGPT: Give Your Chatbot an AI Army*, https://levelup.gitconnected.com/hugginggpt-give-your-chatbot-an-ai-army-cfadf5647f98
- Schick, *Toolformer: Language Models Can Teach Themselves to Use Tools*, 2023, https://arxiv.org/abs/2302.04761

- Bran, *ChemCrow: Augmenting Large Language Models with Chemistry Tools*, 2023, https://arxiv.org/abs/2304.05376

- Cui, *Chatlaw: A Multi-Agent Collaborative Legal Assistant with Knowledge Graph Enhanced Mixture-of-Experts Large Language Model*, 2023, https://arxiv.org/abs/2306.16092v2

- Hamilton, *Blind Judgement: Agent-Based Supreme Court Modelling With GPT*, 2023, https://arxiv.org/abs/2301.05327

- Cheng, *Exploring Large Language Model based Intelligent Agents: Definitions, Methods, and Prospects*, 2024, https://arxiv.org/pdf/2401.03428

- Swanson, *The Virtual Lab: AI Agents Design New SARS-CoV-2 Nanobodies with Experimental Validation*, 2024, https://www.biorxiv.org/content/10.1101/2024.11.11.623004v1.full

- Lu, *The AI Scientist: Towards Fully Automated Open-Ended Scientific Discovery*, 2024, https://arxiv.org/abs/2408.06292

- Fossi, *SwiftDossier: Tailored Automatic Dossier for Drug Discovery with LLMs and Agents*, 2024, https://arxiv.org/abs/2409.15817

- Si, *Can LLMs Generate Novel Research Ideas? A Large-Scale Human Study with 100+ NLP Researchers*, 2024, https://arxiv.org/abs/2409.04109

- Raieli, *AI Planning or Serendipity? Where Do the Best Research Ideas Come From?*, https://ai.gopubby.com/ai-planning-or-serendipity-where-do-the-best-research-ideas-come-from-f8e5e6692964

- Raieli, *A Brave New World for Scientific Discovery: Are AI Research Ideas Better?*, https://levelup.gitconnected.com/a-brave-new-world-for-scientific-discovery-are-ai-research-ideas-better-5692c5aa8182

- Schmidgall, *Agent Laboratory: Using LLM Agents as Research Assistants*, 2024, https://arxiv.org/abs/2501.04227

- Tang, *ChemAgent: Self-updating Library in Large Language Models Improves Chemical Reasoning*, 2025, https://arxiv.org/abs/2501.06590

- Raieli, *Can AI Replace Human Researchers*, https://levelup.gitconnected.com/can-ai-replace-human-researchers-50fcc43ea587

- *European Cloud Computing Platforms*, https://european-alternatives.eu/category/cloud-computing-platforms

- IBM, *What is Multi-tenant?*, https://www.ibm.com/topics/multi-tenant

- Gan, 2023, *Model-as-a-Service (MaaS): A Survey*, https://arxiv.org/pdf/2311.05804

- Abe, *A Data as a Service (DaaS) Model for GPU-based Data Analytics*, 2018, https://arxiv.org/abs/1802.01639

- Forbes, *AI Agents: The Next Frontier In Intelligent Automation*, `https://www.forbes.com/councils/forbestechcouncil/2025/01/02/ai-agents-the-next-frontier-in-intelligent-automation/`

- World Economic Forum, *Why Should Manufacturers Embrace AI's Next Frontier – AI agents – Now?*, `https://www.weforum.org/stories/2025/01/why-manufacturers-should-embrace-next-frontier-ai-agents/`

- Deng, 2023, *Mind2Web: Towards a Generalist Agent for the Web*, `https://arxiv.org/abs/2306.06070`

10
Building an AI Agent Application

In the previous chapter, we discussed how an LLM can extend its capabilities by using other tools. We also saw some examples of how the use of multiple agents at the same time (instead of one) can be used to solve more complex tasks. We extensively discussed how these approaches can be used in various industries and how they can be revolutionary for so many applications. However, we also highlighted two of the limitations of agents: scalability and the complexity of connecting an agent with different tools.

In this chapter, we will expand on these challenges and show how we can overcome them. We will pick up from these two limitations. So far, we have treated multi-agent systems as standalone entities running on a personal computer. In the final section of the previous chapter, we explored the exciting new business paradigms emerging with AI. Agents are poised to play a significant role across industries in the future, but for that to happen, agent systems must be ready for production deployment. Getting a multi-agent system into production means we'll have to solve the previously mentioned scalability and complexity issues to avoid harming the customer experience.

We will follow a progressive approach in this chapter. We will use Streamlit, which is a simple but flexible framework that allows us to manage the entire process of creating an application around our agents. It allows us to conduct rapid prototyping of our application, testing different options until we reach a proof of concept. With Streamlit, we can seamlessly work with both the backend, where agents operate, and the frontend, which shapes the user experience—all within a single framework.

Next, we will discuss in more detail the whole set of operations that are necessary to make an LLM and agents functional. Irrespective of whether you have the opportunity to train a model from scratch, this section will help you understand how to improve scalability and how the industry is handling the complexity of the process. In addition, we will address asynchronous programming and containerization, two concepts that are useful for scaling not only a multi-agent application but any machine learning project.

In this chapter, we'll be covering the following topics:

- Introduction to Streamlit
- Developing our frontend with Streamlit
- Creating an application with Streamlit and AI agents
- Machine learning operations and LLM operations
- Asynchronous programming
- Docker

Technical requirements

Most of the code in this chapter can be run on CPUs. The *Introduction to Streamlit* and *Frontend with Streamlit* sections do not require GPUs. The libraries to install are as follows:

- **Streamlit**: For managing the frontend and backend of our app
- **pandas**: For handling DataFrames
- **Matplotlib**: For plotting graphs
- **Folium**: For plotting maps
- **time**: For monitoring runtime
- **NumPy**: For numerical computation
- **pydeck**: For map representation
- **OpenAI**: For building agents using its LLMs
- **Sentence Transformer**: To conduct embeddings

The *Creating an application with Streamlit and AI agents* section can be run on a CPU, but it would be preferred if it were run on a GPU.

The OpenAI library requires the use of an OpenAI token, and you should register with OpenAI to obtain it. The next sections can be run on CPUs and are mainly based on the use of the AsyncIO library. The code can be found on GitHub: https://github.com/PacktPublishing/Modern-AI-Agents/tree/main/chr10.

Introduction to Streamlit

If readers are familiar with Streamlit, they can move on to the *Creating an application with Streamlit and AI agents* section directly.

Companies have invested heavily in data science and AI. The models that are trained can guide business decisions and provide different insights. Training a model, using it, and extracting insights requires expertise that not everyone has. A model that is truly useful for a company must provide results that must then be used by other stakeholders as well. For example, when you train a model, it should generate results that are usable by other people. It is possible to create static visualizations of the data (exporting graphs), but they convey only limited information. One could provide information in a Jupyter notebook but not everyone is capable of using such a tool. One option that might allow easier access by others is to create a dashboard or web application.

This is where Streamlit comes in.

Starting with Streamlit

Streamlit is a web application framework that allows one to easily and intuitively create web applications with Python. Its library provides a number of built-in components for both the backend and the frontend. It is also compatible with leading machine learning, graph, and plotting libraries.

The objective of this section is to understand how Streamlit works and how it can be a powerful tool.

One of the advantages of Streamlit is its ease of use and installation. Streamlit can simply be installed from the terminal and is present in Anaconda distributions:

```
pip install streamlit
```

Organizing an app with Streamlit is a simple Python script that typically contains both the backend and the frontend. This script can then be run either locally or in the cloud. For example, my_app.py should contain within it all the elements to build a web app. In the simplest cases, with just a few lines of code, we can build a web app. Once we define our app, running it locally is really simple:

```
streamlit run my_app.py
```

What we need to do is call Streamlit and the name of our app (obviously, if we are using a terminal, we need to be in the right directory). Actually, the script does not have to be in your local directory; it can be on the internet. For example, our script is in our repository on GitHub, and we want to run it locally:

```
streamlit run https://raw.githubusercontent.com/streamlit/my_apps/master/my_app.py
```

Under the hood, Streamlit runs through the file and executes the elements it finds sequentially. After that is done, a local Streamlit server will be initialized and your app will open in a new tab in your default web browser. Note that everything we write is in Python, and no other language is required. When we make a change, we must save our source. Streamlit detects any modifications and prompts us to rerun the app. This allows for quick iterations while immediately observing the effects, ensuring a seamless feedback loop between writing and running the application.

An example of a simple app is the following:

```python
import streamlit as st
import pandas as pd
import matplotlib.pyplot as plt

# Title for the app
st.title("Simple Streamlit App with Box Plot")
# Create a sample DataFrame
data = {
    'Category': ['A', 'A', 'A', 'B', 'B', 'B', 'C', 'C', 'C'],
    'Values': [10, 20, 15, 25, 30, 20, 35, 40, 45]
}
df = pd.DataFrame(data)
# Display the DataFrame
st.write("Here is the sample DataFrame:")
st.dataframe(df)
# Create a box plot
fig, ax = plt.subplots()
df.boxplot(column='Values', by='Category', ax=ax, grid=False)
plt.title("Box Plot of Values by Category")
plt.suptitle("")  # Remove the automatic subtitle
plt.xlabel("Category")
plt.ylabel("Values")
# Display the plot in Streamlit
st.pyplot(fig)
```

The app we generated simply does three things: it creates a DataFrame with pandas, plots it, and then produces a box plot. In a few lines of code, we have created a mini web application that is accessible on our browser. Once we have written it, we just have to run it and then Streamlit takes care of everything else.

Simple Streamlit App with Box Plot

Here is the sample DataFrame:

	Category	Values
0	A	10
1	A	20
2	A	15
3	B	25
4	B	30
5	B	20
6	C	35
7	C	40
8	C	45

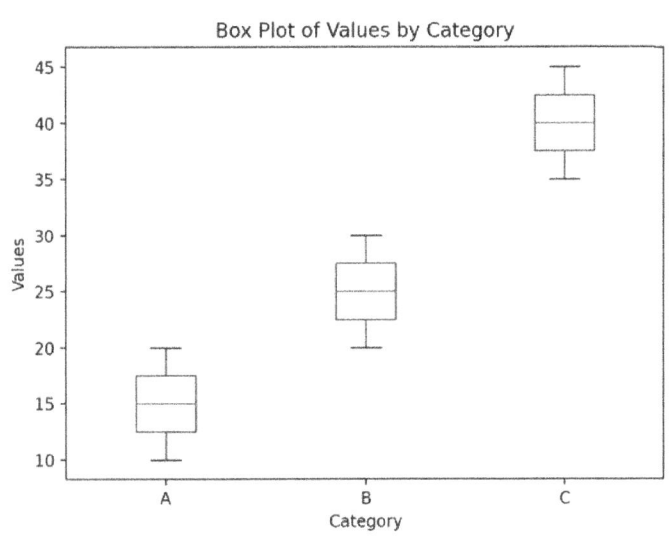

Figure 10.1 – Example of a web application

Let's look at the code block in a bit more detail:

- `st.title`: This is a text element that allows us to display the title of our app. It is a good idea to always include it in an app.
- `st.write`: This is considered the Swiss army knife of Streamlit. Its main purpose is to write both textual and other elements. In this case, we have shown how passing a DataFrame is written to the app in nice formatting. In addition, this element is interactive. In other words, its behavior depends on the input given to it. The `write()` function is not limited to text but can be used with images, other Python elements (such as lists and dictionaries), templates, and so on. It also allows us to insert commands with HTML if we want to edit our text.

- `st.pyplot`: This displays a Matplotlib figure – in our case, a box plot. As you can see, we generated our figure first and then called `pyplot()` for the subsequent plotting. The figure is generated before being actually shown. In other words, the figure is already present in memory; we need `pyplot()` to display the figure to the user in the app. Actually, we could also call plotting directly with Matplotlib, but this is not recommended because it could lead to unexpected behavior.

Note that we have only shown some basic commands, but Streamlit is quite flexible. For example, the DataFrame can be written to the app in different ways. Using `st.write()` is just one way: `st.dataframe()` does the same as `st.write()`, `st.table()` allows us to render the table statically, and writing `'df'` directly acts as if we were using `st.write()`. It is recommended to use one of the built-in methods because the behavior is known and we can also use additional arguments to handle the output.

For example, we can use the flexibility provided by the built-in method, `st.dataframe()`, to highlight elements in our DataFrame:

```
df = pd.DataFrame(data)
st.dataframe(df.style.highlight_max(axis=0))
```

Here is sample DataFrame:

	Category	Values
0	A	10
1	A	20
2	A	15
3	B	25
4	B	30
5	B	20
6	C	35
7	C	40
8	C	45

Figure 10.2 Change in style in the DataFrame rendering

In addition, Streamlit also makes it easy to add maps to our application. Just provide the coordinates, and `st.map()` magically allows us to have a map in our application (a map that we can enlarge and move). In this case, we provided the coordinates of some Sicilian cities:

```
city_data = {
    'City': ['Palermo', 'Syracuse', 'Catania', 'Agrigento'],
    'latitude': [38.1157, 37.0757, 37.5079, 37.2982],
    'longitude': [13.3615, 15.2867, 15.0830, 13.5763]
}

city_data = pd.DataFrame(city_data)
st.map(city_data)
```

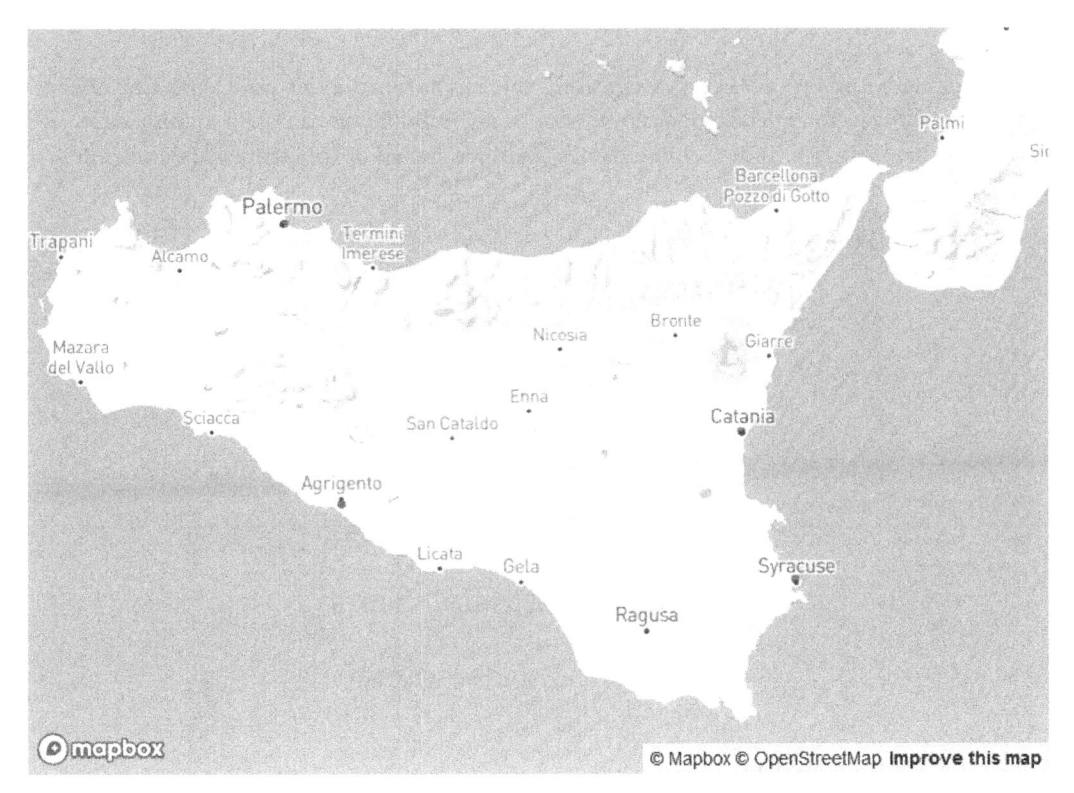

Figure 10.3 – Plotting a map with Streamlit

As can be seen, we have added some elements and made some changes to our app (adding a map). Whenever we modify the code, we should remember to save the changes to the script; then, we go to our app and press the *R* key, which will reload the app with the updates.

If there are any errors, Streamlit will provide us with error messages indicating what we need to correct. An example of an error is shown in the following figure (in this case, about the variable name to use):

StreamlitAPIException: Map data must contain a column named "latitude" or "lat".

Traceback:

```
File "my_app.py", line 34, in <module>
    st.map(city_data)
```

Figure 10.4 – Example of an error

For debugging, we use `st.write()` extensively; this simple function can print almost any Python object by guiding us to understand what the error is. For example, we can use it in this case. As we can see, we have an error in the column names (*Latitude* should be lowercase; so, we substitute it with the correct name):

```
st.write(city_data)
```

	City	Latitude	longitude
0	Palermo	38.1157	13.3615
1	Syracuse	37.0757	15.2867
2	Catania	37.5079	15.0830
3	Agrigento	37.2982	13.5763

Figure 10.5 – Using st.write() to debug

Caching the results

Caching allows our app to remain performant even if data is loaded from the web (we will discuss how to add data from the web or the user later). It also allows it to manipulate large datasets or use machine learning models. So far, we have been using small datasets and hence we could load anything, but what if we start putting models of millions of parameters inside our app? Our app might crash. If we use models or other elements that require long computations, we need to focus on optimizing our app's efficiency by caching results in memory and avoiding redundant calculations. We can see the cache as a kind of short-term memory, where we keep information that we use often or think will be useful to safeguard. Caching allows us to reuse this information and save computation. If we have a function that performs a large computation, we can use two alternatives:

- `st.cache_data`: This is a decorator in Streamlit that is used to cache the results of a function so that the function need not be recomputed every time the app is rerun (such as when a user interacts with widgets or the app reloads). This decorator is recommended for cache computations that return data. One should use `st.cache_data` when a function returns a serializable data object (e.g., `str`, `int`, `float`, `DataFrame`, `dict`, or `list`). When a function is wrapped with `@st.cache_data`, the first time the function is called, Streamlit stores the result in memory or a disk cache, depending on the configuration. On subsequent calls with the same arguments, Streamlit returns the cached result, which is much faster than recomputing it. It speeds up the app by preventing redundant work, especially for functions that take a long time to execute. If the inputs to the function change, Streamlit will invalidate the cache and recompute the function.

- `st.cache_resource`: This is another decorator in Streamlit, introduced to handle the caching of resources – specifically, objects or expensive operations that do not depend on the function arguments but instead represent reusable resources that can be cached for the lifetime of the app. While `st.cache_data` is used for caching the results of computations or data loads based on the inputs, `st.cache_resource` is designed to cache resources such as database connections, model objects, or any other object that is expensive to create or initialize but doesn't change with each function call. Use this for caching resources such as database connections, machine learning models, network connections, or any expensive resource that needs to be reused across multiple runs of the app. If an object or resource (e.g., a pre-trained model) is expensive to create, you can use `st.cache_resource` to avoid reloading or reinitializing it multiple times.

For example, for `st.cache_data`, in the following code, we are simulating a slow operation and showing how caching is saving time:

```
import streamlit as st
import time
# Use @st.cache_data to cache the result
@st.cache_data
def load_data():
    time.sleep(3)  # Simulate a slow operation (e.g., loading a large dataset)
    return "Data loaded!"
# Call the function
st.write(load_data())
in a similar way for st.cache_resource:
import streamlit as st
import time
```

```
# Example: A resource-intensive function (e.g., loading a model)
@st.cache_resource
def load_model():
    time.sleep(5)  # Simulate a slow operation like loading a model
    return "Model loaded!"  # This could be a model object in a real scenario
# Call the function
st.write(load_model())
```

In the preceding snippet, under the hood, before running a function, Streamlit checks its cache for a previously saved result. If it finds one, it uses that instead of running the function; if it doesn't find it, it runs the function and saves it in the cache. The cache is updated during execution, especially if the code changes.

By default, Streamlit doesn't save the information between app reruns, but with each rerun, it reruns the app from top to bottom. Normally, Streamlit reruns the entire script whenever there's an interaction (e.g., when a user adjusts a slider or clicks a button). With session state, you can store data that persists during these reruns so you don't lose values when the script reruns. Each user gets their own independent session state, so data stored in the session state is isolated from other users. You can use the session state to store things such as form inputs, counters, authentication data, or intermediate computation results.

Let's try building an app that makes a shopping list; we will show how to save information about the session:

```
import streamlit as st
# Define a list of grocery items (the initial list of items to buy)
grocery_items = ['Apple', 'Banana', 'Carrot', 'Milk', 'Eggs']
# Streamlit app interface
st.title('Grocery List App')
# Text input to add a new item to the list
new_item = st.text_input("Add a new item to your grocery list:")
# Button to add the new item to the list
if st.button('Add Item'):
    if new_item:
        grocery_items.append(new_item)
        st.success(f"'{new_item}' has been added to your list!")
    else:
        st.warning("Please enter an item to add.")
# Display the current list of grocery items
st.write("### Items to Buy:")
for item in grocery_items:
    st.write(f"- {item}")
```

This is our initial app; we will see immediately afterward how we can view information saved by the user:

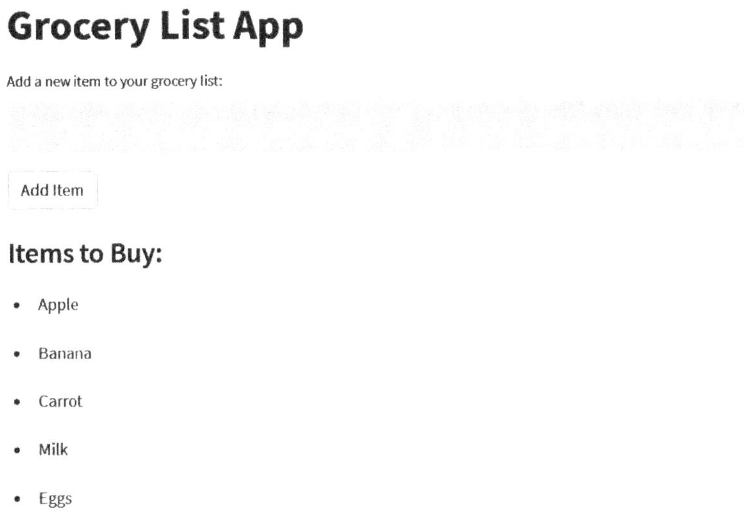

Grocery List App

Add a new item to your grocery list:

Add Item

Items to Buy:

- Apple
- Banana
- Carrot
- Milk
- Eggs

Figure 10.6 – Example of grocery list app

If we add objects by clicking on **Add Item**, they will be added to the list (at this time, the information is not saved; it remains only for the session):

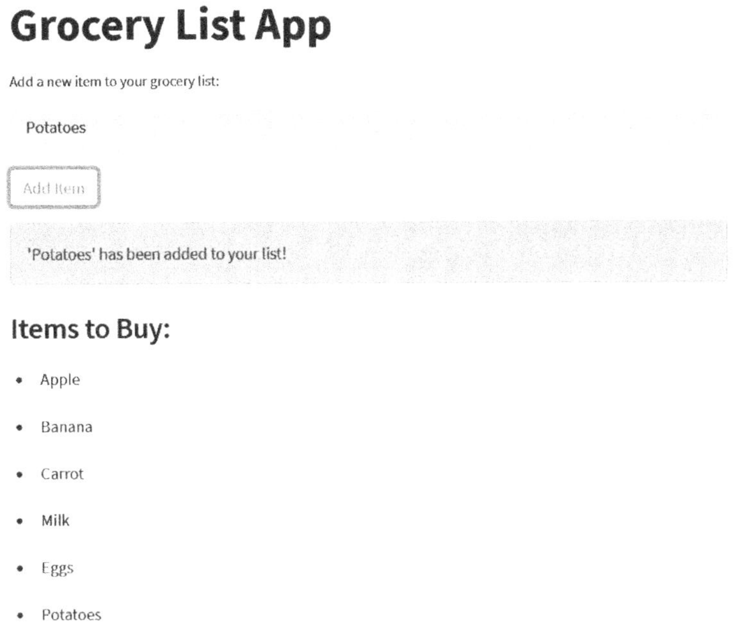

Grocery List App

Add a new item to your grocery list:

Potatoes

Add Item

'Potatoes' has been added to your list!

Items to Buy:

- Apple
- Banana
- Carrot
- Milk
- Eggs
- Potatoes

Figure 10.7 – Example of adding objects to the grocery list app

However, if we press *R* and rerun our app, we will lose this information, and the elements will disappear (because the information is not saved anywhere).

Now, let's try `session_state`:

```
import streamlit as st

# Initialize session state for grocery_items if it doesn't exist yet
if 'grocery_items' not in st.session_state:
    st.session_state.grocery_items = ['Apple', 'Banana', 'Carrot', 'Milk', 'Eggs']

# Streamlit app interface
st.title('Grocery List App')

# Text input to add a new item to the list
new_item = st.text_input("Add a new item to your grocery list:")

# Button to add the new item to the list
if st.button('Add Item'):
    if new_item:
        # Append the new item to the list stored in session state
        st.session_state.grocery_items.append(new_item)
        st.success(f"'{new_item}' has been added to your list!")
    else:
        st.warning("Please enter an item to add.")

# Display the current list of grocery items
st.write("### Items to Buy:")
for item in st.session_state.grocery_items:
    st.write(f"- {item}")
```

When we use `st.session_state`, the items we add will be preserved during the current session. On the first run, the list will contain the initial elements, and as the user adds more items, the list will grow accordingly.

However, once the page is reloaded or the session ends, the list will reset unless we store the data in a persistent location (e.g., a file or database).

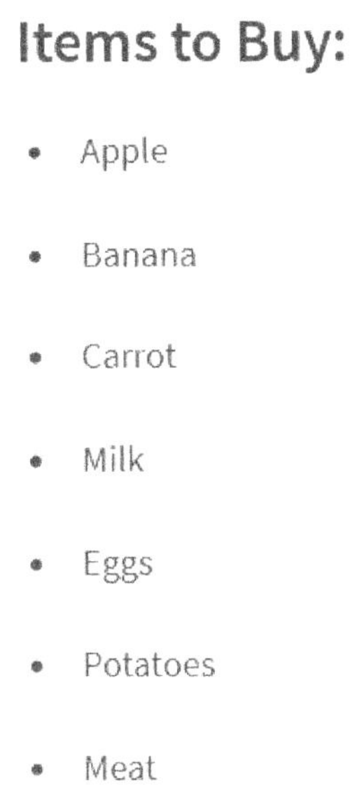

Items to Buy:

- Apple
- Banana
- Carrot
- Milk
- Eggs
- Potatoes
- Meat

Figure 10.8 – Updated list

While using `st.session_state` allows temporary storage of values during a user session—gradually filling up as interactions occur—this data is lost upon a full page reload or app restart. In contrast, `st.connection` enables Streamlit to maintain persistent access to external resources, ensuring that data remains available across sessions and reloads. This makes it ideal for applications that require consistent interaction with long-lived data, overcoming the limitations of in-memory session state. `st.connection` allows the connection to external services to be maintained and reused and does so efficiently with each user interaction.

Let's see how `st.connection` works in practice:

```
import streamlit as st
conn = st.connection("my_database_sql")
df = conn.query("select * from my_beautiful_table")
st.dataframe(df)
```

In this section, we discussed the main components of a Streamlit application. In the next one, we will discuss how to beautify our app and make the user experience better.

Developing our frontend with Streamlit

In this section, we will begin to discuss some of the elements that allow us to improve the user experience when interacting with our app.

We will show the various frontend elements and how to combine them for complex apps.

Adding the text elements

To improve our user experience, we can start by improving the text elements. The first elements we add are the following:

- `st.title()`: This sets the main title of your Streamlit app. It's the largest text element and is typically used for the main heading of your app. Every app should have at least one title, and this is shown in the GitHub-flavored Markdown. This function obviously takes a string.
- `st.header()`: This adds a header to your app. It's smaller than the title but still stands out as an important section heading. This also has a counterpart in GitHub and is similar in purpose. One attribute you can add is `divider`, which shows a colored divider below the header (we can specify a color). Also, we can add a `help` string that provides a tooltip next to the header.
- `st.subheader()`: This adds a subheader, which is smaller than the header and is typically used for subsections or to provide additional structure to the content. The subheader can also have a colored divider if you want one. A help `string` is also possible.

Here are some examples of how to insert these elements:

```
st.title("Your Title Here")
st.header("Your Header Here")
st.header("Your Header Here", divider=True, help ="bla bla")
st.subheader("Your Subheader Here")
```

Now, we can test them directly in our app:

```
import streamlit as st
# Initialize session state for grocery_items if it doesn't exist yet
if 'grocery_items' not in st.session_state:
    st.session_state.grocery_items = ['Apple', 'Banana', 'Carrot', 'Milk', 'Eggs']
# Streamlit app interface
st.title('Grocery List App :banana: :apple: :egg:')  # Main title of the app
# Display a header for the section where the user can add items
st.header('Add new item')
# Text input to add a new item to the list
new_item = st.text_input("Type an item to add to your grocery list:")
# Button to add the new item to the list
if st.button('Add Item'):
    if new_item:
        # Append the new item to the list stored in session state
        st.session_state.grocery_items.append(new_item)
        st.success(f"'{new_item}' has been added to your list!")
    else:
```

```
        st.warning("Please enter an item to add.")
# Display a subheader for the current grocery list
st.subheader('Current Grocery List')
# Display the current list of grocery items
for item in st.session_state.grocery_items:
    st.write(f"- {item}")
```

This code shows how to start inserting stylistic elements into our app. The following figure shows the result after these improvements:

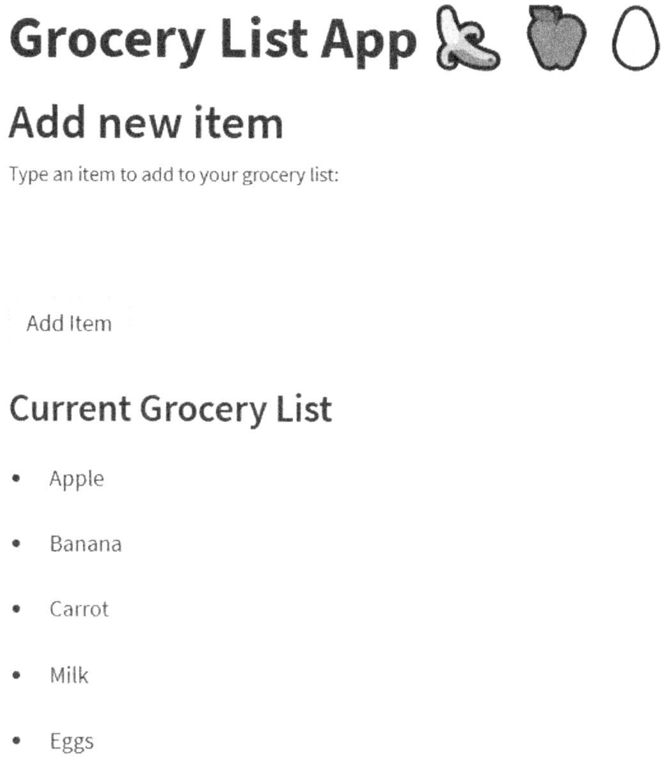

Grocery List App 🍌 🍎 🥚

Add new item

Type an item to add to your grocery list:

Add Item

Current Grocery List

- Apple

- Banana

- Carrot

- Milk

- Eggs

Figure 10.9 – Updated app

Inserting images in a Streamlit app

Next, we begin the customization of our app, adding both a logo and an image. To do this, we will use several elements:

- `st.set_page_config(...)`: This function is used to configure the Streamlit app's page settings, such as the title of the page, favicon (icon in the browser tab), and layout preferences. In this case, we will use it to add a small icon that will be seen as a browser tab element.

- `st.image(...)`: This function displays an image in the Streamlit app. It takes the URL or path of the image and can adjust its width to fit the screen with `use_column_width=True`. As input, `st.image` takes either a URL (as we are doing in this case) or a path to a local image or `numpy.array` (the image can be in number format).

  One of the keywords is `caption`, which allows us to provide a caption for the image directly. In our case, however, we will add the caption separately.

- `st.caption(...)`: This function adds a small caption or descriptive text below elements, such as images or charts. In our app, it provides the image credit.

- `st.sidebar.image(...)`: This places an image in the sidebar, which will be the collapsible menu on the left side of the app. The sidebar is useful for placing navigation, settings, or additional content.

We will now insert an image:

```
# Set the page configuration to include a logo
st.set_page_config(page_title="Grocery List App", page_icon="https://
github.com/SalvatoreRa/tutorial/blob/main/images/vegetable_basket_
logo.jpg?raw=true")
# Display the title image
st.image("https://github.com/SalvatoreRa/tutorial/blob/main/images/
vegetables.jpg?raw=true", use_column_width=True)
st.caption("Image from [here](https://unsplash.com/it/@randyfath)")
# Add logo to the sidebar
st.sidebar.image("https://github.com/SalvatoreRa/tutorial/blob/main/
images/vegetable_basket_logo.jpg?raw=true", use_column_width=True)
```

The preceding code shows how to insert an image with the proper caption. The following figure shows the results:

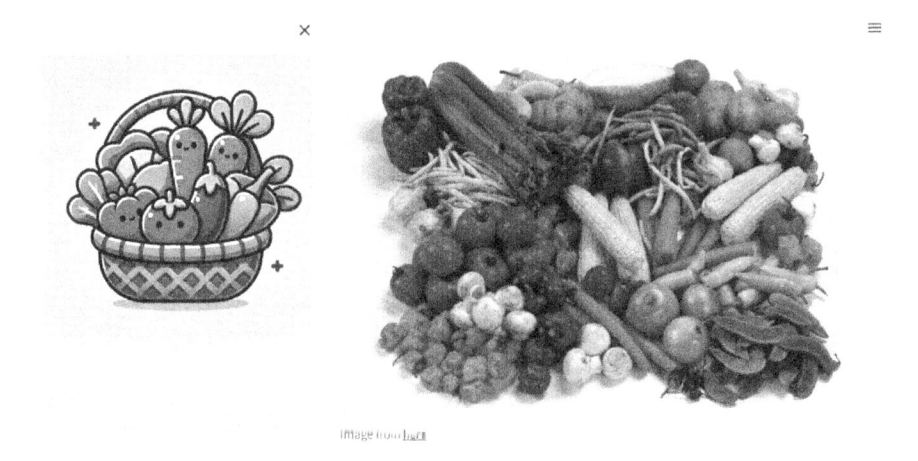

Figure 10.10 – Changes in appearance in the app

Here is our browser icon:

Figure 10.11 – The browser icon

Thus far, we have explored the basic features of Streamlit and used them to build a simple and static app. Now it's time to move beyond and start exploring what makes a Streamlit app dynamic, responsive, and connected to real use.

Creating a dynamic app

We can further modify our app to make it more dynamic. So far, our user can only add items to their list, and then the list is shown. This app is of little use, so we want to make it more dynamic and allow the user to add quantities. So, we're going to do the following:

- Allow the user to add an item to buy. Once the item is added, two sliders are created that represent the quantity the user has at home and how much they have to buy. To avoid creating an endless list, we will use two columns. In addition, we will add a button to select whether or not the user has taken the ingredient.

- Make an interactive display of a table with ingredients, showing how much to buy, how much was taken, and whether it was taken, as well as a completion bar that shows how many items have been taken and how many are missing.

- In the sidebar, add a button to download the list.

Let's start by displaying the grocery list items in a structured manner using two columns, ensuring a more compact and visually balanced layout:

```
data = []
for i, item in enumerate(st.session_state.grocery_items):
    with col1 if i % 2 == 0 else col2:
        st.markdown(f"**{item}**")
        quantity_at_home = st.slider(f"Quantity at home", 0, 12, st.session_state.quantity_at_home[item], key=f"home_{item}")
        st.session_state.quantity_at_home[item] = quantity_at_home
        quantity_to_take = st.slider(f"Quantity to take", 0, 12, st.session_state.quantity_to_take[item], key=f"take_{item}")
        st.session_state.quantity_to_take[item] = quantity_to_take
        taken = st.checkbox(f"Taken", st.session_state.taken[item], key=f"taken_{item}")
        st.session_state.taken[item] = taken
        data.append([item, quantity_at_home, quantity_to_take, "Yes" if taken else "No"])
```

For each item, we determine whether it should be placed in the first column (`col1`) or the second column (`col2`) based on whether the index, `i`, is even or odd. This ensures that items are distributed evenly between the two columns, preventing a long vertical list.

Inside the selected column, the item name is displayed in bold using `st.markdown()`. Below the name, two sliders are created: one for the quantity the user has at home and another for the quantity they need to take. Each slider is assigned a unique key based on the item name to ensure proper tracking and persistence of values. The values from these sliders are stored back into the session state so they remain updated across app interactions. In addition, a checkbox is included for each item. The collected data for each item, including its name, the selected quantities, and whether it has been taken or not, is appended to the data list.

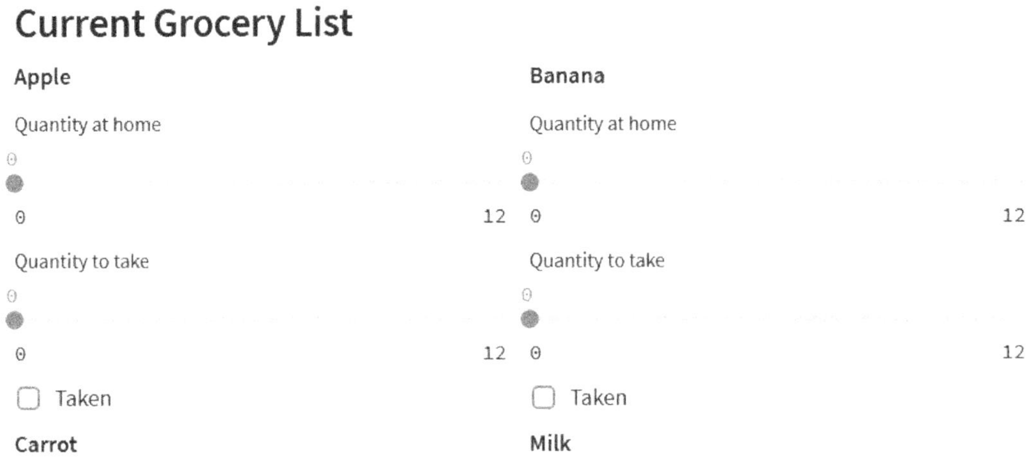

Current Grocery List

Apple

Quantity at home

0 — 12

Quantity to take

0 — 12

☐ Taken

Carrot

Banana

Quantity at home

0 — 12

Quantity to take

0 — 12

☐ Taken

Milk

Figure 10.12 – Restyling of the app

Notice that the app is interactive (we can interact with sliders):

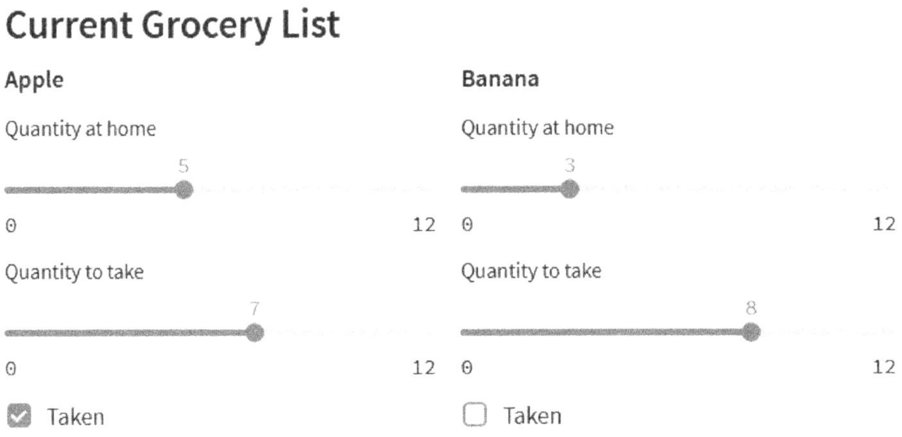

Current Grocery List

Apple

Quantity at home

5

0 — 12

Quantity to take

7

0 — 12

☑ Taken

Banana

Quantity at home

3

0 — 12

Quantity to take

8

0 — 12

☐ Taken

Figure 10.13 – Interactive elements

The preceding figure shows us how to insert interactive elements and how we can interact with them. Streamlit allows this in the background, without the need for us to code these complex elements, and we can use simple commands.

We can then display the table:

```
df = pd.DataFrame(data, columns=["Name", "Quantity at Home", "Quantity to Take", "Taken"])
st.table(df)
```

	Name	Quantity at Home	Quantity to Take	Taken
0	Apple	5	7	Yes
1	Banana	3	8	No
2	Carrot	0	9	No
3	Milk	0	4	No
4	Eggs	9	0	Yes
5	Potato	1	5	No

Figure 10.14 – Table obtained

At this point, we can create our progress bar:

```
# Progress bar
taken_count = sum(1 for item in st.session_state.taken.values() if item)
total_items = len(st.session_state.grocery_items)
progress = taken_count / total_items if total_items > 0 else 0
st.subheader("Grocery Completion Progress")
st.progress(progress)
st.write(f"{taken_count} out of {total_items} items taken ({progress*100:.2f}%)")
```

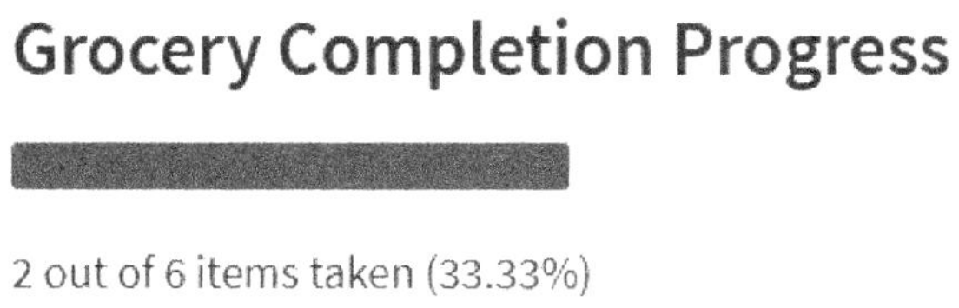

Grocery Completion Progress

2 out of 6 items taken (33.33%)

Figure 10.15 – Progress bar

Next, we define a function, `generate_pdf()`, which creates a PDF document containing the grocery list data and allows users to download it:

```
# Function to generate PDF
def generate_pdf():
    pdf = FPDF()
    pdf.set_auto_page_break(auto=True, margin=15)
    pdf.add_page()
    pdf.set_font("Arial", size=12)
    logo_path = "logo.jpg"  # Add logo to PDF

    response = requests.get(logo_url)
    with open(logo_path, "wb") as f:
        f.write(response.content)
    pdf.image(logo_path, 10, 10, 30)  # Position and size of the logo
    pdf.cell(200, 10, "Grocery List", ln=True, align='C')
    pdf.ln(20)  # Added extra spacing to prevent text overlapping the logo
    for index, row in df.iterrows():
        pdf.cell(0, 10, f"{row['Name']} - At Home: {row['Quantity at Home']} - To Take: {row['Quantity to Take']} - Taken: {row['Taken']}", ln=True)
    pdf_output = os.path.join(os.getcwd(), "grocery_list.pdf")
    pdf.output(pdf_output)
    return pdf_output

# Directly download the PDF when the button is clicked
if st.sidebar.button("Download List as PDF"):
    pdf_file = generate_pdf()
    with open(pdf_file, "rb") as f:
        st.sidebar.download_button("Download Grocery List PDF", f, file_name="grocery_list.pdf", mime="application/pdf", key="download_pdf", on_click=None)
```

First, we initialize an `FPDF` object with automatic page breaks and add a new page. The font is set to `Arial` with a size of `12` for consistent formatting. To enhance the PDF visually, the `generate_pdf()` function downloads a logo from a specified URL, saves it locally as `logo.jpg`, and embeds it in the top-left corner of the page. A centered title, `Grocery List`, is added, followed by some spacing to ensure the text does not overlap with the logo. The function then iterates through the grocery list stored in `DataFrame (df)`, adding each item's name, quantities at home and to take, and whether the item has been marked as taken. Once the document is populated, it is saved in the current working directory as `grocery_list.pdf` and returned.

Download List as PDF

Figure 10.16 – The PDF button

Here is the generated PDF:

Grocery List

Apple - At Home: 5 - To Take: 7 - Taken: Yes

Banana - At Home: 3 - To Take: 8 - Taken: No

Carrot - At Home: 0 - To Take: 9 - Taken: No

Milk - At Home: 0 - To Take: 4 - Taken: No

Eggs - At Home: 9 - To Take: 0 - Taken: Yes

Potato - At Home: 1 - To Take: 5 - Taken: No

Figure 10.17 – The obtained PDF file

Our users may want to add notes; for this, we can take advantage of the fact that Streamlit allows other pages to be added to create a section for notes. Note that we now have a second page that we can access through our sidebar. This way, we can enter notes and then save them:

```
elif page == "Notes":
    st.title("Notes")
    st.session_state.notes = st.text_area("Write your notes here:", st.session_state.notes)
    if st.button("Save Notes"):
        st.success("Notes saved successfully!")
```

418 Building an AI Agent Application

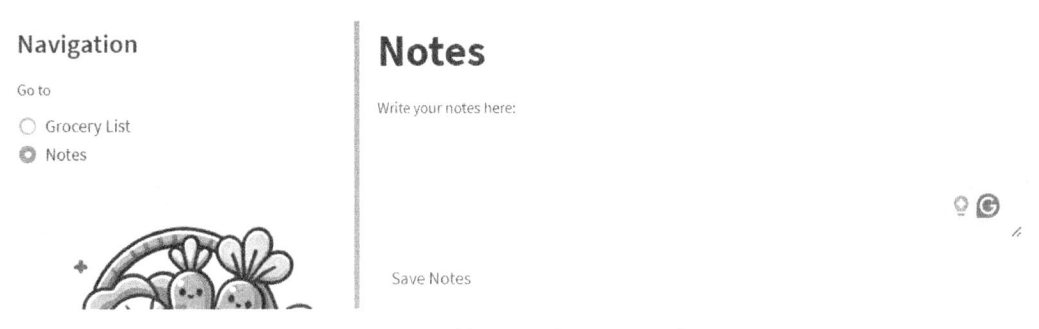

Figure 10.18 – Adding another page to the app

Now, we can also note that the information has been updated in our PDF:

Figure 10.19 – Updated PDF

If our users want to know where the nearest supermarkets are, we could add the following functionality to our app:

```
elif page == "Find Supermarkets":
    st.title("Find Nearby Supermarkets (OSM)")
        # Get user's location
    location_input = st.text_input("Enter your location (City, Address, or Coordinates):")
        if st.button("Find Supermarkets") and location_input:
        geolocator = Nominatim(user_agent="grocery_app")
        location = geolocator.geocode(location_input)
        if location:
            st.success(f"Location found: {location.address}")

            # Create map
            m = folium.Map(location=[location.latitude, location.longitude], zoom_start=14)
            folium.Marker([location.latitude, location.longitude], tooltip="Your Location", icon=folium.Icon(color="blue")).add_to(m)
            # Use Overpass API to find nearby supermarkets
            overpass_url = "http://overpass-api.de/api/interpreter"
```

```
            overpass_query = f"""
            [out:json];
            node["shop"="supermarket"](around:5000,{location.
latitude},{location.longitude});
            out;
            """
            response = requests.get(overpass_url, params={'data':
overpass_query})
            data = response.json()
            for element in data["elements"]:
                lat, lon = element["lat"], element["lon"]
                name = element.get("tags", {}).get("name", "Unnamed
Supermarket")
                folium.Marker([lat, lon], tooltip=name, icon=folium.
Icon(color="green")).add_to(m)
            folium_static(m)
        else:
            st.error("Location not found. Please try a different
input.")
```

In the code, we are adding a new page to the Streamlit app where users can find nearby supermarkets using **OpenStreetMap** (OSM). First, we display a title for the page and add a text input field where users can enter their location, which could be a city name, an address, or coordinates. When the user clicks the **Find Supermarkets** button, we use the Nominatim geocoder from the geopy library to convert the location input into latitude and longitude coordinates. If a valid location is found, we confirm this to the user and create an interactive map centered at the given coordinates using Folium. A marker is added to indicate the user's location. Next, we use the Overpass API, which queries OSM data, to find supermarkets within a 5-kilometer radius. We send a request to the Overpass API and parse the JSON response to extract the coordinates and names of nearby supermarkets. Each supermarket is then added as a green marker on the map. Finally, we display the generated map inside the Streamlit app using folium_static. If the location input is invalid or not found, we show an error message prompting the user to try again.

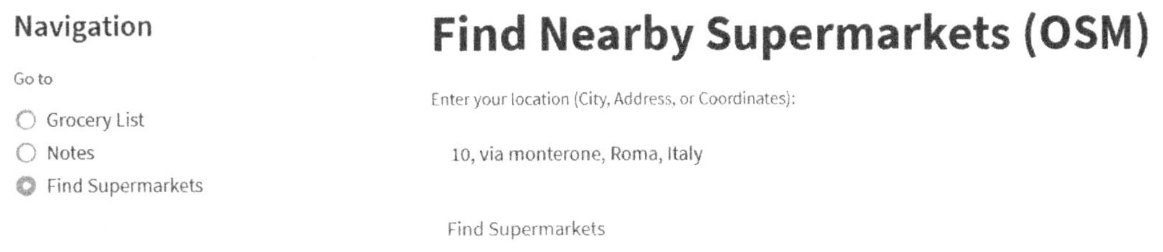

Figure 10.20 – Find Supermarkets page

When we click **Find Supermarkets**, we get the following:

> Location found: Via Monterone, Sant'Eustachio, Municipio Roma I, Roma, Roma Capitale, Lazio, 00186, Italia

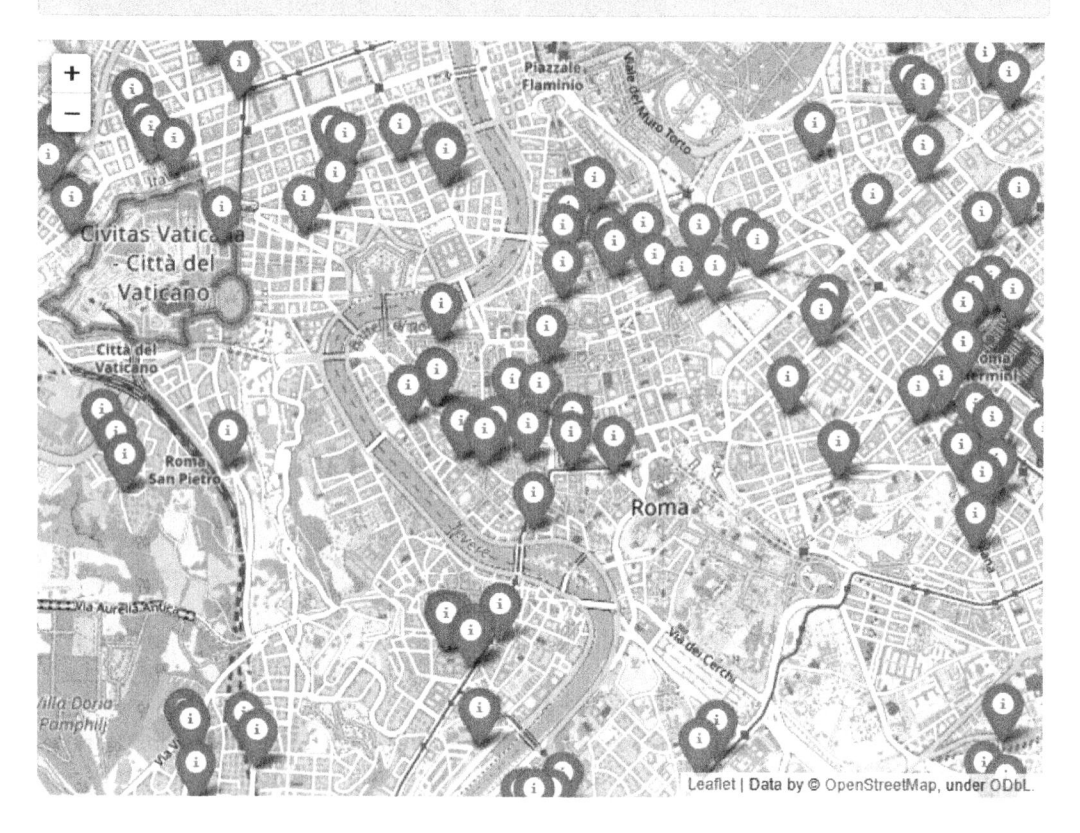

Figure 10.21 – Supermarket map

Now that we know how to build an app, we can build one with agents.

Creating an application with Streamlit and AI agents

In this section, we will look at integrating the multi-agent system described in *Chapter 9* into an app with Streamlit. Here, we will describe only the code parts we change; the structure remains the same. In the previous chapter, we built a script that allowed a travel program to be defined; in this chapter, the output is the same, but the system is encapsulated in an app. In other words, our app will run in the browser and can be used even by a user who does not know programming.

As a brief recap, the multi-model *Travel Planning System* is an AI-driven assistant that integrates multiple specialized models to generate personalized travel plans. It consists of four key agents:

- `WeatherAnalysisAgent`: Predicts the best travel months using historical weather data
- `HotelRecommenderAgent`: Uses a transformer model to find accommodations that match user preferences
- `ItineraryPlannerAgent`: Employs GPT-2 to generate detailed day-by-day travel plans
- `SummaryAgent`: Creates professional trip summaries and cost estimates

The system follows a structured data flow, where the user inputs their destination, preferences, and duration, and the agents collaborate to deliver a complete travel plan. The core AI models include `RandomForestRegressor` for weather predictions, `SentenceTransformer` for hotel recommendations, and GPT-2 for itinerary and summary generation.

To better understand the internal structure of the *Travel Planning System*, this section provides three UML diagrams. These visualizations illustrate the architecture, execution flow, and system interactions of the application described in this chapter:

- **Class diagram**: The following class diagram shows the main components of the application, including the core AI agents (such as `WeatherAnalysisAgent` and `ItineraryPlannerAgent`), the underlying models (RandomForest, SentenceTransformer, and OpenAI GPT), and the Streamlit app that connects the user interface to the backend logic:

422　Building an AI Agent Application

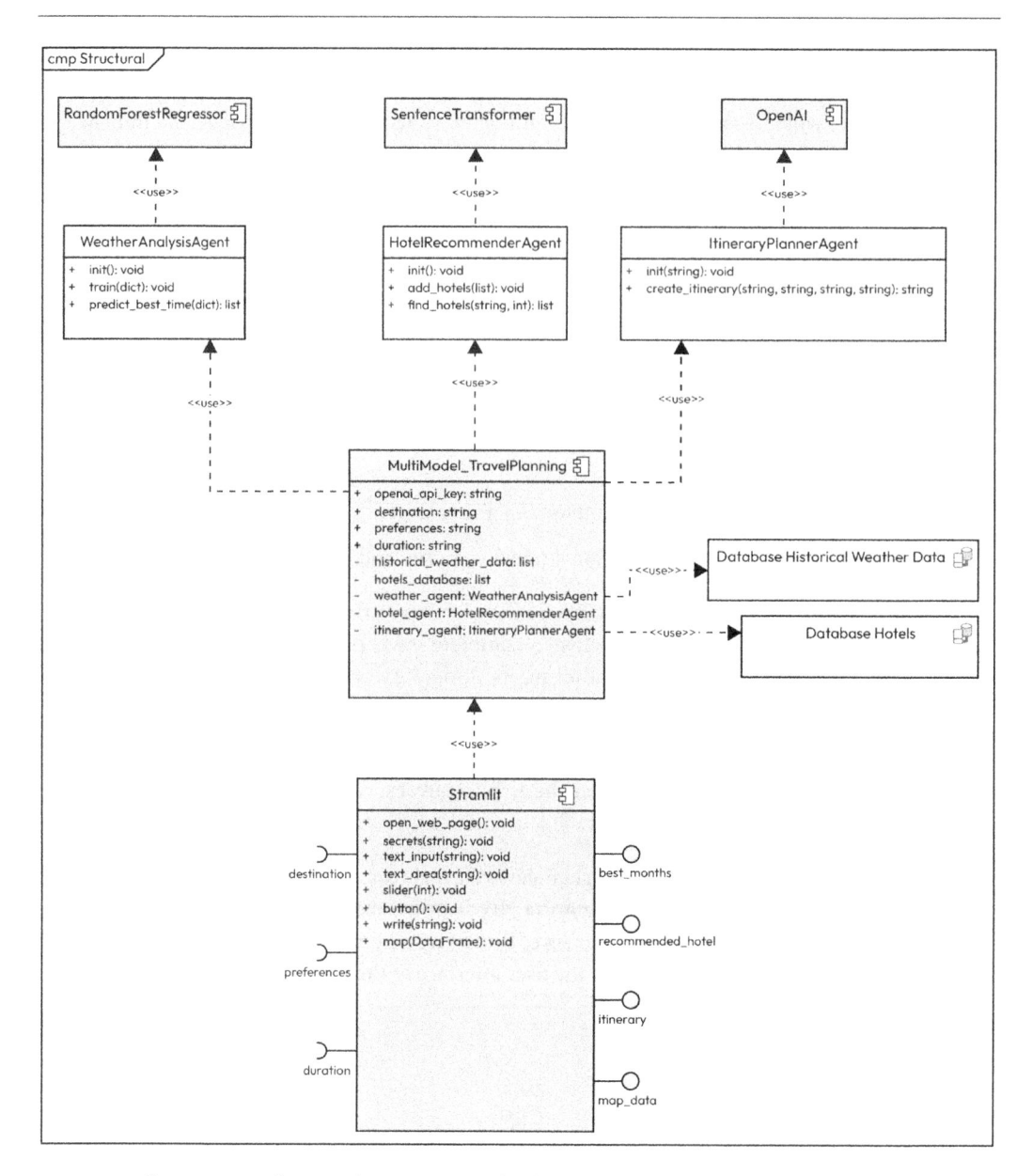

Figure 10.22 – Structural UML Diagram for the multi-model Travel Planning System

- **Activity diagram**: The activity diagram describes the control flow of the application, starting from user input collection through to the generation of a complete travel plan. It illustrates how each agent is triggered and how their outputs are merged:

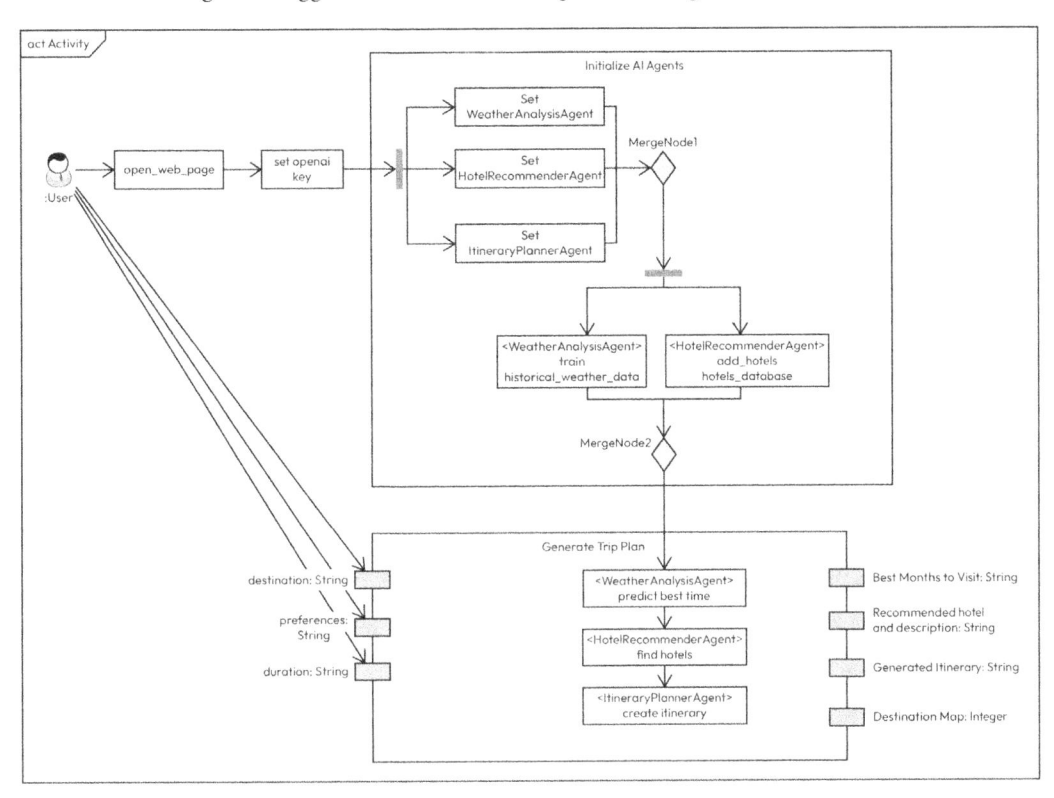

Figure 10.23 – UML activity diagram for the multi-model Travel Planning System

- **Sequence diagram**: Finally, the sequence diagram outlines the time-based interactions between the Streamlit frontend, the database, and the AI agents. It shows the order of method calls, the data exchanged, and the points where the system waits for responses. It makes clear when and how each agent is called:

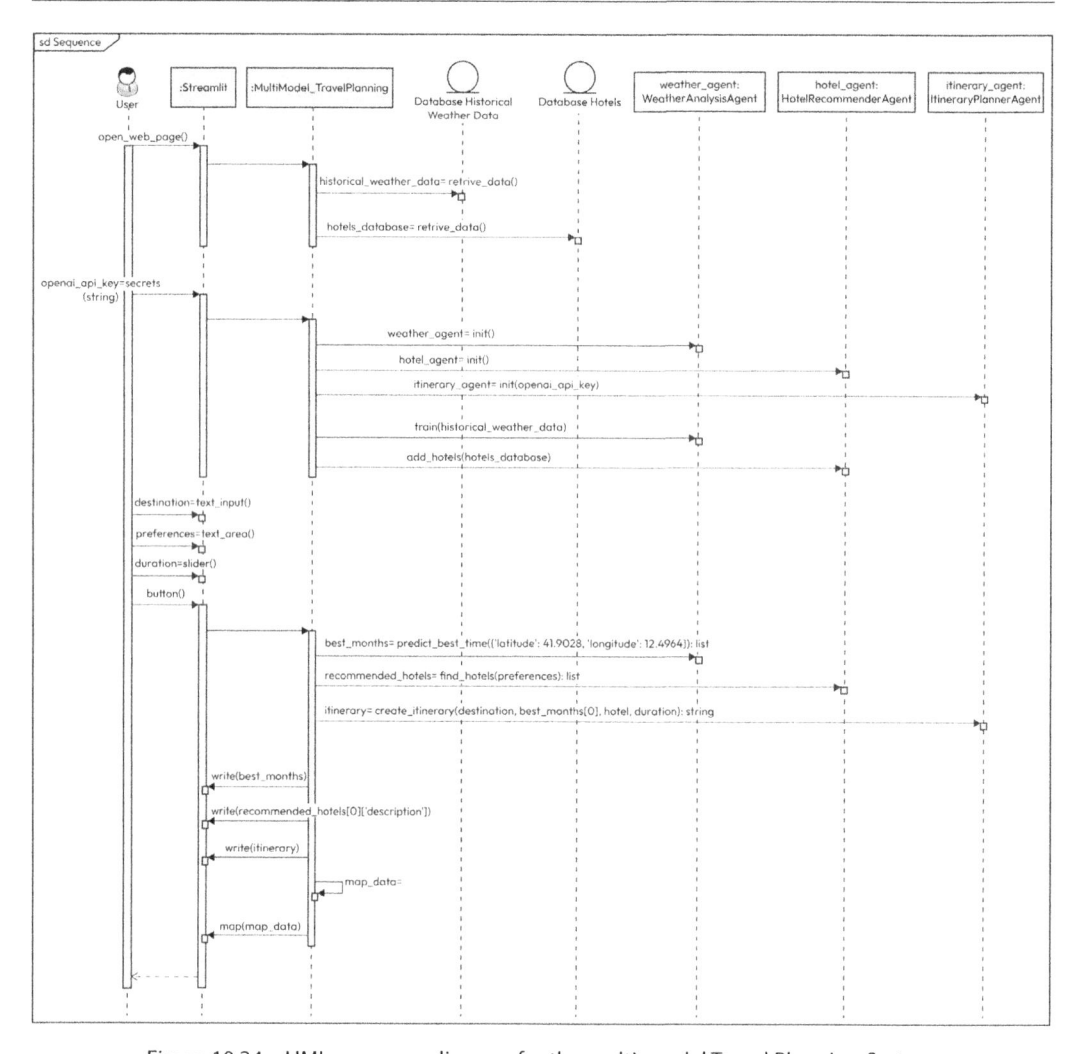

Figure 10.24 – UML sequence diagram for the multi-model Travel Planning System

First, we start by importing the libraries we need:

```
import streamlit as st
import numpy as np
import pandas as pd
import pydeck as pdk
import openai
from sklearn.ensemble import RandomForestRegressor
from sentence_transformers import SentenceTransformer
```

- `streamlit`: Our library to create the interactive web application
- `numpy`: A library for all the numerical operations

- `pandas`: A library to handle DataFrames
- `pydeck`: A visualization library built on top of Deck.gl, specifically for rendering large-scale geographical data
- `openai`: The OpenAI Python library, which provides access to models such as GPT-3.5 and GPT-4 for **natural language processing** (**NLP**) tasks.
- `RandomForestRegressor`: The scikit-learn model we use in our app
- `SentenceTransformer`: The library for the embeddings (see the previous chapter)

The code for agents is the same, except for `ItineraryPlannerAgent`. For a better and smoother response, we use OpenAI's GPT-4 model here:

```
class ItineraryPlannerAgent:
    def __init__(self, api_key):
        self.api_key = api_key

    def create_itinerary(self, destination, best_month, hotel, duration):
        client = openai.OpenAI(api_key=self.api_key)

        prompt = f"""
        Create a {duration}-day travel itinerary for {destination} in the best month: {best_month}.
        Recommended Hotel: {hotel['name']}.
        """

        response = client.chat.completions.create(
            model="gpt-4",
            messages=[
                {"role": "system", "content": "You are an expert travel planner."},
                {"role": "user", "content": prompt}
            ],
            max_tokens=300
        )
        return response.choices[0].message.content
```

The operation is the same: it takes in a travel destination, the best time to visit, a recommended hotel, and the trip duration, following which a structured itinerary is generated. Note that we need to use an API key to authenticate requests to OpenAI's API. Again, the agent does nothing more than generate an itinerary based on the same inputs: travel location, the best months to travel, hotel details, and the number of travel days. GPT-4 also works similarly to GPT-2: we have to provide a prompt with the information and the model then autoregressively generates the travel itinerary

Here again, we provide the same data that we provided to our system previously (you can find it in the repository):

```
# -------------------------------
# Sample Data
# -------------------------------
historical_weather_data = [
    {'month': i, 'latitude': 41.9028, 'longitude': 12.4964, 'weather_score': np.random.rand()} for i i
]
hotels_database = [
    {'name': 'Grand Hotel', 'description': 'Luxury hotel in city center with spa.', 'price': 300},
    {'name': 'Boutique Resort', 'description': 'Cozy boutique hotel with top amenities.', 'price': 250
    {'name': 'City View Hotel', 'description': 'Modern hotel with stunning city views.', 'price': 200}
]
```

Figure 10.25 – Screenshot of the code

At this point, we can initialize our agents, each with its own different purpose:

```
openai_api_key = st.secrets["general"]["openai_api_key"]
weather_agent = WeatherAnalysisAgent()
hotel_agent = HotelRecommenderAgent()
itinerary_agent = ItineraryPlannerAgent(api_key=openai_api_key)

weather_agent.train(historical_weather_data)
hotel_agent.add_hotels(hotels_database)
Your API should be in a file TOML, like this:
[general]
openai_api_key = "YOUR_API"
```

Note, `openai_api_key = st.secrets["general"]["openai_api_key"]` uses Streamlit's secrets manager to securely access the OpenAI API key. In fact, `st.secrets` is a way to store and retrieve sensitive credentials in Streamlit apps. The API key is stored under `st.secrets["general"]["openai_api_key"]`, indicating it is saved inside a `"general"` section within the `secrets` configuration. The purpose of `st.secrets` is to prevent sensitive credentials from being hardcoded in the script, reducing the risk of privacy breaches.

Now, let's start building our interface:

```
st.title("AI Travel Planner ✈")
st.write("Find the best time to travel and discover the perfect hotel!")

destination = st.text_input("Enter your destination (e.g., Rome):", "Rome")
preferences = st.text_area("Describe your ideal hotel:", "Luxury hotel in city center with spa.")
duration = st.slider("Trip duration (days):", 1, 14, 5)
```

First, we add a title: `st.title()` sets the title of the Streamlit web app. This title will appear at the top of the page. At this point, we use `st.write()` to give a brief explanation of the app's purpose. Next, `st.text_input()` is used to create a box where the user can enter their destination. Note that we are providing a hint about what the user can enter – `"Enter your destination (e.g., Rome):"` – and there is a default value of `"Rome"` (if the user doesn't input anything, it defaults to Rome). `st.text_area()` creates a multi-line text box where users can describe their ideal hotel. We use `text_area` to allow users to provide detailed hotel preferences. `st.slider()` creates a slider input for selecting the trip duration (there are parameters that define a minimum duration of `1` day and a maximum of `14`, with a 5-day trip being the default duration).

AI Travel Planner ✈

Find the best time to travel and discover the perfect hotel!

Enter your destination (e.g., Rome):

Rome

Describe your ideal hotel:

Luxury hotel in city center with spa.

Trip duration (days):

5

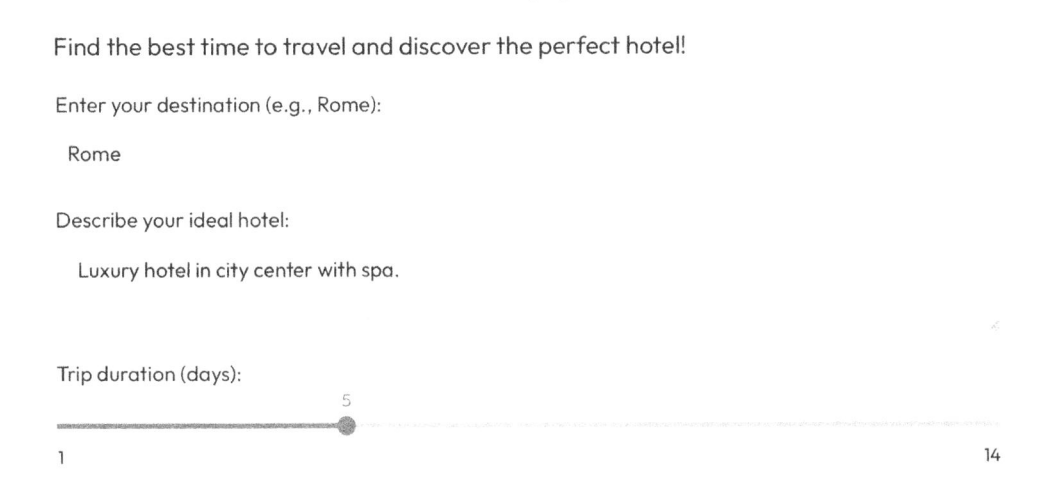

1   14

Figure 10.26 – Input preferences in the app

At this point, we will deal with what happens after the user adds the information and presses a button. To recap, the system predicts the best travel months based on weather conditions (through the use of historical data and random forest algorithms), finds a hotel that matches the user's preferences (using data on hotels and similarity of embeddings), and finally, creates a personalized itinerary using OpenAI's GPT-4.

We have created the framework to be able to visualize the results: the best months to visit, the recommended hotel, the AI-generated itinerary, and finally, a map visualization of the destination. All this happens only when our user presses the button, which we will create next:

```
if st.button("Generate Travel Plan ✈"):
    best_months = weather_agent.predict_best_time({'latitude':
41.9028, 'longitude': 12.4964})
    best_month = best_months[0]['month']
    recommended_hotels = hotel_agent.find_hotels(preferences)
```

```
        itinerary = itinerary_agent.create_itinerary(destination, best_
month, recommended_hotels[0], duration)

        st.subheader("🗓 Best Months to Visit")
        for m in best_months:
            st.write(f"Month {m['month']}: Score {m['score']:.2f}")

        st.subheader("🏨 Recommended Hotel")
        st.write(f"**{recommended_hotels[0]['name']}** - {recommended_
hotels[0]['description']}")

        st.subheader("📋 Generated Itinerary")
        st.write(itinerary)

        # ------------------------------
        # Interactive Map
        # ------------------------------
        st.subheader("🗺 Destination Map")
        map_data = pd.DataFrame(
            {'lat': [41.9028], 'lon': [12.4964]},
        )
        st.map(map_data)
```

`if st.button("Generate Travel Plan 🧳"):` creates an interactive button labeled **Generate Travel Plan 🧳** and defines a block of actions that are executed when the user clicks the button. First, the best month to visit the city is predicted: `best_months = weather_agent. predict_best_time({'latitude': 41.9028, 'longitude': 12.4964})`. Note that we entered the destination's latitude (`41.9028`) and longitude (`12.4964`) for Rome, got our best months based on the weather score, and selected the best month. At this point, we identify the best hotels based on our user's preferences with `hotel_agent.find_hotels(preferences)`. This agent will return a list of hotels matching the user's description.

Since we have all the details, we can generate our itinerary. `itinerary = itinerary_agent. create_itinerary(destination, best_month, recommended_hotels[0], duration)` does exactly that; it takes the inputs defined earlier and produces a structured AI-generated itinerary. Once we have our itinerary, we start the display of it for the user. We use `st.subheader(" 🗓 Best Months to Visit")` to create a subsection and then iterate over `best_months` and print each month with its weather score. At this point, we show the best hotels in an additional subsection after `st.subheader(" 🏨 Recommended Hotel")`. Finally, `st.subheader(" 📋 Generated Itinerary")` allows us to create a subsection where our itinerary will be inserted. In the last part, we show the city map.

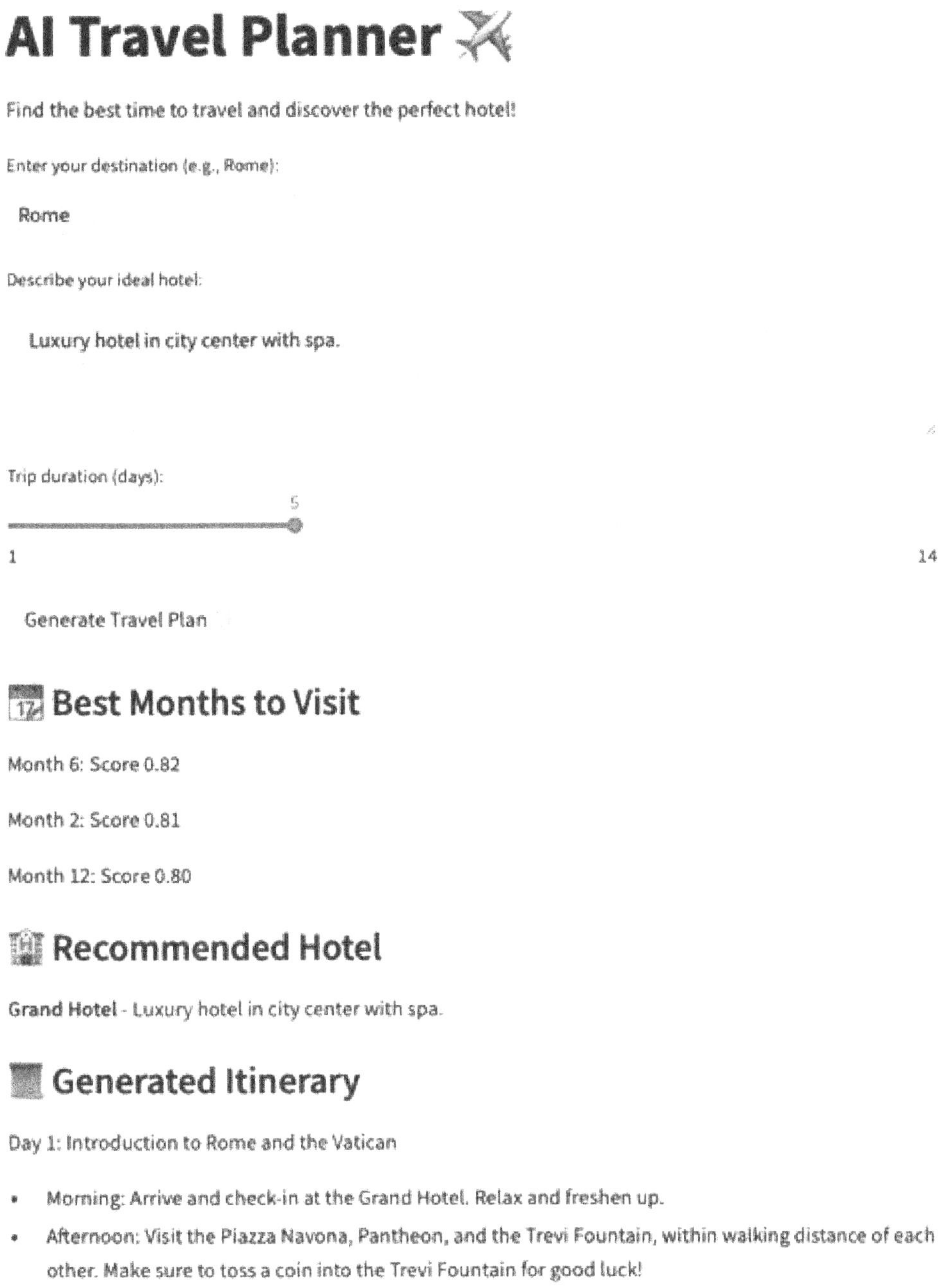

AI Travel Planner ✈

Find the best time to travel and discover the perfect hotel!

Enter your destination (e.g., Rome):

> Rome

Describe your ideal hotel:

> Luxury hotel in city center with spa.

Trip duration (days): 5

1 — 14

Generate Travel Plan

📅 Best Months to Visit

Month 6: Score 0.82

Month 2: Score 0.81

Month 12: Score 0.80

🏨 Recommended Hotel

Grand Hotel - Luxury hotel in city center with spa.

📜 Generated Itinerary

Day 1: Introduction to Rome and the Vatican

- Morning: Arrive and check-in at the Grand Hotel. Relax and freshen up.
- Afternoon: Visit the Piazza Navona, Pantheon, and the Trevi Fountain, within walking distance of each other. Make sure to toss a coin into the Trevi Fountain for good luck!

Figure 10.27 – Generated output (part 1)

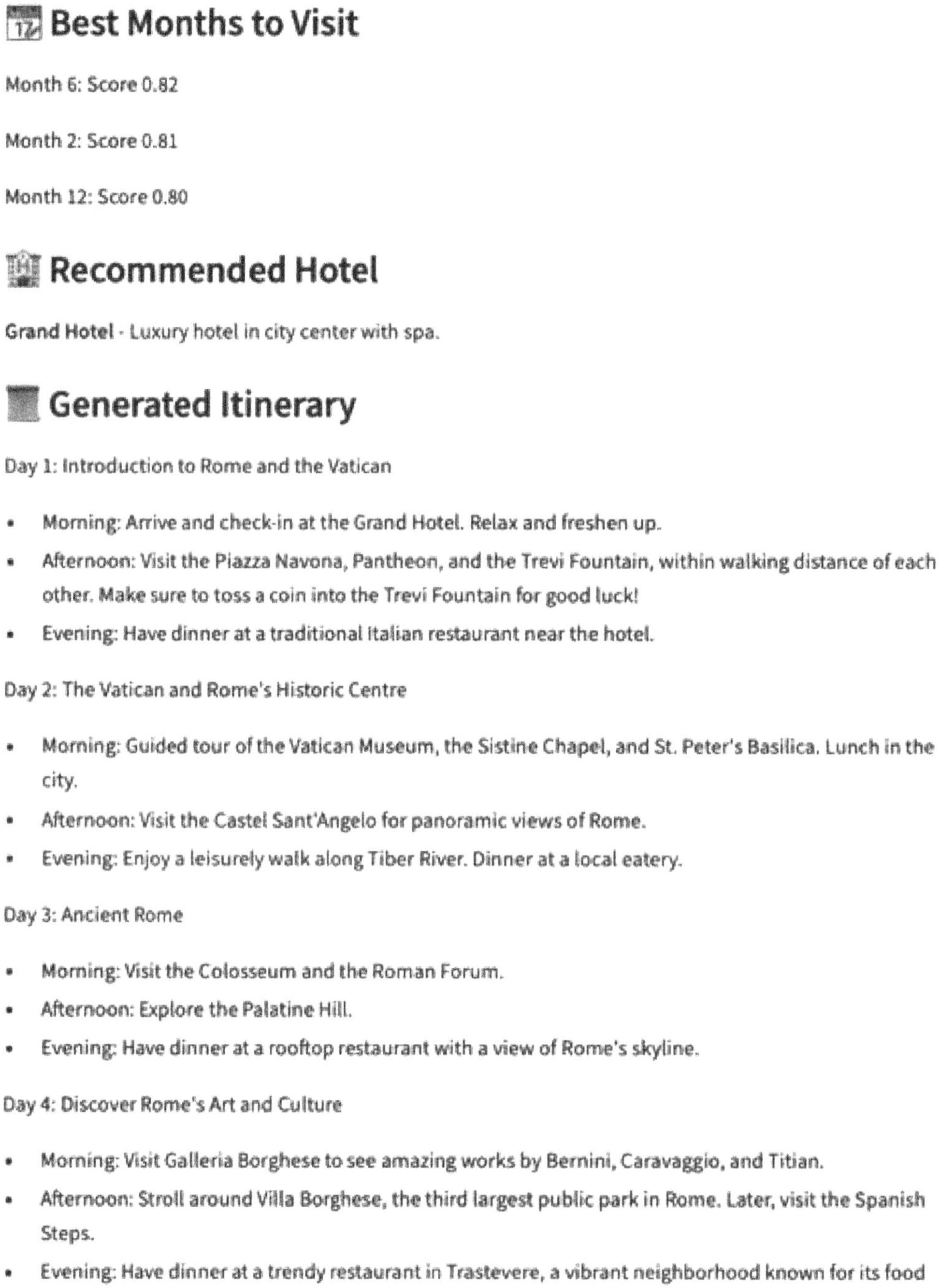

Best Months to Visit

Month 6: Score 0.82

Month 2: Score 0.81

Month 12: Score 0.80

Recommended Hotel

Grand Hotel - Luxury hotel in city center with spa.

Generated Itinerary

Day 1: Introduction to Rome and the Vatican

- Morning: Arrive and check-in at the Grand Hotel. Relax and freshen up.
- Afternoon: Visit the Piazza Navona, Pantheon, and the Trevi Fountain, within walking distance of each other. Make sure to toss a coin into the Trevi Fountain for good luck!
- Evening: Have dinner at a traditional Italian restaurant near the hotel.

Day 2: The Vatican and Rome's Historic Centre

- Morning: Guided tour of the Vatican Museum, the Sistine Chapel, and St. Peter's Basilica. Lunch in the city.
- Afternoon: Visit the Castel Sant'Angelo for panoramic views of Rome.
- Evening: Enjoy a leisurely walk along Tiber River. Dinner at a local eatery.

Day 3: Ancient Rome

- Morning: Visit the Colosseum and the Roman Forum.
- Afternoon: Explore the Palatine Hill.
- Evening: Have dinner at a rooftop restaurant with a view of Rome's skyline.

Day 4: Discover Rome's Art and Culture

- Morning: Visit Galleria Borghese to see amazing works by Bernini, Caravaggio, and Titian.
- Afternoon: Stroll around Villa Borghese, the third largest public park in Rome. Later, visit the Spanish Steps.
- Evening: Have dinner at a trendy restaurant in Trastevere, a vibrant neighborhood known for its food

Figure 10.28 – Generated output (part 2)

- Afternoon: Visit the Castel Sant'Angelo for panoramic views of Rome.
- Evening: Enjoy a leisurely walk along Tiber River. Dinner at a local eatery.

Day 3: Ancient Rome

- Morning: Visit the Colosseum and the Roman Forum.
- Afternoon: Explore the Palatine Hill.
- Evening: Have dinner at a rooftop restaurant with a view of Rome's skyline.

Day 4: Discover Rome's Art and Culture

- Morning: Visit Galleria Borghese to see amazing works by Bernini, Caravaggio, and Titian.
- Afternoon: Stroll around Villa Borghese, the third largest public park in Rome. Later, visit the Spanish Steps.
- Evening: Have dinner at a trendy restaurant in Trastevere, a vibrant neighborhood known for its food

Destination Map

Figure 10.29 – Generated output (part 3)

In this section, we created a multi-agent system and embedded it within an app. In this way, even users with no programming knowledge can interact with our system. The system can be run by a user by clicking a simple button.

We discussed an app as an isolated system; in the next section, we will see how a model is not an isolated concept but part of an ecosystem. This complexity must be taken into account, and in the next section, we will discuss the life cycle of a model, from conception to deployment.

Machine learning operations and LLM operations

We have seen how to create an app containing a multi-agent system. When we create a script with Python, we create an element that can run on our computer, but this is not a product. Turning a script into an app allows a user to be able to interact with our app even if they do not know how to program. Streamlit allows us to be able to run a quick prototype of our app. This is not optimal for a product, especially if it is to be used by several users. In this section, we will discuss all those operations necessary to make our model function as a product.

Machine Learning Operations (**MLOps**) is a set of practices and tools designed to streamline and manage the life cycle of **machine learning** (**ML**) models in production. It combines ML, DevOps, and data engineering practices to ensure the **continuous integration/continuous delivery** (**CI/CD**), monitoring, and scaling of ML systems.

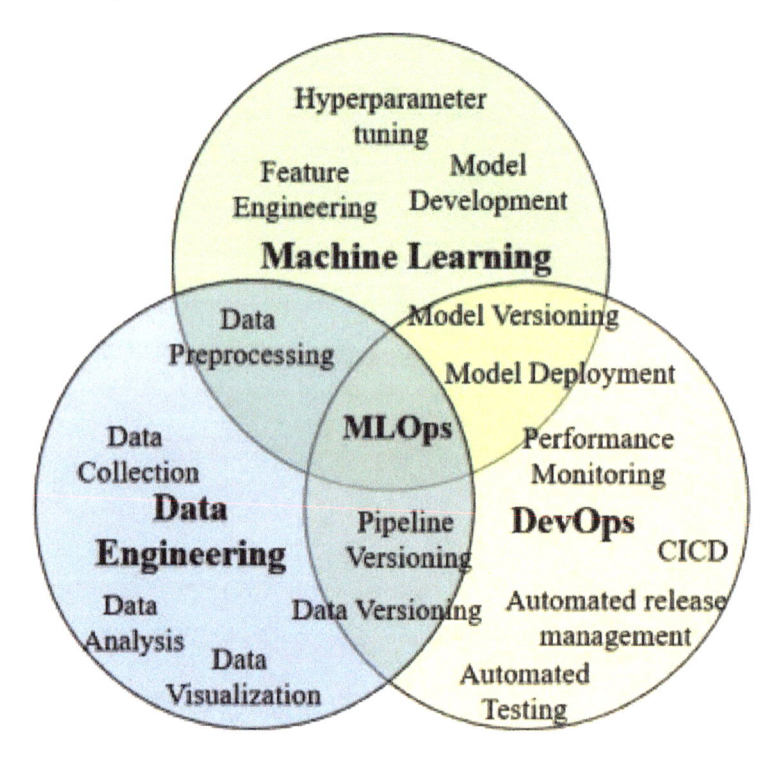

Figure 10.30 – MLOps combination (https://arxiv.org/pdf/2202.10169)

MLOps plays a key role in turning a model into a useful application in the real world. In short, MLOps encompass the development, monitoring, and maintenance of models in a production environment, enabling the transition from a research product to a functional product. Here are the various stages involved:

1. **Model development**: This is the first step, in which an ML model is designed and trained. Typically, at this stage, both data scientists and data engineers collaborate on the choice of model, datasets, and training and testing process.

2. **Testing**: Normally, the testing phase is part of model development; however, today, there is a greater emphasis on testing the model. Hence, we consider it a separate stage. In fact, complex models in particular can exhibit unexpected behaviors, so testing is often considered a separate phase.

3. **Deployment**: Once the model has been developed and tested, it can be deployed in a production environment. This delicate step requires that the model be integrated with other existing systems (which have been developed previously) and that it can be used in real time.

4. **Monitoring and maintenance**: Once the model is deployed, we must ensure its performance doesn't degrade and prevent operational problems. At the same time, we may need to update the model or ensure compatibility with new system elements.

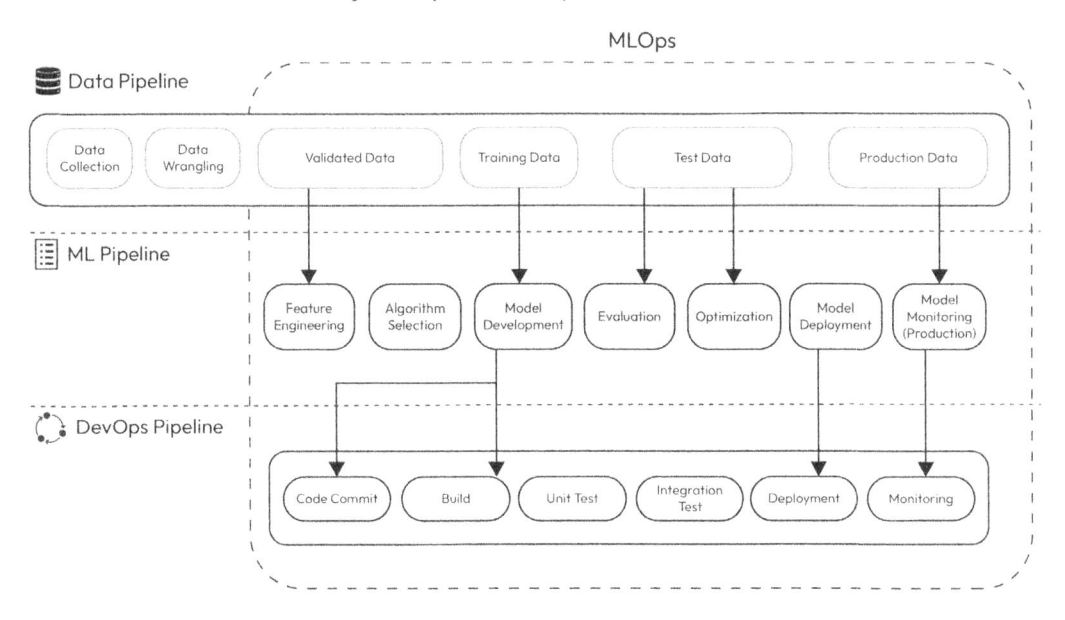

Figure 10.31 – High-level process view of MLOps (https://arxiv.org/pdf/2202.10169)

Large Language Model Operations (**LLMOps**) is an extension of MLOps specifically focused on the deployment, maintenance, and management of LLMs. It incorporates the principles of MLOps but also addresses the unique challenges and needs associated with working with large-scale NLP models.

However, LLMOps adds additional complexity. Here's why:

- **Model size and complexity**: In MLOps, models can vary in size and complexity, but they typically don't require as much computational power or memory as LLMs. Models may include traditional ML algorithms, smaller deep learning models, or specialized models for structured data. LLMs can be in the order of billions of parameters and thus require optimized infrastructure (often involving specialized hardware such as GPUs or TPUs) or distributed training. This means more expertise and dedicated infrastructure (dedicated hardware and storage), which can be very expensive.

- **Training and fine-tuning**: In MLOps, training is much more manageable. Many of the models are small in size and can therefore be easily retrained. Retraining itself can be conducted programmatically. Fine-tuning LLMs is more complex and resource-intensive. Collecting and processing the datasets needed for an LLM is resource-intensive.

- **Scalability and deployment**: In MLOps, deploying models to production is usually straightforward. Scaling LLMs, on the other hand, requires dedicated infrastructure that can ensure necessary support when there is high demand. In fact, latency can increase considerably when there are many users. Optimizing latency during inference can be a delicate process that risks degrading performance.

- **Monitoring and maintenance**: Monitoring ML models in production involves tracking key metrics such as accuracy, precision, and recall, as well as model drift or data drift. Monitoring LLMs involves not only the usual performance metrics but also the quality of text generation, user feedback, and ethical concerns such as biased or harmful outputs. While it is straightforward to evaluate an output in terms of accuracy, it is more complex to assess whether an LLM produces hallucinations or inappropriate or harmful content. Some biases might be subtle but still be noticed by users.

- **Model governance and compliance**: While governance and compliance are critical in any ML deployment, MLOps primarily focuses on ensuring data privacy and model transparency, especially when dealing with sensitive or regulated data. For LLMOps, there is not only privacy, but it can also be used to generate text on a wide variety of topics with the risk of generating inappropriate content. With regulations in development, assessing bias, fairness, and ethical issues is complex and evolving.

Here's an example of the added complexity involved when performing LLMOps. If we wanted to train a model from scratch, we would have to retrieve a corpus of at least 1B tokens. These tokens would have to be collected from different sources (books, websites, articles, code repositories, and so on). In MLOps, we usually create a model when a dataset is already present (e.g., through user interactions with our site). The steps of preprocessing a dataset for a classical model (images or tabular) are much simpler than a large corpus (steps such as debiasing, eliminating duplicates, and so on). Also, since our dataset can be over hundreds of terabytes in size, there is more complexity. While we can train an ML model easily (even on a consumer computer), this is no longer possible with an LLM. Especially for larger ones, we have to use dedicated infrastructure, and we cannot do many experiments (testing different hyperparameters or different architecture combinations). Similarly, fine-tuning will be preferred to having to retrain our model.

Testing also no longer relies on simple measures (such as accuracy) but requires human-in-the-loop evaluations. Given the language-centric nature of the system, a metric such as accuracy gives us only partial information about the output of our model. Only humans (even if we use other LLMs to check at scale) can evaluate the output of an LLM in terms of creativity, bias, quality, and the presence of inappropriate content. Also, after pre-training, there is usually a step where human feedback is used to be able to further improve the output of a model. In addition, we must then continue to evaluate our LLM, because the traffic may grow or there may be evolutions in the language and knowledge that our model must have. For example, an LLM for medical use needs to be updated on new therapies.

In the next section, we will start with the complexities of developing a model as complex as an LLM.

Model development

The development of a model starts with the collection of a corpus. This collection is generally divided into two types: general data and specialized data. General data represents data such as web pages, books, and conversational text. Specialized data, on the other hand, is data that is designed for a specific task, such as multilingual data, scientific data, and code:

- **General data**: Considering the large amount of data on the internet, it is now common for data collection to start with using datasets of downloaded pages or even conducting crawling to collect new data. In addition, there are also datasets of conversations (such as discussions on Reddit or other platforms), chats with LLMs, and other sources. Books are another popular source for training, as they generally contain coherent, quality text on disparate topics. These datasets contain a mixture of quality data (such as Wikipedia and blog posts) but also a large amount of data that needs to be removed, such as spam, toxic posts, and so on.

- **Specialized text data**: Today, it is common to add a multilingual corpus to improve the language capabilities of LLMs (e.g., PaLM covers 122 languages due to the addition of a multilingual corpus).

  Adding scientific text enables improved performance in scientific and reasoning tasks. Huge datasets of articles exist today that are ready to use and can be directly added. Almost all modern pre-training datasets also insert code. The addition of code and other structured data appears to be related to an increase in performance in some reasoning tasks.

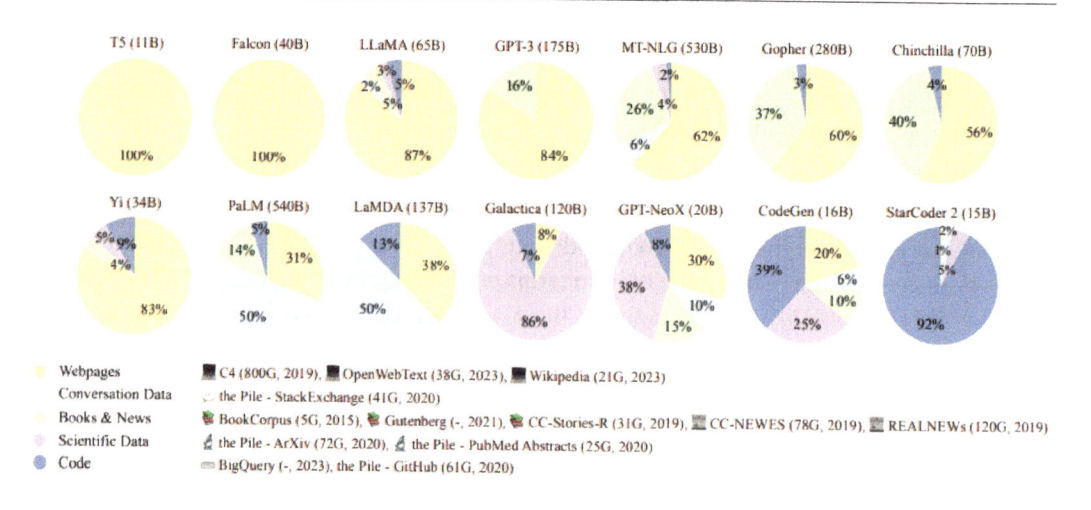

Figure 10.32 – Ratios of various data sources in the pre-training data for existing LLMs (https://arxiv.org/pdf/2303.18223)

Once the data has been collected, it must be preprocessed to remove unnecessary tokens such as HTML tags or other presentation elements, reduce text variation, and eliminate duplicate data. Today, we try to eliminate data that is of low quality, using either heuristic algorithms or classifiers. For example, we can train a classifier on quality data such as Wikipedia to recognize what content we want to preserve. Heuristic algorithms, on the other hand, rely on a set of rules that are defined upstream (such as statistical properties, the presence or absence of keywords, and so on). Deduplication is an important step because it impacts model diversity and training stability. Typically, different granularities, such as sentence or document level, are used to avoid repetitive word patterns. In addition, another common step today is privacy reduction, in which an attempt is made to remove **personally identifiable information** (PII), often through a set of rules that are defined upstream. Once these steps are conducted, tokenization can be done. Tokenization is considered a crucial step because it largely impacts model performance. **Byte-pair encoding** (BPE) tokenization is generally one of the most widely used methods.

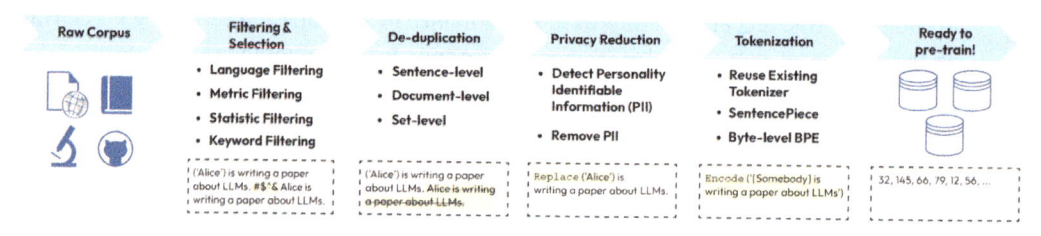

Figure 10.33 – Illustration of a typical data preprocessing pipeline for pre-training LLMs (https://arxiv.org/pdf/2303.18223)

Once we have preprocessed the corpus, we can train the model in the next phase. To train the model, we need to define a strategy to schedule the multi-sources (different types of data such as Wikipedia, text from the internet, books, etc.) previously introduced. In fact, two important aspects are decided: the proportion of each data source (data mixture) and the order in which each data source is scheduled for training (data curriculum). Since each type of data has an impact on performance, the data must be mixed in a precise distribution. This distribution can be global or local (at certain training steps). To do this, we can then decide to conduct upsampling and downsampling of the various sources in order to respect the mixture we have decided on. For example, in the case of LLaMA pre-training, the authors chose to train with the following proportion (based on experimental results, which have shown that this proportion works well): 80% web pages, 6.5% code-related data from GitHub and Stack Exchange, 4.5% from books, and 2.5% of scientific data sourced from arXiv. These values do not sum to exactly 100%, as the remaining portion includes other minor sources not explicitly detailed in the original paper. Today, this recipe has been used for many different types of LLMs, while LLMs with a specific purpose have a different proportion of code and scientific articles.

Generally, a heterogeneous corpus is preferred, as diversity enhances a model's ability to generalize across domains. In contrast, an overly homogeneous dataset can hinder generalization. Additionally, the sequence in which data is presented—often referred to as a data curriculum—is crucial. The training data is thus typically organized to first develop foundational skills, followed by more specialized capabilities.

To do this, you first use easy/general examples and then add examples that are more complex or more specific. For example, for models that are code-specific such as `CodeLLaMA-Python`, the order is as follows: 2T general tokens, 500B code-heavy tokens, and 100B Python-heavy tokens.

In general, it is important that we create pipelines that allow us to collect and organize data. Generally, these kinds of pipelines are called **extract, transform, load** (**ETL**) pipelines. So, if we want to download a set of web pages, we will need to create an ETL pipeline that allows us to download the pages and load them into a database along with a set of metadata. The metadata will then be used both to clean the data and for data scheduling. Once the data is downloaded it needs to be transformed. Because our corpus contains different types of data, it is good to have different pipelines for preprocessing the different types (removing HTML tags from web pages, removing comments from code, and so on).

In addition, data is an important resource, and access must be controlled. Indeed, we need to prevent data leakage and ensure that our corpus complies with regulations such as the **General Data Protection Regulation** (**GDPR**). Often, **role-based access control** (**RBAC**) is also implemented, where different users have control over a different corpus of data. For example, administrators or analysts may have different privileges so as to avoid contamination or problems with the data.

Once we have our data and have cleaned it, we create features (i.e., the data that will be used for training). The feature store is typically a database that is optimized to enable training. The idea is to have a dedicated database that we can efficiently use for training.

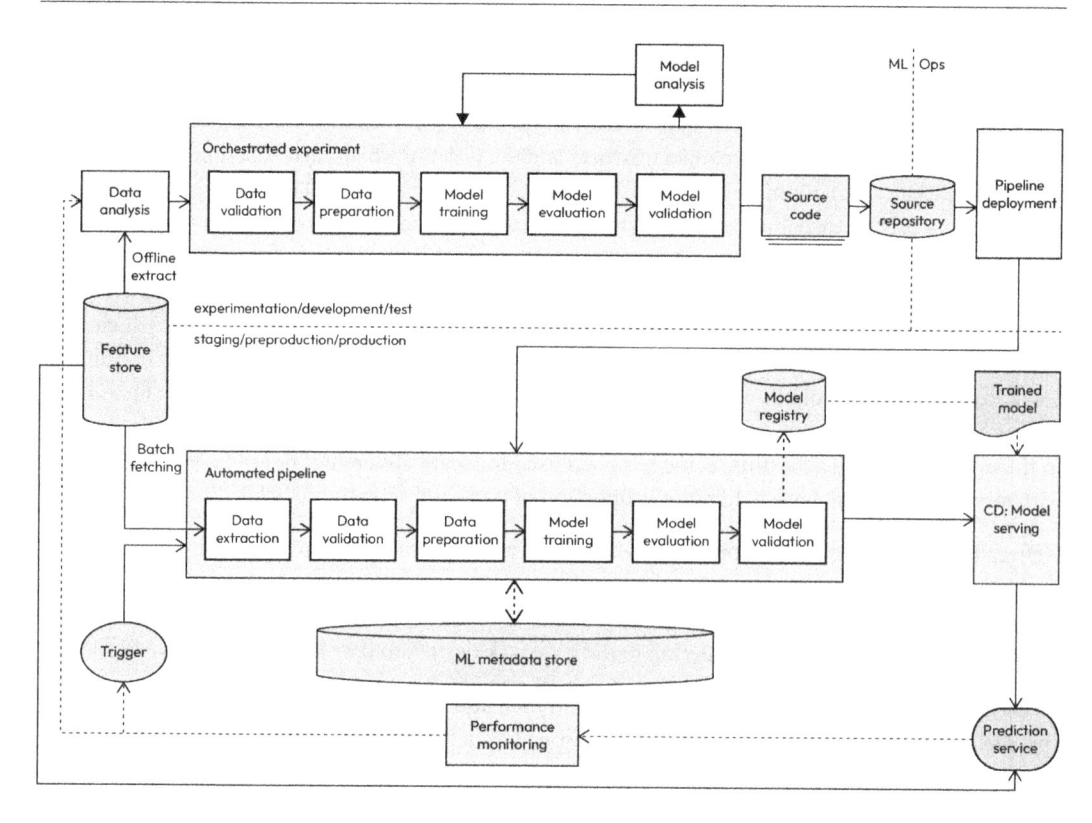

Figure 10.34 – Automation of the ML pipeline for continuous training (https://cloud.google.com/architecture/mlops-continuous-delivery-and-automation-pipelines-in-machine-learning)

Model training

Once we have our features, we need to decide what our foundation model will be. There are two alternatives: use an LLM that has already been trained or conduct fine-tuning of an already trained model. In the first case, most models today are causal decoders (as we saw in *Chapters 2* and *3*). Although the structure remains the base, there are now different alternatives and modifications (such as the mixture of experts architecture) and modifications to the attention mechanism to increase context and reduce computational cost. Training an LLM from scratch is very expensive, however, so most companies focus on using a pre-trained model and conducting fine-tuning.

Therefore, choosing the foundation model will be an important task. First, we must choose a model that has the desired performance in terms of output quality. Obviously, the chosen model must be compatible with the resources available to us (hardware and cost). In addition, we may want to choose a model that exhibits lower performance on general benchmarks but superior performance on some other aspects. For example, if our application focuses on having a coding assistant, it is better to have an LLM with superior performance on coding benchmarks than an LLM that has better wide-ranging capabilities.

When choosing a model, we need to take into account that its size impacts both its memory footprint and its storage. A larger size means higher costs in general, especially if we use a cloud provider. Also, not all models can be used for all applications (for example, we cannot use large models for specific devices). In addition, a larger model also has higher latency (the time to process an input and produce an output). A high latency disrupts the user experience and may lead the user to choose a competitor. As we saw in *Chapter 3*, techniques (distillation, quantization, and pruning) to reduce model size while maintaining performance exist today. Another important point is the licensing of the model. Not all models have an open source license; some models may be available in repositories but may not be commercially usable.

Fine-tuning is intended to enable the model to acquire specific skills or some particular knowledge. In the former case, it is often referred to as instruction tuning. Instruction tuning is a subcategory of the supervised training process that aims to make the model more capable of following instructions or being trained for specific tasks. In repositories, there are often models that have been simply pre-trained or ones that have already undergone an instruction-tuning step. If we want the model to acquire a specific set of skills, it might be more interesting for us to collect a dataset for instruction tuning. Again, some caveats apply:

- **Data distribution**: Instruction tuning considers a mix of different tasks, so our dataset should respect this principle and contain several examples. Ideally, these examples should be of different topics, different contexts, different lengths, different styles, and different types of tasks.

- **Dataset quality**: Generally, in this step (quality check), it is important to use examples that are correct not only in terms of factual correctness but also in terms of ensuring that the task is done correctly and is well explained. For example, chain-of-thought examples are used today, where the intermediate thinking is explained instead of just the solution. The examples are human-generated; however, to save costs, a larger model can be used initially to create the dataset for instruction tuning. For instance, a 70-billion-parameter model could be used to prepare the dataset for tuning a 7-billion-parameter model.

- **Complexity**: In general, we want our model to acquire capabilities. Through simple examples, the model will learn structure and gain a general understanding of the task. However, there should also be examples in the dataset that are difficult, require multi-step reasoning, or are complex in nature. These examples reflect the complexity of real-world problems and have been seen to help the model improve its reasoning skills.

- **Quantity**: There is also a discourse associated with quantity. According to some studies, larger models need fewer examples. For example, models with 70 billion parameters might require as few as 1,000 quality examples. In contrast, smaller models might need many more examples. Smaller models may need many examples just to understand the task and many more to master it. A 7 billion model may use up to a million examples.

Building a dataset of thousands of examples can be particularly expensive. In many studies, only a small portion is created by humans. To reach the desired number of examples, one can either use a model to generate them or integrate already available datasets. Hugging Face contains many datasets for instruction tuning, for both general purposes as well as specific domains.

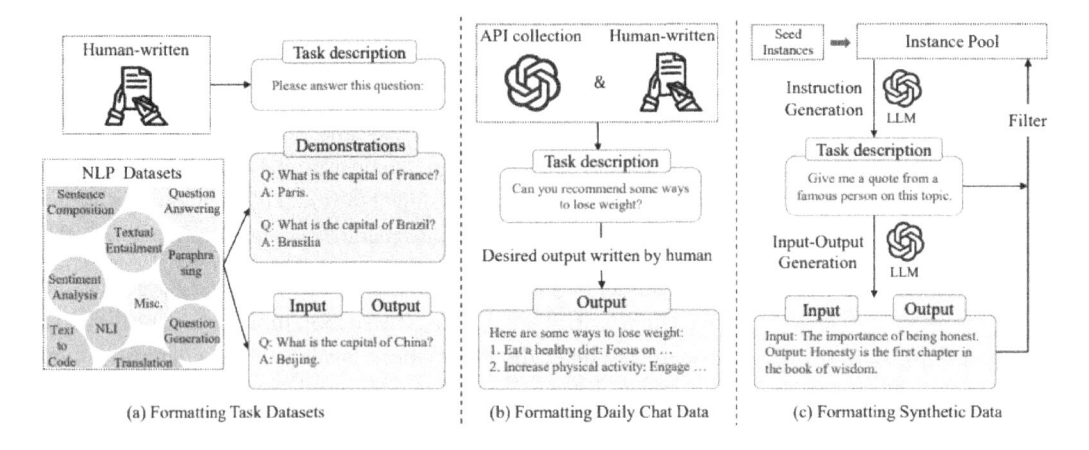

Figure 10.35 – Constructing an instruction-tuning dataset (https://arxiv.org/pdf/2303.18223)

The construction of these datasets, especially for particular domains, also requires the presence of experts (for example, if the dataset is for finance or medicine, collaboration with experts in the field or other institutions is common). Similar to a pre-training dataset, this dataset will undergo preprocessing. For example, examples of poor quality will be filtered out (one of the most commonly used methods is to have a list of keywords that indicate inappropriate content, off-topic examples, and so on), and filters will be used for length (e.g., examples that are too short or too long for the model) and for format (for some tasks, examples are formatted in a particular way, and examples that do not comply are removed). This dataset will also be deduplicated, and examples that are too similar are also often removed (if you ask an LLM to generate the examples, it might happen that examples that are too similar are generated). Patterns such as embeddings can be used for this task, where examples that have too high a similarity are filtered out. **MinHash** is another popular alternative to reduce the computational cost of the task. MinHash generates compact representations of patterns (of vectors), which are then compared with a similarity function.

Because we are interested in model performance for specific tasks, an additional step is also conducted: **data decontamination**. This is a process in which we ensure that our instruction-tuning dataset does not contain examples that are the same or too similar to those in the evaluation or test set. In fact, once we have instruction-tuned our model, we want to test it on test sets that we set aside. If there were examples that were too similar, we could not verify overfitting or storage phenomena. Data decontamination is conducted with techniques similar to data deduplication.

Before proceeding to the actual training, an additional step, **data quality evaluation**, is usually conducted. The dataset is evaluated for several criteria such as quality, accuracy, and complexity. Usually, some statistical parameters (such as the loss) are calculated and some examples are manually inspected. Recently, it has become increasingly popular to use **LLM-as-a-judge**, a strategy in which an LLM evaluates the quality of some examples. In such cases, an LLM is given a kind of template to check the quality of the examples by providing a score. Alternatively, today, there are also specific templates trained to provide a quality score. For example, reward models such as **ArmoRM-Llama3-8B-v0.1** are trained to produce an output that represents the quality of a text in terms of helpfulness, correctness, coherence, complexity, and verbosity.

Model testing

Once we have our dataset, we can conduct fine-tuning. Fine-tuning allows us to steer the capabilities and knowledge of our LLM. We must keep in mind that fine-tuning is not a magic potion; it has both risks and benefits. For example, fine-tuning exploits pre-existing knowledge of the model, but also conducts a refocus for a specific domain. This can lead to performance degradation and hallucinations. For this reason, in *Chapters 5–7*, we looked at alternatives (RAG and GraphRAG). In *Chapter 3*, we saw that there are now also efficient fine-tuning techniques such as LoRA and QLoRA that make the process much less expensive. Today, different libraries can conduct fine-tuning of these models, such as TRL (a library created by Hugging Face), Unsloth, and Axolotl based on Unsloth; these libraries also have additional features.

After training, the key step is LLM evaluation. In general, evaluation is carried out in three stages:

- **During pre-training**: During this step, the training of the model is monitored, and, in general, metrics such as training loss (a metric based on cross-entropy), loss on the validation set, perplexity (the exponential of training loss, one of the most commonly used metrics), and gradient norm (which indicates whether there were any instabilities in the training) are evaluated.

- **After pre-training**: Once pre-training is completed, a capability analysis is conducted on the benchmark datasets. In these datasets, both model knowledge and the ability to solve certain problems are evaluated. For example, MMLU tests model knowledge on a large number of domains, while datasets such as HellaSwag test the model on reasoning skills.

- **After fine-tuning**: After instruction tuning, qualities such as the LLM's ability to follow instructions, converse, and use tools, for example, are usually evaluated. Since fine-tuning allows you to adapt the model to a specialized domain, it is beneficial to use specialized benchmarks in such cases. For example, for medical knowledge, a dataset such as Open Medical-LLM Leaderboard can be used, or for coding skills, BigCodeBench Leaderboard is a popular choice.

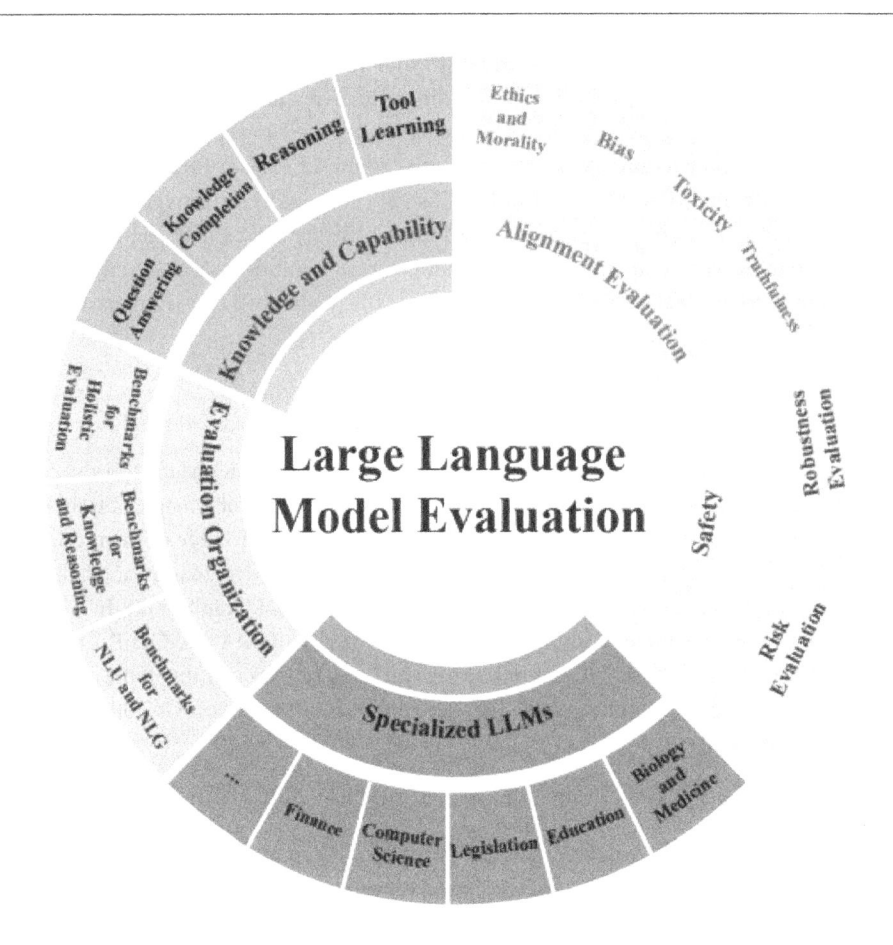

Figure 10.36 – Taxonomy of LLM evaluation (`https://arxiv.org/pdf/2310.19736`)

The last two steps (*After pre-training* and *After fine-tuning*) can also be conducted by manual inspection or using LLM-as-a-judge. For example, for open-ended text generation, it is more difficult to evaluate the capabilities of a model with standard metrics. Moreover, evaluating a model's capabilities in a specific domain requires more in-depth analysis.

If our LLM is a component of a system such as RAG, not only should the capabilities of the LLM be evaluated but the whole system as well. Indeed, we can evaluate the reasoning or hallucination capabilities of a model alone, but since the model will then be part of a system, we need to evaluate the whole product. For example, we should evaluate the whole RAG system for accuracy in retrieval and response generation. Even for RAG, there are both metrics and specific libraries for evaluating the system. For example, RAGAS (Retrieval-Augmented Generation Assessment) uses an LLM to evaluate the RAG response. ARES (Automatic RAG Evaluation through Synthetic data) is a comprehensive tool that takes advantage of synthetic data generation to assess model quality.

Inference optimization

Our LLM has to be deployed and will consume resources; our goal now is to optimize the inference process to avoid users encountering latency and reduce costs for us. Basically, three processes occur in inference:

1. **Tokenization and embedding**: Input is transformed into a numerical representation and then vector.
2. **Computation**: A key and value are computed for each multi-head attention.
3. **Generation**: Output is produced sequentially.

The first two steps are expensive but are easily parallelized on GPUs. The third step, on the other hand, is sequential because each output token depends on the previous token. The purpose of inference optimization is to speed up these three steps, and in this subsection, we will look at some techniques.

Model inference optimization

To produce a token output, we need all the previous context. For example, for the 15th token produced, we should calculate the **key-value** (**KV**) product of all tokens, 1 through 14. This makes the process very slow, reducing over time such that the attention has a quadratic cost ($O(n^2)$). The KV cache caches and reuses the key (K) and value (V) tensors from previous tokens, allowing faster computation of attention scores. This reduces memory and computational cost, enabling near-linear time ($O(n)$) inference. Typically, the process works like this: for the first token, we compute and store (K,V). For the second, we find (K,V) again and add K,V. In other words, attention is applied only to the new tokens. As we saw in *Chapter 2*, this is the calculation of attention:

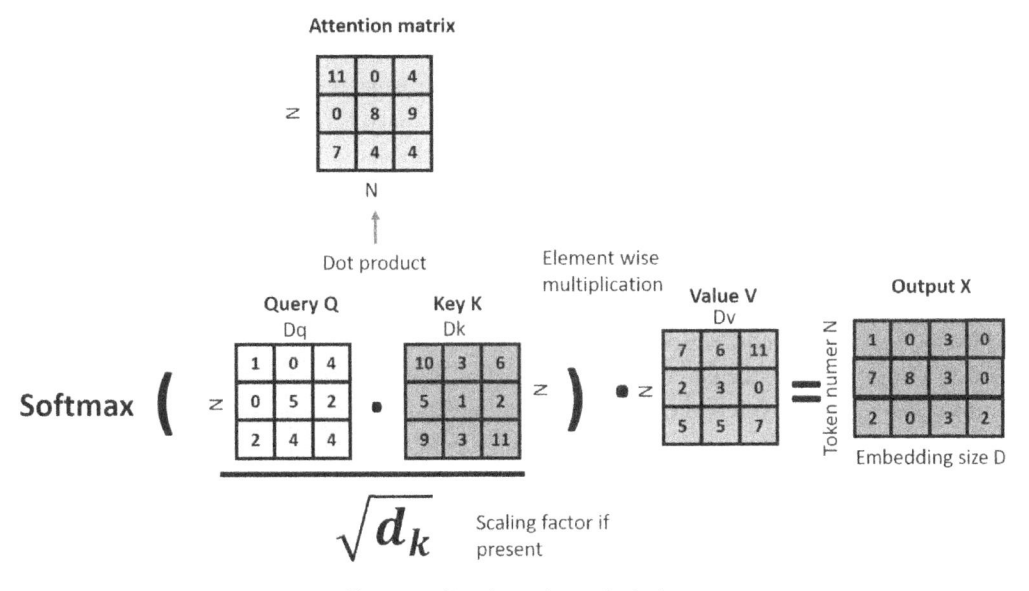

Figure 10.37 – Attention calculation

In the KV cache, we calculate the KV product, and then we save the product result in memory. At the time of a new token, we retrieve this information (the KV product) and calculate the KV product only for that token.

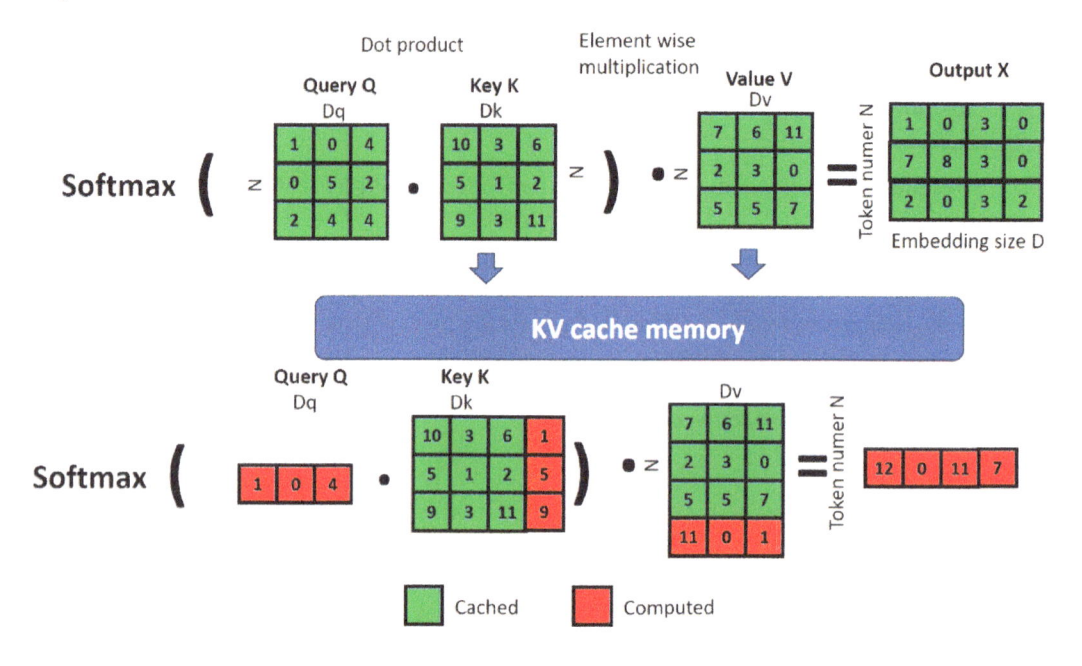

Figure 10.38 – KV cache process

The KV cache speeds up inference by eliminating some redundant computation (it prevents us from reprocessing all the previous parts of the sequence), scales well with long context windows, and is now optimized for major libraries and hardware. Of course, using the KV cache means we use more memory. In fact, it means that we have to keep in memory each KV cache per token, per attention head, and per layer. This, in practice, also places a limit on the size of the context window we can use. Obviously, during model training, it is of little use because we have to conduct parameter updates. Therefore, today, there are approaches that try to compress the KV cache so as to reduce the cost in terms of memory.

Another technique used to speed up inference is **continuous batching**. The main purpose of this technique is to parallelize the various queries, then divide the model memory cost by the batch and transfer more data to the GPU. Traditional batching leads to slower input processing and is not optimized for inference, where the various queries may differ in size. Continuous batching, on the other hand, allows multiple user requests to be handled dynamically, allowing multiple inference requests to be processed in parallel, even if they arrive at different times. Requests that arrive at a different time are dynamically grouped into a series of batches, instead of having a fixed batch to fill. A batching engine merges multiple users' prompts into a single batch. Instead of waiting for an entire batch, new tokens are processed when resources are available. This technique also works well with the KV cache; some tokens may have already been processed and we can recall what is in memory to further speed up the process. Continuous batching thus allows lower latency, allows streaming for several users at the same time, and improves resource utilization. Of course, it is more complex than the standard implementation of attention and requires a different implementation: we have to manage users optimally, and numerous requests are made to the KV cache.

Speculative decoding is another optimization technique used in autoregressive language models to accelerate text generation. Classic LLMs generate only one token at a time, and token generation is not parallelizable, leading to inefficient inference. In speculative decoding, we have two models working together:

- A small, faster "draft" model that generates multiple candidate tokens
- The main, larger LLM that verifies the candidates and either accepts or corrects them

The draft model (a small model of the same LLM architecture as the main one, but with fewer parameters) generates multiple speculative tokens at once. The main LLM checks these proposed tokens; if they match those of the larger LLM's output, they are accepted. If, however, there is no match, the LLM discards them and continues to generate. The process is iterative until the output is finished. Speculative decoding makes it possible to reduce the number of sequential steps in inference, speed up the response, and maximize GPU consumption without losing quality. Of course, the draft model must generate good candidates; if the small model is not accurate, we lose the advantage in speedup, which means we would require another model. This approach works better with long-form than small outputs.

Another way to speed up inference is to use specific forms of attention. **Paged attention** is an optimized memory management technique for handling large KV caches efficiently during LLM inference. It works like a virtual memory system by dynamically managing memory allocation and preventing fragmentation. It is inspired by the management of memory systems in computers, and instead of storing KV caches in a continuous memory block (which can lead to fragmentation), it stores them in smaller memory pages. This allows faster retrieval of information (and only necessary information) from the KV cache. Paged attention thus prevents GPU memory fragmentation, makes the system more efficient for long context (reduces memory consumption for long chats between the user and the system), and decreases latency by allowing easier fetching from the KV cache. **FlashAttention** is another way to make the inference process more efficient, allowing faster processing of attention with decreased memory consumption. It achieves this by processing attention in small blocks instead of storing large intermediate matrices. In this way, it makes more efficient use of GPU resources. In FlashAttention, only small blocks of various tokens are stored in the RAM. Today, many models use forms of attention during training that are aimed at faster reasoning. **Multi-grouped attention** (**MGA**) is a hybrid between **multi-head attention** (**MHA**) and sparse attention. Instead of each attention head attending to all tokens, MGA groups multiple heads together to enable more efficient computation. In MGA, the heads are not separated but grouped into specific clusters and process a group of characters. This makes it possible to reduce computational costs, is more flexible for sparse attention forms, and makes it possible to speed up training and reasoning. Another popular alternative is **multi-head latent** attention (**MLA**), which is used in modern LLMs. In standard MHA, we explicitly compute attention for all heads. In MLA, we use latent heads that indirectly encode relationships between tokens without the need for a full pairwise computation of attention. In this way, the model has better generalization by learning a compressed representation without sacrificing accuracy. This requires less attention during inference and saves memory.

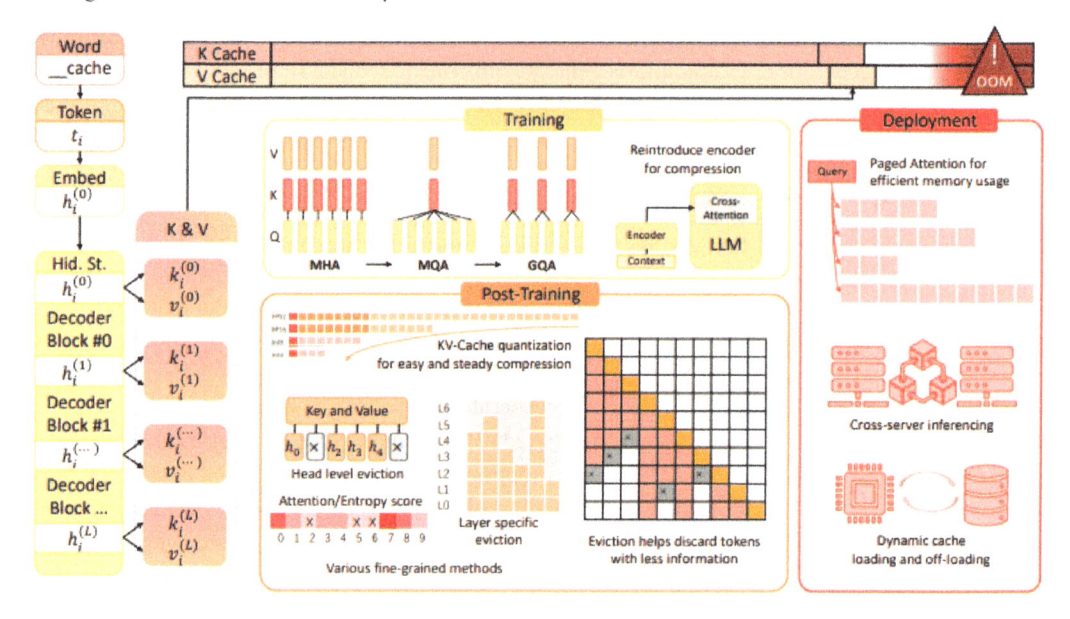

Figure 10.39 – Overview of methods for speeding inference
(https://arxiv.org/pdf/2407.18003)

These techniques, as illustrated in *Figure 10.39*, demonstrate how inference efficiency can be improved across multiple stages—compression, caching, and memory optimization. With this foundation, we can now explore how such optimizations are applied in real-world deployment scenarios.

Data, pipeline, and tensor parallelism

Another way to make training more efficient is to parallelize it. **Model parallelism** for a neural network is to distribute the model across multiple devices (such as GPUs or TPUs) to overcome memory and computation limitations. While this can be useful to speed up training, in other cases, it is necessary because the model is too large to fit on a single device. There are several ways to parallelize a model, as we will see next:

- **Data parallelism** is considered the simplest approach, in which replicas of the model are distributed across multiple computing devices (e.g., GPUs, TPUs, or even different machines), and different subsets of the training dataset are fed into each replica. During training, averaging of the gradients of the various GPUs is conducted; this is used for model updates. Then, each model is replicated across workers (GPUs/TPUs), and the input data batch is split into mini-batches assigned to different workers. During the forward pass, each worker computes predictions and losses for its mini-batch. Subsequently, each worker calculates gradients for its assigned data. These gradients are aggregated either by averaging or using a more complex method, and the aggregated gradients are used to update all model replicas, ensuring synchronization across workers. Data parallelism can be implemented in several ways, the most common being synchronous data parallelism, in which all devices compute the gradient before synchronization. Once all gradients are available, averaging is conducted. Although this approach ensures that there is consistency, a worker can slow down the training. To overcome this, we have asynchronous data parallelism, where each device conducts the local model update independently, at the risk of introducing stale gradients (outdated updates). An intermediate approach (stale-sync data parallelism) is also available, where workers perform multiple local updates before synchronizing with others. Data parallelism can also be centralized with a central server or decentralized with the various workers exchanging gradients in a ring topology. Data parallelism allows the workload to be distributed among different devices, increasing the speed of training, scales well when you have several devices, is not complex to implement, and is efficient because the model stays on the various devices and is not swapped. On the other hand, gradient synchronization can be slow due to communication overhead, especially if communication is inefficient. Variations in device speed, such as using different hardware or GPU versions, can further exacerbate this issue. Additionally, large batch sizes may cause convergence problems, and managing synchronization becomes increasingly complex as the number of devices grows.

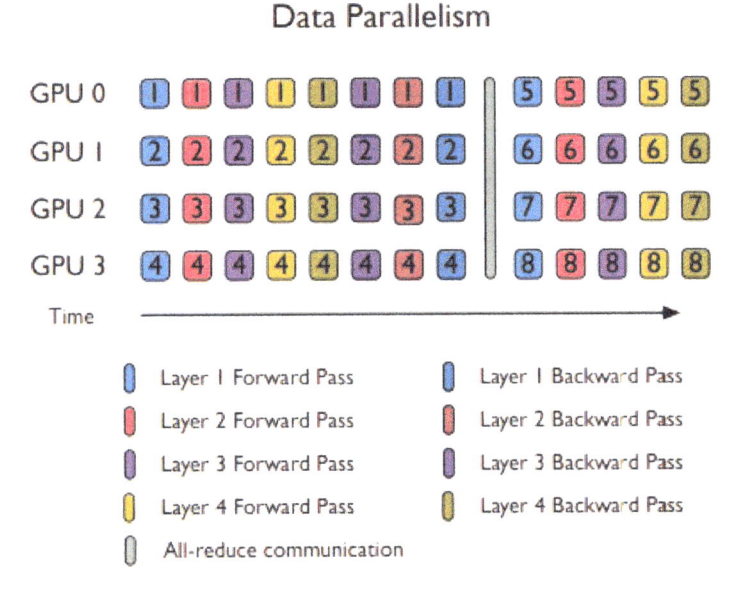

Figure 10.40 – Processing of mini-batches over time in data parallelism. Each GPU has a copy of all the layers (shown in different colors) and different mini-batches (numbered) are processed by different GPUs (`https://arxiv.org/pdf/2111.04949`)

- **Pipeline parallelism** is a distributed training technique where different layers of a deep learning model are assigned to different devices (e.g., GPUs or TPUs), and mini-batches are processed sequentially through the pipeline. This technique helps in training extremely large models that do not fit into a single device's memory. Pipeline parallelism is commonly used in transformer models such as GPT-3, GPT-4, LLaMA, and DeepSeek, where model sizes exceed the memory capacity of a single GPU. The model is divided into multiple stages, where each stage represents a subset of consecutive layers and is assigned to a different GPU. A batch is split into mini-batches, and a mini-batch is split into micro-batches. One micro-batch is then processed from the first stage and passed to the next. The second micro-batch starts being processed before the first micro-batch has finished all the stages (as soon as the first stage clears, it can start processing the second micro-batch, without the first micro-batch having to pass all the layers, thus allowing the process to be parallelized in an efficient manner). The backward pass follows the same pipeline as the forward pass but in reverse order; the gradient starts from the last stages to the first stages. Once all micro-batches are completed, the model update can be conducted.

Figure 10.41 – Forward and backward update for a single micro-batch (https://arxiv.org/pdf/2403.03699v1)

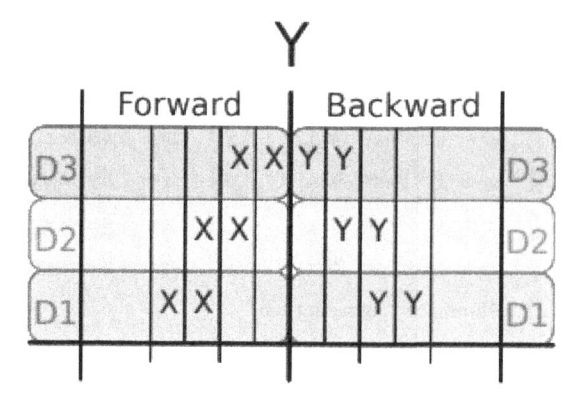

Figure 10.42 – Forward and backward update for two micro-batches in parallel (https://arxiv.org/pdf/2403.03699v1)

Pipeline parallelism can be conducted in different manners such as **one forward, one backward (1F1B)** scheduling, in which each GPU conducts one forward pass and one backward pass at the same time. Alternatively, each device could contain multiple model partitions and thus conduct more flexible scheduling. Pipeline parallelism allows the training of very large models that do not fit into a single GPU, allows better utilization of the various devices (each device constantly processes micro-batches), reduces the risk of memory bottlenecks, and is well adapted to transformers. On the other hand, it is a more complex system, where one has to manage the stages so that some of them do not have more computation-heavy layers and thus become bottlenecks (careful layer partitioning to balance the workload among the various devices). In the first iterations, the system is less efficient as it waits to be filled with micro-batches (the first stage starts working before the other stages), communication is more complex due to gradient aggregation, and there is increased complexity in designing the system.

- **Tensor parallelism** is a model parallelism technique where individual weight tensors (matrices) within a model are split across multiple GPUs. Unlike traditional model parallelism, which assigns entire layers to different GPUs, tensor parallelism breaks down the computations within a single layer and distributes them across multiple devices. This approach is particularly useful for large-scale transformer models where certain operations (such as matrix multiplications in attention layers) require enormous memory and computational power. Instead of computing and storing entire weight matrices on a single GPU, tensor parallelism divides them among multiple GPUs. For example, a fully connected layer applies a weight matrix, W, to an input, X, to obtain an output, Y. If W is too large for a single GPU, we can divide it among multiple GPUs. Each GPU will then conduct only part of the computation, producing part of the output, which is then later aggregated. Similarly, during the backward pass, we must then redistribute the gradient computation to allow proper updates of the weights of the various matrices, W. Column-wise tensor parallelism is among the most widely used for transformers, where the weight matrix is split column-wise across GPUs, and each GPU then computes part of the output, which is then concatenated. Considering the self-attention mechanism of a model, the query (Q), key (K), and value (V) matrices are split column-wise across multiple GPUs. Each GPU then computes a partial attention score, following which the various results are aggregated across GPUs to reconstruct the finished output. The advantage of this approach is that instead of storing entire weight matrices, each GPU stores only a portion. Also, the multiplication of large matrices can be distributed and thus make the computation faster, making it particularly efficient for large models. On the other hand, there is always the risk of communication overhead (GPUs must frequently exchange partial results, which can slow down training), it can be complex to implement, and it is not worthwhile except for large models.

TP
Workflow

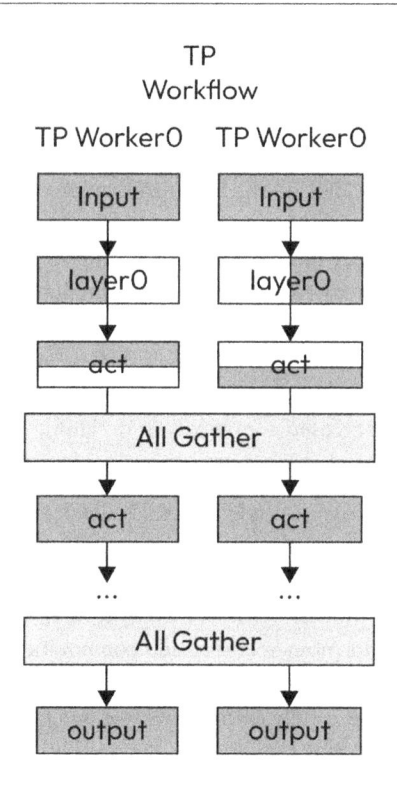

TP Worker0   TP Worker0

Input → layer0 → act → All Gather → act → ... → All Gather → output

Figure 10.43 – Tensor parallelism (`https://arxiv.org/pdf/2311.01635`)

The following table compares tensor parallelism, data parallelism, and pipeline parallelism across key dimensions such as memory usage, communication overhead, and complexity:

Feature	Tensor parallelism	Data parallelism	Pipeline parallelism
How it works	Splits individual tensors across GPUs	Replicates full model on each device; splits data	Splits model layers across GPUs
Memory usage	Low (weights are sharded)	High (full model stored on each GPU)	Medium (layers distributed)
Communication overhead	High (frequent cross-GPU communication)	High (gradient synchronization)	Moderate (micro-batch passing)
Best for	Very large models with huge weight matrices	Medium-sized models with large datasets	Deep models such as transformers
Complexity	High	Low	Medium

Table 10.1 – Comparison of tensor, data, and pipeline parallelism in large-scale model training

Hybrid parallelism integrates different types of parallelism trying to optimize training across multiple GPUs. Generally, the various approaches can be combined, although this requires more complexity. For example, data parallelism ensures that GPUs process different batches while model parallelism (tensor or pipeline parallelism) ensures that the model is optimized across multiple GPUs. For example, if the model is too large for a single GPU, we can use model parallelism and split the model across multiple GPUs. We can then use 16 GPUs to split a batch of data across 4 copies of the model.

So far, we have explored how to build a fully working AI-driven Streamlit app that integrates multiple agents and external APIs such as OpenAI. However, when an application moves from development to production, some important challenges need to be taken into account.

Handling errors in production

In this section, we'll explore some of the approaches we can adopt to handle issues that may occur when an application moves from development to production. Typical problems you might encounter include:

- The OpenAI API is temporarily unavailable
- Intermittent network failures or exceeding rate limits
- Incomplete or missing logging system

Let's see how we can mitigate these issues effectively:

- **The OpenAI API is temporarily unavailable**: One simple and effective way to start handling these issues is by wrapping your API calls in `try`/`except` blocks. Here's an example of how you can handle different types of errors when calling the OpenAI API:

```
try:
    response = client.chat.completions.create(
        model="gpt-4",
        messages=[...],
        timeout=10          # optional timeout
    )
    return response.choices[0].message.content
except openai.RateLimitError:
    st.error("Rate limit exceeded. Please try again later.")
except openai.APIError as e:
    st.error(f"OpenAI API error: {str(e)}")
except Exception as e:
    st.error(f"Unexpected error: {str(e)}")
```

- **Temporary issues**: When there are intermittent network failures or momentary unavailability of external APIs, instead of immediately failing, the app can retry the operation a few times:

  ```
  import time
   import random
  def call_openai_with_retry(prompt, retries=3):
      for i in range(retries):
          try:
              return client.chat.completions.create(
                  model="gpt-4",
                  messages=[ {"role": "user", "content": prompt}]
              )
          except openai.APIError:
              wait = 2 ** i + random.random()
              time.sleep(wait)
      st.error("Failed after multiple retries.")    return None
  ```

- **Logging system**: Using st.write() is fine for quick debugging, but in production, you need a more persistent and structured way to track what's happening in your app.

  A basic logging system helps you record important events and catch errors that may not appear in the UI:

  ```
  import logging
   logging.basicConfig(level=logging.INFO)
   logger = logging.getLogger(__name__)
  try:
      logger.info("Calling OpenAI API")
      response = client.chat.completions.create(...)
  except Exception as e:
      logger.exception("API call failed")
      st.error("Something went wrong.")
  ```

Security considerations for production

Applications deployed in production often involve API keys and potentially sensitive user data, so security must be carefully addressed from the beginning.

One of the most fundamental practices is to avoid hardcoding credentials such as API keys directly into the source code. Instead, credentials should be managed securely using environment variables or a dedicated secrets management system.

Security in production typically involves three key areas:

- Managing secrets
- Data exposure prevention
- Securing your deployment environment

Let's discuss these next.

Managing secrets in production

There are two common ways to securely manage secrets in production environments:

- **Using** `st.secrets`: This is ideal for applications deployed on Streamlit Cloud
- **Using environment variables**: This is recommended for Docker containers or local server deployments

Both approaches allow you to keep sensitive information out of your source code, but the right choice depends on your deployment context.

Here are some examples for each method:

- **Using** `st.secrets`: When using Streamlit, create a `.streamlit/secrets.toml` file that lets you define secrets into it. Here is an example:

    ```
    [general]
    openai_api_key = "application-api-key"
    ```

    Access it in your code like this:

    ```
    import openai
    openai.api_key = st.secrets["general"]["openai_api_key"]
    ```

- **Using environment variables**: For Dockerization or local deployments, it is recommended to store secrets as environment variables, keeping them separate from the source code. To use environment variables, you must define them in your terminal or deployment environment before running your application.

    For example, in a Unix-based terminal (Linux, macOS, or WSL), you can define the variable like this:

    ```
    export OPENAI_API_KEY="your-api-key"
    ```

    Then, in your Python code, access the variable as follows:

    ```
    import os
    openai.api_key = os.getenv("OPENAI_API_KEY")
    ```

The `export` command sets an environment variable only for the current terminal session. This means it will remain active only until you close the terminal. To launch your app using the variable, you must run it in the same shell session:

```
export OPENAI_API_KEY="your-api-key"
  streamlit run app.py
```

To make the variable available every time you open a terminal, you can add it to your shell's startup file.

On Linux, this file is usually called ~/.bash_profile.

These are called initialization scripts. They are automatically executed every time you start a new terminal session and are used to configure the shell environment, including setting environment variables, aliases, and paths.

To add the API key to ~/.bash_profile, open the terminal and run the following:

```
nano ~/.bashrc
```

Then, save and close it. From now on, your app will automatically find the API key every time it is launched from a new terminal session.

Data exposure prevention

In production, one of the most overlooked security risks is the unintentional exposure of sensitive data through logging, error messages, or misconfigured URLs.

While logging is essential for debugging and observability, it can easily become a liability if secrets, tokens, or user data are captured without proper filtering.

Here are a few best practices to minimize the risk:

- **Avoid logging secrets**: Never print API keys, access tokens, or passwords to logs, even in debug mode. This applies to both client-side and server-side logs.

- **Sanitize user data**: If your application logs inputs or error traces that include user-provided data (e.g., form submissions, headers, and payloads), be sure to mask or strip sensitive fields (such as email addresses, credit card numbers, or personal identifiers).

- **Configure logging levels appropriately**: Use different log levels (e.g., INFO, WARNING, ERROR, or DEBUG) and restrict debug-level logs in production. Enable only what is necessary to diagnose issues without overexposing internals.

- **Handle errors**: Avoid sending raw stack traces or system error messages directly to users. These can leak details about your backend, framework, or database.

Preventing data exposure is about designing systems that assume that secrets and user data must always be protected, even in edge cases or failures.

Securing your deployment environment

Even if your code avoids data exposure and your secrets are properly managed, your application can still be vulnerable if the environment in which it runs is misconfigured.

For example, in modern workflows, containerization is one of the most common ways to package and deploy applications. In fact, containers offer portability and consistency across environments, but they also introduce specific security risks.

A wrong or poor Dockerfile configuration can introduce multiple vulnerabilities, such as the following:

- Increased exposure to known exploits if the image includes unnecessary packages or tools
- Credential leaks if secrets are stored directly in the image
- Privilege escalation if the container runs as the root user
- Unsafe access to host resources if volumes are not properly restricted

To mitigate these risks, it is important to follow a set of container security best practices. Let's look at a few simple guidelines to make your Docker-based deployment more secure and production-ready:

- **Bloated images = more attack surface**: Using a full `python:3.11` image instead of `python:3.11-slim` can include dozens of unnecessary system tools. If any of these have known vulnerabilities, they become an unintentional attack, even if your app doesn't use them.

- **Secrets in the image = easy leaks**: Hardcoding API keys or copying `.env` files into the Docker image allows anyone with access to the image to extract and appropriate them.

- **Running as `root` = dangerous escalation**: If no user is specified, containers run as `root`, and combined with an exploit in a Python dependency, this could give an attacker full control of the container and possibly the host too.

- **Unsafe volume mounting = host access**: Mounting critical paths gives containers access to critical host files including SSH keys and system configuration. If the container is compromised, the host is compromised as well. Examples of critical paths include the following:

    - `/`: Root of the host filesystem. Grants full access to the entire filesystem of the host, including sensitive system directories, user data, and configuration files.

    - `/etc`: System configuration directory. Contains critical configuration files, including `/etc/passwd`, `/etc/shadow`, network settings, and user permissions. Exposing this can allow manipulation of how the host system behaves.

    - `/var/run/docker.sock`: Docker daemon socket. Gives the container direct control over the Docker engine running on the host. This lets the container start, stop, and manage other containers, including mounting volumes and executing code on the host.

Here is an example of a minimal and secure Dockerfile:

```
# Minimal python image
 FROM python:3.11-slim
WORKDIR /app
COPY requirements.txt .
 RUN pip install --no-cache-dir -r requirements.txt
COPY . .
# Create and use a non-root user through the keyword USER
 RUN useradd -m appuser
 USER appuser
CMD ["streamlit", "run", "app.py"]
```

To inject secrets securely at runtime, use environment variables passed with `docker run` or use secret management tools such as **Docker secrets**:

```
# Runtime execution
 docker run -e OPENAI_API_KEY="your-api-key" my-streamlit-app
```

MLOPs and LLMOPs are important concepts for anyone who wants to use an ML model or LLM in production. In the next section, we will discuss other important concepts in production deployment, such as asynchronous programming, which allows us to handle multiple concurrent user requests.

Asynchronous programming

So far, you've seen examples where tasks are executed one after the other. But what if some tasks don't need to block the flow of the entire program while waiting? That's where asynchronous programming comes in.

Asynchronous programming allows tasks to cooperatively share the CPU. Instead of each task waiting for the previous one to finish, tasks can voluntarily pause and let others run, making better use of the single processor's time. This does not imply simultaneous execution; instead, it indicates a smart interleaving of their operations.; this is especially useful when waiting for things such as I/O operations.

Think of it as multiple conversations happening with one person switching between them, efficiently and politely. In Python, this is achieved using the `asyncio` module, which supports cooperative multitasking on a single CPU.

As you'll see in the comparison table, asynchronous code is different from using threads or multiple processes. It runs on just one core, but it can still feel fast, especially when dealing with many I/O-bound tasks.

Python module	Number of CPUs	Task switching style	Switching decision
`asyncio`	Single	Cooperative multitasking	Tasks yield control voluntarily through the `await` keyword
`threading`	Single	Preemptive multitasking	OS decides when to switch threads
`multiprocessing`	Multiple	Preemptive multitasking	Separate processes run independently, but on the same machine; the OS decides when to switch

Table 10.2 – Concurrency mechanisms in Python: differences between asyncio, threading, and multiprocessing

Concurrency is particularly useful in two types of scenarios: when a program is waiting for responses from external systems (I/O-bound), and when it is handling a high computational workload (CPU-bound).

In I/O-bound situations, a script spends most of its time waiting for data to arrive from a source, such as a filesystem, a network connection, a database, or an API. During this time, the CPU is often idle, making it a perfect opportunity to run other tasks concurrently.

In contrast, CPU-bound tasks keep the processor fully occupied with calculations such as rendering images, parsing large datasets, or performing cryptographic operations. In these cases, concurrency helps by distributing the workload across multiple CPU cores, enabling true parallel execution. This form of concurrency (better described as parallelism) can significantly reduce total processing time for heavy computations.

Type of task	Main limitation	Examples	Concurrency benefit	Execution style
I/O-bound	Slow external systems	Reading files, API requests, database queries	Keeps CPU busy while waiting for I/O	Cooperative (`asyncio`)
CPU-bound	Intensive computation	Data crunching, image processing, encryption	Distributes load across multiple cores for real parallelism	Preemptive (`threading`, `multiprocessing`)

Table 10.3 – I/O-bound vs. CPU-bound: task types and optimal concurrency models

The following diagram illustrates how task execution differs between synchronous and asynchronous when dealing with I/O-bound operations.

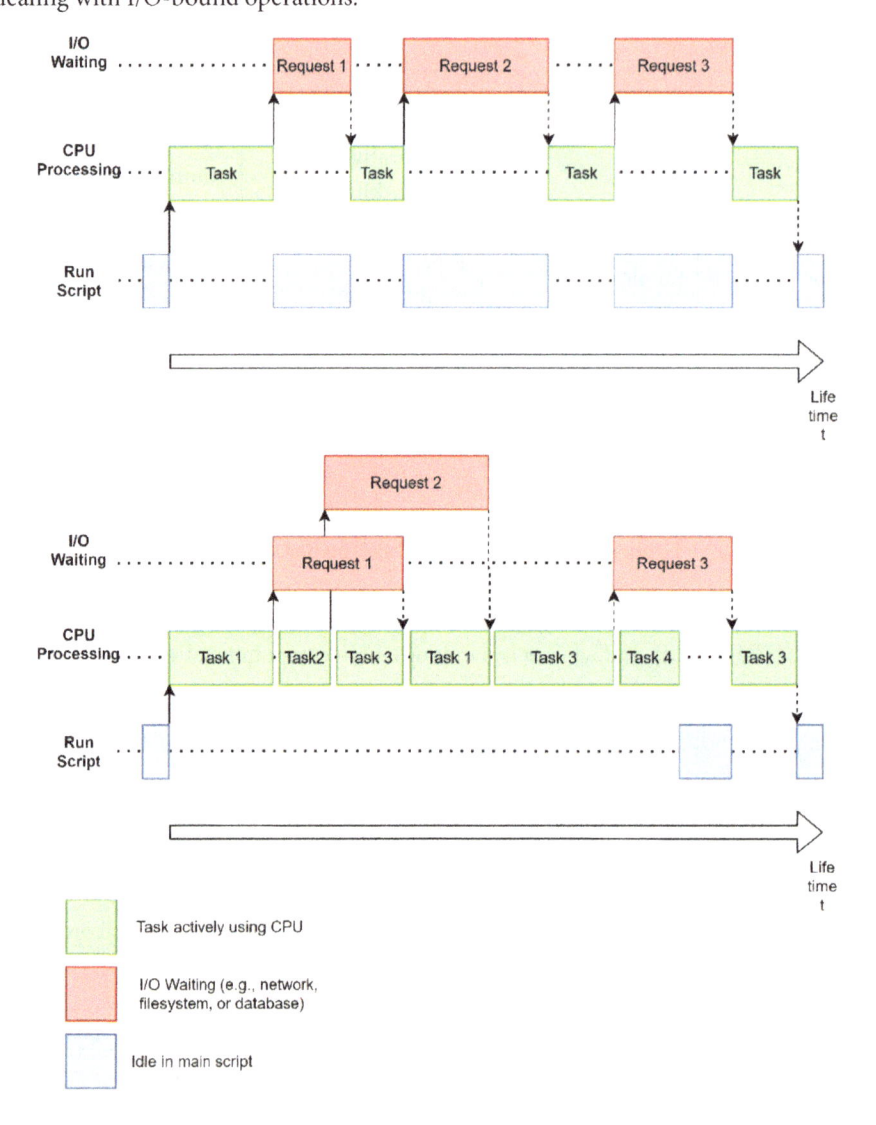

Figure 10.44 – Comparison of blocking vs non-blocking I/O execution

In the first row, each request blocks the CPU until the I/O completes. In the second row (async), the CPU switches between tasks during I/O wait times, improving efficiency on a single core and minimizing the idle time.

When multiple I/O-bound requests arrive in sequence, using a single thread to handle each of them one after the other would block the program during I/O waits.

To improve responsiveness, the `threading` module can be used to delegate each request to a separate thread.

In the following diagram, each incoming request is assigned to one of four worker threads. The actual workload (T1, T2, T3, ...) represents short bursts of CPU activity interleaved with I/O waits:

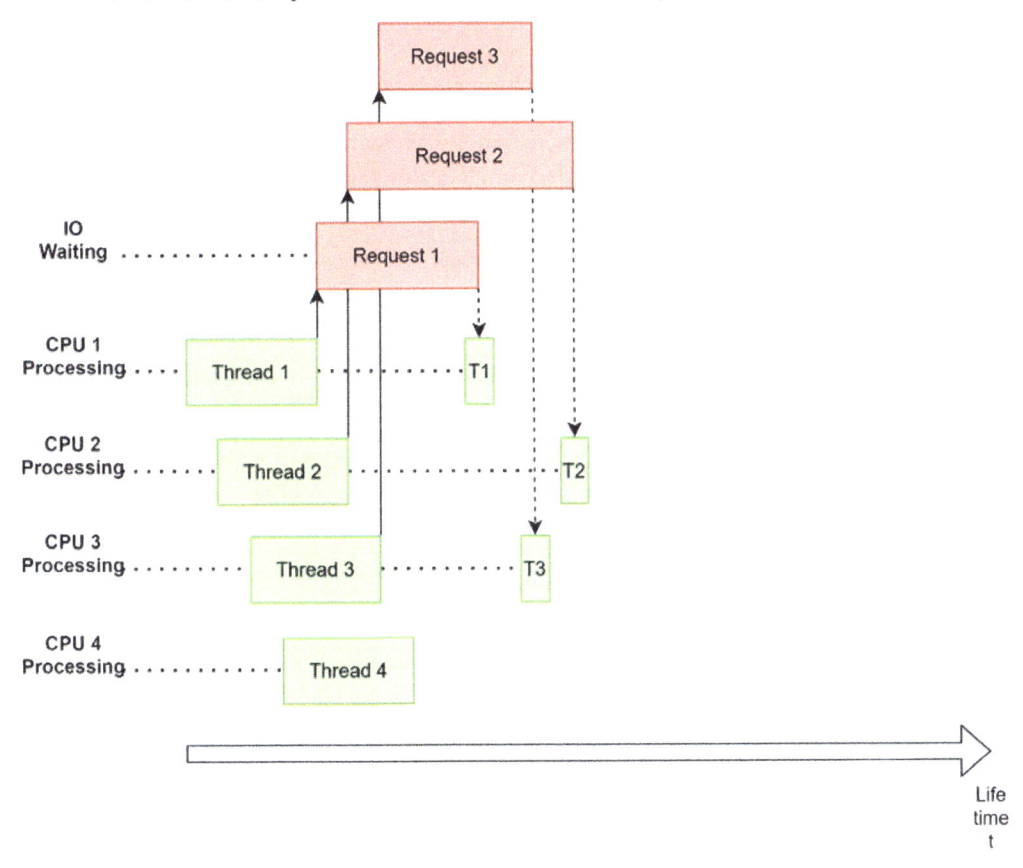

Figure 10.45 – Concurrent request handling with four worker threads and interleaved CPU/I/O workloads

This pattern is useful when your program must remain responsive while interacting with slow external systems such as APIs, databases, filesystems, or even GUIs.

Asynchronous programming is a type of parallel programming that allows programs to perform tasks concurrently, without blocking the main execution thread. For example, when we have multiple users interacting with the system at the same time, we will have more tasks to handle at the same time, with some tasks taking more time by blocking our agent. In traditional synchronous programming, tasks are executed one after the other, where each task must wait for the previous one to finish before it can begin; tasks are executed sequentially in the order in which they are written. Each task must complete fully before the next begins, which can lead to delays if a task involves waiting, such as for file I/O or network operations. Asynchronous programming, on the other hand, allows tasks that may block execution to be initiated and handled concurrently. Instead of waiting for a task to finish, the program can move on to other tasks, returning to the blocked task once it is ready. This approach improves efficiency by making better use of system resources, particularly in scenarios involving high-latency operations, such as web requests or database queries, enabling more responsive and performant applications.

There are some key concepts for discussing asynchronous programming:

- **Concurrency**: This refers to the ability to handle different tasks at the same time; however, this does not mean that tasks are handled simultaneously. Tasks are started and completed in overlapping time periods, but not simultaneously.

- **Parallelism**: This refers to the ability to accomplish tasks at exactly the same time, usually by using multiple processors or cores. While concurrency may or may not involve parallelism, parallelism always involves concurrency.

- **Blocking operations**: These are operations that wait for a task to complete before starting a new operation (e.g., reading a file from disk before starting to process text).

- **Non-blocking operations**: This refers to the ability to start a task and continue the program with other tasks without waiting for the task to complete (making an HTTP request and continuing to generate more text with an LLM while waiting for the response).

- **Callbacks**: These are functions passed as arguments to other functions that are executed when a task completes.

- **Promises and futures**: These are abstractions that represent the eventual result of an asynchronous operation. A promise is a value (or result) that may be unavailable at that time but will be available at some later point. A future is the same thing but is commonly used in languages such as Python and Java.

- **Event loop**: This is the fundamental component of an asynchronous program, where tasks, events, or signals are listed and scheduled for execution when the resources are available. In other words, we use an event loop to allow tasks to run without blocking the main program. The event loop waits for an event to occur and calls an appropriate callback function at this point.

- **Coroutines**: These are special functions that can be paused and then resumed during their execution. In other words, a function can start and then be paused to wait for the result of another task. For example, when we start an analysis of some documents, the function pauses while we conduct an HTTP request to find more information that is needed to accomplish our function. When the results of the HTTP request arrive, the function resumes.

It may seem counterintuitive how asynchronous programming makes code execution faster (after all, no additional resources are being used). I have made extensive changes here for conciseness and clarity. Please confirm whether your intended meaning has been retained. In the synchronous format, she completes each game one at a time before moving to the next. With each move taking her 10 seconds and her opponent 60 seconds, a full game of 30 moves per player (60 moves total) takes 2,100 seconds. Playing all 24 games sequentially requires 50,400 seconds, or roughly 14 hours.

In contrast, the asynchronous format has Judit moving from board to board, making one move per game while each opponent thinks during her rotation. One full round of 24 moves takes 240 seconds, and since each player takes 60 seconds to respond, Judit returns to each board just as the opponent is ready. Over 30 rounds, the entire session lasts only 7,200 seconds, or approximately 2 hours—making asynchronous play significantly more time-efficient.

In async programming, we do exactly the same, the event loop allows us to manage the various tasks in an optimal time management manner. A function that would block other tasks can be optimally blocked when we need to run other tasks, allowing optimized management of the entire program. Here, we do not want to optimize the time of each game but the whole performance.

We can then manage multiple processes at the same time in different ways:

- **Multiple processes**: A process is an independent program in execution. Each process has its own memory, resources, and execution context. In the simplest way, we can manage different processes at the same time (for example, several players playing the 24 games is a simple example of multiple processes occurring at the same time during performance). In the case of programming, this means that different scripts or processes can run at the same time (e.g., four functions and each of them runs on a different CPU). However, this approach is very inefficient.

- **Multiple threads**: This is a variation of the previous approach. A thread is the smallest unit of execution within a process. Multiple threads can be within the same process and share the same memory, but each thread has its own execution stack. In this case, several threads are executed at the same time.

- **Asynchronous programming**: In this case, we have a single process and a single thread but conduct several things at the same time. In Python, `asyncio` does exactly this by exploiting coroutines and futures to simplify asynchronous code.

Asynchronous programming, therefore, improves performance when some tasks are time-consuming and can block the execution of a program. In this way, the system can continue executing other tasks while it waits for them to complete. It also allows better utilization of system resources (for example, while waiting for a network request, the program can perform calculations or handle other requests). Asynchronous programming also helps to achieve systems that are more scalable and can handle multiple requests in parallel, reducing the number of threads.

asyncio

asyncio is a Python library that allows you to write concurrent code using the `async/await` syntax. It provides a framework for running asynchronous operations, without relying on multithreading or multiprocessing. The heart of `asyncio` is the event loop, which schedules and executes asynchronous tasks (called coroutines) in the background. A coroutine is similar to a generator in Python: it can pause execution and let other tasks run and then resume later. It is the event loop that tracks the state of these coroutines and their results, which are presented as `futures`.

Here is a basic example of a coroutine:

```
import asyncio
async def my_coroutine():
    print("Hello, world!")
# Create an event loop and run the coroutine
asyncio.run(my_coroutine())
```

While this code shows how to define and run a coroutine by using the event loop, it does not yet take advantage of concurrent execution. In fact, to execute multiple asynchronous tasks concurrently, we can use either `asyncio.gather()` or `asyncio.create_task()`.

While `gather()` is useful when you want to run several coroutines and wait for all of them to finish together, `create_task()` provides more flexibility. It allows you to launch coroutines in the background and decide when (or whether) to await their results later in your program. Let's look at some examples together.

The following example uses `asyncio.gather()` to execute multiple coroutines concurrently:

```
async def task1():
    await asyncio.sleep(2)
    print("Task 1 completed!")
async def task2():
    await asyncio.sleep(1)
    print("Task 2 completed!")
async def main():
    await asyncio.gather(task1(), task2())  # Run both tasks concurrently
asyncio.run(main())
```

In this case, both tasks are executed concurrently, and the total execution time will be close to 2 seconds: the time taken by the longest task.

We can achieve the same result using `asyncio.create_task()`, which offers more control over task scheduling. Unlike `asyncio.gather()`, which groups coroutines and waits for all of them together, `create_task()` lets us launch coroutines individually and decide when to await their results. This is particularly useful when we want to run background tasks while doing other work.

Here is the same example rewritten with `create_task()`:

```
import asyncio
async def task1():
    await asyncio.sleep(2)
```

```
    print("Task 1 completed!")
async def task2():
    await asyncio.sleep(1)
    print("Task 2 completed!")

async def main():
    t1 = asyncio.create_task(task1())
    t2 = asyncio.create_task(task2())

    # Both tasks start running in the background immediately
    await t1
    await t2

asyncio.run(main())
```

Each call to `create_task()` returns a `Task` object, which represents the running coroutine and can be awaited, cancelled, or monitored.

The result is the same: both tasks run concurrently, and the output is printed once each finish. However, with `create_task()`, we gain more flexibility.

For example, we can start several background tasks and continue executing other logic in `main()`. Then, we can await only the results we need at a specific point in the workflow. This flexibility makes `create_task()` especially useful in complex workflows where not all tasks are equally important or time-sensitive.

To better understand the real-world impact of asynchronous programming, let's compare an example of synchronous versus asynchronous execution. Specifically, we will simulate fetching data from a website using HTTP requests by using Python `requests` library. This will highlight how asynchronous code can significantly improve performance when dealing with I/O-bound tasks such as network calls.

Here is the synchronous code:

```
import requests
import time

def fetch_url(url):
    response = requests.get(url)
    return f"Fetched {url}"

def sync_fetch():
    urls = ['https://httpbin.org/get'] * 5  # Simulating 5 requests to the same URL
    results = [fetch_url(url) for url in urls]
    for result in results:
        print(result)
```

```
def main():
    start_time = time.time()
    sync_fetch()
    end_time = time.time()
    print(f"Synchronous version took {end_time - start_time:.4f} seconds")
# Run the synchronous example
main()
```

Here is the asynchronous code:

```
import asyncio
import aiohttp
import time

async def fetch_url(session, url):
    async with session.get(url) as response:
        await response.text()  # Simulate processing the response
        return f"Fetched {url}"

async def async_fetch():
    urls = ['https://httpbin.org/get'] * 5  # Simulating 5 requests to the same URL
    async with aiohttp.ClientSession() as session:
        tasks = [fetch_url(session, url) for url in urls]
        results = await asyncio.gather(*tasks)
        for result in results:
            print(result)
async def main():
    start_time = time.time()
    await async_fetch()
    end_time = time.time()
    print(f"Asynchronous version took {end_time - start_time:.4f} seconds")
# Directly calling the asynchronous function in Jupyter
await main()
```

The following figures show the output of the synchronous and asynchronous implementations described above, respectively. As we can see, the synchronous version performs the HTTP requests one after the other, resulting in a longer total execution time. The asynchronous version, on the other hand, sends all requests concurrently, significantly reducing the total time required.

```
Fetched https://httpbin.org/get
Fetched https://httpbin.org/get
Fetched https://httpbin.org/get
Fetched https://httpbin.org/get
Fetched https://httpbin.org/get
Synchronous version took 4.9810 seconds
```

Figure 10.46 – Synchronous result

```
Fetched https://httpbin.org/get
Fetched https://httpbin.org/get
Fetched https://httpbin.org/get
Fetched https://httpbin.org/get
Fetched https://httpbin.org/get
Asynchronous version took 1.2333 seconds
```

Figure 10.47 – Asynchronous result

Asynchronous programming and ML

Conjugating asynchronous programming with ML in Python can be a powerful combination. Asynchronous programming can improve performance by allowing non-blocking operations, such as loading large datasets, running hyperparameter tuning, or interacting with APIs. For example, we can see different possibilities:

- **Data loading**: In ML workflows, especially when working with large datasets, loading and preprocessing data can often be a bottleneck. Asynchronous programming can help speed this up by loading different parts of the data concurrently. For example, you can asynchronously load multiple chunks of a dataset while concurrently performing some I/O-bound tasks (such as data augmentation, cleaning, or transformation).

- **Hyperparameter tuning**: The tuning of hyperparameters is one of the most time-consuming and slowest processes, which can benefit from conducting some tasks asynchronously. For example, when performing a grid or random search on hyperparameters, different configurations can be evaluated simultaneously rather than sequentially.

- **Asynchronous inference**: You can use asynchronous programming to create a non-blocking API to serve trained ML models. This is especially useful when deploying a model for real-time inference and wanting to handle multiple queries simultaneously.

- **Model training**: Although training is usually conducted on different GPUs/CPUs in parallel, asynchronous scheduling can be conjugated to allow better loading and preprocessing of data while training appears in parallel. This is particularly useful when we have different data to retrieve.

We can observe a classic example of hyperparameter tuning. In this simple example with the classic Iris dataset and a simple model, we'll show how using `asyncio` saves some time.

Here is the synchronous code:

```
import time
from sklearn.ensemble import RandomForestClassifier
from sklearn.datasets import load_iris
from sklearn.model_selection import train_test_split
from sklearn.metrics import accuracy_score
def train_and_evaluate_model(n_estimators, max_depth, min_samples_split, min_samples_leaf):
    # Load dataset
    data = load_iris()
    X_train, X_test, y_train, y_test = train_test_split(data.data, data.target, test_size=0.2, random_state=42)
        # Initialize and train the model
    model = RandomForestClassifier(
        n_estimators=n_estimators,
        max_depth=max_depth,
        min_samples_split=min_samples_split,
        min_samples_leaf=min_samples_leaf
    )
    model.fit(X_train, y_train)
     # Evaluate the model
    predictions = model.predict(X_test)
    accuracy = accuracy_score(y_test, predictions)
        return (n_estimators, max_depth, min_samples_split, min_samples_leaf, accuracy)

def tune_hyperparameters():
    n_estimators_values = [10, 50, 100, 150, 200]   # Hyperparameter values to tune
    max_depth_values = [5, 10, None]
    min_samples_split_values = [2, 5]
    min_samples_leaf_values = [1, 2, 4]

    results = []
    for n_estimators in n_estimators_values:
        for max_depth in max_depth_values:
            for min_samples_split in min_samples_split_values:
                for min_samples_leaf in min_samples_leaf_values:
                    results.append(train_and_evaluate_model(n_estimators, max_depth, min_samples_split, min_samples_leaf))
        # Find the best hyperparameters and accuracy
```

```
    best_params = max(results, key=lambda x: x[4])
    print(f"Best hyperparameters: {best_params[:4]} with accuracy:
{best_params[4]:.4f}")
# Measure time for synchronous execution
start_time = time.time()
tune_hyperparameters()
end_time = time.time()
print(f"Synchronous version took {end_time - start_time:.4f} seconds")
```

In the preceding script, we run an ML model and search for the best parameters. This script shows how even a small model takes a lot of time to be executed.

```
Best hyperparameters: (10, 5, 2, 1) with accuracy: 1.0000
Synchronous version took 21.7035 seconds
```

Figure 10.48 – Synchronous result

Here is the asynchronous code:

```
import asyncio
import time
from sklearn.ensemble import RandomForestClassifier
from sklearn.datasets import load_iris
from sklearn.model_selection import train_test_split
from sklearn.metrics import accuracy_score

async def train_and_evaluate_model(n_estimators, max_depth, min_
samples_split, min_samples_leaf):
    # Load dataset
    data = load_iris()
    X_train, X_test, y_train, y_test = train_test_split(data.data,
data.target, test_size=0.2, random_state=42)
    # Initialize and train the model
    model = RandomForestClassifier(
        n_estimators=n_estimators,
        max_depth=max_depth,
        min_samples_split=min_samples_split,
        min_samples_leaf=min_samples_leaf
    )
    model.fit(X_train, y_train)
    # Evaluate the model
    predictions = model.predict(X_test)
    accuracy = accuracy_score(y_test, predictions)
    return (n_estimators, max_depth, min_samples_split, min_samples_
leaf, accuracy)
```

```
async def tune_hyperparameters():
    n_estimators_values = [10, 50, 100, 150, 200]  # Hyperparameter values to tune
    max_depth_values = [5, 10, None]
    min_samples_split_values = [2, 5]
    min_samples_leaf_values = [1, 2, 4]
    tasks = []
    for n_estimators in n_estimators_values:
        for max_depth in max_depth_values:
            for min_samples_split in min_samples_split_values:
                for min_samples_leaf in min_samples_leaf_values:
                    tasks.append(train_and_evaluate_model(n_estimators, max_depth, min_samples_split, min_samples_leaf))
    results = await asyncio.gather(*tasks)
    # Find the best hyperparameters and accuracy
    best_params = max(results, key=lambda x: x[4])
    print(f"Best hyperparameters: {best_params[:4]} with accuracy: {best_params[4]:.4f}")
# Measure time for asynchronous execution
start_time = time.time()
await tune_hyperparameters()
end_time = time.time()
print(f"Asynchronous version took {end_time - start_time:.4f} seconds")
```

In this case, we trained the same model using asynchronous programming. This approach allowed us to save time and thus reduce the execution time.

```
Best hyperparameters: (10, 5, 2, 1) with accuracy: 1.0000
Synchronous version took 21.7035 seconds
```

Figure 10.49 – Asynchronous result

This can also be applied to an LLM as an agent. Traditionally, function calls block LLM inference, making the process inefficient as each function call must complete before moving to the next. Some authors propose instead to implement an async approach even with LLMs (or generate tokens and execute function calls concurrently) when tools are connected like in agents. For example, one can consider interruptible LLM decoding, where the function executor notifies the LLM asynchronously, allowing it to continue generating tokens while waiting for function call results. The purpose of this approach is to reduce latency by conducting an overlap of function execution and token generation.

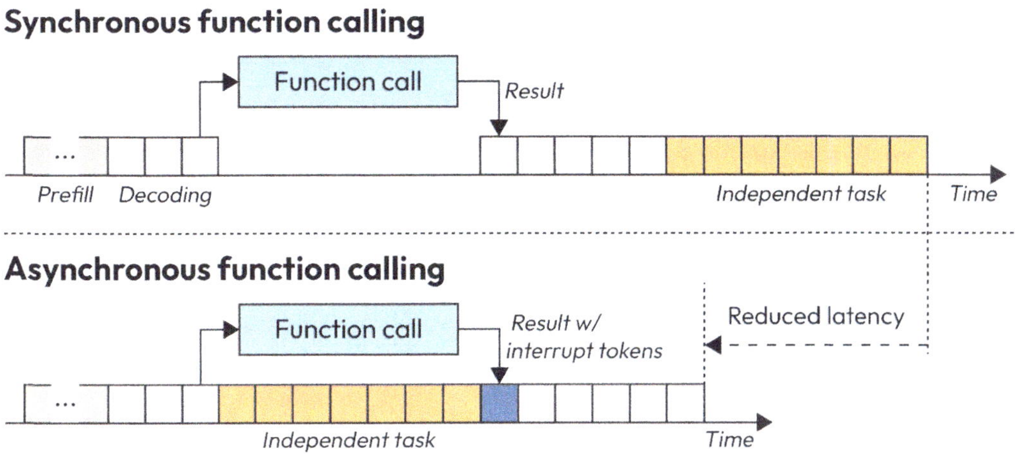

Synchronous function calling

Asynchronous function calling

Figure 10.50 – Synchronous vs. asynchronous function calling (https://arxiv.org/pdf/2412.07017)

So, in theory, we can have three approaches for an LLM agent:

- **Synchronous LLM function calling**: Each function is executed one after the other. An LLM must wait for each function to complete before it can continue with the next one. This approach is the simplest, but it adds latency to the system since it must wait for each operation to finish (e.g., reading HTML, reading XLS files, generating tokens, etc.) before it can continue. This leads to high inefficiency, especially if there are many functions or some functions lose a lot of time.

- **Synchronous LLM function calling with parallel optimization**: This process tries to optimize each task in parallel (e.g., reading HTML, reading XLS, and reading text simultaneously), but each task still blocks the next one. The advantage over the previous approach is that each function can be conducted concurrently, with an increase in speed over the previous one. Synchronization is required to conduct the tasks in the right order. Although the tasks are optimized, they are still synchronous, so we have to wait for a function to finish before completing some tasks.

- **Asynchronous LLM function calling**: In this approach, tasks are executed asynchronously, meaning that functions do not block one another. The system can read HTML, read XLS, and read text while simultaneously performing other operations (such as summarizing or saving data). This leads to a noticeable improvement in latency, improving the use of resources. The system ensures that dependent tasks (e.g., summarizing and saving PDFs) are only performed once the necessary data (e.g., reading text) is available. Dependencies are managed dynamically without halting other operations. Multiprocessing parallelization (the previous approach) creates different processes or threads in order to handle tasks concurrently, thus allocating resources and memory. This leads to more resource consumption than in an asynchronous version, and consumption can explode depending on how many functions we have. Also, this approach is more scalable.

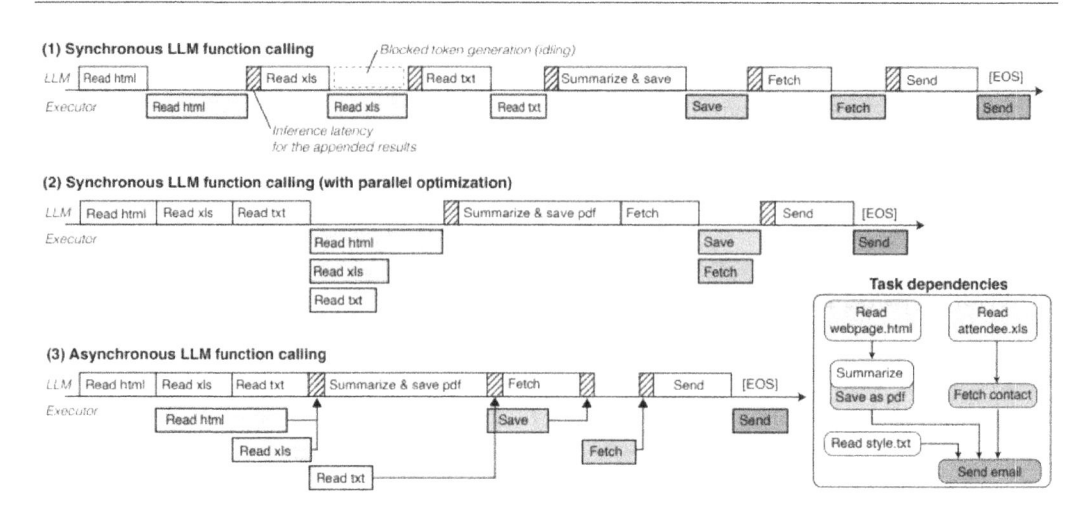

Figure 10.51 – Comparison of LLM-executor interactions (https://arxiv.org/pdf/2412.07017)

Once we have made our system (our application) efficient, it should be placed in isolation to avoid external problems. In the next section, we will explain in detail exactly how Docker allows us to do this.

Docker

Docker is an open source platform that enables developers and system administrators to create, deploy, and run applications in containers. Containers allow software to be packaged along with all its dependencies (such as libraries, configurations, etc.) and run consistently across different environments, whether it's a developer's laptop, a test server, or a production machine.

Containers can then be viewed as virtual machines, allowing for reduced overhead and better utilization of resources and the system itself (especially if we have to use a single model on several systems). The idea is that our software (of which our model or an LLM plus agents is a component) can run in isolation to prevent problems from arising that impact its execution and performance. The use of virtual machines is an example of how a system can run in a guest **operating system** (**OS**) and use resources. Optimizing a system for a guest OS, however, requires considerable resources. Containers try to reduce resource consumption and overhead in order to run the application. Containers offer a way to package an application to make it abstract from the environment in which it runs. This decoupling then allows a container to run in any target environment, predictably and isolated from other applications. At the same time, the container provides the ability to control our environment in a granular manner. Docker containers are lightweight and portable and ensure that the application behaves the same way everywhere. Given these benefits, Docker containers have been adopted by many companies.

Docker is based on a few main concepts:

- **Containers**: These are the basic units of Docker and contain an application and its dependencies in a single package that can be easily moved between environments. A container also contains the OS kernels, to reduce the resources needed. Unlike a virtual machine that contains the entire OS, Docker containers contain only the information needed to run the application. This makes Docker containers much faster and more efficient to run.
- **Images**: An image is a read-only template used to create containers. It contains the application code, runtime, libraries, and environment variables. Docker images contain the blueprint of the application – all the information to be able to execute a code. There are many ready-made images in Docker Hub that can be used to efficiently create containers and reduce the need to start from scratch.
- **Docker Engine**: This is the component responsible for managing and running containers (runtime environment for Docker). Docker Engine runs on both Linux and Windows OSs.
- **Dockerfile**: A Dockerfile is a script containing instructions on how to build a Docker image. This file specifies which base image to use, how to install dependencies, environment configurations, and other details.
- **Docker Compose**: This is a tool for defining and running multi-container Docker applications.

Docker containers thus have a number of advantages:

- **Portability**: Docker containers encapsulate an application and its dependencies in a single, portable unit. In this way, the system abstracts away differences between environments, making it more reliable and consistent in deployment.
- **Efficiency**: The system is more efficient compared to traditional virtual machines. By using only the kernel, the system uses far fewer resources, thus making it easier to deploy and more scalable. Docker integrates well with other orchestration tools, such as Kubernetes and Docker Swarm, making it easier to scale an application both horizontally (more containers) and vertically (increasing the resources available to containers).
- **Isolation**: Docker provides strong isolation between containers, allowing them to run independently and not interfere with each other, thus improving security and avoiding conflicts between different applications.
- **Version control and reproducibility**: A container allows you to store, share, and deploy specific versions of an application, ensuring that a single version is used in different environments, thus improving reproducibility.

Like any system, there are also disadvantages:

- **Security concerns**: It can introduce some vulnerabilities, especially if you're not shrewd and handy with Docker. It has a certain learning curve, especially if you want to use the system efficiently.
- **Data management**: Containers are ephemeral by design, meaning that any data inside a container will be lost if the container is destroyed. Although there are solutions to this problem, it requires more complexity than traditional systems.
- **Complexity**: Docker makes deploying and managing individual containers easy; scaling and orchestrating large numbers of containers across many nodes can become complex. Docker's networking model, while flexible, can be difficult to set up and manage, particularly when containers are spread across multiple hosts. In addition, complexities increase if there are several containers and associated tools. Also, the OS kernel is limited, making debugging and implementing certain features more complex.

While Docker containers offer many advantages such as portability, efficiency, isolation, and scalability, they also come with challenges, especially related to security, complexity, and data management.

Sometimes, our system can be particularly complex and have more than one container; in the following subsection, we will discuss Kubernetes, which allows us to orchestrate multiple containers.

Kubernetes

Kubernetes is an open source container orchestration platform that automates the deployment, scaling, management, and operation of containerized applications. It manages and orchestrates containers in production environments.

In Kubernetes, a Pod is a group of one or more containers that are tied together and share resources such as networks and storage. The containers in a Pod are always deployed together and share the same environment. A Service is an abstraction that defines a logical set of Pods and a policy to access them. Services allow us to manage how our Pods are connected internally or are open to the outside world (during production deployment). A node, on the other hand, is a physical or virtual machine that runs containers in the Kubernetes cluster. Each node in the cluster runs at least one kubelet (the agent that runs containers) and a kube-proxy (networking proxy for managing communication between containers). A group of nodes is called a cluster, and clusters are the backbone of a Kubernetes environment that provides resources such as CPU, memory, and storage to applications. Kubernetes facilitates the deployment and maintenance of containers, allowing easier scaling and production of applications. It also allows us to better manage sensitive data configuration and data management in general.

Kubernetes is widely used to deploy, manage, and scale microservices-based applications. It is also a popular choice in DevOps practices due to its ability to automate deployments and scale applications.

Docker with ML

Over the years, Docker has been extensively used with ML models, both for running models and for ML-based creations. It allows you to set up a workspace that is ready to code, where all the dependencies needed are managed so that the process of using a model is expedited. Docker also allows for improved reproducibility of models, both for training and inference.

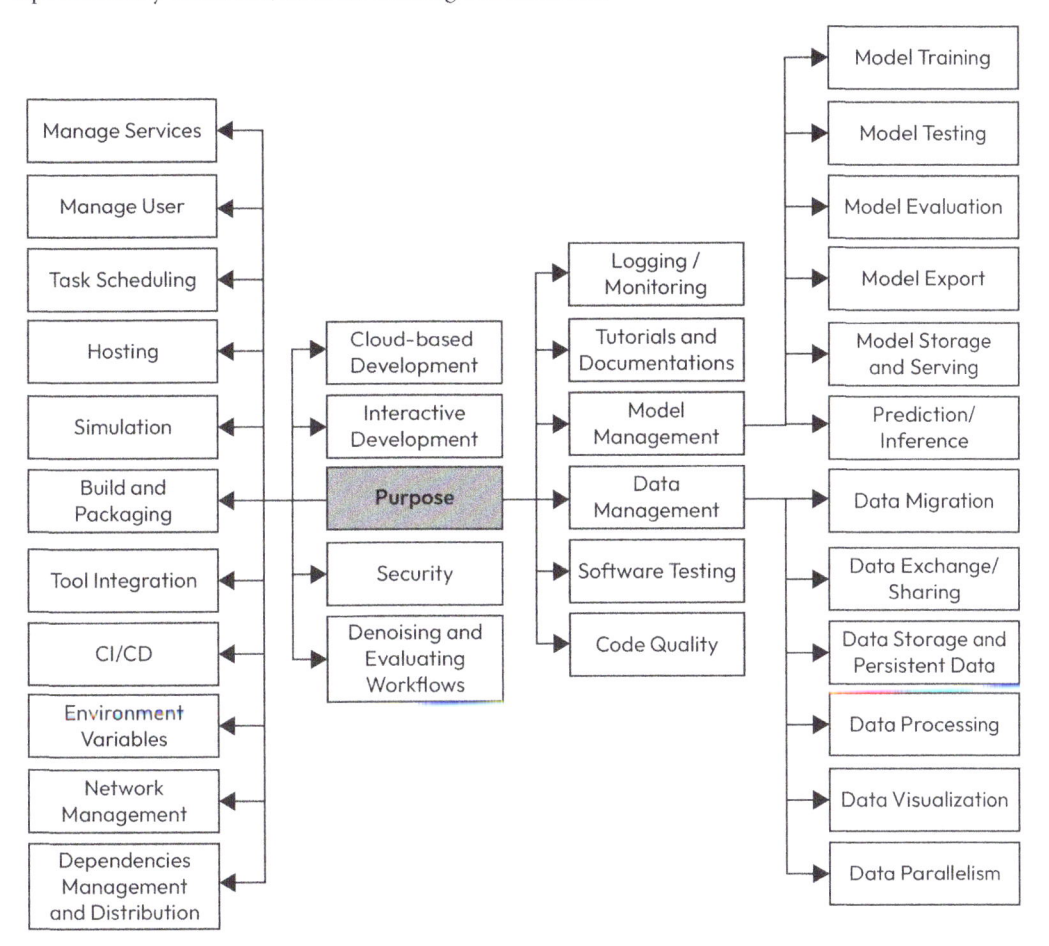

Figure 10.52 – Overview of the purposes of using Docker for ML-based software projects (`https://arxiv.org/pdf/2206.00699`)

Docker can be used with any ML application, including using LLMs and agents. For example, Ollama has its own Docker image available on Docker Hub, thus making it easy to create applications with LLMs and be able to directly deploy them to a server. Our application can also contain RAG or other components.

Also, as Docker containers are now used in various applications and LLMs are used to generate code, an LLM can be used to address the challenges of environment configuration in software development, particularly when using Docker for containerization. In fact, many software repositories require specific dependencies to function properly, and setting up the environment correctly is error-prone, time-consuming, and difficult for users. Docker allows the process to be more robust and reproducible, but Dockerfiles must be configured manually and can be complex when a project has many dependencies or when the configuration involves multiple steps that need to be executed in a specific order. Therefore, it was proposed to use an LLM to act as an intelligent agent that understands the dependencies and requirements of a repository and can generate a fully automated configuration that works in a Docker container. **Repo2Run** is an approach that leverages an LLM as an agent to control the process and ensure that the environment is properly configured before being deployed.

Repo2Run automatically generates Dockerfiles, which are used to configure Docker containers. Dockerfiles contain a set of instructions for setting up a Docker container environment, including installing dependencies and setting up necessary configurations. The system inspects a given Python repository, detects its dependencies (e.g., from files such as `requirements.txt` or Pipfile), and then formulates a Dockerfile to recreate the necessary environment. The core innovation in Repo2Run lies in its use of LLMs to drive the configuration process. The LLM intelligently understands the structure of the repository and its dependencies, reducing the need for manual intervention. It automates steps that are traditionally tedious and prone to errors, such as dependency resolution and configuration setup.

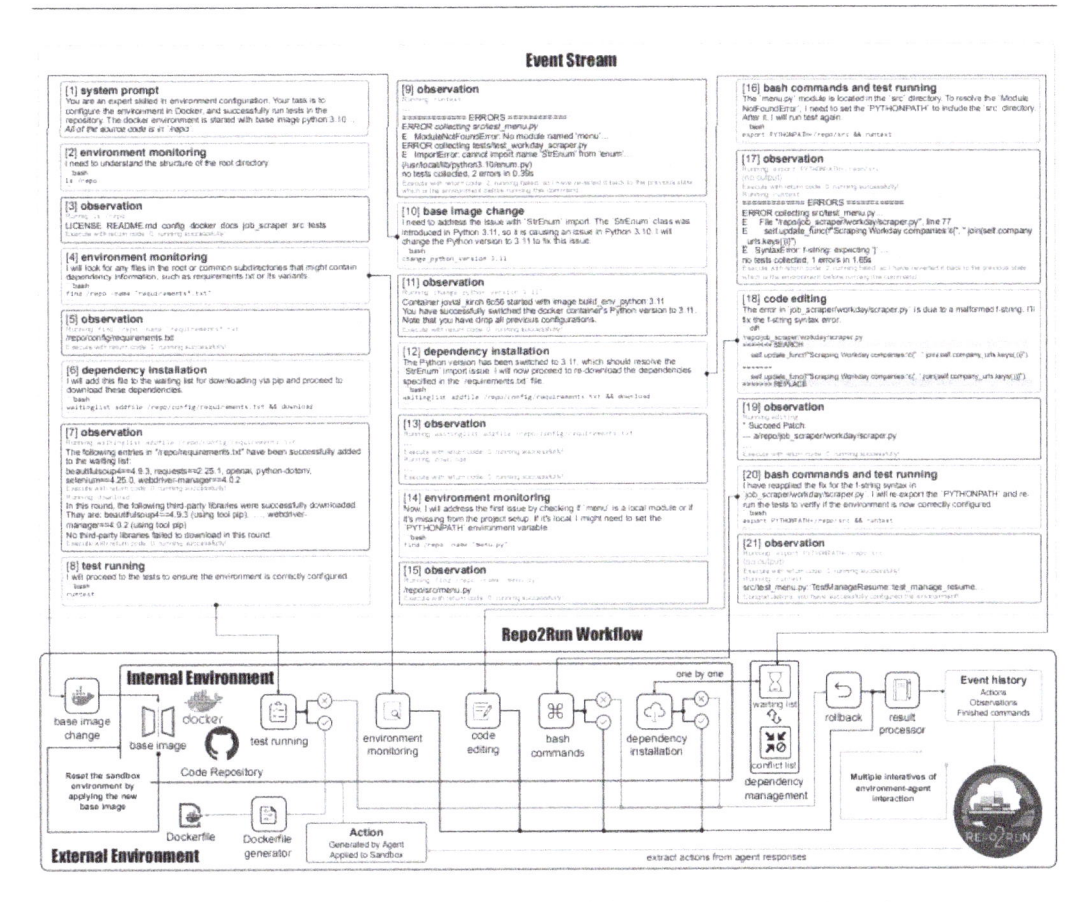

Figure 10.53 – Example process of Repo2Run (https://www.arxiv.org/pdf/2502.13681)

Moving Docker containers to Kubernetes requires a set of configuration files that describe how applications run within Kubernetes clusters (Kubernetes manifests). This migration can be complex, especially for large applications that contain several containers and services. Conducting this process can be error-prone, time-consuming, and difficult to manage, especially for teams without in-depth Kubernetes expertise. Therefore, some works (such as Ueno, 2024) propose to use an LLM to assist in this process and generate the manifest.

The **LLMSecConfig** framework aims to address a critical problem in the security of containerized applications and **container orchestrators** (**COs**) such as Kubernetes. CO tools are used to manage the deployment, scaling, and networking of containerized applications. However, due to their complexity, many possible misconfigurations can expose security vulnerabilities. For instance, misconfigured access controls, improper resource limitations, or insecure network policies can leave applications open to attacks.

These misconfigurations are common because the process requires a high level of expertise and is manual. **Static analysis tools** (**SATs**) are used to detect misconfigurations by analyzing the configuration files of containerized applications, such as Kubernetes YAML files or Dockerfiles. Although SATs are a good solution for detecting vulnerabilities, they lack automation and require manual effort. LLMSecConfig proposes to use RAG and LLMs to find relevant information from external sources to identify misconfigurations. The goal then is to make the process automated, in which vulnerabilities are identified and fixed at the same time while maintaining operational containers.

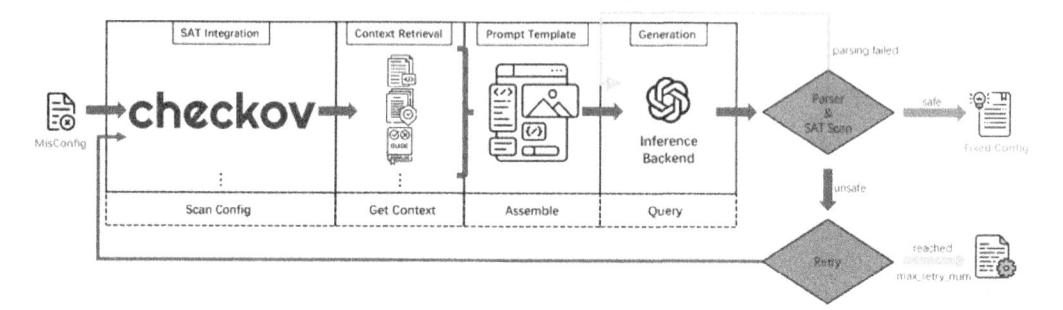

Figure 10.54 – Architecture overview of the LLMSecConfig framework for automated Kubernetes security configuration (`https://arxiv.org/pdf/2502.02009`)

These approaches show that not only can Docker be used for LLM applications but also, conversely, LLMs can be used to enhance the use of containers, especially when the application goes into production.

Summary

This chapter focused on an important aspect of how we plan a multi-agent system. Whatever form our system takes, it must eventually go into production and be used by users. The experience for users is pivotal to whatever project we have in mind. That is why we started by using Streamlit, a framework that allows us to experiment quickly and get an initial proof of concept. Being able to get a prototype of our system allows us to understand both strengths and weaknesses before investing large resources in scaling. The advantage of Streamlit is that it allows us to analyze both the backend and the frontend, enabling us to interact with an application as if we were one of the users. Streamlit allows us to test what a complete product may look like before we conduct scaling and system optimization.

Obviously, an application will then have to pass this prototype stage to enter production. This step requires that we conduct scaling of our application. LLMs are complex products that need a lot of resources, so during the second half of the chapter, we dealt with all those operations that enable the training and what happens afterward. Although we kept a main focus on LLMs, everything we saw can be useful for any ML application.

In the next and final chapter of the book, we will discuss the perspectives of a field that is constantly evolving. We will discuss some important open questions and some of the future opportunities and developments that the exciting field of agents holds for us.

Further reading

- Hewage, *Machine Learning Operations: A Survey on MLOps Tool Support*, 2022, `https://arxiv.org/abs/2202.10169`
- Park, *LlamaDuo: LLMOps Pipeline for Seamless Migration from Service LLMs to Small-Scale Local LLMs*, 2024, `https://arxiv.org/abs/2408.13467`
- Zhao, *A Survey of Large Language Models*, 2023, `https://arxiv.org/abs/2303.18223`
- Chang, *A Survey on Evaluation of Large Language Models*, 2023, `https://arxiv.org/abs/2307.03109`
- IBM, *LLM evaluation: Why Testing AI Models Matters*, `https://www.ibm.com/think/insights/llm-evaluation`
- Guo, *Evaluating Large Language Models: A Comprehensive Survey*, 2023, `https://arxiv.org/abs/2310.19736`
- Shi, *Keep the Cost Down: A Review on Methods to Optimize LLM's KV-Cache Consumption*, 2024, `https://arxiv.org/abs/2407.18003`
- Li, *A Survey on Large Language Model Acceleration based on KV Cache Management*, 2024, `https://arxiv.org/abs/2412.19442`
- Zhou, *A Survey on Efficient Inference for Large Language Models*, 2024, `https://arxiv.org/abs/2404.14294`
- Leviathan, *Looking Back at Speculative Decoding*, 2024, `https://research.google/blog/looking-back-at-speculative-decoding/`
- Determined AI, *Tensor Parallelism in Three Levels of Difficulty*, `https://www.determined.ai/blog/tp`
- Geeksforgeeks, *asyncio in Python*, `https://www.geeksforgeeks.org/asyncio-in-python/`
- Gim, *Asynchronous LLM Function Calling*, 2024, `https://arxiv.org/abs/2412.07017`
- *Asynchronous Computation*, `https://d2l.ai/chapter_computational-performance/async-computation.html`
- Openja, *Studying the Practices of Deploying Machine Learning Projects on Docker*, 2022, `https://arxiv.org/abs/2206.00699`
- Muzumdar, *Navigating the Docker Ecosystem: A Comprehensive Taxonomy and Survey*, 2024, `https://arxiv.org/abs/2403.17940`
- Saha, *Evaluation of Docker Containers for Scientific Workloads in the Cloud*, 2019, `https://arxiv.org/abs/1905.08415`

- Ru, *An LLM-based Agent for Reliable Docker Environment Configuration*, 2025, `https://www.arxiv.org/abs/2502.13681`
- Ueno, *Migrating Existing Container Workload to Kubernetes -- LLM Based Approach and Evaluation*, 2024, `https://arxiv.org/abs/2408.11428v1`
- Ye, *LLMSecConfig: An LLM-Based Approach for Fixing Software Container Misconfigurations*, 2025, `https://arxiv.org/abs/2502.02009`
- Docker, *LLM Everywhere: Docker for Local and Hugging Face Hosting*, `https://www.docker.com/blog/llm-docker-for-local-and-hugging-face-hosting/`

11
The Future Ahead

In this book, we started with how a neural network could digest text. As we have seen, neural networks do not do this natively but require the text to be processed. Simple neural networks can be used for some basic tasks such as classification, but human language carries an enormous amount of complex information.

In *Chapters 2* and *3*, we saw how we need sophisticated models in order to use semantic and syntactic information. The emergence of transformers and LLMs has made it possible to have models capable of reasoning and storing enormous amounts of factual knowledge. These multipurpose knowledge and skills have enabled LLMs to solve tasks for which they have not been trained (coding, solving math problems, and so on). Nevertheless, LLMs have problems such as a lack of specialized domain knowledge, continual learning, being able to use tools, and so on. Thus, from *Chapter 4* onward, we described systems that extend the capabilities of LLMs and which are designed to solve LLMs' problems.

In this chapter, we will discuss how some problems remain to be solved and what lies ahead in the future. We will start by presenting how agents can be used in different industries and the revolution that awaits us thanks to agents. Then, we will discuss some of the most pressing questions both technically and ethically.

In this chapter, we'll be covering the following topics:

- AI agents in healthcare
- AI agents in other sectors
- Challenges and open questions

AI agents in healthcare

One of the most exciting prospects for AI development is the possibility of having autonomous systems capable of conducting scientific discoveries on their own. This new paradigm is referred to as the *AI scientist*. Throughout this book, we have seen some examples of systems that are thought to be in accordance with this idea (ChemCrow, the virtual lab, and so on). In this section, we will discuss this paradigm in more detail: where the research is heading, the challenges faced, and future developments.

The idea behind an AI agent is to exploit LLMs in combination with tools (agents), as we have seen so far. In the future, researchers would like to add an experimental platform (an autonomous system able to conduct experiments by itself) to these systems so that they can conduct experiments independently. The complexity of biology could then be approached in a series of actionable tasks, where an LLM could break down a problem into a series of subtasks and autonomously solve them. The goal then would be to achieve discoveries not only more quickly but also more efficiently. The AI scientist would then be able to produce research at a speed and scale that would otherwise be impossible for humans.

In the first phase, humans would be at the center of the project. Scientists would provide input and criticism to the LLMs, and the models would incorporate this feedback into the process. During this iterative process, the model would analyze the problem, search the internet for information, and devise a plan, under human supervision (or otherwise using handcrafted prompts to guide it through the process). In such a scenario, an LLM would be an assistant to humans, where it proposes solutions and hypotheses. The ultimate goal would be to have an autonomous agent.

This vision is the culmination of a process that has been ongoing for decades in biomedical research. In fact, since the early 1990s, people have been talking about a new paradigm: the use of data-driven models. This paradigm shift has occurred because of technological advances and the vast availability of data. Biomedical research produces a large amount of data, and in the last three decades, this information has begun to be centralized in a series of databases. Simultaneously with this integration and new accessibility of information, all sorts of tools have been developed by researchers. At first, these computational tools were models and statistical methods, but gradually, biomedical research has also benefited from machine learning and AI models. In a sense, the successes of one propelled the successes of the other, and vice versa. The more data was centralized and made available to the community, the more this allowed new models to be developed. Discoveries obtained through new models and methods prompted the production of new experiments and new data. For example, transcriptomics experiments allowed for large datasets, which were perfect for developing new machine learning models and tools. These models allowed some biological questions to be answered, and these answers led to new experiments and thus new data. AlphaFold2 was only possible because of the millions of structures on the **Protein Data Bank** (**PDB**). AlphaFold2 allowed researchers to produce new hypotheses, later confirmed by new experiments and new structures on the PDB. In addition, the limitations of AlphaFold2 led researchers to collect new data for specific questions. These new data and experimental verifications led to new models, creating positive feedback.

As you can see, when the LLMs arrived, fertile ground for further revolution was already present. First, a vast amount of data (millions of articles and huge databases of experimental data) was available, thus allowing models either to be trained on this data or to be able to search for information through dedicated databases. For example, a model could search for information it missed on biological sequences through dedicated APIs. Or, an LLM could use RAG to search for information on new articles. Second, the community produced thousands of models to solve specific tasks. An LLM does not need to know how to solve a task; there is a curated list of resources it can use for a whole range of subtasks. An LLM then does not need additional training but only needs to know how to orchestrate these specific task tools and models. At this point, we have everything we need to be able to create an agent system. Agents can be found at every step of the biomedical research process, thus enabling future drug development in a shorter time frame and saving important resources.

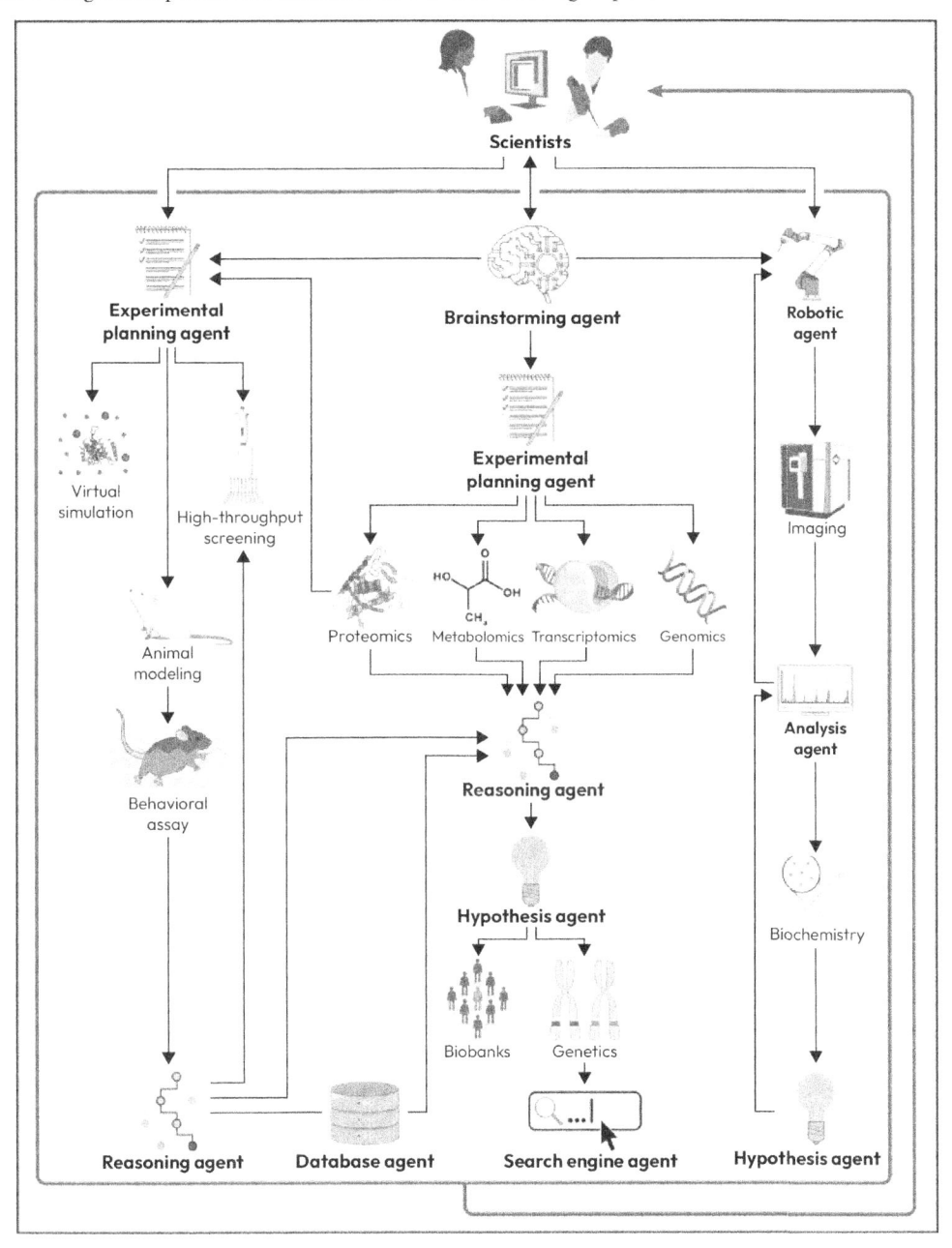

Figure 11.1 – Empowering biomedical research with AI agents (https://www.cell.com/cell/fulltext/S0092-8674(24)01070-5)

Biomedical AI agents

ChemCrow is an example of this type of agent, defined for a specific case and domain. The reasoning of the system is limited to the specific tasks; the agent must use the experimental data and existing knowledge. It is the researcher who defines both the hypothesis and the tasks; the system only has to complete them. Level 1 can be considered orchestrators under the supervision of a human being.

For example, ChemCrow has demonstrated concrete outcomes in research automation: according to a study published in *Nature Machine Intelligence*, ChemCrow autonomously planned and executed the synthesis of an insect repellent and three organocatalysts, and guided the screening and synthesis of a novel chromophore (*Nature Machine Intelligence*, 2024). Additionally, by integrating 18 specialized tools, ChemCrow has streamlined complex chemical research processes, significantly increasing efficiency and accessibility for both expert and non-expert users (*ScienceDaily*, 2024).

Most agent approaches are based on the use of a central LLM. An LLM is pre-trained with general knowledge and then aligned to human preferences to make the most of its knowledge and the skills it has learned during pre-training. The biomedical field requires specialized expertise and knowledge. Therefore, various experiments have often been conducted where an LLM has been fine-tuned to specialize in medicine (e.g., BioGPT, NYUTron, and MedPalm). This approach is clearly expensive, and a model becomes outdated quickly (thousands of papers are published every day). So, different approaches have been sought in which it is not necessary to conduct repeated rounds of fine-tuning.

One option is to try and use one model (one LLM) but with different professional expertise (assigning a specific role at each round). The idea is to use one model, but craft prompts to assign a role to the LLM (biologist, clinician, chemist, and so on). There are also other alternatives, for example, using instruction tuning to create an expert for a domain (so rather than aligning the model on specific knowledge, align it on specific tasks that would be an expert's). For example, we can ask a model to perform a task (*Write a sequence for a protein X that has a function Y*) or provide it with a specific role (*You are a biologist specializing in proteomics; your task is: write a sequence for a protein X that has a function Y*). A complex task can be performed by more than one specialist; for example, we can provide the model with the task directly (*Identify a gene involved in the interaction of the Covid virus with a respiratory cell; design an antibody to block it*) or break it down into several subsequent tasks (a first task with a first role such as *You are a professional virologist with expertise on the Covid19 virus; your task is: identify a gene involved in the interaction of the Covid virus with a respiratory cell* and then assign the model a second task: *You are a computational immunologist with expertise in designing blocking antibodies; your task is: design an antibody to block it*). In contrast to the previous approach to learning, a methodology (solving tasks) does not quickly become outdated like domain knowledge. Other authors suggest that one can instead simply use in-context learning.

This strategy means providing the model in context with a whole range of information that would be needed to play the role of a specialist (specific information about the role the model is to impersonate: definition, skills, specific knowledge, and so on). This strategy is very similar to assigning a role by prompt, but we give much more information. Although these prompts are full of information and instructions, the model does not always follow them. Also, it is difficult to describe in a prompt what a specialist's role is. So, an additional strategy is that the model independently generates and refines the role prompt.

Agents may therefore have different tools at their disposal and different purposes. The rationale for this multi-role approach is that an LLM does not have a deep understanding of planning and reasoning but still shows acquired skills. So, instead of one agent having to handle the whole process, we have a pool of agents where each agent has to take care of a limited subtask. Typically, in addition to the definition of different types of agents, there is also the definition of working protocol (for example, in the virtual lab, in addition to agents, a protocol of team and individual meetings was defined).

In any case, although there is so much expectation about a multi-agent approach where there is an LLM acting with several people, some studies give mixed results. In fact, some authors say that what are formally called "personas" (assigning a role to an LLM) do not give a particular advantage, except in rare cases. In any case, to date, it is necessary for these prompts to be precisely designed to be effective (and it is a laborious, trial-and-error process).

Since LLMs have good critical thinking skills, it has been suggested that they can be used in brainstorming. Although LLMs have no reasoning skills and limited creativity, they can conduct a quick survey of the literature. Agents can then be used to propose ideas, evaluate the best, refine and prioritize, provide critique, and discuss feasibility. One interesting possibility is to use a pool of agents where each agent has different expertise, which mimics the brainstorming discussion process.

Different frameworks can be created where agents interact with humans or with each other. For example, leveraging critique capabilities can facilitate the creation of agents with distinct goals to foster debate. One group of agents could focus on critiquing and challenging ideas, while another could aim to persuade and advocate for their viewpoints. Each agent could have different expertise and have different tools at their disposal. This approach, therefore, evaluates a research proposition from different perspectives. A research idea can then be viewed as an optimization problem where agents try to arrive at the best solution. In addition to a setting where agents are competing, the possibility of cooperation can also be exploited. Agents provide feedback sequentially on a proposition with the purpose of improving an idea. The two frameworks are not necessarily opposites but can be reconciled in systems where each idea goes through feedback loops and critique. Because the frameworks are organized with natural language prompts, multi-agent systems provide unique flexibility.

Similarly, it is not necessary that all agents be equal peers; hierarchical levels can be organized. For example, one agent may have the role of facilitating discussion or having greater decision-making weight. In the virtual lab, there is an agent that has the role of principal investigator, which initiates the discussion and has decision-making power. Thus, multiple decision-making levels can be instituted that are managed by sophisticated architecture.

Note that agents can then design experiments and, conjugated with experiential tools, these experiments can be accomplished. This would provide a new level of capability, toward a process that becomes end to end.

In this regard, Gao (https://www.cell.com/cell/fulltext/S0092-8674(24)01070-5) defined three levels of autonomy for an agent system in biomedical research:

- **Level 0**: A machine learning model is used as a tool by a researcher. The researcher defines the hypothesis, uses the model for a specific task, and evaluates the output. *Level 0* systems are tools such as models for making predictions in the biological field.
- **Level 1**: This is also defined as *AI agent as a research assistant*; the researcher defines a hypothesis, specifies the tasks that need to be conducted to get to the goal, and the agent uses a restricted set of tools. ChemCrow is an example of this type of agent, defined for a specific case and domain. The reasoning of the system is limited to the specific tasks; the agent must use the experimental data and existing knowledge. It is the researcher who defines both the hypothesis and the tasks; the system only has to complete them. *Level 1* can be considered orchestrators under the supervision of a human being.
- **Level 2**: Also referred to as *AI agent as a collaborator*, the system helps a researcher redefine the hypothesis thanks in part to its large set of tools. Despite its contribution to the hypothesis, its ability to understand scientific phenomena and generate innovative hypotheses remains limited. What differentiates it from *Level 1* is participation in hypothesis improvement and task definition to test it.
- **Level 3**: This is the last level and is defined as *AI agent as a scientist*. In this case, an agent must be able to develop and extrapolate novel hypotheses and define links between findings that cannot be inferred solely from the literature. A *Level 3* agent then collaborates as an equal to a researcher or can propose hypotheses on its own, defines tasks to test hypotheses, and completes them.

To date, we have no agents beyond *Level 1*, and we will probably need new architectures and training systems for *Levels 2* and *3*. *Level 0* is then a set of tools that are used by researchers but lack any autonomy. A *Level 1* agent can write code to conduct a bioinformatics analysis to process data, conduct statistical analysis, or use other tools. A *Level 1* agent uses *Level 0* tools to carry out these tasks, allowing it to test a hypothesis. A *Level 2* agent should not just perform narrow tasks on human indications but should be able given an initial hypothesis to refine it, decide, and perform tasks autonomously. We expect a *Level 2* agent, after being given the hypothesis, to be able to also refine experiments, and then critically evaluate to maximize a goal. A *Level 3* agent, on the other hand, should collaborate with humans to generate hypotheses, and can practically be considered its peer. A *Level 3* agent should be able to evaluate existing challenges and anticipate future research directions. In addition, a *Level 3* agent should integrate with experimental platforms to be able to conduct the entire process end to end.

AI agents in other sectors

In this section, we will discuss how LLM agents are having and will have a global impact across a range of industries.

Physical agents

Physical AI agents (for example, robots) are LLM agents that are capable of navigating the real world and performing actions. Thus, they can be considered systems that are embodied and integrate AI with the physical world. LLMs in these systems provide the backbone for reasoning and contextual understanding. On this backbone, other modules such as memory, additional skills, and tools can be added.

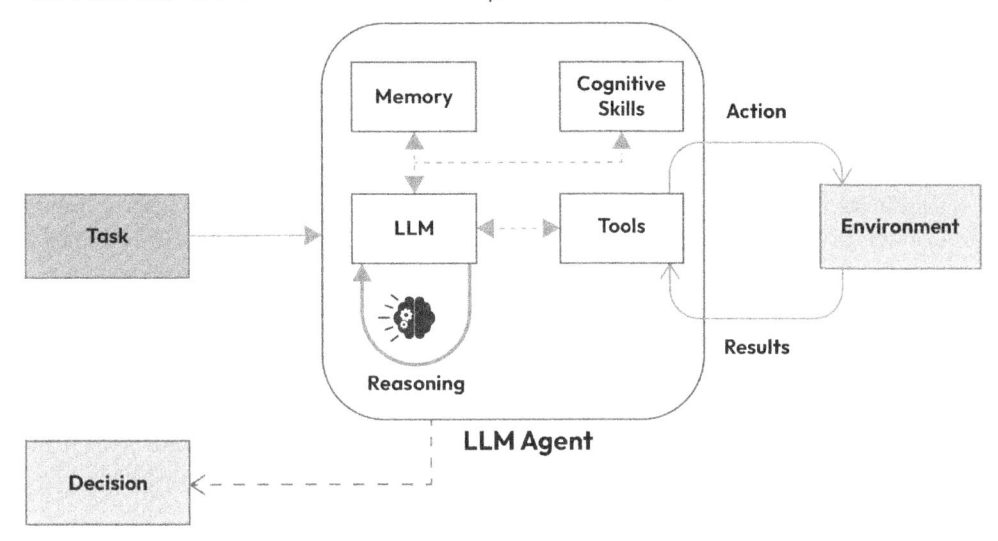

Figure 11.2 – LLM-based agent (`https://arxiv.org/pdf/2501.08944v1`)

Unlike a virtual agent, a physical AI agent must also understand and adapt to physical dynamics such as gravity, friction, and inertia. Being able to understand physical laws allows it to be able to navigate the environment and perform tasks.

There are several advantages to using an LLM for a physical agent:

- **Human interaction**: LLMs allow humans to interact more easily through the use of natural language. In addition, the use of LLMs allows for better communication and better management of emotions, allowing for easier acceptance. Likewise, people are already accustomed to collaboration with LLMs, thus predisposing users to collaborate more easily with robots to solve problems, generate plans, and perform tasks.
- **Flexibility and adaptation**: LLMs today are multi-purpose with generalist capabilities, which allows them to adapt more easily to different tasks and circumstances. In addition, for specific tasks and environments, LLMs can be fine-tuned to acquire new skills and knowledge needed to operate in different environments. LLMs also have reasoning skills and the ability to find information; this knowledge and these skills acquired during pre-training can be used to solve tasks for which they were not programmed. In addition, LLMs can be guided to perform a task through natural language, making it easy to explain to robots the tasks they need to accomplish.

- **Multimodal capabilities**: Today, several LLMs are capable of taking different types of modalities as input. This capability allows them to integrate information from different types of sensors, so they can understand their surroundings.

In recent years, the idea of combining LLMs and robots has already been explored. For example, PaLM-SayCan was an experiment in which they used Google PaLM to command a robot. Later, Google used a PaLM-E model, which is itself multimodal. In addition, new alternatives are being tested today in which **reinforcement learning** (**RL**) is used to improve the interaction of LLMs with the environment.

Several challenges remain at present for robots controlled by LLMs:

- **Datasets and training**: LLMs require extensive training with large amounts of data. Collecting these datasets is not easy; to date, there are no quality datasets to train a robot in an environment (datasets that require large amounts of images and text). A robot would have to be trained with task descriptions and how to perform them, making it expensive to acquire these multimodal datasets. Using RL requires that you acquire datasets in which you have information about the actions taken by the system and the effect on the environment. Datasets used for one task may not be useful for training in another. For example, a dataset used for training a dog robot cannot be used for training a humanoid robot). Robot training requires interaction with the environment; this is a laborious and time-consuming process. Efforts are being made to overcome this problem with the use of games and simulations. However, this alternative is a simplification of the real environment and may not be enough.
- **Structure of the robot**: A robot can be of an arbitrary shape. Today, motion robots are designed with human shape, but this is not strictly necessary. In fact, robots for particular applications might have different shapes. For example, a robot thought of as a chef might have a better shape if designed for its specific environment.
- **Deployment of the LLM**: The optimum in these systems is to place an LLM inside the robot. Deployment inside the robot is one of the limitations of current LLMs. Many LLMs require considerable hardware resources (different GPUs for a single LLM), which makes deployment inside a local brain not feasible. In contrast, today, the robot's brain resides in the cloud. This obviously has several limitations, especially when there is signal loss.
- **Security**: LLMs have biases and misconceptions that result from pre-training. In addition, LLMs can also hallucinate or commit errors. These factors can manifest themselves in errors while performing a task. An LLM who can control physical actions could then cause harm. For example, a robot could burn down a house while cooking. At the same time, LLMs can be hacked, posing the risk of private data leakage or intentional damage.

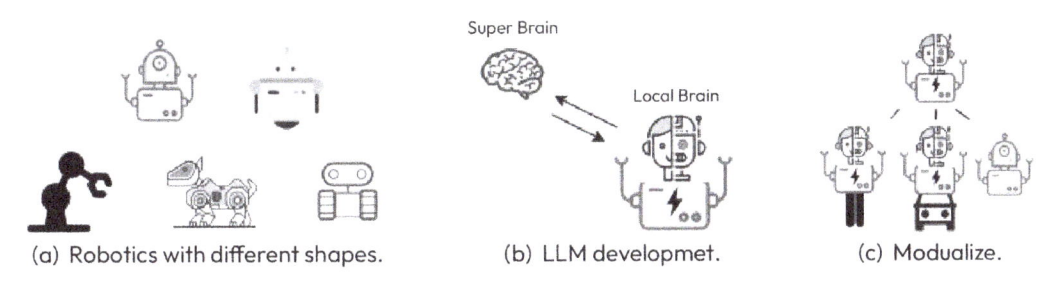

Figure 11.3 – Challenge in embodied intelligence (https://arxiv.org/pdf/2311.07226)

LLM agents for gaming

LLM-based AI agents for gaming are another interesting frontier, where the reasoning capabilities of the model are used to interact with the environment (the game). In general, a framework dedicated to gaming requires a set of components such as an LLM, memory, and tools to interact with the game. Often, the system is trained using RL (where a game is an episode). An LLM can then analyze the moves conducted in previous games and reason about what the best action is.

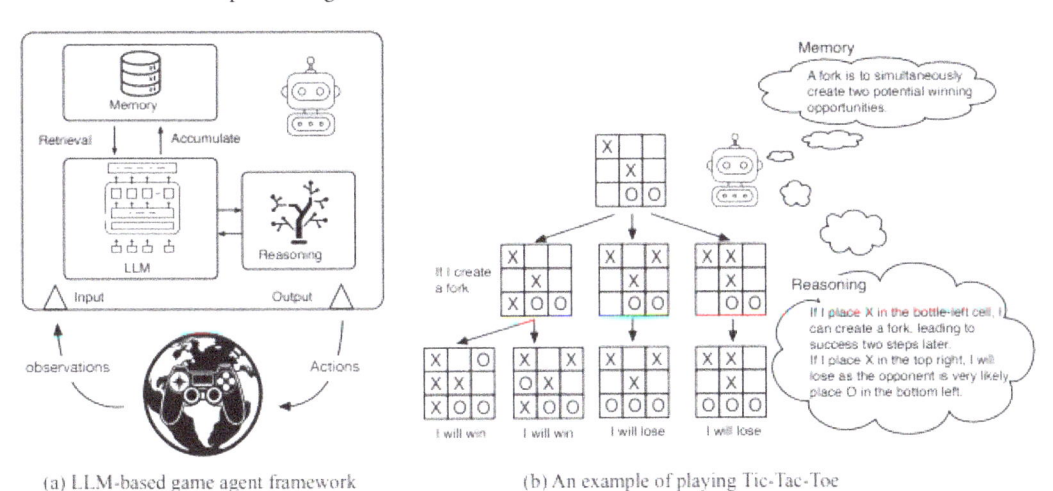

Figure 11.4 – Overall framework for LLM-based game (https://arxiv.org/pdf/2404.02039)

Especially today, many games are quite complex and there is sophisticated interaction with the environment and other characters. An LLM can then reason about the richness of textual information (object descriptions, task descriptions, dialogues with characters, etc.) to decide on a plan of action or strategy. For example, in Pokémon battles, each player has several Pokémon of different species. Each species has different abilities and statistics; knowledge of the game is necessary in order to win a battle. Using an LLM can allow you to leverage the model's implicit knowledge to be able to select an effective strategy (such as using an electric attack does not bring damage to a ground-type Pokémon).

In addition, an LLM can exploit techniques such as chain-of-thought (CoT) to integrate different elements into action choices (especially if it has to think several moves ahead).

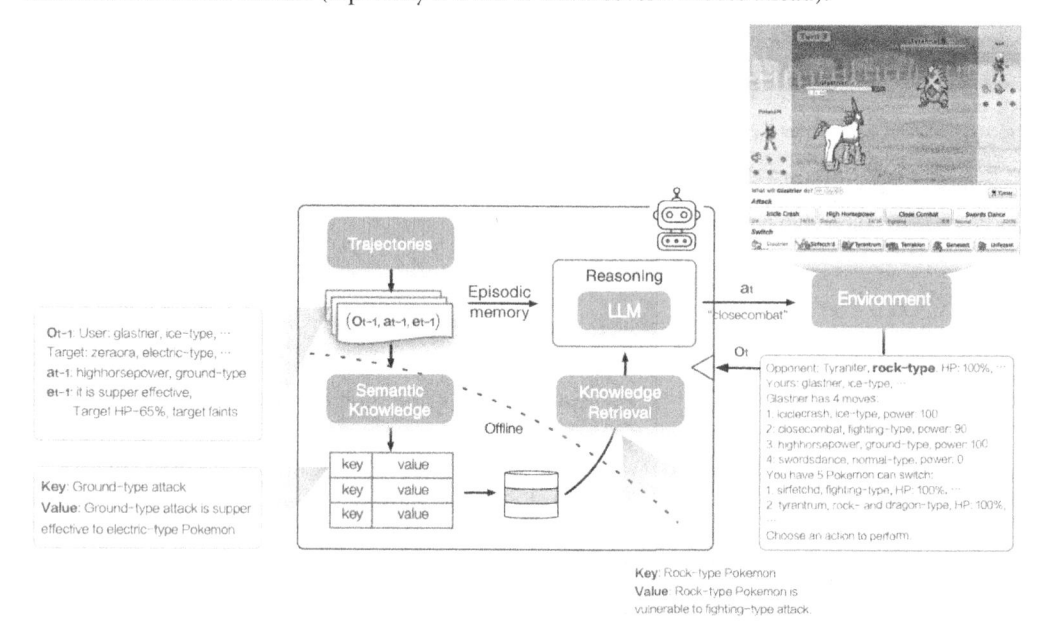

(a) An example of playing Pokémon Battles

Figure 11.5 – Use of semantic knowledge for devising an effective strategy (https://arxiv.org/pdf/2404.02039)

LLM-based agents are an interesting prospect for the game because they could enrich the players' experience. For example, LLMs could create characters who discuss more naturally with players, provide hints during the game, cooperate with them, and guide them through the adventure. Or they could be used to generate antagonists that are more complex and match the player's level.

Web agents

Web agents are AI agents designed explicitly to interact with the web and assist humans in tedious and repetitive tasks. Thus, the purpose of these agents is to automate these tasks and improve productivity and efficiency. Again, the brain is an LLM, which allows reasoning and task understanding to be conducted. The architecture of a web agent is similar to that seen in this book. A web agent has a module dedicated to perception (input from the web), reasoning (LLM), and a module dedicated to interaction with the web. The perception module requires interaction with the web via either HTML (text-based agents that read the HTML document and process it) or via screenshots of websites (use of multimodal LLMs). Once an LLM receives a task, it can then browse the web, schedule subtasks, retrieve information from memory, and execute the plan.

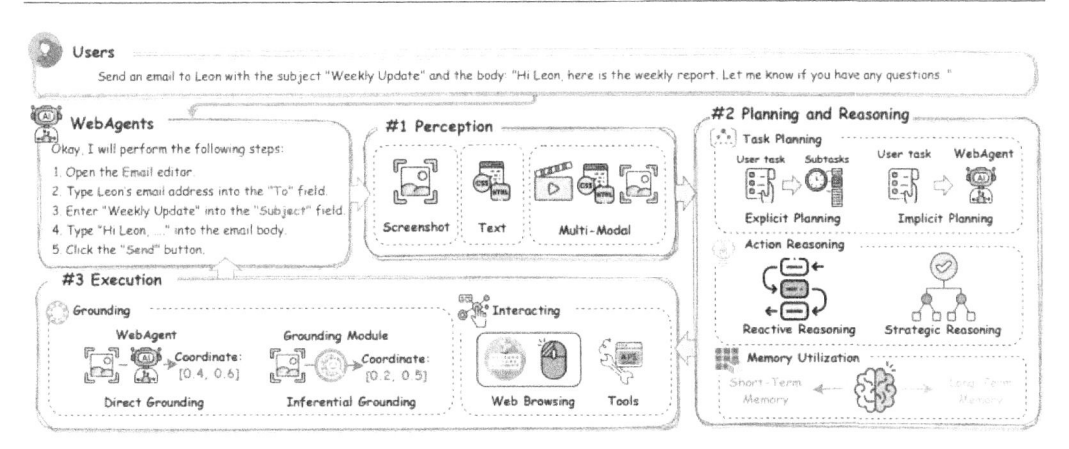

Figure 11.6 – Web agent framework (https://arxiv.org/pdf/2503.23350)

AI agents are a new frontier for AI, one that is poised to have a rapid practical impact. Despite their potential, several challenges and issues remain, which we will address in the next section.

Challenges and open questions

In this section, we will address several open questions about both agents and the capabilities of LLMs. Despite advances in the field, several points remain to be resolved for the safe use of AI agents.

Challenges in human-agent communication

Once they are deployed in the real world, agents can perform actions that lead to problematic failures. For example, a shopping agent might spend money unexpectedly or inadvertently leak sensitive information. Coding agents might execute or produce viruses, delete important files, or push repositories into production that are full of bugs. Communication with the user is key to avoiding such problems. The use of agents should be based on two key principles: transparency and control. Indeed, there must be an alignment between the user's goals and the agent's behavior; the user must then be able to control the process and have access to its progress. Communication between humans and agents allows us to advance these two principles, but some open challenges remain.

Modern agents are not yet completely perfect and can make mistakes (especially for goals that are complex or include several steps). Therefore, it is important that we can verify the agent's behavior, both the result of its work and that it has understood the task. Therefore, a way must be found to verify that the agent has understood the goal and that its plan and actions are directed toward this goal. Verifying that the agent has truly understood the goal allows us to avoid costly errors and save computation and time.

In addition, LLMs have a component that is stochastic. This component arises from the probabilistic nature of the model output functions (stochastic decoding) and the complex natures of interactions that can evolve during the task (unanticipated events). Therefore, the output and behavior of the model may not be consistent. Even in a deterministic setting (temperature 0), changes in the environment during task execution may lead to unexpected or unintended results. Inconsistencies may also emerge from the outdated model knowledge or imperfect world model present within an LLM. For example, an agent might buy an item that is out of budget or different from a user's needs, due to misalignment of its knowledge of the real world.

Similarly, interactions with the user and the outside world generate a great deal of information. This broad context is important for directing the agent's behavior, which can then be learned from past interactions. Although this context is fundamental to being able to perform the task effectively, it risks becoming far too wide and manageable over time. At the same time, modern LLMs have a noise problem and struggle to find relevant information when it is scattered in unnecessary detail. Therefore, effective ways must be found for an agent to focus on the relevant part of the last interaction with the user. Also, some of the information should not be able to be reused (privacy and ethical concerns), so one would need to find an easy way to manage, edit, and remove the past information.

What we have discussed are the general challenges of user-agent communication. We can also define open challenges that are in the communication between user and agent, and vice versa. First, we need to make sure that we can design agents that enable effective communication by the user by addressing these points:

- **Clear goal acquisition**: The focus of the system is for the agent to understand the goal and for the user to be able to provide it clearly. To avoid costly mistakes, we need to design agents for which users can define goals unambiguously. Some possibilities have been studied in some areas: sets of logical rules and the use of formal languages. To make this technology usable for everyone, we need to use natural language. Natural language is rich in both nuance and ambiguity, however, and allows complex goals to be defined with vague and incomplete definitions. Hence, mechanisms must be defined to disambiguate unclear goals or allow the agent to infer from context (or past interactions).

- **Respect for user preferences**: One can achieve a goal with several paths, but some are more optimal than others (both for efficiency and for respecting a user's preferences). User preferences may not be aligned with LLM values (during post-training, the model is aligned with human preferences, which do not necessarily reflect the preferences of a general user but only of a selected pool of annotators). For example, if a user requests a route, they may prefer a more eco-friendly means of transportation. The agent should adhere to these preferences when possible, or interrupt the process to inform the user when it cannot. Model alignment may be one possible approach to take user preferences into account. However, current alignment approaches primarily consider aggregate preferences, and methods for accommodating individual preferences remain undeveloped. In more general terms, an agent can also achieve a goal by generating harm (even in an unintended way), and this risk is greater if it has the ability to use tools.

- **Incorporating feedback**: We know agents are error-prone, and while we can develop strategies to reduce errors, completely eliminating them may not be possible. An agent might continue to use suboptimal tools (not understanding the goal or setting the wrong plan) in repeated interactions, frustrating the user. One way to correct this behavior is to provide feedback from the user. There is now research on how to incorporate this feedback and how to represent it in a more effective form for the agent (e.g., turn it into first-order logic).

There are also challenges that are associated with how the agent communicates to the user, especially pertaining to their capabilities, what actions they take or will take, goal achievement, and unexpected events:

- **Capabilities of the agent**: The user must be able to understand the full capabilities (and limitations) of an agent in order to conduct informed decision-making. It should be clear what information the agent has access to, how it will use this information, how it can modify the external environment, what tools it has access to, and whether it can connect to the internet.

- **What actions the agent will take**: To solve the goal, an agent can detail a complex plan, which can be particularly costly (time, resources, or money) and may violate some of the user's preferences. The user then should be aware of the actions an agent takes and be able to provide feedback. Of course, an effective form of communication must be found to avoid irrelevant details being communicated and the user not fully understanding the agent's actions. In addition, it should be clarified whether some actions require the user's explicit approval.

- **Monitor progress**: For an agent moving in a dynamic environment, a plan to complete a task requires several steps; it is useful for a user to be aware of what the agent is doing and whether it is necessary to modify the process or stop it. An agent conducting multiple actions at the same time could lead to unexpected and harmful behavior. For example, an agent who builds news reports and invests in the market might read fake news and conduct a series of bad investments.

- **Changes in the environment and side effects**: An agent must monitor the changes in the environment or potential side effects of its operations. Take, for example, an agent tasked with buying a product online at the lowest price available. The agent could search online and find the product at a very competitive price and order it. However, the offer might require a subscription or other hidden costs that would make the purchase much more expensive than the user's preferences or budget. The user must be aware of the side effects that are generated by the agent's behavior.

- **Goal attainment**: The user specifies a goal, and the agent plans actions and executes them. At the end of this process, the user must be clear whether the agent has achieved the goal or not (or partially). Thus, a way is needed to evaluate that a goal has been achieved. For example, the goal might be to buy the cheapest possible cell phone with a certain type of performance. The agent could lead the purchase, but we need to assess whether the agent has met the other conditions as well. Thus, we need a way to verify that the goal has been fully and satisfactorily achieved.

Communication with agents is a complex but critical topic. Miscommunication can lead to system failure and is an important point to consider. In this section, we have provided a list of important elements to evaluate user-agent communication from different perspectives. In the next subsection, we will see whether or not the use of multi-agents is superior to the single agent. Some studies question this perspective.

No clear superiority of multi-agents

As mentioned earlier, an LLM-based agent can be identified as an entity that has an initial state (usually a description in the prompt specifying its initial state), can track what it produces (state), and can interact with the environment through the use of tools (action). A **multi-agent system (MAS)** is defined as a collection of agents that interact with each other in a coordinated manner to solve a task.

MASs are an extension of single-agent systems, designed to create a more sophisticated framework capable of addressing complex problems. Obviously, this means a higher computational cost (more LLM calls in inference). This higher computational cost should be justified by a substantial performance gain. In fact, some studies show that this is not the case. MASs offer only marginal gains in performance compared to single-agent systems.

It is useful to outline the architectural trade-offs between single-agent and multi-agent designs. While MASs offer potential advantages in modularity and parallelism, they also introduce additional complexity, coordination overhead, and cost. The following table summarizes the key differences:

	Single-Agent Design	**Multi-Agent Design**
Cost	Lower: fewer inference steps and less orchestration	Higher: more agents, and more LLM calls and tool usage
Latency	Generally lower, streamlined single flow	Potentially higher due to inter-agent communication
Fault tolerance	Lower: failure in the agent often breaks the system	Higher: failures can be contained within individual agents
Modularity	Monolithic and harder to extend	Modular: agents can be added or replaced independently
Scalability	Limited: the agent handles all logic	Higher: parallel agents allow distributed problem-solving
Communication overhead	None (internal reasoning)	Significant: explicit agent-to-agent messaging required
Interpretability	Easier: single decision chain	Harder: distributed reasoning may reduce transparency

Table 11.1 – Potential causes of multi-agent system failure

As shown in the preceding table, multi-agent architectures introduce a set of trade-offs that must be carefully balanced. While they offer modularity and potential fault isolation, they often suffer from increased latency, communication overhead, and coordination challenges. These trade-offs are reflected in empirical evaluations of MASs.

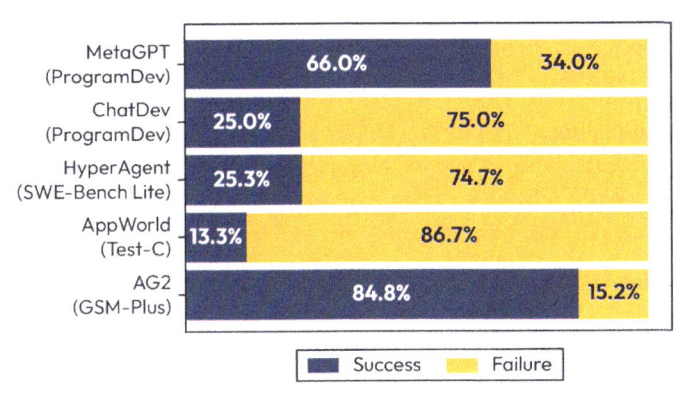

Figure 11.7 – Failure rates of five popular multi-agent LLM systems (https://arxiv.org/pdf/2503.13657)

MASs should bring numerous benefits, such as greater accuracy and the ability to handle more complex tasks, create more complex plans, or find better solutions. If MASs do not bring all these benefits and indeed often fail, we need to understand why. In a recent study, Cemri et al. (2025) set out to conduct a detailed taxonomy of MAS failures with expert annotators by analyzing 150 conversation traces (each averaging over 15,000 lines of text) to identify failures and the causes of these failures. In their work, they identified 14 causes, grouped into 3 main groups:

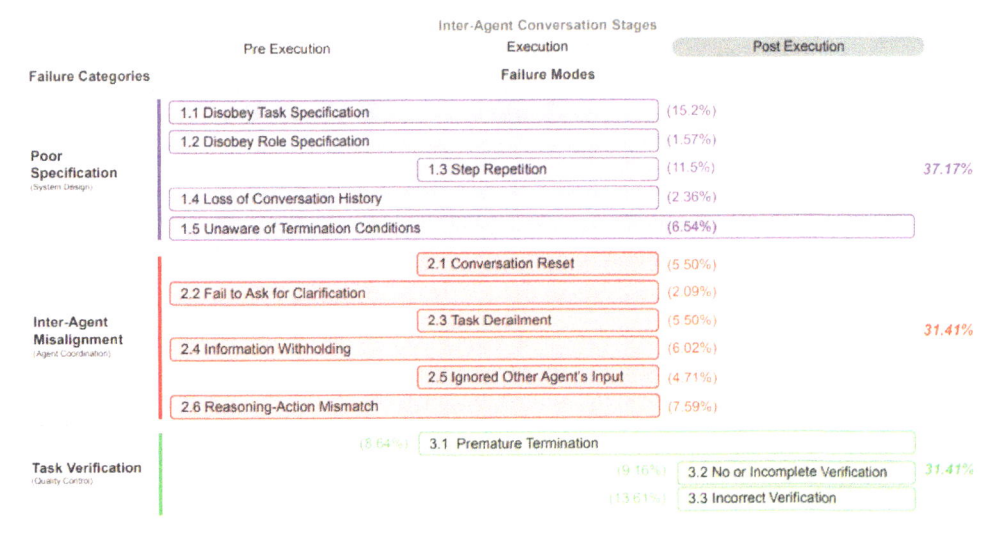

Figure 11.8 – Taxonomy of MAS failure modes (https://arxiv.org/pdf/2503.13657)

The three main categories are thus as follows:

- **Specification and system design failures**: Failure results from deficits in MAS design. For the authors, much of the failure stems from poor choice of architecture, management of conversation between agents, poor task specification, violation of constraints, and poor specification of agent roles and responsibilities. In other words, if the instructions for agents are not clear, the system may fail. Even when instructions are clear, however, the MAS may not be aligned with user instructions.

- **Inter-agent misalignment**: Failure emerges from ineffective communication, little collaboration, conflicting behaviors among agents, and gradual derailment from the initial task. As we mentioned previously, achieving efficient communication between agents is not easy. Therefore, some agents may not communicate efficiently and simply waste resources.

- **Task verification and termination**: A third important category includes failure to complete the task or its premature termination. MASs often lack a verification mechanism that checks and ensures the accuracy, completeness, and reliability of interactions, decisions, and outcomes. Simply put, many systems do not include a dedicated agent (or other mechanism) to monitor the process and verify that the task was successfully executed.

The results of their investigation showed that none of the causes are prevalent but are equally distributed across systems. In addition, some causes are correlated, producing a kind of ripple effect. For example, wrong architecture design can cause inefficient communication between agents.

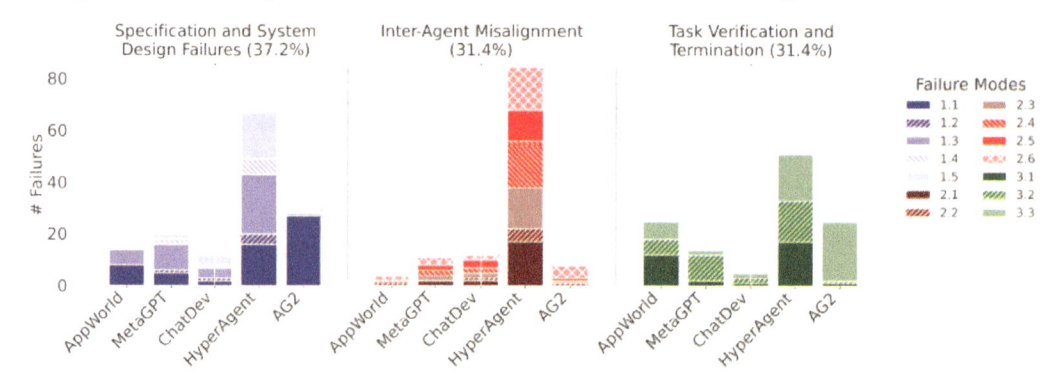

Figure 11.9 – Distribution of failure modes by categories and systems
(https://arxiv.org/pdf/2503.13657)

The results of this work clearly show that failures can be avoided through more careful design. Improving prompts, agent communication, and adding an agent (or other verifier mechanism) allow for noticeably improved performance and lower risk of failure. In two case studies, the authors show how this is the case. On the other hand, these suggestions are not enough to solve all agent problems but will be further technical progress.

In addition to the system itself, many of the limitations of agents also stem from the agent itself (i.e., the model that is used for agents). In the next subsection, we will discuss the reasoning limitations of LLMs.

Limits of reasoning

Reasoning is a fundamental cognitive function of human beings, and it is difficult to give a precise definition. Wikipedia defines reasoning this way: *"Reason is the capacity of consciously applying logic by drawing valid conclusions from new or existing information, with the aim of seeking the truth. It is associated with such characteristically human activities as philosophy, religion, science, language, mathematics, and art, and is normally considered to be a distinguishing ability possessed by humans."*

For a long time, it was said that only human beings are equipped with reasoning. Today, however, it has been shown that primates, octopuses, and birds also exhibit basic forms of reasoning such as making decisions or solving problems. One of the problems with reasoning is the difficulty of being able to evaluate it. Typically, to do this, one assesses the ability to solve complex problems or make decisions. Complex problem-solving requires identifying the problem, dividing it into subproblems, finding patterns, and then choosing the best solution. Decision-making similarly requires identifying problems and patterns and evaluating alternatives before choosing the best solution.

In the case of LLMs, an attempt was made to measure reasoning capabilities through benchmark datasets that assess problem-solving ability (such as GLUE, SuperGLUE, and Hellaswag). Today, on many of these datasets, humans have been outperformed by next-generation LLMs. These new reasoning capabilities would be mainly due to three factors:

- LLMs performing well in all the benchmarks dedicated to reasoning. These benchmarks contain math or coding problems that require reasoning skills. The results in these benchmarks suggest that LLMs are capable of reasoning.

- The emergence of new properties with increasing parameters, number of tokens, and compute budget.

- The use of techniques such as CoT, which allows the model to fulfill its potential.

There are those who question this view, claiming that there are alternative explanations for the performance achieved in these benchmarks. After all, many authors regard LLMs as nothing more than mere stochastic parrots. Jiang, in 2022 (`https://arxiv.org/pdf/2406.11050`), suggested that the models are merely pattern-matching machines: *"A strong token bias suggests that the model is relying on superficial patterns in the input rather than truly understanding the underlying reasoning task."*

In the same study, it was observed that LLMs fail to generalize when they encounter new examples that exhibit patterns different from those seen in the pre-training phase. If we change tokens in the examples, pattern mapping fails (a transformer, through in-context learning, tries to find examples in its knowledge that are similar to the problem posed by the user). When the model fails to find examples, the model fails to solve the question. This fragility and dependence on training examples would explain why the model succeeds in solving complex problems (it finds patterns) and fails even with some very simple questions (it does not find examples). This is confirmed by a correlation between the example's frequency in training data and test performance.

For example, when the model is asked to solve the classic "25 horses" graph theory problem, the model succeeds. If the "horse" token is changed to "bunny," the model fails to solve it. The token change is irrelevant to the problem's underlying logic, yet the model fails to solve it because it has difficulty mapping the problem. Both GPT-4 and Claude have significant performance drops due to perturbations in animal names and numbers.

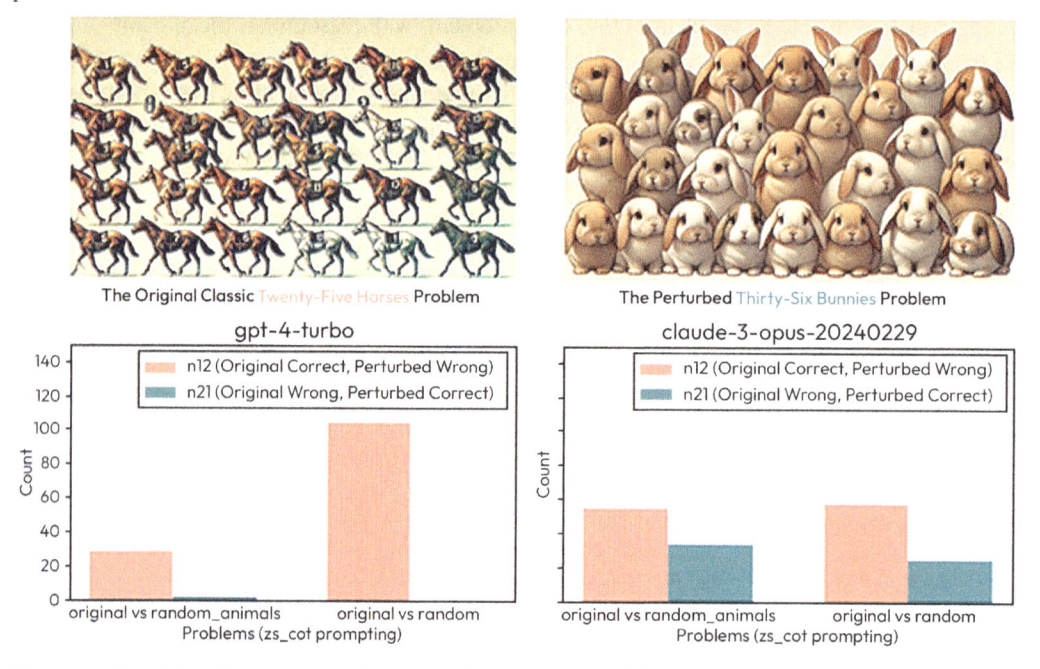

Figure 11.10 – Token bias using the classic problems (https://arxiv.org/pdf/2406.11050)

This phenomenon is called **prompt sensitivity** (a different response to a prompt that is semantically equivalent to another). This is confirmed by the fact that LLMs are sensitive to noise. They are easily distracted by irrelevant context, which makes it more difficult to find patterns. This sensitivity is not resolved by prompting techniques specialized to improve reasoning, suggesting that disturbing pattern-matching activity disrupts reasoning ability. An example of irrelevant context disrupting the pattern but not impacting actual problem-solving follows:

> **Original Problem**
> Jessica is six years older than Claire. In two years, Claire will be 20 years old. How old is Jessica now?
> **Modified Problem**
> Jessica is six years older than Claire. In two years, Claire will be 20 years old. *Twenty years ago, the age of Claire's father is 3 times of Jessica's age.* How old is Jessica now?
> **Standard Answer** 24

Figure 11.11 – Irrelevant context disturbs LLMs (https://arxiv.org/pdf/2302.00093)

Some authors suggest that intelligence can be seen as an emergent property. Biological systems naturally tend to become more complex, and this process is driven by natural selection. Evolution has shown an increase in intelligence over time as it promotes the adaptability of various species. Of course, intelligence is not an economic process, and a larger brain consumes a greater amount of resources (metabolic consumption). Loss function could be seen as evolutionary pressure. From this, it would follow that the increase in model capacity (in terms of the number of parameters) would parallel the increase in neurons in animal brains over time, and that loss function would instead be the evolutionary pressure to push these parameters to be used efficiently. By scaling up models and training (parameters and training tokens), intelligence could also emerge in LLMs. Reasoning then is seen as an emergent property that emerges from scaling the models. However, later studies suggest that emergent properties in LLMs can be a measurement error, and with it, the whole theory is related to the emergence of reasoning.

In the next figure, you can see how some properties seem to emerge as the model size increases.

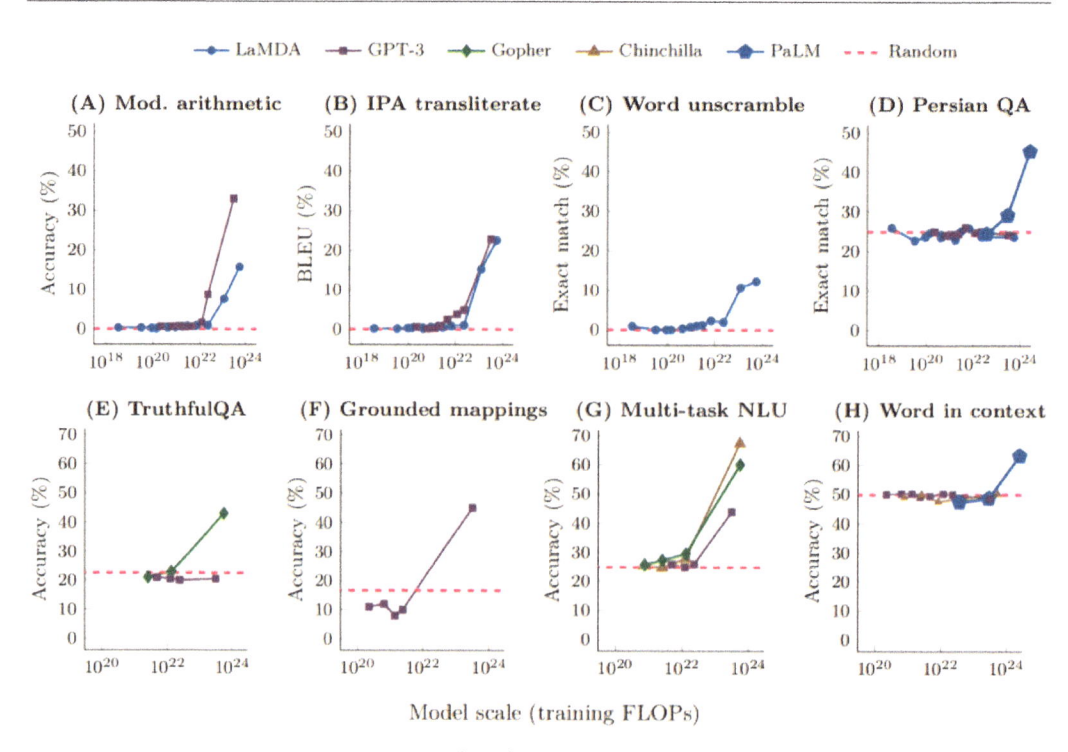

Figure 11.12 – Examples of emerging reasoning properties (https://arxiv.org/abs/2304.15004)

According to other authors, LLMs are capable of reasoning, but it needs to be unlocked. CoT prompting thus helps the model unlock its potential through intermediate reasoning and thus guides it to the correct answer in arithmetic problems. CoT is today's prompt engineering technique and is also used to train deep reasoning models (such as ChatGPT-o1 or DeepSeek R1). In fact, these models are trained on long CoTs that are used to conduct supervised fine-tuning. These models explore different reasoning paths to arrive at an answer, showing high improvements in reasoning benchmarks. However, some studies show that these models suffer from both overthinking and underthinking.

Overthinking is a curious phenomenon in which these models reason longer than necessary when it comes to solving problems that are particularly simple. The model explores different reasoning paths for trivial questions. This indicates that the model is unable to understand which question needs more effort. Underthinking is the opposite, wherein the model may abandon the promising thinking path. This indicates a clear lack of depth of reasoning, where the model does not go all the way to a correct solution.

At the same time, even the benefits of CoT have been questioned (https://arxiv.org/pdf/2409.12183): *"As much as 95% of the total performance gain from CoT on MMLU is attributed to questions containing "=" in the question or generated output. For non-math questions, we find no features to indicate when CoT will help."*

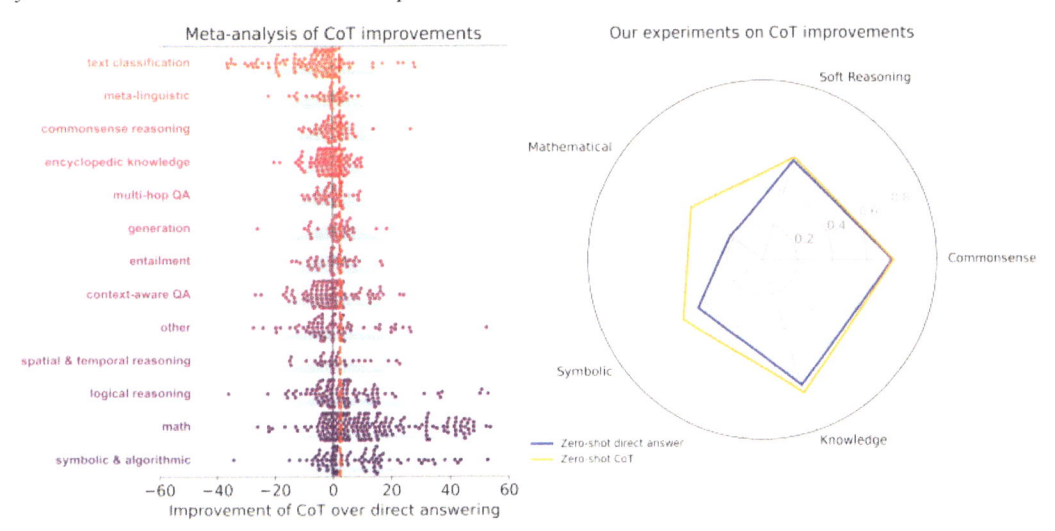

Figure 11.13 – CoT improvements are limited to symbolic and mathematical reasoning (https://arxiv.org/pdf/2409.12183)

CoT would seem to help the model solve problems as it allows it to leverage the skills it learned during pre-training. CoT would simply help develop a plan, but then the LLMs may not be able to execute it. So, CoT can be used to get a plan, but to get the most benefit, an external tool would have to be added (such as a Python interpreter).

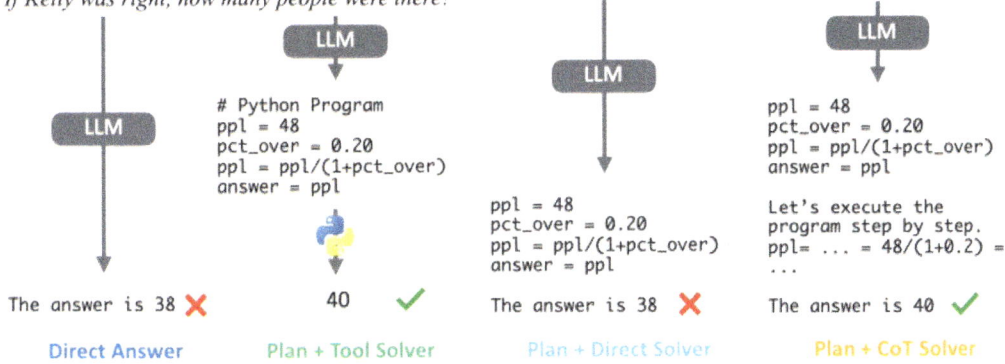

Figure 11.14 – An LLM can devise a plan but needs an external tool to better solve some problems (https://arxiv.org/pdf/2409.12183)

These models are all tested on the same benchmarks as the **Grade School Math 8K** (**GSM8K**) dataset, which provides complex arithmetic problems but is at risk of data leakage (considering how many billions of tokens are used to train an LLM, the model may have already seen the answer in the training).

Therefore, in their study, Mirzadeh et al. modified GSM8K, keeping the same questions but making statistical pattern matching difficult. If the model was capable of true reasoning, it should solve it easily; if, instead, it relied on pattern matching, it would fail.

In the following figure, notice how the GSM8K examples are modified to better control the response of the LLM. Using this dataset, we can formally investigate the LLM's reasoning and highlight that state-of-the-art LLMs exhibit significant performance variations; this shows that LLM reasoning is fragile.

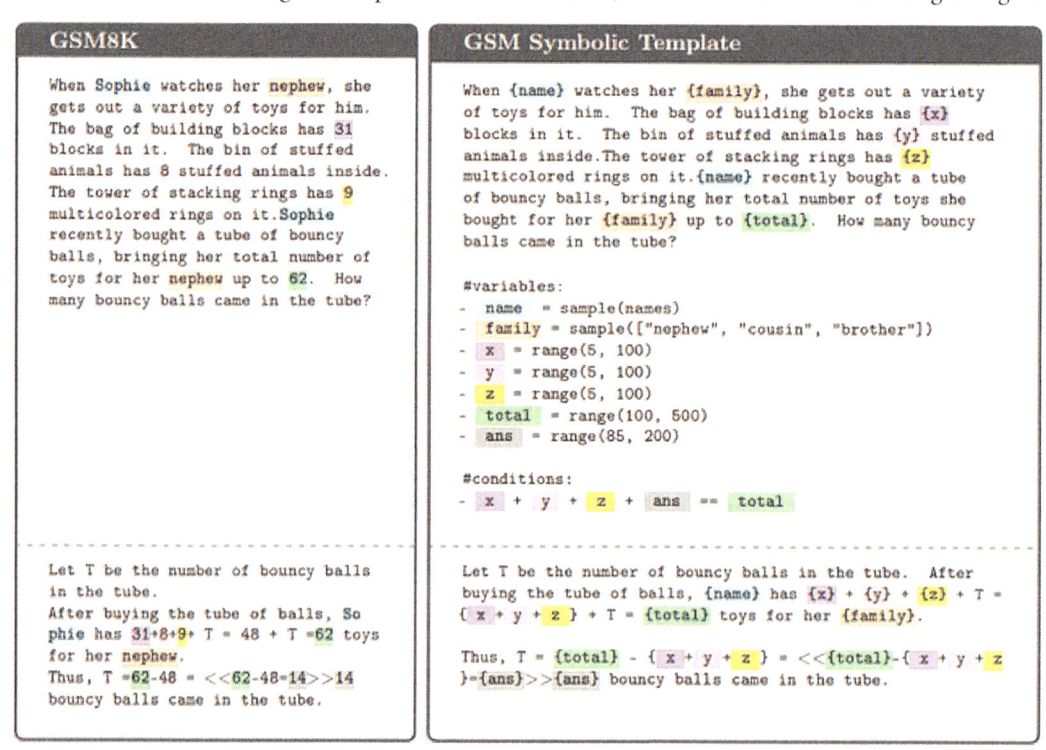

Figure 11.15 – This dataset serves as a tool to investigate the presumed reasoning capabilities of LLMs (`https://arxiv.org/pdf/2410.05229`)

Testing state-of-the-art LLMs, Mirzadeh et al. found no evidence of formal reasoning in language models. The models are not robust and have a drop in performance when numerical values are changed, and their capabilities degrade sharply as the complexity of the problem increases. The model is, in fact, fooled by added phrases that have no relevance. Instead, the model takes them into account, tries to map them, and sometimes turns them into operations. Mirzadeh et al. suggest that this occurs because their training datasets included similar examples that required conversion to mathematical operations: *"For instance, a common case we observe is that models interpret statements about "discount" as "multiplication", regardless of the context. This raises the question of whether these models have truly understood the mathematical concepts well enough."*

```
GSM-NoOp
Oliver picks 44 kiwis on Friday. Then he picks 58 kiwis on Saturday. On Sunday, he picks double the
number of kiwis he did on Friday, but five of them were a bit smaller than average. How many kiwis
does Oliver have?
------------------------------------------------------------------------------------
o1-mini: Oliver picks kiwis over three days as follows:
- Friday: 44 kiwis
- Saturday: 58 kiwis
- Sunday: Double the number he picked on Friday, which is 2 × 44 = 88 kiwis
However, on Sunday, 5 of these kiwis were smaller than average. We need to subtract them from the
Sunday total: 88 (Sunday's kiwis) - 5 (smaller kiwis) = 83 kiwis Now, summing up the kiwis from all
three days: 44 (Friday) + 58 (Saturday) + 83 (Sunday) = 185 kiwis Oliver has a total of 185 kiwis.
------------------------------------------------------------------------------------
Llama3-8B: Let's break it down step by step:
Oliver picks 44 kiwis on Friday. He picks 58 kiwis on Saturday. On Sunday, he picks double the number
of kiwis he did on Friday, which is 2 × 44 = 88 kiwis.
Five of the kiwis picked on Sunday are a bit smaller than average, so we subtract 5 from the total
number of kiwis picked on Sunday: 88 - 5 = 83 kiwis. Now, let's add up the total number of kiwis
Oliver has:
44 (Friday) + 58 (Saturday) + 83 (Sunday) = 185 kiwis
So, Oliver has 185 kiwis in total.
```

Figure 11.16 – Example of error (https://arxiv.org/pdf/2410.05229)

More recent LLMs that have been trained on CoT (such as GPT4-o1) also fail in this task. This suggests that LLMs are elaborate statistical pattern machines but do not possess true reasoning.

Creativity in LLM

Creativity is considered along with reasoning to be one of the skills that makes human beings. If quantifying reasoning is hard, being able to quantify creativity is a much harder task. However, creativity plays a very important role in what makes us human, and it concerns activities such as writing poems or books, creating works of art, or even generating theories and achieving groundbreaking discoveries. That is why the question as to whether an LLM can be creative has been raised.

The problem in investigating the creativity of LLMs is that we do not have an unambiguous definition of creativity. In the field of research, creativity is often used as the definition chosen by Margaret Boden: *"the ability to come up with ideas or artifacts that are new, surprising and valuable."* Although this definition is accepted, it is difficult to evaluate its elements:

- **Value**: This is the easiest element to define. For example, code produced by an LLM can be considered valuable if it works in its own way.
- **Novelty**: For an object to be considered novel, it should be dissimilar to what has already been created. For a text, being novel could be considered the difference in output compared to other texts. One definition might be to generate a text whose embedding is distant from other different texts.
- **Surprising**: This is considered one of the most important and difficult elements to define. Random recombination of words can be considered new (or different) but certainly not surprising (nor valuable). *Surprising* is often understood as something new but not a simple variation or recombination.

Boden at the same time described what she thought were three types of creativity with respect to the concept of surprise:

- **Combinatorial creativity**: The combination of familiar elements in an unfamiliar way (such as two genres that have not been combined previously)
- **Exploratory creativity**: The exploration of new solutions in the way of thinking (such as a new narrative style, or a twist to a narrative style that had not been explored)
- **Transformational creativity**: Changing the current narrative style or the current way of thinking

In line with these definitions, several authors have sought to understand whether LLMs can be creative, and if so, what kind of creativity they can manifest. The main problem with this investigation is trying to quantify the creativity of an LLM. One approach is to assess whether the output of LLMs can be mapped to existing text snippets on the web. Human creativity is influenced by previous writers, but when a writer produces original writing, this cannot be mapped to previous writings. If every text generated by an LLM can be mapped to other texts, it is overwhelming evidence of a lack of creativity. In a recently published study, Lu (2024) analyzed how much of what is produced by an LLM is mappable to texts on the internet. The purpose of this study was precisely to create a creative index and compare LLMs and human beings.

Challenges and open questions 503

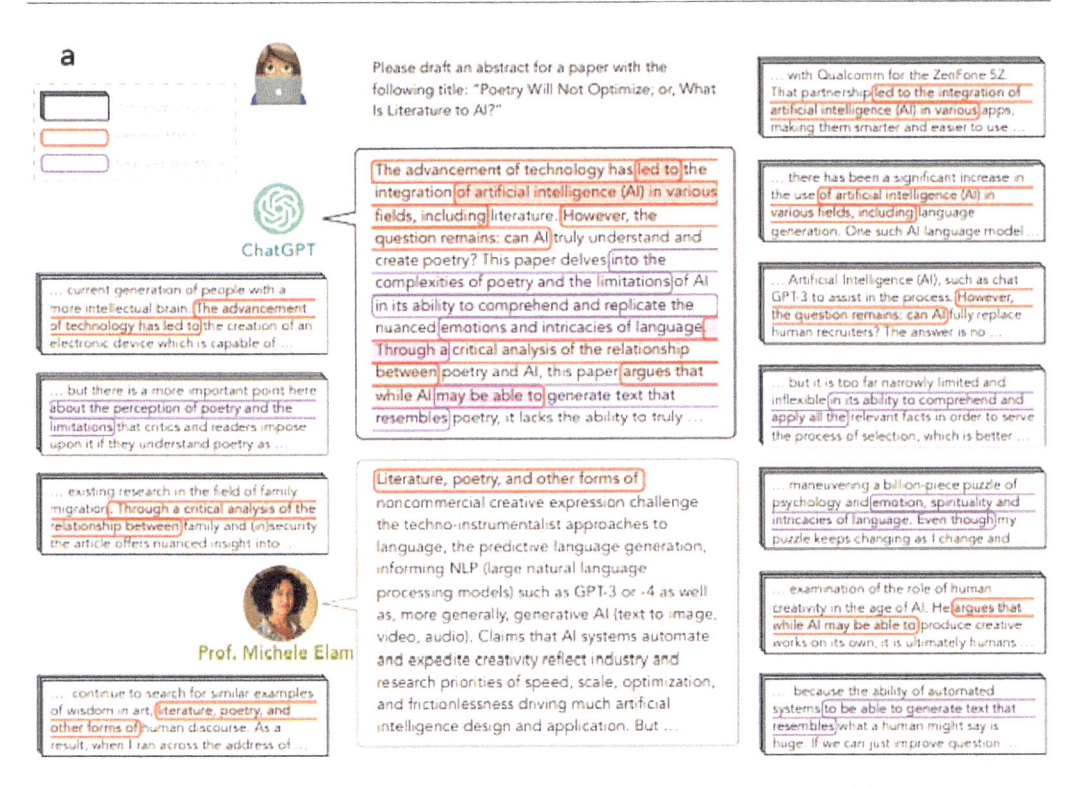

Figure 11.17 – Mapping of LLM output to internet text (https://arxiv.org/pdf/2410.04265)

The results of this approach show that humans exhibit greater creativity (based on unique word and sentence combinations) than LLMs. That small amount of residual creativity in LLMs may simply result from stochastic processes and the fact that we do not know the entire pre-training dataset.

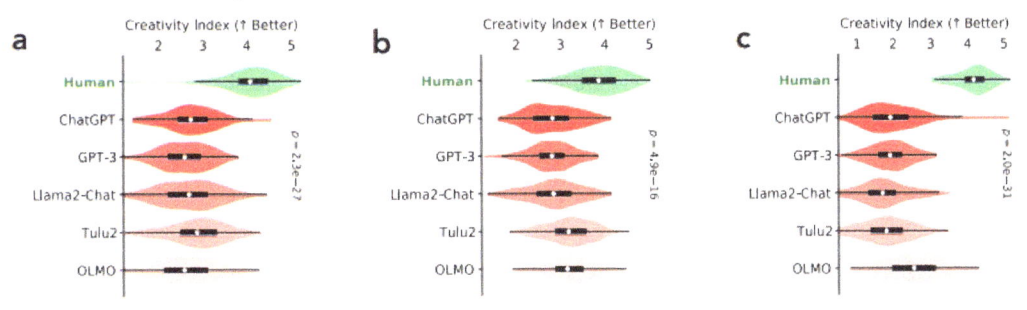

Figure 11.18 – Comparison between the creativity index of humans and that of LLMs (https://arxiv.org/pdf/2410.04265)

Lou et al. suggest an interesting analogy: *"Just as a DJ remixes existing tracks while a composer creates original music, we speculate that LLMs behave more like DJs, blending existing texts to produce impressive new outputs, while skilled human authors, similar to music composers, craft original works."*

Despite LLMs being incapable of true creativity, several studies have tried to increase the pseudo-creativity of models (in the long run, LLMs can be particularly repetitive). There are three potential strategies for doing this:

- **Acting on the hyperparameters of an LLM**: The first strategy coincides with raising the temperature of an LLM. Temperature controls the uncertainty or randomness in the generation process. Adjusting temperature impacts model generation, where at low temperatures (e.g., 0.1–0.5), the model generates deterministic, focused, and predictable outputs. Increasing the temperature generates output that becomes less predictable. Beyond 2.0, the process becomes chaotic and the model generates nonsense. So, for applications that require creativity, you can explore higher temperatures but remember that this also generally leads to a reduction in consistency.

- **Conducting additional training for an LLM**: The use of post-training techniques is an avenue that is being explored widely today. Post-training techniques are used for model alignment and to make the model more receptive to performing tasks. Some authors have proposed using techniques that also incentivize the variety of outputs.

- **Prompting strategy**: Use prompts that try to force the model to be more creative. However, prompting strategies do not seem to have great results.

Mechanistic interpretability

Recent advances in AI have meant rapid advancement in model capabilities. Paradoxically, the paradigm of self-supervised learning means that even if models are designed by humans, the capabilities of LLMs are not designed a priori. In theory, a developer only needs to know the process without understanding how the model works, since the desired properties appear during training. In other words, an LLM is not designed for the properties it shows; these properties were obtained through scaling, and much of how it gets there is unclear. Reconstructing how they appear and the mechanisms behind these abilities is not an easy task, especially after a model of billions of parameters has been trained. These models are considered to be black boxes, and recently, there has been some discussion of how they can be analyzed.

There are several types of interpretability for a model (as described in the following list and figure). Each of these types of interpretability focuses on different aspects.

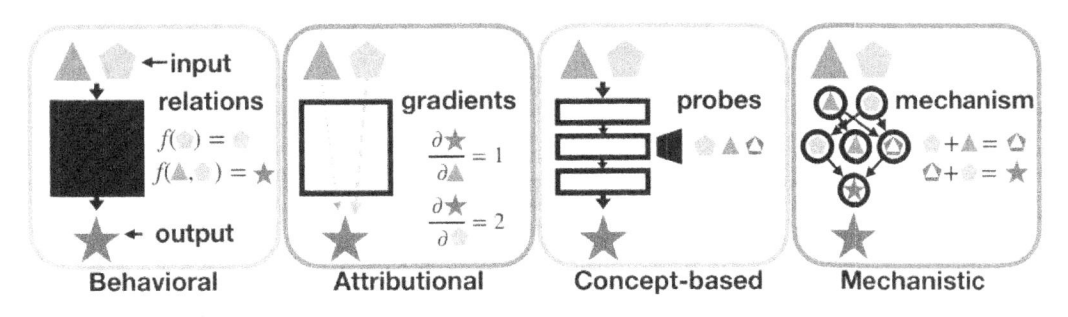

Figure 11.19 – Progressive level of interpretation of a model
(https://arxiv.org/pdf/2404.14082)

We can divide the various types of approaches to interpretability into the following:

- **Behavioral**: One considers the model as a black box and is interested in the relationship between input and output. This paradigm considers those classical approaches to interpretability that are model-agnostic.
- **Attributional**: The approaches try to understand the decision-making processes of the model by tracking the contribution of each component of the input and are based on the gradient shift.
- **Concept-based**: Probes are used to try to better understand the learned representation of the model.
- **Mechanistic**: This is a granular analysis of the components and how they are organized, trying to identify causal relationships.

Mechanistic interpretability aims to uncover the internal decision-making processes of a neural network by identifying the mechanisms that produce its outputs. We focus on this approach because it emphasizes understanding the individual components of a model and how they contribute to its overall behavior. This perspective is valuable as it enables us to analyze the model through a comprehensive and transparent lens.

Mechanistic interpretability goes beyond previous approaches because it seeks to identify causal mechanisms to the generalization of neural networks, and thus the decision-making processes behind them. In response to the growth of models and their increased capabilities, there has been a question of how these models acquire these general capabilities, and thus a need for global explanations.

Although LLMs generate text that resembles that produced by humans, this does not mean that the representation of concepts and cognitive processes are the same. This is demonstrated by the fact that LLMs display superhuman performance on some tasks, whereas in other tasks that are simple for humans, they fail miserably. We need a way to solve this paradox, which is through mechanistic interpretability. To try to resolve this dissonance, reverse engineering of LLMs has been proposed. Reverse engineering (a mechanistic interpretability approach) involves three steps: decomposing the model into simpler parts, describing how these parts work and how they interact, and testing whether the assumptions are correct. While mechanistic interpretability aims to uncover the internal logic and causal mechanisms within the network, concept-based interpretability focuses on understanding how models represent high-level, human-understandable concepts and how these concepts contribute to the model's decisions, providing insights into the reasoning behind predictions and bridging the gap between human cognition and machine learning processes. These two approaches are shown in the following figure:

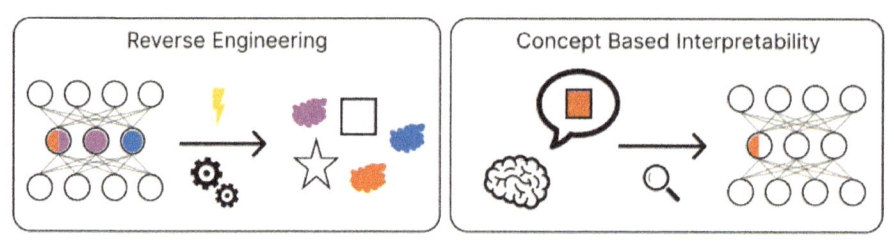

Figure 11.20 – Reverse engineering (https://arxiv.org/pdf/2501.16496)

The problem with this approach is that it is difficult to decompose neural networks into functional components. In fact, in neural networks, neurons are polysemantic and represent more than one concept. So, the interpretation of single components is not very useful, and can instead be misleading. Authors today focus on trying to decompose into functional units that incorporate multiple neurons even on multiple layers. Since these concepts are represented by multiple neurons (superposition hypothesis), attempts are made to disentangle this sparse representation through the use of tools that force sparsity.

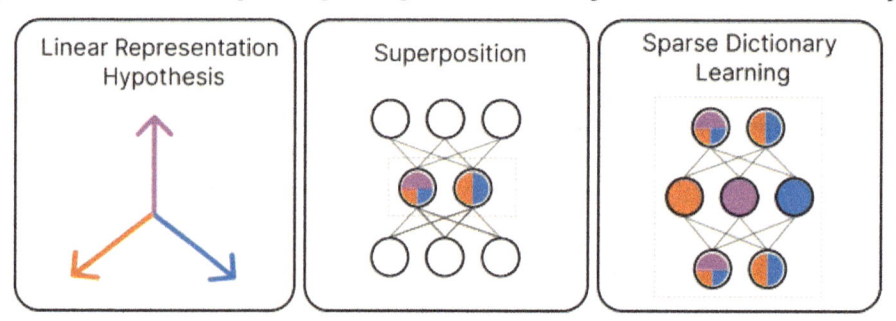

Figure 11.21 – Disentangle superimposed representation with SDL (https://arxiv.org/pdf/2501.16496)

This shift toward decomposing the model into functional units that incorporate multiple neurons and layers requires new techniques.

Sparse dictionary learning (**SDL**) includes a number of approaches that allow a sparse representation of what a model has learned. **Sparse autoencoders** (**SAEs**) are one such approach that allows us to learn sparse features that are connected to model features and make what the model has learned more accessible. SAEs use an encoder and decoder to sparsify the superimposed representation within the model.

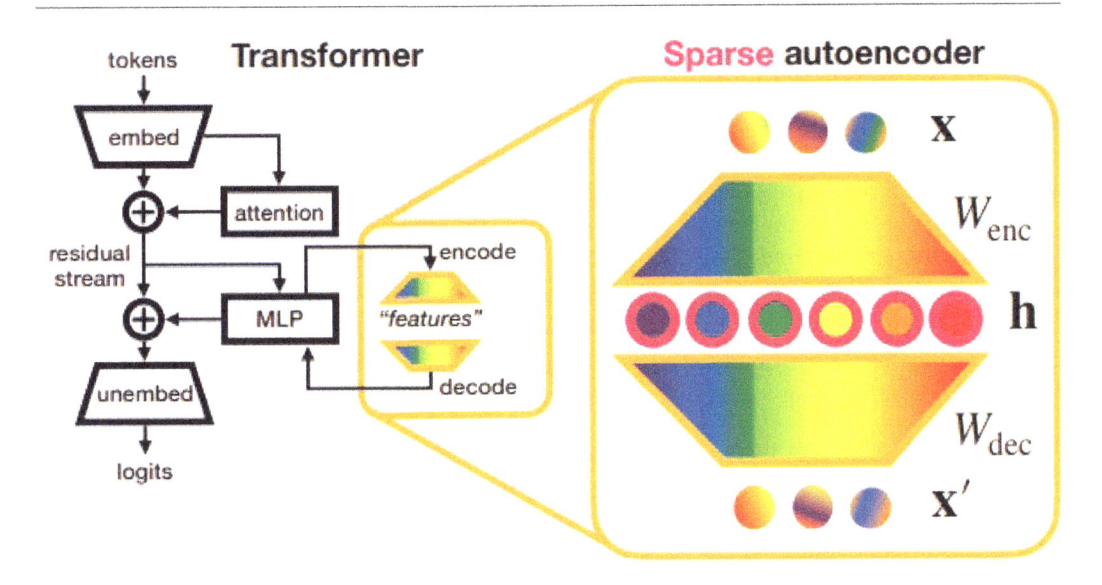

Figure 11.22 – Illustration of an SAE applied to an LLM (https://arxiv.org/pdf/2404.14082)

SAEs allow us to identify features that are human interpretable, and through sparsity, we try to learn a small number of features. At a fundamental level, SAEs can extract features related to individual words or tokens, such as word frequency features (activations that correspond to high-frequency vs. low-frequency words), and part-of-speech features (features that selectively activate for nouns, verbs, or adjectives). SAEs often capture syntactic rules embedded within LLMs, such as activations that fire for certain syntactic patterns (e.g., subject-verb-object structures) or features corresponding to syntactic dependencies, such as whether a word is a noun modifying another noun. In addition, it is also possible to identify high-level features such as neurons that fire for texts about specific domains (e.g., politics, science, or sports) and whether a sentence expresses positive, negative, or neutral sentiment. Lastly, some features can be also related to writing style and discourse structure, such as distinguishing between academic writing and casual conversation, programming languages versus human language, or distinct writing styles of certain authors (e.g., Shakespeare vs. X/Twitter posts).

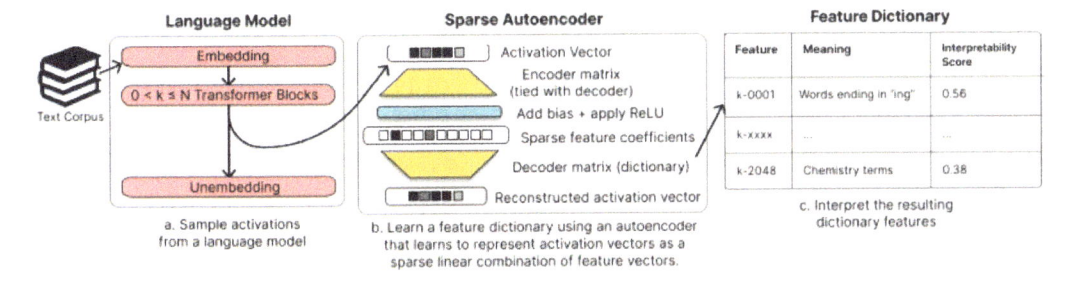

Figure 11.23 – SAE training overview (https://arxiv.org/pdf/2309.08600)

Some features learned by SAEs may not reflect real knowledge but rather random statistical properties of the model's embeddings. In addition, SAEs sometimes learn spurious correlations in hidden layers rather than meaningful conceptual structures. Also, SAEs focus on only one layer at a time, not considering that different neurons in different layers may interact for the same concept. Despite the associated cost, SAEs are considered a promising method for analyzing model behavior. At the same time, it was proposed to train LLMs in a more interpretable and scattered manner. The use of sparsity in the model weights aid interpretability. Techniques such as pruning and other similar techniques introduce zeros into the model weights, effectively erasing them. Sparsity eliminates connections between neurons; this makes it easier to follow the flow of information and better understand the model's decision-making process (or the relationship connecting input and output). Mixture-of-experts has a similar effect and thus makes it more interpretable.

Interpretability techniques are now critical to understanding the behavior of LLMs and preventing dangerous behaviors from emerging, such as deceiving users, showing bias, giving wrong answers especially to please users' beliefs (a phenomenon called "sycophancy"), and learning spurious correlations. As parameters and training have increased, models have become increasingly sophisticated in their responses, increasingly verbose, and persuasive, making it difficult for the user to understand whether an answer is correct. In addition, these models are now deployed with the public, which means users with malicious intentions can conduct attacks such as data poisoning, jailbreaking, adversarial attacks, and so on. Interpretability helps to monitor the behavior of the model in its interaction with the public, highlight where there have been failures, and address them in real time. Interpretability is an important requirement for model safety because it allows us not only to identify problem behaviors but also to identify which components are responsible for them. Once we have identified components associated with unintended behaviors, we can intervene with steering.

In addition, today, there is much more attention to privacy, and *machine unlearning* is the application field that deals with scrubbing the influence of particular data points on a trained machine learning model. For example, regulatory questions may require that we remove information concerning a person from our model. Machine unlearning deals with trying to remove this information without having to train the model from scratch. Machine unlearning is related to interpretability, as decomposition techniques allow us to localize concepts and information in model parameters. More generally, we want to have the ability to be able to edit model knowledge (such as correcting factual errors, removing copyrighted content, or eliminating harmful information like instructions for weapon construction). Editing requires being able to intervene on model parameters in a surgical manner without destroying additional knowledge and other capabilities. Editing is even more complex than unlearning because it means rewriting model knowledge. Interpretability techniques allow us to understand whether editing or unlearning has worked and then to monitor the process.

Interpretability is also useful in trying to predict how the model will perform in new situations, and thus avoid safety risks. Some behaviors of the model may, in fact, appear only in unanticipated situations, and may not manifest themselves when conducting a standard evaluation. For example, we can identify susceptibility or potential backdoors before these are discovered by users. Considering that today's LLMs are increasingly connected to tools, any misuse can have effects that propagate. For example, if an LLM is connected to finance databases, it could be exploited to extract information about users. Or an LLM that shops online could be exploited for fraud and buying fraudulent products. Fine-tuning and other post-training steps can lead to the emergence or exacerbation of behaviors that were not present in the pre-trained model. In addition, some properties seem to emerge at scale and are difficult to predict when we train a smaller model. Often, smaller versions of the final architecture are trained when designing a new architecture. Smaller models may not have problems that emerge only at scale.

Interpretability also has important commendable aspects; understanding the behavior of the model and its components allows us to be able to speed up inference. For example, if some computations are unnecessary, we could turn them off, or use the knowledge gained to distill a more efficient model. In addition, we could identify components that impact either positive or negative reasoning.

Another intriguing aspect of interpretability is that it can be used for new discoveries (commonly called **microscope AI**). In other words, you can investigate a model that has been trained on certain data, and you can use interpretability techniques to gain insights into it. You can use these techniques to identify patterns that might have eluded humans. For example, after AlphaZero's success in defeating humans at chess, researchers considered extracting information from the model to identify concepts about sacrifices that humans could learn. In this paper (`https://arxiv.org/abs/2310.16410`), Schut et al. (2023) identified these concepts or patterns to see how the model had a different representation of the game.

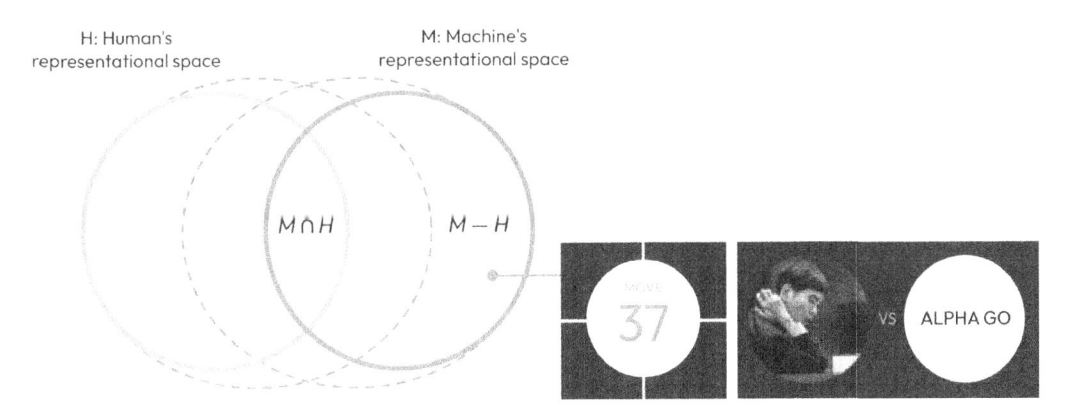

Figure 11.24 – Learning from machine-unique knowledge (`https://arxiv.org/pdf/2310.16410`)

LLMs have a large memory, and humans express themselves through language; this allows them to analyze and conduct hypotheses about human psychology. Interpretability then is an approach that allows us to not only better understand the model but also be able to use models as a tool to better understand humans. In the next section, we will discuss how models can potentially approach human intelligence.

The road to artificial general intelligence

> *"Artificial general intelligence (AGI) is a hypothesized type of highly autonomous artificial intelligence (AI) that would match or surpass human capabilities across most or all economically valuable cognitive work. It contrasts with narrow AI, which is limited to specific tasks. Artificial superintelligence (ASI), on the other hand, refers to AGI that greatly exceeds human cognitive capabilities. AGI is considered one of the definitions of strong AI."*

This is the definition of **artificial general intelligence** (**AGI**) according to Wikipedia. Before imagining AI capable of surpassing humans, one must ask whether AI has caught up with human capabilities. In general, before the advent of ChatGPT, this debate did not begin (at least for the general public). This is because the previous models had superhuman capabilities only for specialized applications. For example, AlphaGo had been able to defeat human champions with relative ease, but no one thought that what makes us human was knowing how to play Go. Models such as DALL-E and ChatGPT, on the other hand, have begun to raise questions in the general audience as well. After all, generating art or creative writing are skills that are generally connected with humans. This feeling was reinforced when ChatGPT and other LLMs were able to pass university or medical and legal licensing exams.

We discussed creativity and reasoning in previous subsections. The current consensus is that LLMs do not exhibit true reasoning or creativity skills. They are sophisticated stochastic pattern machines, and their ability to find patterns in the whole of human knowledge makes them extraordinarily effective.

If LLMs are not capable of showing a level of human intelligence today, one may wonder what that might bring to AGI. Until now, it has been believed that it was possible to achieve AGI simply by scaling parameters and training. According to the idea of emergent properties, reasoning and creativity should appear at some point in the scaling (by increasing the size of the model and the number of tokens used for training, without our being able to predict it, the model should begin to show true reasoning). Today, most researchers do not believe that this is possible, nor that post-training techniques will suffice.

Moreover, scaling is not possible indefinitely. Even if we could invest enormous amounts of money and resources, there is not enough text to create models that grow linearly. In fact, humans generate a limited amount of text, and we are approaching the limit of the stock of text generated by humans.

Projections of the stock of public text and data usage

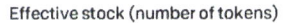

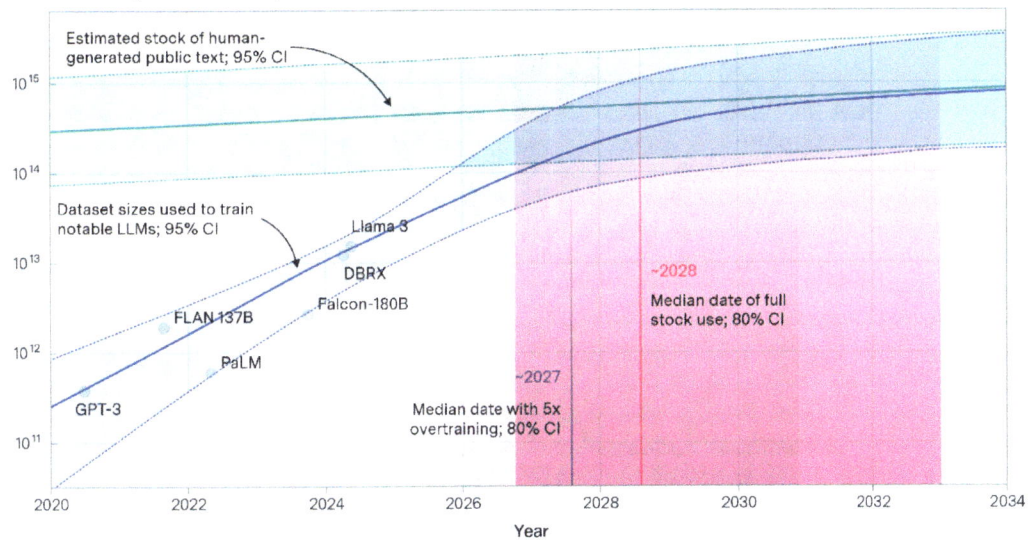

Figure 11.25 – Projections of the stock of public text and data usage (https://epoch.ai/blog/will-we-run-out-of-data-limits-of-llm-scaling-based-on-human-generated-data)

The solution to this could be the use of synthetic data. Synthetic data, however, can be considered a kind of "knowledge distillation" and can lead to model collapse. Models that are trained with synthetic data go into collapse, showing that performance degrades rapidly.

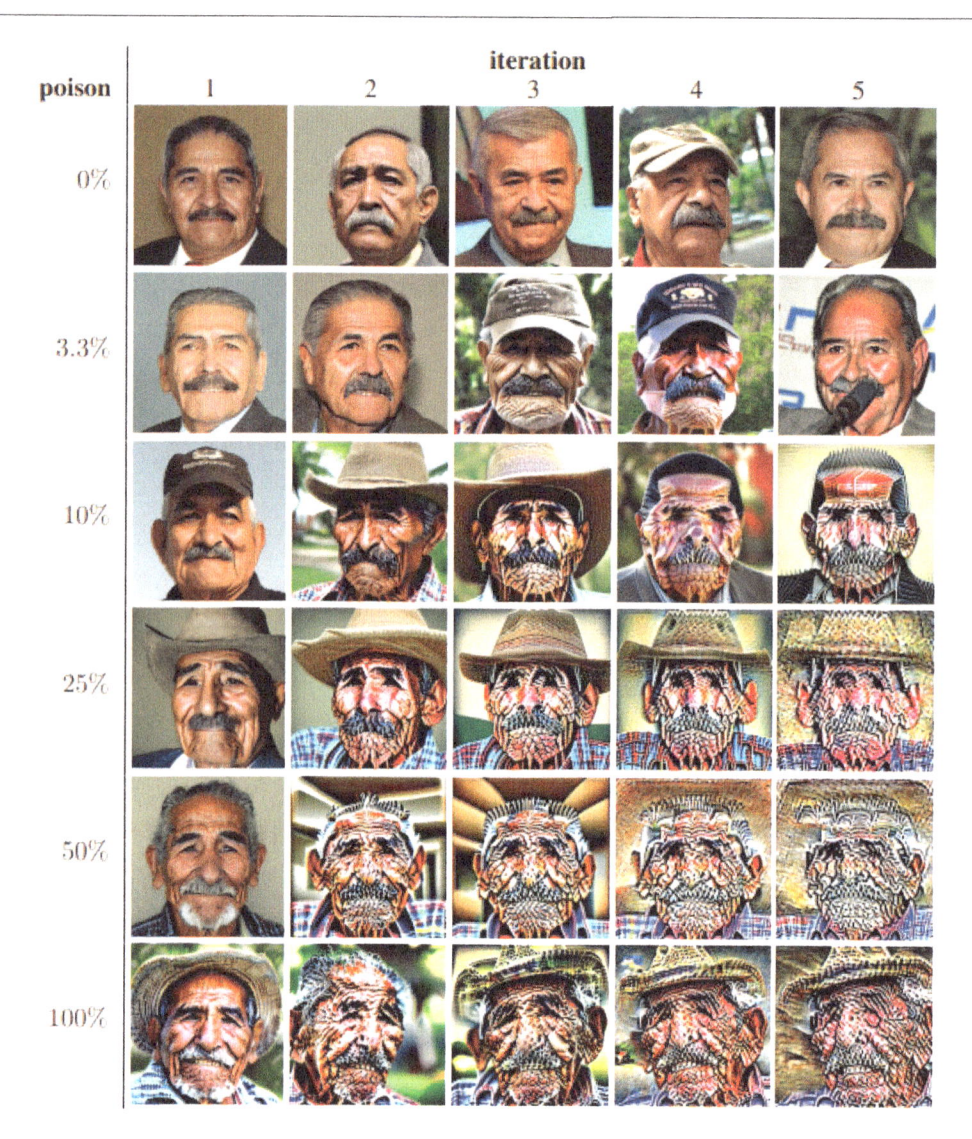

Figure 11.26 – Examples generated after iterative retraining for different compositions of the retraining dataset, from 0% synthetic data to 100 % synthetic data (https://arxiv.org/pdf/2311.12202)

If scaling is not the solution, some researchers propose that the key lies in developing a "world model." That is, much like the human brain constructs an internal representation of the external environment, building such structured representations could be essential to advancing the capabilities of LLMs. This representation is used to imagine possible actions or consequences of actions. This model would also be used to generalize tasks we have learned in one domain and apply them to another. Today, some researchers suggest that LLMs have a rudimentary model of the world and that this can also be

Challenges and open questions 513

visualized. For example, Gurnee (2023) states that LLMs form a rudimentary "world model" during training and that it shows spatiotemporal representations.

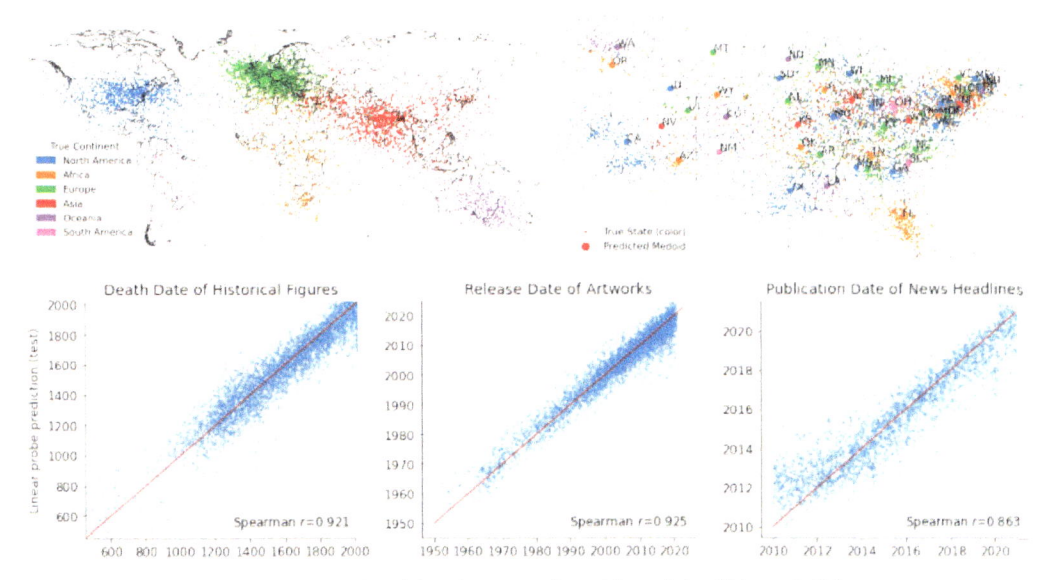

Figure 11.27 – Spatial and temporal world models of Llama-2-70b (https://arxiv.org/pdf/2310.02207)

These spatiotemporal representations are far from constituting a dynamic causal world model, but they seem to be the first elements for its evolution. However, there is no consensus on whether these world models can then evolve into something that is robust and reliable for conducting simulations or learning causal relationships as in humans. For example, in one study (Vafa, 2024), transformers failed to create a reliable map of New York City that can be used to conduct predictions and then used to guide.

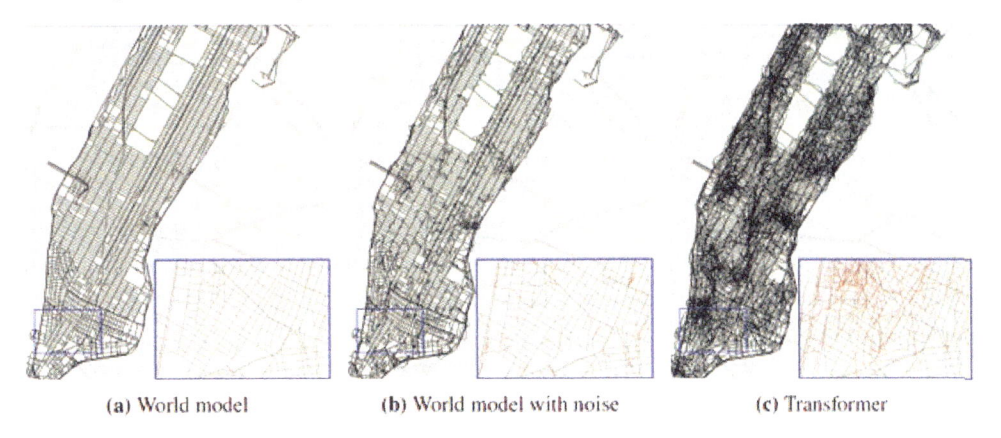

(a) World model (b) World model with noise (c) Transformer

Figure 11.28 – Reconstructed maps of Manhattan from sequences produced by three models (https://arxiv.org/pdf/2406.03689)

Certainly, there is a wealth of information in language that can be learned, and that enables LLMs to be able to solve a large number of tasks. However, some researchers suggest that this is not enough and that models should be embodied (being used in a physical agent and being able to interact physically with the environment) in order to really make a quantum leap (including being able to learn a more robust world model). To date, this is a hypothesis and remains an open question.

Ethical questions

An article was recently published suggesting that fully autonomous AI agents should not be developed (Mitchell, 2025). While this might seem drastic, it still emphasizes the risks that autonomous agents can bring:

> *The development of AI agents is a critical inflection point in artificial intelligence. As history demonstrates, even well-engineered autonomous systems can make catastrophic errors from trivial causes. While increased autonomy can offer genuine benefits in specific contexts, human judgment and contextual understanding remain essential, particularly for high-stakes decisions.*

The authors identify a series of levels for agents, in which humans progressively cede control of a process to the agent until the AI agent takes complete control. Recent developments in AI show how we are moving closer to creating processes where agents are in charge of an entire process.

Agentic Level	Description	Term	Example Code	Who's in Control?
☆☆☆☆	Model has no impact on program flow	Simple processor	`print_llm_output(llm_response)`	👤 Human
★☆☆☆	Model determines basic program flow	Router	`if llm_decision(): path_a() else: path_b()`	👤 Human: How functions are done; 🤖 System: When
★★☆☆	Model determines how functions are executed	Tool call	`run_function(llm_chosen_tool, llm_chosen_args)`	👤 Human: What functions are done; 🤖 System: How
★★★☆	Model controls iteration and program continuation	Multi-step agent	`while should_continue(): execute_next_step()`	👤 Human: What functions exist; 🤖 System: Which to do, when, how
★★★★	Model creates & executes new code	Fully autonomous agent	`create_code(user_request); execute()`	🤖 System

Figure 11.29 – Levels of agents (https://arxiv.org/pdf/2502.02649)

In *Chapter 3*, we discussed the risks associated with LLMs, whereas, in this subsection, we want to discuss in detail the risks that are associated with AI agents. Clearly, many of the risks of agent systems arise from LLMs (an LLM is central to an agent system), but extending an LLM's ability with tools creates or exacerbates new risks.

Before addressing some of the risks in detail, we would like to discuss one of the least underestimated risks of generative AI: namely, the risk of anthropomorphizing agents. As we mentioned previously, LLMs have no level of consciousness nor do they generate real emotions. LLMs emulate the distribution with which they are trained; this makes them appear as though they can emulate emotions (this clearly does not mean that they actually possess or express emotions). This must be taken into account in interactions with chatbots or other social applications in which an LLM is present. These "perceived emotions" affect not only users but also researchers who must interpret the results of agents. Their ability to emulate emotions can be an effective tool for studies that simulate human behaviors, but excessive anthropomorphization risks creating misinformation and misattribution of results. In addition, anthropomorphization can lead to the risk of creating parasocial relationships between users and AI agents (a risk that will become greater when agents are embodied and thus capable of physical interaction).

Linked to the risk of anthropomorphization is the risk of excessive influence on users. There is the risk of a user being over-reliant and over-confident in an agent. Whether it is because of errors (such as hallucinations) or malicious behavior (poisoning or hacking), a user should be sufficiently skeptical of an agent's behavior. Influence risk is considered a group of risks that influence the user's behavior and beliefs:

- **Persuasion**: Refers to the ability of a model to influence a user's behavior. This can be especially problematic when an agent forces a transformative choice on the user or solicits behaviors that are harmful.
- **Manipulation**: Refers to agents that bypass an individual's rational capabilities (such as misrepresenting information or exploiting cognitive bias) to influence decision-making. This behavior could also emerge as a byproduct of poor design choices, creating a product that keeps the user engaged, or personalization for the purpose of creating trust. It is morally problematic because it does not respect the user's autonomy and could force the user into behaviors that are harmful to himself.
- **Deception**: Refers to strategies that cause an individual to form a false belief. This is likely to push a user toward behaviors that could be harmful to themselves because they are confused by false beliefs.
- **Coercion**: Implies an individual choosing something because they have no other acceptable alternative. This risk can be physical (with embodied agents) or psychological (also chatbots).
- **Exploitation**: Implies taking unfair advantage of an individual's circumstances. AI agents can be programmed to be exploitative (we can imagine an AI agent in a casino trying to push users to spend as much as possible).

These behaviors can be exploited by malicious actors. For example, an agent's persuasion skills can be used for the spread of misinformation online. LLMs are capable of generating impressive amounts of text that can seem authoritative. An LLM in itself can generate hallucinations, but it can be used for the purpose of intentionally generating fake news with a specific purpose. The use of agents allows an LLM to use additional tools (generate images and videos and retrieve information) and feed them directly into communication channels. Paradoxically, since this fake news is difficult to intercept by humans, agents can also be used to combat the spread of AI-generated misinformation. Agents can then be used to generate disinformation at scale, with the cost to generate gradually dropping (and is still lower than employing humans). In addition, agents make it possible to search for information about the victim and thus generate customized content to be more effective.

Misinformation can be used to reinforce bias toward individuals or groups. This content (text, images, audio, and video) can be used to influence political elections or drive citizen outrage. In addition, apart from disinformation, agents can also produce other types of harmful content, including depictions of nudity, hate, or violence.

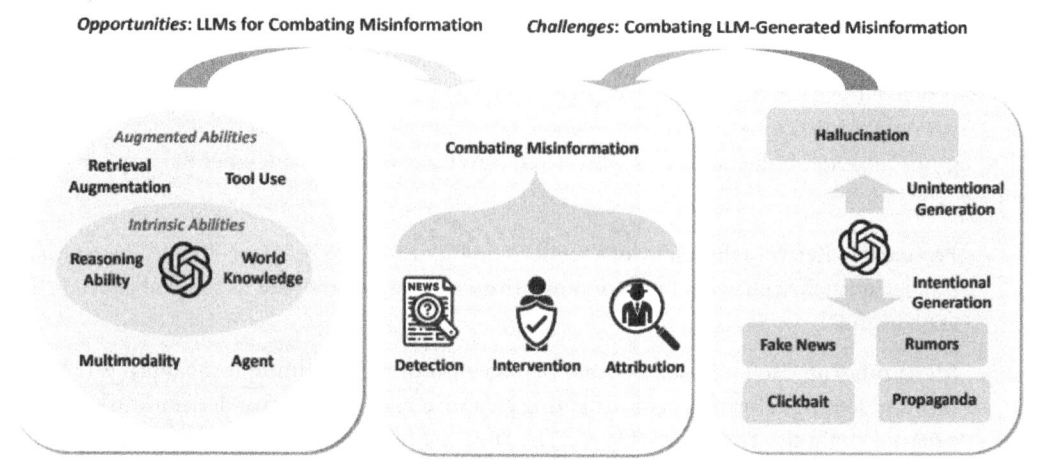

Figure 11.30 – Opportunities and challenges of combating misinformation in the age of LLMs (https://arxiv.org/pdf/2311.05656)

Malicious actors can also use agents for additional purposes such as phishing attacks, cyberattacks, or scams. In fact, LLMs can also generate harmful code that can be used to steal money or information. Chatbots can be used for the purpose of gaining trust and convincing someone to share information or earnings. There are also devious ways to attack an agent; for example, we can imagine an agent who conducts purchases for a user can be infiltrated by a bad actor who poisons the agent and prompts it to conduct fraudulent purchases. The planned deployment of AI assistants in fields such as healthcare, law, education, and science multiplies the risks and severity of possible harm. In addition, many of the AI agents today are natively multimodal (multiple possible types of inputs and outputs) and leverage deep reasoning models that are capable of more reasoning and planning. In addition, unlike LLMs, they also incorporate memory systems, all of which add risk. For example, an agent tasked with conducting a cyberattack could retrieve from memory successful past attacks or discard outdated techniques, search for information on online vulnerabilities, generate and execute code, and devise a multi-step strategy. As has been seen, a malicious actor can interfere with an LLM in several ways, for example, through prompt injection or information extraction. An LLM acquires sensitive information during its training that can be extracted. Agents can be connected to sensitive databases, and there are techniques to make LLMs extract the content. In addition, agent misuse can be conducted by authoritarian governments. For example, governments may use agents to generate misinformation or censorship and may use them for surveillance, tracking, and silencing dissent. Advanced agent systems can extract data from cell phones, cars, the Internet of Things, and more, making it easier to control the population.

Another risk is the economic impact of these agents. AI is expected to impact several aspects of the economy in terms of productivity but also in terms of employment, job quality, and inequality. The use of agents and AI in general have different associated risks:

- **Employment**: Various research estimates that 47 percent of jobs are at risk of automation, especially jobs that are characterized by routines and physical tasks such as driving and manufacturing. Advances in LLMs have also brought alarm to jobs that involve generating and manipulating information, and that are normally associated with higher levels of education such as translators, tax advisers, or even software engineers. AI could therefore accelerate job loss for positions requiring skilled labor, without creating a number of positions with which to absorb displaced jobs.

- **Job quality**: Some initial studies have suggested that the use of AI could make workers more productive and increase the wages of workers. Some studies, however, place emphasis on the possibility that employers may more efficiently monitor their employees with greater stress. Other studies note how the introduction of robots may reduce the physical workload in manufacturing but push workers to work faster, with less human contact and more supervision.

- **Inequality**: On the one hand, technological development has decreased inequality between different countries. At the same time, intra-country income inequality has increased, with a sharper separation of wealth between the richest and poorest. There are few studies looking at how AI may impact inequality, but some studies suggest that firms are best able to draw on AI with increased productivity and earnings, while workers are at risk of displacement and thus reduced income. Some studies suggest that high-income occupations may benefit from using AI, while others will be impacted. For example, AI assistants appear to impact junior positions by reducing them. In addition, most of the leading AI research labs, start-ups, and enterprises are located in certain geographic areas, with the risk of concentration of well-paying positions. Conversely, AI also creates low-paying jobs, especially in data creation and data acquisition.

To date, AI tools are not sophisticated enough to replace humans, but some effects on employment are already visible. Tools such as ChatGPT and DALL-E have already had an impact on the "creative economies" (which includes writers, artists, designers, photographers, content creators, and so on) with reduced positions and earnings.

Another risk is the environmental impact of generative AI. Data and compute underlie the training and use of AI systems. Thus, hardware and infrastructure for storage and processing (including data centers and telecommunications) are required for the creation and use of agents. Creating the necessary hardware has an environmental impact (mining of rare earths, energy to build and ship them, water in plants, and use of chemicals). Then, a model requires energy to be drawn, built, and deployed (operational costs). Beyond training, deployment in inference also requires resources and energy consumption. Energy consumption and corresponding carbon dioxide emissions associated with LLM training are increasing over time. As can be seen in the following figure, carbon dioxide production linearly increases with energy consumption for training (directly related to the number of parameters and the increase in training):

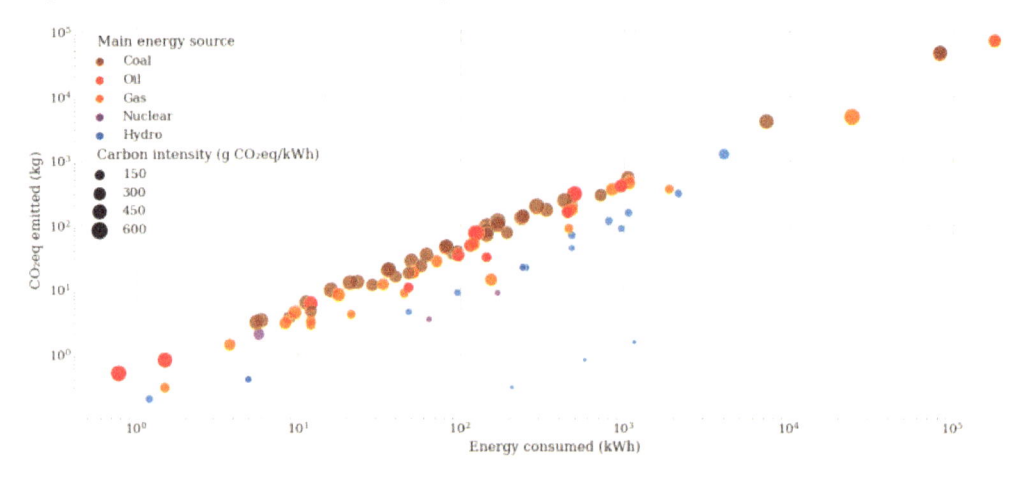

Figure 11.31 – Estimated energy consumed (kWh) and CO2 (kg) by different models (https://arxiv.org/pdf/2302.08476)

Considering the increase in users who use LLMs (or services that include LLMs) on a daily basis, the impact of training on emissions is only a fraction. Today, inference is supposed to be increasingly important (it has been estimated that 60% of machine learning energy use at Google from 2019–2021 was attributable to inference).

These are some of the possible risks with LLMs and agents. To date, strategies are being studied to try to address and mitigate these risks.

Summary

This chapter presented how some industries will be revolutionized by agents. The AI revolution goes beyond these industries and will have a large-scale impact. This book, however, provided a serious and structured introduction to the technical component that will drive this revolution, giving you the tools to understand the future that will come (and is already upon us). Apart from the sense of wonder that this technological revolution may inspire, we wanted to remind you that there are still technical and ethical challenges that should not be overlooked.

This chapter closes this book but leaves open a series of questions and challenges for the future. Readers who have followed us up to this point can find in this final chapter suggestions for leveraging what they have learned at the industry level and at the research level.

Further reading

- Luo, *BioGPT: Generative Pre-trained Transformer for Biomedical Text Generation and Mining*, 2022, `https://academic.oup.com/bib/article/23/6/bbac409/6713511`
- Yao, *Health System-scale Language Models are All-purpose Prediction Engines*, 2023, `https://www.nature.com/articles/s41586-023-06160-y`
- Singhal, *Towards Exper-level Medical Question Answering with Large Language Models*, 2023, `https://arxiv.org/abs/2305.09617`
- Gao, *Empowering Biomedical Discovery with AI Agents*, 2024, `https://www.cell.com/cell/fulltext/S0092-8674(24)01070-5`
- Gu, *A Survey on LLM-as-a-Judge*, 2024, `https://arxiv.org/abs/2411.15594`
- Ning, *A Survey of WebAgents: Towards Next-Generation AI Agents for Web Automation with Large Foundation Models*, 2025, `https://arxiv.org/abs/2503.23350`
- Xu, *A Survey on Robotics with Foundation Models: Toward Embodied AI*, 2024, `https://arxiv.org/pdf/2402.02385`
- Hu, *A Survey on Large Language Model Based Game Agents*, 2025, `https://arxiv.org/pdf/2404.02039`
- Bousateouane, *Physical AI Agents: Integrating Cognitive Intelligence with Real-World Action*, 2025, `https://arxiv.org/pdf/2501.08944v1`
- Zeng, *Large Language Models for Robotics: A Survey*, 2023, `https://arxiv.org/pdf/2311.07226`
- Bansal, *Challenges in Human-Agent Communication*, 2024, `https://www.microsoft.com/en-us/research/uploads/prod/2024/12/HCAI_Agents.pdf`
- Raieli, *The Savant Syndrome: Is Pattern Recognition Equivalent to Intelligence?*, 2024, `https://medium.com/towards-data-science/the-savant-syndrome-is-pattern-recognition-equivalent-to-intelligence-242aab928152`
- Lu, *Fantastically Ordered Prompts and Where to Find Them: Overcoming Few-Shot Prompt Order Sensitivity*, 2022, `https://aclanthology.org/2022.acl-long.556/`
- Zhao, *Calibrate Before Use: Improving Few-shot Performance of Language Models*, 2021, `https://proceedings.mlr.press/v139/zhao21c.html`
- Raieli, *Emergent Abilities in AI: Are We Chasing a Myth?*, 2023, `https://towardsdatascience.com/emergent-abilities-in-ai-are-we-chasing-a-myth-fead754a1bf9`

- Raieli, *A Focus on Emergent Properties in Artificial Intelligence*, 2025, https://github.com/SalvatoreRa/artificial-intelligence-articles/blob/main/articles/emergent_properties.md

- Xu, *Towards Large Reasoning Models: A Survey of Reinforced Reasoning with Large Language Models*, 2025, https://arxiv.org/abs/2501.09686v3

- Sprague, *To CoT or Not to CoT? Chain-of-thought Helps Mainly on Math and Symbolic Reasoning*, 2024, https://arxiv.org/pdf/2409.12183

- Raieli, *To CoT or Not to CoT: Do LLMs Really Need Chain-of-Thought?*, 2024, https://levelup.gitconnected.com/to-cot-or-not-to-cot-do-llms-really-need-chain-of-thought-5a59698c90bb

- Mirzadeh, *GSM-Symbolic: Understanding the Limitations of Mathematical Reasoning in Large Language Models*, 2024, https://arxiv.org/pdf/2410.05229

- Sharkey, *Open Problems in Mechanistic Interpretability*, 2025, https://arxiv.org/abs/2501.16496

- Bereska, *Mechanistic Interpretability for AI Safety -- A Review*, 2025, https://arxiv.org/abs/2404.14082

- Cemri, *Why Do Multi-Agent LLM Systems Fail?*, 2025, https://arxiv.org/pdf/2503.13657

- Raieli, *Creativity in LLMs: Optimizing for Diversity and Uniqueness*, 2025, https://medium.com/data-science-collective/creativity-in-llms-optimizing-for-diversity-and-uniqueness-f5c7208f4d99

- Boden, *The Creative Mind*, 2003, https://www.routledge.com/The-Creative-Mind-Myths-and-Mechanisms/Boden/p/book/9780415314534

- Peeperkorn, *Is Temperature the Creativity Parameter of Large Language Models?*, 2024, https://arxiv.org/abs/2405.00492

- Benedek, *To Create or to Recall? Neural Mechanisms Underlying the Generation of Creative New Ideas*, 2014, https://www.sciencedirect.com/science/article/pii/S1053811913011130

- Raieli, *You're Not a Writer, ChatGPT — But You Sound Like One*, 2024, https://levelup.gitconnected.com/youre-not-a-writer-chatgpt-but-you-sound-like-one-75fa329ac3a9

- Raieli, *How Far Is AI from Human Intelligence?*, 2025, https://levelup.gitconnected.com/how-far-is-ai-from-human-intelligence-6ab4b2a5ce1c

- Villalobos, *Will We Run Out of Data? Limits of LLM Scaling Based on Human-generated Data*, 2022, https://arxiv.org/abs/2211.04325

- Feng, *How Far Are We From AGI: Are LLMs All We Need?*, 2024, `https://arxiv.org/abs/2405.10313`
- Karvonen, *Emergent World Models and Latent Variable Estimation in Chess-Playing Language Models*, 2024, `https://arxiv.org/pdf/2403.15498v2`
- Li, *Emergent World Representations: Exploring a Sequence Model Trained on a Synthetic Task*, 2022, `https://arxiv.org/abs/2210.13382`
- Bowman, *Eight Things to Know about Large Language Models*, 2023, `https://arxiv.org/pdf/2304.00612`
- Shumailov, *AI Models Collapse When Trained on Recursively Generated Data*, 2024, `https://www.nature.com/articles/s41586-024-07566-y`
- LessWrong, *Embodiment is Indispensable for AGI*, 2022, `https://www.lesswrong.com/posts/vBBxKBWn4zRXwivxC/embodiment-is-indispensable-for-agi`
- Tan, *The Path to AGI Goes through Embodiment*, 2023, `https://ojs.aaai.org/index.php/AAAI-SS/article/view/27485`
- Mitchell, *Fully Autonomous AI Agents Should Not be Developed*, 2025, `https://arxiv.org/pdf/2502.02649`
- Diamond, *On the Ethical Considerations of Generative Agents*, 2024, `https://arxiv.org/abs/2411.19211`
- Siqueira de Cerqueira, *Can We Trust AI Agents? An Experimental Study Towards Trustworthy LLM-Based Multi-Agent Systems for AI Ethics*, 2024, `https://arxiv.org/abs/2411.08881`
- Chaffer, *Decentralized Governance of Autonomous AI Agents*, 2024, `https://arxiv.org/abs/2412.17114v3`
- Gabriel, *The Ethics of Advanced AI Assistants*, 2024, `https://arxiv.org/pdf/2404.16244`
- Chen, *Combating Misinformation in the Age of LLMs: Opportunities and Challenges*, 2023, `https://arxiv.org/abs/2311.05656`
- Luccioni, *Counting Carbon: A Survey of Factors Influencing the Emissions of Machine Learning*, 2023, `https://arxiv.org/abs/2302.08476`

Index

Symbols

ε-greedy method 264

A

abstractive question-answering 129
action 114, 115
action agents 115
activity diagram 423
actor-critic algorithm 285, 286
actor-critic architecture 285
adapters 76, 77
adaptive retrieval 186
advanced RAG pipeline 172
   context enrichment 176
   generalization 187, 188
   hierarchical indexing 172-174
   hybrid search 178
   Hypothetical Document Embeddings (HyDE) 175
   hypothetical questions 174, 175
   implementing 193-197
   keyword-based search 178
   query routing 179, 180
   query transformation 177, 178
   reranking 180-183
   response optimization 185
Advantage Actor-Critic (A2C) 287
affine quantization mapping 82
agent 106-108, 185
   autonomy 108
   creating, to search web 129-133
   pro-activeness 108
   reactivity 108
   social ability 108
Agent Laboratory 351-353
AI agents 106
   classifying 115-118
   decomposition-first methods 116
   in healthcare 479, 480
   interleaved decomposition methods 116
   LLM agents, for gaming 487, 488
   physical agents 485, 486
   web agents 488
AI agents, challenges and open questions
   artificial general intelligence (AGI) 510-514
   creativity, in LLM 501-504
   ethical questions 514-518
   human-agent communication 489-491
   limits, of reasoning 495-501
   mechanistic interpretability 504-509
   no clear superiority, of multi-agents 492-494

524 Index

alignment 77, 78
allocational harm 94
AlphaFold 2 346, 347, 480
AlphaGo
   reference link 120
AlphaZero 287-289
Amazon Web Services (AWS) 377
API call prompts 249
approaches, for using prompt in LLM
   API call prompts 249
   manual prompt 249
   self-prompting 249
approximate nearest neighbors
   (ANN) algorithm 157
ArmoRM-Llama3-8B-v0.1 441
artificial general intelligence
   (AGI) 105, 321, 510-514
artificial intelligence (AI)
   text representation 4
Asynchronous Advantage Actor-
   Critic (A3C) method 293
asynchronous programming 456-461
   blocking operations 460
   callbacks 460
   concurrency 460
   coroutines 460
   event loop 460
   futures 460
   non-blocking operations 460
   parallelism 460
   promises 460
   with ML 465-469
asyncio module 457, 461-464
attention 37
   advantages 38
   exploring 36-42
AudioGPT
   reference link 114

auditory input 114
autocompressors 184
autoencoder (AE) 76
AutoGen 127
   advantages 127
   disadvantages 127
autonomous agents 321, 322
autoregressive language modeling 66
average precision (AP) 159

B

bag of words (BoW) 6-8
Bidirectional Encoder Representations
   from Transformers (BERT) 50, 76
bidirectional encoders 51
bi-encoder approach 149
binary quantization 153
Biomedical AI agents 482-484
blocking operations 460
BM25 138, 178
Bootstrapping Language-Image
   Pre-training (BLIP-2) 90
brain 109, 110, 112
Business-to-Business (B2B) 377
Byte-Pair Encoding (BPE) 50, 436

C

caching 404, 405
California Consumer Privacy
   Act (CCPA) 203
callbacks 460
catastrophic forgetting 69
chain-of-thought (CoT) 108, 186, 324
chain-of-thought prompting 99
ChatEngine 183
ChatGPT 510, 517

Chatlaw 345
ChemAgent 342-344
ChemCrow 339-341, 479, 482
chunking
  context-aware chunking 147
  K-means chunking 148
  propositions-based chunking 148
  recursive chunking 147
  semantic chunking 148
  strategies 146-149
chunks 146
class diagram 421
clipped objective function 285
clustering 14
COCO dataset 363
code-like forms 242
collection 136
common-sense knowledge 109
computer vision 27
concurrency 457, 460
conda environment 356, 358
connected data 215
container orchestrators (COs) 475
containers 470
context-aware chunking 147
context enrichment 176
context filtering 184
context length 71
contextual compression 184
contextual hallucinations 209
continual learning 121
continuous batching 444, 445
continuous integration/continuous delivery (CI/CD) 432
Contrastive Language-Image Pre-Training (CLIP) 87-90
contrastive learning 87
conversational AI 71

convolutional neural network (CNN) 26
  for text 27
copyright issue 96
coroutines 460
corpus 4
cosine similarity 16
  properties 16
cosine similarity loss 151
create, read, update, and delete (CRUD) 157
critical scale 69
cross-attention 46
cross-encoders 181
cross-entropy loss 48
current memory gate 26
curse of dimensionality 7
Customer Relationship Management (CRM) 377

D

DALL-E 510, 517
Data as a Service (DaaS) 385, 390
  advantages 386
  advantages (provider) 391
  advantages (user) 392
  disadvantages 386, 387
  disadvantages (provider) 392
  disadvantages (user) 393
data decontamination 440
data deduplication 199
data indexing and retrieval 199
data lake 198
data parallelism 446, 447, 450
data preprocessing and cleaning 199
data quality evaluation 441
data storage 198
debiasing approaches 94

Index

Declarative Self-improving Language Programs in Python (DSPy) 101
decoder 36
Deep Q-Network (DQN) 280
   advantages 281
   architecture 281
   drawbacks 282
deep reinforcement learning (deep RL) 274
   actor-critic algorithm 285, 286
   AlphaZero 287-289
   challenges 289, 290
   Deep Q-Network (DQN) 280, 281
   exploring 277-279
   future direction 289, 290
   model-based methods 275
   model-free methods 275
   off-policy methods 277
   on-policy methods 276
   Proximal Policy Optimization (PPO) 284, 285
   Q-learning 280
   REINFORCE algorithm 282-284
Demonstrate-search-predict (DSP) 189
deployment environment
   securing 455, 456
depth-first search (DFS) 249, 287
DEtection TRansformer (DETR) 364
DETR-ResNet-101 364
digital agents 115
   action agents 115
   interactive agent 115
directed graph 216
Direct Preference Optimization (DPO) 79
distributed data 215
Docker 470
   with ML 473-476
Docker Compose 471

Docker containers 471
   advantages 471
   disadvantages 472
Docker Engine 471
Dockerfile 471
Docker images 471
Docker secrets 456
document model 235
document summarization 71
domain-independent ontologies 221
domain knowledge 109
domain ontologies 221
dot product 15
DuckDuckGo 131
dynamic programming (DP) 273

E

EduChat example 325
embedding 17, 149
   properties 17, 18
   strategies 150-154
embedding databases 155, 157
embedding inversion attacks 203
embedding process 11
embodied action 115
embodied language models 113
embodiment hypothesis 115
emergent properties
   in LLMs 69-71
encoder 36
equal interaction 121
event loop 460
explainable RL (XRL) 310
external planner-aided planning 117
extractive question-answering 129
extract, transform, load (ETL) 437

F

factual hallucinations 93
FAISS (Facebook AI Similarity Search) 157
faithfulness hallucinations 93
feed-forward network (FFN) layer 72
feedforward neural network 20
few-shot prompting 99
figure-of-speech (FoS) detection 71
fine-tuned LLMs 181
fine-tuning 57, 74, 75
   versus RAG 161-163
Flamingo
   reference link 113
FlashAttention 445
forget gate 23
frontend, Streamlit
   dynamic app, creating 413-419
   images, inserting 411, 412
   text elements, adding 410, 411
function composition 126
future 460

G

gated recurrent unit (GRU) 24-26
general data 435
General Data Protection Regulation (GDPR) 203, 437
generalized advantage estimation (GAE) 299
generation module 188
Git LFS 354, 355
   URL 354
Google Serper
   reference link 132
GPT-2 54, 363
GPT-3 67

Grade School Math 8K (GSM8K) dataset 500
gradient X input 55
graph attention networks (GATs) 248
graph-based indexing (G-indexing) 237, 238
graph databases 235
graph-enhanced generation (G-generation) 237
graph formats 241
graph-guided retrieval (G-retrieval) 237, 239-242
Graph Markup Language (GraphML) 242
graph neural networks (GNN) 239, 247, 248
graph of thoughts (GoT) 251
graph reasoning 245, 246
   graph neural networks 247, 248
   knowledge graph embeddings 246, 247
   LLMs reasoning, on knowledge graphs 249-251
graph retrieval-augmented generation (GraphRAG) 236
   applications 242-245
   hybrid granularities 241
   nodes 240
   ongoing challenges 252, 254
   paths 240
   subgraphs 241
   triplets 240
graphs 216
   directed 216
   labeled 217
   multigraph 217
   undirected 216
   weighted 217
graph structure understanding tasks 245
greedy decoding 49

H

Hadamard product 23
hallucinations 93, 94
Hamming distance 153
Haystack 124
   advantages 125
   disadvantages 125
   elements 125
hierarchical clustering 148
hierarchical indexing 172-174
hierarchical KGs 219
Hugging Face Gradio
   URL 361
Hugging Face token 361
HuggingGPT 327-329
   limitations 338
   model execution 333, 334
   model selection 332
   response generation 335-337
   task planning 330, 331
   using, locally 354-360
   using, on web 361-364
   working with 353
hybrid memory 323
hybrid parallelism 451
HybridRAG 244
hybrid search 178, 193
Hypothetical Document Embeddings (HyDE) 175
hypothetical questions 174, 175

I

image decoder 92
image generator 92
in-context learning (ICL) 97-100
   advantages 98

independent training 190
inference optimization 443
   model inference optimization 443-446
InfoNCE 151
information retrieval 136
Infrastructure as a Service (IaaS) 378
innovation-oriented deployment 119
input gate 23
instruction tuning (IT) 80
instructor-executor paradigm 121
interaction
   equal interaction 121
   unequal interaction 121
interactive agent 115
intrinsic rank hypothesis 74
inverse document frequency (IDF) 138
irreducible loss 68
iterative retrieval 186

J

jarvis environment 358
joint encoding 232
joint methods 192

K

k-armed bandit problem 262
key-value (KV) product 443, 444
keyword-based search 178
keyword routers 179
KG ontologies 220
KG taxonomies 220
K-means chunking 148
k-nearest neighbors (kNN) 182
knowledge assessment 230
   metrics 230

knowledge cleaning 231
knowledge creation 222-226
knowledge distillation 61
knowledge enrichment 232, 233
knowledge graph embedding (KGE) 246, 247
knowledge graph question answering (KGQA) 246
knowledge graph reasoning (KGR) 219
knowledge graphs 188 214, 215
   creating, with LLM 221, 226-230
   definition 218, 219
   heuristic search 215
   hosting and deployment 234, 235
   limited rationality 215
   LLMs reasoning 249-251
   ongoing challenges 252-254
   properties 217
   storage alternatives 235
   used, for retrieving information 236, 237
knowledge search 226
kubelet 472
kube-proxy 472
Kubernetes 472
Kullback-Leibler (KL) divergence 78

L

labeled graph 217
LangChain 123, 131
   advantages 124
   components 123
   disadvantages 124
LangServe 123
LangSmith 123
language modeling 66
language translation 71

Large Language Model Operations (LLMOps) 433
   model governance and compliance 434
   model size and complexity 434
   monitoring and maintenance 434
   scalability and deployment 434
   training and fine-tuning 434
large language models (LLMs) 65, 66, 258
   alignment 77, 78
   context length 71
   emergent properties 69-71
   fine-tuning 74, 75
   instruction tuning (IT) 80
   knowledge graph, creating with 221, 226-230
   scaling law 66-69
   used, for retrieving information 236, 237
layer normalization 45
lemmatization 4
life cycle-oriented deployment 120
linguistic knowledge 109
LlamaIndex 126
   advantages 126
   disadvantages 126
LLM agent framework
   selecting 128
LLM-as-a-judge 441
LLM-augmented KGs 224
LLM-based agents 107, 109
   action 107, 114, 115
   brain 107, 109-112
   for gaming 487, 488
   perception 107, 113, 114
LLM-based application
   brain 122
   interface 122
   perception modules 122

530 Index

prompts 123
tools 122
LLM-based autonomous agents, modules
   action module 324, 325
   memory module 323
   planning module 324
   profiling module 323
LLM-enhanced RL 305
   applications 311
   decision-maker 309
   generator 310, 311
   information processor 306
   reward designer 307
LLM function calling router 179
LLM interactions, with RL models 304
   LLM-enhanced RL 305
   RL-enhanced LLMs 304
LLM router 202
LLMSecConfig framework 475
LLMs for reranking 181
   listwise methods 181
   pairwise methods 181
   pointwise methods 181
logical routers 179
logit vector 48
long-context LLM (LC-LLM) 206
LongLLMLingua 184
long short-term memory (LSTM) 22, 23
   properties 24
Low-Rank Adaptation (LoRA) 74
   advantages 76

M

machine learning (ML) community 328
machine learning (ML) models 97, 432

Machine Learning Operations (MLOps) 432, 433
   deployment phase 433
   high-level process view 433
   model development 433
   monitoring and maintenance 433
   testing phase 433
machine translation
   issues 42
machine unlearning methods 96
manual prompt 249
Markov decision processes (MDPs) 270-273
masked language modeling (MLM) 50, 51, 232
Matryoshka Representation Learning 154
mean average precision (MAP) 159
mean reciprocal rank (MRR) 160
MedGraphRAG 243
membership inference attacks (MIAs) 204
memory-augmented planning 118
memory module 188
metrics, LLM
   answer correctness 160
   answer relevance 161
   coherence 161
   context entities recall 160
   context precision 160
   context recall 160
   context relevancy 160
   faithfulness 160
   fluency 161
   summarization score 160
microscope AI 509
Mind2Web 326
MinHash 440
misinformation 94-96

mixture of experts (MoE) 72, 73
  advantages 73
  disadvantages 73
  gate network 72
  sparse MoE layers 72
Model as a Service (MaaS) 380, 381, 390
  advantages 383
  advantages (provider) 391
  advantages (user) 392
  disadvantages (provider) 392
  disadvantages (user) 393
  drawbacks 384
  elements 382
model collapse 69
model development 435-437
model inference optimization 443-446
model knowledge
  common-sense knowledge 109
  domain knowledge 109
  linguistic knowledge 109
model parallelism 446
model testing 441, 442
model training 438-440
modular RAG 188, 189
Monte Carlo Tree Search (MCTS) 287, 324
  backpropagation 288
  expansion 288
  selection 287
  simulation 288
movie recommendation agent
  building, with RAG 163-166
MTEB leaderboard
  reference link 152
multi-agent systems
    (MASs) 120, 365-377, 492
  for healthcare applications 346-353
  for law 344-346
multi-armed bandit problem 262-269

Multi-Criteria Decision-Making
    (MCDM) 376
multi-factor authentication (MFA) 203
Multi-Genre Natural Language Inference
    (MultiNLI) corpus 150
multigraph graph 217
multi-grouped attention (MGA) 445
multi-head attention (MHA) 445
multi-head latent attention (MLA) 446
multi-head self-attention 40
multi-judge system 345
multimodal entity 219
multimodal LLMs (MMLLMs) 208
multimodal models 84-93
multimodal RAG 207-209
multi-plan selection approach 117
multiple-agent systems
  ability 119-121
multiple negatives ranking loss 151
multiple processes 461
multiple threads 461
multiprocessing module 457
multi-tenant software architecture 379
multi-vector rerankers 181

N

naïve RAG 136-143
  issues 170-172
named entity recognition (NER) 222
natural language 241
natural language processing
    (NLP) 4, 35, 65, 222, 304, 425
natural language tasks 66
NeMo Guardrails 204
neural network 12
next sentence prediction 51
next-word prediction 66

non-blocking operations 460
Non-Negative Matrix Factorization (NMF) 56
non-parametric retrievers 239
normalized discounted cumulative gain (NDCG) 152
normalized dot product 16

O

one forward, one backward (1F1B) scheduling 449
one-hot encoding 4-6
ontologies 221
    domain-independent ontologies 221
    domain ontologies 221
OpenAI key 361
OpenStreetMap (OSM) 133, 419
optimal brain surgeon (OBS) 83

P

paged attention 445
PaLM-E
    reference link 113
parallelism 460
parent document retriever 176
perception 113, 114
personally identifiable information (PII) 436
physical AI agents 485, 486
pipeline parallelism 448-450
Platform as a Service (PaaS) 377
Pod 472
poisoning RAG 204
positional encoding 42
post-processing techniques 182
post-retrieval strategies 180

precision 158
precision-recall curve 159
prefix tuning 77
preprocessing 29
pretraining 57
principal component analysis (PCA) 14, 56
Principal Investigator (PI) 348
principal libraries
    AutoGen 127
    exploring 122, 123
    Haystack 124, 125
    LangChain 123, 124
    LlamaIndex 126
    Semantic Kernel 126, 127
privacy issue risk 96
process 461
production environment
    data exposure prevention 454
    error handling 451, 452
    secrets, managing 453, 454
    security considerations 452
promise 460
prompt compression 183
prompt engineering 97, 185
prompt injection attacks 203
prompt sensitivity 497
prompt tuning 77
propositions-based chunking 148
Protein Data Bank (PDB) 480
Proximal Policy Optimization (PPO) 78, 284, 285
pruning 82, 84

Q

Q-Former 90
Q-learning 280
    example 280

Q-network 281
Q-table of State-Action values 280
quantization 81, 82
query 136
query expansion 178
Querying Transformer (Q-Former) 113
query rewriting 177
query routing 179, 180, 193
query transformation 177, 178, 193
question and answer (Q&A)
    systems 66, 71, 125

R

random sampling 49
rank 74
reasoning 495
Reasoning and Acting (ReAct) 131
recurrent neural network (RNN) 19-21
  issues 37
recursive chunking 147
recursive retrieval 186
reference citations 183
reflection and refinement 118
reflection tokens 186
regular expression (regex) 147
REINFORCE algorithm 282-284
reinforcement learning from human
    feedback (RLHF) 78, 304
reinforcement learning
    (RL) 78, 257-259, 486
  actions 260
  agent 259, 260
  elements 259, 260
  exploration, versus exploitation 259
  global goal, achieving 259
  k-armed bandit problem 262
  Markov decision processes (MDPs) 270-273

multi-armed bandit problem 262-269
overview model 262
policy 261
reward 261
value function 261
video game, playing with 290-292
relational databases 235
relation extraction (RE) 222
Repo2Run 474
representational harm 93
reranker 193
reranking 180-183
reset gate 25
ResNet-101 364
response optimization 185
response synthesizer 185
Results as a Service (RaaS) 387, 390
  advantages 388
  advantages (provider) 391
  advantages (user) 392
  disadvantages 388, 389
  disadvantages (provider) 392
  disadvantages (user) 393
retrieval-augmented generation
    (RAG) 118, 135
  generation 144
  hallucinations, reducing ways 210
  indexing 144
  parallel processing 199-201
  retrieval 144
  scalability 197
  security and privacy 202-205
  training-based approach 190
  training-free approach 190
  used, for building movie
      recommendation agent 163-166
  versus fine-tuning 161-163

534 Index

RL-enhanced LLMs 304
RoBERTa 60
role-based access control (RBAC) 437
rounding 82
routing module 188

S

sampling
    methods 49
scaling law 66-69
SciBERT 60
search module 188
secrets
    managing, in production environment 453, 454
self-attention
    advantages 41
    exploring 36-42
self-consistency 100
self-consistent CoT (CoT-SC) 324
self-prompting 249
self-reflective retrieval-augmented generation (Self-RAG) 189
self-supervised manner 48
semantic chunking 148
Semantic Kernel 126, 127
semantic metadata 215
semantic router 180
semantic search 178
semi-structured data 197
sentence window retrieval 176
sentiment analysis
    performing, with embedding and deep learning 28-33
separated encoding 232
seq2seq model 36
sequence diagram 423

sequential training 190
    LLM-first 190, 191
    retriever-first 190
Service 472
similarity measures 15
single-agent systems
    ability 119-121
Single Responsibility Principle (SRP) 372
small language model (SLM) 81
softmax layer 48
Software as a Service (SaaS) 377-379, 389
    advantages 379
    advantages (provider) 391
    advantages (user) 392
    disadvantages (provider) 392
    disadvantages (user) 393
    limitations 380
SpanBERT 60
span extraction 145
span extractor 145
span labeling 145
sparse autoencoders (SAEs) 506-508
sparse dictionary learning (SDL) 506
specialized text data 435
speculative decoding 445
static analysis tools (SATs) 476
statistical merging 148
stemming 4
step-back prompting 177
Streamlit 399
    results, caching 405-409
    working with 400-404
Streamlit, and AI agents
    application, creating 421-428
structured data 198
structured pruning 82
Structured Query Language (SQL) 235
st.secrets 453

summarization 193
supervised fine-tuning (SFT) 78, 249
supervised learning 29, 58
SwiftDossier 341, 342
syntax tree 242

T

task-adaptable module 188
task-oriented deployment 119
t-distributed stochastic neighbor
    embedding (t-SNE) 14
t-distributed stochastic neighbor embedding
    (t-SNE) visualization 139
teacher forcing 48
temperature sampling 50
temporal difference (TD) error 286
temporal KG 219
tensor parallelism 449, 450
term 136
term frequency-inverse document
    frequency (TF-IDF) 8-11
term frequency (TF) 138
text encoder 92
text normalization 4
text representation, for AI 4
    bag of words (BoW) 6-8
    one-hot encoding 4-6
    term frequency-inverse document
        frequency (TF-IDF) 8-11
text segmentation 4
text-to-image models 91
threading module 457
tokenization 4, 29
ToolBench 325
Toolformer 326, 328
top-k sampling 49
top-p sampling 50

training-based approaches, RAG
    independent training 190
    joint methods 192
    sequential training 190
transfer learning 57
transformer-based architecture 364
transformer block 43
transformer model 42-47
    applying 57-64
    internal mechanisms, visualizing 52-57
    training 47-50
tree of thoughts (ToT) 100, 324
triplet stores 235
Trust Region Policy Optimization
    (TRPO) 284

U

undirected graph 216
unembedder 48
unequal interaction 121
U-Net 92
Uniform Manifold Approximation
    and Projection (UMAP) 14
unstructured data 197
unstructured pruning 82
update gate 25
Upper Confidence Bound for Trees
    (UCT) formula 287
Upper Confidence Bound (UCB) 268

V

validation module 189
vector database 155
vectorization 5, 30
vector search 178

video game, playing with RL 290-292
   components, connecting 297-304
   environment, setting up 294
   model, defining 294, 295
   model training 296
   scripts description 293
   system testing 297
video input 113
ViLT-B/32-Finetuned-VQA 364
Virtual Lab 347-351
Vision-and-Language Transformer (ViLT) 364
vision-language model (VLM) 90
Vision Transformer (ViT) 84-86, 363
visual input 113
Visual Question-Answering (VQA) tasks 364
ViT-GPT2-COCO-EN 363

W

web
   agent, creating to search 129-133
web agents 488
WebShop example
   reference link 325
weighted graph 217
Wide Web principles
   connected data 215
   distributed data 215
   semantic metadata 215
Word2vec 12-14, 86
word embeddings 11

Z

zero-shot classification 89, 179
zero-shot CoT prompting 100
zero-shot prompting 99
z-score 139

‹packt›

packtpub.com

Subscribe to our online digital library for full access to over 7,000 books and videos, as well as industry leading tools to help you plan your personal development and advance your career. For more information, please visit our website.

Why subscribe?

- Spend less time learning and more time coding with practical eBooks and Videos from over 4,000 industry professionals
- Improve your learning with Skill Plans built especially for you
- Get a free eBook or video every month
- Fully searchable for easy access to vital information
- Copy and paste, print, and bookmark content

At www.packt.com, you can also read a collection of free technical articles, sign up for a range of free newsletters, and receive exclusive discounts and offers on Packt books and eBooks.

Other Books You May Enjoy

If you enjoyed this book, you may be interested in these other books by Packt:

AI Agents in Practice

Valentina Alto

ISBN: 978-1-80580-135-1

- Master core agent components like LLMs, memory systems, tool integration, and context management
- Build production-ready AI agents using frameworks like LangChain with code
- Create effective multi-agent systems using orchestration patterns for problem-solving
- Implement industry-specific agents for e-commerce, customer support, and more
- Design robust memory architectures for agents with short and long-term recall
- Apply responsible AI practices with monitoring, guardrails, and human oversight
- Optimize AI agent performance and cost for production environments

Generative AI with LangChain

Ben Auffarth, Leonid Kuligin

ISBN: 978-1-83702-201-4

- Design and implement multi-agent systems using LangGraph
- Implement testing strategies that identify issues before deployment
- Deploy observability and monitoring solutions for production environments
- Build agentic RAG systems with re-ranking capabilities
- Architect scalable, production-ready AI agents using LangGraph and MCP
- Work with the latest LLMs and providers like Google Gemini, Anthropic, Mistral, DeepSeek, and OpenAI's o3-mini
- Design secure, compliant AI systems aligned with modern ethical practices

Packt is searching for authors like you

If you're interested in becoming an author for Packt, please visit `authors.packtpub.com` and apply today. We have worked with thousands of developers and tech professionals, just like you, to help them share their insight with the global tech community. You can make a general application, apply for a specific hot topic that we are recruiting an author for, or submit your own idea.

Share Your Thoughts

Now you've finished *Building AI Agents with LLMs, RAG, and Knowledge Graphs*, we'd love to hear your thoughts! Scan the QR code below to go straight to the Amazon review page for this book and share your feedback or leave a review on the site that you purchased it from.

`https://packt.link/r/1-835-08706-X`

Your review is important to us and the tech community and will help us make sure we're delivering excellent quality content.

Download a free PDF copy of this book

Thanks for purchasing this book!

Do you like to read on the go but are unable to carry your print books everywhere?

Is your eBook purchase not compatible with the device of your choice?

Don't worry, now with every Packt book you get a DRM-free PDF version of that book at no cost.

Read anywhere, any place, on any device. Search, copy, and paste code from your favorite technical books directly into your application.

The perks don't stop there, you can get exclusive access to discounts, newsletters, and great free content in your inbox daily

Follow these simple steps to get the benefits:

1. Scan the QR code or visit the link below

   `https://packt.link/free-ebook/978-1-83508-706-0`

2. Submit your proof of purchase
3. That's it! We'll send your free PDF and other benefits to your email directly

Made in the USA
Las Vegas, NV
27 September 2025